Tenth edition
Copyright © November 2006
Alastair Sawday Publishing Co. Ltd

Published in 2006
Alastair Sawday Publishing,
The Old Farmyard,
Yanley Lane, Long Ashton
Bristol BS41 9LR
Tel: +44 (0)1275 395430
Fax: +44 (0)1275 393388
Email: info@specialplacestostay.com
Web: www.specialplacestostay.com

The Globe Pequot Press
P. O. Box 480, Guilford,
Connecticut 06437, USA
Tel: +1 203 458 4500
Fax: +1 203 458 4601
E-mail: info@globepequot.com
Web: www.globepequot.com

Design:
Caroline King

Maps & Mapping:
Maidenhead Cartographic Services Ltd

Printing:
Butler & Tanner, Frome, UK

UK Distribution:
Penguin UK, 80 Strand, London

ISBN-10: 1-901970-76-0
ISBN-13: 978-1-901970-76-0

**Alastair Sawday has asserted his right
to be identified as the author of this
work.**

Paper and Printing: We have sought the
lowest possible ecological 'footprint' from
the production of this book, using super-
efficient machinery, vegetable inks and
high environmental standards. Our printer is
ISO 14001-registered.

ALASTAIR SAWDAY'S
SPECIAL PLACES TO STAY

FRENCH
BED &
BREAKFAST

Contents

Index by département

Photo Corel

Alastair Sawday Publishing

Our main aim is to publish beautiful guidebooks but, for us, the question of who we are is also important. For who we are shapes the books, the books shape your holidays, and thus are shaped the lives of people who own these 'special places'. So we are trying to be a little more than 'just a publishing company'.

New eco offices

In January 2006 we moved into our new eco offices. With super-insulation, underfloor heating, a wood-pellet boiler, solar panels and a rainwater tank, we have a working environment benign to ourselves and to the environment. Lighting is low-energy, dark corners are lit by sun-pipes and one building is of green oak. Carpet tiles are from Herdwick sheep in the Lake District.

Environmental & ethical policies

We make many other gestures: company cars run on gas or recycled cooking oil; kitchen waste is composted and other waste recycled; cycling and car-sharing are encouraged; the company only buys organic or local food; we don't accept web links with companies we consider unethical; we bank with the ethical Triodos Bank.

We have used recycled paper for some books but have settled on selecting paper and printing for their low energy use. Our printer is British and ISO14001-certified and together we will work to reduce our environmental impact.

In 2005 we won a Business Commitment to the Environment Award and in April 2006 we won a Queen's Award for Enterprise in the Sustainable Development category. All this has boosted our resolve to promote our green policies. Our flagship gesture, however, is carbon offsetting; we calculate our carbon emissions and plant trees to compensate. In future we will support projects overseas that plant trees or reduce carbon use.

Carbon offset

SCAD in South India, supports the poorest of the poor. The money we send to offset our carbon emissions will be used to encourage village tree planting and, eventually, low-carbon technologies. Why India? Because the money goes a long way and admin costs are very low.
www.salt-of-the-earth.org.uk

Ethics

But why, you may ask, take these things so seriously? You are just a little publishing company, for heaven's sake! Well, is there any good argument for not taking them seriously? The world, by the admission of the vast majority of scientists, is in trouble. If we do not change our ways urgently we will

Who are we?

doom the planet and all its creatures – whether innocent or not – to a variety of possible catastrophes. To maintain the status quo is unacceptable. Business does much of the damage and should undo it, and provide new models.

Pressure on companies to produce Corporate Social Responsibility policies is mounting. We are trying to keep ahead of it all, yet still to be as informal and human as possible – the antithesis of 'corporate'.

The books – and a dilemma

So, we have created fine books that do good work. They promote authenticity, individuality and good local and organic food – a far cry from corporate culture. Rural economies, pubs, small farms, villages and hamlets all benefit. However, people use fossil fuel to get there. Should we aim to get our readers to offset their own carbon emissions, and the B&B and hotel owners too?

We are gradually introducing green ideas into the books: the Fine Breakfast scheme that highlights British and Irish B&B owners who use local and organic food; celebrating those who make an extra environmental effort; gently encouraging the use of public transport, cycling and walking. This year we are publishing a *Green Places to Stay* focusing on responsible travel and eco-properties around the globe.

Our Fragile Earth series

The 'hard' side of our environmental publishing is the Fragile Earth series: *The Little Earth Book, The Little Food Book* and *The Little Money Book*. They consist of bite-sized essays, polemical, hard-hitting and well researched. They are a 'must have' for anyone who seeks clarity about some of the key issues of our time. This year we have also published *One Planet Living.*

Lastly – what is special?

The notion of 'special' is at the heart of what we do, and highly subjective. We discuss this in the introduction. We take huge pleasure from finding people and places that do their own thing – brilliantly; places that are unusual and follow no trends; places of peace and beauty; people who are kind and interesting – and genuine.

We seem to have touched a nerve with thousands of readers; they obviously want to stay in special places rather than the dull corporate monstrosities that have disfigured so many of our cities and towns. Life is too short to be wasted in the wrong places. A night in a special place can be a transforming experience.

Alastair Sawday

Acknowledgements

Few would think of Leeds, for all its modern pazzazz, as a hotbed of Special Places. But it was from Leeds that Emma Carey, the editor of this wonderful book, nurtured it during the last two years. She is one of our highly-valued remote workers, those wielding as much influence from afar as the rest of us in Head Office.

Emma has done this before, and does it brilliantly – with a rare mix of humanity, verve, wisdom and enthusiasm. She loves France, speaks the language well and is quick to generate empathy. She has thus guided this book through its many subtle changes.

Helping her has been Kate Shepherd, young and dynamic – and equally enthusiastic. She has got her career in travel publishing off to a terrific start. We also have to thank a small army of helpers: Florence, Rebecca, Jo, and all those in Accounts and Production who have woven their support through the very fabric of this complex project. Their names appear opposite, along with Jackie King's – the Managing Editor who skilfully guides all our *Special Places To Stay* projects through the labyrinths of their daily lives.

Alastair Sawday

Series Editor Alastair Sawday

Editor Emma Carey

Assistant to Editor Kate Shepherd

Editorial Director Annie Shillito

Writing Jo Boissevain, Ann Cooke-Yarborough, Viv Cripps, Abigail Hole, Helen Pickles, Aideen Reid

Inspections Katie Anderson, Rose Angas, Richard & Linda Armspach, Helen Barr, Miranda Bell, Emma Carey, Elizabeth Carter, Meredith Dickinson, Penny Dinwiddie, Sue Edrich, John & Jane Edwards, Valerie Foix, Georgina Gabriel, Denise Goss, Diana Harris, Suzanne & Barney Lenheim, Jo-Bell Moore, Clarissa Novak, Annette Parker, Kate Shepherd, Elizabeth Yates

Accounts Bridget Bishop, Christine Buxton, Sandra Hasell, Sally Ranahan

Editorial Jackie King, Jo Boissevain, Florence Oldfield, Maria Serrano, Rebecca Stevens, Danielle Williams

Production Julia Richardson, Rachel Coe, Tom Germain, Rebecca Thomas, Allys Williams

Sales & Marketing & PR Siobhán Flynn, Andreea Petre Goncalves, Sarah Bolton

Web & IT Russell Wilkinson, Chris Banks, Joe Green, Brian Kimberling

Previous Editors Ann Cooke-Yarborough, Annie Shillito

Thanks to those people who did a few inspections or had a go at a write-up!

Our first book on French B&B, 13 years ago, was a trumpet blast for the few great B&Bs out there, for the few French people who had crossed the Rubicon into a world where their houses would be prised open and their privacy invaded. It was exhilarating to discover an old château with a charming chatelaine who loved sharing it with visitors, an ancient farm whose owners happily mixed feeding animals and feeding guests, a Provençal house with as much human warmth as style.

It has caught on. The French, who for centuries have taken guests to the café next door rather than invite them in, are enjoying visitors as much as the English do – so much so that thousands and thousands of them are opening up their houses. Many of them are doing it well. Of course they are charging, but it is nevertheless fairly daft to do B&B if you don't enjoy your fellow humans.

Our job is possibly more difficult now. It is easy to be beguiled into inspecting places that look good but feel, upon inspection, less so. Separating the marvellous from the merely good is a daunting task. We have to be fully attuned to the nuances, the subtleties of human behaviour. We have, in short, to stick to our guns and only select the places that we feel really *are* special. We have to weed out the houses that are fraying at the edges just that bit too much, the owners who think of themselves first and foremost as businesspeople rather than B&B owners.

I think we have succeeded again, for this is a truly captivating collection of houses and their people. Most of them have been with us in previous editions, of course, but the additions are as dynamically seductive as ever. You can now find B&Bs in towns and cities as never before. There are younger owners making their mark. And we even have our first self-consciously 'boutique' B&B – luxurious yet awash with solid values (eg. home-grown food) and superb taste.

Alastair Sawday

Photo Tom Germain

Introduction

CHAMBRES D'HÔTES STILL OFFERS EXCEPTIONAL
VALUE FOR MONEY. WHERE ELSE CAN YOU STAY
IN A CHÂTEAU, SLEEP IN ONE TOWER, AND BATH
IN ANOTHER FOR LESS THAN £50 FOR TWO?

This is the tenth edition of the first guide in our series, *Special Places to Stay*. It goes from strength to strength – and runs along unexpectedly new tracks. Looking back to that day in January 1994 when we held the first copy of *French Bed & Breakfast* in our hands is like looking back to another century, so great are the changes within both our working environment and the world of *chambres d'hôtes*. Where once we had a couple of photographs to give us a visual idea of a house (sometimes none were provided at all and we used holiday snaps instead), now we are assaulted with CDs containing dozens of images.

Where once we had one book, one computer, one database, now we have 20-odd titles and a data-churning monster machine. Once we used to leaf through reams of hand-written letters, now we are flooded with emails and web site links. The internet revolution has happened and the expectations of B&B owners and users have changed for ever.

Remember the authentic old-style *chambres d'hôtes* dinners at the communal table in the family kitchen? The farmer's wife did B&B to bring in some extra cash and to open a door between two worlds: the narrow agricultural sphere of her daily life and the foreign-urban exoticism that breezed in with her guests. Such places filled the pages of the early guides. We – and our readers – still love these places, but they are thin on the ground. Now the farmer's sideline is hounded by an ever-growing mountain of rules and regulations, younger web-educated travellers are demanding stylish rooms and gadgets galore, and farmers' offspring are less inclined than before to live off the land. We must cherish the authentic *chambres d'hôtes* when and where we find them.

Photo left La Roussière, entry 529
Photo right Cabalus, entry 114

Introduction

In their place comes a burgeoning species of up-market B&Bs, many of them started by couples grown tired of the rat race and seeking purer, quieter waters. Some belong to young French families who have given up the worlds of finance or media to move to rural France and be "nearer to heaven"; others to the Dutch, Belgian, British. All have led interesting lives, enjoy meeting new people and are passionate about their adopted corner of France.

I must add here that we keep a close eye on the proportion of foreign to French owners, and favour the latter. Our title is *French Bed & Breakfast*; our intention is to introduce French families and their way of life to English-speaking travellers. Of course, we could write a book entitled *British Bed & Breakfast in France*... but this is not that book.

So what distinguishes this escalating trend? First and foremost, the new generation B&Bers expect their businesses to provide them with a viable source of income. So they may provide five rooms for guests (the maximum number allowed under the category 'chambres d'hôtes') – not the two vaguely refurbished now the children have flown the nest. They may have invested heavily in the renovation and introduced interiors sufficiently chic to appear in glossy magazines (some have!). They may take their food seriously, too; some new owners have a background in the catering world, others are so passionate about food that they run cookery courses alongside their B&B.

In 2005 a flurry of articles appeared in the British press about the new wave of British B&B: stylish furnishings, underfloor heating, rain showers, roll top baths, perhaps a trained chef cooking fabulous meals – you know the kind of thing. The French have been doing this for years, extremely well, and at a fraction of the price you find in Britain.

But things are changing on the French accommodation scene. And now the hotel lobby's decade-long campaign against its more modest rivals – 'unfair competition', in their view – is due to bring out its big

Photo La Ferme de Beaupré, entry 9

legislative guns. Owners are having to pay higher taxes and contributions, to declare themselves to the local authorities, to put up fences, introduce fire exits, even to apply for licences to serve coffee at breakfast. As the mountain of paperwork grows, the business of *chambres d'hôtes* begins to look less appealing, and less profitable. We can only pray the government departments concerned will come to their senses before they lose the special jewel that is French B&B.

What to expect and how we choose our Special Places
There is a wider-than-ever variety of places and prices in this edition but we seek good value for money whatever the price. *Chambres d'hôtes* still offers exceptional value for money. Where else can you stay in a château, sleep in one tower, bathe in another and breakfast on home-hive honey and brioche for less than £50 for two?

Remember to interpret what you see and read in this book. If you opt for a working farm, expect cockerels to crow or tractors to set off at dawn. If you choose a 'rambling château with old-fashioned bathrooms', there could be some draughty corridors and idiosyncratic plumbing. If 'antique beds' sounds seductively authentic, remember they are liable to be antique sizes, too (190cm long,

doubles 140cm wide, singles 80 or 90cm wide). Check on anything that is really important to you before confirming your booking, eg. whether the swimming pool will be ready to use at Easter, whether the bicycles have been booked by others.

We love B&Bs with a family welcome, and we won't exclude a superb farmhouse because of a few cobwebs or a bit of family chaos. Instead, we write honestly so that you can decide for yourselves. As one reader wrote, "Nothing was too much trouble, and our hostess made everyone feel really at home. Who cares about the odd speck of dust with such a welcome."

Special green entries
We have chosen, very subjectively, half a dozen places that are making a particular effort to be eco-friendly.

Photo Un Ange Passe, entry 717

Introduction

We have given them a full page and an extra photo to illustrate what they're up to. We are keen to celebrate pro-actively eco-friendly owners in France, so please let us know if you discover any.

B&Bs are not hotels

If you are expecting anonymity, room service or a key to your bedroom door, then *chambres d'hôtes* are not for you! We all run our homes differently and so do our hosts, so expect to fit in with their norm, however informal and family-orientated. You may expect to feel a privileged guest and to gain a fascinating glimpse of a French way of life, but don't expect your beds to be made or your towels to be changed daily, your children's toys to be gathered or your late request for a vegetarian meal to produce anything more exciting than an omelette. Let your hosts know of any special needs well ahead and take your own tea bags if you are fussy. Owners love guests to stay more than one night and it's really worth doing so for genuine contact, but they often expect you to be out during the day – they have their own lives to lead and cannot be on hand all the time. If they are happy for you to be around, check which parts of the house or garden you may use during the day.

Photo Le Château de Marcenac, entry 587

Problems

Do discuss any problem with your hosts at the time. They are the ones who can do something about it immediately and would be mortified to discover, too late, that you were cold in bed when extra blankets could have been provided.

If you find anything we say misleading (things can change in the lifetime of a guide), or you think we miss the point – if, for example, you thought you'd chosen a child-friendly house and were surprised by white carpets and ornaments at toddler height – please let us know.

Breakfast

The range of what you might be given for breakfast is becoming more diverse. You may 'just' be offered pain de campagne with apricot jam and a bowl of coffee but more choice has crept in. As one reader discovered: "His breakfasts were 'to die for'! He offered the best choice of things to eat: home-squeezed orange and apple juice, cereal, brioche, pain au raisin, homemade jams and marmalades as well as three different kinds of bread."

Dinner – *table d'hôtes*

Again, this varies hugely: from simple farmhouse meals to four courses cooked by a professionally trained chef. We have not attempted to go into details, although price

Introduction

may be a guide. *Table d'hôtes* is a wonderful opportunity to eat fresh, even gourmet, food in an authentic family atmosphere. Don't expect a choice: *table d'hôtes* means the same food for all and absolutely must be booked ahead; do say what your dietary needs are when you book. Meals probably won't be available every day, and may only be prepared for a minimum number of guests, but do turn up if you have booked – it's distressing to prepare a meal that no one comes to enjoy. Few places offer lunch but occasionally picnics can be provided. Sadly, changing lifestyles mean that fewer people are prepared to do evening meals. Do make the most of those that are available.

Meals: en famille or not?

Traditionally they would be, but practically, there are good reasons why they won't always be. Two of these reasons will make sense to a lot of you:
• the owners' young children need their parents' presence at dinner and for homework time and/or are not considered 'civilised' enough to dine with guests
• Your hostess is minding her figure!

If there is no *table d'hôtes*, we give an idea of other places to eat, but beware: rural restaurants stop taking orders at 9pm and close at least one day a week (often a Sunday or a Monday).

Wine

When wine is included this can mean a range of things, from a standard quarter-litre carafe per person to a barrel of table wine; from a decent bottle of local wine to an excellent estate wine. Whatever it is, it is usually good value but please do not abuse your hosts' *vin à volonté* (unlimited wine with meals). And do check prices – some estates may use meals to showcase their wines and this can make for an expensive meal.

Do be considerate about keeping hosts up late... some simply love to stay and chat; others find it hard to say when they feel they should be turning in. (The boot can, of course, be on the other foot!).

Photo Le Mas de Câpriers, entry 676

How to use this book
Bedrooms and how we describe them:
- double: one double bed
- twin: two single beds
- twin/double: two single beds that can become a large double
- triple or 'family room': any mix of beds (sometimes sofabeds) for 3, 4 or more people
- 'suite': either one large room with a sitting area or two or more interconnecting rooms, plus one or more bathrooms
- 'apartment': similar to a suite but with an independent entrance and often a small kitchen
- 'studio': bedroom, bathroom, sitting and cooking areas

Extra beds and cots for children, at an extra cost, can often be provided; ask when booking.

Under certain entries we mention that two rooms share a bathroom and are 'let to same party only'. Please do not assume this means you must be a group of friends or a family to apply; it simply means you will not be sharing a bathroom with strangers.

Bathrooms
There is a wonderful array of washing arrangements in French homes. We've done our best to make the layouts clear: if a room has no bathroom details mentioned, you can assume that the bath/shower

room is en suite. We only mention shared or separate bathrooms.

Most, but not all baths have shower attachments. Bathrooms are generally good but if you are wary of quirky arrangements go for the modernised places (which may be more expensive).

Prices
The prices in this book are not guaranteed but are presumed to be for 2007. Check our web site for those up-dates that we have received from owners. Many places offer reductions for longer stays; good half-board rates, special prices for children: ask when you book.

Photo St Mare, entry 144

Introduction

Symbols
Symbols and their explanations are listed on the last page of the book. Use them as a guide rather than an unequivocal statement of fact and double-check anything that is important to you.

Children
Our ♀ symbol is given to owners who accept children of any age. They are unlikely to have cots, highchairs, safety equipment or all the paraphernalia you need, so check. Elsewhere, they may be welcome with restrictions as indicated in italics at the end of the description eg. babies only, because of an unfenced pool.

Photo above Domaine de la Mouthe, entry 477
Photo right La Grenade, entry 564

Smoking
Our ✗ symbol shows the houses where there's no smoking anywhere indoors.

Pets
Our 🐕 symbol tells you which houses allow pets in the bedroom but not on the bed – but you must check whether this includes the size and type of your pet. Your hosts will expect animals to be well-behaved and you to be responsible for them at all times.

Practical Matters
Telephoning/faxing/emailing
All phone numbers in France have ten digits
eg. (0)5 05 25 35 45.
You should know that:
• the zero (bracketed above) is for use when telephoning from inside France only, eg. dial 05 15 25 35 45 from any private or public telephone;
• when dialling from outside France use the international access code, then the country code for France (33) then the last 9 digits of the number you want, eg.
00 33 5 15 25 35 45;
• numbers beginning (0)6 are mobile phone numbers;
• to telephone from France to Great Britain: 00 44 then the number without the first 0;
to North America: 00 1 then the number without the first 0.

Télécartes (phone cards) are widely available in France and there are plenty of telephone boxes, even in the countryside (they often only take cards).

Don't automatically expect a rapid response to emails, particularly at busy times of the year.

Booking

It is essential to book well ahead for July and August, and wise for other months. You may receive a Contrat de Location (Tenancy Contract) as confirmation. It must be filled in and returned, probably with a deposit, and commits both sides to the arrangement.

Photo La Griottière, entry 87

Remember not to telephone any later than 9pm or 9.30 at the latest – you may disturb those that go early to bed – and that Ireland and the UK are one hour behind the rest of Europe. And please remember that owners count on you to stay as long as you have booked for. If you don't, they may feel justified in applying a cancellation charge.

Deposits

Some owners ask for a deposit. Many readers have found it difficult or ridiculously expensive to do this by direct transfer but you can send an ordinary cheque which the owner will destroy when you arrive (so no one pays the charges); when you leave, they will ask you for cash for your whole stay.

Paying

Most B&B owners do not take credit cards but those who do have our credit card symbol. Virtually all ATMs in France take Visa and MasterCard. Euro travellers' cheques should be accepted; other currency cheques are unpopular because of commission charges.

Taxe de séjour

This is a small tax that local councils can levy on all visitors paying for accommodation. Some councils do, some don't: you may find your bill increased by a euro or two per person per day.

Tipping

B&B owners would be taken aback by a tip but if you encounter unusual kindness you may feel a thank-you letter, Christmas card or small gift would be appropriate.

Arriving

Most owners expect you to arrive between 5pm and 7pm. If you come earlier, rooms may not be ready or your hosts may still be at work. If you are going to be late (or early, unavoidably), please telephone and say so.

No-shows

Owners hope you will treat them as friends by being sensitive and punctual. It's obviously upsetting for them to prepare rooms, even meals, and to wait up late for 'guests' who give no further sign of life. So if you find you are not going to take up a booking, telephone right away. There is a tacit agreement among some B&B owners that no-show plus no-call by 8pm, even 6pm in some cases, can be taken as a refusal of the booking and they will re-let the room if another guest turns up.

Subscriptions

Owners pay to appear in this guide. Their fee goes towards the high costs of a sophisticated inspection system and producing an all-colour book. We only include places and owners that we find positively

special. It is not possible for anyone to buy his/her way into our guides.

Internet

www.specialplacestostay.com
Our web site has online entries for all the places featured here and in our other books, with up-to-date information and direct links to their own e-mail addresses and web sites. You'll find more about the site at the back of this book.

Disclaimer

We make no claims to pure objectivity in choosing our Special Places to Stay. They are here because we like them. Our opinions and tastes are ours alone and this book is a statement of them; we hope that you will share them. A huge Thank You to those of you who take the time and trouble to write to us about your *chambres d'hôtes* experiences – good and bad – or to recommend new places.

Photo Eth Berye Petit, entry 557

Introduction

This is what we do with them:

• Do bear with us at busy times; it's difficult to respond immediately.
• Recommendations are followed up with inspection visits where appropriate. If your recommendation leads us to include a place, you receive a free copy of the edition in which it first appears.
• Owners are informed when we receive substantially positive reports about them.
• Poor reports are followed up with the owners in question: we need to hear both sides of the story. Really bad reports lead to incognito visits, after which we may exclude a place.

We have done our utmost to get our facts right but apologise unreservedly for any mistakes that may have crept in. We would be grateful to hear of any errors that you find.

You should know that we do not check such things as fire alarms, swimming pool security or any other regulation with which owners of properties receiving paying guests should comply. This is the responsibility of the owners.

And finally
Feedback from you is invaluable and we always act upon comments. With your help and our own inspections we can maintain our reputation for dependability.

We value your letters and comments which make a real contribution to this book, be they on our report form, by letter or by email to info@sawdays.co.uk. or visit the web site and contact us from there.

Bon Voyage – Happy Travelling

Emma Carey

Photo above Domaine de l'Oiseau, entry 88
Photo left Mas Pichony, entry 672

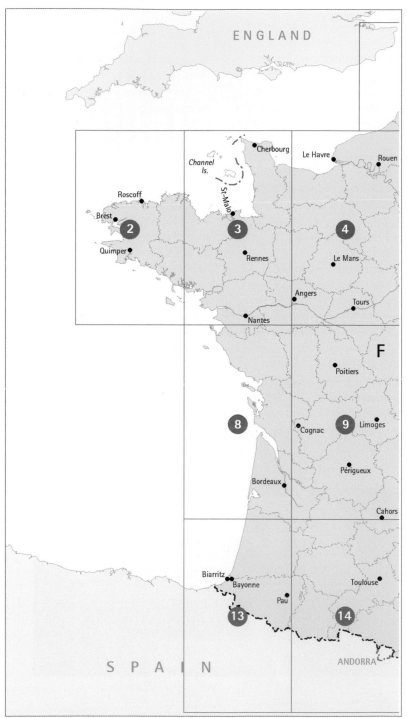

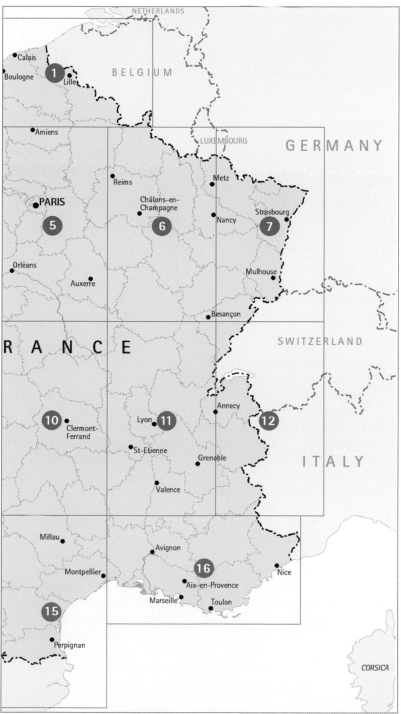

©Maidenhead Cartographic, 2006

Tips for Travellers

Use our maps as a guide only

Our maps are designed for B&B flagging only – you will be deeply frustrated if you try to use them as road maps! Take a **good detailed road map** or atlas such as Michelin or Collins.

The numbered flags are simply indications of position on the ground, not accurate markers. You will find specific directions in the relevant entry.

Reading our directions:

Except in the case of two-way motorway junctions, our directions take you to each house from one side only. French roads are identified with the letters they carry on French maps and road signs:
A = Autoroute. Motorways (mostly toll roads) with junctions that generally have the same name/number on both sides.
N = Route Nationale. The old trunk roads that are still fairly fast, don't charge tolls and often go through towns.
D = Route Départementale. Smaller country roads with less traffic.

Our directions are as succinct as possible.
For example: From A7 exit Valence Sud A49 for Grenoble; exit 33; right D538a for Beaumont 2.5km; right again at sign 800m; house on right.
Interpretation: Take A7 motorway going north or south; leave at junction named 'Valence Sud' and get onto motorway A49 going towards Grenoble; leave this road at junction 33 and turn right onto road D538a (the 'a' means there are probably roads numbered 538b, 538c... in the vicinity) towards Beaumont for 2.5km until you meet a meaningful sign (often 'Chambres d'Hôtes', the name of the house or a pictogram of a bed under a roof); turn right at this sign; the house is 800 metres down this road on the right.

Roads & driving

Current speed limits are: motorways 130 kph (80 mph), RN national trunk roads 110 kph (68 mph), other open roads 90 kph (56 mph), in towns 50 kph (30 mph). The road police are very active and can demand on-the-spot payment of fines.

One soon gets used to driving on the right but complacency leads to trouble; take special care coming out of car parks, private drives, one-lane roads and coming onto roundabouts.

Directions in towns

The French drive towards a destination and use road numbers far less than we do. Thus, to find your way à la française, know the general direction you want to go, i.e. the towns your route goes through, and when you see *Autres Directions* or *Toutes Directions* in a town, forget road numbers, just continue towards the place name you're heading for or through.

Map 1

29

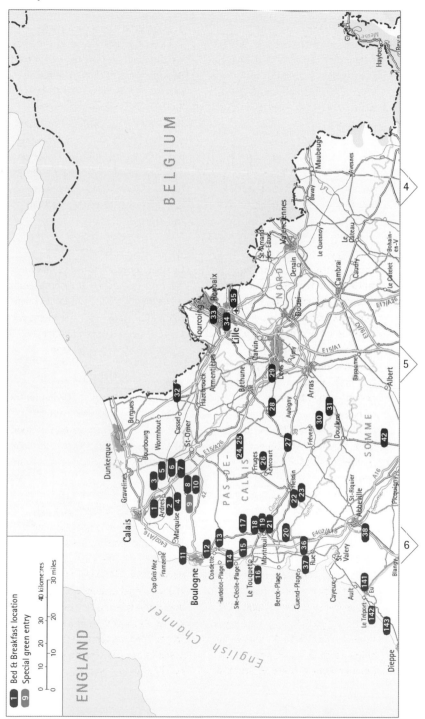

©Maidenhead Cartographic, 2006

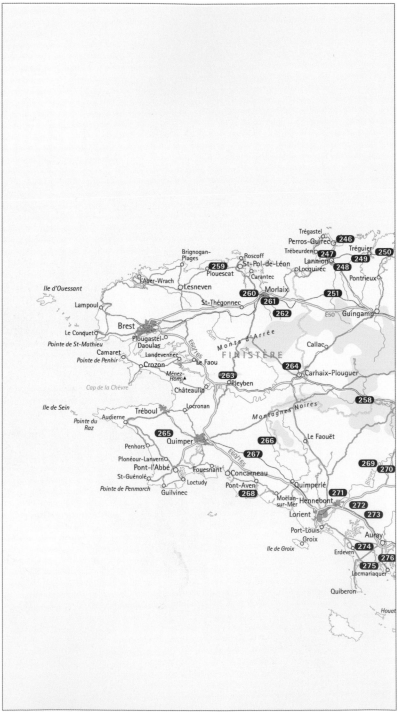

Map 3

31

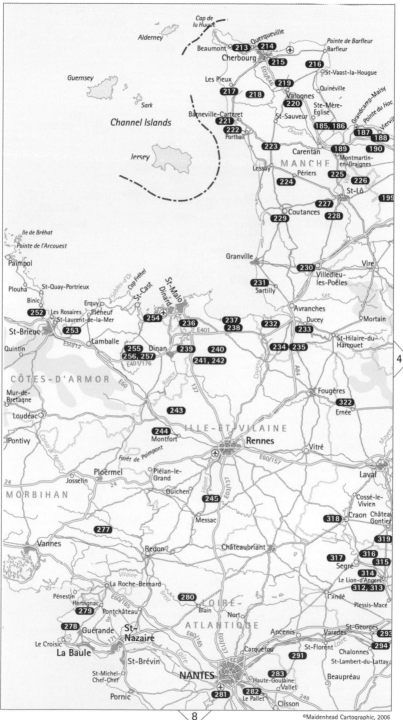

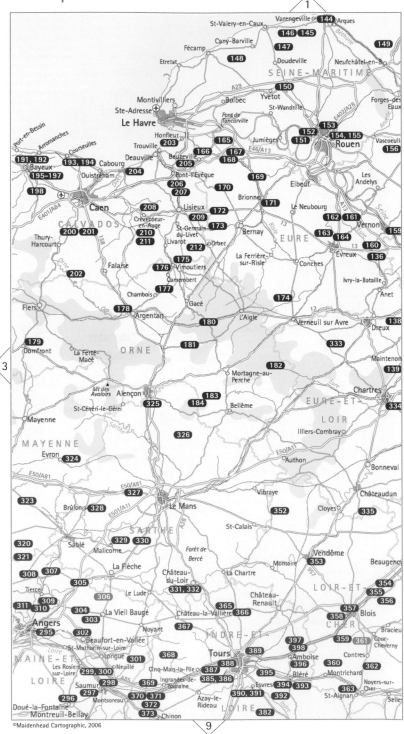

Map 5

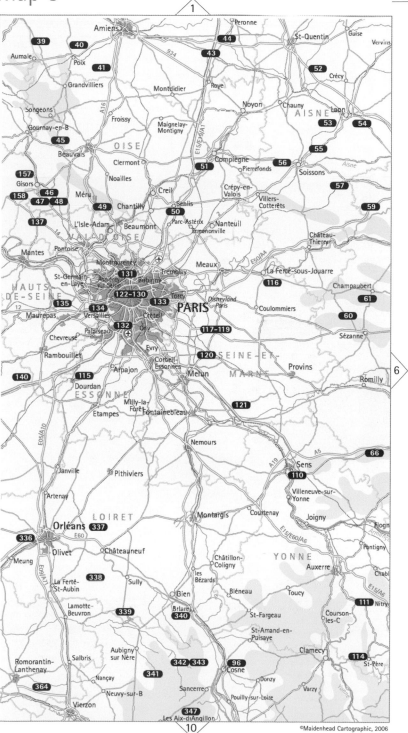

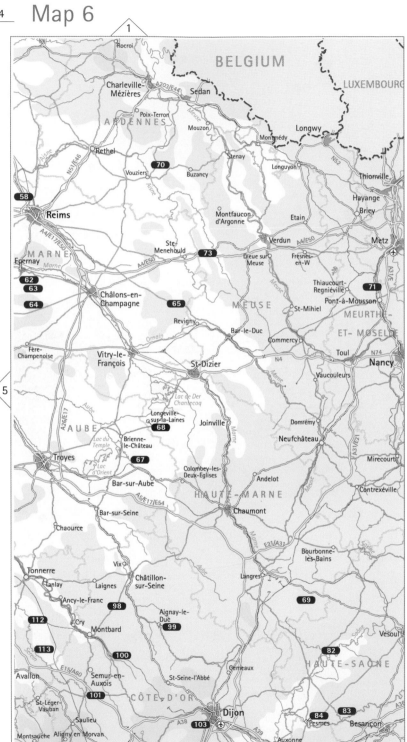

Map 7

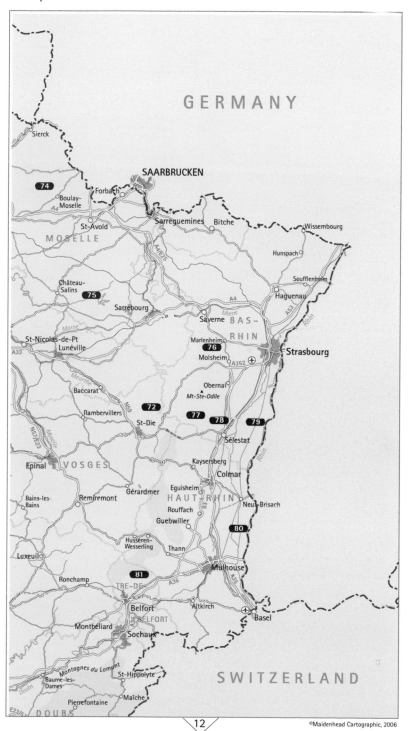

Map 8

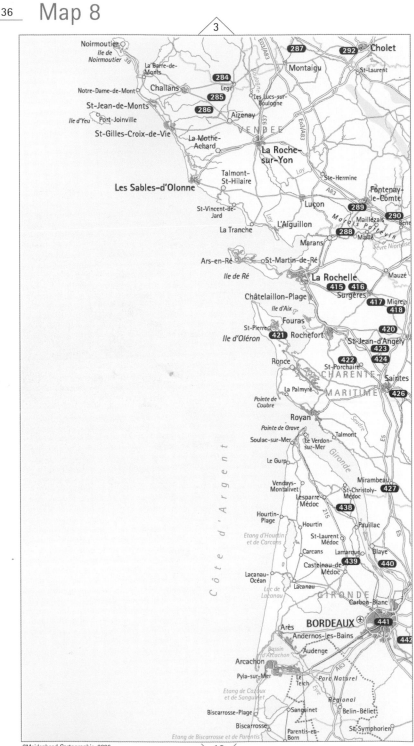

Map 9

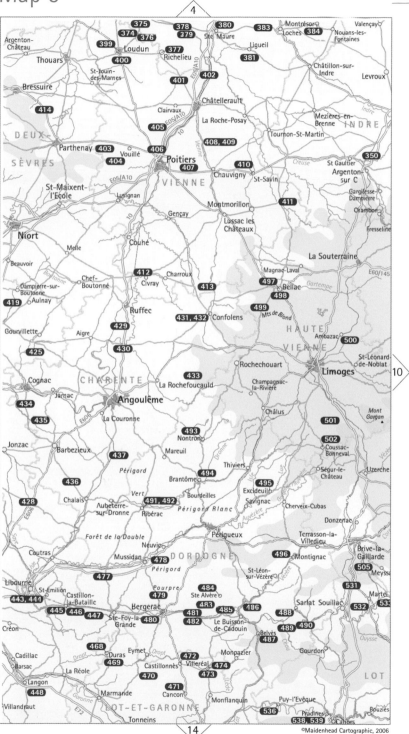

©Maidenhead Cartographic, 2006

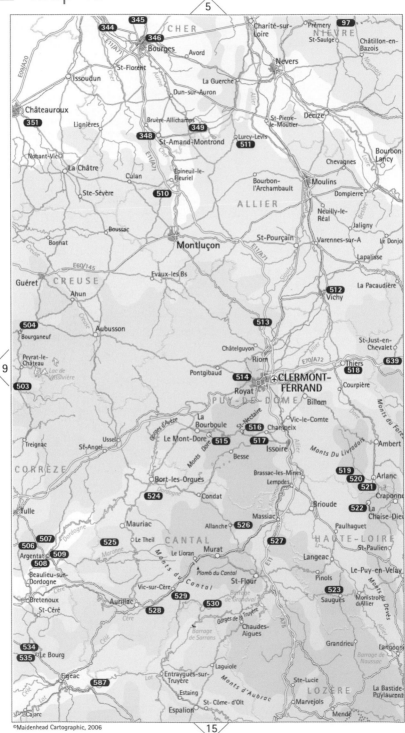

Map 11

39

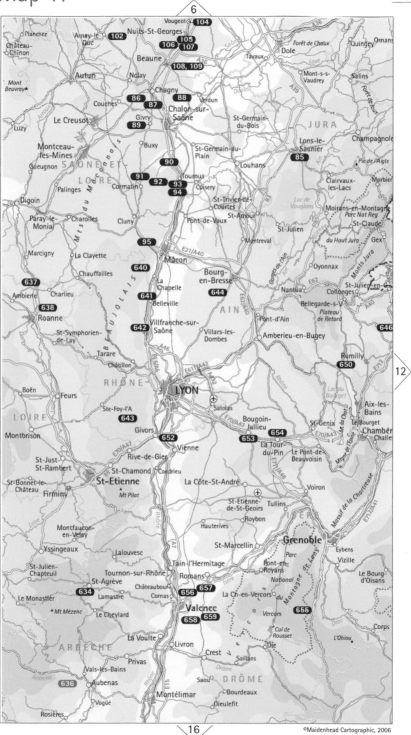

Map 12

Map 13

41

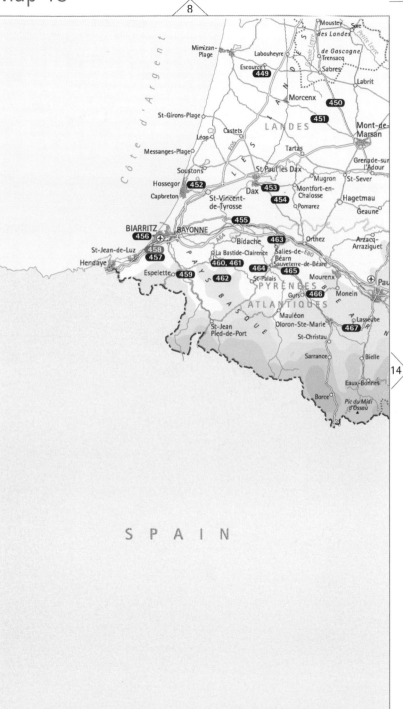

Map 14

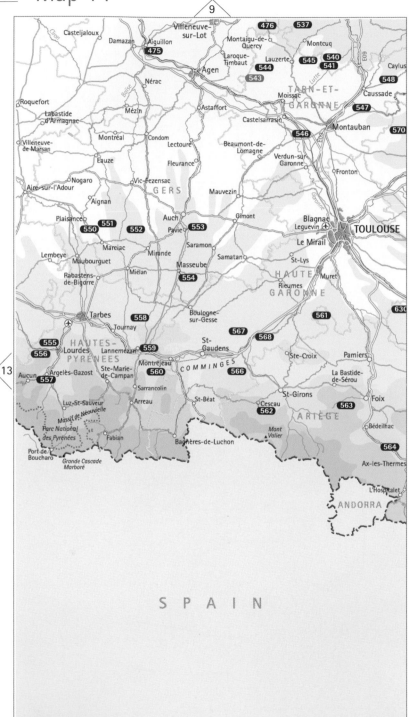

Map 15

43

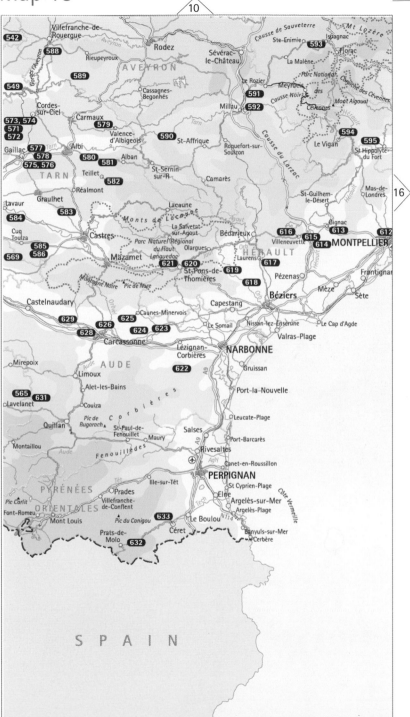

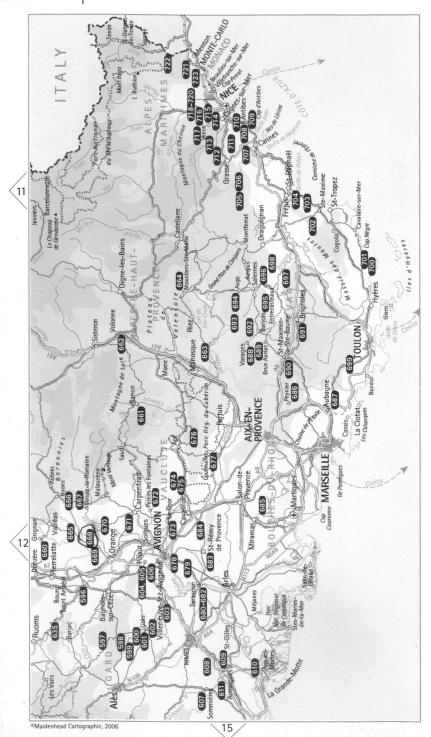

The North
Picardy

Manoir du Meldick

The 1930s house awaits behind electronic gates. Big panelled bedrooms have floral touches and other fantasies, pictures and *objets* are arranged with artistic care and the *lumière du Nord* spreads its amber glow at the end of the day. Madame has huge energy and does everything to perfection, including breakfasts. Another warming highlight is the gorgeously yellow and low-ceilinged dining room with monastery table and family oils. Sitting rooms are generous and comforting, the garden is minimalist, the kennels house 40 hounds and the beach across the windblown plain is wild and wonderful.

rooms	4: 2 doubles, 1 twin, 1 quadruple.
price	€60.
meals	Restaurant 5km.
closed	Rarely.
directions	From A16 exit 48 for Marck; 2nd roundabout exit Le Fort Vert; through Marck; right D119; house 1km on right.

Jean & Danièle Houzet
Manoir du Meldick,
2528 avenue du Général de Gaulle,
Le Fort Vert, 62730 Marck,
Pas-de-Calais

tel   +33 (0)3 21 85 74 34
fax   +33 (0)3 21 85 74 34
email   jeandaniele.houzet@free.fr
web   www.manoir-du-meldick.com

Map 1 Entry 1

La Motte Obin

Madame Breton is irreplaceable: a lovely old lady in a deep-country farmhouse, she talks lots, in French, and otherwise relies on radio and telly for company. Hers is an endearing, piecemeal family house with old-fashioned furniture, masses of photographs (19 grandchildren), lots of crochet and very steep stairs. Simple rooms have good beds and windows to fields of peace. Madame loves cooking country dishes for visitors and readers have praised her hospitality (and her breakfasts). Ask to see the exquisite vaulted stables – built for cows and carthorses, fit for thoroughbreds and prize-winners.

rooms	2: 1 double, 1 family room.
price	€45.
meals	Dinner with wine, €20.
closed	November-March.
directions	From A26 exit 2 for Tournehem, over N43, follow to Muncq Nieurlet, on for Ruminghem. House on left approx. 1.5km after leaving Muncq Nieurlet, at sign.

Mme Françoise Breton
La Motte Obin,
62890 Muncq Nieurlet,
Pas-de-Calais

tel   +33 (0)3 21 82 79 63

Map 1 Entry 2

Les Draps d'Or

The 'Cloths of Gold' has been an inn since 1640 and Christine's open and vivacious welcome fits the tradition – she adores receiving guests, the youngest included. She uses colour joyfully too: the warm, bright little dayroom in the guest wing is a reflection of her dynamic personality. Bedrooms upstairs – blue, yellow, green, white – are equally fresh and bright; the twin has bedheads festooned in muslin, studded with fairy lights, gathered with red raffia. All give onto the cobbled street but Ardres, a delightful little town, is quiet at night while the perfect town garden gives a country feel at the back.

rooms	3: 2 doubles, 1 twin, each with shower & separate wc. Extra twin for children.
price	€52.
meals	Restaurants within walking distance.
closed	Rarely.
directions	From Calais A16, exit 46; N43 to Ardres; right after church; house on corner.

Christine & François Borel
Les Draps d'Or,
152 rue Lambert d'Ardres,
62610 Ardres, Pas-de-Calais
tel   +33 (0)3 21 82 20 44
fax   +33 (0)3 21 82 20 44
email   christine@drapsdor.com
web   www.drapsdor.com

Map 1   Entry 3

Le Manoir de Bois en Ardres

After 200 years of conversions, this house of history and unusual character stands, connected by glazed arches, cloister-like round its sheltered, intimate garden and old stone pond. Beyond, ponies graze beneath the mature trees of the ten acre park: come to commune with nature. Inside, strikingly attractive cottage-contemporary rooms are a hymn to Françoise's stencil and furniture-painting skills and the fruit of Thierry's collecting flair (his antiques and bric-a-brac shop occupies an old stable), the whole atmosphere an echo of this warm, eager couple's joie de vivre. Breakfasts are a delight.

rooms	5: 1 twin, 2 suites for 4; 2 triples (1 with separate wc on floor below).
price	€59-€64.
meals	Restaurant 1km.
closed	Rarely.
directions	From Calais A16, exit 46 for St Omer N43. Pass Les Attaques, Pont d'Ardres, 1st r'bout at Bois en Ardres; before 2nd r'bout left Rue de St Quentin for 1km; green gate.

Françoise & Thierry Roger
Le Manoir de Bois en Ardres,
1530 rue de St Quentin,
62610 Ardres, Pas-de-Calais
tel   +33 (0)3 21 85 97 78
mobile +33 (0)6 15 03 06 21
email   roger@aumanoir.com
web   www.aumanoir.com

Map 1   Entry 4

The North

Les Fuchsias

There is something touchingly mixed-up-Victorian about this unusual house with its gingerbread cutouts, variegated roofs and copsy garden of woodland thrown against lawns and fields with quantities of migrating birds flying past. Monsieur is chatty (in English), charming and informative; Madame is quieter but very attentive: ever busy with needle or paintbrush, she tends her house with loving care and embroidered samplers. Guests have their own cosy colourful sitting and breakfast rooms. Bedrooms have fresh modern furnishings – pretty duvets, wicker armchairs – and simple washing arrangements.

rooms	3: 1 suite for 4; 1 twin, 1 family room sharing separate wc.
price	€46–€50.
meals	Choice of restaurants 2km.
closed	Rarely.
directions	A16 exit 46; N43 for Ardres & St Omer. In Bois en Ardres, 2nd left after r'bout; house on this road.

Bernadette Balloy
Les Fuchsias,
292 rue du Général de St Just,
62610 Bois en Ardres, Pas-de-Calais

tel	+33 (0)3 21 82 05 25
fax	+33 (0)3 21 82 05 25
email	lesfuchsias@aol.com
web	www.lesfuchsias-ardres.fr.fm

Map 1 Entry 5

The North

La Bohême

Extrovert Sonia loves music, painting, cooking and spoiling her guests. White walls, dark wooden doors, floors and beams, solid, good-looking furniture – it's 'French rustique'. The bedroom under the eaves is prettily decorated in red toile de Jouy and looks onto the garden; the suite, in stylish white and grey with a good big bathroom, is in a separate building and perfect for a family (but watch the stairs). You'll adore the garden, bursting with life, full of secret corners. This is walking and pony-trekking country and if you'd like to trade car for horse, Sonia's daughter will happily organise rides.

rooms	3: 2 doubles, 1 family suite.
price	€50.
meals	Dinner with wine, €22.
closed	Rarely.
directions	From A26 exit 2; N43 for Zutkerque; past Chatêau de Cocove; house on right on entering village, signed.

Sonia Benoît
La Bohême,
1947 rue de la Grasse Payelle,
62370 Zutkerque, Pas-de-Calais

tel	+33 (0)3 21 35 70 25
mobile	+33 (0)6 16 18 71 22
email	sonia-benoit-la-boheme@wanadoo.fr
web	perso.wanadoo.fr/sonia-la-boheme/

Map 1 Entry 6

La Ferme de Wolphus

The family, who speak excellent English, do wine-tastings and will sell you wine and honey, are delightful but this is more gîte (three so far) than homely B&B. All is straightforward and simple, breakfast is in your own quarters (or the family kitchen for very early starts), where basic pine furniture and slatting grace the smallish, under-the-eaves rooms and some windows give onto the garden. The closeness to ferry ports is seductive, though the nearby main road may disturb some. Lake, old trees, sheep and peacocks hug both farmhouse and outbuildings. Basic, busy, friendly – and great value.

rooms	3: 1 quadruple; 2 triples, each with shower, sharing wc on floor below. Extra bed available.
price	€41–€45. Triple €54–€58. Quadruple €70.
meals	Restaurants nearby.
closed	Rarely.
directions	From A26 exit 2 onto N43 for Calais. Wolphus on left 1km after junction, with woods beside road. Be careful turning in.

Jean-Jacques Behaghel
La Ferme de Wolphus,
62890 Zouafques,
Pas-de-Calais

tel	+33 (0)3 21 35 61 61
fax	+33 (0)3 21 35 61 61
email	ferme.de.wolphus@wanadoo.fr
web	perso.wanadoo.fr/ferme-wolphus/

Map 1 Entry 7

Le Manoir

The trompe l'oeil and frescoed friezes are lavish, from the panelling in the dining room to the 'marble' up the stairs. Sylvie is restoring her old house with artistry and flair. Known in the village as Le Château, it's not really big but, with so many original details intact, it's a historian's delight. The attic rooms are romantic country-modern, those on the first floor elegantly French – deep mauve and moss green fabrics and papers and some spectacular carved wardrobes and beds. A great atmosphere, excellent *table d'hôtes*, gardens with box parterre and views, and a very charming young family.

rooms	5: 3 doubles, 1 triple, 1 suite for 4.
price	€60. Triple €90. €100 for 4.
meals	Dinner with wine, €25–€40.
closed	Rarely.
directions	From A26 exit 2; left D217 for Zouafques, Tournehem then Bonningues; house on right just after entering village.

Sylvie & Pierre Breemersch
Le Manoir,
40 route de Licques,
62890 Bonningues lès Ardres,
Pas-de-Calais

tel	+33 (0)3 21 82 69 05
email	pierre.breemersch@wanadoo.fr
web	www.lemanoirdebonningues.com

Map 1 Entry 8

La Ferme de Beaupré

129 rue de Licques, 62890 Bonningues lès Ardres, Pas-de-Calais

This organic dairy farm is run with passion by hosts who welcome you into their gorgeous old house at the end of the tree-lined drive and ply you with fine home-grown food (just try the breakfast jams). Lut, from Belgium, is a gracious and unpretentiously warm mother of two boys – her welcome will touch you. Your perfect, peaceful bedroom, a study in taupes and off-whites, is papered in toile de Jouy; a tiny room off it has a bed for a child, and a useful fridge. You get sole use of the living room, and the garden bursts with peonies, lupins, roses and cherries. An adorable, very special place.

A buzz of activity here, the addition of a beehive being the most recent step in a journey towards self-sufficiency that began 22 years ago. The compassion this couple have for the planet runs deep. Everything is now done the organic way: animals are selected for longevity and hardiness, crops are diverse and the soil, nourished by compost alone, contains all that plants need. Care of this rich pasture land sees it brimming with good things, all brought to the table for your tastebuds' delight.

rooms	2 doubles.
price	€52.
meals	Dinner with wine, €20.
closed	Rarely.
directions	From A26 exit 2 for Licques; through Tournehem & Bonningues lès Ardres; left after village to farm.

Lut & Jean-Michel Louf-Degrauwe
tel   +33 (0)3 21 35 14 44
mobile +33 (0)6 88 81 38 62
email   lut.degrauwe@nordnet.fr

SPECIAL GREEN ENTRY
see page 15

Map 1 Entry 9

The North

27 route de Guémy

It's new, brand new. So is the garden. But Madame, a long-standing B&B owner, will soon bring her young house to life, inside and out. Quiet and confident, she simply loves having guests. You have the run of the upper floor, where all rooms look long and far over green hills, are fairly minimalist in décor with white walls and clothes racks, and share a big spanking bathroom. Downstairs, a conservatory for a good friendly breakfast and rooms full of light. It's excellent value, so come and watch as the trees begin to grow and the house learns to breathe under Madame's ministrations.

rooms	1 suite for 2-6.
price	From €39.
meals	Choice of restaurants 5-10km.
closed	Rarely.
directions	From Calais A26 for Paris; exit 2 Licques; left D217 for Zouafques & Clerques; right opp. church in Clerques for La Chapelle St Louis 500m; house with columns.

Christiane Devines
27 route de Guémy,
Le Hamel, 62890 Clerques,
Pas-de-Calais

tel	+33 (0)3 21 82 40 65
fax	+33 (0)3 21 82 40 65
email	Chrisdevines@aol.com
web	maisonhotes.free.fr

Map 1   Entry 10

The North

La Goélette

A great place from which to explore the 'Opal Coast', made fashionable by the British in the Thirties, or to spend your first or last night of a trip to France. *Monsieur Hulot's Holiday* is a perfect image of the little seaside town and this exuberant house on the front. Mary's décor is soberly luxurious, in keeping with the period: white linen, wooden floors, carefully chosen fabrics and furniture, lots of books. She and Franck are charming and Mary, who used to work for Eurostar, speaks excellent English. One room is snug and two, both huge, share the breakfast's rooms ravishing sea views.

rooms	4: 2 doubles, 2 twins.
price	€80-€130.
meals	Dinner with wine, €45.
closed	Rarely.
directions	From A16 exit 3 to Wimereux. There, go to sea front. House about halfway along promenade, 100m left of Hôtel Atlantic (your back to sea). Parking not easy.

Mary Avot
La Goélette,
13 Digue de Mer, 62930 Wimereux,
Pas-de-Calais

tel	+33 (0)3 21 32 62 44
fax	+33 (0)3 21 33 77 54
email	mary@lagoelette.com
web	www.lagoelette.com

Map 1   Entry 11

Rue de l'Église

The golden stone of the oldest farmhouse in the village is easy on the eye. Flowers flourish to the front, the garden and orchard run down to the stream, and the retired horses are happy in their stables (the stud farm is further away). Madame is discreetly friendly and obliging, and gives you delicious breakfasts at marble-topped tables. The bedrooms, in an outbuilding that looks out onto the courtyard and wooded hills, have straightforward modern décor; the new triple sports a wrought-iron four-poster with leopard-skin cover, and a bathroom pretty with mosaics. The living room, too, is spotless and cosy.

rooms	5: 2 doubles, 2 twins, 1 triple.
price	€43–€55.
meals	Auberge in village.
closed	Christmas–January.
directions	From Boulogne D940 to St Léonard; at 2nd lights, left on small road to Echinghen (no sign); in village centre, left in tiny street immed. after sharp bend; left 1st gateway.

Jacqueline & Jean-Pierre
Boussemaere VÉRONIQUE
Rue de l'Église,
62360 Echinghen,
Pas-de-Calais

tel   +33 (0)3 21 91 14 34
fax   +33 (0)3 21 91 06 41
email   jp-boussemaere@wanadoo.fr

Map 1   Entry 12

---

127 rue du Breuil

The shield on the front is a *notaire's* badge of office: his is a house of generous proportions with original 18th-century features and a courtyard at the back in a lovely garden. Matching your hosts' quiet good breeding, a certain old-world formality clings to the heavy dark antiques downstairs; upstairs, the big, prettily traditional French rooms are lighter with more antiques and good rugs on wooden floors. There's a highly original attic salon for guests with all the furniture gathered in the centre. A chance to experience a valuable bourgeois facet of France in an unspoilt village. *Minimum stay two nights.*

rooms	3: 2 twins, 1 family room.
price	€45–€60.
meals	Restaurant 5km.
closed	Rarely.
directions	From Boulogne N1 S for St Léonard & Montreuil approx. 15km. In Samer, take road that goes down to right of church; house on left, near top of hill.

Joëlle Maucotel
127 rue du Breuil,
62830 Samer,
Pas-de-Calais

tel   +33 (0)3 21 87 64 19
fax   +33 (0)3 21 87 64 19

Map 1   Entry 13

Le Moulin

No more milling at the moulin, but the lake is there and it's good to throw open a window and watch the ducks. This is a classically French B&B with black leather easy chairs in the living/dining/sitting room, an enticing velvet chair or two in the bedrooms and painted white tables against candy-stripe walls. Delicious breakfasts are shared with guests from the sprinkling of gîtes in the grounds. All is warm and inviting in this big, reassuring, lakeside mill house, built in 1855. Christine is reserved but very welcoming – and you are a spade's throw from the local sand beach.

La Longue Roye

This remote but fabulous set of buildings was a Cistercian farm and the 13th-century barn – a 'harvest cathedral' – is worth the detour alone. Old arches spring, the brickwork dazzles, the courtyard focuses properly on its duckpond, the guest quarters – country-cottage bedrooms (most with space for a sofabed), big breakfast room with stone country fireplace and little tables – are in a beamy outbuilding and the place still breathes monastic peace. Your farming hosts work hard to maintain their precious legacy, work the land and breed pheasants as well as take in guests. Breakfasts are modest.

rooms	3 doubles.
price	€50–€55.
meals	Restaurants 5km.
closed	Rarely.
directions	A16 exit Neufchâtel Hardelot & Ste Cécile; D940 for Boulogne & Le Touquet; house near church on entering Dannes.

rooms	6: 4 doubles, 2 twins.
price	€58.
meals	Restaurants nearby.
closed	Rarely.
directions	From Calais A16 for Amiens; exit 25, N1 for Montreuil; left for Longvillers; signed.

Christine Lécaille
Le Moulin,
40 rue du Centre, 62187 Dannes,
Pas-de-Calais
tel	+33 (0)3 21 33 74 74
fax	+33 (0)3 21 33 74 74
email	christine.lecaille@free.fr
web	www.au-moulin.com

Anne & Jean-Philippe Delaporte
La Longue Roye,
62630 Longvillers,
Pas-de-Calais
tel	+33 (0)3 21 86 70 65
fax	+33 (0)3 21 86 71 32
email	longue-roye@la-longue-roye.com
web	www.la-longue-roye.com

Map 1 Entry 14

Map 1 Entry 15

Birdy Land

These two are fabulously alive, attentive and cultivated. Georges, a painter, is a majestic figure, well able to talk at the same time as charming Marie... an irresistible double act. The well-proportioned house is an architectural flourish, the contents a classic mix of antique and modern, and there's a new dayroom/bar for guests. Two bedrooms share a balcony terrace and a separate entrance, the third is smaller; all are cosily cossetting with chintz quilts and the odd antique. The landscaped crescents and avenues are restful, the sea is ten minutes away, the garden tended and beautiful. Perfect for families.

rooms	3: 1 double, 1 twin, 1 triple.
price	€75.
meals	Choice of restaurants within walking distance.
closed	Rarely.
directions	From A16 Le Touquet exit; through Étaples; follow signs for Le Touquet centre. After 4th lights, 2nd right for Holiday Inn. 2nd house on right.

Georges & Marie Versmée
Birdy Land,
Avenue du Maréchal Foch,
62520 Le Touquet, Pas-de-Calais

tel	+33 (0)3 21 05 31 46
fax	+33 (0)3 21 05 95 07
mobile	+33 (0)6 80 66 55 88
email	georges.versmee@wanadoo.fr

Map 1 Entry 16

---

14 rue de l'École

Madame once dealt in antiques and now makes pastries (delicious ones), Monsieur potters creatively in his workshop, both are a delight to meet. The guest rooms in the long, low farmhouse are warm, old-fashioned, comfy and clean; those in the cottage are fresher in style – and perfectly private for two families. Generous breakfast is brought when you want it, to a long friendly table. Outside is gravel, grass, crazy paving and space for run-around children, all protected from the passing road. Come for coastline walks, farmhouse cheeses in the village, and a hugely kind and very French welcome.

rooms	2 + 1: 2 doubles. 1 cottage for 2-10.
price	€50.
meals	Restaurants 2-10km.
closed	Never.
directions	From Calais South A16 exit 27 to Neufchatel-Hardelot on D308; 6km D113 to Le Turne. House on left in centre of hamlet, 1.5km before village of Frencq.

M & Mme Delabie
14 rue de l'École,
Le Turne,
62630 Frencq,
Pas-de-Calais

tel	+33 (0)3 21 06 10 96

Map 1 Entry 17

Le Vert Bois

Ancient peace, delightful people, fields as far as the eye can see. And it's majestic for a farm — the house, outbuildings and courtyard are immaculately preserved. Young Étienne, Véronique and their family grow cereals, keep cows and look after guests — charmingly — in a converted cowshed. Upstairs are a cosy double and a pretty twin; ceilings slope, walls are spotless, bedcovers quilted, bathrooms pristine. A log-fired day room with a kitchen and sofas is in the offing. The rampart town of Montreuil is minutes away for shops, restaurants and "astonishing points of view".

rooms	2: 1 double, 1 twin.
price	€50.
meals	Choice of restaurants nearby.
closed	Rarely.
directions	From Montreuil, arriving in Neuville, right opp. antique shop; after 0.5km left at fork; signed.

	Étienne & Véronique Bernard
	Le Vert Bois,
	62170 Neuville sous Montreuil,
	Pas-de-Calais
tel	+33 (0)3 21 06 09 41
fax	+33 (0)3 21 06 09 41
email	etienne.bernard6@wanadoo.fr
web	gite.montreuil.online.fr

Map 1   Entry 18

La Rodière

Behind a grand old façade in lovely Montreuil hides the wonder of an free-standing wooden staircase, a local speciality in the 17th century. Two spacious rooms up here with high ceilings, parquet floors: the twin over the street has elegant original cupboards; the double over the back is cosily alcoved. Families will like the privacy of the snugger room across the yard: pretty blue head cushions and duvet-clothed bunks. There's a softly lit guest sitting room, too. The baths could fill more speedily but the buffet breakfasts are plenteous and Madame is the calmest, smiliest, most unobtrusive hostess.

rooms	4: 2 doubles, 1 twin, 1 family room.
price	€55–€60.
meals	Restaurant 50m.
closed	Rarely.
directions	In Montreuil, drive to top, Place Darnétal; house on right facing square.

	Mme Louchez
	La Rodière,
	77 rue Pierre Ledent,
	62170 Montreuil sur Mer,
	Pas-de-Calais
tel	+33 (0)3 21 81 54 68
mobile	+33 (0)6 84 01 36 84
email	louchez.anne@wanadoo.fr
web	www.larodiere.com

Map 1   Entry 19

Ferme du Saule

Readers have called Le Saule "a little treasure". And we know that the Trunnets' smiles are genuine, their converted outbuilding handsome and perfectly finished (down to mosquito nets on windows), the ground-floor rooms solidly traditional, the beds excellent, the dayroom proud of its beautiful armoire and you get your own little table for breakfast. Monsieur and his son are only too happy to show you the flax production process (it's fascinating); young Madame looks after the baby and cares beautifully for guests. Proclaimed "the best cowshed I've ever stayed in" by one happy guest.

rooms	5: 1 double, 3 family rooms for 3, 1 suite for 4.
price	€50.
meals	Restaurants 6km.
closed	Rarely.
directions	From A16 exit Montreuil; just before town right at lights; left D349 to Brimeux; left at junction, pass church, house on right, sign. From N39 exit Campagne les Hesdin.

Famille Trunnet
Ferme du Saule,
20 rue de l'Église,
62170 Brimeux, Pas-de-Calais
tel   +33 (0)3 21 06 01 28
fax   +33 (0)3 21 81 40 14
web   perso.wanadoo.fr/fermedusaule

Map 1 Entry 20

L'Overgne

A calm unaffected welcome and not even a cockerel to disturb the peace. Madame is as self-assured and down-to-earth as you would expect of someone who brought up nine children on the farm. The farmhouse, built in 1724, has a natural family feel. Rooms are simple and dated, shower rooms basic. The twin in the main house has country fabrics and a wooden floor; the double in the old stables is more intimate. Good breakfasts include cheese and homemade jam on fresh baguettes and croissants. Madame is a fount of local knowledge and loves getting to know her guests properly. Best in summer.

rooms	2: 1 double, 1 twin.
price	€45-€50.
meals	Restaurants 3km.
closed	December-February.
directions	From A16 exit 26 to Montreuil; D349 for Hesdin; through Beaumerie St Martin; 1st right at sign.

Francis & Jeanne-Marie
Locqueville
L'Overgne,
62170 Beaumerie St Martin,
Pas-de-Calais
tel   +33 (0)3 21 81 81 87
email   jmarie.locqueville@wanadoo.fr

Map 1 Entry 21

La Hotoire

New owners have arrived at the farmhouse by the village church – along with two donkeys, one cockerel, a clutch of hens, a cat and a dog. The farmhouse was built in Picardian style around a central courtyard and now the outbuildings house the guests. Ground-floor rooms have wonky timbers, cream tiled floors, pastel colours, modern bathrooms, private entrances and are decently spacious. There's also a light-filled day room for breakfast. Walk in the hills and woods behind and spot the wild deer – maybe one of the sweet donkeys will accompany you – or rent bikes in Hesdin. Ideal for young families.

rooms	7: 1 double; 2 triples, 4 quadruples, each with kitchenette, shower & separate wc.
price	€46. Suite €68.
meals	Restaurants 3-4km.
closed	Rarely.
directions	From Hesdin D928 for St Omer; 1st left D913 through Huby St Leu to Guisy; signposted.

Christophe & Emmanuelle Buisine
La Hotoire,
2 place de la Mairie,
62140 Guisy,
Pas-de-Calais

tel	+33 (0)3 21 81 00 31
fax	+33 (0)3 21 81 00 31
email	a.la.hotoire@wanadoo.fr
web	www.lahotoire.com

Map 1 Entry 22

Ferme Prévost de Courmière

The farmhouse is old: 1680 is depicted in black flint on the façade. Here are comfort and peace in great measure: fine white and floral bed linen, freshly draped bedheads and oriental rugs. With the house restoration behind them, your ex-Parisian hosts are turning their stylish attention to the central (concreted) courtyard, reviving the old orchard and calmly embarking on B&B. Bedrooms (one on the ground floor, the suite spread over two) are pure, fresh, new and extremely charming. Breakfast is a moveable feast; dinner promises Flemish dishes served at a large table in a light, lofty room.

rooms	2: 1 double, 1 suite for 4, each with sitting room.
price	€50-€70.
meals	Dinner with wine, €24.
closed	Rarely.
directions	From Calais; A16 south, exit 26, N39 to Montreuil; N1 to Abbeville, 8km; left N39 to Hesdin, 26km. From Hesdin, D928, 3km; D135 right, 1km to Capelle lès Hesdin. House at end of village, signed.

Annie Lombardet
Ferme Prévost de Courmière,
510 rue de Crécy,
62140 Capelle lès Hesdin,
Pas-de-Calais

tel	+33 (0)3 21 81 16 04
fax	+33 (0)3 21 81 16 04
email	ferme-prevost-de-courmiere@wanadoo.fr
web	prevostdecourmiere.monsite.wanadoo.fr

Map 1 Entry 23

The North

Ferme de la Vallée

This is a real farm, so don't expect pretty-pretty – but Madame is a character and her welcome's top class. Readers return, for the atmosphere and the food. Amazing how much space lies behind the simple frontage of this streetside farmhouse, and every little corner is crammed with 40 years' worth of collecting: porcelain, plates, jugs, baskets of crystal decanter stoppers, collectable plastics – the list is long. Come for comfy beds, spacious dayroom areas, billiards, table football (a vintage table) and games. It's intrinsically French despite the eccentricities – and Madame is huge fun.

rooms	3: 1 twin, 1 triple, 1 suite.
price	€42.
meals	Dinner with wine, €16.
closed	Rarely.
directions	Exit Thérouanne from A26; then D341 for Arras; after 'Vert Dragon' r'bout, 1st on right.

Brigitte de Saint Laurent
Ferme de la Vallée,
13 rue Neuve,
62190 Auchy au Bois,
Pas-de-Calais

tel	+33 (0)3 21 25 80 09
fax	+33 (0)3 21 25 80 09
email	brigitte.de-saint-laurent@wanadoo.fr
web	fermedelavallee.free.fr

Map 1 Entry 24

The North

Les Cohettes

Elegant and vivacious Gina cares deeply that everyone be happy, adores her guests and does brilliant *table d'hôtes*. A full house makes quite a crowd and when B&B and gîte guests come together there can be over a dozen at table. But the spacious garden opens its arms to all and has some comforting mature trees under which guests may link up for summer pétanque. Pretty and cosy bedrooms in the attic of the long low farmhouse are colour coded, while the garden suite is snug with its own little patio. No cockerels, no barking dogs, just an affectionate tabby cat basking in the sun. Readers love it all.

rooms	4: 2 doubles, 1 twin, 1 family suite for 4.
price	€50-€55.
meals	Dinner with wine, €22.
closed	Rarely.
directions	From Calais A26, exit 4 to Thérouanne; D341 to Auchy au Bois, 12km. Right at Le Vert Dragon restaurant. 1st left; 2nd house on right after church.

Gina Bulot
Les Cohettes,
28 rue de Pernes,
62190 Auchy au Bois,
Pas-de-Calais

tel	+33 (0)3 21 02 09 47
mobile	+33 (0)6 07 06 65 42
email	temps-libre-evasion@wanadoo.fr
web	www.chambresdhotes-chezgina.com

Map 1 Entry 25

La Gacogne

Enter a 1750 arched orangery (the tower) filled with a very long table, an open fire and 101 curiosities. Alongside teddies… chain-mail bodices, longbows, crossbows and similar armoured reminders of nearby Agincourt greet the eye. It is a treat to be received in this most colourful and eccentric of parlours for hearty continental breakfasts and hostly diligence. Motherly Marie-José and knightly Patrick have lived here for years. Small bedrooms in the outbuilding are farmhouse simple with heavy-draped medieval touches, a lush garden melts into a conifer copse and your hosts are charmingly eccentric.

rooms	4: 3 doubles, 1 triple.
price	€54. Triple €65.
meals	Restaurant 1km, choice 6-15km.
closed	Rarely.
directions	From St Omer D928 for Abbeville. At Ruisseauville left for Blangy-Tramecourt; at next x-roads, left for Tramecourt; house 100m along.

Patrick & Marie-José Fenet
La Gacogne,
62310 Azincourt,
Pas-de-Calais
tel   +33 (0)3 21 04 45 61
fax   +33 (0)3 21 04 45 61
email fenetgeoffroy@aol.com
web   www.gacogne.new.fr

Map 1 Entry 26

Le Loubarré

What an exciting building. The period of each piece shows on its face, so you expect the elegantly coffered ceilings, the deeply carved woodwork, the vast Louis XIII dresser – but nothing prepares you for the '1830s-medieval' fireplace! In the converted stables, bedrooms are simple and modern, each with pretty fabrics, some old furniture, a neat shower room. Madame loves telling tales of the house and its contents, has a few goats in the quiet garden (a weekend racetrack in the valley, though), and will do anything for her guests. Both your hosts work constantly on their beloved house – good people.

rooms	5: 2 doubles, 3 twins.
price	€44.
meals	Restaurants within walking distance.
closed	Rarely.
directions	From St Pol sur Ternoise, D343 NW for Fruges. Just after entering Gauchin Verloingt, right Rue de Troisvaux; right Rue des Montifaux. House on right.

Marie-Christine & Philippe Vion
Le Loubarré,
550 rue des Montifaux,
62130 Gauchin Verloingt,
Pas-de-Calais
tel   +33 (0)3 21 03 05 05
fax   +33 (0)3 21 41 26 76
email mcvion.loubarre@wanadoo.fr
web   www.loubarre.com

Map 1 Entry 27

La Maison de Campagne

Perched on a hill with delightful views over garden and meadow to valley beyond, a newish house and super B&B. Many people drive straight through this area so take the chance to know it with people who belong; after years as a librarian, Madame has thrown herself into local tourism and loves taking guests on visits – particularly horticultural ones. You enter through the conservatory, every window has the view and bedrooms, one up, one down, are simple but welcoming. Children love it here, farm trips are possible, and you might be treated to homemade brioche, walnut wine and genuine French cooking.

rooms	2: 1 family suite; 1 double with separate wc.
price	€40.
meals	Dinner with wine, €20.
closed	Rarely.
directions	From Calais, exit 5, D916 for St Pol/Ternoise. In Cauchy à la Tour, D341 left to Arras, Division, Houdain. At 'STOP' in Houdain; D86 right to Magnicourt en Comté. In village, follow signs 'Mairie, École, Eglise'.

Jacqueline Guillemant
La Maison de Campagne,
6 rue de l'Europe,
62127 Magnicourt en Comté,
Pas-de-Calais

tel +33 (0)3 21 41 51 00
fax +33 (0)3 21 04 79 76
email jguillemant@hotmail.com
web www.lamaisondecampagne.com

Map 1 Entry 28

Ferme du Moulin

Terraced houses in front, a perfect little farmyard behind, the friendliest of hosts within – it's a privilege to meet such splendid human beings, retired farmers of old-fashioned simple good manners, he silently earthy, tending his garden, she comfortably maternal, delighting in her freedom to indulge her wanderlust at last. Their pretty, old-fashioned French farmers' house is stuffed with collections of bric-a-brac; their genuine *chambres d'hôtes* are family-furnished, floral-papered, draped with all sorts and conditions of crochet. Breakfasts are good and you are perfectly placed for those battlefields.

rooms	2: 1 double, 1 triple, each with shower & separate bath, sharing wc.
price	€38.
meals	Restaurants 500m.
closed	Rarely.
directions	A26 from Calais, exit Aix-Noulette for Liévin. Head for 'centre ville'; for Givenchy. House 300m past little park.

M & Mme François Dupont
Ferme du Moulin,
58 rue du Quatre Septembre,
62800 Liévin,
Pas-de-Calais

tel +33 (0)3 21 44 65 91

Map 1 Entry 29

The North

Château de Grand Rullecourt

An exceptional mix of place and people. This dynamic family, all eight of them, have almost finished rebuilding their monumental château and brightening their coat of arms while being publishers in Paris and brilliant socialites – fascinating people, phenomenal energy, natural hospitality that makes up for any residual damp or slight winter chill. Built in 1745, the château has striking grandeur: come play lord and lady in chandeliered, ancestored salons, discover an aristocratic bedroom with big windows and walk the rolling green parkland as if it were your own. Enter another world.

rooms	4 twins/doubles.
price	€90.
meals	Restaurants within 4km.
closed	Rarely.
directions	From Arras N39 for St Pol & Le Touquet 5km; left D339 to Avesnes le Comte; D75 for Doullens & Grand Rullecourt 4km. Château in village square; sign.

	Patrice & Chantal de Saulieu
	Château de Grand Rullecourt,
	62810 Grand Rullecourt,
	Pas-de-Calais
tel	+33 (0)3 21 58 06 37
fax	+33 (0)1 41 27 97 30
email	c.de.saulieu.gr@tiscali.fr
web	www.chateaux-chambres-hotes.com

Map 1 Entry 30

The North

Château de Saulty

The re lifted stately face looks finer than ever in its great park and apple orchards. Inside, it's a warm, embracing country house with a panelled breakfast room, an amazing, museum-worthy, multi-tiled gents cloakroom and, up the wide old stairs, quietly luxurious bedrooms, some very big, furnished with printed fabrics and period pieces. Be charmed by wooden floors and plain walls in sunny tones, perhaps an old fireplace or a mirrored armoire. Quiet and intelligent, Sylvie will make you feel deeply welcome while serenely concocting delicious jams and managing her young family.

rooms	4: 1 double, 1 triple, 2 suites for 4.
price	€55. Suites €80.
meals	Choice of restaurants 1-9km.
closed	January.
directions	From Doullens N25 towards Arras 17km. In L'Arbret, 1st left to Saulty; follow signs.

	Emmanuel & Sylvie Dalle
	Château de Saulty,
	82 rue de la Gare, 62158 Saulty,
	Pas-de-Calais
tel	+33 (0)3 21 48 24 76
fax	+33 (0)3 21 48 18 32
mobile	+33 (0)6 14 13 16 69
email	chateaudesaulty@nordnet.fr

Map 1 Entry 31

Heerenhuys

Helped by the innate character of the solid old house, Béatrice has applied her artist's talent to the interiors. Tempting ground-floor rooms brim with pictures, antique porcelains, original frieze and pieces handed down from previous generations; bedrooms sing with bright but gentle colours. All are light and harmonious with marble fireplaces, hand-painted furniture and big shower rooms. Roger is as relaxed and generous as his wife; their three teenagers are well-mannered, their dinners are based on real Flemish specialities. The garden is bustling-English-landscape style with formal touches.

Château de Courcelette

From a small-town back street you enter unexpected 18th-century elegance — pilasters, panelling, marble, medallions — then cross a beautiful brick and cobble terrace into an acre of superb walled garden: bliss on the doorstep of Lille and the oldest château left standing in the area. Your hosts will enchant you with their courtesy and deep love for Courcelette, their energy in preserving its classical forms, their care for your comfort; Madame bubbles and chats, Monsieur charms quietly. Pale bedrooms with original doors and handsome antiques set the tone for this quietly luxurious and deeply civilised house.

rooms	4: 2 doubles, 2 triples.
price	€70.
meals	Occasional dinner €25. Wine from €5.
closed	Rarely.
directions	From A25 exit 28 on N225 & A25 for Lille; exit 13 on D948 for Poperinghe; immed. right to Goderwaersveld; D139 to Boeschepe; house on left, just after windmill.

rooms	4: 1 twin/double, 2 doubles, 1 suite for 4.
price	€84.
meals	Dinner with wine €30.
closed	Never.
directions	On Villeneuve d'Ascq road; exit Roubaix Est. for Wattrelos; left at 2nd r'bout to Lys Lez Lannoy; after 100m left to Lannoy; at x-roads follow 'les orchidées', right at Rue St Jacques, 2nd right, right into blind alley.

Roger & Béatrice Maerten
Heerenhuys,
340 rue de la Gare,
59299 Boeschepe,
Nord
tel   +33 (0)3 28 49 45 73
email   info@boeschepe.com
web   www.boeschepe.com

Famille Brame
Château de Courcelette,
17 rue César Parent,
59390 Lannoy, Nord
tel   +33 (0)3 20 75 45 67
fax   +33 (0)3 20 75 45 67
email   contact@chateau-de-courcelette.com
web   chateau-de-courcelette.com

Map 1 Entry 32

Map 1 Entry 33

28 rue des Hannetons

Jeanine Hulin's townhouse reflects her warm, colourful, informal personality and painter's eye. Bright kitchen, snug salon and flowering conservatory – step by step towards the little garden – show masterly use of colour; old tiles, stripped pine doors, masses of plants add atmosphere. Sprightly and dynamic, she adores receiving guests and is a mine of tips for antique and brocante trawlers. Bedrooms are interestingly unsmart: matching sleigh bed, wardrobe and desk, antique bed linen and mirrors, claw-footed bath downstairs for the double (bathrobes supplied). *Will collect from railway station.*

rooms	2: 1 twin; 1 twin with shower, sharing wc on floor below.
price	€55–€60.
meals	Choice of restaurants in town.
closed	August.
directions	From Calais/Dunkirk A25 exit 3 for Faches Thumesnil/Ronchim. At r'bout, 1st right. After 2km, right onto rue Armand Carrel. 2nd right at traffic lights and immed. right onto rue Lesage Senault. Right onto rue des Hannetons.

Jeannine Hulin
28 rue des Hannetons,
59000 Lille,
Nord
tel +33 (0)3 20 53 46 12
fax +33 (0)3 20 53 46 12
email janinehulin@wanadoo.fr

Map 1 Entry 34

Ferme de la Noyelle

The 17th-century archway leads into a typical enclosed farmyard where you feel sheltered and welcomed: these attentive dairy farmers and their young family love having guests. Once installed, you can hardly believe that this patch of countryside is surrounded by shopping outlets and transport links. Guest rooms in the old stables – the standard conversion job includes a kitchen – are in simple cottagey style with careful colour matches and wide showers. Another wing houses a modest restaurant open at weekends. Good value, lovely people – and Belgium five minutes away. *Direct metro to Lille.*

rooms	4: 1 double, 1 twin, 1 triple, 1 family room.
price	€42.
meals	Dinner with wine, €15. Guest kitchen.
closed	Rarely.
directions	A16 from Calais to Dunkerque; A25 to Lille; A1 to Paris, after 1km follow A22 Bruxelles for 1km; exit 2 Cysoing/cité scientifique. At Sainghin follow the signs for Chambres d'Hôtes.

Dominique & Nelly Pollet
Ferme de la Noyelle,
832 rue Pasteur,
59262 Sainghin en Mélantois,
Nord
tel +33 (0)3 20 41 29 82
mobile +33 (0)6 74 85 61 79
email dominique-nelly.pollet@wanadoo.fr
web perso.wanadoo.fr/dpollet/

Map 1 Entry 35

Picardy

La Bergerie

That simple face hides character and riches: a pink, beamed living room, marble floor, old fireplace and some good antiques; an overwhelmingly pretty breakfast room full of *objets trouvés* and plants; two smart, mostly pink bedrooms, one reached by a steep spiral outside stair, which can also be a suite: fine linen, good bathrooms, beams and views over the 12th-century church and the large lush garden. Your hosts are a touch French-formal yet terrifically friendly and interesting. Outside, a summer kitchen/diner, an avenue of poplars swishing, a pony grazing, bantams scuttling – what a picture!

rooms	2 doubles, each with extra single bed.
price	€60-€65.
meals	Restaurants 5km.
closed	Rarely.
directions	From Paris A16 exit 24 (25 from Calais); N1 for Montreuil 25km; in Vron left to Villers; right Rue de l'Église (opp. café); at end of road, left unpaved lane; house left up poplar tree avenue.

Pierre & Sabine
Singer de Wazières
La Bergerie,
80120 VIllers sur Authie,
Somme
tel +33 (0)3 22 29 21 74

Map 1 Entry 36

Picardy

Le Thurel

The open mansion and enclosed farmyard (horses welcome) announce gentle contrasts and that deceptively simple sobriety that turns every patch of colour, every rare object into a rich reward. The minimalist basics of your delightful artistic hosts are white, ivory, sand; floors are pine with ethnic rugs by big new beds; blue, ginger or red details shine out, the setting sun fills a round window, great-grandfather's Flemish oil paintings are perfect finishing touches. Drink in the white-panelled, open-hearthed, brown-leather sitting room, revel in the pale, uncluttered dining room, good food – and a games room.

rooms	4: 3 doubles, 1 suite for 4.
price	€85-€150.
meals	Dinner €29. Wine €8-€35.
closed	1-15 January.
directions	From A16 exit 24 for Boulogne through Bernay en Ponthieu then 1st left; through Arry; 1km beyond, left to Le Thurel after great barn.

Claudine & Patrick
van Bree-Leclef
Le Thurel,
Relais de Campagne,
80120 Rue, Somme
tel   +33 (0)3 22 25 04 44
fax   +33 (0)3 22 25 79 69
email lethurel.relais@libertysurf.fr
web   www.lethurel.com

Map 1 Entry 37

Picardy

Château des Alleux

A horn of plenty. The potager gives artichokes, asparagus, peaches and pears, the farmyard chickens, the fields lamb, the woods game... and they make their own cider. The château has been in the family since the Revolution; its pretty blue and yellow guest room has a four-poster and overlooks that munificent garden. Rooms in the cottage are modern, low-ceilinged and softly lit; both have kitchenettes, ideal for families, and the mezzanine suite has a log fire. Dense trees protect from distant motorway hum; home-produced dinners and local wines, shared in the château with your engaging hosts, are a treat.

rooms	3: 2 doubles, 1 family suite (2 with kitchenettes).
price	€55–€65.
meals	Dinner with wine, €20.
closed	Rarely.
directions	From Calais A16 for Abbeville onto A28 for Rouen 4km; exit Monts Caubert 3; right at stop sign; D928 to Croisettes; right for Les Alleux not Béhen.

	René-François & Élisabeth de Fontanges Château des Alleux, Les Alleux, 80870 Béhen, Somme
tel	+33 (0)3 22 31 64 88
fax	+33 (0)3 22 31 64 88
email	chateaudesalleux@wanadoo.fr

Map 1 Entry 38

Picardy

3 rue d'Inval

It feels imposing, this very fine house with its extraordinary staircase, but you soon relax into the homely atmosphere created by your calm, hospitable, country hosts – the first in the Somme to open their house for B&B. Aart grows thousands of tulips and dahlias in serried ranks, honey, cider and calvados in superb vaulted cellars. Dorette was mayor for 24 years. Her big uncluttered bedrooms (smaller on the second floor) are comfortable, shower rooms big enough for a third bed, views peaceful, the panelled dining room a proper setting for a good breakfast. A great place to stay, with fishing on the lake.

rooms	4: 1 double, 3 triples, all with shower & basin, sharing wc.
price	€42–€45. Triples €60.
meals	Restaurants 12km. Kitchen available.
closed	Rarely.
directions	From Abbeville A28 for Rouen, 28km, exit 5; left at Bouttencourt D1015 to Sénarpont; D211 for Le Mazis, 4.5km; follow Chambres d'Hôtes signs.

	Dorette & Aart Onder de Linden 3 rue d'Inval, 80430 Le Mazis, Somme
tel	+33 (0)3 22 25 90 88
fax	+33 (0)3 22 25 76 04
email	onderdelinden@wanadoo.fr

Map 5 Entry 39

Picardy

1 rue de l'Église

The garden and ancient farmhouse here glow from the loving attention they receive: Françoise 'learned gardens' in England and has made a timbered shrubby delight of the sloping site, Francis loves working with wood and his respectful creativity shines through the gable-end windows. Their lovely big sitting room with its vast fireplace may be your first stop, then up the steep and narrow stairs to pretty white rooms, not huge but uncluttered, fresh and timbered, with floral quilts and compact bathrooms; one wraps itself round a vast chimney breast. A place of friendly peace with an Erard grand piano in the hall.

rooms	4: 1 triple, 2 family rooms, 1 family room & kitchenette.
price	€50. Triple €58. Family room €66.
meals	Restaurant 6km.
closed	Rarely.
directions	From A16 exit 18 to Quévauvillers; right on D38 & D51 through Bussy lès Poix. Last house on left.

Francis & Françoise Guérin
1 rue de l'Église,
80290 Bussy lès Poix,
Somme
tel   +33 (0)3 22 90 06 73
email guerin.francis@free.fr

Map 5 Entry 40

Picardy

L'Herbe de Grâce

You will get a warm northern welcome. Once a social worker, ever-elegant Madame is at ease with all sorts and has the most infectious laugh. Monsieur, a big-hearted, genuine, chatty countryman, is good company too, though they don't breakfast with guests. Your suite, a splendid attic conversion with small windows and private entrance, is furnished with pretty country bric-a-brac and panache. Sitting room, good modern bathroom and kitchenette make it perfect for families. For summer: a lush garden with wrought-iron furniture, lily pond and hens scratching in a pen behind the flowers.

rooms	1 family suite & kitchenette.
price	€50.
meals	Restaurants in Amiens.
closed	November–April, except by arrangement.
directions	From Amiens for Conty on D210.N1 S to Hébécourt 8km. Opp. church follow 'Chambre d'Hôtes' signs to Plachy Buyon.

Mme Jacqueline Pillon
L'Herbe de Grâce,
Hameau de Buyon,
80160 Plachy Buyon,
Somme
tel   +33 (0)3 22 42 12 22
fax   +33 (0)3 22 42 04 42

Map 5 Entry 41

Picardy

Les Aulnaies

The emphasis here is on country family hospitality and Madame, uncomplicated and several times a grandmother, gives guests a wonderful welcome. The rambling garden has stone love-seats and two ponds, swings and a playhouse – a paradise for children – while the old manor house has the feel of an adventure story. Your quarters are nicely independent beyond the hall and your living room leads down to the bedroom; there's plenty of space, a draped bed, and big square French pillows. Most of European history is at your doorstep, from gothic Amiens to the battlefields of the First World War.

rooms	1 suite for 2-4.
price	€50.
meals	Auberge 6km.
closed	December-March.
directions	From Amiens D929 for Albert. At Pont Noyelles, D115 left for Contay; signs in Bavelincourt.

STOP PRESS
no longer doing B&B

Map 1 Entry 42

Picardy

Château d'Omiécourt

On a working estate, Omiécourt is a proudly grand 19th-century château and elegant family house (the Thézys have four teenage children), with tall slender windows and some really old trees. Friendly if formal, communicative and smiling, your hosts have worked hugely to restore their inheritance and create gracious French château guest rooms, each with an ornate fireplace, each named and furnished for a different period and upholstered in Jouy. Fine workmanship shines through oak staircase and carved fireplaces, too. A house of goodwill where you will be very comfortable.

rooms	5: 2 doubles, 2 family rooms, 1 suite for 3.
price	€80.
meals	Light supper €10-€15. Restaurants 12km.
closed	Rarely.
directions	From A1 south for Paris; exit 13 onto N29 for St Quentin; in Villers-Carbonnel right at lights onto N17 for 9km to Omiécourt; right in village, château on right.

	Dominique & Véronique de Thézy
	Château d'Omiécourt,
	80320 Omiécourt, Somme
tel	+33 (0)3 22 83 01 75
fax	+33 (0)3 22 83 09 56
email	thezy@terre-net.fr
web	www.chateau-omiecourt.com

Map 5 Entry 43

Picardy

1 rue Génermont

A dazzling house whose hill-shaped roof becomes a timbered vault way above swathes of natural stone floor. The Picardy sky pours in and fills the vast minimally furnished living space and your hostess shows pleasure at your amazement... then serves you superb food and intelligent conversation. Bedrooms are pure and peaceful: white walls, patches of colour, stone floors, excellent beds and design-conscious bathrooms, 1930s antiques and touches of fun. Civilised seclusion... and modern European history and the First World War battlefields at your door. *Gourmet weekends can be arranged.*

rooms	4: 2 twins, 1 family room, 1 suite for 4.
price	€55–€58.
meals	Dinner with wine, €22–€25.
closed	Rarely.
directions	From A1 exit 13 on N29 for St Quentin; in Villers-Carbonnel, right at r'bout onto N17 for 5km to Fresnes Mazancourt; house next to church.

Martine Warlop
1 rue Génermont,
80320 Fresnes Mazancourt, Somme
tel +33 (0)3 22 85 49 49
fax +33 (0)3 22 85 49 49
email martine.warlop@wanadoo.fr
web www.maison-warlop.com

Map 5 Entry 44

Picardy

La Ferme du Colombier

In a typical big farmyard in a timber-old village stands a round dovecote. Tradition and roses cling to the place, bedrooms in the old bakery are made of space, simple furniture, an Indian cotton throw at each bedhead, magnificent roof timbers and sober carpets – plus two pretty breakfast rooms. Dinner with your active hosts in their lovely open-plan farmhouse room may, for special occasions, include wild herbs and *légumes anciens*. Picnic lunches are good too, and there's masses to see in this ancient land – gothic cathedrals, medieval villages, thriving markets. *20 minutes from Paris-Beauvais airport.*

rooms	4: 2 doubles, 1 triple, 1 quadruple.
price	€42–€43. Triple €55.
meals	Dinner with wine, €16–€19. Picnic hampers.
closed	Rarely.
directions	From Beauvais N31 for Rouen. Leaving Beauvais follow to Savignies. Farm in village, 50m from church.

Annick & Jean-Claude Leturque
La Ferme du Colombier,
60650 Savignies, Oise
tel +33 (0)3 44 82 18 49
fax +33 (0)3 44 82 53 70
email ferme.colombier@wanadoo.fr
web www.fermecolombier.org/

Map 5 Entry 45

Picardy

La Pointe

King of concrete in 1927, Auguste Perret added a piece of design history to a pretty 18th-century house: an immense living room of squares in squares (panels, shelving, tiles, table) and above, a green and puce Perret-panelled bedroom with a flourish of columns, super 1930s furniture, terrace and vast view. Other rooms have lovely ethnic fabrics, much light, sophisticated bathrooms. Extrovert Monsieur and Madame, who is Scottish, join you for magnificent meals around a vast table. They are mad about horses; the pasture is part of the view. And the train can carry you straight from the village to Paris… and back again.

rooms	3: 1 double, 1 triple, 1 quadruple.
price	€55.
meals	Dinner with wine, €25.
closed	Rarely.
directions	From Calais A16 exit 13 (Méru) for Chaumont en Vexin. In Loconville, left to Liancourt St Pierre; right to post office & follow left into Rue du Donjon (no through road); high gate on left.

Fiona & Luc Gallot
La Pointe,
10 rue du Donjon, 60240
Liancourt St Pierre, Oise
tel   +33 (0)3 44 49 32 08
fax   +33 (0)3 44 49 32 08
email   lucgallot@wanadoo.fr
web   www.la-pointe.com

Map 5 Entry 46

Picardy

La Maison Nature

Doze under the lilacs, gaze over plains, take an aperitif to the terrace. This is lazy, languorous living. Guests stay in two granite cottages but share the lovely rambling garden of this elegant, shuttered, 19th-century house. Charming with whitewash and open-stone walls, wooden and iron bedsteads, floral quilts and snug seats, bedrooms are touched with candles and treats. One bathroom (minimalist-pretty) is perched among the rafters. Breakfast beautifully at the long dining table – or in the view-filled garden where ladders and swings hang from ancient trees. Spirited Claudine, ex-media, is mother of three.

rooms	2 doubles.
price	€80-€95.
meals	Dinner with wine, €18.
closed	Never.
directions	From Gisors D15 to Paris for 4km; right after leisure park to Montjavoult; over x-roads to Le Vouast; 1st right onto Chemin Vert; after small car park house on left, big wooden gates.

Claudine & Patrik Coze
La Maison Nature,
17 rue du Chemin Vert,
Le Vouast,
s60240 Montjavoult, Oise
mobile +33 (0)6 60 75 45 56
email   lamaisonnature@orange.fr
web   www.lamaisonnature.com

Map 5 Entry 47

Picardy

Le Clos

The sprucest of farmhouses, whitewashed and Normandy-beamed, sits in the lushest, most secret of gardens, reached via a door in the wall. Inside, a remarkably fresh, open-plan and modernised interior, with a comfortable sitting room to share. Your bedroom, white, fresh, neat, uncluttered and warm, is above the garage; the bedding is the best, the shower room pretty with coloured towels. Dine with your informative hosts by the old farm fireplace on *tarte aux pommes du jardin* — Monsieur is chef, Madame, a primary school teacher, keeps you gentle company. A peaceful spot, close to Paris.

Picardy

Le Château de Fosseuse

Your window looks over the great landscaped park fading away to wooded hillside (with railway), beneath you is the soft grandeur of 16th-century brick. The grand staircase flounces up to big canopied glorious-viewed bedrooms that are château-worthy (one looks over the private lake) but not posh. The sweetest is the double over the library/breakfast room: open the panelling to find the secret stair. Your hosts are a fascinating, cultured marriage of exquisite French manners and Irish warmth who labour on to save their family home and genuinely enjoy sharing it with guests. *Children over four welcome.*

	Le Clos		Le Château de Fosseuse
rooms	1 family room for 3.	rooms	3: 2 doubles, 1 suite.
price	€50. €62 for 3.	price	€77–€97. Suite €150.
meals	Dinner with wine, €25.	meals	Choice of restaurants 2-10km.
closed	Rarely.	closed	Rarely.
directions	From A16 exit 13 for Gisors & Chaumont en Vexin about 20km; after Fleury left to Fay les Étangs; 2nd left; house on left.	directions	From A16 exit 13 for Esches D923; in Fosseuse, château gate on right at traffic lights.

Philippe & Chantal Vermeire
Le Clos,
3 rue du Chêne Noir,
60240 Fay les Étangs, Oise
tel +33 (0)3 44 49 92 38
fax +33 (0)3 44 49 92 38
email philippe.vermeire@wanadoo.fr
web www.leclosdefay.com

Shirley & Jean-Louis Marro
Le Château de Fosseuse,
60540 Fosseuse,
Oise
tel +33 (0)3 44 08 47 66
fax +33 (0)3 44 08 47 66
email chateau.fosseuse@wanadoo.fr
web www.chateau-de-fosseuse.fr

Map 5 Entry 48

Map 5 Entry 49

Picardy

Château de Saint Vincent

An enchantment for garden lovers who want real old château style but not plush bathrooms. Madame is still repairing her 200-year-old family home and garden, her great love – complete with stream and island – and a work of art. The house is elegantly well-worn, you breakfast in a darkly handsome room, sit in a totally French oak-panelled salon, sleep in 210cm-long antique sleigh beds. The second bedroom is simpler, and the washing arrangements, with continental bath, not American standard. But Madame's passion for house and garden will convince you. *Children over 10 welcome.*

rooms	2: 2 twins. Child's room available.
price	€100.
meals	Auberge 3km.
closed	15 October–15 May.
directions	From Senlis D330 for Borest & Nanteuil for 8km; right at cemetery; 1st right; across Place du Tissard towards big farm; left Rue de la Ferme; gates at bottom: No 1.

Hélène Merlotti
Château de Saint Vincent,
1 rue Élisabeth Roussel,
60300 Borest, Oise

tel   +33 (0)3 44 54 21 52
fax   +33 (0)3 44 54 21 52

Map 5 Entry 50

Picardy

La Gaxottière

The high walls look daunting? Fear not, they protect a secret garden, a goldfish pond, lots of intriguing mementos and a merry laughing lady – a retired chemist who loves her dogs, travelling and contact with visitors. In the old house, the two mellow, beamed, fireplaced rooms are like drawing rooms with old pieces and exquisite fabrics (and kettle, etc); the fine new suite is above. Madame lives in the brilliantly converted barn; all is harmony and warmth among the family antiques. Drink it all in with this great soul's talk of France and the world. Sleep in peace, wake to the dawn chorus and breakfast in the sunshine.

rooms	3: 1 double, 1 twin, 1 family suite.
price	€50–€55.
meals	Restaurants 4–6km.
closed	Rarely. Book ahead.
directions	From A1 exit 10 for Compiègne, 4km. By caravan yard right at small turning for Jaux. 1st right to Varanval, over hill. House on right opp. château gates.

Françoise Gaxotte
La Gaxottière,
60880 Jaux Varanval, Oise

tel   +33 (0)3 44 83 22 41
fax   +33 (0)3 44 83 22 41
mobile   +33 (0)6 87 77 28 05
email   lagaxottiere@tele2.fr

Map 5 Entry 51

Picardy

La Commanderie

Up here on the hill is a Templar hamlet and a millennium of history: an enclosed farmyard, a ruined medieval chapel that frames the sunrise, a magnificent tithe barn with leaping oak timbers – and this modern house. Marie-José, an unhurried grandmother of generous spirit, welcomes genuinely, loves the history and cooks her own produce deliciously. Perfectly clean and equipped bedrooms are in plain farm style but open the window and you fall into heaven, the view soars away on all sides of the hill, even to Laon cathedral. One of the most peaceful places to stay in all Picardy.

rooms	3: 1 double, 1 family suite for 4, 1 family suite for 3.
price	€41–€46.
meals	Dinner with wine, €15.
closed	Rarely.
directions	From Calais A26 for Reims, exit 12 to Crécy-sur-Serre; D35 to Pont à Bucy; 1st left to Nouvion & Catillon; D26 right for La Ferté Chevresis, 4km; small lane left up hill to Catillon. Drive through farm on left. Signs.

Marie-José Carette
La Commanderie,
Catillon du Temple,
02270 Nouvion et Catillon, Aisne
tel   +33 (0)3 23 56 51 28
fax   +33 (0)3 23 56 50 14
mobile   +33 (0)6 82 33 22 64
email   carette.jm@wanadoo.fr

Map 5 Entry 52

Picardy

2 rue St Martin

The village on one side, the expansive estate on the other, the 18th-century wine-grower's house in between. There's a civilised mood here: your smiley hosts so well-mannered and breakfast served with silver and choice china. The guest sitting room has a more antiquated feel. Wake to rooftop views in rooms with soft comfort where, under sloping ceilings, French toile de Jouy is as inviting as English chintz (your hosts spent two years in England) and bathrooms are frilled and pretty. Shrubs hug the hem of the house, a pool is sunk into the lawn behind and Laon trumpets the first gothic cathedral of France.

rooms	3: 1 double, 1 twin; 1 double with separate bath.
price	€55–€60.
meals	Restaurants nearby.
closed	Never.
directions	A26 for Soissons exit 13; after r'bout right to Mons en Laonnois, Clacy & Thierret; from centre of Mons cross flyover; right after 30m.

Mme P Woillez
2 rue St Martin,
02000 Mons en Laonnois,
Aisne
tel   +33 (0)3 23 24 18 58
fax   +33 (0)3 23 24 44 52
email   gitemons@aol.com
web   www.domainedeletang.fr

Map 5 Entry 53

Picardy

Le Clos

Authentic country hospitality is yours in the big old house. Madame is kindly and direct; Monsieur is the communicator, knows his local history and loves the hunting horn. It's welcoming and warmly unposh. Floral curtains are matched, walls are Frenchly papered, original painted wainscotting runs throughout, there are funny old prints in bedrooms, comforting clutter in the living room, and touristic posters on passageway walls. Bedrooms are simple but fine; one has a ship's shower room, all look onto green pastures. And there's a small lake for picnics across the narrow road.

rooms	4 : 2 doubles, 1 twin, 1 suite for 5.
price	€45-€50.
meals	Dinner with wine, €20, except Sundays, Mondays & school holidays.
closed	20 October-February, except by arrangement.
directions	From A26-E17 exit 13 on N2 for Laon; 2nd left to Athies sur Laon; D516 to Bruyères & M. 7km; left D967 for Fismes; Chérêt sign leaving Bruyères; house on left entering Chérêt.

Mme Monique Simonnot
Le Clos,
02860 Chérêt,
Aisne
tel   +33 (0)3 23 24 80 64
email   leclos.cheret@club-internet.fr
web   www.lecloscheret.com

Map 5 Entry 54

Picardy

La Quincy

The old family home, faded and weary, timeless and romantic, is well loved and lived in by this charming, natural and quietly elegant couple. Corridors cluttered with books, magazines and traces of family life lead to an octagonal tower, its great double room and child's room across the landing imaginatively set in the space. A fine antique bed on a fine polished floor, charming chintz, erratic plumbing and two parkland views will enchant you. Shrubs hug the feet of the delicious 'troubadour' château, the garden slips into meadow, summer breakfast and dinner (good wine, book ahead) are in the orangery.

rooms	1 suite for 3.
price	€58.
meals	Dinner with wine, €20.
closed	Rarely.
directions	From A26 exit 13 for Laon; Laon bypass for Soissons; N2 approx 15km; left D423; through Nanteuil for La Quincy; château on right outside village.

Jacques & Marie-Catherine Cornu-Langy
La Quincy,
02880 Nanteuil la Fosse,
Aisne
tel   +33 (0)3 23 54 67 76
fax   +33 (0)3 23 54 72 63
email   laquincy@caramail.com

Map 5 Entry 55

Picardy

Domaine de Montaigu

This inviting 18th-century house has, in its vast 1950s extension, a living room heaving with furniture, fabric flowers, an overpowering stone fireplace, some exquisite collections and antiques. There are books, films, music for a relaxing evening with your delightful, gentlemanly hosts, Philippe retired from business, Christian from the army. Montaigu's periods are reflected in three antique-furnished, frilled and furbelowed rooms in pure French style, another done with the heavy wealth of the George V hotel, and *Colette*, an extraordinary 1950s collector's set of mirror-fronted furniture.

rooms	5: 4 doubles, 1 suite for 4.
price	€75–€85.
meals	Dinner with wine, €25.
closed	Rarely.
directions	From Paris north on A1; exit 9 to Compiègne; N31 for Soissons. 5km after Jauzy right onto D943 to Le Soulier (don't take 1st turning to Ambleny). Signed to Domaine.

Philippe de Reyer
Domaine de Montaigu,
16 rue de Montaigu,
02290 Ambleny, Aisne
tel	+33 (0)3 23 74 06 62
fax	+33 (0)3 23 74 06 62
email	info@domainedemontaigu.com
web	www.domainedemontaigu.com

Map 5 Entry 56

Picardy

Ferme de Ressons

At Ressons, you enter the home of a dynamic, intelligent couple who, after a hard day's work running this big farm (Jean-Paul) or being an architect (Valérie) and tending three children, will ply you in apparently leisurely fashion with champagne, excellent dinner and conversation; they also hunt. The deeply-carved Henri III furniture is an admirable family heirloom; rooms are airy and colour-coordinated, beds are beautiful, views roll for miles and sharing facilities seems easy. An elegant, sophisticated house of comfort and relaxed good manners, bordering the champagne region. *Fishing in small lake.*

rooms	5: 1 double, 1 twin, each with bath, sharing wc; 2 doubles, 1 twin, sharing bath & 2 wcs.
price	€48–€50.
meals	Dinner €19. Wine €14, champagne €18.
closed	Rarely.
directions	From Fismes D967 for Fère en Tardenois & Château Thierry 4km. Don't go to Mont St Martin, on 800m beyond turning; white house on left.

Valérie & Jean-Paul Ferry
Ferme de Ressons,
02220 Mont St Martin,
Aisne
tel	+33 (0)3 23 74 71 00
fax	+33 (0)3 23 74 28 88
mobile	+33 (0)6 80 74 17 01

Map 5 Entry 57

Champagne – Ardenne

Champagne – Ardenne

5 rue du Paradis

The Harlauts love entertaining and are keen to provide good value and, even though they produce their own marque of champagne and bottles are for sale, it is for the authentic country cooking and the atmosphere that guests return. Barbecue dinners are regularly served on the terrace overlooking a vast and lovely garden. There are steep narrow stairs up to the warm, wood-floored, uncluttered guest rooms, two of which share a loo – a minor concern as everything is fresh and spotless and they make an excellent family suite. The village is pretty, typical of the delightful Champagne region.

rooms	2 + 1: 1 double, 1 family suite for 2-4. 1 apartment.
price	€46-€50.
meals	Dinner with wine, €25.
closed	January & Easter.
directions	From A26 exit 15 (Reims La Neuvillette) onto N44 for Laon 2km; left to St Thierry; house in village.

Évelyne & Remi Harlaut
5 rue du Paradis,
51220 St Thierry,
Marne

tel	+33 (0)3 26 03 13 75
fax	+33 (0)3 26 03 03 65
email	contact@champagne-harlaut.fr
web	www.champagne-harlaut.fr

Map 6 Entry 58

Champagne – Ardenne

La Brouilletière

Independent champagne growers, the Aristons delight in showing guests round vineyards and cellars (tastings included). Indeed Madame, a wonderful person, started doing B&B for champagne buyers who did not want to leave after tasting! Through the flower-filled courtyard and up a private stair to lovely, light, airy, attic bedrooms with fresh white walls, beams, matching curtains and covers; one has its own kitchenette and the showers are excellent. Breakfast is served in the characterful old family house. A treat to be so near Reims. *Latest bookings 7pm. Minimum stay two nights in family room.*

rooms	4: 3 doubles; 1 family room for 3 & kitchenette.
price	€50-€55. Family room €75 (min. 2 nights).
meals	Choice of restaurants 11km.
closed	3rd week in August.
directions	From A4 exit 22 on N31 Fismes to Jonchery sur Vesle; left D28 to Savigny sur Ardres; right D386 to Crugny 3km; left D23 to Brouillet; house on right, sign.

Remi & Marie Ariston
La Brouilletière,
4 & 8 Grande Rue,
51170 Brouillet, Marne

tel	+33 (0)3 26 97 43 46
fax	+33 (0)3 26 97 49 34
email	contact@champagne-aristonfils.com
web	www.champagne-aristonfils.com

Map 5 Entry 59

Champagne – Ardenne

Ferme de Désiré

A strong, brave woman of character and hidden humour will welcome you to this majestic double-yarded 17th-century farm where she still grows 360 acres of cereals as well as providing real hospitality and good food. It is all simple and real. In the converted stables, guests have a living room with original mangers, log fire and kitchenette, then steep stairs up to two simply decorated, warmly carpeted, roof-lit rooms. You breakfast next to the kitchen but dine at the big old table in the family salon on home-grown vegetables, eggs, poultry and fruit. Fabulous walks to be had in the great Forêt du Gault nearby.

rooms	2: 1 double, 1 twin.
price	€49–€52.
meals	Dinner with wine, €27.
closed	Rarely.
directions	From Calais A26 to St Quentin; D1 to Montmirail; D373 for Sézanne, 7km. On leaving Le Gault left at silo; sign.

Anne & David Chéré-Boutour,
Ferme de Désiré,
51210 Le Gault Soigny,
Marne

tel +33 (0)3 26 81 60 09
fax +33 (0)3 26 81 60 09
email domaine_de_desire@yahoo.fr

Map 5 Entry 60

Champagne – Ardenne

Ferme de Bannay

Bannay bustles with hens, ducks, guinea fowl, turkeys, donkey, sheep, cows, goats… the chatter starts at 6am. Children love this working farm, and its higgledy-piggledy buildings too; school groups come to visit. The house brims with beams, the rooms dance in swags, flowers and antique bits; the piano swarms with candles and photographs and one bathroom is behind a curtain. Our readers have loved the house, the family and the food. Little English is spoken but the welcome is so exceptional, the generosity so genuine, that communication is easy. Superb outings in the area for all.

rooms	3: 1 triple, 1 quadruple, 1 suite for 2-3.
price	€49–€60.
meals	Dinner with wine, €28; with champagne €34.
closed	Rarely.
directions	From Épernay D51 for Sézanne; at Baye, just before church, right D343; at Bannay right; farm before small bridge.

Muguette & Jean-Pierre Curfs,
Ferme de Bannay,
1 rue du Petit Moulin,
51270 Bannay, Marne

tel +33 (0)3 26 52 80 49
fax +33 (0)3 26 59 47 78
email mjpcurfs@aliceadsl.fr

Map 5 Entry 61

Champagne – Ardenne

189 rue Ferdinand Moret

This courageous, endearing couple have flung their rich welcome out into the woods with four newly-redone cottage-cosy bedrooms on top of the lovely big room in their own house 2km away. Éric is a creative handyman, both are ardent trawlers of brocante stalls, the results are an exquisite personal mix of antique styles set against pastel paints, polished floorboards and gorgeously dressed beds. There's a handsome old-fitted kitchen/diner, too, in the house in the woods, plus piano, bar billiards and a big new garden. Sylvie and Éric bend over backwards to bring you delicious, fresh meals and their sparkling presence.

rooms	5: 2 doubles, 1 twin/double, 1 suite for 4. House in woods: 1 double with separate bath & wc.
price	€55–€60. Suite €90–€95.
meals	Restaurants nearby. Guest kitchen.
closed	December-February.
directions	From Épernay, Place de la République, D3 for Châlons; right at 1st r'bout, right at 2nd r'bout for Avize; 1st right for Cramant.

Sylvie & Éric Charbonnier
189 rue Ferdinand Moret,
51530 Cramant, Marne

tel +33 (0)3 26 57 95 34
mobile +33 (0)6 12 09 67 79
email eric-sylvie@wanadoo.fr
web www.ericsylvie.com

Map 6 Entry 62

Champagne – Ardenne

Le Vieux Cèdre

The façade and trees are grand, the interior is gorgeous – the huge, original-panelled dining room looks straight through its 'fireplace window' to a grassy slope – the atmosphere is hospitably informal, a mix of old and new, French and English, champagne and motor-biking. With flair and drive, Imogen has created brilliant bedrooms: two have space, light and luxurious sitting/bathrooms; the smaller has a richly canopied bed, an oriental air, a great claw-footed bath. She is a lively mother of two; Didier makes the champagne and continues his fine restoration work.

rooms	3: 2 doubles, 1 twin.
price	€56.
meals	Restaurants in Epernay, 8km.
closed	2 weeks in September, 2 weeks in August & Christmas.
directions	From Calais A26 to Reims; N51 to Épernay; follow for Châlons en Champagne then to Avize; head for Lycée Viticole, house opp. lycée.

Imogen & Didier Pierson Whitaker
Le Vieux Cèdre,
14 route d'Oger,
51190 Avize, Marne

tel +33 (0)3 26 57 77 04
fax +33 (0)3 26 57 97 97
email champagnepiersonwhitaker@club-internet.fr

Map 6 Entry 63

La Madeleine

The quiet is so deep that the grandfather clock ticking inside – and the doves cooing in the trees outside – can seem deafening. A timeless feel wafts through the new house from that clock, the pretty, traditionally decorated bedrooms (sleigh beds and Louis Philippe furniture), the piano and a lovely old sideboard. Huguette and her husband, who runs the dairy farm, are generous hosts offering traditional unpretentious farmhouse hospitality; they take gîte guests, too. You can opt for champagne from their son-in-law's nearby vineyard, with a meal to match the quality of the wine and the welcome.

rooms	3: 2 doubles, 1 triple.
price	€46.
meals	Dinner with wine, €20; with champagne €30.
closed	Rarely.
directions	From Châlons en Champagne D933 to Bergères (29km); right D9 through Vertus; left, follow signs to La Madeleine 3km.

	Huguette Charageat
	La Madeleine,
	51130 Vertus, Marne
tel	+33 (0)3 26 52 11 29
fax	+33 (0)3 26 59 22 09
mobile	+33 (0)6 85 20 57 92
email	charageat.la.madeleine@wanadoo.fr

Map 6 Entry 64

5 rue St Bernard

Natural, unsophisticated country folk in deep rural France: Madame fun and an excellent cook (lots of organic and farm-grown ingredients); Monsieur a whizz on local history; both proud of their country heritage, wonderful with children, deeply committed to 'real B&B'. In a sleepy village, they chose this roadside house to retire to, did the guest rooms in brave youthful colours that perfectly set off the mix of old and new furniture on lino floors, fitted lovely linen, good mattresses, clean-cut bathrooms. Two rooms have their own ground-floor entrance, the third is upstairs in their 'wing'. All plain sailing.

rooms	3: 1 double, 1 suite for 4, 1 quadruple.
price	€38-€42.
meals	Dinner with wine, €16, Monday-Friday.
closed	Christmas & 1 January.
directions	From A4 exit Ste Menehould D982 (382 on some maps) to Givry en Argonne; left D54 to Les Charmontois (9km).

	M & Mme Bernard Patizel
	5 rue St Bernard,
	51330 Les Charmontois, Marne
tel	+33 (0)3 26 60 39 53
fax	+33 (0)3 26 60 39 53
email	nicole.patizel@wanadoo.fr
web	www.chez.com/patizel

Map 6 Entry 65

Domaine du Moulin d'Eguebaude

The secluded old buildings house two owner families, a fish-tasting restaurant, several guest rooms and 50 tons of live fish – it's a fish farm! Fishers may gather on Sundays to catch trout in the spring water that feeds the ponds. Delicious breakfast and *table d'hôtes* are shared with your enthusiastic hosts, who created this place from an old mill 40 years ago; groups come for speciality lunches. Bedrooms under the eaves are compact, small-windowed, simply furnished, prettily decorated in rustic or granny style, the larger annexe rooms are more motellish. Great fun for children, and good English spoken.

rooms	6: 2 doubles, 1 twin, 1 triple, 2 family rooms.
price	€60–€70.
meals	Dinner with wine, €20.
closed	Rarely.
directions	From Paris A5 exit 19 on N60 to Estissac; right on to Rue Pierre Brossolette; mill at end of lane (1km).

Alexandre & Sandrine Mesley
Domaine du Moulin d'Eguebaude,
36 Rue Pierre Brossdette,
10190 Estissac, Aube
tel   +33 (0)3 25 40 42 18
fax   +33 (0)3 25 40 40 92
email   eguebaude@aol.com

Map 5 Entry 66

Les Épeires

This was the château family's summer house for two centuries and has been their main house for one: Madame will show you the family books, lovely old furniture and mementos and tell you the stories (of Louis XIV's envoy to Peter the Great who was an ancestor…) in incredibly fast French. She does her own bookbinding, adores her rose garden – a jungle of perfume and petals – and has a couple of horses in the paddock; there are racehorses elsewhere. A blithe and extrovert soul, she serves delightful, ever-so-French dinners before a log fire, and offers you a simple bedroom as country-cosy as the old house.

rooms	1 triple.
price	€46. Triple €61.
meals	Dinner with wine, €22; with champagne €28.
closed	Rarely.
directions	A26 to junc. 22 (Troyes); N19 to Bar sur Aube; D384 to Ville sur Terre. Follow for Fuligny. House on long main street.

Nicole Georges-Fougerolle
Les Épeires,
17 rue des Écuyers,
10200 Fuligny,
Aube
tel   +33 (0)3 25 92 77 11
fax   +33 (0)3 25 92 77 11

Map 6 Entry 67

Champagne – Ardenne

Domaine de Boulancourt

This large and splendid farmhouse is irresistible. For fishermen there's a river, for birdwatchers a fine park full of wildlife (come for the cranes in spring or autumn); for architecture buffs, the half-timbered churches are among the "100 most beautiful attractions in France". Bedrooms are comfortable and attractive; afternoon tea is served in the elegant panelled salon; dinner, possibly home-raised boar or carp, is eaten communally or separately but not with your hosts, delightful as they are: they live in another wing and prefer to concentrate on their good *cuisine maison*.

rooms	5: 2 doubles, 2 twins, 1 suite.
price	€60-€70. Suite €70. Singles €55-€65.
meals	Dinner with wine, €25.
closed	30 November-15 March.
directions	From Troyes D960 to Brienne; D400 for St Dizier; at Louze D182 to Longeville; D174 for Boulancourt; house on left at 1st crossroads, sign 'Le Désert'.

Philippe & Christine Viel-Cazal
Domaine de Boulancourt,
Le Désert,
52220 Longeville sur la Laines,
Haute-Marne
tel   +33 (0)3 25 04 60 18
fax   +33 (0)3 25 04 60 18
email dom.boulancourt@wanadoo.fr

Map 6 Entry 68

Champagne – Ardenne

Massin Perrette

While restoring the old house, the Poopes were enchanted to 'meet' the former owners in the shape of old photographs in the attic. These inspired the décor of each plush and classically French bedroom; Évelyne and Michel adore doing B&B, are natural hosts and do all they can to make you feel at home. Breakfast, served at separate tables, is deeply local: yogurt from the farm, honey from the village and Évelyne's jam; dinner in the pastel-panelled dining room is wonderful value. Michel is chief pastry-cook, lawn-mower and hedge-cutter; the garden, too, is impeccably tended.

rooms	5: 1 double, 1 twin, 2 triples, 1 suite for 4.
price	€50-€65.
meals	Dinner with wine, €16.
closed	Christmas.
directions	From A31 exit 7 to north Langres; N19 for Vesoul for 40km. Right at Chambres d'Hôtes sign to Pressigny; just after pond on left.

Évelyne & Michel Poope
Massin Perrette,
24 rue Augustin Massin,
52500 Pressigny, Haute-Marne
tel   +33 (0)3 25 88 80 50
fax   +33 (0)3 25 88 80 49
email e.m.poope@wanadoo.fr
web   www.massin-perrette.com

Map 6 Entry 69

Champagne – Ardenne

La Montgonière

Knee-high wainscotting, opulent fabric, hand-painted wallpaper discovered in the attic: some of the treats in store at this village mansion built in 1673. The first owner was seen off during the Revolution and the house was later sold to the family of the current one – smiling, self-assured Madame who, in 2001, swapped law for B&B and has no regrets. Book-lined walls and elegant fauteuils encourage cogitation under the eaves, French windows open to a delightful walled garden and the passageways are lined with oriental rugs. Refined living, with a relaxed mood and Élisabeth is an accomplished cook.

rooms	3: 2 doubles, 1 suite for 3.
price	€80–€90.
meals	Dinner with wine, €20.
closed	Never.
directions	From Reims D980; D947 for Luxembourg; Harricourt is 18km after Vouziers, 2km before Buzancy.

Élisabeth Regnault de Montgon
La Montgonière,
1 rue St Georges, 08240 Harricourt,
Ardennes

tel	+33 (0)3 24 71 66 50
fax	+33 (0)3 24 71 66 50
email	regnault.montgon@wanadoo.fr
web	www.lamontgoniere.net

Map 6 Entry 70

Lorraine
Alsace
Franche Comté

Lorraine

Château de Jaulny

On a rocky hilltop overlooking green valleys and woods, the fortified castle comes with dungeon, keep and four storeys of underground cellars did Joan of Arc live here? Portraits were discovered beneath wattle and whitewash during the French Revolution...
Today the noble swathe of stone stair is embellished with a wrought-iron banister and spacious guest rooms are decorated in luxurious 19th-century style. Anna, brought up here, now raises her own family and warmly serves breakfast before a great fireplace; Hugues helps restore, and invites schools for archery and courses in medieval life. Amazing!

rooms	3 doubles.
price	€55–€75.
meals	Dinner with wine, €30.
closed	Never.
directions	A4; exit 32 Fresne en Woëvre for Pont à Mousson; Thiaucourt; Jaulny.

Anna Collignon & Hugues Drion
Château de Jaulny,
4 rue du Château,
54470 Jaulny,
Meurthe-et-Moselle
tel   +33 (0)3 83 81 93 04
email   jaulnychateau@free.fr
web   jaulny-chateau.com

Map 6 Entry 71

Lorraine

Les Champs Grandmère

Utter country quiet, inside and out (no telly, many books), views sailing away to the Vosges hills behind, across Judith's lovely rose arbour, herb beds, rock garden and reed-ringed lake in front (fancy a swim with the trout?). She sells her own herb-scented soaps. The 1960s chalet, open-plan downstairs, carpeted up, is spotless throughout. Here, it's bed, breakfast and afternoon tea and cake... and apparently the cake is superb. Bedrooms have good repro furniture typical of the region and new beds. Breakfast can be French, German or English – you choose. Supremely peaceful house, place and person.

rooms	2 doubles, sharing bath & wc.
price	From €55.
meals	Occasional dinner with wine, €25.
closed	Rarely.
directions	From Strasbourg A352 & N420 to St Blaise la Roche 45km; right D424 14km to La Petite Raon; right after church for Moussey; 3rd left after café on to Rue Gen. Leclerc up steep hill; then left, left & left to house.

Judith Lott
Les Champs Grandmère,
Thiamont,
88210 La Petite Raon, Vosges
tel   +33 (0)3 29 57 68 08
mobile   +33 (0)6 88 55 19 37
email   judelott@aol.com
web   leschampsgrandmere.free.fr

Map 7 Entry 72

Lorraine

Villa Les Roses

Monsieur's seemingly endless restoration of these venerable buildings — one house 400, the other 300 years old — is finished, and very nicely too: fine woodwork, stylish furniture, an intriguing gas chandelier in the dining room, elegant terraces and a super garden with a children's play area. Madame is charmingly lively; her attractive rooms have goodnight chocolates, kettle kits, smallish shower rooms and lots of religion on view (bedside Bibles are French Catholic, not American Gideon). Hers is a genuine welcome.

Lorraine

51 rue Lorraine

Alina came from Poland with a bundle of talents: a professional gardener, she paints, embroiders, decorates; Gérard, a retired French architect, has won a prize for his brilliant conversion of this dear little 200-year-old house; their skills and taste for contemporary and ethnic styles shine through the house, their thoughtful, artistic personalities enliven the dinner table, their environmentalist passion informs their lives. Expect superb vegetarian food if you ask for it (delicious meaty things too), pretty rooms with excellent beds and linen, a lovely garden and patio, relaxed and unpretentious intelligence.

rooms	5: 2 doubles, 1 twin, 1 family room.
price	€55-€80.
meals	Restaurants nearby.
closed	Rarely.
directions	From A4 exit Ste Menehould; N3 for Verdun-Chalons; sign in La Vignette, hamlet before Les Islettes; 1st building on left.

rooms	2: 1 double, 1 triple.
price	€54-€56.
meals	Dinner with wine, €21-€22 (meat or fish) or €18-€19 (vegetarian).
closed	Rarely.
directions	From Metz D3 NE for Bouzonville approx. 21km; right on D53a to Burtoncourt. On left in main street.

	Mme Christiaens Villa Les Roses, La Vignette, Les Islettes, 55120 Clermont en Argonne, Meuse
tel	+33 (0)3 26 60 81 91
fax	+33 (0)3 26 60 23 09
email	gites-christiaens@wanadoo.fr

	Alina & Gérard Cahen 51 rue Lorraine, 57220 Burtoncourt, Moselle
tel	+33 (0)3 87 35 72 65
fax	+33 (0)3 87 35 72 65
email	ag.cahen@wanadoo.fr
web	www.maisonlorraine.com

Map 6 Entry 73

Map 7 Entry 74

Lorraine

Château d'Alteville

A solidly reassuring family château in a peaceful, privileged setting. Bedrooms are *vieille France*; not large (bar one, special for its view onto fantastic old trees) but with the patina of long history in carved armoires, Voltaire armchairs, bedhead draperies, pastel fabrics and plush. Bathrooms are endearingly Fifties. The real style is in the utterly French many-chaired salon and the dining room – reached through halls and hunting trophies – with its huge square table. Here you may share elegant meals with your charming host. A morning chorus of birds – and always, fresh flowers.

rooms	5: 4 doubles, 1 twin.
price	€68-€91.
meals	Dinner €31-€38.50. Wine €10.
closed	15 October-15 April.
directions	From Nancy N74 for Sarreguemines & Château Salins. At Burthecourt x-roads D38 to Dieuze; D999 south 5km; left on D199F; right D199G to château.

David Barthélémy
Château d'Alteville,
Tarquimpol,
57260 Dieuze, Moselle

tel	+33 (0)3 87 05 46 63
fax	+33 (0)3 8705 46 64
mobile	+33 (0)6 72 07 56 05
email	chateau.alTeville@caramail.com

Map 7 Entry 75

Alsace

86 rue du Général de Gaulle

A real old Alsatian farmhouse in the wine-growing area where you can be in a bustling village street one minute and your own peaceful little world the next. It is on a busy main road but the bedrooms, in the separate guest wing, are at the back. Their simplicity is reflected in the price. Your hosts retired from milk and wine production in order to have more time for guests; Marie-Claire still teaches German, Paul serves breakfast in the garden or in the dining room. A useful place to know at the start of the Route des Vins, and very close to gorgeous, expensive Strasbourg.

rooms	3 doubles.
price	€35-€38.
meals	Restaurant 200m.
closed	Rarely.
directions	From Saverne A4, exit 45 onto N404 & N4 for Strasbourg, 16km. Farm in middle of Marlenheim on left, before post office.

Paul & Marie-Claire Goetz
86 rue du Général de Gaulle,
67520 Marlenheim,
Bas-Rhin

tel	+33 (0)3 88 87 52 94
email	goetz.paul@wanadoo.fr

Map 7 Entry 76

Alsace

Maison Fleurie

Bubbling, friendly and generous, Doris has been receiving guests for years: she learnt the art at her mother's knee and will greet you with the warmest welcome. Her peaceful chalet is a real home, surrounded by breathtaking views of the mountains and forests. Both she and her husband are upholsterers so furnishings in the neat, traditional bedrooms are... perfect, strong colours giving depth to modernity. Guests have their own quarters, with a log fire in the breakfast room, tables laden with goodies in the morning – try the homemade organic fruit jams and Alsace cake – and geraniums cascading.

rooms	3: 2 doubles, 1 twin.
price	€48-€52.
meals	Choice of restaurants nearby.
closed	Rarely.
directions	From Colmar A35 & N83 Sélestat (exit 17); N59 & D424 to Villé; D697 to Dieffenbach au Val. Careful: ask for exact address as two other Engels do B&B!

Doris Engel-Geiger
Maison Fleurie,
19 route de Neuve Église,
Dieffenbach au Val, 67220 Villé,
Bas-Rhin
tel   +33 (0)3 88 85 60 48
fax   +33 (0)3 88 85 60 48
email engel-thierry@wanadoo.fr
web   www.lamaisonfleurie.com

Map 7 Entry 77

Alsace

34 rue Maréchal Foch

At the centre of a working vineyard in gorgeous old Dambach is a typical, geranium-dripping Alsatian house, built by the first Ruhlmann wine-grower in 1688. Wine buffs enjoy visiting the wine cellar and non-drinkers can taste the sweet water springing from the Vosges hills. The charming rooms, in the guest wing under the sloping roof, have new carpets and old family furniture (there are two gloomy overflow rooms; in use, all four rooms share one wc); no sitting room, but a huge relic-filled guest dayroom: a wine press, a grape basket, a superb ceramic stove. Your friendly hostess speaks excellent English.

rooms	2 doubles, sharing wc.
price	€46.
meals	Restaurants within walking distance.
closed	15 September-15 March.
directions	From Sélestat N on D35, 8km. House in village centre, about equidistant between town gates on main road.

Jean-Charles & Laurence
Ruhlmann
34 rue Maréchal Foch,
67650 Dambach la Ville,
Bas-Rhin
tel   +33 (0)3 88 92 41 86
fax   +33 (0)3 88 92 61 81
email vins@ruhlmann-schutz.fr
web   www.ruhlmann-schutz.fr

Map 7 Entry 78

Alsace

Ambiance Jardin

Shielded from the road by this typical Alsatian house, the guest barn overlooks Pierrette's amazing garden. Tended with passion and knowledge, it expresses her spirit in flourishes of roses, cobbled alleys, meanders of cropped lawn and Jean-Luc's wood-iron-stone sculptures. Her enthusiasm flows from family house to well-converted barn where three big, pretty bedrooms have balconies, the fourth flies up to the rafters and a constant antique hunt furnishes it all joyously: a chandelier hanging from a rafter, antique watering cans and china pieces abounding. Superb breakfast, too, in your open-plan dayroom.

rooms	4: 2 doubles, 2 twins.
price	€70-€80.
meals	Restaurant 200m.
closed	Never.
directions	From Colmar, exit Sélestat Nord; after Ebersheim right for Ebersmunster; in centre of Hilsenheim left for Bindernheim. At x-roads turn left to Diebolsheim. Straight at r'bout; 1st left: Rue d'Eglise.

Pierrette & Jean-Luc Kieny
Ambiance Jardin,
12 rue de l'Abbé Wendling,
67230 Diebolsheim,
Bas-Rhin

tel	+33 (0)3 88 74 84 85
mobile	+33 (0)6 70 55 01 42
email	pierrette@ambiance-jardin.com
web	www.ambiance-jardin.com

Map 7 Entry 79

Alsace

Domaine Thierhurst

Bénédicte and Jean-Jacques are so welcoming in their sturdily luxurious modern house: he, quiet and courteous, runs the farm; she, dynamic and initially a touch formidable, opens her soul – and all the doors of her house – to make you feel at home. She knows the delights of Alsace and nearby Germany intimately, concocts scrumptious authentic Alsatian food in the octagonal kitchen-diner and loves your amazement at the upstairs 'bathroom-extraordinaire' with its vast Italianate rain shower. Pale, Turkey-rugged suites have all contemporary comforts and the large young garden matures a little every day.

rooms	2: 1 double, 1 suite.
price	€100.
meals	Dinner with wine, €35.
closed	Never.
directions	From A36 for Colmar, exit Neuf-Brisach. Through Hirtzfelden-Fessenheim; between Balgau & Heiteren, turn right. Follow 'Pèlerinage Notre-Dame de la Thierhurst'.

Bénédicte & Jean-Jacques Kinny
Domaine Thierhurst,
68740 Nambsheim,
Haut-Rhin

tel	+33 (0)3 89 72 56 94
fax	+33 (0)3 89 72 90 78
email	jean-jacques.kinny@wanadoo.fr
web	www.kinny.fr

Map 7 Entry 80

Franche Comté

Champs Bayeux

The house is a gallery for Madame's hand-painted stencils (she'll teach you if you like). She and her artistic daughter often paint quietly on the landing. Their new house is just around the corner from their old, right up on the edge of the forest. Spacious bedrooms are attic-cosy and full of French flourishes. Dinner with your generous hosts and possibly their grown children is a model of conviviality… and they should charge extra for their company and conversation! The garden leads out to forest, deer, red squirrels; nearby are golf, skiing and the Ballons des Vosges Regional Park.

rooms	3: 2 doubles, 1 suite for 2-4. Extra beds available.
price	€54-€65.
meals	Dinner with wine, €21.
closed	Rarely.
directions	From A36 exit 14 N83 for Mulhouse; in Les Errues left for Anjoutey & Étueffont; at r'bout right for Rougemont; left at 1st bend; house at end.

Astride & Daniel Elbert
Champs Bayeux,
10 rue de la Chapelle,
90170 Étueffont,
Territoire de Belfort
tel   +33 (0)3 84 54 68 63
email   daniel.elbert@wanadoo.fr
web   perso.wanadoo.fr/chambres-tourisme

Map 7 Entry 81

Franche Comté

Le Château

As part of its vast 100m2 suite, this château has one of the most extraordinary bathrooms this side of the Saône: panels hung with old engravings, a sunken bath and an Italian chandelier making an atmosphere of exceptionally elegant luxury; bedroom and sitting room are just as amazing. All this and a family feel. Antiques, attention to detail, a charming hostess with an easy laugh, make it a very special place. Dinner, carefully chosen to suit guests' tastes (if you want snails, you'll have to ask), is exquisitely presented on Gien porcelain, on the terrace in summer. Untouched 18th-century living.

rooms	1 suite for 3.
price	€68.
meals	Dinner with wine, €20.
closed	September-mid-May.
directions	From A36 exit 3 D67 to Gray 35km; entering Gray right D474; fork left D13 to Beaujeu & Motey sur Saône; left to Mercey; signposted in village.

Bernadette Jantet
Le Château,
70130 Mercey sur Saône,
Haute-Saône
tel   +33 (0)3 84 67 07 84

Map 6 Entry 82

Franche Comté

Les Egrignes

Refinement, loving care and high craftsmanship: you are welcomed to this exquisite house by a couple who have breathed new life into the lovely old stones and mouldings. Quiet Roland combs auctions for fine rugs, old mirrors and modern paintings; bubbly Fabienne puts thick curtains, pretty desks, carved armoires and soft sofas in vast pale-walled bedrooms and deluxe bathrooms. He gardens passionately (the half-wheel potager is breathtaking), she cooks brilliantly. Remarkable hosts, interior designers of much flair, they are fun and excellent company. Here is value indeed. *Minimum stay two nights June-August.*

rooms	3: 1 twin/double, 2 suites for 2-5.
price	From €80.
meals	Dinner with wine €25.
closed	Rarely.
directions	From Troyes A31 exit 6 Langres-Sud through Longeau; D67 through Gray for Besançon. Cult on right 21km after Gray; signposted in village.

Mme Fabienne Lego-Deiber
Les Egrignes,
70150 Cult,
Haute-Saône

tel	+33 (0)3 84 31 92 06
fax	+33 (0)3 84 31 92 06
email	lesegrignes@wanadoo.fr
web	les-egrignes.com

Map 6 Entry 83

Franche Comté

La Maison Royale

The gaunt exterior, part of the town's 15th-century fortress, imposes — but wait. Madame, charming, cultured, friendly, bought the two-metre-thick walls and built a house within them — her pride and joy. The courtyard has small gardens and a fountain; the huge ground-floor rooms, open to the public, are gorgeous; bedrooms, all artistically marvellous, have luxury bathrooms and great views — it's like sleeping in a modern palace. It could be overwhelming but Lydie is such a delightful person that it is, in fact, unforgettably moving. And you are in one of the loveliest villages in France. *Children over five welcome.*

rooms	6: 4 doubles, 2 twins.
price	From €70.
meals	Restaurants within walking distance.
closed	Mid-October–March.
directions	From A36 exit 2 onto D475 to Pesmes, 20km. House at top of village on left.

Mme Hoyet
La Maison Royale,
70140 Pesmes,
Haute-Saône

tel	+33 (0)3 84 31 23 23
fax	+33 (0)3 84 31 23 23

Map 6 Entry 84

Franche Comté

Rose Art

The gentlest, most generous couple live here with all the time in the world for you and a delightful art gallery in their vaulted basement: Madame embroiders but shows other artists' paintings and their son holds wine-tasting sessions. It's a fairly average old wine merchant's house but that welcome, the rooms under the roof, a lovely view of orchards and meadows, a brook to sing you to sleep after a fine meal, make it special. Plus a particularly pretty village full of old winemerchants' homes of character, a tempting garden with a playhouse for children, a piano anyone may play – or golf down the road.

rooms	2: 1 twin, 1 suite for 4-5.
price	From €50.
meals	Dinner €15. Wine €10–€12.
closed	Rarely.
directions	In Lons le Saunier for Chalon; right before SNCF station D117 for Macornay; D41 to Vernantois; left before houses & follow signs.

Monique & Michel Ryon
Rose Art,
8 rue Lacuzon,
39570 Vernantois,
Jura

tel	+33 (0)3 84 47 17 28
fax	+33 (0)3 84 47 17 28
email	rose.art@wanadoo.fr

Map 11 Entry 85

Burgundy

Burgundy

La Messalière

Done with passion and panache, the variegated bedrooms – classic, mock medieval, Provençal, Jouy-romantic – in the venerable wine-grower's house (some of it 600 years old) are part of a full French experience. Your hostess, a friendly outgoing person who loves to chat with guests, used to have a dress shop: the old wedding-gowned models in some bedrooms and changing-room doors in the smallish bathrooms (one is low if you're tall) were part of this past life. She does it all herself and you will be intrigued by curios in the heavily-draped salon, tempted by genuine Burgundy dinners and candlelight.

rooms	4: 3 doubles, 1 suite for 2.
price	€85–€140. €160 for 3.
meals	Dinner with wine, €30.
closed	November–March.
directions	From A6 for Autun exit Chalon N; at St Léger sur Dheune; 1st right in centre of village for Santenay & Chagny.

Mireille Marquet
La Messalière,
29 rue du 8 mai 1945,
71510 St Léger sur Dheune,
Saône-et-Loire

tel	+33 (0)3 85 45 35 75
fax	+33 (0)3 85 45 40 96
email	reservations@saintlegersurdheune.com
web	www.saintlegersurdheune.com

Map 11 Entry 86

Burgundy

La Griottière

That pale ochre stone warms this converted barn inside as well – exposed walls among the lime-washed plaster, a delicious bathroom alcove – giving the house an air of serenity. A few well-matched colours help: château grey, rich beige, various reds, all fresh and clean with soft quilts and draped bedheads but nothing riotous in the inviting rooms. Generous and jovial, Monsieur helps a wine-grower friend and willingly takes you wine-tasting. Madame quietly cares for her house and pretty stream-fed garden. Fontaines has a remarkable collection of 19th-century public washhouses.

rooms	2: 1 double, 1 twin/double.
price	€75–€89.
meals	Dinner with wine, €30.
closed	Rarely.
directions	From A6 Paris to Lyon exit Chalon sur Saône Nord; for Autun 5km to Fontaines; signposted.

Serge Doumenc
La Griottière,
7 Les Fontaines,
71150 Fontaines,
Saône-et-Loire

tel	+33 (0)3 85 91 48 47
mobile	+33 (0)6 72 37 49 21
email	lagriottiere@infonie.fr
web	lagriottiere.chez-alice.fr

Map 11 Entry 87

Burgundy

Domaine de L'Oiseau

Lovely 18th-century buildings frame a courtyard, peeping out from under low slanting eaves and climbing plants. The end-of-village setting is secluded riverside woodland; feast by the pool on food *and* views. Bedrooms sing with serenity and good taste: the suite, graceful and feminine, in the old bakery, the rest peacefully in the Pavilion. Each has its own dressing room, small perfect bathroom and enchanting old *tommette* floor. Relax in the glorious beamed barn – the guests' library; sample the domaine's fine wines in the cellar below with friendly, extrovert Monsieur. An exceptional place.

rooms	4: 2 twins/doubles; 1 suite for 3, 1 suite for 4, each with separate wc.
price	€130. Suites €140–€160.
meals	Dinner with wine, from €50.
closed	December–March.
directions	From Gergy through village, past pharmacy on right; towards Complex Sportif; signs to Domaine de L'Oiseau. House on left on leaving village.

Dominique & Philippe Monnier-Pictet
Domaine de L'Oiseau,
17 chemin Chariot, 71590 Gergy,
Saône-et-Loire

tel	+33 (0)3 85 91 61 26
mobile	+33 (0)6 23 46 59 07
email	info@domoiseau.com
web	www.domoiseau.com

Map 11 Entry 88

Burgundy

Manoir du Clos de Vauvry

A ceramic stove as big as two men dominates the breakfast room of this charming 17th-century royal hunting lodge. Summer breakfasts are on the terrace. The whole place has an air of exaggeration: over-generous stairs, ingenious double windows, voluptuous ceilings, all totally French with floral wallpapers and embroidered bedcovers in magnificent bedrooms, 1930s tiled bathrooms (one whirlpool) and immaculate linen. This adorable couple know everyone in wine growing and Marie helps you all she can over another cigarette. Burgundy has so much to offer, as well as superb wines... wonderful.

rooms	3: 1 twin, 1 suite for 4, 1 suite for 5.
price	€65–€76. Suites €122–€140.
meals	Dinner with wine, €25.
closed	Rarely.
directions	From Chalon Sud, N80 for Montceau les Mines 9km; D981 exit Givry; follow Complexe Sportif signs, rue de Sauges; 2nd on left.

Marie & Daniel Lacroix-Mollaret
Manoir du Clos de Vauvry,
3 rue des Faussillons,
71640 Givry Poncey,
Saône-et-Loire

tel	+33 (0)3 85 44 40 83
fax	+33 (0)3 85 44 40 83
email	daniel.mollaret@wanadoo.fr
web	www.clos-de-vauvry.com

Map 11 Entry 89

Burgundy

Abbaye de la Ferté

Immense grandeur with no trace of original Cistercian austerity: the abbot's palace is all that's left of the former abbey and you may glimpse the oversized staircase on your way to family breakfast in the 'small dining room'. Guests sleep in the highly original pigeon loft with its amazing round nest-holed bathroom or in the new and enchanting coach house suite dressed with old materials and tremendous flair. Both suites have log fires and tea trays, art books and a bottle of local wine. It's a short walk to breakfast where your young hosts, the easiest of people, make it all pleasingly eccentric and fun.

Burgundy

La Ferme

Children may be able to watch the goats being milked in the clean, enclosed farmyard, and help if they (and the nannies) like. There are horses too. Your hard-working hosts, with three children of their own and sensitive to the needs of families, have made a two-bedroomed family suite at the top of the old stone farmhouse. Bathrobes are provided for grown-ups, so everyone feels cared for. All is sparkling and charmingly simple. People return, not only for the relaxing experience but also to stock up on the homemade cheeses, mouthwatering jams and local wines that the family make and sell.

rooms	2: 1 suite for 2-4, 1 suite for 4.
price	€66-€97.
meals	Dinner with wine, €25, July & Aug.
closed	Rarely.
directions	From A6 exit Chalon south, N6 for Varrennes le Grand; D6 for Le Lac de Laives to La Ferté; at crossroads marked La Ferté, press intercom at large iron gates.

rooms	4: 2 twins; 2 family suites, each with kitchen.
price	€58-€70.
meals	Restaurant nearby.
closed	Rarely.
directions	From Tournus D14 for Cluny. At Chapaize, D314 to Bissy sous Uxelles. House next to church.

Jacques & Virginie Thenard
Abbaye de la Ferté,
71240 St Ambreuil,
Saône-et-Loire
tel   +33 (0)3 85 44 17 96
email   abbayedelaferte@aol.com
web   www.abbayeferte.com

Pascale & Dominique
de La Bussière
La Ferme,
71460 Bissy sous Uxelles,
Saône-et-Loire
tel   +33 (0)3 85 50 15 03
fax   +33 (0)3 85 50 15 03
email   dominique.de-la-bussiere@wanadoo.fr
web   www.m-fjsolutions.com/BB/

Map 11 Entry 90

Map 11 Entry 91

Burgundy

Château de Nobles

Oceans of history behind it (a prehistoric *menhir* stands in the grounds) and owners bursting with more restoration ideas and passionate about it. Monsieur cultivates the vines and the wine: wine production started here in the 10th century. The bedrooms, in a renovated building near the main, dreamlike, 13th-15th-century château, are fresh and unfussy in the stylish way so many are in France – the bigger one is a gem, with its superb beams, vast mezzanine, little veranda, huge new bath. Breakfast is in the château, a delightfully lived-in listed monument. Irresistible.

rooms	3: 1 double, 1 triple, 1 family room.
price	€81.
meals	Restaurants within 5km.
closed	November-March.
directions	From Tournus D14 for Cormatin. Passing Brancion on right continue on main road for 1.5km. Towers opposite on bend.

Bertrand & Françoise de Cherisey
Château de Nobles,
71700 La Chapelle sous Brancion,
Saône-et-Loire

tel +33 (0)3 85 51 00 55
email cheriseyb@free.fr

Map 11 Entry 92

Burgundy

Le Pré Ménot

Open-minded and wise after years abroad, a man of many parts and full of mirth who punctuates his phrases with a bemused chuckle and a puff of tobacco, Monsieur appears to read unspoken wishes – and cannot put enough out for breakfast. In deep wine-growing country, his traditional Mâconnais house, thrown open for conviviality, appears to wear typical French décor, then you notice the contemporary paintings, tapestries, pottery, antique African sculpture – fascinating. Bedrooms and bathrooms have the same heart-warming mix of ancient, modern and attention to detail. The church is a Romanesque jewel.

rooms	2 doubles.
price	€50.
meals	Restaurant 5km.
closed	Rarely.
directions	From Tournus D14 for Cormatin 12km; left D163 for Grévilly 200m; right to Grévilly; across T-junc.; house 100m on left, outside village, just below church.

Claude Depreay
Le Pré Ménot,
71700 Grévilly,
Saône-et-Loire

tel +33 (0)3 85 33 29 92
fax +33 (0)3 85 33 29 92

Map 11 Entry 93

Burgundy

Le Tinailler

Jean-Paul runs a theatre company with the local actor-winegrowers and he and Régine, a musician, combine their farmhouse B&B with an in-house art gallery and vibrant summer theatre. Interesting, artistic people who live in the main house, they create an atmosphere of relaxed energy, take their B&B seriously and offer wonderfullly warm, fresh bedrooms in the converted tithe barn: deep rose or cool blue walls, beautiful old wooden beds, immaculate bathrooms and, generously, Grand-père's excellent cubist paintings. A friendly welcome at all times, and alfresco dining and theatrical novelty in June and July.

rooms	5: 4 doubles, 1 twin.
price	€54-€58.
meals	Restaurants 6km.
closed	November-March.
directions	From A6 exit Tournus; D56 for Lugny. 3km after Chardonnay right on D463 & follow signs to Chambres d'Hôtes & Théâtre Champvent.

Régine & Jean-Paul Rullière
Le Tinailler,
Manoir de Champvent,
71700 Chardonnay,
Saône-et-Loire
tel   +33 (0)3 85 40 50 23
fax   +33 (0)3 85 40 50 18

Map 11 Entry 94

Burgundy

Le Tinailler d'Aléane

The lovely stones and cascading geraniums outside, the silk flowers, frilly lampshades and polished furniture inside have an old-world charm. The breakfast room is cosily stuffed with bric-a-brac, bedrooms are family-simple. Madame was a florist: she arranges her rooms as if they were bouquets, is always refreshing them and might put a paper heart on your pillow wishing you *bonne nuit*. She doesn't refuse children but may well be happier if you arrive with a little dog under your arm. She or her husband can do winery visits for non-French speakers. Ask for the larger room; the smaller feels cramped.

rooms	2 doubles.
price	€48.
meals	Choice of restaurants 3-5km.
closed	Sundays in winter.
directions	From A6-N79 Cluny-Charolles exit La Roche Vineuse. At junction, left to Charnay & Mâcon; left at r'bout for Sommeré; at village square, up hill follow EH signs, house at top on left, bell by gate.

Éliane Heinen
Le Tinailler d'Aléane,
Sommeré,
71960 La Roche Vineuse,
Saône-et-Loire
tel   +33 (0)3 85 37 80 68
fax   +33 (0)3 85 37 80 68

Map 11 Entry 95

Burgundy

Habitation Beauvilliers

You can do a day's canoeing on the Loire and disembark at the bottom of the garden for aperitifs and boules beneath the plane trees – classy. Your hosts leave you the run of their fine French garden – box hedges and central pond – and classically symmetrical house with its unusual double stairway. Casually elegant and a whizz at interiors, Madame came from Switzerland to study fine art and loves living here. Bedrooms are light and airy, one of them with a dreamy river view and a step-down bathroom disguised as a cupboard. Breakfast is in the super kitchen, decorated with printed teacloths.

rooms	2 suites.
price	€70–€85.
meals	Dinner with wine, €23.
closed	November-Easter.
directions	From Cosne sur Loire for Bourges; r'bout before bridge take exit after exit for Bourges (do not cross river); right after 30m; left after 50m following river upwards; after 3km road turns to left; follow wall on right; gate 100m on right.

Marianne & Daniel Perrier
Habitation Beauvilliers,
Port Aubry,
58200 Cosne sur Loire, Nièvre
tel	+33 (0)3 86 28 41 37
mobile	+33 (0)6 89 37 06 31
email	habitationbeauvilliers@hotmail.com

Map 5 Entry 96

Burgundy

Domaine des Perrieres

Make the most of seasonal *produits de ferme* and traditional French food: the visitors' book is plump with praise. Madame the farmer's wife loves cooking (delectable patisserie and jams) and making folk feel at home. Wheat fields wave to the horizon, farm and cows are next door, this is deepest France. Inside, simple, straightforward rooms, green friezed walls, a bathroom in blue; all is airy and light, cheerful and double-glazed. No sitting room to share, but after a day on horses or bikes (the cross-country trails are inspiring) and a long, leisurely supper, most guests retire gratefully to bed.

rooms	2: 1 double, 1 twin.
price	€55.
meals	Dinner with wine, €20.
closed	Rarely.
directions	From Brinon/Beuvron D34 or Premery D977b. Between Crux-la-Ville and Streverien, follow D34. Signed.

Pascale Cointe
Domaine des Perrieres,
58330 Les Perrières Crux-La-Ville, Nièvre
tel	+33 (0)3 86 58 34 93
fax	+33 (0)3 86 58 26 00
email	pascale.benoit.cointe@wanadoo.fr
web	perso.wanadoo.fr/domainedesperrieres

Map 10 Entry 97

Burgundy

Rue Hoteaux

A master stone mason built this house in the 19th century and left many marks of his consummate skill in stairs and fireplaces as well as his quarry at the back where the Escots have made a sheltered flower-filled rock garden, Madame's passion. They are a relaxed, generous couple, she bubbly and proud of her many grandchildren, he shyer but a mine of information; both love having people to stay. In the converted barn, the big ground-floor stable room has a finely clothed bed, white slatted walls and good yellow wallpaper, or climb the lovely winding stairs to the pretty pink and beamed attic room.

rooms	2: 1 family room, 1 triple.
price	€80-€95.
meals	Restaurants 3-7km.
closed	November-mid-April.
directions	From Montbard D980 for Chatillon; right in village of Puits. House on right next to large tree.

	Gilberte & Jean Escot
	Rue Hoteaux,
	21400 Puits,
	Côte-d'Or
tel	+33 (0)3 80 93 14 83
email	gilbertemichel@free.fr
web	chambrepuits.free.fr

Map 6 Entry 98

Burgundy

Manoir de Tarperon

Tarperon is uniquely French and an ageless charm breathes from the ancient turrets, fine antiques, paintings and prints. Soisick is modern and good fun, with her sense of humour and her unstuffy formality – if you can't find her, walk in and make yourself at home, she's not far. The rooms are full of family furniture in an uncontrived, fadedly elegant, lived-in décor; the bathrooms are family style, with lots of unusual bits. Dinner, superbly cooked by Claudine and Soisick, is a treat. Also: lovely gardens, fly-fishing (25 a day), painting courses. *Whole house for rent. Minimum stay two nights.*

rooms	5: 3 doubles, 1 twin, 1 triple.
price	€65. Triple €82-€90.
meals	Dinner with wine, €25.
closed	2 November-March.
directions	From Dijon N71 for Châtillon sur Seine, 62km; D901 right for Aignay le Duc. Tarperon sign on D901.

	Soisick de Champsavin
	Manoir de Tarperon,
	21510 Aignay le Duc,
	Côte-d'Or
tel	+33 (0)3 80 93 83 74
fax	+33 (0)3 80 93 83 74
mobile	+33 (0)6 07 89 26 13
email	manoir.de.tarperon@wanadoo.fr

Map 6 Entry 99

Burgundy

Villa le Clos

French country hospitality at its finest, meals you will remember for ever (people copy Madame's recipes), a sun trap by the summer house for your own barbecue, stupendous valley views over historic Alésia where Caesar fought Vercingétorix in 52BC (brush up your Asterix), great walks, medieval villages and a modern house set among bright tulips, terraced features and birdsong. Inside, beyond the Alpine mural, you find spotless rooms, good mattresses and bathrooms, a colourful chintzy décor – all endearingly French. Above all, you will remember these wonderfully warm, kind and thoughtful people.

rooms	2: 1 double, 1 twin, each with curtained shower, sharing wc.
price	€45.
meals	Dinner with wine, €20.
closed	November-Easter, except by arrangement.
directions	From Dijon N71 for Châtillon sur Seine; after Courceau D6 left & follow signs; house on D19A near junction with D6. (50km from Dijon.)

Claude & Huguette Gounand
Villa le Clos,
Route de la Villeneuve,
21150 Darcey, Côte-d'Or

tel	+33 (0)3 80 96 23 20
fax	+33 (0)3 80 96 23 20
email	claude.gounand@libertysurf.fr
web	perso.wanadoo.fr/claude.gounand/

Map 6 Entry 100

Burgundy

Château de Beauregard

A brief history of France, 17th-century Beauregard was built on a medieval stronghold overlaying a 5th-century Gallo-Roman settlement – and owned by one of Napoleon's generals who left a couple of sphinxes. The delightful, sociable Bonorons have been restoring the grand old house, its roofs piled high with old tiles, and the beautiful, sadly neglected garden for 15 years. They're also passionate about local wine-growing. Rooms are superb: fairly floral, proper old-style France with copies of original colours and wallpapers, and the suite has a bath you could swim in. A splendid place.

rooms	3: 2 doubles, 1 twin.
price	€100-€130.
meals	Restaurant 5km.
closed	December-January.
directions	From A6 exit at Bierre lès Semur; right for Précy sous Thil; D170 left for Dijon. At tile factory with large chimney right, signed.

Bernard & Nicole Bonoron
Château de Beauregard,
21390 Nan sous Thil,
Côte-d'Or

tel	+33 (0)3 80 64 41 08
fax	+33 (0)3 80 64 47 28
email	beauregard.chateau@wanadoo.fr
web	perso.wanadoo.fr/beauregard.chateau

Map 6 Entry 101

Burgundy

La Monastille

Stunning flagstones in the breakfast room (where pancakes and homemade jams are served) and wooden doors that creak open to cosy rooms. La Monastille is old, built in 1750 as a wealthy farmhouse, and feels like a miniature castle. Generous Madame is passionate about history, antiques, food and loves her English guests. Supper at the big table might be *pot-au-feu* with chicken from the farm next door. Wines flow. Bedrooms are a soothing mix of muted walls, dark old furniture and flowery bed covers, the dear little room in the tower is reached via many steps and outside is a lovely garden.

rooms	4 doubles.
price	€62.
meals	Dinner with wine, €25.
closed	Rarely.
directions	From Beaune D970 to Bligny sur Ouche; after village left to Écutigny; right to Thomirey; house with terracotta flower pots by church.

Françoise Moine
La Monastille,
21360 Thomirey,
Côte-d'Or
tel   +33 (0)3 80 20 00 80
fax   +33 (0)3 80 20 00 80
email   moine.francoise@wanadoo.fr
web   www.monastille.com

Map 11 Entry 102

Burgundy

34 rue de Mazy

You cannot forget the lifeblood of Burgundy: wine buffs will love the twisting drive along the *Route des Vins* into the gravelled courtyard of this fine old wine-grower's house. Your courteous host knows a lot about wine and loves to practise his English, so sample an aperitif in his atmospheric stone-arched cellar; there are locally-pressed fruit juices too. The house has a classic stone staircase and generous windows, the comfortable and homely bedrooms are reached by outside steps, the breakfast room has flagstones and ochre-coloured walls. In summer, breakfast is in the well-kept, willow-draped garden.

rooms	2: 1 double, 1 family room.
price	€50-€56.
meals	Restaurant 300m.
closed	Rarely.
directions	From Lyon N on A6 exit Nuits St Georges; N74 for Dijon. After approx. 13km left to Marsannay.

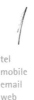

Jean-Charles & Brigitte Viennet
34 rue de Mazy,
21160 Marsannay la Côte,
Côte-d'Or
tel   +33 (0)3 80 59 83 63
mobile   +33 (0)6 82 11 43 31
email   viennet.jean-charles@wanadoo.fr
web   perso.wanadoo.fr/gite.marsannay

Map 6 Entry 103

Burgundy

La Closerie de Gilly

The generous warmth of the green-shuttered façade reaches indoors, too, where a beautiful Alsatian ceramic stove stands beside huge plants in the sunny breakfast room and the guest rooms are airy and florally friezed. Interesting prints on the walls too. Your hosts are chatty and friendly. Monsieur teaches economics, Madame gave up a high-powered marketing job to care for two small children and the visitors she so enjoys receiving. The entrance to the fine gardens and house may seem narrow but don't get it wrong: you are very welcome and can always leave the car outside.

rooms	3: 1 double, 1 triple, 1 family suite & kitchenette.
price	€75–€85.
meals	Restaurant 1km.
closed	Christmas.
directions	From A31 exit Nuits St Georges; N74 for Dijon; at Vougeot r'bout head for Gilly centre; 1st right after bridge.

André & Sandrine Lanaud
La Closerie de Gilly,
16 avenue du Recteur Bouchard,
Gilly lès Cîteaux, 21640 Vougeot,
Côte-d'Or

tel	+33 (0)3 80 62 87 74
fax	+33 (0)3 80 62 87 74
email	info@closerie-gilly.com
web	www.closerie-gilly.com

Map 11 Entry 104

Burgundy

Les Hêtres Rouges

A pretty old Burgundian hunting lodge, 'Copper Beeches' stands in a walled garden full of centenarian trees and has an unexpected air of Provence inside: beautifully judged colour schemes (Madame paints and knows about colour), fine furniture, numerous *objets*, burning incense, two cats and the odd sprig of flowers: soothing and reviving. Your hosts extend a warm, genuine yet ungushing welcome to the weary traveller – up a steep stair are low ceilings and superb bed linen, while the guest cottage is nicely independent. Breakfast has the savour of yesteryear: yogurt, fresh bread and homemade jam.

rooms	3: 1 double, 1 twin. Cottage: 1 twin/double.
price	€88. Cottage €117.
meals	Choice of restaurants 8km.
closed	Rarely.
directions	From A31 exit 1 on D35 for Seurre 3km; right to Quincey then Antilly, 4km. House on right.

Jean-François & Christiane Bugnet
Les Hêtres Rouges,
Antilly, 21700 Argilly, Côte-d'Or

tel	+33 (0)3 80 62 53 98
fax	+33 (0)3 80 62 54 85
email	leshetresrouges2@wanadoo.fr
web	www.leshetresrouges.com

Map 11 Entry 105

Burgundy

Maison des Abeilles

Madame, a genuine Burgundian with family in all the surrounding villages, believes in simplicity, quality and conviviality, and is gradually renovating all her rooms in the 19th-century barn and adjacent workers' cottages. Each has an outside door, two are up an outside stair, bathrooms are snug, some with half baths, and the décor is getting brighter by the month: newly-whitewashed stone walls, fresh fabrics, wooden ceilings and floors, some bits of rustic rough plaster. Breakfast is at one big table in the broad open kitchen looking onto hollyhocks and a fig tree: super atmosphere, excellent value.

rooms	5: 3 doubles, 2 family suites for 4.
price	€47–€53.
meals	Occasional dinner with wine, €24. Restaurant 3km.
closed	Rarely.
directions	A6; exit Beaune à St Nicolas; D974 for Dijon. In Ladoix-Serrigny, left at Chemist for Magny Les Viliers; in village, 1st left onto rue du Lavoir; at tree-lined square, left to Pernand for 2-3m, park alongside trees.

Jocelyne Gaugey
Maison des Abeilles,
Route de Pernand Vergelesses,
21700 Magny les Villers,
Côte-d'Or
tel   +33 (0)3 80 62 95 42
email   joel.gaugey@wanadoo.fr
web   perso.wanadoo.fr/maison-des-abeilles/

Map 11 Entry 106

Burgundy

Place de l'Église

Ancient rafters, white-swathed roof windows, little florals, and a supper salon on the landing. The bedrooms, one on the ground floor in pink, yellow and lime green, another with a rickety ladder up to the mezzanine, are French-traditional, just like the wide flowery terrace where breakfast is served on fine days. The Dufouleur wine is good – Monsieur comes from generations of vignerons and may keep you enthralled for hours (in French!). This house stands on the remains of the Duke of Burgundy's 13th-century castle and the little church is floodlit at night. *Wine-tasting cellar. Children over 10 welcome.*

rooms	4: 1 double, 2 triples; 1 double with mezzanine for children.
price	€70–€75.
meals	Light supper €18. Wine from €11.50.
closed	Rarely.
directions	From A31 exit Nuits St Georges for Gerland-Seurre 3km; right to Quincey; house opposite church.

Chantal Dufouleur
Place de l'Église,
21700 Quincey,
Côte-d'Or
tel   +33 (0)3 80 61 13 23
fax   +33 (0)3 80 61 13 23
email   dufouleurchantal@wanadoo.fr
web   perso.wanadoo.fr/gite.nuits-saint-georges/

Map 11 Entry 107

Burgundy

14 avenue Charles Jaffelin

If your French is imperfect but you fancy becoming fluent in the lore of Burgundy – the region and its wine – this is the place for you. Indeed, Jonathan and Susie have worked in practically every wine-growing region of France over the past 20 years. Just outside the ramparts of the old town, peeping over high walls, the house has two creeper-clad wings joined by a tower. Once inside, guests have their own door up to super bedrooms on two floors and wcs in a tower. The walled garden behind has a child-safe pool, and you will be welcomed on arrival with a glass (or two) of something local. Cosy, friendly, relaxing.

rooms	2: 1 double, 1 suite for 2-4.
price	€90–€120.
meals	Restaurants within walking distance.
closed	Rarely.
directions	On one-way road round ramparts of Beaune, exit for Auxerre (RN, not m'way); house on right after 200m, big white gates.

Susie & Jonathan Lyddon
14 avenue Charles Jaffelin,
Route de Bouze, 21200 Beaune,
Côte-d'Or

tel	+33 (0)3 80 26 90 98
fax	+32(0) 2 6 47 38 93
email	enquiries@routedebouze.com
web	www.routedebouze.com

Map 11 Entry 108

Burgundy

Les Planchottes

If you find yourself in the Mecca of Wine, surely you should stay with a family of winegrowers like the Bouchards? – and sip your aperitif in the courtyard looking out over their organic vineyards. They are charming people, passionate about food, wine and matters 'green'; Cécile's breakfasts linger long in the memory. The townhouse – once three cottages – is immaculate inside. The craftsmanship of new oak and stone, the quiet good taste of the colours, the space in the comfortable bedrooms, the sparkling lights in the bathrooms – they beat most three-star hotels into a cocked hat. The garden is a hidden gem.

rooms	2: 1 double, 1 twin.
price	€95.
meals	Restaurants 100m.
closed	January-February.
directions	On one-way road round ramparts of Beaune, 200m after War Memorial, right at 2nd traffic light; Rue Sylvestre Chauvelot starts at Peugeot garage.

Christophe & Cécile Bouchard
Les Planchottes,
6 rue Sylvestre Chauvelot,
21200 Beaune, Côte-d'Or

tel	+33 (0)3 80 22 83 67
fax	+33 (0)3 80 22 83 67
email	lesplanchottes@voila.fr
web	lesplanchottes.free.fr

Map 11 Entry 109

Burgundy

La Maison d'Aviler

On each floor, eight tall windows look down on the resplendent garden that shelters Aviler from noise. At the back is the Yonne where barges peacefully ply: what a setting. The house was originally a workhouse – destitution in 18th-century France had its compensations. Your hosts were interior decorators by trade and collectors by instinct, so expect subtle but sumptuous detail in elegantly French bedrooms and advice on the best local auctions. Monsieur will even help you bid! Sens has a memorable cathedral, a tempting market, and the shops and restaurants of this lovely town simply yell 'quality'.

rooms	3: 1 double, 1 suite for 3; 1 twin with separate shower.
price	€66–€77.
meals	Restaurants in Sens.
closed	Rarely.
directions	From A19 exit Sens, St Denis les Sens towards Sens Centre Ville. Right between Mercedes garage and restaurant. Left at river, follow road on right bank to No. 43. Green iron gates.

Bernard Barré
La Maison d'Aviler,
43 quai du Petit Hameau,
89100 Sens, Yonne
tel   +33 (0)3 86 95 49 25
email   daviler@online.fr
web   www.daviler.online.fr

Map 5 Entry 110

Burgundy

Le Moulinot

The handsome millhouse, surrounded by herons, kingfishers and a rushing river, is reached via a narrow, private bridge. Wander the beautiful grounds or settle yourself in the most inviting sitting room, complete with roaring log fire when it's cold. Leigh and Cinda are charming hosts who delight in sharing their watery world. There's a canoe and a lake where Leigh has sunk a brilliant natural-looking swimming pool; and balloon flights can be arranged. The big, light bedrooms are freshly decorated with good bathrooms and the mill race is generally noisier than the road. Wonderful. *Children over eight welcome.*

rooms	6: 5 doubles, 1 twin.
price	€55–€80.
meals	Restaurants nearby.
closed	Rarely.
directions	From Auxerre N6 for Avallon, 22km; just before Vermenton village sign, sharp right, double back & over bridge.

Leigh & Cinda Wootton
Le Moulinot,
89270 Vermenton,
Yonne
tel   +33 (0)3 86 81 60 42
email   lemoulinot@aol.com
web   www.moulinot.com

Map 5 Entry 111

Burgundy

Le Calounier

These young owners have brought vitality to their handsome old house with a clever conversion that lets in stacks of light – perfect for exhibiting artists' work. Busy Corinne has created comfortable, colour coordinated bedrooms and good bathrooms; the suite, with inter-connecting rooms, has a sitting room downstairs. Meals, prettily candlelit, are worth booking, there are courses for groups interested in traditional French cooking, and you may choose from Pascal's Yonne wines (not cheap!). A sail provides welcome shade in the pretty little garden. The remote village is tiny, the peace a balm.

rooms	4: 1 double, 1 twin, 1 family room, 1 suite for 4.
price	€61.
meals	Dinner with wine, €17-€23.
closed	January & February.
directions	From A6 exit Nitry for Tonnerre for 7km; right at x-roads sign Chambres d'Hôtes 1.5km; left for Môlay to Arton; house opposite 'lavoir' (wash hut).

Corinne & Pascal Collin
Le Calounier,
5 rue de la Fontaine-Arton,
89310 Môlay, Yonne
tel   +33 (0)3 86 82 67 81
fax   +33 (0)3 86 82 67 81
email info@lecalounier.fr
web   www.lecalounier.fr

Map 6 Entry 112

Burgundy

Maison Crème Anglaise

They named the gracious old house after their desserts, served with *crème anglaise*. From a Tin-Tin collection to Custard the dog, this mellow old place is full of surprises. Swallows nest in a medieval archway, a staircase winds up a tower and the garden falls steeply away giving unforgettable views. Meals are accompanied by candles and flowers, bedrooms are airy and appealing and the charming bathroom is shared. Graham and Christine, open and friendly, hold recitals, art exhibitions and summer *salons de thé* in the courtyard. The hilltop village is historic; tranquility abounds.

rooms	3: 1 double, 1 twin, 1 children's twin sharing bath.
price	€49.
meals	Dinner with wine, €18.
closed	Never.
directions	In Montréal towards church; through arch, house on right.

Graham & Christine Battye
Maison Crème Anglaise,
22 grande rue,
89420 Montréal, Yonne
tel   +33 (0)3 86 32 07 73
fax   +33 (0)3 86 32 07 73
email grahambattye@maisoncremeanglaise.com
web   www.maisoncremeanglaise.com

Map 6 Entry 113

Burgundy

Cabalus

Inimitable. You are on the top of the 'eternal hill' at the centre of one of the most revered historic sites in France; ancient and atmospheric, the old pilgrims' hospice stands in the shadow of the Basilica. A gallery of quietly intriguing, tempting objects and a much-loved coffee shop occupy the 12th-century vaulted hall but guests have that vast fireplace to themselves for organic breakfasts. Rooms are simple, artistic, authentic. Eccentric Monsieur Cabalus is the perfect gentleman with a fine sense of humour, younger Madame is a most welcoming artist. And the morning mists hang in the valley.

rooms	4: 2 doubles; 2 doubles, each with shower, sharing wcs.
price	€58–€75.
meals	Dinner with wine, €20.
closed	Rarely.
directions	In Vézelay centre take main street up to Basilica. Park, walk down main street, ring at 2nd door on right.

	M Cabalus
	Cabalus,
	Rue Saint Pierre,
	89450 Vézelay, Yonne
tel	+33 (0)3 86 33 20 66
mobile	+33 (0)6 13 71 08 20
email	contact@cabalus.com
web	www.cabalus.com

Map 5   Entry 114

Meals, booking and cancelling

Dinner

Do remember that table d'hôtes is a fixed-price set menu that has to be booked. Very few owners offer dinner every day. Once you have booked dinner, it is a question of common courtesy to turn up and partake of the meal prepared for you. Dining in can be a wonderful opportunity to experience both food and company in an authentic French family atmosphere. Or it may be more formal and still utterly French. Some owners no longer eat with their guests for family and waistline reasons.

Rooms

We have heard of chambres d'hôtes hopefuls arriving unannounced at 7pm and being devastated to learn that the house was full. For your own sake and your hosts', do ring ahead: if they can't have you, owners can usually suggest other places nearby. But arriving without warning at the end of the day is asking for disappointment.

Cancelling

As soon as you realise you are not going to take up a booking, even late in the day, please telephone immediately. The owners may still be able to let the room for that night and at least won't stay up wondering whether you've had an accident and when they can give up and go to bed.

By the same token, if you find you're going to arrive later than planned, let your hosts know so that they won't worry unnecessarily or... let your room to someone else.

Paris – Ile de France

Paris – Ile de France

Le Logis d'Arnières

Several centuries shaped this old hunting lodge, then it was determinedly 'modernised' in the 1920s Art Deco style: high-windowed, fully-panelled dining room with extraordinary dressers, fabulous bathroom fittings. It is exuberantly sober and shapely with Versailles parquet and fine fireplaces as well. Tae, from Chile, uses her perfect sense of style and colour to include these respected elements in her décor alongside richly baroque Chinese chairs and lots of South American pieces and paintings. Quiet spot, vast natural garden, joyous hosts, perfect for Chartres, Paris, Versailles.

rooms	2 suites for 5.
price	€70. €105 for 4.
meals	Restaurant 200m.
closed	Rarely.
directions	From A10 exit 10 to toll gate, right after toll; right again on D27 to St Cyr; continue for Arpajon; 1st house on left.

Claude & Tae Dabasse
Le Logis d'Arnières,
1 rue du Pont-Rué,
91410 St Cyr sous Dourdan,
Essonne

tel   +33 (0)1 64 59 14 89
fax   +33 (0)1 64 59 07 46
email   taedabasse@aol.com
web   www.dabasse.com/arniere/

Map 5 Entry 115

Paris – Ile de France

Le Clos de la Rose

For birdwatchers and garden lovers (masses of roses, age-old trees), history vultures and cheese tasters (Brie on the doorstep, lovely Provins nearby), Jean-Paul's gorgeous green retreat from crazed Paris is cool, quiet, elegantly homely and has been restored with fine respect for an old flint house: limewash, wood, terracotta and a great collection of books, paintings, prints. He works from home and looks after guests with care and intelligence, Martine still works in town. Bedrooms have pretty colours and mixed-style furniture, a big new apartment is planned, the adorable cottage is ideal for a longer stay. *Minimum stay two nights.*

rooms	2 + 1: 2 doubles. 1 cottage for 2.
price	€64-€138.
meals	Restaurant 5-minute drive.
closed	Rarely.
directions	From Paris A4 for Reims; exit 18 to La Ferté sous Jouarre; D407 for Montmirail; through woodland to Montapeine (6 km from r'bout in La Ferté); D68 for St Ouen; 1.8 km right; 400m to black gate.

Martine & Jean-Paul Krebs
Le Clos de la Rose,
11 rue de la Source, L'Hermitière,
77750 St Cyr sur Morin,
Seine-et-Marne

tel   +33 (0)1 60 44 81 04
fax   +33 (0)1 60 24 40 84
email   infos@rosa-gallica.fr
web   www.rosa-gallica.fr

Map 5 Entry 116

Paris – Ile de France

Le Portail Bleu

The high blue doors open onto a pair of low stone buildings round a narrow courtyard, the apse of the medieval church can be espied over the wall. The Laurents are friendly, easy-going, generous with ever a new project to hand (the marble bathroom is not their doing!). They have two children who adopt stray cats, keep miniature ponies and will do all they can to make your stay peaceful and fruitful. Flexible breakfasts are served in a bistro-like breakfast room, and bedrooms are 1930-style and inviting. Pleasing bric-a-brac, paintings and old lace at windows; one room has doors to the garden.

rooms	4: 1 triple, 1 suite for 5, 1 suite for 6; 1 suite for 4 & kitchen.
price	€56–€65. Triple €77. Suites €97–€137.
meals	Dinner with wine, €20.
closed	Rarely.
directions	From A4 exit 13 to Villeneuve le Comte; right on D96 through Neufmoutiers to Châtres. House in village centre to left of church.

Dominique & Pierre Laurent
Le Portail Bleu,
2 route de Fontenay,
77610 Châtres, Seine-et-Marne

tel	+33 (0)1 64 25 84 94
fax	+33 (0)1 64 25 84 94
email	leportailbleu@voila.fr
web	www.leportailbleu.com

Map 5 Entry 117

Paris – Ile de France

Manoir de Beaumarchais

It's charmingly bourgeois, and the welcome is warmly French. The house is an architectural cuckoo: an 'Anglo-Norman' face concealing an unspoilt 1920s interior. Fascinating (great arched windows, crested tiles), elegant, comfortable, beautifully furnished. Views are of stretching pastures. Your suite is as untouched as the aqua-panelled salon: pretty, intimate and stylish, with a boudoir sitting room in the tower. Big breakfasts appear at the long dining table; in good English, your retired hosts enjoy telling the history of grandfather's hunting lodge (they still organise shoots).

rooms	1 suite.
price	€130.
meals	Restaurants nearby.
closed	Rarely.
directions	From A4 exit 13 to Villeneuve le C.; right D96 for Tournan; after Neufmoutiers, 1st left small road 1.5km; white gates on left.

Hubert & Francine Charpentier
Manoir de Beaumarchais,
77610 Les Chapelles Bourbon,
Seine-et-Marne

tel	+33 (0)1 64 07 11 08
fax	+33 (0)1 64 07 14 48
email	hubert.charpentier@wanadoo.fr
web	www.le-manoir-de-beaumarchais.com

Map 5 Entry 118

Paris – Ile de France

Bellevue

The big informal garden merges into fields: don't worry about those new houses, there's green space for everyone. Space in the high-beamed dayroom too, and at the magnificent breakfast table made of ancient oak. Upstairs, the simple, softly-coloured rooms, each with two beds on a mezzanine, are ideal for families. A dash of colour adds character, and shower rooms are cleverly designed. The two temptingly independent lodges are quietly stylish, with antique mirrors, modern checks and terraces. Isabelle and Patrick have all the time in the world for their guests and speak English well.

rooms	5: 1 triple, 4 quadruples.
price	Triple €72–€91. Quadruples €87–€106.
meals	Choice of restaurants 4km.
closed	Rarely.
directions	From A4 exit 13 to Villeneuve le Comte; follow signs to Neufmoutiers en Brie then Chambres d'Hôtes signs.

Isabelle & Patrick Galpin
Bellevue,
77610 Neufmoutiers en Brie,
Seine-et-Marne
tel   +33 (0)1 64 07 11 05
fax   +33 (0)1 64 07 19 27
email   ipgalpin@domaine-de-bellevue.net
web   www.domaine-de-bellevue.net

Map 5 Entry 119

Paris – Ile de France

Ferme de Vert St-Père

Cereals and beets grow in wide fields and show-jumpers add a definite touch of elegance to the landscape. A generous farmyard surrounded by beautiful warm stone buildings encloses utter quiet and a genuine welcome from hosts and labradors alike, out here where Monsieur's family has come hunting for 200 years (his great-grandfather was a surgeon with Napoleon's army). Family furniture (the 1900s ensemble is most intriguing) in light-filled rooms, spotless mod cons and a vast sitting room for guests with piano and billiard table. All this, and a Michelin-starred auberge in the village.

rooms	1 + 2: 1 family room for 3. 2 apartments for 4.
price	€58. Apartments €92.
meals	Restaurant in village.
closed	Christmas week.
directions	From A5 exit 15 on N36 towards Meaux, 200m; 2nd right to Crisenoy after TGV bridge, through village for 'Tennis/Salle des Fêtes'; 1.5km to farm.

Philippe & Jeanne Mauban
Ferme de Vert St-Père,
77390 Crisenoy,
Seine-et-Marne
tel   +33 (0)1 64 38 83 51
fax   +33 (0)1 64 38 83 52
email   mauban.vert@wanadoo.fr
web   vert.saint.pere.free.fr

Map 5 Entry 120

Paris – Ile de France

L'Atalante

Cocooned behind the garden walls, one of two hideaways leads straight off the garden. The uncluttered, open-plan space is fresh and bright with its cool cream floors, nautical stripes and pale walls, and, with its curtained-off sitting area and fire, most inviting. Up under the eaves is a fresh two-bedroomed suite overlooking the beautiful peonies and pathways. Tinkle the ivories in the *salon de musique*, stretch out on the flower-freckled lawn. You can use the kitchenette if you want to be independent or join your charming, interested and interesting hosts for dinner. One of our favourites.

Paris – Ile de France

Montmartre district

In the 'village' that is Montmartre – bustling boulevard below, fabric shops next door, Sacré Cœur above – barrister Valérie and her architect husband have created a super-chic studio off their charming cobbled courtyard. The double bed is dressed in dramatic dark red against the white walls, the dining table is an oval antique, the kitchen space a little pine and steel gem, the shower generous, the mirror framed in red. Valérie's discreet decorative flourishes speak for her calm, positive personality and her interest in other lands.
A delicious Paris hideaway you can call your own. *Minimum stay two nights.*

rooms	2: 1 suite for 2-5, 1 suite for 2-4.
price	€55.
meals	Dinner with wine, €22. Guest kitchen.
closed	Rarely.
directions	From A5 exit 17 on D210 for Provins 2km; right D133 1km; left for Gardeloup. Left to Grand Buisson.

rooms	1 studio & kitchenette.
price	€95 (€570 per week).
meals	Breakfast not included. Restaurants nearby.
closed	Rarely.
directions	Metro: Anvers Sacre Coeur (2). Metro/ RER: Gare du Nord. Bus: 30, 31, 54, 85. Car park: Rue Fentrier.

Florence & Georges Manulelis
L'Atalante,
8 rue grande du Buisson,
77148 Laval en Brie,
Seine-et-Marne
fax   +33 (0)1 45 82 94 02
mobile +33 (0)6 86 18 54 98
email   latalante@free.fr
web   latalante.free.fr

Valerie Zuber
Montmartre district,
75018 Paris
fax   +33 (0)1 42 58 47 40
mobile +33 (0)6 30 93 81 35
email   studiodamelie@wanadoo.fr
web   www.paris-oasis.com

Map 5 Entry 121

Map 5 Entry 122

Paris – Ile de France

Belleville district

The street throbs with a motley, multicultural crowd but from the top of this clean modern block you can stretch your eyes across Paris to the scintillating towers of La Défense or the Parc de Belleville, a surprising green hillside above the city. Your pretty room lets in fabulous sunsets over the Eiffel Tower and no noise. The flat is all white walls, modern parquet floors and fine old family furniture, lots from Provence where your very proper elderly hostess used to live. Madame serves fresh pastries at breakfast and tells you all about everything with great verve. *Minimum stay two nights. Spanish spoken.*

rooms	1 double.
price	€69.
meals	Restaurant within walking distance.
closed	Rarely.
directions	Metro: Belleville (2, 11) 200m: 15 mins to centre. Parking & directions: ask owners. Lift to 9th floor.

Danièle de La Brosse
Belleville district,
75019 Paris
tel   +33 (0)1 42 41 99 59
fax   +33 (0)1 42 41 99 59
email   dan.delabrosse@wanadoo.fr

Map 5 Entry 123

Paris – Ile de France

Belleville district

Sabine, artist and art therapist, "feeds people with colours". Jules makes the organic bread with a dazzling smile and big, beautiful Taquin, his guide dog, loves people. Kindly and artistic, they live calmly in this bit of genuine old Paris between two tiny gardens and a tall house. The simple guest room, with good double bed and flame-covered sleigh-bed divan, a welcome tea-maker and an old-fashioned bathroom, shares a building with Sabine's studio. Healthfoody continental breakfast is in the cosy family room in the main house or outside under the birdsung tree. Such peace in Paris is rare. *Minimum stay two nights.*

rooms	1 triple.
price	€66.
meals	Choice of restaurants within walking distance.
closed	July-August.
directions	Metro: Jourdain (11) or Place des Fêtes (11). Parking: Place des Fêtes. Bus: 26, 48, 60.

Sabine & Jules Aïm
Belleville district,
75019 Paris
tel   +33 (0)1 42 08 23 71
fax   +33 (0)1 42 40 56 04
email   jules.aim@wanadoo.fr

Map 5 Entry 124

Paris – Ile de France

Port des Champs-Elysées

Could a room in Paris be more special? It has a panorama of half the city's monuments, the evening twinkles with the Eiffel Tower's hourly brilliance, France's MPs congregate just across the water. A great gilt-framed mirror greets you as you embark, a companionway leads to a simple, cosy bedroom, you have a full bathroom. The airy, wood lined ship has books all round its family-worn, well-loved living room where breakfast is served: Alain and Rita brought up four boys here. A jovial, quick-witted art lover, he will point you to an insider's view of Paris. A real treat (for the nimble-footed).

rooms	1 double.
price	€150.
meals	Restaurants within walking distance.
closed	Rarely.
directions	Metro: Concorde (1, 8, 12); Assemblée Nationale (12). Bus: 24, 42, 52, 72, 84, 94.

Alain Carlier & Rita Leys
Pytheas Vivas,
Port des Champs-Elysées,
75008 Paris
tel   +33 (0)1 42 68 05 85
mobile   +33 (0)6 88 84 47 92
email   agcarlier@orange.fr
web   bed-breakfast-paris.eu

Map 5 Entry 125

Paris – Ile de France

National Assembly / Invalides district

In a provincial-quiet city street, classy dressed stone outside, intelligence, sobriety and style inside. Madame takes you into her vast, serene apartment: no modern gadgets or curly antiques, just a few good pieces, much space and light-flooded parquet floors. Beyond the dining room, the cosy biscuit-coloured bedroom gives onto a big, silent, arcaded courtyard. Your hosts have lived all over the world; Monsieur, a retired engineer, spends his days studying. Madame, as quiet and genuine as her surroundings, lives for her country garden near Chartres and the company of like-minded visitors – she is worth getting to know.

rooms	1 twin/double.
price	€85.
meals	Choice of restaurants within walking distance.
closed	Rarely.
directions	Metro: Solférino (12), Assemblée Nationale (12) or Invalides (8). Parking: Invalides. Lift to 2nd floor.

Mme Élisabeth Marchal
National Assembly/Invalides district
75007 Paris
tel   +33 (0)1 47 05 70 21/
          +33 (0)2 37 23 38 19

Map 5 Entry 126

Paris – Ile de France

Châtelet district

You will be staying with a most civilised couple, she bubbly and interested, he quiet and studious, a university professor, in their very personal, gently refined apartment where original timbers, saved from the renovator's axe, divide the living room and two friendly cats proclaim the cosiness. It is beautifully done, like a warm soft nest, antique-furnished, lots of greenery, interesting art. Madame greatly enjoys her guests and is full of tips on Paris. The attractive, compact guest quarters down the corridor are nicely private with good storage space, pretty quilts and lots of light. *Minimum stay two nights.*

rooms	1 twin.
price	€85.
meals	Restaurants nearby.
closed	Summer holidays.
directions	Metro: Châtelet (1, 4, 7, 11, 14) or Pont-Neuf (7) (between Louvre & Notre-Dame). Parking: Conforama car park, via Rue du Pont Neuf then Rue Boucher. Lift to 3rd floor.

Mme Mona Pierrot
Châtelet district,
75001 Paris
tel   +33 (0)1 42 36 50 65

Map 5 Entry 127

Paris – Ile de France

Notre Dame district

At the end of the street are the Seine and the glory of Notre Dame, her buttresses flying through history. In a grand old building, the unaffected tall-windowed rooms, separated by flights of 17th-century stone stairs, look down to a little garden and peace. The low-mezzanined family room has a bathroom off the private landing where simple breakfast is served beside a spiral staircase. The second, smaller, room has the bed in the corner and a fresh new décor. Madame is polyglot, active in the city, and eager to help when she can – she and her daughter enjoy guests and the variety of contact they bring.

rooms	2: 1 double; 1 quadruple with separate bathroom.
price	€75-€90.
meals	Restaurants nearby.
closed	Rarely.
directions	From street, enter 2407. In courtyard, ring house bell on left. Metro: Maubert-Mutualité (10). RER/Metro: St Michel. Book parking ahead.

Mme Brigitte Chatignoux
Notre Dame district,
75005 Paris
tel   +33 (0)1 43 25 27 20
email   brichati@hotmail.com

Map 5 Entry 128

Paris – Ile de France

Montparnasse district

Filled with books, paintings and objects from all over the world, the Monbrisons' intimate little flat is fascinating. Lively American Cynthia, an art-lover, and quintessentially French Christian, knowledgeable about history, wine and cattle-breeding, offer great hospitality and will take guests on special evening tours to historical landmarks. Their guest room, quiet, sunny, snug, has a king-size bed and its own bathroom. Twice a week, the street market brings the real food of France to your doorstep; shops, cafés and restaurants abound; you can walk to the Luxembourg Gardens. *Enquire about their B&B in south-west France.*

rooms	1 twin/double.
price	€79.
meals	Occasional dinner with wine.
closed	August.
directions	Metro: Edgar Quinet (6) or Montparnasse (4, 6, 12, 13). Airport buses from Orly & Charles de Gaulle to Montparnasse (5 minutes' walk).

Christian & Cynthia de Monbrison
Montparnasse district,
75014 Paris
tel +33 (0)1 43 35 20 87
fax +33 (0)1 45 38 68 72
mobile +33 (0)6 27 20 74 44

Map 5 Entry 129

Paris – Ile de France

Montparnasse district

A little white blue-shuttered house in a cobbled alley? Just behind Montparnasse? It's not a dream and Janine, a fascinating live-wire cinema journalist who has lived in Canada, will welcome you of an evening to her pretty wood-ceilinged kitchen/diner (she's a night bird so breakfast will be laid for you to do your own). The guest room across the book-lined hall is a good, square room with a highly pleasing mix of warm fabrics, honeycomb tiles, white walls, old chest and contemporary paintings. The new white and pine bathroom has space, all mod cons and good cupboards. Ideal. *Minimum stay two nights.*

rooms	1 double.
price	€54.
meals	Restaurants nearby.
closed	July-September.
directions	Metro: Gaîté (13). RER: Denfert-Rochereau; airport buses nearby. Bus: 28 58.

Janine Euvrard
Montparnasse district,
75014 Paris
tel +33 (0)1 43 27 19 43
fax +33 (0)1 43 27 19 43
email euvrard@club-internet.fr

Map 5 Entry 130

Paris – Ile de France

10 rue Denfert Rochereau

You can be close to the centre of Paris but still relax in a sweet, gnomy garden under the gazebo. Cecilia is Anglo-French and loves having people to stay in her comfortable 1950s suburban house. She enjoys a chat over the breakfast table, helping you plan the day ahead. Green is clearly her favourite colour. Rooms open directly to the garden and are light and airy with replica tapestry wall hangings, chintzy curtains with net drapes, onyx figurine bedside lamps, potted plants and, I need hardly say, green carpets. *Six minutes from centre of Paris by train. Minimum stay two nights.*

Paris – Ile de France

Le Clos des Princes

Ten minutes on the train and you're in Paris. Here, behind wrought-iron gates in an elegant suburb, the French mansion sits in an exuberant town garden of pergolas, box bushes and mature trees. Your kind, attentive hosts – she an ex-English teacher, he with a passion for Prudhomme – give you the poet/philosopher's two-room first-floor suite; he lived here in 1902. Polished floorboards, pretty prints, choice antiques, decorative perfume bottles by a claw-footed tub – all dance to the 19th-century theme. Breakfast unveils gorgeous porcelain and delicious homemade muffins and jams.

rooms	1 quadruple & kitchenette.
price	€60-€90. Breakfast €5 p.p.
meals	Restaurants nearby.
closed	Occasionally.
directions	From the Paris Périphérique, exit Porte d'Asnières through Levallois, across Seine. Ask for map. Train: from St Lazare, *Banlieue* direct train to Bécon Les Bruyères.

rooms	1 suite for 2-3 with separate bath.
price	€105.
meals	Restaurant 400m.
closed	15 July-August.
directions	From the Paris Périphérique, exit Porte d'Orléans onto N20; A86 after Bourg la Reine to Versailles; exit 28 for Châtenay Malabry; over at Salvador Allende r'bout; right at 2nd r'bout; house on left.

	M & Mme Bobrie
	10 rue Denfert Rochereau,
	92600 Asnières sur Seine,
	Hauts-de-Seine
tel	+33 (0)1 47 93 53 60
fax	+33 (0)1 47 93 53 60
email	ceciliasguesthouse@hotmail.com

	Christine & Eric Duprez
	Le Clos des Princes,
	60 ave Jean Jaurès, 92290
	Châtenay Malabry,
	Hauts-de-Seine
tel	+33 (0)1 46 61 94 49
mobile	+33 (0)6 70 33 19 16
email	christine.eric.duprez@noos.fr

Map 5 Entry 131

Map 5 Entry 132

Villa Mansart

Wind your way up the handsome staircase and nudge open the attic door. The guest salon has sunny walls, mustard sofas and ethnic rugs on pristine floors. Slim, arched bedrooms are blue or vanilla-and-orange with family furniture and windows that peep over the rooftops. Breakfast on fresh fruit and mini-pastries in an elegant dining room or on the terrace. Marble steps, rescued from a local demolition, sweep down to a huge, immaculate lawn; a curtain of trees shields you from the suburbs. All is peace and calm yet only 20 minutes from the centre of Paris. *Garage available. Minimum stay two nights Mar-Oct.*

rooms	2: 1 double, 1 triple. Extra single bed in salon.
price	€79. Triple €105. Singles €55.
meals	Restaurants close by.
closed	Rarely.
directions	From Paris A4; exit 5 for Pont de Nogent; at exit keep left, don't take tunnel; along viaduct; at 2nd lights under bridge; Av. L. Rollin for Le Perreux centre; next lights straight on; 2nd left 200m.

Françoise Marcoz
Villa Mansart,
9 allée Victor Basche,
94170 Le Perreux sur Marne,
Val-de-Marne

tel	+33 (0)1 48 72 91 88
fax	+33 (0)1 48 72 91 88
email	francoisemarcoz@hotmail.com
web	www.villamansart.com

Map 5 Entry 133

27 rue de Beauvau

The new owners of this townhouse have brought it new, gorgeously minimalist white life. Their three well-mannered teenagers add to the lively atmosphere; all happily chat to guests with comfortable informality. The one smallish second-floor guest room is as uncomplicated as the rest with honey-coloured floorboards, red/beige Jouy curtains and bedcover and two deep red lampshades to focus the eye. In the big double salon original mouldings and fireplaces gleam palely, its one painting a modern splash of colour. A sumptuous breakfast and intimate garden finish the picture. *Minimum stay two nights.*

rooms	1 double with separate wc.
price	€80.
meals	Choice of restaurants nearby.
closed	Rarely.
directions	From Paris A13 for Rouen; after 7km exit for Versailles on D186 & Bd St Antoine to r'bout: Place de la Loi; opp. rue Colonel de Bauge; right at lights, 3rd right, rue Beauvau; house 3rd on right.

Philippe & Christine Agostini
27 rue de Beauvau,
78000 Versailles,
Yvelines

tel	+33 (0)1 39 50 16 43
mobile	+33 (0)6 20 64 38 89
email	p.agostini1@libertysurf.fr

Map 5 Entry 134

Paris – Ile de France

7 rue Gustave Courbet

Behind the modest façade – on this lush, private housing estate – is a generous interior where Madame's interesting paintings (she once taught art) stand in pleasing contrast to elegant antiques and feminine furnishings. Picture windows let the garden in and the woods rise beyond. The larger guest room is soberly classic in blue, with a fur throw and big bathroom; the smaller one with skylight and bathroom across the landing is excellent value. Madame, charming and communicative, sings as well as she paints and enjoys cooking refined dinners for attentive guests; she is very good company. Usefully close to Paris.

rooms	2: 1 double; 1 double with separate bath.
price	€50–€65.
meals	Dinner with wine, €18.
closed	Rarely.
directions	From Paris A13 on A12 for St Quentin en Yvelines; exit N12 for Dreux; exit to Plaisir Centre; 1st exit off r'bout for Plaisir Les Gâtines, 1st left for 400m; right into Domaine des Gâtines; consult roadside plan.

	Mme Hélène Castelnau
	7 rue Gustave Courbet,
	Domaine des Gâtines,
	78370 Plaisir, Yvelines
tel	+33 (0)1 30 54 05 15
fax	+33 (0)1 30 54 05 15
mobile	+33 (0)6 79 21 86 44
email	hcastelnau@club-internet.fr

Map 5 Entry 135

Paris – Ile de France

La Saussaye

In the Seine valley, a civilised distance from Paris, is this beautifully restored old farmhouse. The long warm-looking house, its white shutters garlanded by scented climbers, is home to this young energetic couple and their five children. Perrine brought her Parisian chic to the country and generous guest rooms in a private wing are tributes to her artistic creativity. Crisp striped cotton covers, smooth bed linen, polished floors, white walls – it is charming and restful. At breakfast, starched tablecloths fall to the floor and pretty painted chairs with flirty finials inject a romantic, very French air.

rooms	3 doubles.
price	€60–€80.
meals	Dinner with wine, €15.
closed	Christmas.
directions	From Paris; A13 exit 15 to Chaufour; right to Blaru; 1st left to La Saussaye; house 500m on left.

	Perrine & Stanislas Ripert
	La Saussaye,
	78270 Blaru, Yvelines
tel	+33 (0)1 34 76 23 42
mobile	+33 (0)6 21 24 01 61
email	stanislasripert@hotmail.com
web	www.lasaussaye.com

Map 4 Entry 136

Paris – Ile de France

Château d'Hazeville

Utterly original, a meld of brimming creativity and scholarship, Hazeville dazzles. Your artist host uses his fine château-farm, dated 1400s to 1600s, as a living show of his talents: huge abstract paintings, hand-painted plates and tiles, a stunning 'Egyptian' reception room (and loos), and now photography. The old stables house hi-tech artisans. Beautifully finished guest rooms in the *pigeonnier* are deeply luxurious; generous breakfasts come on china hand-painted by Monsieur to match the wall covering; he also knows the secret treasures of the Vexin. *Children over seven welcome. Hot-air ballooning possible.*

rooms	2: 1 double, 1 twin.
price	€125.
meals	Choice of restaurants within 5-10km.
closed	Weekdays & school term time.
directions	From Rouen N14 for Paris. 20km before Pontoise, at Magny en Vexin, right D983 to Arthies; left D81 through Enfer; château on left.

Guy & Monique Deneck
Château d'Hazeville,
95420 Wy dit Joli Village,
Val-d'Oise
tel   +33 (0)1 34 67 06 17
fax   +33 (0)1 34 67 17 82
email guy.deneck@free.fr

Map 5 Entry 137

Paris – Ile de France

La Ferme des Tourelles

A straightforward welcome, an unpretentious house with that friendly, lived-in air — what matter if sometimes it's the oilcloth on the table. These amiable, down-to-earth farmers love having children and guests around and lead a sociable life. Low-beamed bedrooms are modest but comfortable with imitation parquet floors and very good mattresses. In summer, meals can be taken under canvas in the flower-filled courtyard. Readers have told of hilarious evenings in approximate French and English over honest, family meals, often made with home-grown vegetables. Usefully near Paris.

rooms	2 doubles.
price	€48.
meals	Dinner with wine, €19.
closed	Rarely.
directions	From Dreux N12 to Broué; D305 to La Musse (La Musse between Boutigny & Prouais); Chambres d'Hôtes signs.

Serge & Jeanne-Marie Maréchal
La Ferme des Tourelles,
11 rue des Tourelles, La Musse,
28410 Boutigny Prouais,
Eure-et-Loir
tel   +33 (0)2 37 65 18 74
fax   +33 (0)2 37 65 18 74
mobile +33 (0)6 74 52 39 79
email   la-ferme.des-tourelles@wanadoo.fr

Map 4 Entry 138

Paris – Ile de France

Les Chandelles

At the end of a pretty village, a converted farmhouse behind high gates. Jean-Marc teaches golf to all ages and levels, Catherine is full of infectious enthusiasm and advice for visitors. They, their son and two big sloppy dogs receive you with alacrity in the old beamed kitchen then send you up steep barn stairs to simple white rooms where patches of bright colour punctuate the space. The two lovely new rooms, bigger, higher and more luxurious in fabric and fitting, are good for families, and there's a wood-clad sitting room for guests, its sofa spread with an African throw. *Lake for watersports nearby.*

rooms	5: 1 double, 2 twins, 2 family rooms.
price	€60-€80. Family room €115.
meals	Restaurants in Nogent le Roi & Maintenon.
closed	Rarely.
directions	From Paris A13, A12, N12, exit Gambais for Nogent le Roi. Entering Coulombs, left at lights for Chandelles; left at x-roads 1.5km; house on right.

Catherine & Jean-Marc Simon
Les Chandelles,
19 rue des Sablons, Chandelles,
28130 Villiers le Morhier,
Eure-et-Loir

tel	+33 (0)2 37 82 71 59
fax	+33 (0)2 37 82 71 59
email	info@chandelles-golf.com
web	www.chandelles-golf.com

Map 4 Entry 139

Paris – Ile de France

Château de Jonvilliers

Delightful hosts: Virginie beautifully French, Richard a gentle Europeanised American, and their two sons. Down a wooded drive and set in a big leafy garden, the family house has tall windows, fine proportions and the air of a properly lived-in château: elegance and deep armchairs by the marble fireplace under crystal chandeliers. The top floor has been converted into five good rooms with sound-proofing, big beds, masses of hot water, rich, bright colour schemes… and just the right amount of family memorabilia: oils, engravings, lamps, old dishes. It feels easy, intelligent and fun.

rooms	5: 4 doubles, 1 triple.
price	€60-€70.
meals	Restaurants 5km.
closed	Rarely. Book ahead.
directions	From A11 exit Ablis on N10 for Chartres. At Essars, right to St Symphorien, Bleury & Ecrosnes. There right & immed. left to Jonvilliers, 2.5km. White château gates straight ahead.

Virginie & Richard Thompson
Château de Jonvilliers,
17 rue Lucien Petit,
28320 Jonvilliers,
Eure-et-Loir

tel	+33 (0)2 37 31 41 26
fax	+33 (0)2 37 31 56 74
email	information@chateaudejonvilliers.com
web	www.chateaudejonvilliers.com

Map 5 Entry 140

Normandy

Normandy

Manoir de Beaumont

In the old hunting lodge for guests, a vast, boar- and stag's-headed dayroom with log fire, chandelier and bedrooms above – ideal for parties. In the main house (charming, *bourgeoise*, colourful), the huge Jouy'd room for four; from the garden, wide hilltop views. Monsieur manages the Port and is a mine of local knowledge; Madame tends house, garden and guests, masterfully. Proud of their region, naturally generous, elegant, poised, they are keen to advise on explorations: nature, hiking, historical visits, wet days, dry days… Legend has it that Queen Victoria 'stopped' at this very gracious house.

rooms	3: 1 quadruple. Lodge: 1 double, 1 family suite (triple + bunks).
price	€47-€55. Triple €50-€55.
meals	Restaurants 2-4km.
closed	Rarely.
directions	D49 to Eu; before Eu left for Forest of Eu & Route de Beaumont; house 3km on right.

Catherine & Jean-Marie Demarquet
Manoir de Beaumont,
76260 Eu, Seine-Maritime
tel +33 (0)2 35 50 91 91
fax +33 (0)2 35 50 19 45
email catherine@demarquet.com
web www.demarquet.com

Map 1 Entry 141

Normandy

Prieuré Sainte Croix

It's 100m into town but, by some sort of magic, no bustle intrudes. The buildings are evocative: built in 1850 as part of the Château d'Eu, this is where all the king's horses and all the king's men were stabled and housed. Off the arched courtyard is the guest wing – lusciously creeper-clad. Bedrooms, and self-catering apartment below, are old-fashioned with sturdy antiques but not a sign of wear and tear -perfectionist Madame would not allow that! Breakfast tables have coffee machines and flowers, the small garden bursts with roses, and views reach to grazed pastures, copse and wooded horizon.

rooms	4: 3 doubles, 1 twin.
price	€48-€60.
meals	Restaurants in Le Tréport, 2km.
closed	Rarely.
directions	From Dieppe D925 for Le Tréport; at Étalondes left at r'bout for Le Tréport; at 2nd r'bout 1st right; 100m, signposted.

Romain & Nicole Carton
Prieuré Sainte Croix,
76470 Le Tréport,
Seine-Maritime
tel +33 (0)2 35 86 14 77
fax +33 (0)2 35 86 14 77
email carton.nicole@wanadoo.fr
web prieuresaintecroix.free.fr

Map 1 Entry 142

Le Clos Mélise

In a charming village on the edge of a green, a dear little cottage in a big sloping garden. Madame is a quietly-spoken, welcoming and attentive hostess, keeps a spotless and pretty house, and joyfully paints with oils; her love of colour is reflected inside and out. The attic bedroom, up a steep stair, may be small but is delightfully cosy; the other two, one large, one small, are on the ground floor of an adjacent wing, each with a door to the garden. Walls are toile de Jouy'd, floorboards are polished, fluffy towels are tied with bright bows, and breakfasts are delicious.

rooms	3 doubles.
price	€43.
meals	Restaurant in village.
closed	Rarely.
directions	From Le Tréport D925 for Dieppe 15km; in Biville sur Mer right Rue de l'Église, No. 14 faces you in middle of fork in road.

Marie-José Klaes
Le Clos Mélise,
14 rue de l'Église,
76630 Biville sur Mer,
Seine-Maritime

tel	+33 (0)2 35 83 14 71
mobile	+33 (0)6 79 71 07 68
email	closmelise@wanadoo.fr

Map 1 Entry 143

St Mare

A fresh modern house under a steep slate roof in a lush green sanctuary; it could not be more tranquil. The garden really is lovely and worth a wander — a tailored lawn, a mass of colour, huge banks of rhododendrons for which the village is renowned (three of its gardens are open to the public). Claudine runs home and B&B with effortless efficiency and gives you homemade brioches for breakfast; smiling Remi leads you to guest quarters in a freshly wood-clad house reached via stepping stones through the laurels. Bedrooms are comfortable, sunny, spotless, shining and utterly peaceful — two are big enough to lounge in.

rooms	3: 1 suite for 2, 1 suite for 4; 1 suite for 2 & kitchenette.
price	€60-€70. €95-€105 for 4.
meals	Restaurants 20-minute walk.
closed	Rarely.
directions	From Dieppe D75 to Varengeville sur Mer, 8kms; 1st left after entering village onto chemin des Petites Bruyères. Entrance to house on left.

Claudine Goubet
St Mare, Le Quesnot,
Chemin de Petites Bruyères,
76119 Varengeville sur Mer,
Seine-Maritime

tel	+33 (0)2 35 85 99 28
mobile	+33 (0)6 18 92 28 20
email	claudine.goubet@aliceadsl.fr
web	www.chsaintmare.com

Map 4 Entry 144

Normandy

179 chemin du Bel Évent

Informal elegance, French charm from 1864, a dose of American antiques and masses of warmly impressionistic paintings. Boston-born Daniel adopted France, married chiropractor Virginie, had three children and chose these two houses, one for B&B, one for the family, in an area they both love; then his mother, a prolific painter, joined them. They put books everywhere and create a youthful, easy atmosphere. The guest-house dining, sitting and music rooms have a period feel: superb floors, high ceilings, views to the delicious garden (tennis court too); bedrooms are generous and mattresses new.

rooms	4 doubles. Extra child beds.
price	€50–€55.
meals	Bistro-épicerie in village.
closed	Rarely.
directions	From Dieppe D925 for St Valéry en Caux; 3.5km after Le Bourg Dun, left for La Chapelle sur Dun; opp. church, left at café go to end; enter on left.

Daniel Westhead
179 chemin du Bel Évent,
76740 La Chapelle sur Dun,
Seine-Maritime
tel +33 (0)2 35 57 08 44
mobile +33 (0)6 11 10 00 80
email info@chaletdubelevent.com
web www.chaletdubelevent.com

Map 4 Entry 145

Normandy

Château du Mesnil Geoffroy

This gloriously restored 1640 château is surrounded by gardens designed by a pupil of Le Nôtre's: a hornbeam maze, lime tree avenues and 2,457 perfectly tended roses. The Prince (Syrian father, French mother) knows every one of them; the Princess makes rose-petal jelly for breakfast. She is also a devotee of 17th-century dishes. Bedrooms are dreamy with fireplaces and panelling, canopies and lavender, fat duvets and fine linen; dressing closets have been transformed into bathrooms. A sophisticated dining room, an elegant sitting room, and a lovely log fire (perhaps even a cat) to keep you company.

rooms	5: 2 doubles, 1 twin, 2 suites for 3.
price	€95–€140. €170 for 3.
meals	Dinner with wine, €42. Saturday only.
closed	Rarely.
directions	From A13 exit 25 Pont de Bretonne & Yvetot. Through Yvetot for St Valéry en Caux. 2km after Ste Colombe, right for Houdetot. Château 2km on left.

Prince & Princesse Kayali
Château du Mesnil Geoffroy,
76740 Ermenouville,
Seine-Maritime
tel +33 (0)2 35 57 12 77
fax +33 (0)2 35 57 10 24
email contact@chateau-mesnil-geoffroy.com
web www.chateau-mesnil-geoffroy.com

Map 4 Entry 146

Normandy

Le Gui Nel

Brace yourself for the last lap home or, better still, unwind in this leafy Norman oasis, neatly set between Dieppe and le Havre. Welsh cob ponies graze in the lee of a little Norman church and bantams strut by this beautifully restored farmhouse. A deep pitched roof caps the attractive timbered façade, the stout oak doors and the high windows. Comfortable, immaculate ground-floor rooms have their own entrance. If up and about early you may meet Etienne, a doctor, as he dashes off to work, or chat to Catherine about her beloved cobs as you breakfast on French pastries in the handsome dining room.

Normandy

Le Clos du Vivier

The lush garden shelters fantails, ducks, bantams, frilly black swans, sleek cats and a phenomenal variety of shrubs and flowering plants. While Monsieur works in town, Madame tends all this, and her guests, with respect for everyone's privacy, guidance on hiking, tennis or fishing nearby. An intelligent, active and graceful person, her bedrooms are cosily colourful, her bathrooms big and luxurious, her breakfast richly varied. After a jaunt, you can read their books, relax among their lovely antiques or make tea in their breakfast room. And the cliffs at Étretat are 20 minutes away.

rooms	2 doubles.
price	€75.
meals	Restaurant 2km.
closed	Never.
directions	From Dieppe D925 to Veules les Roses; D142 to Fontaine le Dun; D89 Bourville to Canville les Deux Églises. Do not go into Bourville; entrance on right next to small church set back from road.

rooms	2: 1 triple, 1 suite.
price	€90–€100.
meals	Restaurants in Valmont, 1km.
closed	Rarely.
directions	From Dieppe D925 W for Fécamp 60km; left D17 to Valmont centre; left D150 for Ourville 1.2km; right chemin du Vivier; house 2nd entrance on right (no. 4), signed 'Fleur de Soleil'.

Catherine Stevens
Le Gui Nel,
4 rue de Canville,
76740 Bourville,
Seine-Maritime

tel	+33 (0)2 35 57 02 31
mobile	+33 (0)6 70 55 26 39
email	contact@gui-nel.com
web	www.gui-nel.com.

Dominique Cachera
& François Greverie
Le Clos du Vivier,
4-6 chemin du Vivier,
76540 Valmont, Seine-Maritime

tel	+33 (0)2 35 29 90 95
fax	+33 (0)2 35 27 44 49
email	le.clos.du.vivier@wanadoo.fr
web	www.leclosduvivier.com

Map 4 Entry 147

Map 4 Entry 148

Château Le Bourg

Luxury and sophistication are the nouns, friendly and intelligent the adjectives. Leonora's refined mix of English mahogany and French fabrics is as high-class as her sumptuous dinners. Having finished the soberly elegant bedrooms and scintillating bathrooms of her grand 19th-century mansion, she is turning her attention to the garden: it will undoubtedly delight. A brilliant hands-on hostess, she is independent and generous, talks with passionate knowledge about art and has a mass of books for you to browse through on your return from walking the old railway line or exploring the coastal cliffs.

rooms	2 doubles.
price	€70–€100.
meals	Dinner with wine, €30–€65.
closed	Rarely.
directions	A16 from Calais; exit 23 to A28, exit 6 for Londinières. D12 for 8km to Bures en Bray. House opposite church, with high iron gates between red & white brick pillars.

Leonora Macleod
Château Le Bourg,
27 Grande Rue,
76660 Bures en Bray,
Seine-Maritime
tel   +33 (0)2 35 94 09 35
email   leonora.macleod@wanadoo.fr

Map 4 Entry 149

La Ferme de la Rue Verte

The 300-year-old house stands in a classic, poplar-sheltered Seine-Maritime farmyard, its worn old stones and bricks and the less worn flints bearing witness to its age, as does the fine timberwork inside. Otherwise it has been fairly deeply modernised, but your retired farmer hosts and the long lace-clothed breakfast table before the winter log fire are most welcoming. Madame was born here, has a winning smile and loves to talk – in French. Her pleasant rooms are in good, rural French style and the only sounds are the occasional lowing of the herd and the shushing of the poplars.

rooms	4: 1 double, 1 triple; 2 doubles sharing shower & wc.
price	€45.
meals	Auberge 1km. Restaurant 4km.
closed	Rarely.
directions	From Dieppe N27 for Rouen 29km; right N29 through Yerville, cont. 4.5km; left D20 to Motteville; right to Flamanville. Rue Verte behind church. Farm 300m on left; signposted.

Yves & Béatrice Quevilly Baret
La Ferme de la Rue Verte,
No. 21,
76970 Flamanville,
Seine-Maritime
tel   +33 (0)2 35 96 81 27

Map 4 Entry 150

Normandy

Le Brécy

Jérôme has happy childhood holiday memories of this large 17th-century manor house; he and Patricia moved in some years ago to join his *grand-mère*, who had been living alone in a few rooms for years. A long path flanked by willows leads down to the Seine: perfect (when not mud-bound!) for an evening stroll. Your suite (twin room, small sitting room) is on the ground floor, in classically French coral and cream, its windows opening to a walled garden. Breakfast is when you fancy: brioches, walnuts, fresh fruit in a pretty green-panelled room. Ask Patricia about the Abbey. *Tow-path walks 1km.*

rooms	1 suite & kitchenette.
price	€75.
meals	Choice of restaurants 1km.
closed	Rarely.
directions	From A13 exit 24 'Maison Brulée' for La Bouille-Bas to Sahurs; left for St Martin de Boscherville; after Quevillon, 2nd left for Le Brécy; signposted.

Jérôme & Patricia Lanquest
Le Brécy,
72 route du Brécy,
76840 St Martin de Boscherville,
Seine-Maritime

tel	+33 (0)2 35 32 69 92
fax	+33 (0)2 35 32 00 30
email	jlanquest@tele2.fr
web	home.tele2.fr/lebrecy

Map 4 Entry 151

Normandy

Manoir de Captot

Gracious living is declared at the pillared gates, the drive curves through slow horse pastures to a serene 18th-century mansion, the forest behind may ring with the stag's call, the heads and feet of his kin decorate the hall. Peacefully formal, it is a fine classic French interior: gorgeous primrose-yellow dining room with an oval mahogany table for breakfast, collection-filled drawing room, one superb high bedroom with the right curly antiques and pink Jouy draperies, one attic twin plus little twin for children. Madame cherishes her mansion and resembles it: gently friendly with impeccable manners.

rooms	3: 1 double, 1 twin/double, 1 children's twin.
price	€70-€75. Children's twin €35.
meals	Restaurants nearby.
closed	Rarely.
directions	From Rouen D982; north side of river Seine going west 3km to Canteleu on left; D351 for Sahurs; entrance on right 900m after church, big iron gates.

Mme Michèle Desrez
Manoir de Captot,
42 route de Sahurs,
6380 Canteleu,
Seine-Maritime

tel	+33 (0)2 35 36 00 04
mobile	+33 (0)6 63 51 34 57
email	captot76@yahoo.fr
web	www.captot.com

Map 4 Entry 152

Normandy

22 rue Hénault

The elegant, black-doored face hides a light, stylish interior with soul-lifting views across old Rouen to the spires of the cathedral. Dominique, a cultured Egyptologist and delightful hostess, has a flair for decoration – as her paintings, coverings and mix of contemporary and country furniture declare. Oriental rugs on parquet floor, French windows to balcony and garden, bedrooms feminine but not frilly. Nothing standard, nothing too studied, a very personal home and leisurely breakfasts brimming with homemade surprises. The house's hillside position in this attractive suburb is equally special. Such value!

rooms	3: 1 double; 2 doubles, each with bath, sharing wc.
price	€55. Singles €38.
meals	Restaurant 1km.
closed	October-November.
directions	In Rouen follow Gare SNCF signs; Rue Rochefoucault right of station; left Rue des Champs des Oiseaux; over 2 traffic lights into Rue Vigné; fork left Rue Hénault; black door on left.

Dominique Gogny
22 rue Hénault,
76130 Mont St Aignan,
Seine-Maritime
tel +33 (0)2 35 70 26 95
mobile +33 (0)6 62 42 26 95
email chambreavecvue@online.fr
web chambreavecvue.online.fr

Map 4 Entry 153

Normandy

45 rue aux Ours

You are in a privileged position in the heart of old Rouen, 100m from the cathedral. This building of character, built around a cobbled courtyard, is maintained like a museum, its beamed and passaged interior a treasure trove of curios and antiques, ethnic pieces, ecclesiastical art and salvage and family memorabilia. Once he has warmed to you, wry Monsieur enjoys sharing – in English, German or Norman – the history of Rouen. Bedrooms are dated but warm, bathrooms just adequate, breakfast generous and good, and Madame kindly attentive. *Car park a short walk.*

rooms	1 + 1: 1 double. 1 apartment for 5.
price	€58.
meals	Choice of restaurants.
closed	Rarely.
directions	On cathedral-side embankment: at Théâtre des Arts, take Rue Jeanne d'Arc; Rue aux Ours 2nd on right but NO parking: leave car in Bourse or Pucelle car park & walk.

Philippe & Annick
Aunay-Stanguennec
45 rue aux Ours,
76000 Rouen,
Seine-Maritime
tel +33 (0)2 35 70 99 68

Map 4 Entry 154

Le Clos Jouvenet

It is a privilege to stay in these refined city surroundings, safely inside a serene walled garden above the towers of Rouen (from one bath you can gaze at the cathedral spire). The garden is as elegantly uncomplicated as the house and its Belgian owners, the décor classic sophisticated French to suit the gentle proportions: there are pretty pictures and prints, lots of books, handsome antique furniture and on cold mornings breakfast is served in the kitchen, warmed by slate and oak. Madame is charming, Monsieur enjoys guests too, and you wake to birdsong and church bells. *Minimum stay two nights at weekends & high season.*

rooms	4: 2 doubles, 2 twins/doubles.
price	€80–€88.
meals	Restaurants within walking distance.
closed	Rarely.
directions	From train station for Bd de L'Yser for Boulogne-Amiens; take Neufchatel road in same direction, 1st right rue du Champ du Pardon; Rue Jouvenet; left at lights; 2nd right.

Catherine de Witte
Le Clos Jouvenet,
42 rue Hyacinthe Langlois,
76000 Rouen, Seine-Maritime

tel	+33 (0)2 35 89 80 66
fax	+33 (0)2 35 98 37 65
email	cdewitte@club-internet.fr
web	www.leclosjouvenet.com

Map 4 Entry 155

Château de Fleury la Forêt

A huge place that breathes comfort – and a challenge for the young Caffins: half the château's 65 rooms have yet to be restored. They live in one wing, you in another; a museum sits in between. The handsome guest suite is pale-panelled and red-brocaded, with a separate room for children; the double elegantly and creamily draped. The immense entrance hall has a giant dolls' house and a multitude of antlers; there are stylish lawns to the front and majestic trees, stables for the show-jumpers, a maize-maze for you. Breakfast is at a vast table in a kitchen lined with blue porcelain. *Giverny a 40-minute drive.*

rooms	2: 1 double, 1 family suite for 4.
price	€72. Suite €115.
meals	Choice of restaurants 6km.
closed	Rarely.
directions	From Gournay en Bray N31 for Rouen 17km; left D921 to Lyons la Forêt; D6 for Étrépagny; 1st left for Château de Fleury; left at fork; 5km, house on right, signposted.

Kristina Caffin
Château de Fleury la Forêt,
27480 Lyons la Forêt, Eure

tel	+33 (0)2 32 49 63 91
fax	+33 (0)2 32 49 71 67
email	info@chateau-fleury-la-foret.com
web	www.chateau-fleury-la-foret.com

Map 4 Entry 156

Normandy

La Lévrière

It's aptly named: the garden laps at the river bank where ducks and moorhens nest. Trout swim, birds chirrup, deer pop by – a dreamy village setting. Madame is charming and takes everything (including escaped horses in the garden!) in her stride and her entire young family love it when guests come to stay. Breakfast is at an oak table with blue-painted chairs; garden loungers tempt you to stay all day. Two bedrooms are in the granary, one up, one down, the third in the attic of the coach house. Creamy walls, sweeping floors, rafters, toile de Jouy, fresh flowers. Stay for a long while.

rooms	3: 1 triple, 1 suite for 3, 1 suite for 4.
price	€55-€60.
meals	Restaurant opposite.
closed	Never.
directions	From Gisor; right by château for St Denis; at St Paër right onto D17 into St Denis; house on right, signed.

Sandrine & Pascal Gravier
La Lévrière,
24 rue Guérard, 27140
St Denis le Ferment, Eure
tel   +33 (0)2 32 27 04 78
fax   +33 (0)2 32 27 04 78
email   pascalgravier@hotmail.com
web   www.normandyrooms.com

Map 5 Entry 157

Normandy

Les Ombelles

Madame's home is old-fashioned cosy. To one side are pretty old houses and church; behind, a cottagey garden that runs down to the Epte – the river that Monet diverted at Giverny (35km) for his famous ponds. Madame, poised and intelligent, shares her great knowledge of all things Norman, including food, and has devised her own detailed tourist circuits. Smallish roadside bedrooms have antiques and traditional wallpaper, a pretty hand-painted wardrobe from Lorraine and an Art Deco brass bed. No day room for guests, but you may share the owner's sitting room.

rooms	3: 1 double, 1 suite; 1 double with separate bath & wc.
price	€55-€60.
meals	Dinner with wine, €20.
closed	15 November-14 March.
directions	From Dieppe D915 to Gisors. Cross Gisors; D10 for Vernon. In Dangu, Rue du Gué is beside River Epte.

Nicole de Saint Père
Les Ombelles,
4 rue du Gué,
27720 Dangu, Eure
tel   +33 (0)2 32 55 04 95
mobile   +33 (0)6 31 67 50 61
email   vextour@aol.com
web   vextour.ifrance.com

Map 5 Entry 158

Normandy

La Réserve

Big and beautiful, old and new, refined, relaxed and unpretentious. The Brunets, as delightful as their house, have the lightness of touch to combine the fresh best of modern French taste with an eye for authenticity, in a brand new house. Light floods in through recycled château windows on both sides of the classically narrow *maison de campagne*; soft limewash walls hemmed by lavender outside, matt grey woodwork inside, handsome rugs on polished floors, gorgeous fabrics by fine antiques all add up to the château feel. Exquisite style, massive comfort, perfect hosts – and wild deer on occasional visits.

rooms	5: 2 doubles, 3 twins.
price	€110–€170.
meals	Restaurants 1.5km–4km.
closed	December–March, except by arrangement.
directions	From A13, exit 16 to Giverny; left rue Claude Monet; after church & Hotel Baudy, 1st left rue Blanche Hoschedé Monet; chemin du Grand Val, 1.2km; left on white arrow, immed. right on track 800m, left to house.

Didier & Marie Lorraine Brunet
La Réserve,
27620 Giverny,
Eure

tel	+33 (0)2 32 21 99 09
fax	+33 (0)2 32 21 99 09
email	ml1reserve@aol.com
web	www.giverny.fr/article24.html

Map 4 Entry 159

Normandy

L'Aulnaie

Michel and Éliane invested seven years and much natural good taste in restoring this lovely 19th-century farmhouse in a particularly pretty village. Guests share a self-contained part of the house with its own dayroom and breakfast area, and there's lots of space to settle in, with books, music and open fire. Bedrooms are gentle, beautiful, fresh, with toile de Jouy fabrics, plain walls and honey-coloured floors. Naturally welcoming and elegant Éliane is an amateur painter and passionate gardener, pointing out the rich and the rare; lawns sweep down to a stream that meanders beneath high wooded cliffs.

rooms	2: 1 double, 1 twin.
price	€65.
meals	Choice of restaurants nearby.
closed	Rarely.
directions	A13 exit 16 for Cocherel; after 10km to Chambray; left at monument; left after 100m to Fontaine sous Jouy. In centre right Rue de l'Ancienne Forge for 800m; Rue de l'Aulnaie on right.

Éliane & Michel Philippe
L'Aulnaie,
29 rue de l'Aulnaie, 27120
Fontaine sous Jouy, Eure

tel	+33 (0)2 32 36 89 05
fax	+33 (0)2 32 36 89 05
email	emi.philippe@worldonline.fr
web	chambre-fontaine.chez.tiscali.fr

Map 4 Entry 160

Normandy

Manoir de la Boissière

Madame cooks great Norman dishes with home-grown ingredients served on good china. She has been doing B&B for years, is well organised and still enjoys meeting new people when she's not too busy. Guest quarters, independent of the house, have pretty French-style rooms, good bedding and excellent tiled shower rooms while the caringly-restored, listed 15th-century farm buildings, the animated farmyard (peacocks, ducks, black swans) and the furniture – each item carefully chosen, some tenderly hand-painted – all give it character. Near the motorway yet utterly peaceful: an exceptional situation.

rooms	5: 2 doubles, 2 twins, 1 triple.
price	€49. Triple €66.
meals	Dinner with cider, €22. Guest kitchen.
closed	Rarely.
directions	From Rouen N15 for Paris 40km; at Gaillon right D10 for La Croix St Leufroy about 7km; in La Boissaye, Chambres d'Hôtes signs.

Clotilde & Gérard Sénécal
Manoir de la Boissière,
Hameau la Boissaye,
27490 La Croix St Leufroy, Eure
tel   +33 (0)2 32 67 70 85
fax   +33 (0)2 32 67 03 18
email   chambreslaboissiere@wanadoo.fr
web   www.chambres-la-boissiere.com

Map 4 Entry 161

Normandy

4 sente de l'Abreuvoir

The big flowery garden flows down to the river and the old farmhouse and yesteryear buildings are as neat as new pins. Sweet Madeleine devotes herself to home and guests. Bedrooms are neat, clean, pretty, sober and relaxing; the double's French windows open to the garden, the perfect small suite sits under the eaves. Expect antique lace, silver snuff boxes (Madame dealt in antiques), a kitchen/salon for guests and fine breakfasts with garden views. A form of perfection in a privileged and peaceful spot: woods and water for walking, canoeing, fishing; Giverny – or Rouen – a half-hour drive.

rooms	2: 1 double, 1 suite for 3.
price	€50–€56..
meals	Choice of restaurants 5km. Guest kitchen.
closed	Rarely.
directions	A13 exit 19 for Louviers & Évreux; 2nd exit N154 to Acquigny; D71 through Heudreville for Cailly to La Londe; left; house on right.

Madeleine & Bernard Gossent
4 sente de l'Abreuvoir,
La Londe,
27400 Heudreville sur Eure, Eure
tel   +33 (0)2 32 40 36 89
mobile   +33 (0)6 89 38 36 59
email   madeleine.gossent@online.fr
web   www.lalonde.online.fr

Map 4 Entry 162

Normandy

Domaine de Broc Fontaine

The highlight of Broc Fontaine is the lovely tailored, immaculate garden, and the star turn, the remarkable colour-coded organic potager where Deborah grows blue leeks, scarlet chard and masses of berries. In the 300-year-old farmhouse, your friendly hosts entertain together and treasure their contact with guests. Bedrooms, with a fine personal mix of antique furniture and fabrics, are welcoming and private; the pretty garden cottage with its kitchen is perfect for families. American Deborah adopted France and French food 25 years ago and is an excellent cook who now gives courses.

rooms	2 + 2: 1 double, 1 suite for 2-6. 1 cottage for 2-4, 1 cottage for 2-5.
price	€75-€95.
meals	Dinner with wine, €30-€40.
closed	Rarely.
directions	From Rouen A13 for Paris; exit 18 for Louviers; A154 for 7km; N154 for 3km; exit Acquigny; D61 7km; D52 to Brosville. 1st house after bakery on left.

Deborah Pivain
Domaine de Broc Fontaine,
36 rue St Fiacre,
27930 Brosville, Eure
tel   +33 (0)2 32 34 61 78
fax   +33 (0)2 32 24 14 72
email   brocfontaine@aol.com
web   giverny.org/hotels/pivain

Map 4 Entry 163

Normandy

Clair Matin

Handsomely carved Colombian furniture, strong colours, interesting prints – not what you expect to find inside an 18th-century manor with a Norman cottage face and a surprising turret. Your charming Franco-Spanish hosts raised five children in South America before renovating their French home – it joyfully vibrates with echoes of faraway places. Bedrooms, not huge, are solidly comfortable; bathrooms are immaculate. There are fresh breads and homemade jams at the huge Andean cedar breakfast table, and good conversation. Jean-Pierre is a passionate gardener and his plantations are maturing beautifully.

rooms	3: 1 double, 1 family room, 1 suite.
price	€55-€70. €85 for 4.
meals	Auberges 6km.
closed	Rarely.
directions	From A13 exit 17 for Gaillon D316 for Évreux through Autheuil, St Vigor & up hill 11km; right to Reuilly; house on road, 200m past Mairie on right.

Jean-Pierre & Amaia Trevisani
Clair Matin,
19 rue de l'Église,
27930 Reuilly,
Eure
tel   +33 (0)2 32 34 71 47
fax   +33 (0)2 32 34 97 64
email   bienvenue@clair-matin.com

Map 4 Entry 164

Normandy

Les Basses Terres

For breakfast, *viennoiseries* and home honey. For dinner, mouthwatering Cordon Bleu. Andrew – more French than English – loves to use the best seasonal produce, including the perfect dandelion leaves for his salads. In deep, lush Normandy he and Bernard are throwing themselves into their new orchard-garden and delectable B&B. Meals are taken in a *gentilhommière* interior of fine fabrics and seagrass floors; conversation flows, winter logs smoulder. Overlooking woodland and fields, each charming, stylish cottage suite has its own little pocket of garden. Bliss for couples – or small families.

rooms	2 suites for 2-4.
price	€120.
meals	Dinner with wine, €30-€35.
closed	Rarely.
directions	From Pont Audemer D810 to Le Havre/Pt de Tancarville for 4km; D100 to St Samson/Bouquelon; at Bouquelon left onto D90; on for 5km through woods; at fork right; cont. 800m; gates on right.

Bernard Ducher
& Andrew Urquhart
Les Basses Terres,
27680 St Samson de la Roque,
Eure
tel   +33 (0)2 32 41 54 62
mobile +33 (0)6 86 55 11 67
email   bernard.arthur@wanadoo.fr

Map 4 Entry 165

Normandy

Le Moulin

You will warm to this courteous, kind, very French couple who, whatever they turn their hand to – once farm and DIY store, now garden and *chambres d'hôtes* – turn it to perfection. The lovely half-timbered mill, operating from 1769 to 1965, is in working order still – ask Monsieur to give you a demo at breakfast. Bedrooms (polished floorboards, gentle hues) are neat, pretty, comfortable and enticing, two with bird's-eye garden views and dormer windows that open to the sound of trickling waters. The setting is bucolic, there's gourmet dining in Conteville, and a sweet, simple restaurant up the road.

rooms	2: 1 double, 1 family suite for 4.
price	€55. Suite €60.
meals	Restaurants 2km.
closed	Never.
directions	From Le Havre exit Tancarville, N178, 10km; 1st right to Foulbec. Signed.

Mme Derouet
Le Moulin,
27210 Foulbec, Eure
tel   +33 (0)2 32 56 55 25
web   www.location-honfleur.com/FR_detail_chambre.asp?numeroauto=37

Map 4 Entry 166

Normandy

Les Sources Bleues

A privileged setting on the banks of the Seine just below Rouen... once every four years the great armada comes sailing by. The garden is 50m from the water's edge and there are binoculars for birdwatching – this is a Panda (WWF) house (the owners live in the cottage next door). Bedrooms, though in need of a lick of paint, are old-fashioned and charming, with family rooms squeezed into the attic. You get beams and panelling and windows onto that stunning view, a kitchen/diner, a surprisingly elegant sitting room. Monsieur cooks and Madame has all the time in the world for you.

rooms	4: 2 suites for 3, 2 quadruples.
price	€55-€68. Singles €48. €78 for 4.
meals	Dinner €20. Wine €12-€14, cider €5. Guest kitchen.
closed	Rarely.
directions	From Pont Audemer D139 NE for 10km to Bourneville & D139 to Aizier. There, left at Mairie for Vieux Port, D95; on right.

Yves & Marie-Thérèse Laurent
Les Sources Bleues,
Le Bourg,
27500 Aizier, Eure
tel   +33 (0)2 32 57 26 68
fax   +33 (0)2 32 57 42 25
web   www.les-sources-bleues.com

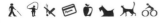

Map 4 Entry 167

Normandy

L'Aufragère

This generous couple run food-and-wine breaks and cookery courses: you'll eat well. Nicky is English and a Cordon Bleu cook, Régis is French with great taste in all departments, and there's nothing nicer than waking up in one of the sedate, antique-furnished rooms of their superbly renovated farmhouse (those in the attic are more ethnic in flavour). The dining room has a long table and fine panelling, the sitting room wraparound red sofas and a gentle black lab, and the grassed farmyard just gets prettier, strutted by poultry, mown by black-headed sheep. Come and indulge in everything. *Minimum stay two nights.*

rooms	5: 2 doubles, 3 twins.
price	Half-board €120.
meals	Half-board only.
closed	Rarely.
directions	In Fourmetot turn for Corneville by church for 1km; 50m after small r'bout left through 2 round brick pillars.

Régis & Nicky Dussartre
L'Aufragère,
La Croisée,
27500 Fourmetot, Eure
tel   +33 (0)2 32 56 91 92
email   regis@laufragere.com
web   www.laufragere.com

Map 4 Entry 168

Normandy

Les Aubépines

That lovely timber frame embraces a heart-warming antique clutter spread over original bricks, beams, tiles and carved family furniture. Guests share this marvellous space as family; Madame welcomes and cooks with delight (maybe over an open fire) and tends the intimate paradise of her garden whence views glide over forested hills; Monsieur smiles, charms and mends everything. The delicious bedrooms are subtly lit by dormer windows, country-furnished, pastel-hued and comfortably bathroomed; the suite has steep rafters and a smart new shower room. A dream of a place; they deserve a medal.

rooms	3: 2 twins/doubles, 1 suite for 4.
price	€55–€60.
meals	Dinner with wine, €20.
closed	October-March, except by arrangement.
directions	From Paris A13 exit 26 for Pont Audemer D89; at 'Médine' r'bout. on for Évreux & Appeville Annebault 4km; left immed. after Les Marettes sign, follow Chambres d'Hôtes signs.

Françoise & Yves Closson Maze
Les Aubépines,
Aux Chauffourniers, 27290
Appeville dit Annebault, Eure
tel +33 (0)2 32 56 14 25
fax +33 (0)2 32 56 14 25
email clossonmaze@wanadoo.fr
web perso.wanadoo.fr/lesaubepines

Map 4 Entry 169

Normandy

Le Coquerel

Jean-Marc overflows with ideas for varied stays and love for his garden, modern art and lingering dinners with guests. He has transformed the old cottage, surrounded by soft pastures, into a country gem, and the garden is exuberant with flowers. Inside, a mix of the sober, the cultivated, the frivolous and the kitsch: old and modern pieces, rustic revival and leather, paintings and brocante. Bedrooms stand out in their uncomplicated good taste, bathrooms are irreproachable, but it's your host who makes the place: duck in cider, strawberry soup and laughter, butterflies alighting on the table at breakfast.

rooms	5: 1 twin, 1 double, 1 triple, 2 family rooms.
price	€54–€58. Triple €65. Family room €78.
meals	Dinner with wine, €21. Picnic possible.
closed	Rarely.
directions	From Pont Audemer D810 for Bernay 12km; right through St Siméon; up hill for Selles; house on left at top.

Jean-Marc Drumel
Le Coquerel,
27560 St Siméon,
Eure
tel +33 (0)2 32 56 56 08
fax +33 (0)2 32 56 56 08
email moreau-drumel@wanadoo.fr
web perso.wanadoo.fr/chambreshotes/

Map 4 Entry 170

Normandy

Manoir d'Hermos

The sedately old-French panelled rooms with good antiques and satin touches are up the grand staircase of this 16th-century house where brick and sandstone sit in peace by birdy orchard, pastoral meadows and spreading lake. Madame is a most welcoming hostess, full of spontaneous smiles, who puts flowers everywhere and whose family has owned the house for 100 years. She also organises seminars (not when B&B guests are here), serves breakfasts and brunches at pretty tables and gardens brilliantly: trees are being planted to Napoleonic plans discovered in the archives.

rooms	2: 1 triple, 1 quadruple.
price	€53–€66. Triple €72–€85. Quadruple €104.
meals	Choice of restaurants 2-8km.
closed	Never.
directions	From A13 take A28, exit 13. Take N138 on left for 400m, right to D92; on for 1km, signed.

Béatrice & Patrice Noël–Windsor
Manoir d'Hermos,
27800 St Éloi de Fourques,
Eure

tel	+33 (0)2 32 35 51 32
fax	+33 (0)2 32 35 51 32
email	contact@hermos.fr
web	www.hermos.fr

Map 4 Entry 171

Normandy

La Charterie

One of the most delicious houses we know, with the bonus of fine *table d'hôtes*. It is the new-found delight of your courteous and endearing hosts, ex-Parisiens. Hidden amid the fields of the Normandy plains, the 18th-century *maison de maître* stands in a dream of a garden, overgrown here, brought to heel there, flanked by a majestic walnut and age-old pears, filled with shrub roses; the odd forgotten bench adds to the Flaubertian charm. Inside, Marie-Hélène, bright-eyed and eager, has used Jouy cloth and elegant colours to dress the country-French bedrooms that fill the first floor. Enchanting.

rooms	4: 2 doubles, 1 twin, 1 triple.
price	€60.
meals	Dinner with wine, €23.
closed	Rarely.
directions	From Évreux N13 for Lisieux 50km; entering Duranville right D41 for St Aubin de Scellon 2.5km; drive on right.

Marie-Hélène François
La Charterie,
27230 St Aubin de Scellon,
Eure

tel	+33 (0)2 32 45 46 52
mobile	+33 (0)6 20 39 08 63
email	la.charterie@wanadoo.fr
web	monsite.wanadoo.fr/la.charterie

Map 4 Entry 172

Normandy

Château du Grand Bus

A many-shuttered house of sturdy grandeur, it feels like a family home inside: up the monumental oak staircase to big comfortably French bedrooms with family furniture (old washstands, carved wardrobes, a billiard table…), views of grazing cattle and Madame's own wallpapering. Tall, sophisticated, relaxed and welcoming, she finds it normal that everyone sit together in the ochre and scarlet breakfast room. There's a family-friendly common room with picnic table and refrigerator. No finery, a touch of faded grandeur and all-pervasive warmth characterise this splendidly unsmart house of friendship.

rooms	4: 1 double, 1 twin, 2 family rooms.
price	€50.
meals	Choice of restaurants in Orbec.
closed	Rarely.
directions	From Lisieux N13 for Évreux 18km to Thiberville; D145 for Orbec 10km. On right about 50m after sign 'Le Grand Bus'.

Bruno & Laurence de Préaumont
Château du Grand Bus,
Saint Germain la Campagne,
27230 Thiberville, Eure

tel	+33 (0)2 32 44 71 14
fax	+33 (0)2 32 46 45 81
email	bruno.laurence.depreaumont@libertysurf.fr
web	perso.libertysurf.fr/depreaumont

Map 4 Entry 173

Normandy

Le Vieux Château

Alone on its tiny island, the 'ancient' fortress is 40 years old and the rickety rail-less bridge made of 60s sleepers; goats and fowl roam the courtyard. Downstairs, a collector's clutter of pictures, porcelain and old shoes. Up a corkscrew staircase in the tower to classic bedrooms, irreproachably clean, with starched linen and lace. Madame, extraordinary and bohemian, changes from scatty gardener to lady-at-gracious-candlelit-dinner – enjoy conversation about the arts illuminated with flashes of outrageous humour. One loo between three rooms is a small price to pay for such fun.

rooms	3: 2 doubles, 1 twin, each with bath or shower, sharing wc.
price	€65.
meals	Dinner with wine, €23.
closed	January-February.
directions	From Breteuil D141 for Rugles; through forest; at Bémécourt, left 300m after lights into Allée du Vieux Château.

Mme Maryvonne Lallemand-Legras
Le Vieux Château,
27160 Bémécourt,
Eure

tel	+33 (0)2 32 29 90 47

Map 4 Entry 174

Normandy

L'Orangerie

Madame Gran has a talent for enjoying things: painting, bridge, languages, music — and people. The faded blue signs lead to a feudal-feel hamlet (church, presbytery, mairie, house) where this very elegant orangery is the only trace of the old estate. Breakfast in the large, sunny, familial kitchen, enjoy opera and wine on the terrace, sink into a smart deep sofa; Madame loves you to feel at home. Bedrooms are simpler, with small mansard windows, rugs on parquet floors and old-style beds. The lovely grounds summon you out to Norman woods, walks, horses (yours too, if you wish) — and peace.

rooms	4: 2 doubles; 1 double, 1 triple sharing bath.
price	€60–€70.
meals	Restaurants 12km.
closed	Never.
directions	From Vimoutiers for Orbec; D248 for Pontchardon; follow signs for Avernes. House immed. on left after church.

Marie-Christine Gran
L'Orangerie,
61470 Avernes St Gourgon,
Orne
tel   +33 (0)2 33 67 48 37
mobile   +33 (0)6 22 69 35 55
email   marie-christine.gran@wanadoo.fr

Map 4 Entry 175

Normandy

Le Prieuré St Michel

An atmospheric time warp for the night: the timbered 14th-century monks' storeroom (you are on the St Michel pilgrim route here) with tapestry wall covering and antiques, or the old dairy or perhaps a converted stable; a huge 15th-century cider press for breakfast in the company of the Ulrichs' interesting choice of art; a chapel for yet more art, a tithe barn in magnificent condition for fabulous receptions, perfectly stupendous gardens (to rival Giverny?). Your hosts are totally devoted to their fabulous domain and its listed buildings and deeply happy to share it with guests who appreciate its historical value.

rooms	4: 2 doubles, 2 suites for 3.
price	€90–€135.
meals	Restaurant 4km.
closed	Rarely.
directions	From Lisieux D579 for Livarot & Vimoutiers. D916 for Argentan. Right 3km after Vimoutiers D703 for Crouttes. Le Prieuré is 500m after village.

Jean-Pierre & Viviane Ulrich
Le Prieuré St Michel,
61120 Crouttes, Orne
tel   +33 (0)2 33 39 15 15
fax   +33 (0)2 33 36 15 16
email   leprieuresaintmichel@wanadoo.fr
web   www.prieure-saint-michel.com

Map 4 Entry 176

Normandy

Les Gains

There's homemade elderflower cordial if you arrive on a hot day, or the smell of fresh bread may greet you: this converted manor farm with its pigeon tower and duck stream has a lived-in family feel. Your hosts have 800 sheep and 300 apple trees, work hard and are thoroughly integrated, as are their daughters. Bedrooms in the old cheese dairy are pretty, painted in light colours with touches of *fantaisie* and Diana's decorative stencils. Breakfast is superb, dinner with your lovely hosts is for lingering over; both happen under the pergola in fine weather. Laid-back, rural and bucolic.

rooms	3: 1 double, 1 twin, 1 triple.
price	€55–€60.
meals	Dinner with wine, €25.
closed	November–March.
directions	A28 exit 16; into Gacé; D13 to Chambois & Trun for 10km; opp. bar/restaurant D26 to Vimoutiers; house signed at entry to Survie. Tricky to find.

Diana & Christopher Wordsworth
Les Gains,
Survie, 61310 Exmes, Orne
tel   +33 (0)2 33 36 05 56
fax   +33 (0)2 33 35 03 65
email   lesgains@tiscali.fr
web   www.lesgains.co.uk

Map 4 Entry 177

Normandy

Le Mesnil

There are fresh flowers everywhere and your hosts, retired farmers, offer true country hospitality. Peace is the norm not the exception in this deeply rural spot, racehorses graze in the pasture and you are unhesitatingly received into a warm and lively extended family. The rooms, in a converted outbuilding, have an appropriately rustic air with beams, old wardrobes and micro-kitchens. The ground-floor room has a little private garden; up steepish stairs the bedroom is bigger. Breakfast is in the family dining room, with tiled floors and a large fireplace. Children are welcome to visit the family farm next door.

rooms	2: 2 doubles, each with kitchenette.
price	€42.
meals	Restaurant 5km.
closed	Rarely.
directions	From Argentan N158 for Caen; after sign 'Moulin sur Orne', left; house 800m on left; sign (3.5km from Argentan).

Janine & Rémy Laignel
Le Mesnil,
61200 Occagnes,
Orne
tel   +33 (0)2 33 67 11 12

Map 4 Entry 178

Normandy

Château de La Maigraire

Built in 1870, it stands in pretty grounds with its own little carp-filled lake. Monsieur (an interior designer) fell for it, took it on (with his cousin) and did a brilliant restoration. You get an elegant drawing room with a rosewood baby grand, a cosy sitting room filled with books, and three sunny bedrooms furnished with antiques, one with its own terrace. Bathrooms come with oodles of towels "for the English"; croissants and homemade jams are presented on antique Limoges: Monsieur loves to please. Guests are encouraged to lounge around during the day, and you may picnic in the grounds.

Normandy

La Bussière

It's angular inside too, the pitch-pine staircase elbowing its way right up to the guests' top floor where the sky rushes in. The house was built by Monsieur's parents in 1910 in open-plan American style. Sliding glass partitions give grandly generous dining and sitting rooms; bedrooms are excellent, much-windowed, soft-coloured and -bedded, marble-fireplaced, old-mirrored. Impeccable and full of personality, the house is the pride and joy of your intelligent hostess who laughs easily and manages her home, family and guests expertly. In the steeply sloped garden, a sandpit and trikes. *Please arrive from 6pm.*

rooms	3: 1 double, 1 suite for 3, 1 suite for 4.
price	€95–€115.
meals	Restaurants in the area.
closed	Rarely.
directions	From D962, between Flers & Domfront, D260 for Forges de Varennes & Champsecret for 1.5km; left into La Maigraire hamlet.

rooms	2: 1 twin, 1 suite for 4.
price	€59.
meals	Dinner with wine, €26.
closed	December–February.
directions	From Argentan N26 E for 37km. Entrance 4km after Planches on right by small crucifix; long lime-bordered drive.

Jean Fischer
Château de La Maigraire,
61700 St Bômer les Forges, Orne
tel   +33 (0)2 33 38 09 52
fax   +33 (0)2 33 38 09 52
email   la.maigraire@wanadoo.fr
web   chateaudelamaigraire.monsite.wanadoo.fr

Antoine & Nathalie Le Brethon
La Bussière,
61370 Ste Gauburge Ste Colombe, Orne
tel   +33 (0)2 33 34 05 23
fax   +33 (0)2 33 34 71 47
mobile   +33 (0)6 03 84 78 07
email   la.bussiere.61@free.fr

Map 4 Entry 179

Map 4 Entry 180

Normandy

Le Marnis

This is Barbara's "corner of paradise" and her delight is contagious. In utter peace among the cattle-dotted Norman pastures, here is one brave, outspoken woman, her horses, dogs and cats in a low-lying farmhouse, beautifully rebuilt "from a pile of stones", where old and new mix easily and flowers rampage all around. The lovely sloping garden is all her own work too – she appears to have endless energy. The pastel guest rooms, one upstairs with orchard views, the other down, with doors to the garden, are pleasantly floral. The village provides everything, and Sées is nearby. *Children over 10 welcome.*

rooms	2: 1 double, 1 twin.
price	€55.
meals	Restaurant in village, 1.5km.
closed	Rarely.
directions	From Courtomer, past Mairie right after last building for Tellières. Left at wayside cross for Le Marnis. 2nd lane on right.

Barbara Goff
Le Marnis,
Tellières le Plessis,
61390 Courtomer,
Orne
tel   +33 (0)2 33 27 47 55
email   barbara.goff@wanadoo.fr

Map 4 Entry 181

Normandy

Château de la Grande Noë

Trompe-l'œil marble and Wedgwood mouldings inherited from an Adam-inspired ancestor who escaped the French Revolution; chamber music in the log-fired drawing room; breakfast in the dining room wrapped in oak panelling inlaid with precious woods; elegant, alcoved bedrooms full of antiques, books, ancestral portraits, much soft comfort, a bathroom through a secret door, a loo in a tower: it's a fascinating, human place. And the delightful Longcamps are a civilised, friendly couple, she vivaciously cultured and musical, he a retired camembert-maker who enjoys his estate. Walks start 2km away.

rooms	3: 2 doubles, 1 twin.
price	€100–€115.
meals	Restaurants 5km.
closed	December–March, except by arrangement.
directions	From Verneuil sur Avre, N12 SW 24km to Carrefour Ste Anne. Left D918 for Longny au Perche for 4.5km; left D289 for Moulicent. House 800m on right.

Jacques & Pascale de Longcamp
Château de la Grande Noë,
61290 Moulicent, Orne
tel   +33 (0)2 33 73 63 30
fax   +33 (0)2 33 83 62 92
email   grandenoe@wanadoo.fr
web   www.chateaudelagrandenoe.com

Map 4 Entry 182

La Simondrière

Your English hosts take great care of you in the Percheron farmhouse they have rescued and restored – and enjoy sharing their enthusiasm for this beautiful, undiscovered, horse-breeding region. Feel free to potter on their land or to venture further afield, then come back to a friendly cup of tea and a truly delicious supper in the dining room. Bedrooms are beamy, cosy and uncomplicated, with good mattresses and warm duvets; in the big square sitting room are books, maps and voluminous easy chairs. A super country place in a forested region, and Rex and Helen are wonderful company. Readers are full of praise.

Le Tertre

Pilgrims have trudged past towards Mont St Michel since the 1500s and the search for inner peace continues: groups come for yoga, tai chi and meditation but never overlap with B&B. Anne talks brilliantly about her exotic travels, is active in the village and also pours her creative energy into her house, with the help of an excellent restorer. Each room has its own clear personality, good beds and sitting space, antiques, soft colours and privacy. One has a six-seater jacuzzi, another a fine set of ivory-backed brushes, the third an impressive bureau. Super breakfast in the big kitchen, served with love.

rooms	3: 1 double, 1 twin, 1 family room.
price	€60.
meals	Dinner with wine, €25.
closed	December.
directions	From Mortagne au Perche D931 for Mamers for 8km; right on D650 for Coulimer at small x-roads. House 800m on left, last of small hamlet of houses.

rooms	3: 2 doubles, 1 twin.
price	€72-€130.
meals	Choice of restaurants 6km.
closed	January.
directions	From Alençon D311 for Mamers, left for Contilly & Montgaudry D113, 5km. Follow signs.

Helen Barr
La Simondrière,
61360 Coulimer, Orne

tel	+33 (0)2 33 25 55 34
fax	+33 (0)2 33 25 49 01
mobile	+33 (0)6 83 45 32 18
email	helenbarr@wanadoo.fr

Anne Morgan
Le Tertre,
61360 Montgaudry, Orne

tel	+33 (0)2 33 25 59 98
fax	+33 (0)2 33 25 56 96
email	annemorgan@wanadoo.fr
web	www.french-country-retreat.com

Map 4 Entry 183

Map 4 Entry 184

Normandy

Ferme-Manoir de la Rivière

Breakfast by the massive fireplace may be candle- or oil-lamp-lit on dark mornings in this 13th-century fortress of a dairy farm, with its ancient tithe barn and little watchtower. Madame is proud of her family home, its flagstones worn smooth with age, its high vaulted stone livingroom ceiling with the second-floor rooms, one narrow with a shower in a tower, one with exposed beams, furnished with *ciel de lit* drapes. Her welcome is warm, her energy boundless; she is ever improving her rooms and cooking imaginative Norman cuisine – much supported by Gérard. A great team. *Out-of-season cookery weekends.*

rooms	3: 1 double, 2 triples.
price	€60–€75.
meals	Dinner with cider or wine, €25, during low season.
closed	Rarely.
directions	From Bayeux N13 30km west; exit on D514 to Osmanville & on for Grandchamp, 5km; left for Géfosse Fontenay; house 800m on left before church.

Gérard & Isabelle Leharivel
Ferme-Manoir de la Rivière,
14230 Géfosse Fontenay,
Calvados

tel	+33 (0)2 31 22 64 45
fax	+33 (0)2 31 22 01 18
email	leharivel@wanadoo.fr
web	www.chez.com/manoirdelariviere

Map 3 Entry 185

Normandy

L'Hermerel

Some sort of perfection? A round pigeon tower and a private chapel complete the picture of this charming fortified working farm, parts of which are 15th-century. The lofty beamed rooms and vast fireplaces have been carefully restored and it all feels unpretentiously stylish with a friendly, relaxed atmosphere. Up the old worn stone stair of the interconnecting wing to green velvet armchairs, taffeta drapes and vases of wild flowers: these bedrooms have been decorated quite beautifully. Breakfasts of compotes, special jams and *viennoiserie*, a walled garden to share and the sea a short walk away.

rooms	4: 1 double, 1 twin, 1 family room, 1 suite.
price	€70.
meals	Choice of restaurants in Grandcamp Maisy.
closed	November–March.
directions	From Bayeux N13 30km west; exit on D514 to Osmanville & on for Grandcamp 4km; left D199a for Géfosse Fontenay 400m; follow yellow signs on right.

François & Agnès Lemarié
L'Hermerel,
14230 Géfosse Fontenay,
Calvados

tel	+33 (0)2 31 22 64 12
fax	+33 (0)2 31 22 76 37
email	lemariehermerel@aol.com
web	www.manoir-hermerel.com

Map 3 Entry 186

Normandy

Le Château

At the end of the road stands the original old château, built in 1580. Here, two beamy bedrooms give onto the arched outbuildings round the yard, restored to tremendous shape and character and now a garden area for guests. In the main house, as well as two other rooms, you can admire the astounding roof timbers through a trap window. Rooms are pretty, pastelly, restful and private. Madame is a warm, well-read person, Monsieur is a trawler master; they travel lots, speak good English, love having guests and can discourse at fascinating length about the Vikings, the Inuits, the Dukes of Normandy...

rooms	4: 2 doubles, 1 twin, 1 suite for 5.
price	€70–€85.
meals	Choice of restaurants within walking distance.
closed	November–15 March.
directions	From Cherbourg N13; D514; exit for Grandcamp Maisy; at edge of village continue on D514 for Vierville sur Mer; just after water tower & football field, right (signposted tennis club). House at end of lane, 400m.

Dominique Marion
Le Château,
Chemin du Château,
14450 Grandcamp Maisy, Calvados
tel	+33 (0)2 31 22 66 22
mobile	+33 (0)6 72 14 95 70
email	marionbandb@wanadoo.fr
web	perso.wanadoo.fr/alain.marion/gbindex.html

Map 3 Entry 187

Normandy

Le Mouchel

An interesting couple, she natural, strong and brave, he softly-spoken and communicative, they have been busy doing B&B for 20 years now as well as running a large dairy herd. Their 300-year-old farmhouse contains two of the guest rooms; the family room is in the more recent extension with a somewhat café-like breakfast room that leads onto a pretty patio. There's also a largish grassy area for run-around children. Rooms are floral, shiny floorboarded and have excellent beds and shower rooms. D-Day Omaha Beach lies near the small village of St Laurent sur Mer.

rooms	3: 1 double, 1 triple, 1 family suite for 4.
price	€50.
meals	Restaurants in St Laurent sur Mer, 4km.
closed	Rarely.
directions	From Cherbourg N13 S 76km; exit Formigny for St Laurent sur Mer; after church right 800m: entrance on left.

Odile & Jean-Claude Lenourichel
Le Mouchel,
14710 Formigny,
Calvados
tel	+33 (0)2 31 22 53 79
fax	+33 (0)2 31 21 56 55
mobile	+33 (0)6 15 37 50 80
email	odile.lenourichel@wanadoo.fr

Map 3 Entry 188

Normandy

Château de Vouilly

Previously renovated in the 16th and 18th centuries...the glorified farm has 30 rooms with fabulous parquet and classic French décor. At its heart: the sun-streamed, panelled dining room (a press room for correspondents during WWII), its French windows opening to a bridge over the moat – then formal gardens with swings and myriad plants, and an orangery. Breakfast is at separate tables here. Come for ancient and modern history, a pigeon tower in the courtyard, woodcarvings made by Monsieur's father and bedrooms splendidly, classically French. Madame is a gracious and outgoing hostess. *Pets by arrangement.*

rooms	5: 2 doubles, 1 family room, 1 suite for 4, 1 suite for 5.
price	€70–€90.
meals	Choice of restaurants 7-12km.
closed	December-March.
directions	From Cherbourg N13 to Isigny; right D5 for Le Molay; left opposite Vouilly church, D113; château on right.

Marie-José & James Hamel
Château de Vouilly,
Vouilly, 14230 Isigny sur Mer,
Calvados

tel	+33 (0)2 31 22 08 59
fax	+33 (0)2 31 22 90 58
email	chateau.vouilly@wanadoo.fr
web	www.chateau-vouilly.com

Map 3 Entry 189

Normandy

La Fresnée

A little bridge over a stream brings you to the impressive 19th-century house, owned by a lovely young farming family. One wing is the old bake house, and the hay barn and stables are for the guests. Rooms are sunny, contemporary and charming – original features, carefully chosen furnishings, pretty touches. Breakfasts are served beautifully in the family dining room where a wall hanging hides a fresco painted by an occupying German soldier. Outside, a garden to play in and an amazing 'Labyrinthe de Bayeux' for families: a five-hectare summertime maize-maze created by Pierre-Yves. A happy find.

rooms	4: 1 double, 1 twin, 1 family for 3, 1 family room for 4.
price	€60.
meals	Restaurant in village, 1km.
closed	January.
directions	From Bayeux N13 for Cherbourg; exit 38; through Tour en Bessin for Mosles; D206 for Blay; over dual carriageway; house signposted 1km on right.

Cathérine & Pierre-Yves Robidou
La Fresnée,
14400 Mosles,
Calvados

tel	+33 (0)2 31 21 04 31
fax	+33 (0)2 31 92 82 36
email	catherine@lafresnee.com
web	www.lafresnee.com

Map 3 Entry 190

Normandy

La Closerie du Phare

Inside this rather suburban modern house you find a genuinely family-friendly couple who have two small children of their own, serve fabulous dinners and make fresh crêpes for breakfast. Although Laurent now runs a business, he is also a keen deep-sea fisherman and used to be a chef. It shows. The sea is celebrated in the décor with the odd ship's wheel or marine wallpaper. Charming Sandrine, who taught IT in Paris, makes sure everything in the big, welcoming rooms works well and is spotless: they built the separate guest rooms especially for B&B and are enjoying it hugely.

rooms	2 family rooms for 3-4.
price	€55.
meals	Dinner with wine, €25-€30.
closed	Never.
directions	From Caen D404 to Courseuilles sur Mer; in Courseuilles straight over r'bout; 2nd r'bout right into port; left at Le P'tit Mousse to Ver; in Ver left at lights with pharmacy on corner; 1st left into rue de la Rivière.

Sandrine & Laurent Melet
La Closerie du Phare,
18 rue de la Rivière,
14114 Ver sur Mer,
Calvados
tel +33 (0)2 31 21 30 34
email sandrine.melet@wanadoo.fr
web www.chambres-hotes-ver-sur-mer.com

Map 4 Entry 191

Normandy

Le Mas Normand

Your young hosts have done a great job on their lovely 18th-century house at the end of the lane. Old stonework and beams, modern showers, decent beds and a modern-rustic style. Mylène has brought Provençal fabrics and handmade soaps from her native Drôme and bedrooms are sheer delight: the sunny double on the ground floor, the charming suites, one with an *armoire de mariage*, across the yard. Christian is Norman and trained as a chef. Chicken, apples, calvados and laughter at dinner; at breakfast, perfect brioches and jams. Ducks, geese and hens roam; there are bikes, fridge and barbecue to borrow.

rooms	3: 1 double, 2 suites for 3-4.
price	€60. Suite €80-€115.
meals	Dinner with wine, €35-€40.
closed	Rarely. Book ahead.
directions	From Caen D7 for Douvres 8km; left D404 5.5km; D79 to Courseulles sur Mer; D514 to Ver sur Mer; at village entrance 1st left Av. Provence; 1st right; 1st left cul-de-sac; at end on right.

Christian Mériel & Mylène Gilles
Le Mas Normand,
8 impasse de la Rivière,
14114 Ver sur Mer, Calvados
tel +33 (0)2 31 21 97 75
fax +33 (0)2 31 21 97 75
email lemasnormand@wanadoo.fr
web www.lemasnormand.com

Map 4 Entry 192

Normandy

La Malposte

It's just plain lovely, this little group of stone buildings with wooden footbridge over the rushing river, trees and flowers and hens. There's the age-old converted mill for the family and the 'hunting lodge' for guests, where Madame's talented decoration marries nostalgic past (antiques, old prints, photographs) and designer-hued present. A spiral stair winds to a sitting/dining room with guest kitchen and homemade jams; sun pours into the suite at the top. Woods for nut-gathering, beaches nearby, table tennis here and that playful stream. Your hosts are sweet and love having families.

rooms	3: 1 double; 1 double, 1 twin sharing shower & wc.
price	€62.
meals	Restaurants 2-3km. Kitchen available.
closed	Rarely.
directions	From Ouistreham D35 through Douvres & Tailleville; over D404; right at r'bout entering Reviers; 2nd Chambres d'Hôtes on left.

Patricia & Jean-Michel Blanlot
La Malposte,
15 rue des Moulins,
14470 Reviers, Calvados

tel	+33 (0)2 31 37 51 29
fax	+33 (0)2 31 37 51 29
email	jean-michel.blanlot@wanadoo.fr
web	www.lamalposte.com

Map 4 Entry 193

Normandy

Le Clos St Bernard

It was the second farmhouse to be built in the village — and named, 400 years later, in honour of the Vandons' dog. Madame loves her house and its history, her family and her guests — and delights in concocting Breton breakfasts of *tergoule*, crêpes, homemade juice, rice pudding. Bedrooms are lovely, with pretty bedcovers and cushions and interesting antiques; showers have embroidered towels and the beamy two-bedroom suite is worth the climb. There's a big guest dining salon (and a kitchenette where the hens once lived) that opens to a garden terraced against salt breezes. Charming, and great value. *Minimum stay two nights.*

rooms	3: 2 doubles, 1 family suite.
price	€50. Singles €40.
meals	Dinner with wine, €20, October-March.
closed	15 December-15 January.
directions	From Caen take ring road N; exit 5 for Douvres la Délivrande; 8km, for Courseulles & Mer; at nxt r'bout D35 lft. to Reviers; straight at r'bout; 1st lft. into rue de l'Église; house at top of road.

Nicole Vandon
Le Clos St Bernard,
36 rue de l'Église,
14470 Reviers, Calvados

tel	+33 (0)2 31 37 87 82
fax	+33 (0)2 31 37 87 82
email	leclosbernard@wanadoo.fr
web	www.leclosbernard.com

Map 4 Entry 194

Normandy

Manoir des Doyens

The lovely old house of golden stone is the warmly natural home of interesting people: an extrovert military historian who takes battlefield tours (don't be daunted, you'll learn lots), and his gentle lady, who directs things masterfully and serves her own jams for breakfast. Stone stairs lead to old-fashioned, comfortably casual guest rooms and good, clean bathrooms – nothing swish. The courtyard houses visiting grandchildren's swings, slide, rabbits and games room; the family sitting room is shared. Here is space and a genuine family-friendly feel just 15 minutes' walk from the cathedral.

Normandy

Le Relais de la Vignette

Masses of history and interesting features. A Celtic chieftain was buried here 2,100 years ago; then the Romans stayed a bit; the present wonderful house is 11th-century, rebuilt in 1802. Its brass-railed staircase and salon are gracious but the dining room, relaxed in its yellow and green garb with huge fireplace and modern bar, is the hub. Madame uses colour and style well, mixing bright with soft, antiques with artificial flowers. The comfortable, fluffy bedrooms, raftered in the attic (reached by a steep stone stair) and fireplaced below, look onto wide fields.

rooms	3 triples.
price	€55.
meals	Choice of restaurants 1km.
closed	Rarely.
directions	From N13 exit 37 for Bayeux & St Lô; for Bayeux; 2nd left. Signed.

rooms	4 doubles.
price	€60.
meals	Dinner with wine, €23.
closed	Rarely.
directions	N13 Bayeux-Cherbourg. Exit 38 for Tour en Bessin; thro' village, D100 for Crouay; 1km, house on right.

	Lt-Col & Mrs Chilcott
	Manoir des Doyens,
	Saint Loup Hors,
	14400 Bayeux,
	Calvados
tel	+33 (0)2 31 22 39 09
fax	+33 (0)2 31 21 97 84
email	chilcott@mail.cpod.fr

	Catherine Girard
	Le Relais de la Vignette,
	Route de Crouay, Tour en Bessin,
	14400 Bayeux, Calvados
tel	+33 (0)2 31 21 52 83
fax	+33 (0)2 31 21 52 83
email	relais.vignette@wanadoo.fr
web	perso.wanadoo.fr/relais.vignette/

Map 4 Entry 195

Map 4 Entry 196

Normandy

13 rue aux Coqs

This delicious couple, she softly-spoken and twinkling, he jovial and talkative, have retired from farming and moved into the heart of Bayeux — you can glimpse the cathedral spires from their townhouse, once part of the former bishop's palace. Beyond the wisteria, the door opens onto a lofty beamed living room rejoicing in good antiques and a monumental fireplace – through (yes) another is the kitchen. Up the ancient stone stair to pretty guest rooms – excellent new bedding, pastel-tiled showers – that look quietly over the pocket-handkerchief back garden. History all around, and no need for a car.

Normandy

La Londe

Down a high-bordered lane dotted with violets and cowslips, through a wood, across a stream, to the Ameys — solid country folk who wrap you in blue-eyed smiles. Theirs is an unpretentious welcome full of comfort and warmth, and the garden is a haven for hide-and-seek and dens. Inside, simple country furnishings, bar two superb Norman armoires; walls are pastel, curtains lace, bathroom pink, towels small; all is spotless and tidy. Breakfast brings incomparably good farm butter; later you may be offered a glass of home-brewed *pommeau* and cider. Lovely people, excellent value, and the wisteria blooms.

rooms	3: 2 doubles, 1 twin.
price	€57.
meals	Restaurant 50m.
closed	Rarely.
directions	From Caen N13 to Bayeux; for Gare SNCF; right after traffic lights; over 1st crossroads & traffic lights, park on left; house 50m on right, signposted.

rooms	3 doubles, all with basin, sharing bath & separate wc.
price	€35–€37.
meals	Restaurants 10km.
closed	Rarely.
directions	From Caen A84 for Mt St Michel, exit 46 'Noyers Bocage'. Right D83 for Cheux 1.5km; left to Tessel; signposted.

Louis & Annick Fauvel
13 rue aux Coqs,
14400 Bayeux,
Calvados
tel   +33 (0)2 31 22 52 32
fax   +33 (0)2 31 51 01 90

Paul & Éliane Amey
La Londe,
14250 Tessel, Calvados
tel   +33 (0)2 31 80 81 12
fax   +33 (0)2 31 80 81 57
email paul.amey@wanadoo.fr

Map 4 Entry 197

Map 4 Entry 198

Normandy

La Suhardière

Up the drive, across the spotless (non-working!) farmyard to be met by your charmingly hospitable hostess who delights in gardening and cooking – dinner is a wonderful affair. Beyond the dinky little hall, the salon, with its high-backed chairs, beams and antimacassars, is a good place for a quiet read. The big sunny bedrooms are cosily frilly with quantities of lace, country furniture and gentle morning views over the garden dropping down to the pond (and you may fish). Special are the walks in the pretty rolling countryside, the homemade yogurt and cider, and pillows for the asking. *Small dogs welcome.*

rooms	3: 2 doubles, 1 suite.
price	€45.
meals	Dinner with wine, €20.
closed	Rarely.
directions	From Caen A13 for Cherbourg, exit Carpiquet (airport) & Caumont l'Éventé D9; 500m before Caumont, house signed left.

Alain & Françoise Petiton
La Suhardière,
14240 Livry, Calvados
tel   +33 (0)2 31 77 51 02
fax   +33 (0)2 31 77 51 02
mobile +33 (0)6 19 37 02 11
email   petiton.alain@wanadoo.fr

Map 3 Entry 199

Normandy

Les Fontaines

Just about impossible to fault this big, elegant mansion with lovely, half-kempt garden and pond (unfenced), games room with drums, and excellent meals. Quite often Andrew cooks on the grand open fire, and is a relaxed host; dynamic Elizabeth is present at weekends. Up the lovely elm stair to sleeping and sitting rooms with generous light, glowing parquet, French and English antiques against pale walls; the big new attic bedroom is wonderful for families. The breakfast room is unusually frescoed, the dining room oak-beamed, and both have seriously big tables. Comfortable, civilised, easy.

rooms	5: 2 doubles, 3 family rooms.
price	€65.
meals	Dinner with wine, €23.
closed	December-March.
directions	From Caen ring road exit 13 for Falaise; 9km, right to Bretteville sur Laize; continue to Barbery. House behind field on right, with high, green gates.

Elizabeth & Andrew Bamford
Les Fontaines,
14220 Barbery, Calvados
tel   +33 (0)2 31 78 24 48
fax   +33 (0)2 31 78 24 49
email   information@lesfontaines.com
web   www.lesfontaines.com

Map 4 Entry 200

Normandy

Château des Riffets

The square-set château stands handsome still as the park recovers from the 1987 storm. Taste the wines and "world's best cider" (says Monsieur), admire yourself in myriad gilded mirrors, luxuriate in a jacuzzi, bare your chest to a rain shower, play the piano, appreciate Madame's superb cooking, and lie at last in an antique bed in one of the great, cherished bedrooms. Take a stroll in the 40-acre wooded park, hire a nearby horse or a canoe, hone your carriage-driving skills. Period ceilings, tapestries and furniture make Riffets a real château experience; the people make it very human. *Wine-tastings.*

rooms	4: 2 doubles, 2 suites.
price	€105–€160.
meals	Dinner with wine & calvados, €45.
closed	Rarely.
directions	From Caen N158 for Falaise; at La Jalousie, right D23; right D235 just before Bretteville; signposted.

Anne-Marie & Alain Cantel
Château des Riffets,
14680 Bretteville sur Laize,
Calvados

tel	+33 (0)2 31 23 53 21
fax	+33 (0)2 31 23 75 14
email	acantel@free.fr
web	www.chateau-des-riffets.com

Map 4 Entry 201

Normandy

Arclais

Such very special people, quietly, uncomplicatedly intelligent: what the house lacks in years is made up for tenfold by their timeless, down-to-earth Norman hospitality. Close to all things natural, they plough their big veg patch with a cob horse, provide breakfast on a long table in the family dining room, offer good rooms with walls covered in old-fashioned farming photos, where you wake to soul-lifting views over the hushed hills of La Suisse Normande. Nothing gushy; these are independent, strong, charming people who take you to their bosom and genuinely care for your well-being and that of the land.

rooms	2 doubles.
price	€42.
meals	Occasional dinner with cider, €16.
closed	Rarely.
directions	From Caen D562 for Flers, 35km; at Le Fresne D1 for Falaise, 4km; house on right, signed.

Roland & Claudine Lebatard
Arclais,
14690 Pont d'Ouilly,
Calvados

tel	+33 (0)2 31 69 81 65
fax	+33 (0)2 31 69 81 65
mobile	+33 (0)6 12 92 14 08
email	claudine.lebatard@laposte.net

Map 4 Entry 202

La Cour Ste Catherine

Through the Norman gateway into the sun-drenched courtyard; Liliane and history embrace you. The building was first a convent, then fishermen's cottages, later a *ciderie*. Now this historic quarter is a conservation area and all has been properly restored. Breakfast *viennoiseries* are served in the huge beamed room where the apples were once pressed; in summer you relax in the courtyard with fellow guests. Bedrooms are sunny, airy, impeccable, contemporary, one in the hayloft with its own outside stair. There's a small salon for guests and Honfleur at your feet; charming Liliane knows the town intimately.

rooms	5: 2 doubles, 1 twin/double, 2 family suites. Two rooms have kitchenettes.
price	€70-€90.
meals	Restaurants close by.
closed	Never.
directions	From St Cathérine Church for Hotel Maison de Lucie; after hotel 1st left; left again. Signed.

Liliane & Antoine Giaglis
La Cour Ste Catherine,
74 rue du Puits,
14600 Honfleur,
Calvados
tel   +33 (0)2 31 89 42 40
email   giaglis@wanadoo.fr
web   www.giaglis.com

Map 4 Entry 203

Manoir de la Marjolaine

The Parisian burgher who built Marjolaine in 1850 designed a toes-in-the-water holiday retreat – then the sea retreated 300 metres. So peace reigns here behind the dunes, yet beach and village are within easy walking distance. Your friendly host is genuinely interested in people, chatting easily in his antique-furnished, tapestry-curtained dining room. He has created four good bedrooms with two exotic moods – African (with great balcony views) and Asian (with oriental marriage wardrobe) – and two classic French. Excellent jacuzzi bathrooms, a good feel of bourgeois comfort all over.

rooms	4: 2 doubles, 1 family room, 1 suite for 3.
price	€80-€120. Suite €130.
meals	Restaurants 200m.
closed	Rarely.
directions	From Caen D513 to Cabourg; after Peugeot garage, left into chemin de Cailloue; 100m stop; left, house signposted on left.

Éric Faye
Manoir de la Marjolaine,
5 ave du Président Coty,
14390 Le Home Varaville, Calvados
tel   +33 (0)2 31 91 70 25
fax   +33 (0)2 31 91 77 10
email   eric.faye@orange.fr
web   manoirdelamarjolaine.free.fr

Map 4 Entry 204

Normandy

Les Hauts de la Côte Ransue

Light bounces off the symmetry of this pretty 19th-century farmhouse in its large landscaped setting: quiet harmony outside, striking colour and style inside. Your charming Anglo-French hosts have done a super renovation bringing the original woodwork to life with careful toning, as well as having a baby. Even on grey days the sun shines at breakfast in the airy yellow dining room/kitchen... especially with Catherine's hawthorn berry coulis on fromage frais. Bedrooms are country comfortable in pale green or blue and cream, little sweets appear daily and Catherine's artistic talent is clear.

rooms	2: 1 double, 1 family suite for 4.
price	€70.
meals	Dinner with wine, €25.
closed	April-September.
directions	N175 to Pont l'Evêque; exit Beuzeville, D109 to Quetteville; turn right for 'Les Anglais' & follow road for 3km.

Catherine & Robert Wall
Les Hauts de la Côte Ransue,
D283 La Cote Ransue,
14130 Quetteville, Calvados
tel   +33 (0)2 31 64 69 95
fax   +33 (0)2 31 64 69 95
email   catherinegruvel@hotmail.com

Map 4 Entry 205

Normandy

Clos St Hymer

The approach is down a leafy lane, dotted with primroses in spring. Françoise and Michel have been doing B&B for years, and are ever ready to welcome guests to their typically Norman house where space is well organised and you won't feel crowded in. In the sitting/dining room is a roaring, open-doored woodburning stove, in the double bedroom a patchwork quilt and Louis XIII wardrobe, in the triple an *armoire de mariage* and cupboards stocked with towels. Both bedrooms look onto the pretty garden, complete with table tennis. Utterly French, and friendly.

rooms	2: 1 double, 1 triple.
price	€60-€70.
meals	Dinner with wine, €25.
closed	Rarely.
directions	From Pont l'Évêque D579 for Lisieux. At Le Breuil en Auge r'bout D264 to Le Torquesne. 1st right after church, Chemin des Toutains. House 500m on.

Françoise Valle
Clos St Hymer,
14130 Le Torquesne, Calvados
tel   +33 (0)2 31 61 99 15
fax   +33 (0)2 31 61 99 15
mobile   +33 (0)6 65 50 61 63
email   leclossthymer@wanadoo.fr

Map 4 Entry 206

Château des Parcs Fontaine

A dream of a place for children: five acres of trees, bushes, rides; a 200-year-old lime tree whose branches sweep the ground in a corner of the walled garden, ideal for making a den; join Monsieur at croquet, he's a fiendish player, or badminton, table tennis, billiards, darts, the piano… These are outgoing, enthusiastic, interesting people, she an English teacher, he a journalist. In the breakfast room awash with sunlight you are struck by an enormous Art Deco tiled panel surveying a veritable feast. Bedrooms have the deep luxury of thick carpets, good décor and colour schemes and old-fashioned bathrooms.

rooms	4: 3 doubles, 1 twin.
price	€60–€75.
meals	Restaurants 5km.
closed	Rarely.
directions	Autoroute exit Pont l'Evêque to Lisieux. After 5km, sign on left for property.

M & Mme Rouet
Château des Parcs Fontaine,
Les Parcs Fontaine,
14130 Flerville les Parcs, Calvados
tel   +33 (0)2 31 65 49 70
email rouetch@wanadoo.fr
web   www.parcs-fontaine.com

Map 4 Entry 207

Manoir de Cantepie

It may have a make-believe face, among the smooth green curves of racehorse country, but it is genuine early 1600s; it's amazing from all sides. Inside is an equally astounding dining room built by one Mr Swann and resplendently carved, panelled and painted. Bedrooms have a sunny feel, and are delightful: one with white painted beams and green toile de Jouy, another in yellows, a third with a glorious valley view. All are incredible value. Madame, a beautiful Swedish lady, made the curtains and covers. She and her husband are well-travelled, polyglot and cultured and make their B&B doubly special.

rooms	3: 2 doubles, 1 twin.
price	€60.
meals	Restaurant 1km.
closed	15 November–February.
directions	From Caen N13 for Lisieux 25km; at Carrefour St Jean, D50 (virtually straight on) for Cambremer; 5km from junc., house on right; sign.

Christine & Arnauld Gherrak
Manoir de Cantepie,
Le Cadran,
14340 Cambremer,
Calvados
tel   +33 (0)2 31 62 87 27
fax   +33 (0)2 31 62 87 27

Map 4 Entry 208

Normandy

La Baronnière

The Baron moved on but left a fine house, superb grounds and a stream-fed lake – enchanting. Pet geese gabble, birds triumph, children rejoice (dens in trees, games on lawns, bikes). Christine, who is English, is in heaven caring for the old house and chatting with her guests; her French husband cooks subtle regional meals served in the pretty conservatory. The room in the old pantry has a Louis XIV bed and painted furniture on original honeycomb tiles, the other, up an outside staircase in the handsome timbered barn, is just as pretty. *Watch children near unfenced water. Minimum stay two nights.*

rooms	2 doubles.
price	€60–€70.
meals	Dinner with wine, €38–€43.
closed	Rarely.
directions	From Liseux N13 for Evreux; D145 at Thiberville to la Chapelle Hareng. Follow signs; do not go into Cordebugle.

Christine Gilliatt-Fleury
La Baronnière,
14100 Cordebugle,
Calvados
tel   +33 (0)2 32 46 41 74
fax   +33 (0)2 32 44 26 09
email labaronniere@wanadoo.fr
web   www.labaronniere.connectfree.co.uk

Map 4 Entry 209

Normandy

Manoir du Lieu Rocher

That beautiful 17th-century symmetry is home to a fascinating couple. Born in Bulgaria, Madame is a polyglot classical singer, Monsieur accompanies her on the piano; they are widely travelled and enthusiastic and have a fine sense of humour (recitals are sometimes held here). Their exceptional house, all set about with beams and timbers and bursting with antiques, paintings and portraits, has its original oak stair. Bedrooms are in keeping: big, soft welcoming feel, antiques, lovely views; the suite is perfect for families. The ancient village church peeks into the garden, and rose fans visit in June.

rooms	3: 1 double, 1 twin, 1 suite for 2-5.
price	€65–€80. Suite €130–€150.
meals	Restaurants 5km.
closed	Rarely.
directions	From St Pierre sur Dives D4 for Livarot, 7km; at Boissy D154 to Vieux Pont; continue on D154 towards church. Manoir on right.

M & Mme Grigaut
Manoir du Lieu Rocher,
14140 Vieux Pont en Auge,
Calvados
tel   +33 (0)2 31 20 53 03
fax   +33 (0)2 31 20 59 03
email manoirlieurocher@wanadoo.fr
web   www.castlenormandy.com

Map 4 Entry 210

Normandy

La Ferme de l'Oudon

Madame has hugely enjoyed rescuing this old house, making the modern blend with the ancient, and her enthusiasm is infectious. Her husband is a decorator – it helps. Come and chat in the kitchen conservatory, mingle with this lively couple, admire the potager. Rooms are delightful; one under the eaves, up a worn spiral past the old pigeon niches, has sun-filled roof windows; another has fine beams, a mezzanine and several big desert pictures. Décor is strong green and yellow, warm terracotta or dainty floral; bathrooms are excellent with careful detail and colour splashes. Dining here must be delicious and fun.

rooms	4: 3 doubles, 1 triple.
price	€65–€150.
meals	Dinner with wine, €40, Monday-Thursday.
closed	January.
directions	A13 exit 29a for La Haie Tondue; D16 to Carrefour St Jean; N13 to Crévecoeur (for 3km); D16 to St Pierre sur Dives; from St Pierre sur Dives, D40 to Berville. La Ferme at last x-roads, on left.

Patrick & Dany Vesque
La Ferme de l'Oudon,
12 Route d'Ecots,
14170 Berville L'Oudon, Calvados
tel   +33 (0)2 31 20 77 96
fax   +33 (0)2 31 20 67 13
email   contact@fermedeloudon.com
web   www.fermedeloudon.com

Map 4 Entry 211

Normandy

Côté Jardin

Behind the urbanity of this fine house in the centre of old Orbec (timbers, thatch, cider orchards), you discover the stableyard with the guest rooms, a pretty garden and a lively little stream. Your hosts came back from African jobs in 2002 and the atmosphere over breakfast in the family kitchen is warm and friendly: they enjoy life and laugh a lot. The coachhouse room has an African theme, *naturellement*, and a splendid tiled shower; up a steep outside staircase, the coachman's room is pale green and floral; the other two are equally thoughtful. *Watch children near unfenced water.*

rooms	5: 4 doubles, 1 family room for 3-4.
price	€60.
meals	Choice of restaurants in Orbec.
closed	Rarely.
directions	Orbec 19km south of Lisieux on D519. Turn into village; house on main street on left next to L'Orbecquoise restaurant.

Georges & Véronique Lorette
Côté Jardin,
62 rue Grande,
14290 Orbec, Calvados
tel   +33 (0)2 31 32 77 99
fax   +33 (0)2 31 32 77 99
email   georges.lorette@wanadoo.fr
web   www.cotejardin-france.be

Map 4 Entry 212

Normandy

Eudal de Bas

Old-fashioned hospitality in a modern house. You are just a mile from the (often) glittering sea and Michel, who makes submarines, is happy to share his passion for sailing and might even take you coast-hopping. His shipbuilding skill is evident here: the attic space has been cleverly used to make two snug rooms with showers (one with a kitchenette for evening meals); the landing makes a pleasant sitting area. A brilliantly quiet position, simple décor, spotless rooms and an open, chatty hostess who will rise early for dawn ferry-catchers make it ideal for beach holidays and channel crossing alike.

rooms	2: 1 double; 1 triple & kitchenette.
price	€44.
meals	Restaurants within 2km.
closed	Rarely.
directions	From Cherbourg D901 then D45 W 13km to Urville Nacqueville; 1st left by Hôtel Le Beau Rivage; up hill D22 for 2km; 2nd left; sign.

Michel & Éliane Thomas
Eudal de Bas,
1 rue Escènes,
50460 Urville Nacqueville,
Manche

tel +33 (0)2 33 03 58 16
fax +33 (0)2 33 03 58 16
email thomas.eudal@wanadoo.fr

Map 3 Entry 213

Normandy

36 ave Ducheureuil

Rejoice in this oasis (where nuns lived until 1914) on the built-up edge of bustling Cherbourg. Plants and flowers tumble prettily over the edges of the narrow canal that feeds the sloping horseshoe-shaped pond with rainwater collected from 18th-century roofs. A wide stone stair leads to the walled garden and a multitude of paths, trees, shrubs – and teak furniture to lounge on. Converted farm buildings house guest bedrooms full of light and attractively dressed with striking colours and rug-strewn parquet: not fussy but classy. Like her house and garden, Madame is charming and elegant.

rooms	2: 1 suite for 2-3, 1 suite for 2-4.
price	€90.
meals	Restaurants nearby.
closed	Rarely.
directions	With Cherbourg railway station on right, straight to Équeurdreville for 2km; after tunnel left to Octeville; 200m lights; right to Val Abbé; 3rd right; archway end of road.

Sophie Draber
36 ave Ducheureuil,
50120 Équeurdreville,
Manche

tel +33 (0)2 33 01 33 10
fax +33 (0)2 33 94 12 88
email drabersophie@hotmail.com
web perso.wanadoo.fr/maison-duchevreuil

Map 3 Entry 214

Normandy

Manoir Saint Jean

Standing near the Normandy coastal hiking path, the old stone manor looks proudly across the town and out to sea. Retired from farming, the sociable Guérards welcome guests with courtesy and happily point them towards the (distant!) cliff walks, the nearby blue-green Château of Ravalet and other hidden sights. This is living in French genteel style, everything in its beautiful place, spotless and well-loved, bedrooms spacious and bathrooms simple. You are in quiet country, just 6km from the ferries – the triple room with its outside entrance is ideal for early ferry-catchers and Madame leaves a breakfast tray.

rooms	3: 1 double, 1 twin, 1 triple.
price	€50-€55.
meals	Restaurants 3km.
closed	Rarely.
directions	From Cherbourg D901 to Tourlaville & for St Pierre Église. Right at exit for Château Ravalet & St Jean; up hill to 'Centre Aéré', follow Chambres d'Hôtes signs.

Mme Guérard
Manoir Saint Jean,
50110 Tourlaville,
Manche

tel   +33 (0)2 33 22 00 86

Map 3 Entry 215

Normandy

La Fèvrerie

One of our very best. Your blithe, beautiful, energetic hostess is a delight. Her shyly chatty ex-farmer husband now breeds horses while she indulges her passion for interior decoration: her impeccable rooms are a festival of colours, textures, antiques, embroidered linen. It's a heart-warming experience to stay in this wonderful old building where they love having guests; the great granite hearth is always lit for the delicious breakfast which includes local specialities on elegant china; there is a richly-carved 'throne' at the head of the long table. A stupendous place, very special people.

rooms	3: 2 doubles, 1 twin; children's room available.
price	€62-€70.
meals	Choice of restaurants 3km.
closed	Rarely.
directions	From Cherbourg D901; after Tocqueville right, D10; 1st left.

Marie-France & Maurice Caillet
La Fèvrerie,
50760 Ste Geneviève,
Manche

tel   +33 (0)2 33 54 33 53
fax   +33 (0)2 33 22 12 50
mobile   +33 (0)6 80 85 89 01
email   caillet.manoirlafevrerie@wanadoo.fr

Map 3 Entry 216

Normandy

Le Château

The wonderful granite château with towers, turrets and castellations gives entry to a big safe courtyard – sanctuary during times of invasion – and wild breakers crash on the endless beach 1km away. It is your hosts' mission in life to restore and revive! They and their home are irreproachably French and civilised – books, fine china, panelling, gilt mirrors, plush chairs, engravings. Your two-bedroom suite has ancient floor tiles, new bedding, a loo in a tower. Stay a while, make your own breakfast with homemade jam and fresh eggs – you may use the grand dining room – and get to know your remarkable hostess.

rooms	1 suite for 2-4.
price	€80-€120.
meals	Restaurants 2-3km.
closed	Rarely.
directions	From Cherbourg D650 for Carteret; 3km after Les Pieux, right D62 to Le Rozel; right D117 into village; house just beyond village.

	Josiane & Jean-Claude Grandchamp Le Château, 50340 Le Rozel, Manche
tel	+33 (0)2 33 52 95 08
fax	+33 (0)2 33 02 00 35

Map 3 Entry 217

Normandy

La Lande

A laughing, talkative couple with taste and manners, your hosts give you "the best of France, the best of England" in their fabulous old Norman house. Antiques from both countries and English china inside, wild French hares and owls outside. The guest suites have been recently redone and are enticing – one is under the eaves and full of light, all have deep comfort and oodles of towels. Seductive dining, sitting and reading rooms, too. Breakfast is as beautifully presented as the rest; Ted, an expert on WWII, will take you round the landing beaches. A tremendous atmosphere of friendship and goodwill.

rooms	3: 1 suite for 2, 1 suite for 3, 1 suite for 4.
price	€60-€70.
meals	Dinner with wine, €27. Picnics possible.
closed	Rarely.
directions	From Cherbourg S for Caen; D900 to Bricquebec via Le Pont; on for Valognes, past Intermarché, left at T-junc.; D902 to Valognes; past Super U on left; 1st left, then 1st right.

	Ted & Linda Malindine La Lande, Les Grosmonts, 50260 Bricquebec, Manche
tel	+33 (0)2 33 52 24 78
fax	+33 (0)2 33 52 24 78
email	la.lande@wanadoo.fr

Map 3 Entry 218

Manoir de Bellaunay

Even the smallest bathroom oozes atmosphere through its *oeil de boeuf*. The youngest piece of this fascinating house is over 400 years old; its predecessor stood on the site of a monastery, the fireplace in the lovely *Medieval* bedroom carries the coat of arms of the original owners and your farmer hosts share their energy enthusiastically between a large beef herd, their ancient house and the guests they share it with. They have sought carved marriage wardrobes, lace canopies, footstools for the rooms – and hung tapestry curtains at the windows. Sheer comfort among warm old stones.

rooms	3: 2 doubles, 1 suite for 3.
price	€55-€75.
meals	Choice of restaurants 4km.
closed	November-March.
directions	On RN13 exit at Valognes; follow Route de Quettehou D902; house 3km after Valognes, number 11.

Christiane & Jacques
Allix-Desfauteaux
Manoir de Bellaunay,
50700 Tamerville, Manche

tel	+33 (0)2 33 40 10 62
fax	+33 (0)2 33 40 10 62
email	bellauney@wanadoo.fr
web	www.bellauney.com

Map 3 Entry 219

Le Château

Gravel crunches as you sweep up to the imposing granite château on the Cherbourg peninsula. The beguiling fairytale turrets and Françoise's welcome soon work their magic. External stone stairs lead to the red-velvet charm of the *Chambre Château* (with secret grille where maids peeped into the chapel below); ancient chestnut stairs in the converted farm building lead to simple family rooms. In the morning, as you breakfast generously in a light-flooded, pink-panelled family dining room and sip your café au lait, you might like to nod a grateful 'merci' to Bernard's obliging Normandy cows.

rooms	2: 1 double. Annexe: 1 suite for 4.
price	€50-€80.
meals	Restaurant 500m.
closed	Never.
directions	From Valognes D2 for St Sauveur le Vicomte; left onto D2, 3km; auberge Pont Cochon left before bridge. Driveway on left opp. church.

M & Mme Lucas de Vallavieille
Le Château,
50700 Flottemanville Bocage,
Manche

tel	+33 (0)2 33 40 29 02
fax	+33 (0)2 33 95 23 51
email	contact@chateau-flottemanville.com
web	www.chateau-flottemanville.com

Map 3 Entry 220

Normandy

Manoir de Caillemont

The presence of the first lord of this 1720s manor house still presides; wrought-iron balustrading incorporates his monogram as it sweeps up the fine Valognes white-stone stair of the entrance hall. Loll by the lovely hedged-in pool; congregate in the games room before a civilised aperitif; dine in an open-plan, rush-matted room on deep-cushioned chairs at a table for eight. This house is full of paintings, antiques and collectables and a 1950s jukebox will play music for you; or make your own on the pretty harmonium in the two-roomed, elegantly panelled suite. The Fouchés love sharing their home.

rooms	3: 1 twin/double, 1 suite for 2, 1 suite for 4.
price	€88–€128.
meals	Dinner with wine, €38.
closed	Never.
directions	From Haye du Puits D903 for Barneville Carteret; opp. signs to St Georges, right signed St Maurice du Cotentin; house signed after 200m.

Catherine & Eric Fouché
Manoir de Caillemont,
St Georges de la Rivière,
50270 Barneville Carteret, Manche
tel   +33 (0)2 33 53 25 66
fax   +33 (0)2 33 53 25 66
email manoircaillemont@aol.com
web   www.manoircaillemont.com

Map 3 Entry 221

Normandy

La Roque de Gouey

A fishing, sailing port and a bridge with 13 arches: a pretty place to stay. The restored *longère* is the home of two of our favourite owners: Madame, the same honest open character as ever and Monsieur, retired, who has time to spread his modest farmer's joviality. They give you good French rooms with pretty bedcovers and antiques that are cherished. Your side of the house has its own entrance, dayroom and vast old fireplace where old beams and *tommettes* flourish. The rooms up the steepish outside stairs are small, the ground-floor room larger, and the breakfast tables sport flowery cloths.

rooms	4: 1 double, 1 twin, 1 family for 3, 1 family suite for 5.
price	€45. €60 for 3.
meals	Choice of restaurants 500m. Guest kitchen.
closed	Rarely.
directions	From St Sauveur le Vicomte D15 to Portbail; right just before church Rue R. Asselin; over old railway; house 250m on right.

Bernadette Vasselin
La Roque de Gouey,
Rue Gilles Poërier,
50580 Portbail, Manche
tel   +33 (0)2 33 04 80 27
fax   +33 (0)2 33 04 80 27
mobile +33 (0)6 67 75 31 52

Map 3 Entry 222

Normandy

La Merise

After travelling the world, John and Valerie moved from Australia to this bird lovers' haven (marsh, coastal and woodland species protected by the nature reserve) and are thoroughly integrated in their rural community. A lively, interesting and attentive couple, they understand home comforts and guests easily join them for coffee and chat. Leading off the kitchen, the gently-coloured ground-floor guest room is generous enough for some old-style Normandy furniture, a hand-made quilt and two extra beds. It looks over the pretty garden where chirruping peace is a constant and the sun shines a lot.

rooms	1 double (2 extra children's beds).
price	€46.
meals	Dinner with wine, €22.
closed	Rarely.
directions	From La Haye du Puits; D97 to T-junction, 5 kms; left for Gorges; 1st small lane on right before radio tower, signposted.

Valerie & John Armstrong
La Merise,
13 Village de Haut,
50430 Gerville la Forêt, Manche

tel +33 (0)2 33 45 63 86
mobile +33 (0)6 30 74 42 49
email the.armstrong@free.fr

Map 3 Entry 223

Normandy

Le Pont Sanson

So old it's almost venerable: timbers dated 1600s, a spiral staircase up to big bedrooms full of antiques, personality and paintings, a Vieille Cuisine where fresh orange juice is served before a giant fireplace. Another 'wow' is the garden, planted for a brilliant effect of colour and perspective and sporting a delicious summer room for guests and the Monet-Grouvel Bridge – sense of humour too. Your hosts, she Scottish, he French, enthusiastic about their lovely home, welcome you with real pleasure and give the guided tour to anyone interested in history, architecture and gardens.

rooms	2: 1 double; 1 twin/double with separate bath.
price	€80–€90.
meals	Auberge 3-10km.
closed	Rarely.
directions	From Periers or St Lô D900 take D57 to Feugères; in village left D142 then D533 for Lozon. Blue/green gates on right.

Baron & Baronne Grouvel
Le Pont Sanson,
Feugères, 50190 Periers, Manche

tel +33 (0)2 33 07 79 00
fax +33 (0)2 33 07 79 00
email lalage.grouvel@wanadoo.fr

Map 3 Entry 224

Normandy

La Virmonderie

Sigrid's big country kitchen and crackling fire are the heart of this fine 18th-century granite house and you know instantly you are sharing her home: the built-in dresser carries pretty china, her pictures and ornaments bring interest to the salon and its Normandy fireplace, and she proudly tells how she rescued the superb elm staircase. A fascinating person, for years a potter in England, she has retired to France and vegetarian happiness. Bedrooms have colour and lace, unusual antiques and original beams. Five acres of garden mean plenty of space for children and grown-ups alike. Great value.
Minimum stay two nights.

rooms	3 doubles.
price	€45.
meals	Dinner with wine, from €22. Supper €10. Picnic from €5. Guest kitchen.
closed	January-February.
directions	From Carentan N174 to St Lô. for 12-13km; before major r'bout D377 for Cavigny; 4th house on right.

	Sigrid Hamilton
	La Virmonderie,
	50620 Cavigny,
	Manche
tel	+33 (0)2 33 56 01 13
fax	+33 (0)2 33 56 41 32
web	perso.wanadoo.fr/sigrid.hamilton

Normandy

Le Suppey

The younger Franco-American Buissons have given a thorough internal facelift to this 18th-century farmhouse with its old stables and outbuildings flanking a flowered courtyard. Rooms are sprigged in peach or green, beds have new mattresses, the rustic furniture is locally made with marble tops, the watercolours are done by an aunt. It is all simple, sunny and most welcoming. Jean works during the week; Nancy, perfectly bilingual, is very present and loving her B&B activity. There's a green and secluded garden for picnics, and a small spring that has great damming-up potential for little ones!

rooms	2 doubles.
price	€44.
meals	Restaurants in St Lô 5km.
closed	Rarely.
directions	From Cherbourg, N13 & N174 to St Lô. At St Georges-Montcocq, D191 to Villiers Fossard. In village, right on C7; house is 800m on right.

	Jean & Nancy Buisson
	Le Suppey,
	50680 Villiers Fossard,
	Manche
tel	+33 (0)2 33 57 30 23
email	nancy.buisson@wanadoo.fr
web	perso.wanadoo.fr/nancy.buisson/

Map 3 Entry 225

Map 3 Entry 226

Normandy

Saint Léger

The totally French farmhouse, 19th-century without, modern within, is colourful, neat and immaculate. One room is pink-flavoured, the other blue, each with bits of crochet, a carved armoire (one *charbourgoise*, the other from St Lô) and a clean, compact shower room; the gloriously ostentatious blue bathroom is also yours for the asking – giant tub and plants rampaging. But most special of all is the charming, elegant Madame Lepoittevin, full of smiles and laughter, and actively involved in a walking group in summer – why not join in? You can picnic in the garden or cook your own on the barbecue.

Normandy

La Rhétorerie

Here is old-style, down-to-earth, French country hospitality. Madame, an elderly live wire, full of smiles, humorous chat and spontaneous welcome, plays the organ in the village church. Monsieur, a retired farmer, is quietly interested. Their bedrooms have old family furniture (admire *grand-mère's* elaborately crocheted bedcover), good mattresses, simple washing arrangements. It is all spotless and guests have a large, colourful dayroom, formerly the *pressoir*, with massive beams, lots of plants and a kitchen – the greatstone is now a flower feature outside. Kids can sit on the donkeys and collect the eggs.

rooms	2: 1 double; 1 double with shower & separate wc.
price	€38.
meals	Choice of restaurants 2-10km.
closed	1st two weeks of March.
directions	From St Lô D972 for Coutances, through St Gilles; house sign on left, 4km after St Gilles, on D972.

rooms	2: 1 twin/double, 1 twin, each with shower, sharing wc.
price	€40.
meals	Restaurant 1km, choice 4km. Kitchen available.
closed	Rarely.
directions	From St Lô D999 for Percy, exit 5, 3km; right D38 for Canisy. House 1km along on right.

Jean & Micheline Lepoittevin
Saint Léger,
50570 Quibou, Manche
tel   +33 (0)2 33 57 18 41
fax   +33 (0)2 33 57 18 41
mobile   +33 (0)6 18 93 47 95
email   rico123@hotmail.com

Marie-Thérèse & Roger Osmond
La Rhétorerie,
Route de Canisy,
50750 St Ébremond de Bonfossé,
Manche
tel   +33 (0)2 33 56 62 98

Map 3 Entry 227

Map 3 Entry 228

Normandy

Les Hauts Champs

This place is so French: rich carpeting on floors and walls, highly floral linen, toiletries, bathrobes and bonbons. Monsieur breeds horses and riding is possible for experienced riders; the less horsey can visit the stables which have produced great showjumpers. Madame cooks the food, including bread and croissants, and serves you special meals in the beamed and colombaged kitchen. She and her husband are wonderful hosts, it is all snug and homey (one room up steep wooden stairs), the setting is charming, among hills, woods and fields. Perfect for winter visits, too.

rooms	2: 1 double, 1 twin.
price	€40.
meals	Dinner with wine, €20.
closed	Rarely.
directions	From Coutances D971 for Granville; fork quickly left D7 for Gavray for 1.5km; left D27 to Nicorps; through village; 1st right; house on left, signposted.

M & Mme Posloux
Les Hauts Champs,
La Moinerie de Haut,
50200 Nicorps, Manche
tel   +33 (0)2 33 45 30 56
fax   +33 (0)2 33 07 60 21

Map 3 Entry 229

Normandy

Château des Boulais

There is space and grandeur in this mixed-period château and Madame and her Dutch professor partner have bravely taken up the challenge: the onetime *colonie de vacances* is being licked into stylish shape. The parquet-floored sitting room is vast; bedrooms have antique beds and strong plain colours alongside old wooden floors and fireplaces – it's great fun and the views sail out of those big windows across copses and woods for miles. Your colourful hostess adores meeting new people and hearing about their lives; her four teenagers are a delight and her meals are delicious. Friendly, easy, comfortable.

rooms	3: 2 doubles, 1 suite. Extra beds.
price	€60–€80.
meals	Dinner €15. Wine list.
closed	Christmas & New Year.
directions	From Villedieu les P. N175 & D524 for Vire 1.5km; right D999 for Brécey. After Chérencé le H. left through St Martin B. to sawmill; follow signs to Loges sur Brécey; house 2km, 2nd left after wood.

Nathalie de Drouas
Château des Boulais,
Loges sur Brécey,
50800 St Martin le Bouillant,
Manche
tel   +33 (0)2 33 60 32 20
mobile   +33 (0)6 84 56 33 55
web   www.chateau-des-boulais.com

Map 3 Entry 230

La Haute Gilberdière

Generous, artistic and young in spirit, the Champagnacs are a privilege to meet. Their 18th-century *longère* bathes in a floral wonderland: roses climb and tumble, narrow paths meander and a kitchen garden grows your breakfast – wander and revel or settle down in a shady spot. Inside, bedrooms are perfect with handsome antiques, pretty bed linen and polished floors, or modern with pale wood and bucolic views. The honey-coloured breakfast room is warmly contemporary – all timber and exposed stone; Monsieur's bread comes warm from the oven served with homemade jams. Wonderful. *Minimum stay two nights.*

rooms	3 + 1: 2 doubles, 1 twin, sharing bath. Barn for 2-4.
price	€60 €150.
meals	Restaurants 5km.
closed	November-March.
directions	From Avranches D973 for Granville & Sartilly; left at end of village D61 for Carolles; 800m house on left.

Édith & Pierre Champagnac
la Haute Gilberdière,
50530 Sartilly, Manche

tel	+33 (0)2 33 60 17 44
mobile	+33 (0)6 80 87 17 62
email	champagnac@libertysurf.fr
web	www.champagnac-farmhouse.com

Map 3 Entry 231

Le Petit Manoir

That view is definitely worth the detour, and you can walk to Mont St Michel in two hours. The Gédouins keep cows and pigs; Annick, who used to teach, makes jams, crêpes and delicious breakfast rice pudding (a Breton speciality); Jean is Mayor. Rooms are French country style, without frills or soft touches, just a few little pictures on lightly patterned walls, and spotlessly clean. In the courtyard are passion fruit and figs; two large cider presses brim with geraniums; the old stone bakery will charm you. All is rural peace in this tiny village by the marshes.

rooms	2: 1 double, 1 twin.
price	€38.
meals	Restaurants 500m-2km.
closed	15 November-7 February.
directions	From A84 exit 33 for St Malo & Pontorson on N175 for 9km; right to Servon; at church right for 500m; farm on left.

Annick, Jean & Valérie Gédouin
Le Petit Manoir,
21 rue de la Pierre du lertre,
50170 Servon, Manche

tel	+33 (0)2 33 60 03 44
fax	+33 (0)2 33 60 17 79
email	agedouinmanoir@tiscali.fr
web	chambresgedouin.com

Map 3 Entry 232

Normandy

Les Blotteries

Monsieur, formerly a fire officer, is proud of his restoration of the old farm (the B&B is his project; Madame works in town). He is an attentive, positive host, full of smiles and jokes, and has done a good job. Old granite glints as you pass into the softly-curtained entrance; an original hay rack hangs above. One bedroom is on the first floor, another is in the former stable, a third in the old bakery: a ground-floor family room whose large windows overlook the courtyard. The cream breakfast room is simple and elegant and the fields around are open to all so no need to worry about the road at the front.

Normandy

La Ferme de l'Étang

An authentic farm B&B in a glorious setting. Ivy on walls, beamed attic bedrooms with fresh flowers, woodland walks, lake and château across the way – and a proper farming family. Jean-Paul and Brigitte are friendly, interested people, travel a lot and talk well. He is a dairy farmer and arbitrator; she collects copper and brass. Country meals (quite delicious) are taken round the big table in the dining room with its huge fireplace. A splendid staircase leads you up to the good, snug, cottagey yet unfussy guest rooms. Children love it – there are games galore, swings in the garden and cows all around.

rooms	3: 1 double, 2 family rooms.
price	€65–€70.
meals	Restaurants 1km.
closed	Rarely.
directions	From A84 exit 33; right at r'bout & uphill for about 300m to next r'bout; left then left again, D998 for St James; house on right after 5km.

rooms	4: 2 doubles, 2 family rooms.
price	€45–€48.
meals	Dinner with wine, €16.
closed	Rarely.
directions	From Cherbourg A84 exit 34 for Mt St Michel & St Malo 600m; exit for Mt St Michel & Rennes D43 for Rennes. At r'bout D40 for Rennes, 5.5km; D308 left; signposted.

	Laurence & Jean-Malo Tizon
	Les Blotteries,
	50220 Juilley,
	Manche
tel	+33 (0)2 33 60 84 95
email	bb@les-blotteries.com
web	www.les-blotteries.com

	Jean-Paul & Brigitte Gavard
	La Ferme de l'Étang,
	Boucéel, Vergoncey,
	50240 St James, Manche
tel	+33 (0)2 33 48 34 68
fax	+33 (0)2 33 48 48 53
email	jpgavard@club-internet.fr

Map 3 Entry 233

Map 3 Entry 234

Normandy

La Gautrais

Come for a slice of French farmhouse life. Madame is quietly friendly, "makes a superb soufflé" and mouthwatering Norman cuisine – she loves it. She and Monsieur cook, serve, clear, and always find time for a glass of calvados with their guests. The old granite stable block, built in 1622, was last modernised in the 1970s. Polished floors, spare furnishings, cots in the attic rooms, a couple of kitchenettes and a welcoming dining room with big table make this suitable for families on a budget. The poetically-named but perfectly ordinary Two Estuaries motorway now provides quick access one kilometre away.

rooms	5: 2 doubles, 1 twin, 2 suites for 4–5. Some rooms have kitchenette.
price	From €48.
meals	Dinner with wine, €18.
closed	Rarely.
directions	From A84 exit 32 at St James then D12, following signs for Super U store for Antrain, 1km. On right.

François & Catherine Tiffaine
La Gautrais,
50240 St James,
Manche

tel	+33 (0)2 33 48 31 86
fax	+33 (0)2 33 48 58 17
email	ctiffaine@hotmail.fr

Map 3 Entry 235

Brittany

Brittany

Les Mouettes

House and owner are imbued with the calm of a balmy summer's morning, whatever the weather. Isabelle's talent seems to touch the very air that fills her old family house. Timeless simplicity reigns; there is nothing superfluous: simple carved pine furniture, an antique wrought-iron cot, dhurries on scrubbed plank floors, palest yellow or mauve walls to reflect the ocean-borne light, harmonious striped or gingham curtains. Starfish and many-splendoured pebbles keep the house sea-connected. The unspoilt seaside village, popular in season, is worth the trip alone.

rooms	5: 4 doubles, 1 twin.
price	€48.
meals	Choice of restaurants in village.
closed	Rarely.
directions	From St Malo, N137 for Rennes. 6km after St Malo, right on D117 to St Suliac (3km from N137 exit to village entrance). Road leads to Grande Rue down to port; house at top on right.

Isabelle Rouvrais
Les Mouettes,
17 Grande Rue,
35430 St Suliac, Ille-et-Vilaine

tel	+33 (0)2 99 58 30 41
email	contact@les-mouettes-saint-suliac.com
web	www.les-mouettes-saint-suliac.com

Map 3 Entry 236

Brittany

La Hamelinais

The lovely farmhouse goes back to 1718 – Madame arrived here at the age of 15. Expect old beams, exposed stones, few mod cons and bags of rustic charm. But it's Marie-Madeleine who makes this place special: up before breakfast to prepare a roaring fire in the magnificent granite fireplace and, in summer, giving her all to garden and orchard. Gentle, bright-eyed Jean says that, tied to the farm, he "travels through his guests". Rooms are old-fashioned and homely (white bedspreads on comfy beds), your hosts know and love their region intimately and the sea is just 3km away. *Stays of 2 nights or more preferred.*

rooms	3: 1 double, 2 triples.
price	€45-€50.
meals	Choice of restaurants 4km.
closed	Rarely.
directions	From St Malo N137 for Rennes 15km; exit N176 for Mt St Michel 12km. At Dol de Bretagne D80 for St Brolâdre 3km; left D85 for Cherrueix; house sign on right before 3rd little bridge.

Jean & Marie-Madeleine Glémot
La Hamelinais,
35120 Cherrueix,
Ille-et-Vilaine

tel	+33 (0)2 99 48 95 26
fax	+33 (0)2 99 48 89 23
mobile	+33 (0)6 17 47 53 49

Map 3 Entry 237

Brittany

Le Presbytère

Solid granite, earth energy: inside its walled garden, the vast old priest's house is warm, reassuring and superbly restored: fine old timbers, antiques, panelling, hangings. Dotted around the house, each bedroom has character... perhaps a sleigh bed or a canopy, a staircase straight or spiral, pretty fabrics, white bedcovers, a garden view; our favourites are those with private entrances. There's a sense of its never ending, there's even a classy mobile home. Madame, a lovely energetic and warmly attentive person, loves cooking. You will leave with new friends in your address book.

rooms	5: 1 double, 1 suite for 3, 2 triples; 1 twin sharing bath.
price	€49. €70 for 3.
meals	Dinner €17–€20. Wine list.
closed	15-31 January.
directions	From Pontorson D219 to Vieux-Viel; follow signs for 'Chambres d'Hôte Vieux-Viel'; next to church.

Madeleine Stracquadanio
Le Presbytère,
35610 Vieux-Viel,
Ille-et-Vilaine
tel +33 (0)2 99 48 65 29
fax +33 (0)2 99 48 65 29
web www.vieux-viel.com

Map 3 Entry 238

Brittany

La Maison Neuve

Fabrice whips up wonderful aperitifs, Nicole spoils you with her cooking – home-baking at breakfast, a feast of surprises at dinner. Set in pretty Breton countryside, close to golf, riding and beaches, the 19th-century farmhouse combines original features with a light, modern style. Fresh, French bedrooms – one with hand-painted furniture, another with a wrought-iron four-poster – are dotted with objects from Japanese travels. On chilly evenings, cosy up to the fire in the grand granite fireplace; in the summer, wander meadow, garden and woodland. A sauna and spa are planned. *Min. stay two nights weekends.*

rooms	5: 2 doubles, 1 twin, 2 family rooms for 3.
price	€70.
meals	Dinner with wine, €25.
closed	Rarely.
directions	N137 from St Malo; exit Miniac Morvan; left onto rue de la Blainerie, 400m after petrol station; on for 800m; left to Bas Gouillon. House 300m on right.

Nicole & Fabrice Barbot
La Maison Neuve,
35540 Miniac Morvan,
Ille-et-Vilaine
tel +33 (0)2 99 58 05 38
fax +33 (0)2 99 58 05 38
email fbarbot@wanadoo.fr
web www.la-maison-neuve.com

Map 3 Entry 239

Brittany

Le Mesnil des Bois

Fringed by lawn in a forest clearing is a cluster of buildings, part of a 16th-century manoir. The manor is awaiting renovation but the Villettes' own long, creeper-covered house has been transformed. They live at one end, guests at the other and the ample living space, full of rugs, books and rich, warm colours, is generously shared. Bedrooms, understatedly luxurious, have paintings and books; a nearby cottage has become a family suite. Home-cooked food and a whole forest to wander in at will… the sense of space is exhilarating and the entire place captivating. *Minimum stay two nights holiday weekends & July / August.*

rooms	5: 1 double, 1 twin, 2 family rooms for 2–3, 1 family suite for 4.
price	€80–€130.
meals	Dinner with wine, €30–€50.
closed	January & February.
directions	From Rennes, exit Miniac Morvan; right to Tressé for Tronchet; at x-roads, right to Lanhélin, D73; forest on right, take forest road. Signed.

Martine Villette
Le Mesnil des Bois,
35540 Le Tronchet,
Ille-et-Vilaine
tel   +33 (0)2 99 58 97 12
fax   +33 (0)2 99 58 97 12
email villette@le-mesnil-des-bois.com
web   www.le-mesnil-des-bois.com

Map 3 Entry 240

Brittany

Le Pont Ricoul

The little lakeside cottage in the old bakery is a dream, far enough from the main house to feel secluded… it is snugly romantic, utterly seductive. The suite off the big house is larger and as pretty, its split levels twinned by a blue-painted stair. Cane chairs, sunny curtains, a granite handbasin, rugs on parquet: a dreamy décor in a bucolic setting. If your need for intimacy is deep, then Catherine will deliver breakfast and dinner (course by course, and delicious) to your hideaway. Nicer still to join them at their artistic table; they are young and delightful and we have received nothing but praise.

rooms	2: 1 suite for 4. Cottage: 1 suite.
price	€50–€89.
meals	Dinner with wine, €20.
closed	Rarely.
directions	From St Malo N137 to St Pierre de Plesguen; by church D10 for Lanhélin 1.5km; signposted on right.

Catherine & François Grosset
Le Pont Ricoul,
35720 St Pierre de Plesguen,
Ille-et-Vilaine
tel   +33 (0)2 99 73 92 65
email pontricoul@aol.com
web   www.pontricoul.com

Map 3 Entry 241

Le Petit Moulin du Rouvre

Escape the modern world for this tranquil 17th-century watermill. Régis has taken over from his grandmother and is an excellent host – professional yet quietly easy-going. The sitting room – vast granite fireplace, leather chairs and sofa – is traditionally, wonderfully cosy, and the bedrooms in the Moulin are typically French, one overlooking the swishing wheel (turned off at night). The rest are very well renovated with a contemporary feel, one with its own woodburner, another with a nautical theme, all with a private entrance. Régis is an excellent chef, loves his wines and opens his restaurant to all.

Château du Quengo

Two fascinating generations of an ancient Breton family welcome you open-armed to their inimitable house where history, atmosphere and silence rule: private chapel, Bio-garden and rare trees outside, carved chestnut staircase, Italian mosaic floor, 1900s wallpaper, about 30 rooms inside. Anne plys you with homemade delights and knows the family history; Alfred builds organs and merrily serves breakfast. The bedrooms have antique radiators and are properly old-fashioned, our favourite the family room. No plastic coathangers, few mod cons – just humorous hosts and a beautiful place.

rooms	5: 2 doubles, 1 family for 3. Annexe: 1 double, 1 family.
price	€65-€68.
meals	Dinner €20.60. Wine list €8-€25.
closed	Rarely.
directions	From Rennes-St Malo N137, exit St Pierre de Plesguen; D10 for Lanhélin: right for 2.5km; signed.

rooms	5: 2 doubles, 2 twins sharing 2 baths, 1 family room for 3.
price	€49-€73.
meals	Choice of restaurants 1.5-5km. Kitchen available.
closed	Rarely.
directions	From N12 for St Brieuc exit at Bédée D72 to Irodouer; 1st right before church to Romillé; château entrance 600m on left, signposted.

	Régis Maillard
	Le Petit Moulin du Rouvre,
	35720 St Pierre de Plesguen,
	Ille-et-Vilaine
tel	+33 (0)2 99 73 85 84
email	maillard.regis@aumoulindurouvre.com
web	www.aumoulindurouvre.com

	Anne & Alfred
	du Crest de Lorgerie
	Château du Quengo,
	35850 Irodouer, Ille-et-Vilaine
tel	+33 (0)2 99 39 81 47
email	lequengo@hotmail.com
web	www.chateauduquengo.com

Map 3 Entry 242

Map 3 Entry 243

Brittany

Château du Pin

Watercolourist and photographer, the brave, artistic Ruans have launched with passionate enthusiasm into renovating a small château with its ruined chapel, stables and thrilling atmosphere. For art and simplicity this is the place. The original staircase curves up to the 'literary' guest rooms: romantic *Proust*, light-flooded *George Sand*, immaculate *Victor Hugo*; each shower is behind a great rafter; the stunning drawing room with antique snooker table wears rich reds. It's brilliant, and great fun. Your gentle hosts will join you for an aperitif – then create a superb dinner for you.

rooms	4: 2 twins, 2 family suites for 4.
price	€75–€120.
meals	Dinner with wine, €30.
closed	Rarely.
directions	From Rennes N12 west to Bédée 23km; D72 to Montfort sur Meu; D125 for St Méen le Grand; château 3km on left.

Catherine & Luc Ruan
Château du Pin,
35370 Iffendic près de Montfort,
Ille-et-Vilaine
tel   +33 (0)2 99 09 34 05
fax   +33 (0)2 99 09 34 05
email   luc.ruan@wanadoo.fr
web   www.chateaudupin-bretagne.com

Map 3 Entry 244

Brittany

Épineu

Fear not, the farm mess is forgotten once you reach the cottage and the long, rural views beyond. Through that timbered porch, a sociable, sprightly and unpretentious lady will lead you into her big, wood-floored and -ceilinged country dining room – warmed in winter by the old stone fireplace. It is uncluttered and soberly French. Bedrooms are a good size, the most characterful one (by far) in the main house. The country garden is tended with love and pride and produces vegetables for dinner. You will be spoiled outrageously at dinner, and Madame will join you if you are just two.

rooms	1 triple.
price	€50. €66 for 3.
meals	Dinner €18. Wine €12.
closed	Never.
directions	From Rennes N137 S exit Poligné D47 for Bourg des Comptes for 4km; left & drive through L'Aubriais to next hamlet, Épineu; right into & across farmyard, down lane 20m, cottage on right.

Yvette Guillopé
Épineu,
35890 Bourg des Comptes,
Ille-et-Vilaine
tel   +33 (0)2 99 52 16 84
mobile   +33 (0)6 25 60 23 22

Map 3 Entry 245

Brittany

41 rue de la Petite Corniche

Enter and you will understand why we chose this modernised house: the ever-changing light of the great bay shimmers in through vast swathes of glass. In guest rooms too you can sit in your armchair and gaze as boats go by. Or take ten minutes and walk to Perros. Guy chose the house so he could see his small ship at anchor (lucky guests may be taken for a sail) and Marie-Clo has enlivened the interior with her patchwork and embroidery. It is calm, light, bright; they are attentive, warm and generous and breakfast is seriously good. Great for family holidays by the sea, but note steep steps on arrival.

rooms	2 doubles, each with sitting area.
price	€60–€65.
meals	Restaurants 400–500m.
closed	Never.
directions	From Lannion D788 N to Perros Guirec; follow signs to Port; coastal road round bay for approx. 1km; left at sign. (Will fax map or collect you from railway station.)

Marie–Clotilde Biarnès
41 rue de la Petite Corniche,
BP 24, 22700 Perros Guirec,
Côtes-d'Armor

tel	+33 (0)2 96 23 28 08
mobile	+33 (0)6 81 23 15 49
email	marieclo.biarnes@wanadoo.fr
web	perso.wanadoo.fr/corniche/

Map 2 Entry 246

Brittany

Manoir du Launay

A fine beech avenue leads to the reconstructed *maison bourgeoise*, the original stone family crest above its front door. Your very welcoming hosts renovated the old place superbly, then rag-rolled and stencilled each airy room. Bedrooms are colour themed and serene; a painted fireplace, a mistletoe-sprigged duvet, a simple armoire; luxurious bathrooms ooze big fluffy towels. In the peachy dining room plenteous breakfasts are served at three tables before an impressive stone fireplace: *far breton* cake, crêpes, homemade jams. There's a games room for children and a salon for you.

rooms	5: 4 doubles, 1 suite for 4-5.
price	€80–€110.
meals	Choice of restaurants nearby.
closed	Rarely.
directions	From Lannion D65 for Trébeurden; at r'bout signs for Servel, 3km; right into wooded driveway; signposted.

Florence & Ivan Charpentier
Manoir du Launay,
Lannion, 22300 Servel,
Côtes-d'Armor

tel	+33 (0)2 96 47 21 24
mobile	+33 (0)6 87 61 91 13
email	manoirdulaunay@wanadoo.fr
web	www.manoirdulaunay.com

Map 2 Entry 247

Brittany

Manoir de Kerguéréon

Such wonderful, gracious hosts with a nice sense of humour: you feel you are at a house party; such age and history in the gloriously asymmetrical château: tower, turrets, vast fireplaces, low doors, ancestral portraits, fine furniture; such a lovely garden, Madame's own work. Once you have managed the worn spiral staircase you find bedrooms with space, taste, arched doors, a lovely window seat to do your tapestry in, good bathrooms; and the great Breton breakfast can be brought up if you wish. An elegant welcome, intelligent conversation, delightful house – and their son breeds racehorses on the estate.

rooms	3: 2 doubles, 1 triple.
price	€95.
meals	Choice of restaurants 7-10km.
closed	Never.
directions	N12 exit Bég Chra & Plouaret (bet. Guingamp & Morlaix); Plouaret D11 for Lannion; after 5.5km left at crossroads for Ploumilliau, D30; over railway, after 3km left to 'Kerguéréon', 100m left to end.

M & Mme Arnauld de Bellefon
Manoir de Kerguéréon,
Ploubezre,
22300 Lannion,
Côtes-d'Armor
tel +33 (0)2 96 38 80 59
fax +33 (0)2 96 38 91 46
mobile +33 (0)6 03 45 68 55

Map 2 Entry 248

Brittany

Château de Kermezen

A very special place, aristocratic Kermezen has been in the family for 600 years and feels as if it will stand for ever in its granite certainty. Its 17th-19th century 'modernisation' is a masterpiece of high ceilings, generous windows, a granite-hearthed, tapestried guest sitting room where old books and family portraits remind you this is "just an ordinary family house". Madame, dynamic and adorable, loves her visitors. All the bedrooms, from traditional to timber-strewn to yellow-panelled, have a laid-back charm. Plus private chapel, old mill, vast lawns and trees…An enduring favourite, worth every penny.

rooms	5: 3 doubles, 2 twins.
price	€88–€104.
meals	Restaurant and crêperie in village.
closed	Rarely.
directions	From St Brieuc N12 to Guingamp; D8 for Tréguier; at Pommerit Jaudy left at lights; signposted.

Comte & Comtesse de Kermel
Château de Kermezen,
22450 Pommerit Jaudy,
Côtes-d'Armor
tel +33 (0)2 96 91 35 75
fax +33 (0)2 96 91 35 75
mobile +33 (0)6 83 05 26 60
email micheldekermel@kermezen.com

Map 2 Entry 249

Brittany

Manoir de Coat Gueno

The 15th-century manor house, only a few minutes' drive from the fishing ports, headlands and long sandy beaches, is cocooned in countryside. Wrapped in a rich fluffy towel, gaze out of your lavishly furnished bedroom onto the lawns below. You may hear the crackling of the log fire in the vast stone hearth downstairs, lit by your perfectionist host, the splash and laughter of guests in the pool or the crack of billiard balls echoing upwards to the tower. The games room and one gorgeous suite are in separate buildings in the grounds. *Gosford Park*, à la Bretonne. *Children over eight welcome. Minimum two nights.*

rooms	3: 1 double, 1 suite for 3, 1 suite for 4.
price	€85–€95. Suite €115–€140.
meals	Dinner €25. Wine €15. Restaurants nearby.
closed	September–April.
directions	From Paimpol for Lézardrieux; after bridge left to Pleudaniel; right for Pouldouran; thro' Prat Collet & Passe Porte to sign for Croas Guezou; left; 1st track right 800m. Not easy to find!

Christian de Rouffignac
Manoir de Coat Gueno,
Coat Gueno, 22740 Pleudaniel,
Côtes-d'Armor

tel	+33 (0)2 96 20 10 98
mobile	+33 (0)6 80 75 75 67
email	coatguen@aol.com
web	mapage.noos.fr/coatgueno

Map 2 Entry 250

Brittany

L'Ancien Presbytère

Inside an enclosed courtyard, a charming village presbytery. Walled gardens and an orchard for picnics complete the peaceful, private mood. The comfy, lived-in rooms are stuffed with personal touches; the biggest is the lightest, high and stylish with an amazing, 1950s/Deco bathroom. The cosy, cottagey, low-beamed attic rooms have very small shower rooms. Madame, easy and approachable, loves gardening and her two elderly cats, and knows the area "like her pocket". She has itineraries for your deeper discovery of secret delights, so stay awhile. You may eat here but make sure your dinner booking is firm.

rooms	3: 1 double, 2 twins.
price	€60–€65.
meals	Dinner with wine, €23.
closed	October–February.
directions	From Guingamp N12 for Morlaix, exit Louargat. From Louargat church, D33 to Tregrom (7km). House in village centre opp. church & bell tower (blue door in wall).

Nicole de Morchoven
L'Ancien Presbytère,
Tregrom, 22420 Plouaret,
Côtes-d'Armor

tel	+33 (0)2 96 47 94 15
fax	+33 (0)2 96 47 94 15
email	nicole.de-morchoven@wanadoo.fr
web	tregrom.monsite.wanadoo.fr

Map 2 Entry 251

Brittany

56 rue de la Ville Éveque

A wonder at every turn: a life-size bronze panther, seahorses flowing up the oak stairs, a zebra-covered throne for an Arab prince, the stone, bronze and marble works of sculptor Pierre Roche whose summer retreat this was. Yours now, in all its Breton austerity, and its superb gardens falling away to the bluebell wood, its private lane to the shore, its owners' eclectic collection of furniture, *objets* and art, Monsieur's amazing Egyptian photographs, its quilty, lacey bedrooms on different themes. Ask your hosts about the history of the house and its previous occupants: they'll regale and delight you.

rooms	4: 3 doubles, 1 family room.
price	€70–€100.
meals	Restaurants 2-4km.
closed	Rarely.
directions	RN12 west of St Brieuc; D768, exit Les Rampes for Pordic; at 2nd r'bout for Pordic centre; right at church; left at r'bout past Mairie, 700m; 3rd right; 1st left.

Isabelle & Jean-Yves Le Fevre
56 rue de la Ville Éveque,
22590 Pordic,
Côtes-d'Armor
tel +33 (0)2 96 79 17 32
mobile +33 (0)6 87 41 48 32
email keryos@wanadoo.fr
web www.keryos.com

Map 3 Entry 252

Brittany

Château de Bonabry

An extraordinary old château, built in 1373 by the Viscount's ancestor, with vastly wonderful bedrooms, a lively, lovable couple of aristocratic hosts bent on riding, hunting and entertaining you, fields all around and the sea at the end of the drive. Breakfast till ten on crêpes, croissants and quince jam. Madame is using her energy and taste in renovating some of the 30 rooms; in one suite, a canopied bed, colourful rugs and a stag's head on a lustrous wall. Windows tall, portraits ancestral, chapel 18th century, roses myriad – and bathrooms with hand-embroidered towels. Incomparable.

rooms	3: 2 suites; 1 double with separate bath.
price	€90–€135.
meals	Choice of restaurants within 10km.
closed	October-Easter.
directions	From St Brieuc N12 for Lamballe, exit Yffigniac-Hillion; left D80 to Hillion; D34 for Morieux, 200m to roadside cross on left by château gates.

Vicomtesse Louis
du Fou de Kerdaniel
Château de Bonabry,
22120 Hillion, Côtes-d'Armor
tel +33 (0)2 96 32 21 06
fax +33 (0)2 96 32 21 06
email bonabry@wanadoo.fr
web www.bonabry.fr.st

Map 3 Entry 253

Brittany

Le Clos Saint Cadreuc

Your warm hosts put good Breton dishes on your plate, and pour good organic wines – they create a welcoming atmosphere in their stone farmhouse. The very French rooms in the converted stables – two just finished: spacious, lovely, with huge walk-in showers – are enlivened by primitive West Indian paintings. More colour and space in the open-plan dining/sitting room: a good place to spend time in. Between house and stables is a pretty sheltered garden for picnics and DIY barbecues – great for families. Real peace in this quiet hamlet just 2km from the coast and a stone's throw from Mont St Michel.

rooms	4 + 2: 3 doubles, 1 twin. 2 apartments for 4-6.
price	€60. Apt €66.
meals	Dinner with wine, €22. Restaurants 4km.
closed	Rarely.
directions	From St Malo D168 for St Brieuc. At 1st r'bout after Ploubalay D26 for Plessix Balisson for 4km to hamlet; house on right, signposted.

Brigitte & Patrick Noël
Le Clos Saint Cadreuc,
22650 Ploubalay,
Côtes-d'Armor

tel	+33 (0)2 96 27 32 43
mobile	+33 (0)6 82 14 94 66
email	clos-saint-cadreuc@wanadoo.fr
web	www.clos-saint-cadreuc.com

Map 3 Entry 254

Brittany

La Besnardière

Fresh oysters, vegetables from the potager, local cheeses, Annie's gâteaux. Traditional home cooking is a highlight of staying at this Breton longère. Annie and Daniel charmingly host the meal – beneath a raftered ceiling – and share their knowledge of the area. Spacious guest rooms, each with a separate entrance, mix period details with a contemporary feel: breezy colours, tiled floors, an elegant writing desk, a carved bedhead. Come for walks, horse riding and beaches, a garden soft with stream, fruit trees and quiet corners, and breakfasts at a fine old wagon wheel topped with glass.

rooms	3: 1 twin/double, 1 family room for 4, 1 family room for 5.
price	€70.
meals	Dinner with wine, €22.
closed	Rarely.
directions	From Dinan N176 for St Brieuc; exit Plélan le petit centre; through village; for St Méloir des Bois; 50m before St Méloir sign take right; continue to junction; left at cross. House 1st on right.

Annie & Daniel Besnard
La Besnardière,
Les Biez,
22980 St Michel de Plélan,
Côtes-d'Armor

tel	+33 (0)2 96 82 13 49
email	labesnardiere@wanadoo.fr
web	www.labesnardiere.com

Map 3 Entry 255

Brittany

La Corbinais

The grand old family house, a 15th-century Breton *longère*, has a cosy, farm atmosphere, utterly delightful owners who are generous with their time and talk, plus a nine-hole golf course and all the trappings (clubhouse, lessons, socialising), carp ponds for those with rods and imaginative decoration. Madame, who paints, has a flair for interiors and uses velvet and florals, plants, paintings, sculptures and photographs – her rooms are appealingly personal and very comfortable. The old Breton bread oven is working again for the baking of bread. Birds cavort in the trees.

rooms	3: 2 doubles, 1 family room.
price	€58.
meals	Restaurant 4km.
closed	Rarely.
directions	From Dinan N176 west; north on D734 for Corseul; D44 for St Michel de Plelan; farm just outside village, map in village.

Odile & Henri Beaupère
La Corbinais,
22980 St Michel de Plélan,
Côtes-d'Armor

tel	+33 (0)2 96 27 64 81
fax	+33 (0)2 96 27 68 45
email	corbinais@corbinais.com
web	www.corbinais.com

Map 3 Entry 256

Brittany

Malik

The everyday becomes remarkable in these people's hands: we seldom consider modern houses but sensitively-designed Malik sailed in. Clad in red cedar, open-plan to provide space for six children, its wood, metal and sliding glass doors are in harmony with the dense trees, and every detail is taken care of. Plain white covers on good beds, eastern-style cushions and wall hangings on plain walls, monogrammed towels and lovely soaps. Breakfast, *un peu brunch*, is carefully attended to, and breads and jams homemade. Lovely people and an exquisitely serene house that seems to hug its garden to its heart.

rooms	2: 1 suite & salon, 1 suite for 4 (2 bedrooms).
price	€72. €112 for 4.
meals	Restaurants within walking distance.
closed	December-March.
directions	From Dinan N176 W for St Brieuc for about 12km. Exit right to Plélan le Petit. Follow signs to Centre & Mairie; at Mairie right for St Maudez then 2nd right.

Martine & Hubert Viannay
Malik, Chemin de l'Étoupe,
22980 Plélan le Petit,
Côtes-d'Armor

tel	+33 (0)2 96 27 62 71
mobile	+33 (0)6 09 92 35 21
email	bienvenue@malik-bretagne.com
web	www.malik-bretagne.com

Map 3 Entry 257

Brittany

Toul Bleïz

Have breakfast in the courtyard of this traditional Breton cottage serenaded by birds. There may be standing stones, badgers and wild boar on the moors behind but civilisation is a five-minute drive – perfect. An art teacher in her other life, Julie takes people out painting while Jez runs vegetarian cookery courses. Inside: exposed stone walls, renovated wood, comfy white sofas, quiet good taste. The ground-floor bedroom has a patchwork quilt, lace pillows and doors onto the garden; the new room in the attic has velux windows and high rafters. You'll love this place. *Children over 12 welcome.*

rooms	2: 1 double, 1 twin.
price	€48.
meals	Dinner with wine, €18.
closed	Rarely.
directions	From N164 D44 for Gorges du Daoulas; left at junction for Allées Couvertes; continue through hamlet; past lay-by on right; Toul Bleïz next track on right.

Julie & Jez Rooke
Toul Bleïz,
22570 Laniscat,
Côtes-d'Armor
tel   +33 (0)2 96 36 98 34
email   jezrooke@hotmail.com
web   www.phoneinsick.co.uk

Map 2   Entry 258

Brittany

Kernévez

Squarely planted in its Breton soil, this is a family house open to guests, not a purpose-converted affair. The children run the farm and the Gralls, genuine Breton-speaking Bretons, have time for visitors. After a peaceful night – rooms have warm traditional décor, excellent mattresses, family pieces – and a bucolic awakening to birdsong in the fields, come down to Madame's homemade crêpes or Breton cake at the long table. She's a lovely lady dressed in Breton dress, the perfect hostess. Prepare your own meals in the guest kitchenette, eat out in the garden that looks down to the sea. *Minimum stay two nights July/August.*

rooms	2: 1 twin, 1 family room.
price	€45.
meals	Restaurant 2.5km. Guest kitchen.
closed	Rarely.
directions	From St Pol de Léon D10 W to Cléder, right at 2nd r'bout. Arriving in Cléder, take road to sea for 2km; left following signs to Ferme de Kernévez.

François & Marceline Grall
Kernévez,
29233 Cléder,
Finistère
tel   +33 (0)2 98 69 41 14
mobile   +33 (0)6 10 65 27 80
web   www.kernevez.fr.fm

Map 2   Entry 259

Brittany

Manoir de Coat Amour

A dramatic, steep, shrubby drive brings you to a grand old house guarded by stone elephants and a spectacular gem of a chapel. strength and spirit. Set in a paradisical park, the Taylors' house overlooks Morlaix yet the traffic hum is minimal, the seclusion total. Chandeliers and antiques, polished floors, Jouy prints and strong colours add to the house-party atmosphere, refined yet comfortable. Jenny and Stafford (she taught textiles) have enjoyed doing their beautiful house in their own style and chat delightedly about it all. Super bedrooms, some connecting, a high colourful guest salon, simple luxury.

rooms	6: 2 doubles, 1 triple, 1 suite for 4; 2 triples sharing bath.
price	€90–€110.
meals	Dinner with wine, €30; 4 courses €45.
closed	Never.
directions	From Morlaix Route de Paris for St Brieuc; at mini-r'bout left up hill; immed. opp. Ford garage sharp left into drive; pale blue gates.

Stafford & Jenny Taylor
Manoir de Coat Amour,
Route de Paris,
29600 Morlaix, Finistère

tel	+33 (0)2 98 88 57 02
fax	+33 (0)2 98 88 57 02
email	stafford.taylor@wanadoo.fr
web	www.gites-morlaix.com

Map 2 Entry 260

Brittany

Manoir de Roch ar Brini

Crow's Rock Manor: sounds wild? It is wonderfully civilised. Built in the 1840s and admirably restored by your young and sociable hosts, who have four young children, it breathes an air of old-style, refined yet understated luxury in big, lofty-ceilinged, antiqued and chandeliered rooms with superb views of the generous grounds. The drawing-room parquet alone is worth the visit; bed linen is exceptional; from one super bathroom you can gaze out to the fields; another has tapestries of... baths. Breakfast may include *far breton* and fresh fruit salad. *Horse riding possible. Minimum stay two nights July/August.*

rooms	2 doubles.
price	€65–€75.
meals	Bistro 1km.
closed	Rarely.
directions	From Port Morlaix follow right bank of river N for Le Dourduff; after 3.6km, 3rd right at Roch ar Brini sign (hairpin bend) 500m. Right for Ploujean; house 3rd on right.

Étienne & Armelle Delaisi
Manoir de Roch ar Brini,
29600 Morlaix Ploujean,
Finistère

tel	+33 (0)2 98 72 01 44
fax	+33 (0)2 98 88 04 49
email	rochbrini@aol.com
web	www.brittanyguesthouse.com

Map 2 Entry 261

Brittany

La Grange de Coatélan

Yolande is a smiling, helpful mother of five, Charlick the most sociable workaholic you could find. Having beautifully renovated their old Breton weaver's house, they are converting other ruins as well as running the small auberge that serves traditional dishes and meats grilled on the open fire. They are active, artistic (he paints) and fun. The rooms have clever layouts, colour schemes and fabrics and brilliant use of wood, all informed by an artist's imagination; superb rustic elegance. Deep in the countryside, with animals and swings for children's delight.
Minimum stay two nights in summer.

rooms	5: 2 doubles, 3 quadruples.
price	€48–€68.
meals	Dinner €20. Wine €12–€17.
closed	Christmas-New Year.
directions	From Morlaix D9 south to Pougonven; at 2nd r'bout D109 to Coetélan. House on right. Signposted.

Charlick & Yolande de Ternay
La Grange de Coatélan,
29640 Plougonven,
Finistère

tel	+33 (0)2 98 72 60 16
fax	+33 (0)2 98 72 60 16
email	la-grange-de-coatelan@wanadoo.fr
web	www.lagrangedecoatelan.com

Map 2 Entry 262

Brittany

Domaine de Rugornou Uras

The two most memorable things here are Marie-Christine's smile as she talks about her native Brittany, and the crispness of the décor. Guest rooms are in the old cider-press – pretty and fresh with skylight windows and country antiques, and shower rooms immaculate. Breakfast, perhaps with Breton music in the background (to make the Breton costumes dance?), is prepared in the guest dayroom and eaten at the refectory table, with views of the garden and books all around. Dinner is at an auberge run by Madame's daughter, a walk away. It is quiet and comfortable and you can be quite independent.

rooms	2: 1 double, 1 triple.
price	€45–€48. Triple €65. Singles €40.
meals	Dinner with wine, €18.
closed	Rarely.
directions	From Morlaix D785 for Quimper, approx. 35km. 800m before Brasparts, right (on bend) & follow signs.

Marie-Christine Chaussy
Domaine de Rugornou Uras,
Garz ar Bik,
29190 Brasparts, Finistère

tel	+33 (0)2 98 81 47 14/ 46 27
fax	+33 (0)2 98 81 47 14
mobile	+33 (0)6 82 91 37 36
email	marie-christine.chaussy@wanadoo.fr

Map 2 Entry 263

Brittany

Manoir de Kerledan

Everyone loves Kerledan, its gargoyles, sophisticated theatrical décor and owners' enthusiasm. In 2002, they bought a neglected sadness. Peter and Penny, she a designer, have renovated it themselves and made it stunningly original. Sit in the dining room with its great fire, lounge in the young garden (baroque courtyard, orchard, potager) or in your bedroom armchair. Natural colours of sisal and unstained oak, the odd dramatic splash of antique mirror or gilded *bergère* in fake leopard skin bring a calm, minimalist atmosphere; slate-floored bathrooms are perfect, candlelit dinners are legendary.

rooms	3: 1 double, 1 twin, 1 family room.
price	€60–€80.
meals	Dinner, 3 courses with wine, €25–€30.
closed	January–February.
directions	From Boulevard Jean-Moulin (southern bypass of Carhaix); take small lane between Hotel des Impots & Disti-Centre. House signposted 250m on right.

Peter & Penny Dinwiddie
Manoir de Kerledan,
Rue de Kerledan,
29270 Carhaix-Plouguer,
Finistère
tel   +33 (0)2 98 99 44 63
email   pdin@wanadoo.fr

Map 2 Entry 264

Brittany

Domaine du Guilguiffin

Guilguiffin is a powerful, unforgettable experience. The bewitching name of the warring first baron (1010), the splendidness of the place, its opulent, ancestor-hung, Chinese-potted rooms and magnificent grounds, are truly seductive. Built with stones from the 11th-century fortress, it is a jewel of an 18th-century château, inside and out. Passionate about furniture and buildings, especially his ancient family seat, your host applies his intelligent energy to restoring his estate, nurturing thousands of plants and, with Madame's help, charming his guests. Bedrooms are a treat, each more heavenly than the last.

rooms	6: 4 doubles, 2 suites.
price	€135–€160. Suite €170–€220.
meals	Choice of restaurants nearby.
closed	Rarely. Book ahead in winter.
directions	From Quimper D765 W for 5km; left D784 for Landudec 13km; left & follow signs.

Philippe Davy
Domaine du Guilguiffin,
29710 Landudec, Finistère
tel   +33 (0)2 98 91 52 11
fax   +33 (0)2 98 91 52 52
email   chateau@guilguiffin.com
web   www.guilguiffin.com

Map 2 Entry 265

Brittany

Kerloaï

A Breton house with hospitable Breton owners, Breton furniture and a huge Breton brass pot once used for mixing crêpes. Young Madame is welcoming and chatty (in French), Monsieur is full of energy and ideas and grows organic produce for *table d'hôtes*; you may picnic and barbecue. The large, light, country-style rooms are all merrily painted in sunny yellow, fresh green, orange or pink. Copious breakfasts include those crêpes (not mixed in the brass pot) and home-grown kiwi fruit in season. An authentic rural haven between Armor, the land by the sea, and Argoat, the land of the woods. *Wi-fi connection.*

rooms	4: 2 doubles, 2 twins.
price	€45.
meals	Restaurant 4km.
closed	Occasionally.
directions	From Scaër, D50 for Coray Briec; after 3km, left at 'Ty Ru' & follow signs for Kerloaï.

Hervé Thomas & Gabrielle Penn
Kerloaï,
29390 Scaër,
Finistère
tel   +33 (0)2 98 59 42 60
email   ti.penn@wanadoo.fr

Map 2 Entry 266

Brittany

Kervren

The view from all six rooms across fields and wooded hills is perfectly wonderful. In a stone outbuilding separate from the owners' house, each small, neatly modern room, each impeccable, has a double-glazed door-window onto the long terrace where chairs await. Breakfast, with crêpes or croissants, is in a big modern veranda room where a richly carved Breton wardrobe takes pride of place. Madame is efficient, full of information about Breton culture, and very purposeful. *Only suitable for older children who can sleep alone. Small pets welcome. Minimum stay two nights July / August.*

rooms	6: 4 doubles, 2 twins.
price	€44.
meals	Choice of restaurants 10km.
closed	February.
directions	From Quimper D765 for Rosporden. At St Yvi left to Kervren; to end of lane (2.5km).

Odile Le Gall
Kervren,
29140 St Yvi,
Finistère
tel   +33 (0)2 98 94 70 34
fax   +33 (0)2 98 94 81 19
mobile +33 (0)6 08 06 54 93

Map 2 Entry 267

Brittany

Kerambris

Madame is a darling: quiet, serene and immensely kind, she really treats her guests as friends. The long, low, granite house has been in the family for all of its 300 years, enjoying the peace of this wind-blown, bird-sung spot just five minutes from the sea and that gorgeous coastal path and standing stones in the garden! Most of the building is gîtes; the *chambres d'hôtes* are tucked into the far end – small, impeccably simple, like the dining room, with some handsome Breton furniture. With charming Port Manech and good beaches nearby, it is a wonderful holiday spot.

rooms	4: 2 doubles, 2 twins.
price	€45.
meals	Restaurants within walking distance.
closed	Rarely.
directions	From Pont Aven, D77 for Port Manech; right just before sign Port Manech; 1st left. Follow Chambres d'Hôtes signs.

Yveline Gourlaouen
Kerambris,
Port Manech,
29920 Nevez, Finistère
tel   +33 (0)2 98 06 83 82
fax   +33 (0)2 98 06 83 82

Map 2 Entry 268

Brittany

Lezerhy

A heavenly spot, cradled in a quiet hamlet 200 yards from the river in deepest Brittany. Delightful people: Martine looks after old folk and young Melissa, Philippe pots and teaches aikido; both have lots of time for guests. In an outbuilding, you have your own sitting/breakfast room and kitchen and two big, superbly converted, uncluttered attic rooms, decorated with flair in subtle pastels and fitted with good shower rooms. Birds sing; the cat is one of the best ever; the dog will love you. A genuine welcome and possibly a different kind of cake for breakfast every day. Readers' letters are full of praise.

rooms	2 twins.
price	€44.
meals	Choice of restaurants 3km. Guest kitchen.
closed	November-Easter, except by arrangement.
directions	From Pontivy D768 S for 12km; exit to St Nicolas des Eaux; right immed. after bridge; follow signs for Chambres d'Hôtes & Poterie for 3km.

Martine Maignan
& Philippe Boivin
Lezerhy,
56310 Bieuzy les Eaux, Morbihan
tel   +33 (0)2 97 27 74 59
fax   +33 (0)2 97 27 73 11
email boivinp@wanadoo.fr
web   perso.wanadoo.fr/poterie-de-lezerhy/

Map 2 Entry 269

Brittany

Le Rhun

Family-friendly, easy-going, this lovely German couple have done a high-class renovation job on their cluster of buildings, creating a thoughtful guest house in the old stables with living room, dining room and kitchen – just for B&B guests. Up the outside staircase are two well finished bedrooms, their slightly minimalist style lifted by colourful quilts, pretty rugs and one red rocking chair. Clouds scud past the roof windows, cows graze next door (you can watch the milking), the lake attracts birds, and there's a sauna. Simple country pursuits, shared with a number of gîte guests. *Minimum stay two nights.*

rooms	2 twins.
price	€42–€45.
meals	Restaurant 7km. Guest kitchen.
closed	Winter.
directions	From Pontivy D768 south; exit to Pluméliau. In Pluméliau church square left D203 at sign for Gîtes du Rhun, 2.5km.

Eva & Jurgen Lincke
Le Rhun,
56930 Pluméliau,
Morbihan
tel +33 (0)2 97 51 83 48
fax +33 (0)2 97 51 83 48
email eva.lincke@web.de
web www.lerhun.de

Map 2 Entry 270

Brittany

Le Ty-Mat Penquesten

The yellow mansion is a bit surprising in this remote setting of magnificent trees and tumbledown buildings, its renovation as impressive as the house. The Spences were respectful of origins during this huge job: the slightly wormy old staircase has great character; they laid parquet in the grand drawing room, then put down fine Turkey carpets; they limewashed the walls and hung portraits beneath the high ceiling. Play with the animals, try the grand piano or admire the park from the deep windows. Soft blue and cream bedrooms are done in simple, unfussy luxury and Catherine, who's French, is charming.

rooms	4: 3 doubles, 1 twin.
price	€54–€64
meals	Crêperie 3km, restaurant 6km.
closed	Rarely.
directions	From N165 for Inzinzac-Lochrist. At Lochrist, right immediately after 2nd bridge onto D23. After 4km, Ty-Mat on left.

Catherine Spence
Le Ty-Mat Penquesten,
56650 Inzinzac-Lochrist,
Morbihan
tel +33 (0)2 97 36 89 26
fax +33 (0)2 97 36 89 26
email ty-mat@wanadoo.fr
web pro.wanadoo.fr/ty-mat/

Map 2 Entry 271

Brittany

Talvern

Separated from the road by a grassy courtyard, this honest old farmhouse once belonged to the château. A stone wall divides it from its grander neighbour, enclosing a young fruit-treed garden, plenty of space for the Gillots' children – and yours – to play, and a potager; ask gentle Patrick about his vegetables and herbs and his face lights up! He was a chef in Paris (do eat in); Christine teaches English and is the talent behind the quietly original and very fine décor of the bedrooms. There are walks in the woods next door, good cycling, resident peacocks, birdlife all around. Wonderful. *Cookery courses October-March.*

rooms	5: 2 doubles, 1 twin/double, 2 suites.
price	€55. €105 for 4.
meals	Dinner with wine, €20.
closed	Never.
directions	N165 Auray to Lorient; 1st exit to Landévant; after Renault garage, 1st right onto D24 for Baud; after 50m, 1st right; on for 1.2km on rue de Château. House on left.

Patrick Gillot
Talvern,
56690 Landévant,
Morbihan
tel   +33 (0)2 97 56 99 80
mobile   +33 (0)6 16 18 08 75
email   talvern@chambre-morbihan.com
web   www.chambre-morbihan.com

Map 2 Entry 272

Brittany

Keraubert

Dreams drift over Keraubert, the pond mirrors the dragonflies' precious dance, a semi-tropical Breton garden luxuriates. Your hosts create a welcoming, relaxed atmosphere, Bernard's paintings grace walls and he and Jacqueline quickly convey their refreshing optimism and warm delight in the place. Each pretty but untwee guest room has a garden door with table and chairs. The very pink room is small and cosy with garden views, the garage at the end has been converted into a suite. All is to be revived with a lick of paint. Unashamedly homey, with lovely owners and a special garden. *Minimum stay three nights in suite.*

rooms	2: 1 double, 1 suite.
price	€50-€60.
meals	Dinner with wine, €15. Restaurants 6km.
closed	Rarely.
directions	From Rennes N24 for Lorient, exit Baud & Auray; D768 for Vannes 4km; D24 right for Landevant 10km; entrance on left between Lambel & Malachappe.

Bernard & Jacqueline Belin
Keraubert,
56330 Pluvigner,
Morbihan
tel   +33 (0)2 97 24 93 10
fax   +33 (0)2 97 24 93 10
mobile   +33 (0)6 87 46 70 75

Map 2 Entry 273

Brittany

Kerimel

The standing stones of Carnac are minutes away, beaches, coastal pathways and golf course close by. Kerimel is a handsome group of granite farm buildings in a perfect setting among the fields. The bedrooms are beauties: plain walls, some panelling, patchwork bedcovers and pale blue curtains, old stones and beams, sparkling shower rooms and fluffy towels. The dining room is cottage perfection: dried flowers hanging from beams over wooden table, tiled floor, vast blackened chimney, stone walls. Gentle, generous, elegant people... "We talked of flowers", wrote one guest.

rooms	4: 2 twins/doubles, 2 triples.
price	€70.
meals	Restaurants 3km.
closed	Rarely.
directions	From N165 exit for Quiberon & Carnac on D768, 4km; right to Ploemel; D105 W for Erdeven; sign on right, 1.5km.

	Nicola Malherbe
	Kerimel,
	56400 Ploemel,
	Morbihan
tel	+33 (0)2 97 56 83 53
email	chaumieres.kerimel@wanadoo.fr
web	kerimel.free.fr

Map 2 Entry 274

Brittany

Kernivilit

Bang there on the quayside, an oyster farm! Bedrooms touch the view – you may want to stay and capture that lovely, limpid light on canvas while drinking coffee on the balcony, smelling the sea and listening to the chugging of fishing boats. Madame worked in England, Germany and the USA before coming to Brittany to help François farm oysters; he'll take you out there too, if you ask. Hospitable and generous, alert and chatty, she hangs interesting paintings in her rooms, lights a fire on cool days and serves a good French breakfast on a terrace shaded by pines. Unusual and very welcoming.

rooms	2 + 1: 2 twins. 1 apartment for 3.
price	€60-€65.
meals	Restaurant 500m.
closed	Rarely.
directions	From Auray D28 & D781 to Crach & Trinité sur Mer.; right at r'bout before bridge for La Trinité; house 400m along on left, sign 'François Gouzer'.

	Christine & François Gouzer
	Kernivilit,
	St Philibert,
	56470 La Trinité sur Mer, Morbihan
tel	+33 (0)2 97 55 17 78
fax	+33 (0)2 97 30 04 11
email	info@residence-mer.com
web	www.residence-mer.com

Map 2 Entry 275

Brittany

Locqueltas

In a gem of a setting, the modern house looks over the ever-changing blue-green gulf and its islands. The three well-furnished garden-level rooms have eyes to the sea and loos in the corridor.
A carved four-poster reigns imposingly in the room upstairs that leads to an even more startling dayroom with billiard table, books galore, oak altar, 1950s juke box, telescope, baby Louis XV armchair – all neatly arranged as if in a stately home – and the loo. Madame, brisk and practical, has a style that features marked contrasts – you will warm to her – and there's a little beach at the end of the garden for shallow bathing.

rooms	4: 1 double, 1 twin; 2 doubles with basin & bidet, each with separate shower & wc.
price	€60–€75.
meals	Restaurants 1.5km.
closed	Mid-July & August.
directions	From Auray D101 S for Baden; D316 S for Larmor Baden; through village N/NE for Locqueltas; sign on right, house 10m on right.

Mme Marie-Claude Hecker
Locqueltas,
56870 Larmor Baden,
Morbihan
tel   +33 (0)2 97 57 05 85
fax   +33 (0)2 97 57 25 02
email   marie-claude.hecker@wanadoo.fr

Map 2 Entry 276

Brittany

Château de Castellan

Fields and forests and not a house in sight. And, at the end of a lane, this quietly grand château, built in 1732 and a one-time hideout for counter-revolutionaries. Ring the bell and Monsieur or Madame will come running to greet you. Antique church pews, a wide winding stair, pastoral views are the pleasing first impressions. The owners have the right wing, Grandmère has the left and guests are in the middle, on two floors. Be charmed by big restful rooms, antiques, comfy chairs and discreet TVs. Delightful Madame cooks, irons, cleans, and directs you to the prettiest of ancient Breton villages.

rooms	6: 1 double; 1 twin, 1 triple, 1 family room for 4, 1 suite for 4, 1 suite for 6, all with separate wcs.
price	€85–€110. €135–€160 for 4. €164 for 6.
meals	Dinner with wine, €20.
closed	November–March.
directions	From Redon; D873 to La Gacilly; D777 to St Martin; D149; 1.5km for St Congard. Signs to Castellan.

Patrick & Marie Cossé
Château de Castellan,
56200 St Martin sur Oust,
Morbihan
tel   +33 (0)2 99 91 51 69
fax   +33 (0)2 99 91 57 41
email   auberge@club-internet.fr
web   www.castellan.fr.st

Map 3 Entry 277

Western Loire

Western Loire

Le Manoir des Quatre Saisons

Jean-Philippe, his mother and sister (who speaks good English) are engaging hosts and attentive, providing not only robes but drinks beside the pool. Breakfast is a flexible feast, complete with eggs and bacon as well as local choices. Immaculate bedrooms (three in a separate manoir) are colourfully coordinated – Jean-Philippe has an eye for detail. Expect stripes, patterns, French flourishes and distant sea views. Beach, river and town are walkable but children will love just mucking around in the big garden full of secret corners. *Minimum stay two nights July / August.*

Western Loire

Château de Coët Caret

Come for a taste of life with the French country aristocracy – it's getting hard to find. Madame is there to greet you on arrival and on hand during the day, and breakfast is properly formal (at 9am sharp, please!). Your hosts are cultured people, proud of their château tucked into the woods and its 100 hectares of parkland full of rare plants and ferns. Bedrooms are comfortable; *Saumon* is carpeted under the eaves and comes with binoculars for the birds. You are within the Brière Regional Park where water and land are inextricably mingled and wildlife abounds. *Minimum stay two nights. Wi-fi connection.*

rooms	5: 1 double, 4 suites for 2–4 (2 with kitchen).
price	€65–€70. Suites €84–€89.
meals	Restaurants 1.5km.
closed	Rarely.
directions	From Guérande D99 to La Turballe; just before town take D333 at r'bout. House 600m on right.

rooms	3: 2 doubles, 1 twin.
price	€90–€100.
meals	Auberges nearby, 1.5-2km.
closed	Rarely.
directions	From N165, exit 15 D774 for La Baule to Herbignac, 10km; fork left D47 for St Lyphard for 4km; house on right.

Jean-Philippe Meyran
Le Manoir des Quatre Saisons,
744 Bd de Lauvergnac,
44420 La Turballe, Loire-Atlantique
tel   +33 (0)2 40 11 76 16
fax   +33 (0)2 40 11 76 16
email jean-philippe.meyran@club-internet.fr
web   www.manoir-des-quatre-saisons.com

François & Cécile
de La Monneraye
Château de Coët Caret,
44410 Herbignac, Loire-Atlantique
tel   +33 (0)2 40 91 41 20
fax   +33 (0)2 40 91 37 46
email coetcaret@free.fr
web   coetcaret.com

Map 3 Entry 278

Map 3 Entry 279

Western Loire

La Mercerais

These are the sweetest people, even if their somewhat kitschy taste is not everyone's cup of tea! They really do "treat their guests as friends". Madame, bright and sparkling, is proud to show you her decorated books, musical scores and hats with the dried flower and gold spray touch; Monsieur is a retired farmer, quiet, friendly, attached to this place. The house is warm (log fire in winter), cosily country-furnished, the smallish rooms (mind your head on the way up) are as pink as can be. In the immaculately tended garden, a summer kitchen. Breakfast is served in pretty little baskets at the long table.

rooms	3: 2 triples; 1 family room with bath & separate wc.
price	€48. €62 for 3.
meals	Restaurant 3km.
closed	Rarely.
directions	From Rennes N137 for Nantes 63km. Exit at Nozay N171 for Blain 8km. At bottom of hill, left at roadside cross; sign.

Yvonne & Marcel Pineau
La Mercerais,
44130 Blain,
Loire-Atlantique
tel +33 (0)2 40 79 04 30
mobile +33 (0)6 87 90 66 81

Map 3 Entry 280

Western Loire

Château du Plessis-Atlantique

History-loaded Le Plessis belonged to the Roche family who crossed with William in 1066. The Belordes had it in 1632, kept it for centuries, lost it, bought in back 30 years ago. Pure château, it has velvet curtains and high-backed chairs in the salon, silver coffee pots and fresh orange juice at breakfast, 3,000 rosebushes in the garden and bedrooms of huge antique personality. Madame's father was in London with de Gaulle; she loves the English, enjoys cosmopolitan conversation and is proud of her "19th-century desire to please". Not cheap but special – enter another age. *Minimum stay two nights.*

rooms	3: 1 twin, 1 family room, 1 suite for 2-5.
price	€110-€160. €185-€205 for 3. €210-€220 for 4. Singles €80-€105.
meals	Restaurant 800m.
closed	Rarely.
directions	From Nantes leave A83 ringroad on D85 past airport. At T-junc. at Champ de Foire left through Pont St Martin & follow signs to Le Plessis.

M & Mme Belorde
Château du Plessis-Atlantique,
44860 Pont St Martin,
Loire-Atlantique
tel +33 (0)2 40 26 81 72
fax +33 (0)2 40 32 76 67
email chateauduplessis@wanadoo.fr
web monsite.wanadoo.fr/belorde.leplessis

Map 3 Entry 281

Western Loire

Château de la Sébinière

Young, warm, humorous Anne has exquisite taste and a perfectionist's eye; find it in the house of her dreams. The 18th-century château in its pretty park is a light, sunny and harmonious home. Walls are white or red-ochre, ceilings beamed, bathrooms a blend of old and new. There's an extravagant attention to detail – a pewter jug of old roses by a gilt mirror, a fine wicker chair on an ancient terracotta floor. You have your own entrance and the run of the sitting room, log-fired in winter. Your hosts serve real hot chocolate at breakfast, and, if you wish, a glass of wine on arrival. Nearby Clisson is full of charm.

Western Loire

Le Relais de la Rinière

A palm tree grows in the courtyard, hens potter and the views from the grassy garden, big enough to satisfy the liveliest child, stretch across vineyards of Muscadet grapes. Madame is as full of fun and energy as ever and Monsieur, a retired baker, produces delicious cakes at breakfast on the terrace. The bedrooms in the main house are private, traditional and very French with their fine carved armoires and fresh flowers. The other two, up steep external stone stairs, are bright and cheerful, with new pine beds, kitchenettes and sparkling showers. Excellent value, and family-friendly.

rooms	3 doubles.
price	€80–€110.
meals	Dinner with wine, €30.
closed	Rarely.
directions	From Nantes N249 for Poitiers; 2nd exit N149 for Le Pallet; through village, just past wine museum; right, signed.

rooms	5: 4 doubles, 1 twin (2 with kitchenettes).
price	€43.
meals	Choice of restaurants 6km. Guest kitchen.
closed	Rarely.
directions	From Nantes N249 for Poitiers, exit Vallet for Loroux Bottereau & Le Landreau, 5km; 600m before Le Landreau right; signs to La Rinière.

	Anne Cannaferina
	Château de la Sébinière,
	44330 Le Pallet,
	Loire-Atlantique
tel	+33 (0)2 40 80 49 25
fax	+33 (0)2 40 80 49 25
email	info@chateausebiniere.com
web	www.chateausebiniere.com

	Françoise & Louis Lebarillier
	Le Relais de la Rinière,
	44430 Le Landreau,
	Loire-Atlantique
tel	+33 (0)2 40 06 41 44
fax	+33 (0)2 51 13 10 52
email	riniere@netcourrier.com
web	www.riniere.com

Map 3 Entry 282

Map 3 Entry 283

Western Loire

Logis de Richebonne

Monsieur's parents bought this old *logis Vendéen* when he was six. Years later, researching the history of the house, he found his family first owned it in 1670! Madame's family tree, framed in the hall, goes back to the 14th century. But they are both warm and welcoming, not at all grand, and the house is full of personal touches: Madame painted the breakfast china and embroidered the beautiful tablecloths. Bedrooms are vast, with peaceful views and lots of fresh and dried flowers. The suite, and huge grounds, would be ideal for a family but very small children would need watching near the two pretty ponds.

rooms	3: 2 doubles, 1 suite for 5.
price	€65–€70.
meals	Restaurants in nearby village, 500m.
closed	Rarely.
directions	From Nantes through Legé for Challans & Machecoul; on leaving village left after restaurant Le Paradis; Logis 150m left.

Mme de Ternay
Logis de Richebonne,
44650 Legé,
Loire-Atlantique
tel   +33 (0)2 40 04 90 41
fax   +33 (0)2 40 04 90 41
email   adeternay@wanadoo.fr

Map 8   Entry 284

Western Loire

L'Hubertière

Hurry! Here is a lovely quiet farming family with cows that they know by name and a love of the land that is becoming rare. Michelle does the B&B, Gérard and their son run the farm, and the shaggy dog wags his tail. The hub is the open-plan living/dining room with woodburner, while the bedrooms, all small, are comfortable in French country style. It's not four-star but it's lovingly cared for. The two rooms in the separate old sheepfold make up the family room, and the big garden has games for children as well as an immaculate potager – help yourselves! Good, down-to-earth B&B, run by good people.

rooms	3: 2 doubles, 1 family room for 4–5.
price	€44. Family room €54–€84.
meals	Restaurants nearby.
closed	November–April.
directions	From Challans D948 to St Christophe du Ligneron; opposite bakery right D2 for Palluau for 4km; left at sign for house.

Michelle & Gérard Loizeau
L'Hubertière,
85670 St Christophe du Ligneron,
Vendée
tel   +33 (0)2 51 35 06 41
fax   +33 (0)2 51 49 87 43
email   michelle.loizeau@hubertiere-chambrehotes-vendee.fr
web   www.hubertiere-chambrehotes-vendee.fr

Map 8   Entry 285

Western Loire

La Fraternité

The lovely, lively Pikes brim with optimism and pleasure in their adopted country where they grow game birds. Their simple, old-fashioned, easily renovated 1900s farmhouse has a big garden where children play and adults barbecue and, up the outside stairs in the former apple loft, two cheerful, comfortable rooms – good beds, two kinds of pillow – for restful seclusion, all details cared for. Ian manages the farm, lovely, willowy Janty helps with the eggs, they'd do anything for their guests (gîte as well as B&B) and will point you towards the hidden treasures of the area they have come to love.

rooms	2: 1 double, 1 twin. Guest kitchenette.
price	€45.
meals	Restaurant 5km.
closed	Open weekends only mid-September-mid-June, out of season by reservation.
directions	From La Roche sur Yon D948 (25km) through Aizenay; 4km after lake, D94 left for Commequiers, 1km (signs to La Fraternité); 1st left, house immed. on right.

Janty & Ian Pike
La Fraternité,
Maché, 85190 Aizenay,
Vendée

tel	+33 (0)2 51 55 42 58
mobile	+33 (0)6 72 63 41 86
email	janet.pike@wanadoo.fr
web	perso.orange.fr/lafraternite/

Map 8 Entry 286

Western Loire

Le Verger

The Broux' new project is reviving this fine cluster of granite buildings for their family farm and the guests they welcome so well. One small ancient house of low heavy beams and big stones is the new guest quarters: two divans in the sitting area, double room upstairs, hand-painted furniture, loads of personality. Across the yard in the big square family house where noble stone, timber and terracotta also reign, Annick prepares meals at the long bright table – come and chat with her. Outside, horse and goats graze in the field, ducks and geese dabble in the pond, hens and turkeys squabble. Families love it.

rooms	1 suite for 2-4.
price	€42.
meals	Dinner with wine, €16.
closed	Rarely.
directions	From Nantes N249 for Poitiers, exit D763 to Clisson. From Clisson, N149 for Poitiers. At La Colonne, right to D753 direction Tiffauges. Through Tiffauges to Montaigu, 1km. First right, signed Vendee.

Annick & Marc Broux
Le Verger,
85530 La Bruffière,
Vendée

tel	+33 (0)2 51 43 62 02
fax	+33 (0)2 51 43 62 02
email	broux.annick@wanadoo.fr
web	perso.wanadoo.fr/le-verger

Map 8 Entry 287

Western Loire

Le Logis d'Elpénor

Katherine is proud of her lovely house beside the river Vendée – a glorious setting, with all the flavour of this watery area where the sea once lapped, and a fisherman's paradise (pike, roach, bass). There are two boats for exploring the river, a terrace for dry observation, a walled garden for seclusion and fine rooms for guests: rugs on polished floors, charming old pine doors, antique washstands and armoires, brand new bedding. And, a short drive away, the loveliness of La Venise Verte, the marshlands whose villages and waterways, built by 11th-century monks, are protected and largely unspoiled.

rooms	5 doubles.
price	€60–€68.
meals	Dinner with wine, €22, except Saturday.
closed	December-February.
directions	A83 exit Fontenay le Comte; D938 to La Rochelle; for Niort exit 8 to Marans.

Katherine Henry
Le Logis d'Elpénor,
5 rue de la Rivière,
85770 Le Gué de Velluire, Vendée
tel   +33 (0)2 51 52 59 10
fax   +33 (0)2 51 52 57 21
email katherine.henry@wanadoo.fr
web   www.lelogisdelpenor.fr

Map 8 Entry 288

Western Loire

Le Logis de la Clef de Bois

The town, a *ville d'art et d'histoire*, is one of the loveliest in the Vendée. The house, a *chambres d'hôtes* since the children have flown, stands at one end. Madame and Monsieur have an easy elegance and their home overflows with good taste and glamorous touches – from the contemporary mural on the dining room wall to the immaculate fauteuils of the salon. Big paintings, a collection of muslin caps from Poitou, bedrooms that celebrate writers... all point to cultural leanings. 'Rabelais' speaks of the Renaissance, 'Michel Ragon' is flamboyant in red and white checks, 'Simenon' reveals a cool blue charm.

rooms	4: 2 doubles, 2 suites.
price	€96–€116.
meals	Dinner with wine, €30.
closed	Never.
directions	From Nantes for Niort /Bordeaux /Paris; exit 8 for Fontenay le Comte.

Danielle Portebois
Le Logis de la Clef de Bois,
5 rue du Département,
85200 Fontenay le Comte, Vendée
tel   +33 (0)2 51 69 03 49
fax   +33 (0)2 51 69 03 49
email clef_de_bois@hotmail.com
web   www.clef-de-bois.com

Map 8 Entry 289

Western Loire

Le Rosier Sauvage

The pretty village is known for its exquisitely cloistered abbey – and something of the serenity and simplicity of the convent permeates the smallish, spotless bedrooms. The nicest is in a converted loft with the original massive oak door, timbered ceiling, terracotta-tiled floor and hotch-potch of furniture. The breakfast room, reached via the family's kitchen, is the old stable, complete with long polished table, while the old laundry, with vast stone washtub, is now a sitting room. Guests can picnic in the walled garden, overlooked by the abbey. When Christine is busy with her twins, her parents look after guests.

rooms	4: 1 double, 1 twin, 2 triples.
price	€46–€49.
meals	Restaurant & crêperie 100m.
closed	October-April.
directions	From Niort N148 for Fontenay le Comte 20km (or A83 exit 9); after Oulmes right to Nieul sur l'Autise to Abbey; house just beyond on left.

Christine Chastain-Poupin
Le Rosier Sauvage,
1 rue de l'Abbaye,
85240 Nieul sur l'Autise,
Vendée
tel   +33 (0)2 51 52 49 39
fax   +33 (0)2 51 52 49 46
email   rosier.sauvage1@tiscali.fr

Map 8 Entry 290

Western Loire

Le Mésangeau

The Migons, who couldn't be nicer, have expertly renovated their unusual, long-faced house with its barn-enclosed courtyard, two towers and covered terrace. Big, north-facing bedrooms are elegant and comfortable behind their shutters. In the reception rooms: contemporary leather sofas and a suit of armour; blue and green painted beams over antique dining-room furniture; two billiard tables, a piano, a set of drums in the games room. Monsieur collects veteran cars and plays bass guitar – promises of entertaining evenings. Superb grounds with a fishing pond and an 'aperitif gazebo'.

rooms	6: 4 doubles, 1 twin, 1 suite for 3.
price	€80–€110.
meals	Dinner with wine, €35.
closed	Rarely.
directions	From A11 exit 20 on D923. Cross Loire to Liré on D763; right D751 to Drain; left D154 for St Laurent des Autels. In Drain, house 3.5km after church on left.

Brigitte & Gérard Migon
Le Mésangeau,
49530 Drain,
Maine-et-Loire
tel   +33 (0)2 40 98 21 57
fax   +33 (0)2 40 98 28 62
email   le.mesangeau@wanadoo.fr
web   www.anjou-et-loire.com/mesangeau

Map 3 Entry 291

Western Loire

Demeure l'Impériale

A rare survivor of Cholet's imperial past, when the whole town flourished on making handkerchiefs, this elegant townhouse was the orangery of a long-gone château. Nothing imperial about Édith, though, who loves to make guests feel at home. The bedrooms are light and beautiful with fine period furniture and gleaming modern bathrooms. Two give onto the quiet street, the suite looks over the rose-filled, tree-shaded garden. There are two pretty salons and a glass-roofed dining room in the sunken courtyard – excellent dinners here. French style and hospitality at its best.

rooms	4: 3 doubles, 1 suite for 4.
price	€69–€76. Suite €120.
meals	Dinner €23. Wine list €10–€15. Restaurants 50m.
closed	Rarely.
directions	Rue Nationale is one-way street through Cholet centre. No 28 200m down on right, near St Pierre church.

Édith & Jean-René Duchesne
Demeure l'Impériale,
28 rue Nationale, 49300 Cholet,
Maine-et-Loire
tel +33 (0)2 41 58 84 84
fax +33 (0)2 41 63 17 03
email demeure.imperiale@wanadoo.fr
web demeure-imperiale.com

Map 8 Entry 292

Western Loire

Prieuré de l'Épinay

Your hosts are happy, interested, interesting people, and meals are the greatest fun – chicken from the farm, asparagus, raspberries, salads from the potager… all is organic. Facing the larged grassed garden, the ancient priory has changed so little that the monks would feel at home here today – though the swimming pool, large and lovely, might be a surprise. Your hosts happily share their home and its history; lofty ceilings, 15th-century beams, a fascinating *cave*, a rare fireplace. The two-storey guest suites in the barn have simplicity and space, delicious breakfasts are served in the chapel.

rooms	3: 1 suite for 2, 2 suites for 4–5.
price	€75.
meals	Dinner with wine, €30.
closed	30 September–April.
directions	From Angers N23 for Nantes 18km; through St Georges; cont. 1.5km; left after garage. Pass château; house on left. Park outside, walk through gate.

Bernard & Geneviève Gaultier
Prieuré de l'Épinay,
49170 St Georges sur Loire,
Maine-et-Loire
tel +33 (0)2 41 39 14 44
fax +33 (0)2 41 39 14 44
email bernard.gaultier3@wanadoo.fr
web monsite.wanadoo.fr/prieure-epinay/index.jhtml

Map 3 Entry 293

Western Loire

La Rousselière

A fine-columned terrace faces the serenity of an impeccably lovely garden, Monsieur's pride and joy; château-like reception rooms open one into another – glass doors to glass doors, billiards to dining to sitting – like an indoor arcade; family portraits follow you wherever you go; mass is still said in the private chapel on 16 August. But it's never over-grand, bedrooms are highly individual with their hand-painted armoires (Madame's artistic sister) and family antiques, bathrooms are charmingly dated and Madame is the most delightful smiling hostess and fine cook. A hymn to peace and gentle living.

rooms	5: 2 doubles, 1 twin, 1 family room, 1 family suite for 5.
price	€55-€80.
meals	Dinner with wine, €27.50.
closed	Rarely.
directions	From Angers N23 to Nantes; exit St Georges sur Loire; left at 1st r'bout for Chalonnes; left at 2nd r'bout for Chalonnes. Immediately before bridge left to La Possonnière; 1.5km, left, signed.

François & Jacqueline de Béru
La Rousselière,
49170 La Possonnière,
Maine-et-Loire
tel	+33 (0)2 41 39 13 21
fax	+33 (0)2 41 39 13 21
email	larousseliere@unimedia.fr
web	www.anjou-et-loire.com/rousseliere

Map 3 Entry 294

Western Loire

Logis la Roche Corbin

On the 'old' side of Anger river, a secret, special place. Behind a high wall: a cobbled path, a climbing rose, a sweet box hedge, a bunch of lettuces to keep the tortoise happy. Off this delightful courtyard garden is your room, aglow with 18th-century charm; off a French-grey hallway, an exquisite zen-like bathroom. Breakfast is up a magnificent rough-hewn oak stair, in a fine room with a rooftop view. Behind this hugely sympathetic restoration of a 16th-century house are Michael, an American painter with a studio over the road, and Pascale from Paris, warm, relaxed and enthusiastically new to B&B.

rooms	1 double.
price	€80.
meals	Occasional dinner with wine, €15-€30.
closed	Rarely.
directions	A11 to Angers; exit for hospital; opp. hospital (urgences), rue de l'Hommeau. House at end of street on corner of rue de la Harpe.

Michael & Pascale Rogosin
Logis la Roche Corbin,
3 rue de la Harpe,
49100 Angers, Maine-et-Loire
tel	+33 (0)2 41 86 93 70
fax	+33 (0)2 41 86 93 70
mobile	+33 (0)6 14 78 37 06
email	logisdelaroche@wanadoo.fr

Map 4 Entry 295

Western Loire

Troglodyte de la Fosse

The flattish countryside round the oldest house in the village gives little inkling that under your feet are quarries and caves, transformed by the owners into a stylish maze of terraced gardens and courtyards. One cave is now a kitchen for guests and another a gallery for Carole's rustic, artistic glass light fittings and paintings. Three bedrooms open onto the sunny courtyard, the others look down onto a sunken garden with pool (busy in summer). All are simply, attractively decorated; mouthwateringly vibrant colours give an exotic feel to the dining room. A fascinating place. *Children over seven welcome.*

rooms	5: 4 doubles, 1 suite.
price	€58-€66.
meals	Restaurant 3km.
	Kitchen available, small charge.
closed	Rarely.
directions	From Saumur D960 to Doué la Fontaine; 1st right D214 to Forges. Through village; fork left at crucifix. House on left, sign.

Carole Berréhar
& Michel Tribondeau
Troglodyte de la Fosse,
7 la Fosse, Meigné sous Doué,
49700 Forges, Maine-et-Loire
tel   +33 (0)2 41 50 90 09
mobile   +33 (0)6 75 40 50 00
email   info@chambrehote.com
web   www.chambrehote.com

Map 4 Entry 296

Western Loire

La Mascaron

On the banks of the Loire broods old Saumur. Deep inside hides a miniature medieval 'palace' with courtyard and balcony; it is central yet peaceful. A successful blend of old and contemporary is a rare surprise but the architect-owner – inspired, committed – has achieved it in the large, relaxing suite with its own entrance off the street. Beams, shutters, curtains and bedlinen are highly original in colour and design; the fireplace, furniture, pictures and tapestries in the sitting room are of such quality and interest that one feels "this could not have been done better". Madame is knowledgable, gentle and friendly.

rooms	1 suite.
price	€100.
meals	Restaurants in Saumur.
closed	November-March.
directions	From Tourist Office to Église St Pierre; in Place St Pierre, Rue Hte St Pierre on right opp. church.

Marie & Marc Ganuchaud
La Mascaron,
6 rue Haute St Pierre,
49400 Saumur,
Maine-et-Loire
tel   +33 (0)2 41 67 42 91

Map 4 Entry 297

Western Loire

La Chouannière

It's a charming 16th-century house complete with the old *pigeonnier* and its resident owl – he may woo you in from his impressive quarters next to the huge guest dining room. Your smiley, generous hosts, Gilles and Patricia, converted the stables leaving its original beauties in view, all exposed brickwork and tiled floors. Antique French country pieces that they restored themselves are buoyed up by colourful furnishings. Stay for delicious dinner, then take a stroll around the fairytale woodland garden. Readers love this place. *WWF Gîte Panda. Hot tub May-October. Minimum stay two nights July/August.*

rooms	4: 1 double, 1 twin, 1 triple, 1 family room.
price	€55–€59.
meals	Dinner with wine, €22.
closed	Rarely.
directions	From Saumur N147 for Longué; right D938 for Baugé; in Jumelles left at church for Brion; signed.

Patricia & Gilles Patrice
La Chouannière,
Domaine des Hayes,
49250 Brion, Maine-et-Loire
tel   +33 (0)2 41 80 21 74
fax   +33 (0)2 41 80 21 74
email   chouanniere@loire-passion.com
web   www.loire-passion.com

Map 4 Entry 298

Western Loire

Château de Salvert

This highly sculpted neo-Gothic folly is home to a couple of unselfconscious aristocrats and lots of cheerful children. The baronial hall is properly dark and spooky, the dining room and salon elegant and plush with gilt chairs and ancestors on the walls. In the vast suite, a sitting area and a library in an alcove. The double has the shower in one turret, the loo in another (off the corridor). Both are well decorated with fine French pieces and modern fabrics. The park is huge, wild boar roam, spring boarlets scamper, and Madame plays the piano and holds concerts. *Arrivals after 4pm.*

rooms	2: 1 double, 1 suite for 2-5.
price	€110. Suite €180-€250. Suite €370.
meals	Dinner €55. Wine €22-€35.
closed	Rarely.
directions	From A85 exit 'Saumur' on D767 for Le Lude. After 1km, left on D129 to Neuillé. Signed.

Monica Le Pelletier de Glatigny
Château de Salvert,
Salvert, 49680 Neuillé,
Maine-et-Loire
tel   +33 (0)2 41 52 55 89
fax   +33 (0)2 41 52 56 14
email   info@salvert.com
web   www.chateau-de-salvert.fr

Map 4 Entry 299

Western Loire

Château du Goupillon

The whole place sings this lovely lady's independent, youthful and nature-loving personality and her romantic approach to interiors. The suite is superb in rich reds and dramatic blues, the four-poster room is snug, the salon is lofty and beamed. The light pours in as you bask in the harmony of warm, authentic comfort: stripped woodwork, richly clothed walls (all Madame's work), old but not wealthy furniture. Outside the rambling 19th-century château lies a lush magical haven, a ten-acre oasis of semi-wild vegetation where endangered flora and fauna take refuge. Readers love house and owner.

rooms	3: 2 doubles, 1 suite for 2-5.
price	€75-€110. Suite €170 for 4-5.
meals	Restaurants in Saumur, 9km.
closed	In winter, except by arrangement.
directions	From Saumur N147 for Longué to La Ronde; D767 for Vernantes; left D129 for Neuillé; 1km before Neuillé follow Fontaine Suzon; signed.

Mme Monique Calot
Château du Goupillon,
49680 Neuillé,
Maine-et-Loire
tel   +33 (0)2 41 52 51 89
fax   +33 (0)2 41 52 51 89
email chateau-de-goupillon@wanadoo.fr
web   www.chateau-de-goupillon.com

Map 4 Entry 300

Western Loire

La Closerie

Nothing pretentious about this quiet village house – or its owners. Genuine country folk: Carmen, deputy mayor with a great sense of humour, and Hervé, equally jolly, creator of excellent traditional French dinners. Bedrooms in the old farmhouse or off the shady courtyard, two of them with their own entrances, are simply but pleasantly decorated with small shower rooms. One has a magnificent stone fireplace; another, up outside stairs, has old beams, stone walls and pretty yellow and white fabrics. Trees almost engulf the house and the sunny conservatory dining room looks over a bosky garden.

rooms	4: 2 doubles, 1 triple, 1 family room for 4.
price	€48-€50.
meals	Dinner with wine, €22.
closed	Rarely.
directions	From A85 exit 2 (Longué); then N147 for Saumur; at Super U r'bout D53 to St Philbert. House on right in centre of village.

Carmen & Hervé Taté
La Closerie,
Le Bourg,
49160 St Philbert du Peuple,
Maine-et-Loire
tel   +33 (0)2 41 52 62 69
email herve.tate@wanadoo.fr
web   www.bandb-lacloserie.com

Map 4 Entry 301

Le Haut Pouillé

This conversion of farm and outbuildings is impeccably done and Mireille's sense of style and attention to detail are everywhere: perfectly coordinated colour schemes with her own stencilling, new beds, good linen, nice big towels and a living area with fridge and microwave for guests. Wonderful meals, in tune with the season, and well-chosen wines, are served on the patio in summer. The Métiviers love to chat and are fascinating about local history and the environment; but they'll fully understand if you prefer to eat alone. Fantastic value, a lovely garden, and all utterly restful. *Children under two free.*

rooms	2 family rooms, 1 with separate wc.
price	€52.
meals	Dinner with wine, €20.
closed	2 weeks in summer.
directions	From Angers N147 for Saumur; 3km after Corné D61 left for Baugé for 2km past dairy & agricultural co-op; 2nd left at sign. House 1st on right.

Mireille & Michel Métivier
Le Haut Pouillé,
La Buissonnière, 49630 Mazé,
Maine-et-Loire

tel	+33 (0)2 41 45 13 72
fax	+33 (0)2 41 45 19 02
email	labuissonniere@mageos.com
web	www.labuissonniere.fr.st

Map 4 Entry 302

Les Bouchets

Beams, beams and more beams. The house was a ruin when the Bignons found it but they managed to save a wealth of original timber and stone details then added lovely old furniture, open fires, fresh flowers and soft cosy bedrooms. The result is a seductively warm cheerful house. Passionate about food, they used to have a top-class restaurant where Michel was the chef; the signs are everywhere: coppers in the kitchen/entrance hall, loads of memorabilia in the soft family sitting room. Géraldine, bright, friendly and organised, loves needlework… and serving good food.

rooms	2 doubles.
price	€50.
meals	Dinner with wine, €23.
closed	Rarely.
directions	From Bauge D60 for Beaufort en Vallée; at Chartrene right at x-roads; 2nd left. Signed.

Michel & Géraldine Bignon
Les Bouchets,
49150 Le Vieil Baugé,
Maine-et-Loire

tel	+33 (0)2 41 82 34 48
email	bignonm@wanadoo.fr
web	www.lesbouchets.com

Map 4 Entry 303

Western Loire

Le Point du Jour

Down-to-earth, fun-loving and decent, Madame is a splendid woman and hers is authentic farmhouse hospitality. Breakfast is in the cosy living room, alive with the desire to please. The attic has become three well-finished, honest guest rooms and a children's room with a fascinating original *lit de coin*. Great old roof timbers share the space with new beds and inherited armoires. It is simple and clean-cut with discreet plastic flooring, pastel walls, sparkling new showers. Your hosts are delighted to show you their grass-fed brown oxen, have two lively kids and provide toys, games and swings for yours.

rooms	4: 1 double, 1 twin, 1 triple, 1 children's room.
price	€42.
meals	Choice of restaurants 10km.
closed	Rarely.
directions	From Angers N23 to Seiches sur le Loir; right D766 Tours, 9km; right into Jarzé D59 for Beaufort en Vallé. On left 700m after Jarzé.

Véronique & Vincent Papiau
Le Point du Jour,
49140 Jarzé, Maine-et-Loire
tel   +33 (0)2 41 95 46 04
fax   +33 (0)2 41 95 46 04
email veronique.papiau@wanadoo.fr
web   perso.wanadoo.fr/veronique.papiau

Map 4 Entry 304

Western Loire

Château de Chambiers

Another marvellous family château, this one surrounded by a forest of wild boar. Smiling Madame speaks perfect English, is proud of her gardens fronted by topiary sheep and her big, beautiful rooms; she is an original and talented designer. Bedrooms have delicious antiques, one a French-Caribbean mahogany bed (the family owned a banana plantation), floors are 18th-century oak with *terre cuit* borders – exquisite; baths, washstands and fittings are period originals. There's a panelled, fresh-flowered *salon de thé* for breakfast and dinner, and vegetables from the potager. French heaven.

rooms	5 family rooms.
price	€90-€120.
meals	Dinner €28. Wine €15.
closed	Rarely. Book ahead in winter.
directions	From Angers, N23 to Durtal; r'bout, 1st exit to Bangé; after 150m, right to Jarzé; château on left after 3km.

Anne Crouan
Château de Chambiers,
49430 Durtal, Maine-et-Loire
tel   +33 (0)2 41 76 07 31
fax   +33 (0)2 41 76 04 28
email info@chateauchambiers.com
web   www.chateauchambiers.com

Map 4 Entry 305

La Besnardière

Route de Baugé, 49150 Fougeré, Maine-et-Loire

Joyce brims with knowledge about all things horticultural and aromatherapy and is calm personified. She also cooks lovely vegetarian dishes, welcomes art, yoga and meditation workshops in her meditation room and shares her fresh, comforting and comfortable home with great generosity. Beams spring everywhere in the 500-year-old farmhouse – mind your head! – and the two big, warm, book-filled bedrooms are tucked under the rafters, one with steps to a courtyard below. Be charmed by log fires, a soft pink sofa'd sitting room, a garden full of wildflowers, a donkey, goats, ducks, hens and views. Gentle, peaceful heaven.

Joyce's sustainable lifestyle is inspirational – people come here from around the world to learn to create their own organic paradise. The large garden produces a stunning variety of fruit and vegetables, and chamomile, marigold and lavender for massage oils. Woodburning stoves heat the farmhouse in winter, the potash from which is used as a natural fertilizer – along with comfrey, nettles and manure from two goats and a donkey. Drinking water comes straight from the well, and wildlife abounds.

rooms	2: 1 double, 1 triple, sharing bath & wc.
price	€50.
meals	Vegetarian dinner with wine, €20.
closed	Rarely.
directions	A11 to Durtal; D138 to Fougeré; D217 for Baugé; 1.5km; house on left.

Joyce Rimell
tel	+33 (0)2 41 90 15 20
fax	+33 (0)2 41 90 15 20
email	rimell.joyce@wanadoo.fr
web	www.holidays-loire.com

SPECIAL GREEN ENTRY
see page 15

Map 4 Entry 306

Western Loire

La Marronnière

This pretty white-shuttered house overlooking the river has been in the family for ever. The vicomte, vicomtesse and their daughter give you a gracious, smiling welcome and large, serene bedrooms lovingly revived. Choose a bed tucked into a poppy-papered alcove, or butterflies fluttering pinkly on the walls; each room has river views. Madame loves cooking and breakfast is a moveable feast: dining room in winter, terrace in summer. The warmly authentic salon provides a winter fire in a stone hearth, Italian ochres, silk drapes, family portraits and – on warm nights – doors open to the Loire.

rooms	2 doubles.
price	€94-€114.
meals	Dinner €30. Wine €10.
closed	Never.
directions	From Angers A11 to Paris; exit 14b Tiercé; at Tiercé for Cheffes, at r'bout Soulaire & Bourg; 100m after village left; house 300m on right by river Sarthe.

Jean & Marie–Hélène de la Selle
La Marronnière,
49125 Cheffes,
Maine-et-Loire

tel	+33 (0)2 41 34 08 50
fax	+33 (0)2 41 34 07 40
email	jeandelaselle@lamarronniere.com
web	www.lamarronniere.com

Map 4 Entry 307

Western Loire

La Ruchelière

Through the door in the wall, under the tunnel of greenery and lo! a fine presbytery rises from the lawns, fairly well sheltered from the road. The Ruches have done their classic French house in thoughtful, unusual fashion: a taffeta theme throughout with draperies and florals, collections of glass, china, dolls (the Indian puppets on the dining room walls are a joy) and modern paintings under high beautifully beamed ceilings, a piano by the great sitting-room fireplace and a convivial table for breakfast. These are fun, generous people (he's a pilot) with a talent for interior design and a desire to please.

rooms	4 doubles.
price	€50-€115.
meals	Dinner with wine, €25-£35.
closed	Rarely.
directions	From Le Mans A11 exit 11; D859 for Châteauneuf sur Sarthe; D89 for Contigné; house opp. church, signed.

Carole & Oliver Ruche
La Ruchelière,
6 place Jacques Ledoyen,
49330 Contigné, Maine-et-Loire

tel	+33 (0)2 41 32 74 86
fax	+33 (0)2 41 32 74 86
email	rucheliere@wanadoo.fr
web	www.anjou-bnb.com

Map 4 Entry 308

Western Loire

Château de Montreuil

An 1840s neo-gothic delight in a 16-hectare, deer-roamed park, a river for swimming and rowing, an ornamental pool for fishing, and a film set of an interior. The sitting room is splendidly 'medieval', the panelled salon pure 18th century, taken whole from a château, with superb hangings and immensely high doors. This was once a self-sufficient country estate with chapel, dovecote and mill (remains still visible). Large lofty bedrooms have authentic wooden floors and carpets, antique cupboards, bucolic river views. Your hosts are gracious, refined and humorous, always there to receive guests.

rooms	4: 1 double, 1 twin, 2 family rooms.
price	€75–€90.
meals	Dinner with wine, €27–€30.
closed	November-Easter.
directions	From Angers N23 to Seiches sur Loir; D74 for Châteauneuf sur Sarthe 5.5km. Château on right as you leave Montreuil village.

Jacques & Marie Bailliou
Château de Montreuil,
49140 Montreuil sur Loir,
Maine-et-Loire

tel	+33 (0)2 41 76 21 03
mobile	+33 (0)6 66 68 90 29
email	chateau.montreuil@anjou-et-loire.com
web	www.anjou-et-loire.com/chateau

Map 4 Entry 309

Western Loire

Malvoisine

Age-old peace and youthful freshness breathe from the old farmhouse, transformed from tumbledown dereliction to rural idyll for this cultured, artistic, unpretentious couple and their four children. Rooms are decorated with flair and simplicity with strong, warm colours, seagrass flooring and good fabrics. Wonderful meals – Regina's regional recipes are very sought after. A perfect retreat, too, for music, art and nature lovers. This is the family estate: join the Tuesday choir practice at the château, take singing lessons with Patrice's sister. A special place, a delightful hostess.

rooms	3: 1 double, 1 twin, 1 triple.
price	€64.
meals	Dinner with wine, €28.
closed	Rarely.
directions	From Angers for Lion d'Angers; at Montreuil Juigné right on D768 for Champigné; 500m after x-roads at La Croix de Beauvais right up drive to La Roche & Malvoisine.

Patrice & Regina de la Bastille
Malvoisine,
49460 Écuillé,
Maine-et-Loire

tel	+33 (0)2 41 93 34 44
fax	+33 (0)2 41 93 34 44
email	bastille-pr@wanadoo.fr
web	www.malvoisine-bastille.com

Map 4 Entry 310

Western Loire

Château de Montriou

The park will explode your senses – and Monsieur sparkles! He and Nicole are bringing fresh energy to the house along with a passion for gardening: the lake, the famous sequoia, the waves of crocuses in spring, the tunnel of squashes, ravishing at summer's last flush. The 15th-century château has been lived in and tended by the same family for 300 years. A very old stone staircase leads to the properly formal bedrooms whose bold colours were design flavour of the period, and wooden floors, thick rugs and antiques are only slightly younger. And the venerable library is now a guest sitting room. Remarkable.

rooms	4: 2 doubles, 1 double & kitchen, 1 suite for 4 & kitchen.
price	€80–€100. Suite for 4 €145.
meals	Restaurant nearby.
closed	Rarely.
directions	From Angers for Lion d'Angers; at Montreuil-Juigné right on D768 for Champigné; Montriou signposted between Feneu & Champigné at x-roads La Croix de Beauvais; D74 left for Sceaux d'Anjou, on for 300m.

Régis & Nicole de Loture
Château de Montriou,
49460 Feneu,
Maine-et-Loire
tel   +33 (0)2 41 93 30 11
fax   +33 (0)2 41 93 15 63
email   chateau-de-montriou@wanadoo.fr
web   www.chateau-de-montriou.com

Map 4 Entry 311

Western Loire

La Croix d'Étain

Frisky red squirrels decorate the stone balustrade, the wide river flows past the lush garden: it feels like deep country yet this handsome manor has urban elegance in its very stones. Panelling, mouldings, subtly muted floor tiles bring grace; traditional French florals add softness. It looks fairly formal but sprightly Madame adores having guests and pampers them, in their own quarters, with luxury. Monsieur is jovial, makes jam and loves fishing! Expect plush, lacy-feminine, carpeted bedrooms, three with river views, all with sunny bathrooms. The yacht-side setting is stunning – it could be the Riviera.

rooms	4: 2 doubles, 2 twins.
price	€65–€85.
meals	Dinner with wine, €30.
closed	Rarely.
directions	From Angers N162 for Lion d'Angers; 20km to Grieul; right D291 to Grez Neuville. At church, Rue de l'Écluse towards river on left.

Jacqueline & Auguste Bahuaud
La Croix d'Étain,
2 rue de l'Écluse,
49220 Grez-Neuville,
Maine-et-Loire
tel   +33 (0)2 41 95 68 49
fax   +33 (0)2 41 18 02 72
email   croix.etain@anjou-et-loire.com
web   www.anjou-et-loire.com/croix

Map 3 Entry 312

Western Loire

Manoir du Bois de Grez

An old peace lingers over the unique fan-shaped yard, the old well, the little chapel: this place oozes history. Your doctor host, who also loves painting, and his friendly chatty wife, much-travelled antique-hunters with imagination and flair, set the tone with a bright red petrol pump and a penny-farthing in the hall. Generous bedrooms (a superb new family room) hung with well-chosen oriental pieces or paintings are done in good strong colours that reflect the garden light. You share the big sitting room with your charming, interesting hosts, lots of plants and a suit of armour. A lovely garden, too.

rooms	4: 2 doubles, 1 twin, 1 family room.
price	€70-€75.
meals	Light supper €15. Wine from €5. Guest kitchen.
closed	Rarely.
directions	From Angers N162 to Laval; exit Grieul D291 to Grez Neuville; exit village via Sceaux d'Anjou road; 900m right Allée du Bois de Grez.

Marie Laure & Jean Gaël Cesbron
Manoir du Bois de Grez,
Route de Sceaux d'Anjou,
49220 Grez-Neuville,
Maine-et-Loire

tel	+33 (0)2 41 18 00 09
fax	+33 (0)2 41 18 00 09
email	cesbron.boisgrez@wanadoo.fr
web	www.boisdegrez.com

Map 3 Entry 313

Western Loire

Les Travaillères

You cannot fail to warm to Madame's easy vivacity and infectious laugh. She virtually lives in her beloved garden – or in her kitchen in the house opposite, making pastries in the old bread oven. The lovingly preserved Segré farmhouse with its deep roof and curious *outeau* openings (some would have put in modern dormers), has great beams, a big fireplace, exposed stone and new country furniture. Attic bedrooms are neatly rustic: crochet, terracotta, pine, with bathrooms cunningly sneaked in among the rafters. The woods are full of birdlife, cows graze in the field outside one bedroom's window.

rooms	3: 1 double, 2 suites for 4.
price	€38-€40.
meals	Restaurants 2-5km. Kitchen available. Picnic in garden possible.
closed	Rarely.
directions	From Angers N162 to Lion d'Angers; on for Rennes & Segré on D863 3km; right at Chambres d'Hôtes & La Himbaudière sign; under main road; 1km along on left.

Jocelyne Vivier
Les Travaillères,
49220 Le Lion d'Angers,
Maine-et-Loire

tel	+33 (0)2 41 61 33 56
mobile	+33 (0)6 77 86 24 33
web	www.lestravailleres.com

Map 3 Entry 314

Western Loire

Le Rideau Miné

The old country values are at home here: Madame has extended her house with deep respect for the 17th- and 18th-century shapes and materials of her lovely old millhouse (the Mayenne runs through the garden), she grows most of her own fruit and vegetables, delights in preparing local recipes for dinner and a fresh breakfast cake every day, sees that her pretty, beamed, many-windowed bedrooms with their good sitting areas are always spotless. Her sense for softened primary colours on white is remarkable: gentle but not timid. She is an unintrusive but caring hostess, rightly proud of her house and garden.

rooms	3: 1 double, 1 twin; 1 double with separate bathroom.
price	€58.
meals	Dinner with wine, €22.
closed	Rarely.
directions	From Angers for Rennes N162; after Lion d'Angers D770 for Champigné; after river Mayenne over bridge; D287 left for Chambellay; left after 500m. Signed.

Dany Fabry
Le Rideau Miné,
49220 Thorigné d'Anjou,
Maine-et-Loire
tel   +33 (0)2 41 76 88 40
email   lerideaumine@yahoo.fr
web   www.lerideaumine.com

Map 3 Entry 315

Western Loire

Château de la Montchevalleraie

Maurice Chevalier used to rehearse in this elegant house and there's a theatrical mood still — thanks to Christian, who bubbles over with enthusiasm and puts the world at ease. His space is your space, from the elegantly proportioned reception rooms rich in pictures and portraits with a story to tell, to the large orchard and garden where chickens wander in from next door's farm. Guest rooms glow with authenticity: warm orange walls and a boudoir feel in one, a magnificent carved bed in another. Be gratified by fabulous breakfasts, big walk-in showers, richly embossed towels — Christian loves his guests.

rooms	2: 1 double, 1 family suite for 4.
price	€100–€120. €150 for 3.
meals	Restaurant 4km.
closed	October–April.
directions	From Segré D75 to Avrié; entrance to house on left after 4km.

Christian Boulmant
Château de la Montchevalleraie,
49500 Aviré, Maine-et-Loire
tel   +33 (0)2 41 61 32 24
fax   +33 (0)2 41 61 32 24
email   contact@chateaulamontchevalleraie.com
web   www.chateaulamontchevalleraie.com

Map 3 Entry 316

Le Frêne

Unbroken views of the countryside, and not a whisper of the 21st century. The austere topiaried spinning-tops flanking the drive belie the warm, sunny rooms ahead – this house breathes books, music and art. Richard, who once had a book shop in Angers, is charming and funny; Florence runs art courses from home. Built on the ramparts of the old fortified village, the house has a 'hanging' garden whose beds are themed with colour. More in the house: crushed raspberry, lime green, sunny yellow. The attic suite, ideal for families, is big enough to hold a Russian billiard table – and Florence's charming watercolours.

Château de Craon

Such a close and welcoming family, whose kindness will extend to include you, too. It's a magnificent place, with innumerable expressions of history, taste and personality, and Loïk and Hélène, the younger generation, are gracious and treat you like friends. A salon with sofas and a view of the park, an Italianate hall with sweeping stone stair, classic French bedrooms in lavender, blue, cream... an original washstand, a canopied bed, a velvet armchair. Everywhere a feast for the eyes, paintings, watercolours, antiques; outside, 40 acres of river, meadows and lake, and a potager worth leaving home for.

rooms	4: 1 double, 2 twins, 1 suite for 4.
price	€50. Suite €80.
meals	Dinner €17. Wine from €4.
closed	Rarely.
directions	From Angers N162 to Le Lion d'Angers; D863 to Segré; D923; left D863 to l'Hôtellerie de Flée; D180 to Châtelais; 1st left on entering village.

rooms	6: 3 doubles, 1 twin, 1 single, 1 suite. Extra beds for children.
price	€120–€160. Single €100. Suite €240.
meals	Restaurants in village.
closed	Mid-November-mid-March.
directions	From Château Gontier, N171 to Craon; clear signs as you enter town. 30km south of Laval.

Richard & Florence Sence
Le Frêne,
22 rue Saint Sauveur,
49520 Châtelais, Maine-et-Loire

tel	+33 (0)2 41 61 16 45
fax	+33 (0)2 41 61 16 45
email	lefrene@free.fr
web	lefrene.online.fr

Loïk & Hélène de Guébriant
Château de Craon,
53400 Craon,
Mayenne

tel	+33 (0)2 43 06 11 02
fax	+33 (0)2 43 06 05 18
email	chateaudecraon@wanadoo.fr
web	www.chateaudecraon.com

Map 3 Entry 317

Map 3 Entry 318

Western Loire

Le Rocher

Being the Richecours' only guests means free run of Madame's delightful conversation (travel, history, houses, gardens, people), her lovingly designed garden, the old house that they have restored and furnished with care and imagination (she collects antique doors). Your room is in the 17th-century part above the old kitchen, so attractive in its wealth of fitted cupboards and slabs of slate. Character fills the big guest room: original tiles, iron bed, great old timbers (duck!). The meadow sweeps down to the river, the family boat and the little restaurant on the opposite bank awaits. Peaceful elegance and great warmth.

rooms	1 family room for 2-3.
price	€90.
meals	Choice of restaurants within 7km.
closed	Rarely.
directions	From Château Gontier N162 for Laval, 4km; left for St Germain de l'Hommel; immediately right; on to village; left, signed 'no through road', 500m 2nd house called Rocher.

Mme de Richecour
Le Rocher,
St Germain de l'Hommel,
53200 Fromentières, Mayenne
tel +33 (0)2 43 07 06 64
fax +33 (0)2 43 06 51 55
mobile +33 (0)6 76 86 01 78

Map 3 Entry 319

Western Loire

La Gilardière

The ancient oak stairs wind up through the subtly lit interior to fairly sophisticated rooms with low doorways and beautiful colombage, plenty of sitting areas, rooms off for your children or your butler. The French-Irish Drions' restoration of this ancient priory, mostly 14th and 15th century, is a marvel (famous people get married in the chapel). They are a splendidly humorous couple of horse and hunting enthusiasts who greatly enjoy their B&B activity. The huge grounds and discreet pool, safe for children (and grandchildren), lead to open country unspoilt by 20th-century wonders. Very special.

rooms	4: 2 doubles, 2 family rooms.
price	€60-€100.
meals	Dinner with wine, €30.
closed	16 October-April.
directions	From Château Gontier D28 for Grez en Bouère; at Gennes right D15 for Bierné; in St Aignan right before church; house 2km on left.

Ghislain & Françoise Drion
La Gilardière,
53200 Gennes sur Glaize, Mayenne
tel +33 (0)2 43 70 93 03
fax +33 (0)2 43 70 93 03
mobile +33 (0)6 29 37 46 43
email ghislain.drion@wanadoo.fr

Map 4 Entry 320

Western Loire

Château des Lutz

You couldn't help but enjoy yourself at this address — Monsieur's enthusiasm is infectious and, in true *chambres d'hôtes* spirit, he and Madame eat with their guests. The 17th-century hall with ancient *tommettes* sets the tone: walking sticks, boot jacks, hunting prints, garden flowers. You share a dining room for breakfast; a small salon; and a room off the drawing room with billiards (English and French games: Monsieur prefers the English). Elegantly coordinated bedrooms, a long table for poolside dinners, swims in front of the orangery, open farmland views. Comfort, grandeur and sheer joie de vivre.

rooms	5: 2 doubles, 1 twin, 1 triple, 1 suite for 4.
price	€80–€150.
meals	Dinner with wine, €35.
closed	Rarely.
directions	From A11 take Durtal exit; to Château Gontier; D22 to Coudray, property on left after 2km, signed; on for 1km down narrow lane, château on left, private drive.

Louis du Tertre
Château des Lutz,
53200 Daon, Mayenne
tel +33 (0)2 43 06 93 09
mobile +33 (0)6 78 27 23 52
email louis.dutertre@wanadoo.fr
web chateaudeslutz.com

Map 4 Entry 321

Western Loire

La Rouaudière

Prize-winning cows in the fields, prize-winning owners in the house. They are an exceptionally engaging, relaxed couple and their conversation is the heart and soul of this place. Breakfasts in front of the crackling fire are estimable — delicious everything, lashings of coffee; dinners are divine. You'll find a second fire in the salon, a rare magnolia in the garden (Madame is a keen plantswoman) and redecorated bedrooms that are straightforward and simple: plain walls, a few antiquey bits and bobs and pretty window boxes. Madame cannot do enough for her guests, and readers have been full of praise.

rooms	3: 1 double, 1 twin, 1 triple.
price	€46–€58.
meals	Dinner with wine, €20.
closed	Rarely.
directions	From Fougères N12 east for Laval 15km; farm sign on right.

Maurice & Thérèse Trihan
La Rouaudière,
Mégaudais, 53500 Ernée, Mayenne
tel +33 (0)2 43 05 13 57
fax +33 (0)2 43 05 71 15
email therese-trihan@wanadoo.fr
web www.chambresdhotes-auxportesdelabretagne.com

Map 3 Entry 322

Western Loire

Villeprouvé

Of vast age and character – and an ancient, leaning stair – this farmhouse is home to a humorous and talented couple who juggle cattle, children and guests. Delicious dinners end with a flaming presention of *grog maison* to guarantee deep sleep. In the big, soft rooms, every bed is canopied except the single box-bed which is carved and curtained to a tee. There are nooks, crannies and crooked lines, terracotta floors, half-timbered walls, antiques, books on art, tourism, history – and pretty new bathrooms. Ducks paddle in the pond, cows graze, the wind ruffles the trees, apples become cider – bucolic peace.

rooms	4: 2 doubles, 1 triple, 1 family room.
price	€43-€63.
meals	Dinner €13. Wine €8.50.
closed	Rarely.
directions	From Laval N162 for Château Gontier 14km; right through Villiers Charlemagne to Ruille Froid Fonds; left C4 for Bignon 1km; signed.

Christophe & Christine Davenel
Villeprouvé,
53170 Ruille Froid Fonds,
Mayenne
tel   +33 (0)2 43 07 71 62
fax   +33 (0)2 43 07 71 62
email   christ.davenel@wanadoo.fr
web   perso.wanadoo.fr/villeprouve/bb

Map 4 Entry 323

Western Loire

Le Cruchet

In a *gentilhommière* dating from 1640, a stone staircase in a pepperpot tower leads to a massively atmospheric bedroom for three. Downstairs in the fine dining room breakfast is served to the chiming of the church clock; in the garden is the old bread oven. The Nays' family home is well lived in and they love sharing it with guests. Rooms are elegant with antiques and decent bathrooms, the studio is in the stable, and your charming, unintrusive hosts can teach you French, weave baskets or make music. A wonderful atmosphere in delectable countryside – readers have loved the "real character of the place".

rooms	3: 1 double, 1 triple, 1 studio for 2.
price	€40-€45.
meals	Restaurants in village or 3km.
closed	Rarely.
directions	From Laval N157 for Le Mans; at Soulgé sur Ouette D20 left to Evron; D7 for Mayenne. signposted in Mézangers.

Léopold & Marie-Thérèse Nay
Le Cruchet,
53600 Mézangers,
Mayenne
tel   +33 (0)2 43 90 65 55
email   bandb.lecruchet@wanadoo.fr

Map 4 Entry 324

Garencière

The door stands open to welcome all comers or for waving excitedly to the little steam train. This happy, active couple love their farm, small brocante and B&B – he the handyman, she the decorator, mosaic-layer (superb pool in a converted barn) and chef. Dinner is a lengthy, gregarious, generous affair – wonderful for lovers of French family cooking and calvados! The endearingly French guest quarters in the outbuildings have pretty new touches, the suite in the old *boulangerie*, a bedroom on each floor, is charming, and the dining room would suit a banquet. *Well-behaved pets only.*

rooms	5: 2 doubles, 1 twin, 1 triple. Petite Maison: 1 suite for 4.
price	€52-€58.
meals	Dinner with wine or cider, €20-€25.
closed	One week at Christmas.
directions	A28 at Alençon; from Alençon exit 19 N138 S for 4km; left D55 through Champfleur for Bourg le Roi; farm sign 1km after Champfleur.

Denis & Christine Langlais
Garencière,
72610 Champfleur,
Sarthe
tel   +33 (0)2 33 31 75 84
fax   +33 (0)2 33 27 42 09
email   denis.langlais@wanadoo.fr
web   monsite.wanadoo.fr/garenciere

Map 4 Entry 325

Château de Monhoudou

Your hosts are the nicest, easiest of aristocrats, determined to keep the ancestral home alive in a dignified manner – 19 generations on. A jewel set in rolling parkland, sheep and horses grazing under mature trees, swans on a bit of the moat, peacock, deer, boar… it has antiques on parquet floors, charming bathrooms and loos in turrets, ravishing fabrics and polished old doors; an elegant dining room with family silver, a sitting room with log fire, a piano to play, family portraits, a small book-lined library – and do ask to see the chapel upstairs. Hunting trophies, timeless tranquillity, genuine people.

rooms	6: 4 doubles, 1 twin, 1 suite for 3.
price	€95-€150.
meals	Dinner with wine, €39.
closed	Rarely.
directions	From Alençon N138 S for Le Mans about 14km; at La Hutte left D310 for 10km; right D19 through Courgains; left D132 to Monhoudou; signed.

Michel & Marie-Christine de Monhoudou
Château de Monhoudou,
72260 Monhoudou, Sarthe
tel   +33 (0)2 43 97 40 05
fax   +33 (0)2 43 33 11 58
email   monhoudou@aol.com
web   www.monhoudou.com

Map 4 Entry 326

Western Loire

Éporcé

You may think yourself as lucky to stay in this relaxedly luxurious place as the owner and his young family to have inherited it, so fine and genuine inside and out. Pure 17th century with a magnificent avenue of trees, moat, lofty beamed ceilings, three salons for guests, it brims with antiques, books and atmosphere yet never overwhelms. First-floor rooms are proper château stuff, upstairs they are cosier, with pretty oval mansard windows. If you choose the gourmet dinner, your host will set out the family silver and Wedgwood as well as unforgettable food. Wholly delightful. *Chapel & coach house for weddings.*

rooms	6: 4 doubles, 1 twin, 1 suite.
price	€90-€150.
meals	Dinner with wine, €35.
closed	Rarely.
directions	From A11 exit 8, N157 for Laval; D28 for La Quinte; left by church for Coulans; 1km, wayside cross, fork right; entrance on left.

	Rémy de Scitivaux
	Éporcé,
	72550 La Quinte,
	Sarthe
tel	+33 (0)2 43 27 70 22
fax	+33 (0)2 43 27 89 29
email	eporce@wanadoo.fr

Map 4 Entry 327

Western Loire

Château de L'Enclos

The Guillous welcome you into their grand château in its elegant setting as long-lost friends. Sociable and fun – they own a red 1933 Citroen – they will whisk you around their parkland with its fine trees, llamas and donkeys... and plans are afoot for a tree house in the giant sequoia. Inside, a staircase sweeps up to the handsome bedrooms of parquet floors and rich carpets, writing desks and tall windows. Two have balconies. The charming salon opens to a stage-set-perfect garden, and you dine with your hosts in best *table d'hôtes* style. Masses to do in little Brûlon – and a marvellous home to return to.

rooms	3: 2 doubles, 1 twin.
price	€90.
meals	Dinner with wine, €30.
closed	Never.
directions	From A81 Le Mans-Laval; exit 1 to Brûlon. Château on right at end of town. Signed.

	Annie-Claude & Jean-Claude Guillou
	Château de L'Enclos,
	2 ave de la Libération,
	72350 Brûlon, Sarthe
tel	+33 (0)2 43 92 17 85
email	jean-claude.guillou5@wanadoo.fr
web	www.chateau-enclos.com

Map 4 Entry 328

Western Loire

Le Perceau

A happy house, part farm, part *maison bourgeoise*, where the smell of baking may greet you and the delicious results be on the table by the morning: fabulous pastries, breads and cakes. Your easy, amusing hosts have three charming sons and Mr Alfred the donkey – and space indoors for little ones to run their socks off when they tire of the garden. Then it's up the spiral staircase to a serene, chic cassis-and-orange bedroom; or the lavender room where a huge stone fireplace has pride of place. All very rural and river-viewed, yet Malicorne, with its market and restaurants, is a few minutes' meander. Readers return.

rooms	2: 1 double, 1 room for 4.
price	€49.
meals	Restaurants 800m.
closed	Rarely.
directions	From Le Mans N23 for La Flèche; at Fontaine St Martin, D8 for Malicorne sur Sarthe; D23 for Le Mans; house last on left, signed.

Catherine & Jean-Paul Beuvier
Le Perceau,
72270 Malicorne,
Sarthe
tel   +33 (0)2 43 45 74 40
email leperceau@libertysurf.fr
web   leperceau.chez-alice.fr/

Map 4 Entry 329

Western Loire

Château de Montaupin

Following her family's tradition, Marie is a helpful hostess, and her château has an easy family feel. An impressive suspended spiral staircase leads to the upper floors. Some rooms look onto an amazing 400-year-old cedar, others have gorgeous garden views, all have interesting furniture and are being redone (50 windows to replace!). The best suite is up a steep stair, its roof timbers exposed. There are some gratifyingly untidy corners, some small, pretty shower rooms and peaceful loveliness with farmland and woods beyond. For racing buffs, Le Mans is up the road. *Ask about French courses.*

rooms	5: 1 double, 2 triples, 2 suites for 5.
price	€65-€70. Suites €125-€140.
meals	Dinner with wine, €20.
closed	Occasionally. Book ahead.
directions	From Le Mans N23 for La Flèche to Cérans Foulletourte; D31 to Oizé; left on D32; sign to right.

Laurent Sénéchal & Marie David
Château de Montaupin,
72330 Oizé,
Sarthe
tel   +33 (0)2 43 87 81 70
fax   +33 (0)2 43 87 26 25
mobile +33 (0)6 83 56 60 40
email   chateaudemontaupin@wanadoo.fr

Map 4 Entry 330

Western Loire

Le Moulin du Prieuré

It's a brilliantly converted old watermill, this couple's labour of love, down to the smooth cogwheels that turn in the great kitchen. Marie-Claire, who used to live in London, is so relaxed and unflappably efficient, such good company and such fun, it's hard to believe she has four young children; the garden is heaven for little ones. The double-height sitting room bursts with books and videos for all; simple, attractive rooms have good beds, old tiled floors, bare stone walls. The atmosphere embraces you, the country sounds of stream, cockerel and Angelus prayer bells soothe, the unsung area brims with interest.

rooms	5: 4 doubles, 1 family room.
price	€55. Family room €85.
meals	Restaurant opposite.
closed	Rarely.
directions	From Tours N138 for Le Mans 35km to Dissay sous Courcillon; left at lights; mill just past church.

Marie-Claire Bretonneau
Le Moulin du Prieuré,
3 rue de la Gare,
72500 Dissay sous Courcillon,
Sarthe

tel	+33 (0)2 43 44 59 79
mobile	+33 (0)6 20 73 56 11
email	moulinduprieure@wanadoo.fr
web	www.moulinduprieure.fr

Map 4 Entry 331

Western Loire

Le Prieuré

Bushels of history from the beams and vaulted ceilings of the moated priory, snug beneath its old church: built in the 12th, extended in the 16th, it had monks into the 20th century. Christophe loves telling the history, Marie-France does the decorating, brilliantly in keeping with the elegant old house: oriental rugs on old tiled floors, pale-painted beams over stone fireplaces, fine old paintings on plain walls and good modern beds under soft-coloured covers. They are attentive hosts, happy to share their vaulted dining room and peaceful garden, and the road is not an inconvenience. *Ask about local wine tours.*

rooms	4: 2 doubles, 1 twin, 1 suite for 3.
price	€90-€120. Suite €130.
meals	Auberge opposite & restaurants nearby.
closed	November-February, unless booked in advance.
directions	From Le Mans A28 for Tours; exit 26 Château du Loir; N138 to Dissay sous Courcillon; left at lights, property on left.

Christophe & Marie-France Calla
Le Prieuré,
1 rue de la Gare,
72500 Dissay sous Courcillon,
Sarthe

tel	+33 (0)2 43 44 09 09
fax	+33 (0)2 43 44 09 09
mobile	+33 (0)6 15 77 84 48
email	ccalla@club-internet.fr

Map 4 Entry 332

Loire Valley

Loire Valley

Chambre d'hôtes

This was Dagmar's country cottage until she left Paris to settle here. She left her native Germany and adopted France many moons ago. Breakfast is a feast: hot croissants, homemade jams, smoked salmon, farm butter. The cottage garden is cherished and, if you time it right, every old wall is covered with roses. One bedroom is wood-panelled, the other more typical with sloping rafters; fabrics are flowered and the varnished wooden floors are symmetrically rugged. Cosy, friendly and great fun.

rooms	2: 1 double, 1 suite for 3.
price	€46–€56.
meals	Choice of restaurants 8km.
closed	Rarely.
directions	From Verneuil sur Avre D939 for Chartres; in Maillebois left on D20 to Blévy; follow signs to Chambres d'Hôtes.

Dagmar Parmentier
Chambre d'hôtes,
2 route des Champarts,
28170 Blévy, Eure-et-Loir
tel +33 (0)2 37 48 01 21
fax +33 (0)2 37 48 01 21
email parti@club-internet.fr
web www.bab-blevy.com

Map 4 Entry 333

Loire Valley

Maison JLN

Come to enjoy this gentle family and the serene vibes of their old Chartrain house. Up two steep spirals to the attic, through the family's little prayer room, past the stained-glass window, the sweet, peaceful bedroom feels a bit like a chapel with honey floorboards, beds, small windows (no wardrobe). Lots of books; reminders of pilgrimage, just beneath the great cathedral; Madame knowledgeably friendly, Monsieur, who speaks nine languages, quietly amusing, both interested in your travels: they're all happy to sit and talk when you get back. An unusual and welcoming place in a timeless spot. *Tricky parking.*

rooms	1 twin with separate shower & wc on floor below.
price	€47.
meals	Restaurants close by.
closed	Rarely.
directions	Arriving in Chartres follow signs for IBIS Centre; park by Hotel IBIS Centre (Place Drouaise); walk 20m along Rue de la Porte Drouaise to Rue Muret (100m car to house).

Jean-Loup & Nathalie Cuisiniez
Maison JLN,
80 rue Muret, 28000 Chartres,
Eure-et-Loir
tel +33 (0)2 37 21 98 36
fax +33 (0)2 37 21 98 36
email jln.cuisiniez@wanadoo.fr
web monsite.wanadoo.fr/maisonjln/

Map 4 Entry 334

Loire Valley

20 rue Pierre Genet

Caroline has cleverly organised the old 200-year-old farmhouse for herself and her animals to share easily with guests, who have the stable wing: the atmosphere is relaxed and informal, modern comfort and spirit in a deeply French rural husk. She is multi-lingual, having worked with Unesco, does a lot of the restoration herself, weeds her pretty, crazy-paved garden, cooks like an angel and still finds time for art and literature. Bedrooms are big and airy, with pretty rugs and super bathrooms. Up the outside steps, the double has exposed beams and subtle lighting from rooflight and window. Very special.

rooms	2: 1 double, 1 triple.
price	€80.
meals	Dinner with wine, €45.
closed	November–February.
directions	From Paris A1 exit Thivars; N10 to Châteaudun; 3rd r'bout with garage on left, left for Blois 5km; left for Le Mée 5km, left for Le Mée. In village right opp. café; on 100m to No. 20; turn into passage just after wall; into courtyard.

Caroline Vidican
20 rue Pierre Genet,
28220 Le Méc,
Eure-et-Loir
tel   +33 (0)2 37 44 13 77
email mcvidican@gmail.com
web   www.loire-bedandbreakfast.com

Map 4   Entry 335

Loire Valley

18 rue de la Grolle

A cluster of slightly younger siblings huddles up to the original 16th-century house: a lovely higgledy-piggledy family, mothered by your delightful, unintrusive hostess. Since the Moutons came here 30 years ago, Orléans has crept out to meet them but the country sounds still win through (the railway is virtually imperceptible). Crunch over the drive to your room, cosy with books, dried flowers and antiques (Monsieur gathers brocante), or up to sleep under Provençal fabrics beneath the steep roof, then breakfast in the huge salon by the massive fireplace and the bust of a moustachioed *grand-père*.

rooms	3: 2 doubles, 1 double with sofabed for 2 children.
price	€48–€52.
meals	Restaurants within walking distance.
closed	November–March.
directions	In Chaingy N152; left at lights from Blois; right at light from Orléans, Rue des Fourneaux 300m; left Rue de la Grolle. Signposted.

Ursula Mouton
18 rue de la Grolle,
45380 Chaingy,
Loiret
tel   +33 (0)2 38 80 65 68
email ulimout@yahoo.fr
web   chambreshoteschaingy.free.fr

Map 5   Entry 336

Loire Valley

Les Charmettes

This robust 18th-century canalside townhouse has inherited an expansive atmosphere from its wine-merchant builders. They were loading their wine onto barges on the canal that flows under the windows until the 1930s. So much for the past. For the present: you will dine – beautifully – with your refined hosts in the chandeliered dining room, sleep in good, very individual rooms (a bath in one bedroom), breakfast off ravishing Gien china with fruit from the garden, chat with Madame over a glass of local wine. Madame is happy to arrange visits to wine-growers.

rooms	1 + 2: 1 triple. 1 apartment for 4, 1 apartment for 5.
price	€70–€100. Apartments €140–€150.
meals	Dinner with wine, €30.
closed	Rarely.
directions	From Orléans N60 E for Montargis & Nevers; exit to Fay aux Loges; through Fay, cross canal, left D709; house 1st on left arriving in Donnery.

Nicole & Jacques Sicot
Les Charmettes,
45450 Donnery,
Loiret
tel +33 (0)2 38 59 22 50
email n.sicot@wanadoo.fr

Map 5 Entry 337

Loire Valley

Domaine de Sainte Hélène

Sologne used to be the hunting ground of kings and your bubbling, smiling hostess is a huntswoman, hence horses and dogs outside, horns and antlers in. Hers is a typical Solognote house with great beams and lovely flagstones, the talking telly in contemporary contrast. The double room is brilliantly done, small but cosy, with steeply sloping ceilings – no good for the over-stretched; the suite is larger (60m^2); both are differently furnished – this is very much a family house. Madame, genuinely eager to please, cooks only occasionally but will happily drive you to and from the restaurant. *Minimum stay two nights.*

rooms	2: 1 double, 1 suite for 4.
price	€63–€90. Suite €110–€150.
meals	Auberges 1km.
closed	Rarely.
directions	From Orléans N60 E to Jargeau; over bridge through town centre; left on D951 for Tigy; D83 for Isdes, through Vannes; house about 2km on right.

Agnès Célérier
Domaine de Sainte Hélène,
Route d'Isdes,
45510 Vannes sur Cosson, Loiret
tel +33 (0)2 38 58 04 55
mobile +33 (0)6 12 93 09 19
email celerierloiret@hotmail.com
web monsite.wanadoo.fr/hotes.loiret

Map 5 Entry 338

Loire Valley

Les Vieux Guays

If secluded is what you want, this house sits in 200 acres of woods, its grassy garden – larder to legions of fearless rabbits – rambling down to the lake and a constant show of water fowl. Sandrine and Alvaro, a tennis professional, returned from Chile to open the family home to guests. They are a poised and friendly couple easily mixing old and modern, bright and dark, happy for guests to sit in their vast, colourful, galleried salon and breakfast at their long dining table before the bucolic lake view. In another wing, bedrooms are high quality too: antiques, excellent new bedding, plain walls and floral fabrics.

rooms	5: 2 doubles, 2 twins, 1 family suite for 4.
price	€75.
meals	Restaurant 2km.
closed	Rarely.
directions	From Paris de Gien by A6; A77 exit Gien; D940 Argents-Sauldre; D948 to Cerdon; D65 for Clémont; immed. right after level crossing; 1.5km left onto track beside lake on left; straight on.

Sandrine & Alvaro Martinez
Les Vieux Guays,
45620 Cerdon du Loiret,
Loiret
tel +33 (0)2 38 36 03 76
fax +33 (0)2 38 36 03 76
email alydrine@aol.com
web www.lesvieuxguays.com

Map 5 Entry 339

Loire Valley

Domaine de la Thiau

A vast estate by the Loire, a 19th-century house for the family, a 17th-century one for guests, exotic pheasants and peacocks strutting around the splendid garden. Your welcoming young hosts – he is a busy vet, she looks after the house, small children and you with natural elegance – make it feel friendly despite the grand appearance. Guest bedrooms with high ceilings are carefully decorated with carved bedsteads and papered walls – snug, exclusive, peaceful. Breakfast and dinner are served in the guests' house, or on the flowered terrace that borders the château's large, rambling garden.

rooms	3: 2 doubles; 1 suite for 3 & kitchen.
price	€45-€58.
meals	Dinner €26. Wine list €7-€15.
closed	Rarely.
directions	From A6 onto A77 for Nevers, exit Briare; D952 for Gien. Between Briare & Gien: sign by nurseries.

Mme Bénédicte François
Domaine de la Thiau,
45250 Briare,
Loiret
tel +33 (0)2 38 38 20 92
fax +33 (0)2 38 38 06 20
email lathiau@club-internet.fr
web lathiau.club.fr

Map 5 Entry 340

Loire Valley

La Verrerie

Fantastic bedrooms: in a pretty outbuilding, the double, with a green iron bed, old tiled floor and bold bedspread, looks onto the garden from the ground floor; the twin has the same tiles underfoot, beams overhead and high wooden beds with an inviting mix of white covers and red quilts. The Count and Countess, who manage forests, farm and hunt but are relatively new to B&B, are charming and thoroughly hospitable. If you would like to eat in, you will join them for dinner in the main house. Members of the family run a vineyard in Provence, so try their wine.

rooms	2: 1 double, 1 suite for 2-4.
price	€75-€99. Suite €145.
meals	Dinner with wine, €18-€28.
closed	Rarely.
directions	From Paris A6 to A77 exit 19 for Gien. From Bourges D940 to Chapelle d'Angillon; D12 to Ivoy le Pré. At church left D39 for Blancafort, Oizon, Château de la Verrerie for 2.5km; gate on right.

Étienne & Marie de Saporta
La Verrerie,
18380 Ivoy le Pré, Cher
tel   +33 (0)2 48 58 90 86
fax   +33 (0)2 48 58 92 79
email   m.desaporta@wanadoo.fr
web   perso.wanadoo.fr/laverreriedivoy

Map 5 Entry 341

La Brissauderie

Utter peace… this 1970s farmhouse is cradled in tumbling woodland and wrapped in birdsong. Goats softly bleat on the farm below. Madame is chatty and genuine, she still helps out with the animals and can arrange goat visits for children. The downstairs double is functional, the upstairs suites perfect for families: all have stencilled furniture, some good family pieces, tongue-and-groove pine. Walls, ceilings and doors are filled with fun murals: sunflowers shine, bees bumble and butterflies flutter by. Your tasty breakfast comes with honey from a friend's bees and, of course, goat's cheese.

rooms	3: 1 double, 1 suite for 3-5, 1 suite for 4-6.
price	€33-€38. Suite €67-€69.
meals	Choice of restaurants nearby.
closed	Rarely.
directions	From Sancerre D923 for Jars & Vailly sur Sauldre; 2km before Jars right on track into wood, house at end of track, signposted.

Madeleine Jay
La Brissauderie,
18260 Jars, Cher
tel   +33 (0)2 48 58 74 94
fax   +33 (0)2 48 58 74 94
email   madeleine.jay@wanadoo.fr
web   www.labrissauderie.com

Map 5 Entry 342

Loire Valley

Moulin Guillard

Just outside the village of Subligny, not far from Sancerre, is this enchanting blue-shuttered mill. Where once walnut oil was produced is a stylish and delightful B&B. Dorothée, a fascinating and cultured woman who once ran a bookshop in Paris, divides her time between her garden of rare plants and her guests. She offers you a smallish, softly serene double upstairs, and a two-bedroom suite across the way, its private sitting room with piano downstairs. You breakfast between the two, in a converted barn overlooking the stream and Dorothée's several breeds of free-roaming hen. Charming, and fun.

rooms	2: 1 double;
	1 suite for 4 with sitting room.
price	€60–€80.
meals	Dinner €22. Wine list from €15.
closed	Never.
directions	A77; 15km towards Paris.

Dorothée Malinge
Moulin Guillard,
18260 Subligny, Cher
tel   +33 (0)2 48 73 70 49
fax   +33 (0)2 48 73 70 49
email malinge.annig@tiscali.fr
web   moulin-guillard.chez.tiscali.fr

Map 5 Entry 343

Loire Valley

Domaine de l'Ermitage

Deepest Berry, the heartland of rural France, where this articulate husband-and-wife team run their beef and cereals farm, taxi their children to school, make their own jam and still have time for their guests. Laurence is vivacious and casually elegant and runs an intelligent, welcoming house. The big, simple yet stylishly attractive bedrooms of her superior 18th-century farmhouse are of pleasing proportions – one of them is in an unusual round brick-and-timber tower, others have views over the peaceful park. Guests may use the swimming pool, set discreetly out of sight, at agreed times.

rooms	5: 2 doubles, 1 twin, 1 triple,
	1 quadruple.
price	€60–€63. Triple €80–€83.
	Quadruple €100–€103.
meals	Restaurants in village or 6km.
closed	Rarely.
directions	From Vierzon N76 for Bourges through Mehun sur Yèvre; D60 right to Berry Bouy & beyond for about 3km; farm on right.

Laurence & Géraud de La Farge
Domaine de l'Ermitage,
18500 Berry Bouy,
Cher
tel   +33 (0)2 48 26 87 46
fax   +33 (0)2 48 26 03 28
email domaine-ermitage@wanadoo.fr

Map 10 Entry 344

Loire Valley

La Grande Mouline

Your hosts came to this rustic haven, where the natural garden flows into woods and fields, deer roam and birdlife astounds, to raise their new family. Jean is a kindly young grandfather, proud of his efforts in converting his outbuildings for *chambres d'hôtes*. Bedrooms reflect his travels to distant places: Indian rugs, Moroccan brasses, a collection of fossils in an old chemist's cabinet and lots of old farmhouse stuff, nothing too sophisticated. Breakfast is in the main house where family life bustles busily. Return after contemplating Bourges to meditate in this corner of God's harmonious garden.

rooms	4: 2 triples, 1 quadruple, 1 family room.
price	€45.
meals	Restaurant 2.5km.
closed	Rarely.
directions	From Bourges D944 for Orléans. In Bourgneuf left at little r'bout; immed. right & follow signs 1.5km.

Jean Malot & Chantal Charlon
La Grande Mouline,
Bourgneuf,
18110 St Éloy de Gy,
Cher

tel	+33 (0)2 48 25 40 44
fax	+33 (0)2 48 25 40 44
email	jean-m4@wanadoo.fr

Map 10 Entry 345

Loire Valley

Les Bonnets Rouges

Cross the secret garden courtyard and step into this venerable 15th-century guest house. Beyond the dining room, where ancient timbers and niches are exposed in all their mixed-up glory, the knight in shining armour beckons you up the staircase. Bedrooms are elegant with antique beds and new mattresses, marble fireplaces and a claw-footed bath; in the attic, the pretty double is festooned with beams. Your charming hosts live just across the courtyard with two small daughters. Add the privilege of sleeping beneath that unsurpassed cathedral and it feels like a gift from the angels. *Not easy to find.*

rooms	4: 2 doubles, 2 suites for 3-4.
price	€58-€75.
meals	Choice of restaurants within walking distance.
closed	Rarely.
directions	In Bourges towards Cathedral; Rue Moyenne, left onto Rue Louis Pauliat; right, then left onto Rue des 3 Maillets; off Rue Bourbonnoux, on north aspect of cathedral. Park in yard if space permits.

Olivier Llopis
Les Bonnets Rouges,
3 rue de la Thaumassière,
18000 Bourges, Cher

tel	+33 (0)2 48 65 79 92
mobile	+33 (0)6 64 25 94 13
email	bonnets-rouges@bourges.net
web	bonnets-rouges.bourges.net

Map 10 Entry 346

La Reculée

A marriage of 18th-century stone and 20th-century design has created ideal guest quarters in the stables. Pale timber clothes the space with clever features such as the vast staircase leading to the tree-house-like top bedroom. The breakfast/sitting room combines new wood, contemporary artists' work and antiques; bedrooms are all different, the twins on the ground floor: Japanese-style doors and shutters, modern fabrics, lacy linen, crocheted covers. The garden, where guests have a terrace, is full of green and flowery things. Meals are delicious – thanks to chic, gracious Madame.

rooms	5: 3 doubles, 2 twins.
price	€56.
meals	Dinner with wine, €22.
closed	15 November-April.
directions	From Sancerre D955 for Bourges for 16km; D44 left to Montigny & 5km beyond; signposted.

Élisabeth Gressin
La Reculée,
18250 Montigny,
Cher
tel   +33 (0)2 48 69 59 18
fax   +33 (0)2 48 69 52 51
email   e.gressin@wanadoo.fr
web   www.domainedelareculee.fr

Map 5 Entry 347

Domaine de la Trolière

The beautifully proportioned house in its big shady garden has been in the family for over 200 years. The salon is a cool blue-grey symphony, the dining room smart yellow-grey with a rare, remarkable maroon and grey marble table: breakfast is in here, dinner en famille is in the big beamed kitchen. Each stylishly comfortable room has individual character and Madame has a fine eye for detail. She is charming, dynamic, casually elegant and genuinely welcoming. Visitors have poured praise: "quite the most beautiful house we've ever stayed in", "the evening meals were superb".

rooms	4: 3 doubles; 1 double with separate wc.
price	€47-€67.
meals	Dinner with wine, €21, except Saturday.
closed	Rarely.
directions	From A71 exit 8; at r'bout D925 W for Lignières & Châteauroux. Sign 500m on right.

Marie-Claude Dussert
Domaine de la Trolière,
18200 Orval,
Cher
tel   +33 (0)2 48 96 47 45
fax   +33 (0)2 48 96 07 71

Map 10 Entry 348

Loire Valley

La Serre

The two Claudes inspire remarks like: "I learned heaps about Art Deco and gardening", "a wonderful lanky couple full of life, laughter and intelligence", "lovely, artistic, wacky". Conversation flows effortlessly over glass and ashtray. Their 1940s manor is entirely Art Deco with an eclectic collection of modern art. You find good beds in the rooms, can learn how to make a properly formal French garden, have breakfast when you want. Dine until the small hours beneath the huge collage in the congenial, bohemian, fun-loving atmosphere created by your down-to-earth hosts. Out of the ordinary – we love it.

rooms	3: 2 doubles, 1 twin.
price	€76–€90.
meals	Dinner with wine, €23–€35.
closed	Rarely.
directions	From St Amand Montrond, D951 for Sancoin & Nevers. At Charenton Laugère, D953 for Dun sur Auron; house 300m on left.

M & Mme Claude Moreau
La Serre,
18210 Charenton Laugère,
Cher
tel	+33 (0)2 48 60 75 82
fax	+33 (0)2 48 60 75 82
mobile	+33 (0)6 14 90 23 56

Map 10 Entry 349

Loire Valley

La Chasse

This delightful and hard-working English couple came to farm in France, with their two boys, and cattle, too, and invite you to drive 2km down a bumpy track through pretty woods to their comfortable farmhouse. There's a dining room in the sitting room, some old beams still and a stone fireplace, and bedrooms that are big, pale-floored and attractively simple and peaceful: pilgrims to Compostela often stay here. Alison will take wonderful care of you and Robin may tell you tales of shearing French sheep or where to gaze on rare orchids. Argenton, 'Venice of the Indre', is a must.

rooms	3: 1 double; 1 double, 1 family room, sharing bath & separate wc.
price	From €56.
meals	Dinner with wine, €24.
closed	January-March.
directions	From Châteauroux A20 exit 16 to Tendu; 1st left in village. Pass Mairie, fork left at church for Chavin & Pommiers for 1.5km; left up track for 2km.

Robin & Alison Mitchell
La Chasse,
36200 Tendu,
Indre
tel	+33 (0)2 54 24 07 76
fax	+33 (0)2 54 24 07 76

Map 9 Entry 350

Loire Valley

Château de la Villette

Grand hunting lodge rather than château, it stands in acres of parkland before a vast private lake (boating and safe swimming). Karin lovingly tends every inch of it, including the vast picture window that seems to bring the lake into the sitting room. A great staircase leads to a beauty of a Bavarian bedroom with views; the ground-floor room is more modern but equally cosy. Feather duvets cosset you, breakfasts are served at a handsome convent table. Nothing is too much trouble for Madame, gardener, cook and perfect hostess. A gem.

rooms	2: 1 double; 1 double with separate bath.
price	€65–€70.
meals	Dinner with wine, €25.
closed	Rarely.
directions	From Châteauroux D943 to Ardentes; left on D14 for St Août 8km; left at château sign 400m; entrance on right.

Karin Verburgh
Château de la Villette,
Saint Août,
36120 Ardentes,
Indre
tel   +33 (0)2 54 36 28 46
fax   +33 (0)2 54 36 28 46

Map 10 Entry 351

Loire Valley

Carrefour de l'Ormeau

A Bauhaus minimalism from Alain, music lover, painter, craftsman and cultivator of the senses, and Isabelle, who loves to cook. In big bedrooms of monastic simplicity, nothing distracts from the natural warmth of old tiles and Alain's smooth, contemporary, local-wood furniture: all is light, space, harmony. The magnificent room under the rafters is used for recitals and furniture display. Isabelle's lush village garden centres on potager and lily pond and there's a little path through the 'wild' wood beyond: this big house is a meeting of market-place and wilderness where people grow.

rooms	4: 1 double, 2 triples, 1 suite for 4–5.
price	€48. Triple €63. Suite €78–€93.
meals	Dinner with wine, €22. April–September.
closed	November–Easter.
directions	From Le Mans N157 for Orléans 52km; left D921 to Mondoubleau; Carrefour de l'Ormeau is central village junction; house on corner opp. Ford garage.

Alain Gaubert & Isabelle Peyron
Carrefour de l'Ormeau,
41170 Mondoubleau, Loir-et-Cher
tel   +33 (0)2 54 80 93 76
fax   +33 (0)2 54 80 93 76
email   i.peyron1@tiscali.fr
web   www.carrefour-de-lormeau.com

Map 4 Entry 352

Loire Valley

Les Bordes

With its sweeping farmyard, its pond and such a spontaneous welcome, it is, as one reader wrote, "a gem of a B&B". You can see for miles across fields filled with lark song and cereals. The owners are a smiling couple who give you their time without invading your space but are delighted to show you their immaculate farm, orchard and vegetable garden if you're interested. Their spotless rooms have floral walls and firm mattresses. The furniture is simple and rustic, the bedrooms and bathrooms are deeply raftered, the old farmhouse breathes through its timbers. It is peaceful, pretty and a place for picnics.

rooms	3: 1 double; 2 doubles sharing bath & wc.
price	€39-€42.
meals	Dinner with wine, €16.
closed	Rarely.
directions	From Vendôme D957 for Blois 6km. Right to Crucheray & Chambres d'Hôtes. 4km from turning; signposted.

Élisabeth & Guy Tondereau
Les Bordes,
41100 Crucheray,
Loir-et-Cher

tel	+33 (0)2 54 77 05 43
fax	+33 (0)2 54 77 05 43
mobile	+33 (0)6 10 63 89 28
email	ge.tondereau@wanadoo.fr

Map 4 Entry 353

Loire Valley

9 rue Dutems

An old townhouse with a country feel, a lovely walled garden, a majestic chestnut and miniature trees at the bottom to screen the outbuildings. Guests eat at separate tables in a room full of brocante and wonderful pictures collected, and framed, by Joëlle; Claude, a farmer, serves and animates the whole affair. Up the characterful sloping-treaded stairs to light, simple bedrooms and bathrooms decorated in ephemeral greys, whites, creams and yellows – understated and beautiful. There are beams, polished parquet and tiles, billiards in the sitting room and a kitchenette for guests. A fun place to stay.

rooms	5: 1 twin/double, 3 triples, 1 suite.
price	€52-€72.
meals	Choice of restaurants in Mer. Guest kitchen.
closed	January.
directions	From N152 enter Mer & park by church. House is short walk up main street; entrance in picture-framing shop on left. (Car access details on arrival.)

Joëlle & Claude Mormiche
9 rue Dutems,
41500 Mer,
Loir-et-Cher

tel	+33 (0)2 54 81 17 36
fax	+33 (0)2 54 81 70 19
email	mormiche@wanadoo.fr
web	www.chambres-gites-chambord.com

Map 4 Entry 354

Loire Valley

Le Moulin de Choiseaux

Beyond the security gates, a blissful, informal garden — lakes and bridges, nooks and ducks, even a Ginkgo biloba, the hardiest tree on earth — rambles round the old millhouse (a mill stood here in 1455). Inside, a warmly sensitive atmosphere radiates from beautiful old floor tiles, timbered ceilings, lovely family furniture. Your hosts are gently caring about your well-being. Madame uses her innate feeling for history to advise on visits; Monsieur restored the old mill wheel; there are myriad teas for breakfast — and bedrooms, all different, are big, harmonious in fabric and colour and lit by the garden sky.

rooms	5: 2 doubles, 2 triples, 1 suite.
price	€57-€82.
meals	Choice of restaurants within 7km.
closed	Rarely.
directions	From A10 exit 16 N152 for Blois. 3.5km after Mer, right for Diziers - follow Chambres d'Hôtes signs.

Marie-Françoise & André Seguin
Le Moulin de Choiseaux,
8 rue des Choiseaux,
41500 Suèvres, Loir-et-Cher

tel   +33 (0)2 54 87 85 01
fax   +33 (0)2 54 87 86 44
email   choiseaux@wanadoo.fr
web   www.choiseaux.com

Map 4   Entry 355

Loire Valley

L'Échappée Belle

A house of style, originality and lovely surprises, with fascinating people. Madame, an art historian, talks exuberantly and creates beauty with her hands — patchwork, sculpture... Monsieur has a great sense of fun too, yet the house hums with serenity. Rooms are period-themed with family pieces: the 1930s has an old typewriter, a valve radio and an authentic, garish green bathroom; the 1900s has a splendid carved bed. The garden is a mixture of French geometric and English informal, the house set back enough for the road not to be a problem and the Loire a short step from the garden gate.

rooms	3: 1 double, 1 twin, 1 triple.
price	€70.
meals	Restaurant in village.
closed	November-March, except by arrangement.
directions	From A10 exit 16 for Chambord; cross Loire river at Mer; after bridge right D951; house on right at end of village.

Francis & Béatrice Bonnefoy
L'Échappée Belle,
120 rue Nationale,
41500 St Dyé sur Loire,
Loir-et-Cher

tel   +33 (0)2 54 81 60 01
email   fbonnefoy@libertysurf.fr
web   perso.libertysurf.fr/fbonnefoy

Map 4   Entry 356

Loire Valley

La Villa Médicis

Why the Italian name, the Italianate look? Queen Marie de Médicis used to take the waters here in the 17th century: the fine garden still has a hot spring and the Loire flows regally past behind the huge old trees. Muriel, a flower-loving perfectionist of immaculate taste, has let loose her decorative flair on the interior. It is unmistakably yet adventurously French in its splash of colours, lush fabrics and fine details – fresh flowers too. Carved wardrobes and brass beds grace some rooms. The suite is a great 1930s surprise with a super-smart bathroom. You will be thoroughly coddled in this elegant and stylish house.

rooms	6: 2 doubles, 2 twins, 1 triple, 1 suite.
price	€68.
meals	Dinner with wine, €32.
closed	In winter, except by arrangement.
directions	Macé is 3km north of Blois along N152 for Orléans. In village follow signs; 500m on right before church.

Muriel Cabin-Saint-Marcel
La Villa Médicis,
Macé,
41000 St Denis sur Loire,
Loir-et-Cher
tel   +33 (0)2 54 74 46 38
fax   +33 (0)2 54 78 20 27
email medicis.bienvenue@wanadoo.fr

Map 4   Entry 357

Loire Valley

La Petite Fugue

This tranquil townhouse stands on the Loire, away from Blois centre. A small walled rose garden welcomes you in off the street; a private courtyard at the back looks out over the historic town (Houdini's birthplace) and château. Monsieur is an inspired and original cook who visits the markets daily; breakfasts and dinners look as exquisite as they taste. Pale greys, mauves and creams (from mirror frames to quilted covers) tie in perfectly with interesting and original features. Bedrooms are harmonious, views flow over the valley and your hosts are discreet, attentive and charming. *Ask about cookery courses.*

rooms	4: 2 doubles, 1 twin/double, 1 family room for 3.
price	€95-€135.
meals	Dinner with wine, €35-€50.
closed	Never.
directions	A10 exit Blois; into town centre; right-bank.

M & Mme Lescure
La Petite Fugue,
9 quai du Foix,
41000 Blois,
Loir-et-Cher
tel   +33 (0)2 54 78 42 95
email lapetitefugue@wanadoo.fr
web   www.lapetitefugue.com

Map 4   Entry 358

Loire Valley

Le Chêne Vert

A house of endless happy discoveries, an architectural dream marrying 16th-century roots with an ultra-modern, marble-floored open-plan space and a glass walkway five metres overhead. Easy-going Marie-France and her husband live in an oasis of sophisticated rusticity with a few sheep and hens and egg hunts for children. They love the garden, too. The house has a soft, attractive feel and a gorgeous woodsy valley view. A cylindrical shower amazes in one room, a billiard table awaits above another, in a barn; a sense of texture and fabric inhabits them all. And your hosts are a great couple. *Min. two nights in suite.*

rooms	3: 1 double, 1 triple; 1 suite for 5 & kitchen.
price	€64–€90.
meals	Restaurants 800m.
closed	Rarely. Book ahead.
directions	From Blois D751 to Candé, left after bridge for Valaire; pass memorial to Pontlevoy; right at fork; left for Le Chêne Vert; house on left after small bridge.

Marie-France Tohier
Le Chêne Vert,
41120 Monthou sur Bièvre,
Loir-et-Cher
tel   +33 (0)2 54 44 07 28
fax   +33 (0)2 54 44 17 94
email tohier@sci-le-chene-vert.com
web   www.sci-le-chene-vert.com

Map 4 Entry 359

Loire Valley

Prieuré de la Chaise

It's a delight for the eyes: stunning ancient buildings outside, Madame's decorating flair inside. The 13th-century chapel, still used on the village feast day, and the newer manor house (1500s) drip with history, 16th-century antiques, tapestries and loveliness — huge sitting and dining rooms, smallish cosy bedrooms. One has a large stone fireplace, painted beams and successful Laura Ashley fabrics. The setting is superb, fine mature trees shade the secluded garden and you can put your horse in the paddock. You can't fail to like your hosts and their estate wine and they can arrange tastings for you.

rooms	4: 2 doubles, 2 suites.
price	€60–€70. Suite €120–€140.
meals	Choice of restaurants nearby.
closed	Rarely.
directions	St Georges is between Chenonceau & Montrichard on N76. In town centre, up hill to 'La Chaise' (signs); on up Rue du Prieuré. No. 8 has heavy wooden gates.

Danièle Duret-Therizols
Prieuré de la Chaise,
8 rue du Prieuré,
41400 St Georges sur Cher,
Loir-et-Cher
tel   +33 (0)2 54 32 59 77
fax   +33 (0)2 54 32 69 49
email prieuredelachaise@yahoo.fr
web   www.prieuredelachaise.com

Map 4 Entry 360

Les Chambres Vertes

Le Clos de la Chartrie, 41120 Cormeray, Loir-et-Cher

Flowers fill the quadrangle formed by the house (16th- and 19th-century) and an old wall; a fountain adds coolness. Your rooms are in the former stables opposite Sophie's house, each with a slate porch; her's has this slate running its full length, giving shelter from sun and rain. Outside the quadrangle is a covered patio for drinks and delicious meals, overlooking countryside. All this just a stone's throw from the village and with unbroken views of the sea. The rooms, on the ground floor, are uncluttered, exquisitely simple, with attractive no-frills bathrooms. The mood is natural, artistic, delightful.

Everything about Sophie's place breathes awareness of ecology – from the bedroom decoration (original wattle and daub), to the rendering and the oatmeal tones to the many, many books. She was once a dancer and her interest in the arts and harmony with nature blend naturally with her 'green' credentials: organic vegetables from her garden, traditional lime-renderings and hemp insulation, a wood-pellet boiler with underfloor heating, solar panels and a solar oven for summer.

rooms	3: 2 doubles, 1 twin.
price	€55–€60.
meals	Dinner with wine, €22.
closed	November-March.
directions	A10 from Paris exit Blois for Chateauroux D956; 15km from Blois left just before village sign Cormeray; 800m, left. 1st house on left.

	Sophie Gélinier
tel	+33 (0)2 54 20 24 95
fax	+33 (0)2 54 20 24 95
email	sophie@chambresvertes.net
web	www.chambresvertes.net/en

SPECIAL GREEN ENTRY
see page 15

Map 4 Entry 361

Loire Valley

La Rabouillère

Monsieur built the Sologne farmhouse himself. This, and his first project, the delicious little cottage next door, bring together traditional style and modern comfort. Madame, who is charming, furnished the interiors delightfully, and the first-floor suite of the main house is particularly splendid and spacious, with fine views over woodland and park. All the rooms are immaculate and serene, some on ground-floor level. Old family pieces decorate the cottage, with its two bedrooms, kitchenette and rustic feel. Breakfasts are served at tables laid with English china, and include eggs from the farm and homemade jam.

Loire Valley

Le Moutier

The artist's touch and Jean-Lou's paintings vibrate throughout this house of tradition and originality where you are instantly one of the family: a bright and friendly little girl, her congenial artist father, her linguist mother – and Persian Puss. Rooms – two in the main house, two in the studio – are subtle-hued with good family furniture and bold bathrooms. An Aubusson tapestry cartoon too, and understated elegance in the sitting and dining rooms. A joy of a garden, interesting, fun-loving hosts and a welcoming table in the evening. *Painting and French courses.*

rooms	5 + 1: 4 doubles, 1 suite. Cottage for 2-5.
price	€65-€95. Cottage €110-€155.
meals	Restaurants 3-10km.
closed	Rarely.
directions	Leave A10 at Blois for Vierzon, D765; D102 for Contres; after 6km sign for La Rabouillère on left.

rooms	4 doubles.
price	€60.
meals	Dinner with wine, €25.
closed	Rarely.
directions	From Blois D956 to Contres; D675 to St Aignan; over bridge; D17 right to Mareuil sur Cher. House on left in hamlet La Maison des Marchands (just before cat breeder sign) before main village.

	Martine & Jean-Marie Thimonnier
	La Rabouillère,
	Chemin de Marçon,
	41700 Contres,
	Loir-et-Cher
tel	+33 (0)2 54 79 05 14
fax	+33 (0)2 54 79 59 39
email	rabouillere@wanadoo.fr
web	www.larabouillere.com

	Martine & Jean-Lou Coursaget
	Le Moutier,
	13 rue de la République,
	41110 Mareuil sur Cher,
	Loir-et-Cher
tel	+33 (0)2 54 75 20 48
fax	+33 (0)2 54 75 20 48
email	lemoutier.coursaget@wanadoo.fr
web	monsite.wanadoo.fr/lemoutier/

Map 4 Entry 362

Map 4 Entry 363

Loire Valley

La Gaucherie

A beautifully restored, L-shaped farmhouse stashed away in the conifer forests of the Sologne, with plenty of grassed space around it and a pretty orchard. Aurelia, who ran a restaurant and studied art in New York, loves light and simplicity: colours are beige and ecru, furniture wooden and roughly planed. The stable conversion has a rustic sitting room with wood-burning stove and red sofas; floors are terracotta or seagrass, bathrooms are pebbled or mosaic'd. Rejoice in ponies and hens for the children, home-produced eggs and lamb, a pond with boat and a pool. Fresh, young, welcoming.

rooms	4: 1 double.
	Stables: 1 twin/double, 2 doubles.
price	€55–€70.
meals	Dinner with wine, €20.
closed	15 January-15 February.
directions	From Langon: past bakery, for Romorantin; at fork on Rue des Prevosts for Bois aux Frères. Continue for 7km; right to Mery sur Cher; after 500m turn right. 1st right.

Mme Aurelia Curnin
La Gaucherie,
Route de Mery, Dep 76,
41320 Langon, Loir-et-Cher

tel	+33 (0)2 54 96 42 23
mobile	+33 (0)6 88 80 45 93
email	lagaucherie@wanadoo.fr
web	www.lagaucherie.com

Map 5   Entry 364

Loire Valley

20 rue Pilate

In the lovely Loire valley where the intimate and the romantic reign, you have the little house in the garden to yourselves. It has a kitchen and a bathroom downstairs, two bedrooms upstairs and its own piece of flower-filled garden for private breakfasts. Or you can join Madame at the long check-clothed table in her light and cheerful kitchen, baskets hanging from the beams. She is friendly, cultivated and dynamic, involved in tourist activities so an excellent adviser, will cook you refined dinners and is a great maker of jams. It's not luxurious, but elegantly homely, quiet and welcoming.

rooms	Cottage: 2 doubles sharing bath (let to same party only).
price	€50. €90 for 4.
meals	Dinner with wine, €20.
closed	November-March.
directions	A28 exit 27 Neuillé-Pont-Pierre; D766 to Beaumont-la-Ronce; D2 for 1km. House on left on road D2; blue front door, opp. turning to Louestault.

Ghislaine & Gérard
de Couesnongle
20 rue Pilate,
37370 Neuvy le Roi,
Indre-et-Loire

tel	+33 (0)2 47 24 41 48
email	de-couesnongle-neuvy@caramail.com

Map 4   Entry 365

Loire Valley

La Louisière

Simplicity, character and a marvellous welcome make La Louisière special. Madame clearly delights in her role as hostess; Monsieur, who once rode the horse-drawn combine, tends his many roses and his paintings of bucolic bliss line the walls. Both are active in their community – a caring and unpretentious couple. The traditional rooms have subtle, well-chosen colour schemes and sparkling bathrooms; touches of fun, too. Surrounded by chestnut trees, the farmhouse backs onto the gardens of the château and is wonderfully quiet. Tennis to play, bikes to borrow, horses to ride. Great for children.

rooms	3: 1 twin, 1 triple, 1 suite for 5.
price	€48–€50.
meals	Auberge 800m.
closed	Rarely.
directions	From Tours D29 to Beaumont la Ronce. Signs to house in village.

Michel & Andrée Campion
La Louisière,
37360 Beaumont la Ronce,
Indre-et-Loire
tel   +33 (0)2 47 24 42 24
fax   +33 (0)2 47 24 42 24

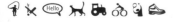

Map 4 Entry 366

Loire Valley

Château du Plessis

Meet Elizabeth, Gil and their château: she charming and full of plans, he an expert on French antiques, their home built by the Lord of Plessis in 1705 (with later additions). It's all warmly civilised and the grounds are delightful – magnificent trees, open lawns, pretty pool, and a play area through the woods. Up the guest staircase are two big rooms, Lilian Gish's (she stayed here) in pale pistachio with large canopied bed, Eugene O'Neill's (he lived here) bathed in light from seven windows, elegant with stripes and chandelier. Breakfasts are prettified by flowers. *Heated pool.*

rooms	2: 1 suite for 2, 1 suite for 4.
price	€130. Suite €210.
meals	Restaurants in Charentilly, 3km.
closed	Never.
directions	From Le Mans for Tours; exit 27 Neuillé Pont Pierre; D938 (former N138) for Tours, 15km; after 'Sportchamp' restaurant on right take left; 2km under bridge, château on right.

Elizabeth & Gil Barrios
Château du Plessis,
37360 St Antoine du Rocher,
Indre-et-Loire
tel   +33 (0)2 47 56 50 69
email   elizabeth@chateauduplessis.com
web   www.chateauduplessis.com

Map 4 Entry 367

Loire Valley

La Butte de l'Épine

A happy marriage of rustic French manor house and immaculate 'English' garden, surrounded by forest. Madame, caring, creative, soignée, is passionate about her flowers, inside and out, and the house has a harmonious feel despite being built so recently... in 17th-century Angevin style with old materials from the château next door. Terracotta tiles, polished oak, big vases of flowers – all is well-ordered peace and harmony in this unusual and refreshingly natural place. Bedrooms are carefully and prettily decorated; the pigeon loft with half-timbered walls and round window is enticing. *Children over 10 welcome.*

rooms	3: 1 double, 2 twins.
price	€60.
meals	Restaurants 2-5km.
closed	December-March.
directions	From Bourgueil; D749 to Gizeux; D15 to Continvoir; left on D64; signposted.

Michel & Claudette Bodet
La Butte de l'Épine,
37340 Continvoir,
Indre-et-Loire

tel	+33 (0)2 47 96 62 25
fax	+33 (0)2 47 96 07 36
email	mibodet@wanadoo.fr
web	www.labutte-de-lepine.com

Map 4 Entry 368

Loire Valley

3 rue du Moulin de Touvois

The brook gently flows and soothes – so relaxing. Myriam and Jean-Claude are interesting and energetic and have renovated their old miller's house with a blend of styles: original stonework, beams and terracotta floors and some funky modern furniture. The Moroccan tiled table with wrought-iron legs works well with the old stone fireplace in the dining room. Simple, pleasantly-decorated bedrooms have parquet floors, good bedding and stylish modern lighting. The garden is a delight with its wide-planked bridge, fruit trees and dessert grapes and Jean-Claude is happy to arrange visits to local wine-growers.

rooms	5: 1 double, 3 twins/doubles, 1 triple.
price	€52-€58.
meals	Dinner with wine, €20.
closed	Mid-December-mid-January.
directions	From A85 exit Saumur; D10 & D35 to Bourgueil; at r'bout on Bourgueil ring road (north), D749 for Gizeux 4km; right immed. before restaurant; 200m on left.

Myriam & Jean-Claude Marchand
3 rue du Moulin de Touvois,
37140 Bourgueil,
Indre-et-Loire

tel	+33 (0)2 47 97 87 70
fax	+33 (0)2 47 97 87 70
email	moulindetouvois@wanadoo.fr
web	www.moulindetouvois.com

Map 4 Entry 369

Loire Valley

Cheviré

Guests at Cheviré stay in the well-converted stable block of an elegant stone house in a quiet little village, all a-shimmer in the Loire's inimitable limpid light – welcome to the protected wetlands between the rivers Loire and Vienne. Your quarters have ancient beams, stone walls, new floors, space to sit or cook, a little terrace; the uncluttered, sizeable rooms show the same happy mix of old and new with some fine pieces. Your hospitable, gentle hosts, proud of their house and area, will direct you to less obvious places of interest. "Very clean, very friendly, very good breakfasts," say our readers.

rooms	3: 1 double, 1 triple, 1 quadruple.
price	€40-€48.
meals	Choice of restaurants 10km.
closed	15 December-15 January.
directions	From Chinon D749 for Bourgueil 6km; left to Savigny en Véron; in village follow 'Camping'; house 1km after campsite on right.

Marie-Françoise & Michel Chauvelin
Cheviré, 11 rue Basse,
37420 Savigny en Véron,
Indre-et-Loire

tel	+33 (0)2 47 58 42 49
fax	+33 (0)2 47 58 42 49
email	chauvelin.michel@wanadoo.fr
web	perso.wanadoo.fr/chevire

Map 4 Entry 370

Loire Valley

La Balastière

Antoinette indulges two loves, bringing people together and caring for nature, in her old vine-surrounded farmhouse on this environmentally-sensitive spit of land. Loire and Vienne meet nearby and the air tingles with watery prisms, spring flowers fill the meadow behind the house, shady trees and tall hollyhocks provide private corners in the large walled courtyard. There are delicious homemade jams for breakfast in the cool, stone-walled, low-beamed dining room with its huge 15th-century fireplace and there is a well-equipped guests' kitchen. Pleasant, comfortable rooms complete the picture. *WWF Gîte Panda. Minimum stay two nights.*

rooms	5: 3 doubles, 1 twin, 1 suite for 3.
price	€42-€56.
meals	Restaurants nearby. Guest kitchen.
closed	January.
directions	From Chinon D749 for Bourgueil; Beaumont r'bout 3rd exit for La Roche Honneur; left at sign to Balastière & continue to La Balastière.

Antoinette Degrémont
La Balastière,
Hameau de Grézille,
37420 Beaumont en Veron,
Indre-et-Loire

tel	+33 (0)2 47 58 87 93
fax	+33 (0)2 47 58 82 41
email	balastiere@infonie.fr
web	balastiere.chez-alice.fr

Map 4 Entry 371

Loire Valley

Domaine de la Blanche Treille

Chic Madame has sparkling eyes and a warm energy; Monsieur is charming and loves gardening; the house (in a wine village) is the last word in luxury. So meticulously furnished are the rooms that, as you sip coffee poured from a silver pot, you may wish you'd abandoned your jeans. No matter; your Parisien hosts love swapping travellers' tales and inspiration from Asia informs the décor – pictures, prints, wicker elephants for tables. Bedrooms ooze comfort: a toile de Jouy quilt, a Directoire bed, linen embroidered by Madame. The garden is being tamed and the vineyards stretch to the hills.

rooms	3: 2 doubles, 1 twin.
price	€90.
meals	Restaurants within walking distance.
closed	Never.
directions	Leave A85 at Bourgueil; D749 to Bourgueil; follow one-way system; D635 to Restigné; in Fougerolles, house on left, after Auger winery.

Aimée Rabillon
Domaine de la Blanche Treille,
56 route de Bourgueil,
37140 Fougerolles,
Indre-et-Loire
tel +33 (0)2 47 97 93 30
email rabillon.c@free.fr

Map 4 Entry 372

Loire Valley

L'Oiselière

Jean d'Arc's passionate call to arms lingers in this medieval hill town. But gentle Micheline's lovely townhouse and large walled garden, shaded by an old sequoia, seem to have absorbed the quiet order and peaceful spirit of the ruined abbey next door. Sounds of children's play and music drifting from the odd open air concert put the past to rest. Inside, up a fine spiral stair, are refreshingly unfussy bedrooms with white walls softened by pretty fabrics, ancient tiles and soft panelling: elegant and charming. Feast at breakfast in the privacy of your own dining room or in the ageless garden.

rooms	2: 1 suite, 1 family suite for 4.
price	€55-€65. €115 for 4.
meals	Kitchen available. Restaurant 500m.
closed	Mid-October-mid-April.
directions	From Chinon centre, past hotel; 1st right to rue Jean-Jacques Rousseau; continue until St Mexme square.

Micheline Dubruel
L'Oiselière,
113 rue Jean-Jacques Rousseau,
37500 Chinon, Indre-et-Loire
tel +33 (0)2 47 98 38 57
mobile +33 (0)6 16 35 18 61
email m.dubruel@wanadoo.fr
web www.loiseliere-mdubruel.com

Map 4 Entry 373

Loire Valley

Le Châtaignier

In the safe garden is a vast and venerable *châtaignier* (horse chestnut), open lawns, swings, boules and fruit trees. The farmhouse is similarly unpretentious, thanks to these hospitable, intelligent hosts. Odile is quietly elegant, Jean-Joseph loves his garden and they set aside two fresh, well-furnished bedrooms for guests. The two bedroom suite is on the first floor, its twin across the landing; the double – walls prettily sponged by artistic Odile – is reached via an outside stair. Sunny, country-elegant sitting and dining rooms (private tables for breakfast) open to the garden, and the fields stretch for miles.

rooms	2: 1 double & sofabed, 1 family suite for 4.
price	€53.
meals	Restaurant 3km.
closed	Never.
directions	From Tours to Chinon; D759 to Loudun. At Beuxes, left to La Roberderie. Left at x-roads in hamlet, 4th house on left.

Odile & Jean-Joseph Crescenzo
Le Châtaignier,
16 rue du Carroi, La Roberderie,
37500 Marcay, Indre-et-Loire

tel	+33 (0)2 47 93 97 09
mobile	+33 (0)6 71 42 22 15
email	crescenzo@wanadoo.fr
web	lechataignier.free.fr

Map 9 Entry 374

Loire Valley

Manoir La Fuye

The gates swing silently open to topiary and this beautifully proportioned house. Step into an opulently tiled hall and a refined sense of light and space. A smiling Buddha stands in a quiet corner, flowers spill over a turquoise chest of drawers and Micheline's serenity fills the house with good cheer. Up a curving 18th-century stair are peaceful, comfortable, petit-château rooms, one with old family furniture and an ornate bedhead, another with a vast balcony terrace. Bathrooms reveal mirrors from oriental travels, the salon a fine reproduction of a Kandinsky and the magical garden hides an antique gazebo.

rooms	5: 2 doubles, 2 twins/doubles, 1 triple.
price	€90-€110.
meals	Dinner with wine, €35.
closed	December-January.
directions	D749 from Chinon to Richelieu; right opp. Château du Rivau. Left at junction after railway crossing; first right; house first on right.

Micheline Trudeau
Manoir La Fuye,
La Fuye, 37500 Ligré,
Indre-et-Loire

tel	+33 (0)2 47 93 99 87
fax	+33 (0)2 47 93 24 91
email	contact@manoirlafuye.fr
web	www.manoirlafuye.fr

Map 9 Entry 375

Loire Valley

Le Clos de Ligré

This solid wine-grower's house sings in a subtle harmony of traditional charm and contemporary chic under thoroughly modern Martine's touch. Terracotta sponged walls, creamy beams and colourful modern fabrics breathe new life into rooms with old tiled floors and stone fireplaces. Windows are flung open to let in the light and the stresses of city living are forgotten in cheerful, easy conversations with your hostess. There is a baby grand piano in the elegant sitting room for the musical, a pool for the energetic and wine-tastings at the vineyard next door. A great place.

rooms	3 doubles.
price	€90.
meals	Dinner with wine, €30.
closed	Rarely.
directions	From Chinon D749 for Richelieu; 1km after r'bout D115 right for 'Ligré par le vignoble' 5km; left to Le Rouilly; left at Dozon warehouse; house 800m on left.

Martine Descamps
Le Clos de Ligré,
Le Rouilly, 37500 Ligré,
Indre-et-Loire
tel   +33 (0)2 47 93 95 59
fax   +33 (0)2 47 93 06 31
email mdescamps@club-internet.fr
web   www.le-clos-de-ligre.com

Map 9 Entry 376

Loire Valley

La Maison

When a diplomat's wife with impeccable taste and a flair for design is let loose on an austere 18th-century townhouse, the result is a treat. The family's antique furniture blends with pieces of art, sculpture and rugs from Africa and the Near East; tall windows, storey'd terracotta floors and an oval oak staircase are the grand backdrop; bedrooms are traditional and sumptuous, overlooking, via window and balcony, a walled formal garden which ends in a semi-wild area of bamboo. All is peace: even the fine chime of the church clock over the wall falls bashfully silent at night. The best house in Richelieu? Yes.

rooms	4: 2 doubles, 2 twins.
price	€100.
meals	Restaurant within walking distance.
closed	Mid-October-mid-April.
directions	From A10, exit Ste Maure de Touraine; left D760 for Noyant; left D58 for Richelieu; in town, cross over la Place des Religieuses, 1st left, signed.

Mme Michèle Couvrat-Desvergnes
La Maison,
6 rue Henri Proust, 37120
Richelieu, Indre-et-Loire
tel   +33 (0)2 47 58 29 40
fax   +33 (0)2 47 58 29 40
email lamaisondemichele@yahoo.com
web   www.lamaisondemichele.com

Map 9 Entry 377

Loire Valley

Domaine de Beauséjour

Dug into the hillside with the forest behind and a panorama of vines in front, this wine-grower's manor successfully pretends it was built in the 1800s rather than 20 years ago. Expect venerable oak beams and stone cut by troglodyte masons. In stylish, sophisticated rooms are carved bedheads, big puffy eiderdowns and old prints; bathrooms are spotless and elegant. There's a terraced pool with a view, a grassy hillside garden at the back, a functional guest sitting room, and wine to taste and buy. Exuberant Marie-Claude looks after you beautifully. *Minimum stay two nights.*

rooms	3: 1 suite for 3-4. Cottage: 2 doubles.
price	€70-€85. €110 for 4.
meals	Choice of restaurants 5km.
closed	Rarely.
directions	From Chinon, D21 to Cravant les Côteaux. On towards Panzoult; house on left after 2km.

Marie-Claude Chauveau
Domaine de Beauséjour,
37220 Panzoult,
Indre-et-Loire
tel   +33 (0)2 47 58 64 64
fax   +33 (0)2 47 95 27 13
email   info@domainedebeausejour.com
web   www.domainedebeausejour.com

Map 9   Entry 378

Loire Valley

Les Bournais

Cats, a small dog and six ponies – your horse-loving hosts encourage you to ride. Philippe and Florence are a great team: easy-going, intelligent, considerate, with many talents. Their old farm, lovingly restored, is set round a pretty courtyard and the bedrooms are in the stables, upstairs and down. Each has brocante finds and striped drapes, sofabeds and armchairs, character, charm and space; spotless floors are black-and-white tiled, showers are walk-in. Excellent traditional dinners with innovative touches are served round a rustic table and breakfasts are moveable feasts. Special.

rooms	4 doubles, each with extra bed.
price	€60.
meals	Dinner with wine, €20.
closed	Rarely.
directions	Leave A10 at Ste Maure de Touraine; D760 to L'Ile Bouchard; cross river; D757 for Richelieu. Les Bournais signposted left just before entering Brizay.

Philippe & Florence Martinez
Les Bournais,
37220 Theneuil,
Indre-et-Loire
tel   +33 (0)2 47 95 29 61
email   les.bournais@orange.fr
web   www.lesbournais.net

Map 9   Entry 379

Loire Valley

La Tinellière

A pretty farmhouse in a hamlet, a gentle goose wandering the garden, a glass of homemade *épine*. Éliane is a welcoming and enthusiastic hostess who loves talking to people about their interests and her own, and is constantly looking for ideas to improve her rooms: the ground-floor, mezzanined quadruple (with ladder steps), and the other larger room in the converted stable. Parts of the house are 17th-century with massive beams and good mixes of new and old furniture, wild and dried flowers, colours and fabrics. The sitting/dining room is darkish, beamed and cosy, the guests' kitchenette brand new.

rooms	2 quadruples.
price	€42–€45.
meals	Auberge nearby. Guest kitchen.
closed	Rarely.
directions	From A10 exit Ste Maure de Touraine; N10 for Tours 6km; right to Ste Catherine de Fierbois; D101 for Bossé; - house 3km.

Mme Éliane Pelluard
La Tinellière,
37800 Ste Catherine de Fierbois,
Indre-et-Loire
tel   +33 (0)2 47 65 61 80

Map 9   Entry 380

Loire Valley

La Ferme Blanche

The rambling, L-shaped White Farmhouse brims with an enchanting light. Outside: flowerbeds, roses and the shade of a white fig tree to bask in and an unobtrusive (unfenced) pool. Parisian Anne, shyly welcoming, has created romantic interiors where Louis XV antiques mingle with charming oddities such as a 19th-century mannequin, and tobacco-brown sofas sit harmoniously beneath cream-beamed ceilings on old pine floors. Rooms are largely white, with hand-painted walls and gauzy canopies over the beds; dinners are 'epicurean gourmet'. Superb.
Minimum stay two nights July/August.

rooms	2: 1 suite for 4, 1 suite for 6.
price	€80–€90
meals	Dinner with wine, €28.
closed	Never.
directions	From A10 exit 25; D59 to Ligueil; D31 to Cussay; in Cussay left opp. post office; behind church lane to left; signed; after La Chaume Brangerie; 1st right. House 1st left.

Anne Fabienne Bouvier
La Ferme Blanche,
La Chaume, Brangerie,
37240 Cussay, Indre-et-Loire
tel   +33 (0)2 47 91 94 43
mobile   +33 (0)6 61 72 68 30
email   af-bouvier@wanadoo.fr
web   www.la-ferme-blanche.com

Map 9   Entry 381

La Chapelle

It is a gothic chapel transformed into a traditional family house, an unselfconscious witness of things past, a place to live in serenity. Up a winding stair in the little tower, the pretty guest rooms owe their marble fireplaces to an earlier conversion, their fine well-sat-in furniture to past generations, their good watercolours to friends and relations, their art books to Dominique himself. A well-travelled artist, he came home when he inherited the house; he is cultured, amusing, very good company and an excellent cook. A place to dawdle in and soak up the timeless charm.

rooms	2 doubles sharing bath (let to same party only).
price	€60.
meals	Dinner with wine, €20.
closed	November-March.
directions	From A10 exit 18; D31 to Bléré; D58 to Cigngné; D83 to Tauxigny. Rue Haute on D82 to St Bauld. House on corner.

Dominique Moreau-Granger
La Chapelle,
53 rue Haute,
37310 Tauxigny,
Indre-et-Loire
tel   +33 (0)2 47 92 15 38
fax   +33 (0)2 47 92 15 38
email   d.moreaugranger@free.fr

Map 4 Entry 382

Le Moulin L'Étang

As brilliant as ever, Sue with her unbeatable eye for colour and decorative detail, Andrew with his kitchen conjuring and dry wit, have turned another old mill into an exceptional B&B. You feel instantly at home – even if your taste doesn't stretch to golden salamander stencils or angels-wing curtains, draped bedheads or lacquered chairs. The overgrown garden has been tamed; the pool is heated and naturally filtered. Do dine with them: superb food and sparkling conversation vie for pride of place. A remarkable couple, a place of character and Loches two miles up the road. *Not for young children: unfenced water.*

rooms	4: 3 doubles, 1 family room.
price	€70-€80.
meals	Dinner with wine, €30.
closed	December.
directions	From Loches N143 for Tours; left before Chambourg sur Indre on road signposted L'Étang; 1 mile, left at T-junction; house on right, first right past Esso garage.

Andrew & Sue Page
Le Moulin L'Étang,
37600 Chanceaux près Loches,
Indre-et-Loire
tel   +33 (0)2 47 59 15 10
mobile   +33 (0)6 17 62 36 53
email   moulinletang37@aol.com
web   www.moulinetang.com

Map 9 Entry 383

Loire Valley

Le Moulin de Montrésor

Do you dream of living in a watermill? Your young hosts have converted theirs, near the magnificent château of Montrésor, in stylish and simple good taste: a wooden staircase leading to a coconut-matted landing, family portraits, super colours, lots of light and original features… and quiet flows the water over the wheel beneath the glass panel in the dining room! Madame is cultured and well-travelled, her family has had the château for 200 years but no-one stands on ceremony and there's a sense of timeless peace here, miles from anywhere. The plain garden has a fenced, child-friendly pool.

rooms	4: 1 double, 1 twin, 2 triples.
price	€60–€65. Under 4s free.
meals	Choice of restaurants within 5km.
closed	Rarely.
directions	From Loches D760 to Montrésor; left for Chemillé; mill on left; signposted.

Sophie & Alain
Willems de Ladersous
Le Moulin de Montrésor,
37460 Montrésor,
Indre-et-Loire
tel   +33 (0)2 47 92 68 20
fax   +33 (0)2 47 92 74 65
email   alain.willems@wanadoo.fr

Map 9 Entry 384

Loire Valley

Château du Vau

Delightful philosopher Bruno and Titian-haired Nancy have turned his family château into a stylish refuge for travellers. The demands of children to be taken to dancing lessons and guests needing sustenance are met with quiet good humour. Generations of sliding young have polished the banisters on the stairs leading to the large, light bedrooms, freshly decorated round splendid brass bedsteads, with seagrass and family memorabilia. Dinners of estate produce, eggs, roast duck and, on summer evenings, gastronomic buffets you can take to a favourite corner of the vast grounds (with new pool).

rooms	6: 4 doubles, 1 triple, 1 family room.
price	€105–€110.
meals	Dinner with wine, €26–€42.
closed	Occasionally.
directions	From Tours A85 (Saumur); 1st exit for Ballan Miré; signs for Château de Vau & golf course at motorway exit. Entrance opp. golf course.

Bruno & Nancy Clément
Château du Vau,
37510 Ballan Miré,
Indre-et-Loire
tel   +33 (0)2 47 67 84 04
fax   +33 (0)2 47 67 55 77
email   chateauduvau@chez.com
web   www.chez.com/chateauduvau

Map 4 Entry 385

Loire Valley

Château du Grand Bouchet

An elegant château, its big windows fore and aft let in floods of light. Guest rooms are large, well-proportioned, airy; there are no unnecessary frills, just a few good-quality pieces of furniture, parquet floors, pretty floral curtains, attractive quilts and good beds. The attentive and very knowledgeable Devants have lived in Touraine for ever, are passionate environmentalists and enjoy this gracious house. A motley collection of 18th- and 19th-century armchairs summons you to the fireside In the guest salon, there are billiards and board games next door, and a tree-rich garden which is their pride and joy.

rooms	4: 2 doubles, 2 suites for 2-4.
price	€100.
meals	Restaurant 3km.
closed	November-Easter.
directions	From Tours D7 for Savonnières & Villandry; turning to house on left 3km after exit from bypass west of Tours.

M & Mme Devant
Château du Grand Bouchet,
Chemin Dugrand Bouchet,
D7 Routes des Vallées,
37510 Ballan-Miré, Indre-et-Loire

tel	+33 (0)2 47 67 79 08
fax	+33 (0)2 47 67 79 08
email	grandbouchet@wanadoo.fr
web	perso.wanadoo.fr/grandbouchet

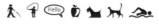

Map 4 Entry 386

Loire Valley

Le Chat Courant

Traditional materials – soft Touraine stone, lime render, wood   and old furniture, pale colours and lots of light make the slate-topped house a stylish welcoming haven by the Cher where the birdsong drowns out the trains. Here live Anne, Éric, their four children and various animals. They have lots of local lore for you, and concoct wonders from their miniature-Villandry garden. Anne adores looking for new recipes and bits of antiquery (your bedhead in the guest room is an adapted Breton *lit clos*), and attends lovingly to every detail. Flowers inside and out – exceptional.

rooms	2: 1 double, 1 family suite for 2-5.
price	€60. €105 for 4.
meals	Occasional dinner with wine, €25.
closed	Rarely.
directions	From Tours D7 to Savonnières; right across bridge; left for 3.5km; on right.

Anne & Éric Gaudouin
Le Chat Courant,
37510 Villandry,
Indre-et-Loire

tel	+33 (0)2 47 50 06 94
email	info@le-chat-courant.com
web	www.le-chat-courant.com

Map 4 Entry 387

Loire Valley

Les Mazeraies

Beautifully sculpted from the same ancient cedar trees that stalked the splendid grounds 100 years ago, this thoroughly contemporary mansion on the old château foundations in the Garden of France is a real delight. Humour, intelligence and love of fine things inhabit this welcoming family and their guest wing is unostentatiously luxurious in rich fabrics, oriental and modern furniture, good pictures and lovely, scented, cedar-lined bathrooms. Ground-floor rooms have a private terrace each, upstairs ones have direct access to the roof garden. Marie-Laurence is utterly charming.

rooms	4: 1 double, 2 twins/doubles, 1 suite for 3.
price	€95.
meals	Choice of restaurants locally.
closed	Rarely.
directions	From Tours D7 for Savonnières; 3km before village left after Les Cèdres restaurant; 800m on left.

Marie-Laurence Jallet
Les Mazeraies,
Route des Mazeraies,
37510 Savonnières,
Indre-et-Loire
tel   +33 (0)2 47 67 85 35
mobile   +33 (0)6 76 94 92 43
email   lesmazeraies@wanadoo.fr
web   www.lesmazeraies.com

Map 4   Entry 388

Loire Valley

7 Chemin de Bois Soleil

High on a cliff above the Loire, it looks over the village across the vines and the valley to a château. It may be modern imitating old, but we chose it for Madame's superb, generous, five-star hospitality. The house is immaculate and meticulously kept; one room is repro Louis XIV, plus orangey carpet and flowery paper. There is a big living area with tiled floor and rugs, an insert fireplace and views over the large sloping garden which peers down over the picturesque village with its church and châteaux. Giant breakfasts, wonderful welcome, great value for the Loire. *Free internet access.*

rooms	3: 2 doubles, 1 suite for 4.
price	€55. Suite €89.
meals	Restaurants in village, 500m.
closed	Rarely.
directions	From Tours A10 for Paris; cross Loire; exit 20 to Vouvray. In Rochecorbon left at lights & right up steep narrow lane; signposted.

Mme Jacqueline Gay
7 Chemin de Bois Soleil,
37210 Rochecorbon,
Indre-et-Loire
tel   +33 (0)2 47 52 88 08
email   jacqueline.gay2@wanadoo.fr
web   perso.wanadoo.fr/hautes-gatinieres

Map 4   Entry 389

Loire Valley

La Lubinerie

Built by Elizabeth's grandfather a hundred years ago, its typical brick and tile face still looking good, this neat townhouse is done in an attractive, spirited mixture of modern and nostalgic: strong colour juxtapositions against family furniture, delicate muslin as a backdrop to a fascinating collection of paintings, prints, old cartoons and teapots. Elizabeth lived for years in England, collected all these things and calls her delicious rooms Earl Grey, Orange Pekoe, Darjeeling. She and Jacques, who is more reserved with a subtle sense of humour, love sharing their stories and knowledge with guests.

rooms	3: 2 doubles, 1 suite for 4.
price	€70–€120. Singles €60.
meals	Dinner with wine, €25.
closed	Rarely.
directions	A10 exit 23 for Loches & Châteauroux; N143; carry straight on to 2nd r'bout; exit for Esvres sur Indre; in village left at stop sign; house opposite nursery school.

Elizabeth Aubert-Girard
La Lubinerie,
3 rue des Écoles,
37320 Esvres sur Indre,
Indre-et-Loire

tel	+33 (0)2 47 26 40 87
mobile	+33 (0)6 15 30 59 66
email	lalubinerie@wanadoo.fr
web	www.lalubinerie.com

Map 4 Entry 390

Loire Valley

Les Moulins de Vontes

Pure magic for all *Wind in the Willows* fans. Three old mills side by side on an unspoiled sweep of the Indre, a boat for messing about in, wooden bridges to cross from one secluded bank to another, a ship-stern view of the river from the terrace. No evening meals so pick up a picnic and your hosts will be happy to provide cutlery, rugs and anything else you need. The airy, elegant, uncluttered rooms have stunning river views (the sound of rushing water is limited to a gentle murmur at night), in various styles – Empire, oriental – and bathrooms sparkle. You may swim, but watch little ones. Sophisticated, magical.

rooms	3: 1 twin; 2 doubles, each with shower & separate wc.
price	€130.
meals	Restaurant 6km.
closed	October–March.
directions	From Tours N143 for Loches for 12km; 500m after Esso garage, right D17 for 1.3km; left to Vontes; left to Bas-Vontes. At end of road.

Odile & Jean-Jacques Degail
Les Moulins de Vontes,
37320 Esvres sur Indre,
Indre-et-Loire

tel	+33 (0)2 47 26 45 72
fax	+33 (0)2 47 26 45 35
email	info@moulinsdevontes.com
web	www.moulinsdevontes.com

Map 4 Entry 391

Loire Valley

Moulin de la Follaine

Follaine is a deeply serene place and feels as old as the hills (actually the Middle Ages: the background farm was used as a hunting lodge by Lafayette). Ornamental geese adorn the lake, the neatly-tended garden has places to sit, colourful bedrooms have antique furniture and lake views, and one opens to the garden. Upstairs is a lovely light sitting room. Amazingly, the old milling machinery in the breakfast area still works – ask and Monsieur will turn it on for you – and there are other relics from the old days. Your hosts, once in the hotel trade, are absolutely charming.

rooms	4: 2 doubles, 2 suites.
price	€65.
meals	Auberge in village, 500m.
closed	Rarely.
directions	From Tours N143 for Loches; left D58 to Reignac; D17 to Azay sur Indre; left opp. restaurant; at fork, left (over 2 bridges); mill below fortified farm on right.

Mme Danie Lignelet
Moulin de la Follaine,
37310 Azay sur Indre,
Indre-et-Loire
tel +33 (0)2 47 92 57 91
fax +33 (0)2 47 92 57 91
email moulindelafollaine@wanadoo.fr
web www.moulindefollaine.com

Map 4 Entry 392

Loire Valley

La Métairie des Bois

Monsieur grew up in a château and some fine family pieces have followed him here – including a Napoleon III billiard table, one of two in France. The small 16th-century farmhouse has been beautifully extended to incorporate an old barn for guest rooms, each one with a pretty patio and a bank of pink roses. Friendly Madame is proud of this comfortable, French-traditional house with its pleasant, rambling garden and fenced, alarmed pool. The estate stretches as far as the eye can see and has its own lake. Help yourself to boats and fishing rods, or set off for the treasures of medieval Loches.

rooms	3: 2 doubles, 1 family suite for 2-4.
price	€60. Suite €90.
meals	Dinner with wine, €25.
closed	Rarely.
directions	From Loches D760 for Ste Maure de Touraine; left D95 for Vou; 1st right at sign 'La Métairie des Bois'.

M & Mme Jean-Claude Baillou
La Métairie des Bois,
37240 Vou,
Indre-et-Loire
tel +33 (0)2 47 92 36 46
fax +33 (0)2 47 92 36 46
email baillou@wanadoo.fr
web www.lametairiedesbois.com

Map 4 Entry 393

Loire Valley

Le Belvédère

From plain street to stately courtyard magnolia to extraordinary marble-walled spiral staircase with dome atop – it's a *monument historique*, a miniature Bagatelle Palace, a bachelor's folly with a circular salon. The light, airy, fadingly elegant rooms, small and perfectly proportioned, are soft pink and grey; lean out and pick a grape from the vine-clad pergola. Monsieur was a pilot and still flies vintage aircraft. Madame was an air hostess and English teacher and is casually sophisticated and articulate about her love of fine things, places and buildings. Wonderful, and a stone's throw from Chenonceau.

rooms	3: 2 double, 1 suite for 4.
price	€90. Suite €140.
meals	Restaurant opposite (must book).
closed	Occasionally.
directions	From Amboise D31 to Bléré through Croix en Touraine; over bridge (Rue des Déportés opp. is one-way): left, immed. right, 1st right, right again. OR collection from private airport 5km.

Dominique Guillemot
Le Belvédère,
24 rue des Déportés,
37150 Bléré, Indre-et-Loire
tel +33 (0)2 47 30 30 25
fax +33 (0)2 47 30 30 25
email jr.guillemot@wanadoo.fr
web thebelvedere.free.fr

Map 4 Entry 394

Loire Valley

Le Pavillon de Vallet

When she moved to this little valley, charming, chatty Astrid had no B&B plans at all – "it happened" and she loves it, taking huge care over the rooms (new beds in all) and breakfast (delicious) – she and her pilot husband are escapees from Paris. The *tuffeau* stone is light and bright, the walled garden runs down to the Cher, country quiet fills the patios. Guests have an antique-furnished living room full of lightness and well-being. The lovely ground-floor bread-oven bedroom is sweet with its flowery wallpaper and painted beams; in another, an enormous four-poster looms beneath its canopy of joists.

rooms	3: 1 double, 2 triples.
price	€60–€70.
meals	Restaurants 4km.
closed	Rarely.
directions	From Tours N76 for Bléré; pass sign for Athée sur Cher, continue to Granlay; immed. left to Vallet; on down lane; left at bottom of hill; last house on right.

Astrid Lange
Le Pavillon de Vallet,
4 rue de l'Acqueduc,
37270 Athée sur Cher,
Indre-et-Loire
tel +33 (0)2 47 50 67 83
fax +33 (0)2 47 50 67 83
email pavillon.vallet@wanadoo.fr
web perso.wanadoo.fr/lepavillondevallet/

Map 4 Entry 395

Loire Valley

Manoir de la Maison Blanche

Your 17th-century manor sits in blissful seclusion yet you can walk into the centre of old Amboise. Annick has bags of energy and enthusiasm and gives you four fabulous, generous, lofty bedrooms in a converted outbuilding. One is tiled and beamed with a small patio overlooking the garden, another, under the eaves, is charming, beamy and reached via an outdoor spiral stair. The youthful garden is full of promise and bursting with roses and irises that often make their way to your room. Look out for the 16th-century pigeon loft – a historical rarity. Wonderful hostess, super rooms, châteaux all around.

rooms	4 doubles.
price	€85.
meals	Choice of restaurants in Amboise.
closed	Rarely.
directions	From Place du Château in Amboise for Clos Lucé; round park; straight on at 1st stop sign, right at 2nd stop sign, 1st left. Signs.

Annick Delécheneau
Manoir de la Maison Blanche,
18 rue de l'Épinetterie,
37400 Amboise, Indre-et-Loire

tel	+33 (0)2 47 23 16 14
mobile	+33 (0)6 88 89 33 66
email	annick.delecheneau@wanadoo.fr
web	www.lamaisonblanche-fr.com

Map 4 Entry 396

Loire Valley

Château de Nazelles

Even the pool is special: a 'Roman' bath hewn out of the hillside with a fountain and two columns, set on one of several garden levels that rise to the crowning glory of vines where grapes are grown by natural methods. The young owners brim with enthusiasm for their elegant, history-laden château, built in 1518 to gaze across the Loire at Amboise. Every detail has been treated with taste and discretion. Rooms, two in the main house, two smaller in the adorable old *pavillon*, are light and fresh with lovely wooden floors – and there's a big living room with books, internet and games.

rooms	4: 3 doubles, 1 suite for 4.
price	€95-€120.
meals	Restaurants in Amboise.
closed	Christmas Day & New Year's Day.
directions	From A10 exit 18 for Amboise 12km; right D1 to Pocé & Cisse & Nazelles Négron; in village centre, narrow Rue Tue la Soif between Mairie & La Poste.

Véronique & Olivier Fructus
Château de Nazelles,
16 rue Tue la Soif, 37530 Nazelles,
Indre-et-Loire

tel	+33 (0)2 47 30 53 79
fax	+33 (0)2 47 30 53 79
email	info@chateau-nazelles.com
web	www.chateau-nazelles.com

Map 4 Entry 397

Le Clos du Golf

All this in one place? There are 14 hectares of heron, wild boar, deer *and* a nine-hole golf course. Mark, a gallicised Englishman, and Katia, an anglicised Frenchwoman, great travellers both, are at rest and in love with their beautiful home. The old farmhouse or *longière* has been masterfully restored and is filled, naturally, with a mix of English and French: pleasing antiques, crisp bright bedrooms beneath old beams, dinners – praised by readers – of fresh seasonal things such as gentle local asparagus. Swimming, tennis and the splendours of the Loire lie just down the road.

rooms	4: 3 doubles, 1 single.
price	€50–€80.
meals	Dinner with wine, €30.
closed	December–January.
directions	From A10 exit 18 on D31 for Amboise to Autrèche; left D55 to Dame Marie les Bois; right D74; 1st house on left after woods.

Mark & Katia Foster
Le Clos du Golf,
Route de Dame-Marie-les-Bois,
37530 Cangey-Amboise,
Indre-et-Loire

tel	+33 (0)2 47 56 07 07
fax	+33 (0)2 47 56 82 12
email	closdugolf@wanadoo.fr
web	www.bonadresse.com/val-de-loire/cangey-amboise.htm

Map 4 Entry 398

Meals, booking and cancelling

Dinner

Do remember that table d'hôtes is a fixed-price set menu that has to be booked. Very few owners offer dinner every day. Once you have booked dinner, it is a question of common courtesy to turn up and partake of the meal prepared for you. Dining in can be a wonderful opportunity to experience both food and company in an authentic French family atmosphere. Or it may be more formal and still utterly French. Some owners no longer eat with their guests for family and waistline reasons.

Rooms

We have heard of chambres d'hôtes hopefuls arriving unannounced at 7pm and being devastated to learn that the house was full. For your own sake and your hosts', do ring ahead: if they can't have you, owners can usually suggest other places nearby. But arriving without warning at the end of the day is asking for disappointment.

Cancelling

As soon as you realise you are not going to take up a booking, even late in the day, please telephone immediately. The owners may still be able to let the room for that night and at least won't stay up wondering whether you've had an accident and when they can give up and go to bed.

By the same token, if you find you're going to arrive later than planned, let your hosts know so that they won't worry unnecessarily or… let your room to someone else.

Poitou – Charentes

Poitou – Charentes

L'Aumônerie

If walls could speak… this old hospital priory beside the original moat (now the boulevard bringing newer neighbours) has eight drama-packed centuries to tell. The L'Haridons have put back several original features and alongside picture windows the old stone spiral leads up to the suite (big warm sitting room, low oak door to fresh beamed bedroom with extra bed); the charming double feels really old. Madame is well-travelled, loves history, old buildings and gardens and is a most interesting and considerate hostess who also has a passion for patchwork. Loudun has restaurants aplenty. *Château de Chinon 25km.*

rooms	3: 1 double, 1 twin, 1 family suite for 4.
price	€38-€50. Suite €48-€105.
meals	Restaurants within walking distance.
closed	Rarely.
directions	From Fontevraud, take Loudun centre; cross traffic lights; at r'bout (Hotel de la Roue d'Or on right) take 1st exit for Thouars. Entrance 200m on right opp. Cultural Centre.

Christiane L'Haridon
L'Aumônerie,
3 boulevard Maréchal Leclerc,
86200 Loudun, Vienne
tel   +33 (0)5 49 22 63 86
mobile   +33 (0)6 83 58 26 18
email   chris.lharidon@wanadoo.fr
web   www.l-aumonerie.biz

Map 9 Entry 399

Poitou – Charentes

Le Bois Goulu

Set proudly at the end of its drive, the finely proportioned 18th century manor is a farming family's house. Five generations of Picards have lived here serenely, where Madame, intelligent, feisty and down to earth, will welcome you as family. Overlooking the chestnut-tree'd garden, the generous bedrooms have handsome wardrobes, good firm mattresses and slightly faded wallpapers. Sunlight streams onto the well-matched beams, white walls and terracotta floor of the huge sitting room, breakfast is in the yellow dining room or on the leafy terrace and there are simple cooking facilities for guests.

rooms	2: 1 double, 1 suite.
price	€45.
meals	Restaurant 600m. Kitchen available.
closed	Rarely.
directions	From Richelieu D58 towards Loudun for 4km; right into drive lined with lime trees.

Marie-Christine Picard
Le Bois Goulu,
86200 Pouant,
Vienne
tel   +33 (0)5 49 22 52 05
fax   +33 (0)5 49 22 52 05

Map 9 Entry 400

Château de la Motte

Nothing austere about this imposing, lovingly restored, 15th-century fortified castle. A wide spiral stone staircase leads to the simply but grandly decorated and high-ceilinged rooms where old family furniture, vast stone fireplaces and beds with richly textured canopies, finely stitched by your talented hostess, preserve the medieval flavour, while bathrooms (also generous) are state of the art. There is an elegant dining room and a huge, lofty, light-filled sitting room for enlightened conversation with your cultured and charming hosts.

La Grenouillère

You will be charmed by these warm, delightful, good-hearted people. Always fresh flowers and lovely colour schemes on the table, good French food and flowing wine, and meals on the shaded terrace in summer. The bedroom in the converted woodshed has beams, pretty curtains, a blue and yellow tiled floor and a view over the rambling garden with its meandering frog pond (hence the name). Further rooms are upstairs in a house across the courtyard where Madame's charming mother lives and makes delicious jam. Stimulating company, a most attractive cluster of old buildings and a rowing boat to mess about in.

rooms	4: 1 twin, 1 triple, 2 suites.
price	€75-€120.
meals	Dinner with wine, €25.
closed	Occasionally.
directions	From Paris A10 exit Châtellerault Nord; at r'bout after toll for Usseau 5km; D749 for Richelieu; D75 to Usseau.

rooms	5: 3 doubles, 2 triples.
price	€43-€49.
meals	Dinner with wine, €20.
closed	Rarely.
directions	From Tours N10 S for Châtellerault 55km. In Dangé St Romain, right at 3rd traffic lights, cross river, keep left on little square. House 200m along on left; signed.

	Jean-Marie & Marie-Andrée Bardin
	Château de la Motte,
	86230 Usseau, Vienne
tel	+33 (0)5 49 85 88 25
fax	+33 (0)5 49 85 88 25
email	chateau.delamotte@wanadoo.fr
web	www.chateau-de-la-motte.net

	Annie & Noël Braguier
	La Grenouillère,
	17 rue de la Grenouillère,
	86220 Dangé St Romain,
	Vienne
tel	+33 (0)5 49 86 48 68
fax	+33 (0)5 49 86 46 56
email	lagrenouillere86@aol.com

Map 9 Entry 401

Map 9 Entry 402

Poitou – Charentes

La Demeure de Latillé

A quiet village, a fine 18th-century coaching inn, a charming courtyard, large garden and mature trees: an oasis of green peace. Attractively restored by Monsieur and his vivaciously welcoming English/French wife, the rooms are airy, light, lovely: Spring – very French with its old cherrywood bed; Summer – brass four-poster and pretty wicker; Winter snow-white canopied bed; Four Seasons – almost English with old-style pine and sweet children's room; and a peach-pink double on the ground floor. Immaculate bathrooms and a sitting room in the old stables. *Babysitting available.*

rooms	5: 1 double, 3 triples, 1 suite for 5.
price	€48-€60.
meals	Restaurant 50m.
closed	23 December-2 January.
directions	From Poitiers N149 W for Nantes 14km; at Vouillé left D62 to Latillé (24km). House largest in main village square.

Maryanne Broquerault
La Demeure de Latillé,
1 place Robert Gerbier,
86190 Latillé, Vienne
tel   +33 (0)5 49 51 54 74
fax   +33 (0)5 49 51 56 32
email maryanne.broquerault@cegetel.net
web   www.chez.com/latille

Map 9 Entry 403

Poitou – Charentes

Château de Masseuil

In the big flagstoned kitchen of the crag-perched château, friends and family chat over the jam-making. Hunting trophies, family portraits, including a mob-capped great-grandmother, adorn the sunny breakfast room; comfortable, fresh bedrooms have old family pieces, a shower each, new beds; charming, unstuffily aristocratic hosts are hugely knowledgeable about local Romanesque art and tell stories of monks and brigands. Medieval castles didn't have en suite loos: there are chamber pots in case you can't face the stairs! Wonderful. *The simple suite can be turned into a gîte.*

rooms	3: 1 double, 1 twin/double, sharing wc; 1 suite & kitchenette.
price	€65.
meals	Restaurants 3km.
closed	Rarely.
directions	From A10 exit Poitiers Nord N149 for Nantes 12km; at bottom of hill left for Masseuil.

Alain & Claude Gail
Château de Masseuil,
86190 Quinçay,
Vienne
tel   +33 (0)5 49 60 42 15
fax   +33 (0)5 49 60 70 15

Map 9 Entry 404

Poitou – Charentes

Château de Labarom

A great couple in their genuine family château of fading grandeur – mainly 17th century, it has a properly aged face. From the dramatic hall up the superbly bannistered staircase, through a carved screen, you reach the salon gallery that runs majestically through the house. Here you may sit, read, dream of benevolent ghosts. Bedrooms burst with personality and wonderful old beds. Madame's hand-painted tiles adorn a shower, her laughter accompanies your breakfast in the splendid family living room; Monsieur tends his trees and is a fund of local wisdom. A warm, authentic place.

rooms	3: 2 twins, 1 suite. Extra children's room.
price	€69-€75.
meals	Auberge nearby, choice 10km.
closed	Rarely.
directions	From A10 Futuroscope exit D62 to Quatre Vents r'bout; D757 to Vendeuvre; left D15 through Chéneché. Labarom 800m on right after leaving Chéneché.

Éric & Henriette Le Gallais
Château de Labarom,
86380 Chéneché, Vienne
tel +33 (0)5 49 51 24 22
fax +33 (0)5 49 51 47 38
mobile +33 (0)6 83 57 68 14
email chateau.de.labarom@wanadoo.fr

Map 9 Entry 405

Poitou – Charentes

La Ferme du Château de Martigny

Madame, vivacious and dynamic, is delighted for you to enjoy her simple, pretty rooms in the converted outbuilding and hugely generous breakfast in the creeper-clad patio or dining room (you can ask for doggy bags). The two rooms sharing kitchen and sitting room are traditional French-furnished. Off the games room, the delightful, two-storey suite has 'rustic' rooms and an intriguing window layout. So close to lovely old Poitiers, even closer to the high-tech Futuroscope, yet only the ping-pong of a little white ball or the splish-splosh of swimmers disturbs the hush of the tiny village.

rooms	3: 1 double, 1 triple, 1 suite for 4-5.
price	€42-€49. Triple €55-€60. Suite €68-€85.
meals	Restaurants 3km. Kitchen available.
closed	Mid November-January.
directions	From A10 exit 28 on D18 for Avanton 2km. Signs in hamlet Martigny.

Annie & Didier Arrondeau
La Ferme du Château de Martigny,
86170 Avanton, Vienne
tel +33 (0)5 49 51 04 57
fax +33 (0)5 49 51 04 57
email lafermeduchateau@wanadoo.fr
web www.lafermeduchateau.fr

Map 9 Entry 406

Poitou – Charentes

Logis du Château du Bois Doucet

Naturally, unstiltedly, aristocratically French, owners and house are full of stories and character: a fine jumble of ten French chairs, bits of ancient furniture, pictures, heirlooms, lamps in the stone-flagged salon, a properly elegant dining room; there are statues indoors and out; large bedrooms bursting with personality; bathrooms too. Monsieur's interests are history and his family, Madame's are art and life – they are a delightful combination of unselfconscious class and flashes of Mediterranean non-conformism. You are very much part of family life in this people- and dog-friendly house.

rooms	3: 1 double, 2 family suites.
price	€70–€80. Suite €130.
meals	Dinner with wine, €30.
closed	Rarely.
directions	From A10 exit Poitiers Nord, N10 for Limoges 7km; left to Bignoux; follow signs to Bois Dousset.

Vicomte & Vicomtesse Hilaire de Villoutreys de Brignac
Logis du Château du Bois Doucet,
86800 Lavoux,
Vienne
tel +33 (0)5 49 44 20 26
fax +33 (0)5 49 44 20 26

Map 9 Entry 407

Poitou – Charentes

La Pocterie

A "passionate gardener" is how Martine describes herself, with a soft spot for old-fashioned roses: they ramble through the wisteria on the walls and gather in beautifully tended beds. The 'L' of the house shelters a very decent pool (now alarmed) while furniture is arranged in a welcoming spot for picnics. Martine works but will see you for breakfast (under the pretty arbour in summer) or in the evening: she's the one with the big smile. A peaceful, welcoming retreat with the Futuroscope literally minutes away. Bikes and tennis nearby, and a huge range of day trips to choose from.

rooms	3: 2 doubles, 1 triple.
price	€50. Triple €60.
meals	Restaurants 3km.
closed	Rarely.
directions	From Châtellerault D749 for Chauvigny & Limoges about 10km; Vouneuil on right; after 750m, left; house down track.

Michel & Martine Poussard
La Pocterie,
86210 Vouneuil sur Vienne,
Vienne
tel +33 (0)5 49 85 11 96
mobile +33 (0)6 76 95 49 46

Map 9 Entry 408

Poitou – Charentes

Les Hauts de Chabonne

A pleasant 'stop off' in an undiscovered area. This sociable couple will spend time with guests after dinner when their children allow. They have converted a fine big barn into guest quarters – older than the main house, it has been well done, muted colour schemes and ethnic rugs in dark and pleasant rooms, a good dayroom with an open fireplace, a superb cobbled terrace inviting you to sit on balmy evenings and gaze across the wide landscape while the wind plays in the poplars. With a nature reserve on the doorstep – dragonflies a speciality – here is an area waiting to be discovered.

rooms	3: 2 doubles, 1 triple.
price	€60.
meals	Dinner with wine, €25.
closed	Rarely.
directions	From Châtellerault D749 to Vouneuil sur Vienne; left in church square & follow Chambres d'Hôtes signs. Last house on right in hamlet of Chabonne.

Florence & Antoine Penot
Les Hauts de Chabonne,
Chabonne, 86210
Vouneuil sur Vienne, Vienne
tel	+33 (0)5 49 85 28 25
fax	+33 (0)5 49 85 22 75
email	penot.antoine@wanadoo.fr
web	www.chabonne.com

Map 9 Entry 409

Poitou – Charentes

Siouvre

The humble bee reigns royal here where honeys and bee products are made and sold. It's a great place for families, with a child-friendly garden, and Jacky and Charline such fun. She is excellent at explaining (in French) the ancient complicity between man and insect over breakfast in the guest building. You get a cheerful dayroom, fronted by great banks of lavender, and two rooms in the converted pigsty: a big, cool, darkish double, and, up steep steps, a suite, with low skylights, colourful décor, sitting space and kitchenette. The third room is behind the main house – small, with its own tiny garden. Great fun.

rooms	3: 2 doubles, 1 family suite for 5 & kitchenette.
price	€43.
meals	Restaurant in St Savin. BBQ available.
closed	15 October-15 March.
directions	From Chauvigny, N151 for St Savin. 2km before St Savin, left to Siouvre; signed.

Charline & Jacky Barbarin
Siouvre,
86310 St Savin,
Vienne
tel	+33 (0)5 49 48 10 19
fax	+33 (0)5 49 48 46 89
email	charline@lafermeapicole.com
web	www.lafermeapicole.com

Map 9 Entry 410

Poitou – Charentes

Le Haut Peu

This delightful farming family are rooted in village life, including the local drama group. Monsieur also shares his time with mayoral duties and his dream of restoring the 12th-century Villesalem priory. Madame, somewhat shyer, embroidered the exquisite samplers. Both enjoy sharing their simple, stylish, much-loved house with cultured, like-minded guests. The suite is in the old coach house, its kitchen in the bread oven. Finely decorated bedrooms blend with the garden and woodlands (golden orioles, hoopoes, wild orchids…). Visit the goats, watch the cheese-making or fish in their big lake.

rooms	3: 2 doubles; 1 suite for 4-5 & kitchen. Extra room for children.
price	€55.
meals	Dinner with wine, €18.
closed	Mid-November-mid-February.
directions	From Poitiers N147 SE to Lussac les Châteaux; D727 E for 21km; left D121 to Journet. There, N for Haims; house 1km on left.

Jacques & Chantal Cochin
Le Haut Peu,
86290 Journet,
Vienne
tel   +33 (0)5 49 91 62 02
fax   +33 (0)5 49 91 22 01

Map 9   Entry 411

Poitou – Charentes

La Théophilière

Jean-Louis, a genial twinkly man, used to farm but now sticks to vegetables, chickens and a role in numerous local events; Geneviève is a perfectionist. Their traditional Poitevin farmhouse, rendered a sunny ochre, has a modern conservatory along its width and rooms opening off either side. You come to it from the back, up a long tree-lined drive, so will be surprised to find it is in the middle of the village. Rooms are fresh and immaculate, with great colours, furniture is suitably old: the canopy over the double bed was made for Madame's great-grandmother's wedding. Real and comforting. *Heated pool.*

rooms	2: 1 family room; 1 twin with shower & separate wc.
price	€48-€55.
meals	Dinner with wine, €12-€18.
closed	Rarely.
directions	From A10 exit Poitiers Sud N10 for Angoulême to Vivonne; 2nd exit D4 to Champagne St H. & Sommières du C.; right D1 for Civray 8km; left to Champniers; signed.

Geneviève & Jean-Louis Fazilleau
La Théophilière,
86400 Champniers,
Vienne
tel   +33 (0)5 49 87 19 04
email   jeanlouis.fazilleau@free.fr
web   chambres-hotes-poitou-
        charente.ifrance.com

Map 9   Entry 412

Poitou – Charentes

Les Écots

The Salvaudons are educated, intelligent farmers, he energetic and down-to-earth, she gentle and smiling, who are committed to the natural way, like swapping travellers' tales and sharing simple, lasting values while providing decent guest rooms in a relaxed and genuine house. There is indeed "more here than the Futuroscope". The farm is fully organic: don't miss Madame's Limousin specialities – lamb, chicken cooked in honey, vegetable pies – round the family table. The sheep pastures lie in rolling, stream-run country beloved of fisherfolk and Monsieur will take children to meet the animals.

rooms	2 doubles, each with shower & basin, sharing wc.
price	€36.
meals	Dinner with wine, €15.
closed	Rarely.
directions	From Poitiers D741 to Civray; D148 east & D34 to Availles; D100 for Mauprévoir, 3km; signed.

Pierre & Line Salvaudon
Les Écots,
86460 Availles Limousine,
Vienne

tel	+33 (0)5 49 48 59 17
fax	+33 (0)5 49 48 59 17
mobile	+33 (0)6 26 39 39 51
email	pierre.salvaudon@wanadoo.fr

Map 9 Entry 413

Poitou – Charentes

Château de Tennessus

It's all real: moat, drawbridge, dreams. Two steep stone spirals to "the biggest bedroom in France": granite windowsills, giant hearth, canopied bed, shower snug; on the lower floors of the keep, the medieval family room: vast timbers, good mattresses, arrow slits for windows. Furniture is sober, candles are lit, fires always laid, and you breakfast at a massive table on 14th-century flagstones. Indeed, the whole place is brilliantly authentic, the charming gardens glow from loving care (medieval potager, modern pool), the views reach far, and Pippa is a bundle of energy and generosity. *Children over six welcome.*

rooms	2: 1 double & kitchenette, 1 family suite for 4.
price	€120-€145.
meals	Restaurant 4km, choice 9km.
closed	Christmas-New Year.
directions	From A10 exit 29 on N147; N149 W to Parthenay; round Parthenay northbound; on N149 for Bressuire; 7km north of Parthenay right at sign for château.

Nicholas & Philippa Freeland
Château de Tennessus,
79350 Amailloux,
Deux Sèvres

tel	+33 (0)5 49 95 50 60
fax	+33 (0)5 49 95 50 62
email	tennessus@csi.com
web	www.tennessus.com

Map 9 Entry 414

Poitou – Charentes

A l'Ombre du Figuier

The old farmhouse, lovingly restored and decorated, is simple, pristine, with biggish, comfortable rooms overlooking a pretty garden where you may picnic (there's a guest kitchen too). They are an interesting couple of anglophiles. Madame knows about nutrition and serves generous organic breakfasts with homemade jam, cheese, yogurt and cereals, all on local pottery. Monsieur teaches engineering in beautiful La Rochelle: follow his hints and discover the lesser-known treasures there. A rural idyll wrapped in birdsong. Good value.
No pets in rooms.

rooms	2: 1 double, 1 room for 2-4. Rooms interconnect.
price	€54-€59.
meals	Occasional dinner with wine, €20. Guest kitchen.
closed	Rarely.
directions	From La Rochelle N11 E for 11km exit Longèves; D112, signed to village. In village, past church; right at 'bar-pizzas', 1st left, signed. 700m on left.

M-Christine & J-François Prou
A l'Ombre du Figuier,
43 rue du Marais,
17230 Longèves,
Charente-Maritime

tel	+33 (0)5 46 37 11 15
fax	+33 (0)5 46 37 11 15
email	mcprou@wanadoo.fr
web	www.alombredufiguier.com

Map 8 Entry 415

Poitou – Charentes

Le Clos de la Garenne

In this lovingly restored 16th-century house lives a lively young family: three children to entertain young visitors, and sophisticated parents, avid collectors, to decorate with elegance and eclectic flair, cook with exotic inspiration and organics, and talk with passion. Old and modern rub happy shoulders: traditional armoires and new beds, disabled facilities in the newer-style cottage, antique treasures and a tennis court. The air is full of warm smiles, harmony breathes from walls and woodwork, your hosts are endlessly thoughtful, families are positively welcome.
Minimum stay three nights July/Aug.

rooms	2 + 1: 1 triple, 1 suite for 6. Cottage for 5.
price	€65. Triple €75. Cottage €125.
meals	Dinner with wine, €25.
closed	Rarely.
directions	From Surgères Gendarmerie & fire station, D115 for Marans & Puyravault 5km, following signs.

Brigitte & Patrick François
Le Clos de la Garenne,
9 rue de la Garenne,
17700 Puyravault,
Charente-Maritime

tel	+33 (0)5 46 35 47 71
fax	+33 (0)5 46 35 47 91
email	info@closdelagarenne.com
web	www.closdelagarenne.com

Map 8 Entry 416

Poitou – Charentes

Les Grands Vents

In a lovely sleepy village in the heart of wine and cognac country, by the road but peaceful, the former *pineau* farmhouse has simple limewashed walls and a traditional French décor. You have your own entrance here you and can be as private as you like – but Valérie and Nicolas are easy, generous hosts and happy for you to have the run of the place. Bedrooms, with views onto a well-pruned garden, are large, fresh and catch the morning or evening sun. There's a lush pool and a new covered terrace for four-course dinners full of laugher and conversation – a great find for families.

rooms	2: 1 triple, 1 suite for 4.
price	€53.
meals	Dinner with wine, €22.
closed	Rarely.
directions	From A10 exit 33 E601 to Mauzé sur le Mignon; D911 to Surgères; D939 12km, right to Chervettes; behind iron gates.

Valérie & Nicolas Godebout
Les Grands Vents,
17380 Chervettes,
Charente-Maritime
tel   +33 (0)5 46 35 92 21
fax   +33 (0)5 46 35 92 21
email   godebout@club-internet.fr
web   www.les-grands-vents.com

Map 8 Entry 417

Poitou – Charentes

La Sauvagerie

Beyond the leafy fruit orchard lies the gem that is La Sauvagerie and inside, lovely Madame, its number one treasure. Close by is Surgères, home to beautiful churches and creamy butter. Equally lovely is the farmhouse, once the cognac store for the neighbouring manor, where, with the right wind, you may still catch a whiff of the amber tipple. Rooms are simple, old-fashioned and themed with family sailing trophies from a lifetime of seafarers. For a magical finale, fish supper in Madame's hearty kitchen is served with *pommes de terre diable* from an ancient clay cooking pot on a roaring log fire.

rooms	4: 1 double, 1 triple; 1 double, 1 suite for 5, each with separate wc.
price	€60.
meals	Dinner with wine, €20.
closed	Never.
directions	From Surgères, D115 to Aulnay. Between St Félix and Migré, left into Les Petites Tannières, house signed to left after 25m.

M & Mme Chambonnet-Bonnet
La Sauvagerie, Les Petites Tannières,
1 rue des Paquerettes,
17330 Migré, Charente-Maritime
tel   +33 (0)5 46 33 26 05
fax   +33 (0)5 46 33 26 05
email   francoise.chambonnet@wanadoo.fr
web   www.lasauvagerie.com

Map 8 Entry 418

Poitou – Charentes

Les Moulins

A wonderful old house and dear hosts who grow endives – what more could one ask? Built in 1600, renovated in 1720, the house stands in a garden of mature trees reaching to the river Boutonne. In clean, fresh bedrooms are good beds and big armoires; in the huge guest sitting room, antiques, armchairs, a French billiards table and… bowls of sweets. French country food is served in ample proportions, breakfast brioche is scrumptious. You might be staying with your favourite granny; Madame is an angel, Monsieur has a wicked sense of humour. Spin off on bike trails, visit fabulous Romanesque churches.

rooms	2: 1 twin/double, 1 suite for 4.
price	€46-€49.
meals	Dinner with wine, €19.
closed	Rarely.
directions	From Gendarmerie in St Jean d'Angély, D127 NE for Dampierre, 8km. In Antezant, 1st right.

Pierre & Marie-Claude Fallelour
Les Moulins,
17400 Antezant,
Charente-Maritime

tel	+33 (0)5 46 59 94 52
fax	+33 (0)5 46 59 94 52
email	marie-claude.fallelour@club-internet.fr

Map 9 Entry 419

Poitou – Charentes

Les Hortensias

Behind its modest, wisteria-covered mask, this 17th-century former wine-grower's house hides a very pretty face and a magnificent garden that flows through orchard to trimmed topiary to potager with blackcurrants for delicious sorbet. Soft duck-egg colours and rich trimmings make it a warm and safe haven. Light, airy bedrooms are immaculate, one with original stone sink, another with pink décor, all with luxurious bathrooms. Your sweet hosts, retired from jobs in agriculture and tourism, have given their all to make it perfect: look at Madame's paintings on the stairwell. Amazing value.

rooms	3: 2 doubles, 1 suite for 4.
price	€52-€58.
meals	Dinner with wine, €22.
closed	Rarely.
directions	From A10 exit 34 on D739 to Tonnay Boutonne; left D114 to Archingeay; left for Les Nouillers; house just after turning, with hydrangea at door.

M-Thérèse & J-Pierre Jacques
Les Hortensias, 16 rue des Sablières,
17380 Archingeay,
Charente-Maritime

tel	+33 (0)5 46 97 85 70
fax	+33 (0)5 46 97 61 89
email	jpmt.jacques@wanadoo.fr
web	www.gite-prop.com/17/5114/

Map 8 Entry 420

Poitou – Charentes

Habitation Léonie

Between the rugged Atlantic coastline and the salty marshes of the Marenne, oyster huts line the shores in a kaleidoscope of colours. Bronzed bodies jet-ski, tinny fishing boats glisten on the water. Your French Algerian host lives by the tides, his passion reflected in the stormy colour schemes inside: seagull-grey and sandy beige teamed with whitewashed woodwork. The chalet-style rooms, each with their own perfect front garden and immaculate bathroom, are separated by sails. Madame gives tennis and dance lessons, Monsieur's breakfasts are a must… before you swan off to the sparkling family-happy pool.

rooms	7: 3 doubles, 4 family suites.
price	€75-€115.
meals	Restaurant 1km.
closed	Never.
directions	A10 south to Saintes; D728 to Marennes; on to Ile d'Oléron; follow D734 to St Pierre d'Oléron; just after town hamlet of St Giles; 1st right, signed.

Jean-Jacques & Bernadette Mazoyer
Habitation Léonie, 5 rue du Moulin, Bois Fleury, 17310 St Pierre d'Oléron, Charente-Maritime
tel +33 (0)5 46 36 88 42
fax +33 (0)5 46 36 88 42
email jean-jacques-mazoyer@wanadoo.fr
web www.oleron.org/habitation-leonie/

Map 8 Entry 421

Poitou – Charentes

La Jaquetterie

Arrive at La Jaquetterie and step back in time: the old virtues of having time for people and living at a gentler pace are here in this well-furnished, old-fashioned house, and it is so comfortable. These kindly farmers are really worth getting to know: Madame keeps a good home-produced table; Monsieur organises outings to distilleries and quarries; both enjoy their guests, especially those who help catch escaping rabbits. Great old armoires loom in the bedrooms, lace covers lovely antique sleigh beds, and one of the bathrooms is highly modern-smart. An authentic country experience with genuinely good, kind people.

rooms	2: 1 triple, 1 suite for 2-4.
price	€47. €65 for 3. €80 for 4.
meals	Dinner with wine, €17.
closed	Rarely.
directions	From A10 exit Saintes N137 for Rochefort & La Rochelle, 11km; D119 to Plassay. House on left on entering village.

Michelle & Jacques Louradour
La Jaquetterie,
17250 Plassay,
Charente-Maritime
tel +33 (0)5 46 93 91 88
fax +33 (0)5 46 93 48 09
email louradour-denis@aviva-assurances.com

Map 8 Entry 422

Poitou – Charentes

Le Moulin de la Quine

A totally French house and a thoroughly English couple. Jenny gardens and writes, with pleasure; John builds his boat for crossing the Atlantic, with dedication; together they have caringly restored their Charentais farmhouse and delight in creating a welcoming atmosphere. Feel free to go your own way, too: you have a separate guest entrance. The beautifully landscaped garden with its pretty windmill (let separately) and croquet lawn has an English feel – but the 'sense of place' remains unmistakably French. And St Savinien is a painter's delight – this really is a lovely part of the country.

rooms	2: 1 double, 1 family for 3-4.
price	€44-€52.
meals	Dinner with wine, €19.
closed	Christmas.
directions	From St Savinien bridge D114 along river, under railway, left D124 for Bords 2km; 2nd left after Le Pontreau sign; 200m on right.

John & Jenny Elmes
Le Moulin de la Quine,
17350 St Savinien,
Charente-Maritime
tel   +33 (0)5 46 90 19 31
fax   +33 (0)5 46 90 19 31
email   elmes@club-internet.fr
web   www.laquine.co.uk

Map 8 Entry 423

Poitou – Charentes

Château Mouillepied

A truly delightful pair, Martine and Pierre rescued Mouillepied ('wet feet'; today's stream-fed moat is mostly dry) and are restoring house and grounds. Large airy bedrooms are charming and uncluttered, with original wooden floors or new boards suitably wide; walls are white, curtains cotton. Breakfast – stewed fruit, croissants, all the coffee or tea you'd like – is in the vast orangery overlooking the gardens. Seek out the fascinating old laundry in the grounds, the pigeon house, bread oven and wine store, pick up a fishing licence at the bakery, stroll along the banks of the Charente. Deeply atmospheric.

rooms	8: 4 doubles, 3 triples, 1 suite for 4.
price	€62-€94.
meals	Occasional dinner. Wine €4.50. Restaurant 2km.
closed	Rarely.
directions	From A10 exit 35 at Saintes; N137 to Rochefort, right to Ecurat D119. Right for Taillebourg D236; D127 to Saint James; right to Saintes D128, right after 300m, signed.

Martine & Pierre Clément
Château Mouillepied,
17350 Port d'Envaux,
Charente-Maritime
tel   +33 (0)5 46 90 49 88
fax   +33 (0)5 46 90 36 91
email   info@chateaumouillepied.com
web   www.chateaumouillepied.com

Map 8 Entry 424

Poitou – Charentes

Le Clos du Plantis

Your hostess brazenly indulges her passion for old buildings in this area of vast architectural wealth. She'll teach you stone wall restoration, the intricacies of the Romanesque style or how to garden beautifully – the creamy local stone is a perfect foil for flowers and the veg is organic. In the old cognac press, the cool, light garden bedrooms are big and uncluttered, effective in their pale colours with a few well-chosen pieces each and exquisite bathrooms. Cognac nearby, the island beaches not too far and such a delightful, intelligent couple, full of fun and sparkle, make this a very special place to stay.

rooms	3: 2 doubles, 1 family suite.
price	€52–€58. Suite €94.
meals	Restaurants 1-2km.
closed	Rarely.
directions	From A10 exit St Jean d'Angély to Matha/Cognac. At Matha, direction Cognac (not Sonnac); follow signs for 'Le Clos du Plantis'. Next hamlet, Le Goulet. Signed.

Frédérique Thill-Toussaint
Le Clos du Plantis,
1 rue du Pont, Le Goulet,
17160 Sonnac,
Charente-Maritime
tel +33 (0)5 46 25 07 91
mobile +33 (0)6 81 99 07 98
email auplantis@wanadoo.fr
web www.auplantis.com

Map 9 Entry 425

Poitou – Charentes

La Rotonde

Stupendously confident, this city mansion seems to ride the whole rich story of lovely old Saintes from its Roman glory days. Soft blue river light hovers into high bourgeois rooms to stroke the warm panelling, marble fireplaces, perfect parquet. The Rougers love renovating their guest house. Marie-Laure, calm and talented, has her own sensitive way with classic French furnishings: appropriately grand, they are feminine yet not frilly, rich yet gentle, just ornate enough. Superb linen and bathrooms, too, little extras and always that elegance.

rooms	7: 4 doubles, 1 twin, 2 studios for 2.
price	€84–€100.
meals	Restaurants in town centre.
closed	Rarely.
directions	A10 exit Saintes; straight ahead to Charente river.

Marie-Laure Rouger
La Rotonde,
2 Rue Monconseil,
17100 Saintes,
Charente-Maritime
tel +33 (0)5 46 74 74 44
fax +33 (0)5 46 74 74 45
email laure@larotonde-saintes.com
web www.larotonde-saintes.com

Map 8 Entry 426

Poitou – Charentes

Les Hauts de Font Moure

The grand house lords it over a tiny hamlet surrounded by walking country and tantalising views. Dinah is English and tends a beautiful garden; Claude's ravishing collection of ornaments and antiques is on display in every room. Inside all is serenity and space; big bedrooms, one of which has a fabulous ormolu wardrobe, are magnificently decorated and scattered with oriental rugs; bathrooms are terrific. Look at the floor tiles in the salon: they were left to dry outside in the woods where they collected imprints of the feet of badgers and birds, before being laid in a church. Delicious pool, too.

rooms	4: 2 doubles, 1 twin, 1 family suite.
price	€66–€73. Family suite €83.
meals	Dinner with wine, €25.
closed	Occasionally.
directions	From A10 exit 37 for Mirambeau. At r'bout pass 'Marché U'; D254 1st right to St Georges des Agoûts; right at church D146; 1st junc. left & follow Chambres d'Hôtes signs.

Dinah & Claude Teulet
Les Hauts de Font Moure,
17150 St Georges des Agoûts,
Charente-Maritime

tel	+33 (0)5 46 86 04 41
fax	+33 (0)5 46 49 67 18
email	cteulet@aol.com
web	www.fontmoure.com

Map 8   Entry 427

Poitou – Charentes

La Font Bétou

Both former market researchers, Londoner Gordon and Parisienne Laure thoroughly enjoy people. Laure cooks because she loves it and breakfast is a spread. The two big, spotlessly clean rooms in the annexe are pretty and welcoming with tea-making stuff and plenty of stone and wood. Sit by the hosts' sitting-room fire or by the pool; the kitchen door is always open. Once a modest inn for train travellers, the house still overlooks the old station, now another house, and there's a frog-filled pond behind. As the owners say, this is not a place that pretends to be anything, it just is. *Minimum stay four nights July/Aug.*

rooms	2: 1 split-level double, 1 twin, each with sitting space downstairs.
price	€60.
meals	Dinner with wine, €25.
closed	January–February.
directions	N10 S; exit Montlieu-la-Garde; D730 for Montguyon. 1km after Orignolles, right to house, signed.

Laure Tarrou & Gordon Flude
La Font Bétou,
17210 Orignolles,
Charente-Maritime

tel	+33 (0)5 46 04 02 52
fax	+33 (0)5 46 04 02 52
email	laure.tarrou@tiscali.fr
web	www.fontbetou.com

Map 9   Entry 428

Poitou – Charentes

La Cochère

Cool off by the lush pool, listen to the clacking and cheering of summer Sundays' boules. Kathy, John, four children and Bob the St Bernard are the proud protectors of this dreamlike place, where the long checked table groans with fresh compôtes, croissants and coffee at breakfast and the tranquil garden – John's delight – is sprinkled with lanterns at dusk. In the old coach house, antique iron beds wear floral quilts and crisp linen, and pretty stone peeps through timeworn render. Who would not fall for this heart-warming blend of sophistication and rusticity in a sleepy farming village?

rooms	4: 2 doubles, 1 twin. Studio: 1 triple (May-Sept only).
price	€55.
meals	Dinner with wine, €25.
closed	Christmas.
directions	A10 to Poitiers; RN10 S from Poitiers; 10km S of exit for Ruffec leave N10 for Salles de Villefagnan on D27; in centre of village by Salles des Fêtes, right to Villefagnan; house after 200m on right.

John & Kathy Anderson
La Cochère,
Le Bourg,
16700 Salles de Villefagnan,
Charente
tel   +33 (0)5 45 30 34 60
email   la.cochere@wanadoo.fr
web   www.lacochere.com

Map 9 Entry 429

Poitou – Charentes

La Fontaine des Arts

Along the narrow street in the bustling town, through the heavy oak gates, under the ancient arch, is a cottage by the Charente with a little boat for trips upriver. Marie-France, beautifully coiffed, combines the glamour of the city with the warmth of a homely country hostess: guests love her. Breakfast in the conservatory alongside Gérard's easel and piano, or in the courtyard by the prettily fountain'd pool. Décor is quintessential French: shiny gold taps, striped and flowered walls, a white dressing table, a shared kitchenette – and a surprising open-gallery bathroom in the double. Great for summer.

rooms	3: 1 double, 1 twin, 1 triple.
price	€59-€66.
meals	Restaurant within walking distance. Guest kitchen.
closed	Rarely.
directions	RN10 between Angoulême & Poitiers, exit Mansle; towards centre ville; between tourist office & L'Hotel Beau Rivage straight on to number 13.

Marie-France Pagano
La Fontaine des Arts,
13 rue du Temple,
16230 Mansle, Charente
tel   +33 (0)5 45 69 13 56
fax   +33 (0)5 45 69 48 66
mobile   +33 (0)6 12 52 39 86
email   mfpagano@wanadoo.fr

Map 9 Entry 430

Lesterie

Visiting children are welcome to share the young residents' playhouse and toys. This English farming family with three friendly dogs lives in a roadside country house with many original delights. Balconies look out onto parkland and Stephen's crops, while a sweeping staircase leads to simple bedrooms and bathrooms. Two are next to the family's, two are in a dormitory-style attic. Your hosts are busy but happy to sit round the candlelit table for companionable dinners. For evenings, a little guest sitting room in soft pinks and greens, for summer, a garden with sunloungers dotted under treees.

rooms	4: 2 doubles, 1 twin; 1 double with shower & sharing wc.
price	€45.
meals	Dinner with wine, €18.
closed	Rarely.
directions	From Confolens, D948 for Limoges for 4km; sign on road.

Stephen & Polly Hoare
Lesterie,
Saint Maurice des Lions,
16500 Confolens, Charente

tel   +33 (0)5 45 84 18 33
fax   +33 (0)5 45 84 01 45
email   polly.hoare@libertysurf.fr
web   www.lesterie.com

Map 9 Entry 431

Le Pit

What an interesting, unexpected place – heaven for walkers. And children, thanks to llamas, wallabies and deer. Pretty, fresh bedrooms are in a converted outbuilding, the larger one overlooking the lake. Dinner is unusual (ostrich pâté perhaps) and delicious, preceded by a chilled glass of homemade *pineau des Charentes*. Alex left hectic London for French farming with a difference (and a thriving farm shop); Hélène loves pergolas, and there are plenty of little corners of rustic charm and colour from which to enjoy the fascinating surroundings. Fun and hugely welcoming.

rooms	2: 1 triple, 1 quadruple.
price	€48. Triple €70. Quadruple €90.
meals	Dinner with wine, €20.
closed	Rarely.
directions	From Poitiers D741 S for Confolens 50km. 10km after Pressac, left on D168 for St Germain de Confolens; sign after 2km.

Alex & Hélène Everitt
Le Pit,
Lessac, 16500 Confolens,
Charente

tel   +33 (0)5 45 84 27 65
fax   +33 (0)5 45 85 41 34
mobile   +33 (0)6 82 30 74 98
email   everitt16@aol.com

Map 9 Entry 432

Poitou – Charentes

La Grenouille

Do look up as you enter the guest house in the old stables: the hall ceiling is marvellous. Breakfast is served here if it isn't fine enough to sit outside. Rooms are good too: white paint and exposed stone make a stunning setting for fine antiques and old beds fitted with new mattresses. Madame, busy breeding horses (gorgeous foals in summer), is full of smiles and always has time to help arrange cognac-distillery visits or invite you to relax in a hammock after a bit of badminton. Monsieur may offer a local aperitif to guests of an evening. A peaceful wooded spot in a very special corner of France.

rooms	2: 1 double, 1 twin.
price	€52.
meals	Restaurants at St Adjutory.
closed	Rarely.
directions	From Angoulême, N141 to La Rochefoucauld; right at 3rd traffic light on D162 to St Adjutory; in village 2nd right & follow signs.

Sylviane & Vincent Casper
La Grenouille,
16310 St Adjutory,
Charente
tel +33 (0)5 45 62 00 34
fax +33 (0)5 45 63 06 41
email sylviane.casper@wanadoo.fr
web www.saint-a.com

Map 9 Entry 433

Poitou – Charentes

Le Chiron

There's an old-fashioned, well-lived-in, much-loved air to this interesting house. The bedrooms have parquet floors, old-style wallpapers, pretty old beds with new mattresses; bathrooms have been modernised. Madame's regional cooking is highly appreciated and dinner is worth coming back for. A conservatory has been built to seat more people round a bigger table where your hosts stay and chat if not too busy serving you. They'll also show you the fascinating old cognac still and on winter weekends you may be able to help with the distilling process. It's a blissful spot, too. *Camping possible. Mobile homes available.*

rooms	6: 2 doubles, 1 twin, 2 triples, 1 family suite for 4.
price	€45. Suite €75.
meals	Dinner with wine, €16.
closed	Rarely.
directions	From A10 Pons exit D700 for Barbezieux Archiac. After Echebrune D148 (1st left) for Lonzac-Celles; right D151 & follow signs.

Micheline & Jacky Chainier
Le Chiron,
16130 Salles d'Angles,
Charente
tel +33 (0)5 45 83 72 79
fax +33 (0)5 45 83 64 80
email mchainier@voila.fr

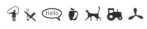

Map 9 Entry 434

Les Collinauds

Some of the most famous Cognac houses in the region use Roland and Geneviève's grapes. After a glass of freshly squeezed grape juice at breakfast, a walk along the tiny white paths between the vines is a blissfully simple start to the day. Les Collinauds is imposing but its owners are as gentle and uncomplicated as the surrounding countryside. Madame is natural and easy, Monsieur dark-eyed with a huge sunny smile. Wood, toile de Jouy and beeswax in the bedrooms; in the dining room, a fantastic heirloom sideboard, a trophy to generations of *chasseurs*; in the garden, an immaculate pool.

rooms	4: 2 doubles, 1 triple, 1 family room for 4.
price	€45.
meals	Restaurants 2-8km.
closed	Never.
directions	From Barbezieux, D1 to Lignières, right on D699 to Banneuil. Signed on right after 5km.

Geneviève & Roland Matignon
Les Collinauds,
16130 Lignières-Sonneville,
Charente
tel   +33 (0)5 45 80 51 23
fax   +33 (0)5 45 80 51 23
email   matignon.les-collinauds@wanadoo.fr
web   www.les-collinauds-charente.com

Map 9 Entry 435

Le Chatelard

This is a gem of a place to stay, both grand and intimate. Béatrice inherited the exquisitely French neo-gothic château and she lovingly protects it from the worst of modernisation (though the hurricane took its toll and trees have had to be replanted). Sleep between old linen sheets, sit in handsome old chairs and be charmed by a bedroom in a tower. The sitting room has that unusual quirk, a window over the fireplace, the dining room a panelled ceiling studded with plates. Béatrice, a teacher, and Christopher, a lecturer in philosophy, are interesting, cultured hosts who enjoy eating with their guests.

rooms	4: 2 doubles, one with separate wc; 1 twin, 1 family suite, each with separate wc.
price	€50-€60.
meals	Dinner with wine, €20.
closed	Rarely.
directions	From A10 exit 36 to Pons, Archiac & Barbezieux; D731 for Chalais 12km. After Passirac, 1st right at roadside cross; up leafy drive.

Béatrice de Castelbajac &
Christopher Macann
Le Chatelard,
Passirac, 16480 Brossac, Charente
tel   +33 (0)5 45 98 71 03
fax   +33 (0)5 45 98 71 03
email   c.macann@wanadoo.fr
web   www.lechatelard.tk

Map 9 Entry 436

Poitou – Charentes

Château de Lerse

François abandoned the sea and Laurie
the law to return to this unspoilt land
of rolling hills and Romanesque chapels.
The château gateway, with its stone
scallop of St Jacques de Compostelle,
tells of medieval pilgrims and timeless
hospitality. Sail down stone stairs to a
magnificent drawing and dining room
under the benevolent eye of family
portraits and top-drawer connections.
François, informal and sociable, conjures
delicious dinners and joins you for a
goblet or two. Later, in traditional
bedrooms softened by Laurie's sure
touch, drift away as muslin stirs in the
soft night air.

rooms	3: 1 double, 2 triples.
price	€80–€100.
meals	Dinner with wine, €25.
closed	October-April.
directions	From Angoulême, N10 south; 10km after Angoulême, exit to Blanzac; D10 for 6km, château on left.

François Lafargue
Château de Lerse,
16250 Perignac,
Charente

tel	+33 (0)5 45 60 32 81
fax	+33 (0)5 45 62 30 98
email	fl.lafargue@wanadoo.fr
web	www.chateaudelerse.com

Map 9 Entry 437

Aquitaine

Aquitaine

Cantemerle

From Brazil, New Zealand, the New Hebrides, the Sahara, Michèle came home to the hacienda-style house built when her family's old wine-growing farm crumbled away. The imitation zebra skins in one living room fit strangely well with the memorabilia and African sculptures. Bedrooms are good traditional, with fine views across oceans of vines. It is relaxed and exotic, the gardens support a fabulous collection of trees and journalist Michèle, lively and fun, knows all there is to know about this area. Their own wine comes with dinner and the nearby ferry comes from Blaye and Royan. *Minimum stay two nights.*

rooms	2: 1 double, 1 twin.
price	€65-€70.
meals	Restaurant 1km.
closed	Rarely.
directions	From Bordeaux bypass exit 7 on D1 to Castelnau; N215 through St Laurent; 4km, D104 to Vertheuil; abbey on right, over level crossing, house 1km on left.

Michèle Tardat
Cantemerle,
9 rue des Châtaigniers,
33180 Vertheuil Médoc, Gironde
tel +33 (0)5 56 41 96 24
fax +33 (0)5 56 41 96 24
email micheletardat@tele2.fr
web www.bbfrance.com/tardat.html

Map 8 Entry 438

Aquitaine

Domaine les Sapins

You couldn't be deeper into wine country than this. Alain is a wine broker and although he doesn't bring his work home, he could probably be persuaded to talk wine of an evening. Natalie's father was born in this house and it is very much a family home, despite its size. Alain and Natalie enjoy having an aperitif and a chat with their guests so they can plan the most congenial seating arrangement at dinner. The house is set back from the village road (ask for one of the quieter rooms) in a large garden with a big and breathtaking pool: jets can be set so it feels like swimming against the current.

rooms	6: 5 twins/doubles, 1 suite for 4.
price	€58-€78. Suite €148.
meals	Dinner €29. Wine from €10.
closed	Rarely.
directions	From Bordeaux A630 exit 7; D1 for Le Verdon sur Soulac; skirt around Castelnau; N215 for St Laurent 1km to Bouqueyran. Sign on left.

Alain & Natalie Genestine
Domaine les Sapins,
62 ave du Médoc,
33480 Moulis en Médoc, Gironde
tel +33 (0)5 56 58 18 26
fax +33 (0)5 56 58 28 45
email domaine-les-sapins@wanadoo.fr
web www.domaine-les-sapins.com

Map 8 Entry 439

Aquitaine

Château de la Grave

Come for three sweeping bedrooms, two balconies with vineyard views, a stone entrance hall — and a wrought-iron terrace for a glass of the Bassereaus' own dry white semillon. They are a hard-working and confident young couple in an 18th-century château with too much good taste to make it sumptuous — thank heavens! It is relaxed and easy — even busy — with three children, decorative bantams all over the garden and deer in the woods. Breakfast is on the terrace, wine-tasting in the magnificent *salle de dégustation*. The small pool is for evening dippers rather than sun-worshippers. Good value.

rooms	3: 1 double, 1 triple, 1 family room for 4.
price	€66–€80. Family room €110.
meals	Choice of restaurants in Bourg.
closed	February & 2 weeks in August.
directions	From A10 exit 40a or 40b through St André de Cubzac; D669 through Bourg for Blaye; quickly right D251 for Berson for 1km; sign on right, up lane.

M & Mme Bassereau
Château de la Grave,
33710 Bourg sur Gironde,
Gironde

tel	+33 (0)5 57 68 41 49
fax	+33 (0)5 57 68 49 26
email	reservation@chateaudelagrave.com
web	www.chateaudelagrave.com

Map 8 Entry 440

Aquitaine

83 rue de Patay

Martine may be new to B&B but she's used to making guests feel welcome: she owns a restaurant in the middle of the old town. Le Loup has been serving local specialities since 1932: you will probably want to pay a visit. This old stone townhouse is a welcome retreat after days visiting the city or those renowned vineyards. Martine has given it a light modern touch which works well. Your bedroom is approached up a curved stone staircase and you have the floor to yourselves. It overlooks a small courtyard garden and has a desk and other pieces stencilled by a friend.

rooms	1 twin/double.
price	€65.
meals	Madame's restaurant near Cathedral.
closed	Rarely.
directions	Take Les Boulevards to Barrière de Pessac; 100m, 1st right, right again onto Rue de Patay.

Martine Peiffer
83 rue de Patay,
33000 Bordeaux,
Gironde

tel	+33 (0)5 56 99 41 74
mobile	+33 (0)6 19 81 22 81
email	mpeifferma95@numericable.fr

Map 8 Entry 441

Aquitaine

Château Lestange

We are filled with admiration for Anne-Marie, who works so hard to keep this proud old place and its vineyards afloat. Built in 1645, it was 'modernised' after the Revolution, but the faded Louis XV paintwork and imperfect tiles merely add to its charm. Beautiful wooden floors, panelled walls and old furniture create a well lived-in feel, and the very private family suites, furnished with mirrors and portraits Anne-Marie is still unearthing from the attic, are capacious. Bathrooms are incongruously modern. Breakfast in a vast room beneath a grand mirror; stroll to dinner in the restaurant down the road.

rooms	2 family suites for 3.
price	€80-€85. €95-€100 for 3.
meals	Restaurant in village.
closed	Rarely.
directions	From Bordeaux take Rocade (ring-road) exit 22; after 6km left at r'bout to Quinsac; on left, signed.

Anne-Marie Charmet
Château Lestange,
33360 Quinsac,
Gironde
tel   +33 (0)8 77 96 49 26
fax   +33 (0)5 56 20 86 14
email charmet@chateau-lestange.com
web   www.chateau-lestange.com

Map 8 Entry 442

Aquitaine

Château Monlot

If you appreciate good wine you will enjoy this coolly restrained, very beautiful manor among the vines, just a mile from St Émilion. It has been in the family for nine generations, though the owners leave their delightful nephew and relaxed manager to look after you. You will almost certainly be invited to taste the goods in the cellars. Charming bedrooms, with plain sandstone or painted walls and sober antiques, offer space, comfort and tranquillity and the shrubby garden has an arch of trees that gives dappled shade as you walk towards the distant statue. Superb wines, good people, relaxed place.

rooms	5: 3 doubles, 1 twin, 1 suite.
price	€70-€120.
meals	Restaurants 2km. Guest kitchen.
closed	Rarely.
directions	From A10 exit St André de Cubzac through Libourne for Bergerac; 3km after Bigaroux left D234E for St Laurent; right before railway for St Hippolyte; house on left.

Bernard & Béatrice Rivals
Château Monlot,
St Hippolyte,
33330 St Émilion, Gironde
tel   +33 (0)5 57 74 49 47
fax   +33 (0)5 57 24 62 33
email mussetrivals@chateaumonlot.com
web   www.chateaumonlot.com

Map 9 Entry 443

Château Millaud-Montlabert

Tradition has deep, proud roots here. Monsieur is a kind and gentle man, his big farmhouse has stood for three centuries, his vines, now tended by the next generation, are mature, his wine superb; the lovely linen, patchwork and lace are family heirlooms and the family has a strong, lively presence. The stone-walled, old-furnished bedrooms (and small bathrooms) have patchwork quilts and immaculate linen, though great beams and attic ceilings reduce your space. You share a guest living room and kitchen – ideal if you're daunted by Saint Émilion's prices. Huge breakfasts are served in the cosy family dining room.

rooms	5: 2 doubles, 2 twins, 1 triple.
price	€55-€60. Triple €75.
meals	Auberge 300m. Kitchen available.
closed	15 January-15 February.
directions	From Libourne D243 for St Émilion; pass Château Girard Bassail on right; 3km before St Émilion left D245 towards Pomerol; house 300m on right.

Claude Brieux
Château Millaud-Montlabert,
33330 St Émilion,
Gironde
tel   +33 (0)5 57 24 71 85
fax   +33 (0)5 57 24 62 78

Map 9 Entry 444

Le Refuge du Peintre

Monsieur has lived all round the world and there are quantities of fascinating souvenirs to tell the tale but this immaculate and comfortable 1750s farmhouse was his family holiday home for years. Madame, pleasant and houseproud, is an artist who used to be a teacher; their combined conversation is stimulating. She does much to please her guests and may serve you delectable walnut cake on hand-painted plates in a dazzling white room. Beautiful bedrooms, simple yet not stark, have white or clean stone walls, the suite has an opulent sunken bath, the garden is rich with roses, the peace is a balm. *Min. stay two nights.*

rooms	2: 1 twin/double, 1 suite for 2-4.
price	€59. Suite €90-€120.
meals	Auberge 300m.
closed	Rarely.
directions	From D670, Bayonne-Toulouse; at Rauzan, D231 direction Frontenac; Right after 2km, D140 to Bellefond.

France Prat
Le Refuge du Peintre,
3 chemin de Courbestey, Lavagnac,
33350 Ste Terre, Gironde
tel   +33 (0)5 57 47 13 74
mobile   +33 (0)6 81 62 42 99
email   france.prat@wanadoo.fr
web   perso.wanadoo.fr/france.prat

Map 9 Entry 445

Aquitaine

Domaine de Barrouil

As befits its calling, this old winegrower's stands in a sea of vines whose liquid fruits you will taste and over which may wander re-enactment battlecries or summer fireworks. Inside this colourful and immaculate house, green, cream and red set off gilt-framed mirrors and bright modern bathrooms. Your hosts believe in big thick towels too. They have lived in French Guiana so Madame's classic French dinners, served in the beautifully tiled dining room, may bring echoes of more exotic lands. She is charming and chatty, a former English teacher; he is more shy but most interesting.

rooms	4: 2 doubles, 1 twin, 1 family suite for 4.
price	€50-€80.
meals	Dinner with wine, €23.
closed	Rarely.
directions	From A10 exit St André de Cubzac to Libourne Bergerac. At Castillon, D17 south for 8kms; at D126 crossroad, turn left; 1st house on the left.

Annie & Michel Ehrsam
Domaine de Barrouil,
Bossugan,
33350 Castillon La Bataille,
Gironde
tel	+33 (0)5 57 40 59 12
fax	+33 (0)5 57 40 59 12
email	info@barrouil.com
web	www.barrouil.com

Map 9 Entry 446

Aquitaine

Château de Carbonneau

Big château bedrooms done in safe pastels over classic dados, a fine old bed in the beige room, huge bathrooms done with rich tiles — here is a quiet, self-assured family house where quality is natural, history stalks and there's plenty of space for four young Ferrières and a dozen guests. Visit Wilfred's winery and taste the talent handed down by his forebears. Jacquie, a relaxed dynamic New Zealander, does all the interior stuff, wields a canny paintbrush and has created a guest sitting room of comfortable furniture, old family pieces and modern lampshades. They breed gorgeous Bearnaise dogs.

rooms	5: 1 double, 2 twins/doubles, 1 twin, 1 suite.
price	€75-€95.
meals	Dinner €22. Wine €4.70-€6.60.
closed	December-February.
directions	D936 to Castillion la Bataille-Bergerac; from Réaux, right to Gensac, Pessac; at r'bout, D18 to Ste Foy le Gde; 2km on right.

Wilfred & Jacquie
Franc de Ferrière
Château de Carbonneau,
33890 Pessac sur Dordogne,
Gironde
tel	+33 (0)5 57 47 46 46
fax	+33 (0)5 57 47 42 26
email	carbonneau@wanadoo.fr
web	www.chateau-carbonneau.com

Map 9 Entry 447

Aquitaine

La Tuilerie

Such a special place. Antoine, a cookery teacher, loves to whip up feasts in his sensational kitchen and offer good wines from his 'trade contacts'. Dinner is at a giant round table, made from an outsize wine barrel, in a 19th-century barn with a cantilevered gallery and a superb two-storey fireplace; good quality rooms are interestingly different. Children are spoilt: sandpit, climbing frame, huge shallow-ended pool, horses to feed, three Laborde children to play with. Canoeing, trips on the lovely Canal du Midi, fishing, riding, cycling are all possible. Readers write reams of praise.

rooms	4: 2 doubles, 1 triple, 1 twin.
price	€63.
meals	Dinner with wine, €27.
closed	Rarely.
directions	From A62 exit 4 onto D9; left for Bazas-Grignols; over m'way bridge; 1st left, 250m after bridge; follow signs Chambres d'Hôtes 3km.

Claire & Antoine Laborde
La Tuilerie,
33190 Noaillac,
Gironde
tel	+33 (0)5 56 71 05 51
fax	+33 (0)5 56 71 05 51
email	claire.laborde@libertysurf.fr
web	www.latuilerie33.com

Map 9 Entry 448

Aquitaine

Maison Cameleyre

Tall pines guard the clearing, tall timbers support the 300-year-old buildings in a world of vertical wood on horizontal green, with ancient oaks for shade and luscious mushrooms. Emma and Thierry's barn conversion is full of peace and natural country finishes (the farmhouse is their space) and has pride of place: lovely big rooms, soft textures, gentle light. Emma, a fitness trainer, loves cooking and gives Aga demos; do book your dinner. They run de-stress weekends too – super people. An ideal country retreat for city-mad adults and families. *Ask about courses in surfing, sailing & cookery.*

rooms	3 twins/doubles.
price	€62.
meals	Dinner with wine, €18.
closed	Mid December-January.
directions	N10 Bordeaux & Bayonne exit 15 for Escource; at r'bout D44 to village; D63 for Mézos; house in Cameleyre on right, after 3km sign at entrance.

Emma & Thierry Bernabeu
Maison Cameleyre,
Quartier Cameleyre,
40210 Escource, Landes
tel	+33 (0)5 58 04 22 02
fax	+33 (0)5 58 04 22 04
email	tbernabe@club-internet.fr
web	www.cameleyre.com

Map 13 Entry 449

Aquitaine

Moulin Vieux

A house to satisfy your soul: lost in a forest, its windows open onto endless oaks and pines with mere and river beyond. Madame, a lovable person, joins you in the warm conservatory for deliciously organic meals. Bedrooms are small and simply furnished with a touch of Liliane's son's artistry in a marbled or frescoed wall; colours are harmonious, shower rooms basic. In the salon: a trompe l'oeil of the Enchanted Forest, a piano and masses of books, in the huge kitchen an open fire. The setting is tremendous and springtime walks yield birdsong and wildflower treasures.

rooms	3: 1 double, 1 twin, 1 family room.
price	€32–€43.
meals	Dinner with wine, €16.
closed	Rarely.
directions	From Mont de Marsan N134 NW to Garein; left D57 for Ygos & Tartas; follow signs: 1km of lane to house.

Mme Liliane Jehl
Moulin Vieux,
40420 Garein,
Landes

| tel | +33 (0)5 58 51 61 43 |
| fax | +33 (0)5 58 51 61 43 |

Map 13   Entry 450

Aquitaine

Domaine d'Agès

In an intriguing mixture of typical brickwork and colonial verandas, this noble manor stands among fabulous old hardwoods and acres of pines. Nature rejoices, cranes fly overhead, thoroughbreds grace the paddock (the Hayes breed horses), hens range free and Madame deploys boundless energy to ply you with exquisite food from the potager, myriad teas, lovely antique-filled, sweet-coloured bedrooms (with her own framed embroidery): she adores entertaining. Monsieur smiles, while teenage Jonathan is all discretion. A huge open fire, baby grand piano and panelled salon tell it perfectly.

rooms	3: 1 double, 1 twin, 1 suite for 2.
price	€60–€80.
meals	Dinner with wine, €25.
closed	Rarely.
directions	N10 Bordeaux & Bayonne exit Morcenx; D38 for Mont de Marsan; in Ygos right to Ousse Suzan; in Ousse pass 'Chez Jojo'; signposted Chambres d'Hôtes; up lane; Domaine 1.5km on left.

Élisabeth Haye
Domaine d'Agès,
40110 Ousse Suzan,
Landes

tel	+33 (0)5 58 51 82 28
fax	+33 (0)5 58 51 82 29
email	haye.eeb@wanadoo.fr
web	www.hotelslandes.com

Map 13   Entry 451

Villa Ty Gias

Golfers rejoice! You look down on the 13th hole of the Seignosse Golf Club; ask Monsieur or Madame to join you in a round. Great surfing is almost as close. Light, birdsong and ocean breezes whisper round this Californian villa and its balmy garden with pool so don't be daunted by the residential area or the steep drive. Up and down go the pale wooden decks connecting living spaces and levels, waves of light wash over natural colours, finishes and fabrics that are gentle on the eye and Madame's exotic pieces. She revels in guests' appreciation of their soft, clean-cut rooms and alfresco brunches. Fabulous.

rooms	3: 1 double, 1 twin, 1 suite for 4.
price	€60-€95. Suite €110-€150.
meals	Choice of restaurants nearby.
closed	Rarely.
directions	From A63 exit 10 for St Vincent de Tyrosse & Seignosse; on for Golf 3km; over r'bout, 800m; left into Av. de Morfontaine, 200m, blue house, signposted.

Jean-Luc & Noëllie Annic
Villa Ty Gias,
1 avenue Hilton Head,
40510 Seignosse, Landes
tel   +33 (0)5 58 41 64 29
fax   +33 (0)5 58 41 64 29
email tygias@wanadoo.fr
web   perso.wanadoo.fr/tygias

Map 13 Entry 452

Château de Bezincam

An atmosphere of dream-like tranquillity wafts over this grand and appealing old French country house, with its elegant doors and polished oak floors. Just outside the park gates is the beautiful River Adour, abundant in bird and wildlife – every ten years or so it comes and kisses the terrace steps. Two of the gilt-mirrored bedrooms overlook the water and a great spread of meadows where animals graze. There is a vast choice for 'flexitime' breakfast on the terrace or in the rustic-chic dining room. Madame, an energetic and interesting hostess, was a publisher in Paris for many years.

rooms	3: 2 doubles, 1 triple.
price	€60-€70.
meals	Choice of restaurants 2-5km.
closed	Rarely.
directions	From A63 exit 8 to St Geours de Maremne; D17 S for 5km to Saubusse; right just before bridge; château 600m on right.

Claude Dourlet
Château de Bezincam,
600 Quai de Bezincam,
Saubusse les Bains,
40180 Dax, Landes
tel   +33 (0)5 58 57 70 27
fax   +33 (0)5 58 57 70 27
email dourlet.bezincam@tiscali.fr

Map 13 Entry 453

Aquitaine

Maison Capcazal de Pachioü

Fall asleep by a crackling fire, wake to the clucking of the hens. Be moved by this house, with original panelling (1610) and contents accumulated by the family for 14 generations. Portraits from the 17th century onwards, spectacular bedrooms with canopied antique beds, strong colours, luscious armoires, embroidered linen. One luminous bathroom has a marble-topped washstand. Dining room and salon are handsome: twin grandfather clocks, terracotta tiles and a huge stone fireplace. François has stepped into his mother's shoes seamlessly, and does brilliant *table d'hôtes*. Exceptional.

rooms	4 doubles.
price	€50–€70.
meals	Dinner with wine, €20.
closed	Rarely.
directions	From Dax D947 for Pau & Orthez; from r'bout at end of town on for 10km; at crossroads on D947 ignore sign for Mimbaste; take next right C16; follow discreet yellow signs for 1km.

François Dufourcet-Alberca
Maison Capcazal de Pachioü,
40350 Mimbaste,
Landes
tel   +33 (0)5 58 55 30 54
fax   +33 (0)5 58 55 30 54

Map 13 Entry 454

Aquitaine

Château de Monbet

The miniature château in its secluded setting rejoices in a fine chestnut staircase, a veranda paved with rare Bidache stone, high ceilings, old prints, a glimpse of the Pyrenees and the call of a peacock. Madame is a gem, gracious and charming – she teaches yoga, paints, is a long-distance walker and a committed vegetarian. Children can roam the 20 hectares of parkland freely – they will love it. The rooms, large and properly decorated, have gorgeous parquet floors and relatively little 'château' furniture. We think the smaller ones give better value.

rooms	2: 1 double, 1 twin.
price	€50–€80.
meals	Restaurant in village 1.3km.
closed	November–March, except by arrangement.
directions	From A10 or A63 exit St Geours de Maremne to Saubusse & Orist. Or, from A64 exit Peyrehorade to Dax. In both cases, 10km to Monbet.

Mme Hubert de Lataillade
Château de Monbet,
40300 St Lon les Mines,
Landes
tel   +33 (0)5 58 57 80 68
fax   +33 (0)5 58 57 89 29
email chateau.de.monbet@wanadoo.fr
web   www.chateaudemonbet.com

Map 13 Entry 455

Aquitaine

Villa Le Goëland

It is lush, lavish, inviting. Dominating the ocean, yards from the beaches of glamorous Biarritz, the only privately owned villa of its kind to have resisted commercial redevelopment has opened its arms to guests. Turrets were added in 1903; Paul's family took possession in 1934; now he and his wife, young, charming, professional, are its inspired guardians and restorers. Be ravished by oak floors, magnificent stairs, tall windows and balconies that go on for ever. Two suites have terraces, beds are king-size, bathrooms are vintage or modern, breakfasts flourish sunshine and *viennoiseries*. Amazing.

rooms	4: 3 doubles, 1 suite for 3.
price	€150–€270.
meals	Restaurant 20m.
closed	November–February.
directions	From place Clemençeau in Biarritz centre follow signs for place Ste Eugénie by Rue Mazagran; after pharmacy 1st right Rue des Goëland. House between antique shop & bar, narrow street.

Paul & Elisabeth Daraignez
Villa Le Goëland,
12 plateau de l'Atalaye,
64200 Biarritz,
Pyrénées-Atlantiques
fax   +33 (0)5 59 22 36 83
mobile   +33 (0)6 87 66 22 19
email   info@villagoeland.com
web   www.villagoeland.com

Map 13   Entry 456

Aquitaine

Bidachuna

Hear the electronic gate click behind you and 29 hectares of forested peace and quiet are yours with their fabulous wildlife. Draw your beautiful curtains next morning and you may see deer feeding; lift your eyes and feast on long, long vistas to the Pyrenean foothills; come down to the earthly feast that is Basque breakfast. Shyly attentive, Isabelle manages all this impeccably and keeps a refined house where everything is polished and gleaming; floors are chestnut, bathrooms marble, family antiques of high quality. A beautifully manicured haven – worth staying several days for serious cossetting.

rooms	3: 2 doubles, 1 twin.
price	€100–€110.
meals	Restaurant 6km.
closed	Occasionally.
directions	From Biarritz railway station to Bassussary & Arcangues; D3 for St Pée; 8km after Arcangues house on left; signposted.

Isabelle Ormazabal
Bidachuna,
Route Oihan Bidea D3,
64310 St Pée sur Nivelle,
Pyrénées-Atlantiques
tel   +33 (0)5 59 54 56 22
fax   +33 (0)5 59 54 55 07
email   isabelle@bidachuna.com
web   www.bidachuna.com

Map 13   Entry 457

Villa Coriolan

Chemin Domintxenea, 64210 Ahetze, Pyrénées-Atlantiques

Superb modern design – 320 square metres of generous space, angles and style softened by curves – and split levels outside. It's 'green' too, with solar heating, insulation and water harvesting. English Alexandra married Georges and they have upended their lives to do this together, with real enthusiasm. A huge white bath, a stand-alone basin, pale yellows and burgundies, Farrow & Ball paints, Sanderson fabrics, oak floors, books, bay windows and views. It is original, comfortable and relaxed, the breakfasts are vast and varied, and you can do real lengths in the pool. *Minimum stay two nights.*

"The greenest house in the Pays Basque," claims our inspector. Not only do Georges and Alexandra harvest rain water, use solar energy to power their house and insulate their walls, their garden too has been designed with the protection of the planet in mind. In their tropical paradise, only exotic plants needing little water are planted and ashes are scattered over the vegetables to prevent the need for chemicals. Local and seasonal ingredients prevail in the kitchen.

rooms	2: 1 double, 1 suite.
price	€85-€150. Breakfast €10 p.p.
meals	Dinner with wine, €35.
closed	Rarely.
directions	From A63 exit 4 Biarritz/St Pée sur Nivelle. From D255; through Arbonne for St Pée; after 2.9km follow sign Uhazaldea, signed.

SPECIAL GREEN ENTRY see page 15

	Georges & Alexandra Guillaume
tel	+33 (0)5 59 41 82 48
fax	+33 (0)5 59 41 82 33
email	georges.guillaume@9online.fr
web	www.villa-coriolan.com

Map 13 Entry 458

Aquitaine

Domaine de Silencenia

The house cornerstone, the magnificent magnolia, the towering pines were all planted on one day in 1881. A pool and lake (with fountain, boat, trout and koi-carp) are set in spacious parkland, and billard room, sauna and fitness area (for a small charge) are on tap. The sensitive restoration includes a Blue Marlin room, canopied pine beds, modern fittings, a desk made from famous wine cases and respect for the original chestnut panelling. Philippe, discreetly helped by his mother with evening meals, knows about wine too: his cellar is brilliant. And there's great walking in the surrounding hills.

rooms	5: 3 doubles, 2 triples.
price	€65–€70.
meals	Dinner with wine, €30.
closed	Rarely.
directions	From A63 exit on D932, on through Ustaritz & Cambo les Bains; left into Louhossoa; straight over crossroads. House 800m on left.

Philippe Mallor
Domaine de Silencenia,
64250 Louhossoa,
Pyrénées-Atlantiques
tel   +33 (0)5 59 93 35 60
fax   +33 (0)5 59 93 35 60
email   domaine.de.silencenia@wanadoo.fr
web   www.domaine-silencenia.com

Map 13 Entry 459

Aquitaine

Maison Maxana

Step through a 17th-century Basque façade into a world of stone-flagged floors and bold African art, subtle lights, soft velour sofas and antiques with a story to tell. Ana mixes styles and textures with panache and the art is collected by banker husband Max. Which bedroom to choose – minimalist chic, Chinese red, lavish silk? One has a terrace, another ancient tiles, all have fat white pillows, hand-made soaps, textured throws. Relax by the pool as Ana pours a glass of chilled rosé and you consider dinner; Ana loves people *and* is a fine cook. The village is charming and Biarritz a short drive.

rooms	5 doubles.
price	€80–€110.
meals	Dinner with wine, €20–€30.
closed	Rarely.
directions	From A64 exit 4 for urt; right onto D936; D123 right at mini-r'bout to La Bastide Clairence. House on main street just past Post Office on left.

Ana Berdoulat
Maison Maxana,
Rue Notre Dame,
64240 La Bastide Clairence,
Pyrénées-Atlantiques
tel   +33 (0)5 59 70 10 10
mobile   +33 (0)6 32 42 65 99
email   ab@maison-maxana.com
web   www.maison-maxana.com

Map 13 Entry 460

Aquitaine

Maison Marchand

A lovely face among all the lovely faces of this superb listed village, the 16th-century Basque farmhouse, resuscitated by its French/Irish owners, is run with well-organised informality. Dinners around the great oak table are lively; local dishes excellent. Rooms each have their own terrace and are light and well-decorated with hand-stencilling and pretty fabrics, beams and exposed wafer bricks, country antiques and thoughtful extras such as good books and bottled water. Breakfast is on the terrace in warm weather. And Gilbert will laugh and teach you *la pelote basque. Minimum stay two nights.*

rooms	3: 2 doubles; 1 double & extra bed for 2 children.
price	€55–€70.
meals	Dinner with wine, €25.
closed	Occasionally.
directions	From A64 junc. 4 for Urt & Bidache; right on D936, right on D123 at mini-island to La Bastide Clairence. House on main street, opp. bakery.

Valerie & Gilbert Foix
Maison Marchand,
Rue Notre Dame,
64240 La Bastide Clairence,
Pyrénées-Atlantiques
tel +33 (0)5 59 29 18 27
mobile +33 (0)6 19 21 21 24
email valerie.et.gilbert.foix@wanadoo.fr
web perso.wanadoo.fr/maison.marchand

Map 13 Entry 461

Aquitaine

Urruti Zaharria

Above the village, this Basque farmhouse is 14th century: the vast lintel stones, heart-of-oak staircase, split levels and crannies speak their great age. A huge hall leads to the salon, leather chairs wait round the open fireplace, views stretch to the hills, and the attic, restored with imagination and colour, is a good mix of old and new. Indulge in these new owners' love of this place, admire their pretty, immaculate garden, sleep deeply (new mosquito screens on windows!) ... and visit the prehistoric caves of Isturitz for a taste of things more ancient still. They open from March to November.

rooms	5: 2 doubles, 3 triples.
price	€53–€62. €69–€97 for 3.
meals	Dinner with wine, €20.
closed	Christmas & New Year.
directions	From A64 Hasparren exit D21 to Hasparren; left D10 for Labastide Clairence for 3km; right D251 through Ayherre to Isturitz. Signed.

Mme Fillaudeau
Urruti Zaharria,
64240 Isturitz,
Pyrénées-Atlantiques
tel +33 (0)5 59 29 45 98
mobile +33 (0)5 59 93 95 03
email urruti.zaharria@wanadoo.fr
web www.urruti-zaharria.fr

Map 13 Entry 462

Aquitaine

La Closerie du Guilhat

Guilhat is one of those sturdy Béarn houses with solid old furniture and traditional décor. Marie-Christine has added her own decorative touches – colourful bedroom wallpapers, small modern bathrooms – and everything is immaculate. She is elegant and energetic, doing nearly all the work here herself and longing to show you her garden – beautifully flowering all year. It has huge old trees, magnolia, azalea, rhododendron, camellia; benches discreetly placed for quiet reading and the Pyrenees as a backdrop. There's table tennis – shared with gite guests – and the spa in Salies is good for swimming all year.

rooms	3: 1 double, 1 twin, 1 suite.
price	€55–€60.
meals	Dinner with wine, €22.
closed	Rarely.
directions	From A64 exit 7; right for Salies '5 tonnes'; next right to Le Guilhat 1.8km; house on left beside nurseries at junction with Chemin des Bois.

Marie-Christine Potiron
La Closerie du Guilhat,
64270 Salies de Béarn,
Pyrénées-Atlantiques
tel +33 (0)5 59 38 08 80
fax +33 (0)5 59 38 08 80
email guilhat@club-internet.fr
web www.holidayshomes.com/guilhat

Map 13 Entry 463

Aquitaine

Manoir de Marsan

Its looks belie its youth: that lovely roof and all beneath it is only 50 years old, the gorgeous garden is André's dazzling ten-year triumph, a haven of peace and natural beauty. He plays the piano pretty well too. He and Nicole are happily present for guests, she bilingual after 20 years in Canada and quietly caring for details, he vibrantly telling you all there is to know. Their renovation is the height of comfort and taste (lots of space, deep sofas, unusual antiques, Turkey carpets), the big, sweetly feminine guest suite feels like a private apartment, garden beauty bursts in through every window.

rooms	1 suite for 2–4.
price	€90.
meals	Restaurants within walking distance.
closed	Rarely.
directions	From RN133 for Centre ville; in village square; Rue Panneceau left of Mairie; at stop sign right; follow green & white signs; ring at gate.

Nicole & André Capdet
Manoir de Marsan,
64390 Sauveterre de Bearn,
Pyrénées-Atlantiques
tel +33 (0)5 59 38 52 75
fax +33 (0)5 59 38 52 75
email andre.capdet@wanadoo.fr
web www.manoir-de-marsan.com

Map 13 Entry 464

Aquitaine

Lou Guit

The nooked and crannied 17th-century farmhouse resides in a hamlet with little passing traffic… through the electric gates and into a big garden with shaded loungers and a lovely pool. Sally's sense of style permeates the house in a comfortable mix of antique and modern. A big, wooden, open-tread stair leads to fresh, lovely bedrooms; the garden suite for two has the whitest of white bed linen and its own super terrace. The sitting room, formal but relaxed, is full of books on history and travel – Sally's passions. She loves her guests and treats you to delicious Mediterranean cooking. *Minimum stay two nights.*

rooms	2: 1 double, 1 suite for 2.
price	€70-€100.
meals	Dinner with wine, €30.
closed	Rarely.
directions	From A64 exit 7; D430 for Saliès de Beam: D933 past Sauveterre; D936 left for Oloron; r'bout right on D23; right for Rivareyte. House 500m on right.

Sally Worthington
Lou Guit,
Quartier Arrive,
64390 St Gladie Arrive Munein,
Pyrénées-Atlantiques
tel   +33 (0)5 59 38 57 76
fax   +33 (0)5 59 38 50 27
email   lou.guit@wanadoo.fr
web   www.lou-guit.com

Map 13 Entry 465

Aquitaine

Maison L'Aubèle

The Desbonnets completely renovated their grand 18th-century village house after finding it and this sleepy village in the Pyrenean foothills: both house and owners are quiet, elegant, sophisticated and full of interest, the furniture a feast for the eyes. Breakfast is a chance to pick their well-stocked brains about the region and do delve into their tempting library (she binds books). The light, airy bedrooms have more interesting furniture on lovely wooden floors. *La Rose* is very chic, *La Verte* is a dream – enormous and boldly coloured with views of the mountains and a 'waltz-in' bathroom.

rooms	2 doubles.
price	€60.
meals	Restaurants 4-10km.
closed	Rarely.
directions	From Navarrenx D2 for Monein to Jasses; right D27 for Oloron Ste Marie; in Lay-Lamidou, left, 1st right, 2nd house on right.

Marie-France Desbonnet
Maison L'Aubèle,
4 rue de la Hauti,
64190 Lay-Lamidou,
Pyrénées-Atlantiques
tel   +33 (0)5 59 66 00 44
fax   +33 (0)5 59 66 00 44
email   desbonnet.bmf@infonie.fr
web   www.ifrance.com/chambrehote/

Map 13 Entry 466

Aquitaine

Maison Rancesamy

Landscape painters love this haven. From terrace and pool you can see for ever into the high Pyrenees – sunlit snowy in winter, all the greens in summer. Beside their 1700s farmhouse, the Brownes' barn conversion shelters artistic, uncluttered, stone-walled bedrooms and incredible views. The superb dining room – Isabelle's trompe-l'œil floor, huge carved table – reflects their origins (Polish, French, South African). They are a happy, relaxed family. On balmy summer evenings, the food (not every night) is deliciously garden-aromatic. *Minimum stay two nights July/August.*

rooms	5: 2 doubles, 1 twin, 2 family rooms.
price	€60–€74. Family room €90–€105.
meals	Dinner, 4 courses with wine, €32.
closed	Rarely.
directions	From Pau N134 S for Saragosse to Gan; right at lights after chemist, D24 for Lasseube 9km; left D324. Follow Chambres d'Hôtes signs; cross 2 small bridges; house on left up hill.

Simon & Isabelle Browne
Maison Rancesamy,
Quartier Rey,
64290 Lasseube,
Pyrénées-Atlantiques
tel   +33 (0)5 59 04 26 37
fax   +33 (0)5 59 04 26 37
email   missbrowne@wanadoo.fr
web   www.missbrowne.com

Map 13 Entry 467

Aquitaine

Manoir de Levignac

Walk through the entrance hall into the handsome country kitchen and thence into the grounds with nature reserve, pond, pool, pines and views. Or stay and dine, in this room with big fireplace, pottery pieces and beautiful carved cupboard doors. In the sitting room, terracotta tiles, kilim rugs, and grand piano give a comfortably artistic air. Adriana is Swiss-Italian, Jocelyn South African; they are warm and lovely and do everything well. You get a lush bedroom with rural views, a sitting room and an immaculate bathroom. Table tennis and space outside, attention to detail within, delicious food.

rooms	1 suite.
price	€70–€80.
meals	Dinner with wine, €20.
closed	Rarely.
directions	From A10 exit St André de Cubzac to Ste Foy La Grande; D708 to Duras; 4km after Duras left C1 to St Pierre.

Jocelyn & Adriana Cloete
Manoir de Levignac,
Saint Pierre sur Dropt,
47120 Duras, Lot-et-Garonne
tel   +33 (0)5 53 83 68 11
email   cloete@wanadoo.fr

Map 9 Entry 468

Aquitaine

La Maison de la Halle

Eighteenth-century elegance in a lovely hilltop village… there are a walled garden, two terraces (the lower with a pool), breathtaking views and sunsets to die for. Fiona is Scottish, Leif, a wonderful raconteur, is Danish; their background: cosmopolitan in film and design; their house: full of paintings, antiques, props from film and theatre productions. Bedrooms, one upstairs, two down, overlook the peaceful old market square, and beige and white luxury reigns – white-painted floors, sumptuous raw linen, fine polished armoires, hugely comfy beds. *Entire house available for self-catering in summer.*

rooms	2: 1 double, 1 twin.
price	€80.
meals	Dinner with wine, €40.
closed	Rarely.
directions	From Marmande D708 for Duras 17km to Lévignac; bear left; head for Centre Ville; house on left behind market hall: two bay trees & white front door.

Leif & Fiona Pedersen
La Maison de la Halle,
47120 Lévignac de Guyenne,
Lot-et-Garonne
tel   +33 (0)5 53 94 37 61
fax   +33 (0)5 53 94 37 66
email   maison.de.la.halle@wanadoo.fr
web   www.lamaisondelahalle.com

Map 9 Entry 469

Aquitaine

Château de Péchalbet

Having lived vibrantly on the Riviera, the Peyres moved here in search of rural peace, then chose to share their love of the place. Glorious public rooms have high rafters, splendid furnishings and sensuous old terracotta tiles. Bedrooms are on the ground floor, off a rag-rolled hall: one with a metalwork four-poster, another bluebell walls and a terrace. Children get bunk beds in an ancient tower. Then there's the fine old kitchen for breakfast, a formal terrace for dining and a view of the lake (illuminated at night). Highly civilised casualness in both house and owners – and acres of wildlife to discover.

rooms	3: 1 family suite, 1 double, 1 twin.
price	€75-€106.
meals	Dinner with wine, €20.
closed	November-March.
directions	From Bergerac D933 for Marmande. 1.5km after Eymet left C1 for Agnac-Mairie; 500m on left.

Françoise & Henri Peyre
Château de Péchalbet,
47800 Agnac, Lot-et-Garonne
tel   +33 (0)5 53 83 04 70
fax   +33 (0)5 53 83 04 70
email   pechalbet@hotmail.com
web   pechalbet.free.fr

Map 9 Entry 470

Aquitaine

Manoir de Roquegautier

In a beautful park with rolling views, the fairytale château is wondrously French. Drapes, swags and interlinings – all done, but never overdone, by Madame – and the rooms in the old tower truly memorable with their own entrance and spiral stone stair. There are claw-footed baths and huge old basins and taps, and each top-floor suite has one round tower room. There are swings and a games room, a discreet pool, gazebos around the garden and mature trees to shade your picnic lunches. Delicious food fresh from the family farm and shared with your hosts – such gentle, friendly people that you'll wish you could stay for ever.

rooms	4: 2 doubles, 1 family suite for 3, 1 family suite for 4.
price	€68. Suites €107–€115.
meals	Dinner with wine, €24, July-August only.
closed	October-April.
directions	From Villeneuve sur Lot N21 north for Cancon, 15.5km. Manoir signed on left 3.5km before Cancon.

Brigitte & Christian Vrech
Manoir de Roquegautier,
Beaugas,
47290 Cancon,
Lot-et-Garonne
tel   +33 (0)5 53 01 60 75
email   roquegautier@free.fr
web   www.roquegautier.com

Map 9 Entry 471

Aquitaine

Domaine des Rigals

A many-gloried 17th-century family château with 15 fabulous hectares of garden and woodland: red squirrels and deer cavort, wild orchids glow, the Babers nurture 400 new trees. Their furniture from Scotland sits graciously in the French rooms, white carpeting spreads deep luxury in the lovely suite, family antiques grace the guest sitting room and they love you to share their welcoming manor. Breakfast generously in the huge kitchen or on the terrace then roam, relax or play: there's a carp lake for fishing, a tennis court, a 16m child-friendly pool. Great hosts, rooms, local markets, restaurants and wines.

rooms	3: 2 doubles, 1 family suite.
price	€100–€130.
meals	Restaurants in Castillonnès.
closed	Christmas & New Year.
directions	From Bergerac N21 for Villeneuve. 1.5km after Castillonnès, pass 'Terres du Sud' on left. After 50m, sign on right before crest of hill.

James Petley,
Patricia & David Baber
Domaine des Rigals,
47330 Castillonnès, Lot-et-Garonne
tel   +33 (0)5 53 41 24 21
fax   +33 (0)5 53 41 24 79
email   babersrigals@wanadoo.fr
web   www.domainedesrigals.com

Map 9 Entry 472

Aquitaine

Colombié

With infectious energy and fluent English, Madame tells her love of her house, land and gently cropping horses. In the old-style *pigeonnier* one bold-coloured, kempt bedroom sits above the other (one with a view to die for), plus tiny children's attic, superb little kitchen, barbecue terrace and log-fired living room. Throw open the shutters, smell the freshness, behold the Pannetier empire of paddocks, pool and lake (for fishing and boating) up to distant hills. After breakfast at the family table, in your dayroom or outside, launch into this area's endless riches. Perfect for families.

rooms	2 twins/doubles, 1 with kitchen.
price	€55.
meals	Use of kitchen €10 per day.
closed	Rarely.
directions	From Villeneuve sur Lot D676 to Monflanquin; D272 towards Monpazier. 1.5km beyond x-roads to Dévillac, left before bridge; 3rd house on right.

Michel & Maryse Pannetier
Colombié,
47210 Dévillac,
Lot-et-Garonne

tel	+33 (0)5 53 36 62 34
mobile	+33 (0)6 86 97 38 95
email	colombie@wanadoo.fr
web	perso.wanadoo.fr/colombie

Map 9 Entry 473

Aquitaine

Domaine du Moulin de Labique

Ponies in the field, ducks on the pond, goats in the greenhouse and food *à la grande-mère* on the plate – the Passebons' place glows with warmth and humour. Shutters are painted with *bleu de pastel* from the Gers and the 13th-century interiors have lost none of their aged charm. In house and outbuildings are chunky roof beams, seagrass mats on ancient tiles, vintage iron bedsteads, antique mirrors and walls flower-sprigged in positive colours (framboise, jade, green). Outside, old French roses and young alleys of trees, a bamboo-fringed stream, a restaurant in the stables and an exquisite pool.

rooms	4 + 1: 4 twins/doubles. 1 apartment for 4.
price	€110. Apartment €160.
meals	Dinner €31. Wine list €19–€30.
closed	Rarely.
directions	From Cancon N21; D124 for Monflanquin; D153 at Beauregard to St Vivien; on right 1km after St Vivien.

Hélène Boulet & François Passebon
Domaine du Moulin de Labique,
St Vivien, 47210 Villeréal,
Lot-et-Garonne

tel	+33 (0)5 53 01 63 90
fax	+33 (0)5 53 01 73 17
email	moulin-de-labique@wanadoo.fr
web	www.moulin-de-labique.fr

Map 9 Entry 474

Aquitaine

Château de Grenier

One minute you're bowling along a fairly busy road, the next you've pulled up at the doors of an 18th- and 19th-century *belle demeure*. Painted wood and dried flowers set the tone of this large, light, comfortable home. Discreet, charming Madame ushers you up to beautifully proportioned bedrooms with tall windows; ask for one facing the garden. Expect pristine white bathrooms, a sun-streamed double, a generous twin with pink walls, a two-room suite off the garden — more basic but ideal for families. Dinners are serenely elegant affairs, your hosts share the cooking. *Ask about furniture painting courses.*

rooms	5: 3 doubles, 1 twin, 1 family suite.
price	€80. Suite €130.
meals	Dinner with wine, €25.
closed	Rarely.
directions	A62; exit 6; D8 N for Agen for approx. 4km; château on right just before river Garonne. Signed.

	Chantal Breton le Grelle
	Château de Grenier,
	47160 St Léger,
	Lot-et-Garonne
tel	+33 (0)5 53 79 59 06
fax	+33 (0)5 53 79 59 06
email	info@chateaudegrenier.fr
web	www.chateaudegrenier.fr

Map 14 Entry 475

Aquitaine

Château de Rodié

Paul and Pippa did the triumphant restoration themselves, with two small children and a passionate commitment to the integrity of this ancient building: brash modernities are hidden (the telephone lurks behind a model ship). |It is breathtaking: an elaborate *pisé* floor set in cabalistic patterns and lit only with candles, two stone staircases, patches of fresco, a vast hall with giant fireplace and table — and a welcome to match. The tower room is unforgettable, so is the pool. The family is veggie-friendly and Pippa cooks sumptuous organic dinners (home-reared lamb...) that last for hours.

rooms	5: 3 doubles, 2 suites.
price	€70–€100.
meals	Dinner with wine, €18.
closed	Rarely.
directions	From Fumel D102 to Tournon; D656 for Agen 300m; left to Courbiac, past church, right at cross for Montaigu 1km; house on left.

	Paul & Pippa Hecquet
	Château de Rodié,
	47370 Courbiac de Tournon,
	Lot-et-Garonne
tel	+33 (0)5 53 40 89 24
fax	+33 (0)5 53 40 89 25
email	chateau.rodie@wanadoo.fr
web	www.chateauderodie.com

Map 14 Entry 476

Aquitaine

Domaine de la Mouthe

The hilltop site, with wide rural views, was carefully chosen to transplant this lovely old barn – once the garden has matured, you'll think it's been here for centuries. Marie-Ange's country furniture looks just right on the old floor tiles beneath the old oak beams; ancient wood and new glass marry beautifully, and the small but fresh bedrooms have views, stylish fabrics and a piece of patio each. Soaps and towels are luxurious. Laze by the heavenly new pool, or contemplate a spot of fishing – the domaine has its own lake. There's riding, too: another member of this charming family runs stables nearby.

Aquitaine

Le Moulin de Leymonie du Maupas

The Kieffers did the utterly successful restoration of their old Dordogne mill themselves, their gardening past speaks softly in the herb-scented patio and the little brook trembles off past grazing horses to the valley. Inside, levels juggle with space, steep stairs rise to smallish rooms of huge character with wood walls, rich rugs and selected antiques. Your sitting room is seductive with its logs on the fire and a forest overhead. Add a relaxed, bubbly welcome, organic dinners served with crisp linen and candles, homemade bread and jams for breakfast, and you have great value.

rooms	5: 2 doubles, 1 twin; 2 doubles & kitchenette.
price	€54–€70.
meals	Restaurants 3km.
closed	Rarely.
directions	From Libourne A89 exit Monpon Ménestérol; right D708 for Ste Foy la Grande 8km. Right in St Rémy, opp. Le Pressoir, D33 for St Martin & Villefranche; follow signs.

rooms	2: 1 double, 1 twin; child's room available.
price	€60.
meals	Dinner €20. Wine €9.
closed	Rarely.
directions	In Mussidan, at church, for Villamblard 4km; follow blue signs left for St Séverin 2km, blue sign on right.

	Marie-Ange Caignard
	Domaine de la Mouthe,
	24700 St Rémy sur Lidoire,
	Dordogne
tel	+33 (0)5 53 82 15 40
fax	+33 (0)5 53 82 15 40
email	lamoutheperigord@wanadoo.fr
web	www.pays-de-bergerac.com/ hebergement/domaine-mouthe

	Jacques & Ginette Kieffer
	Le Moulin de Leymonie du Maupas,
	24400 Issac,
	Dordogne
tel	+33 (0)5 53 81 24 02
email	jacques.kieffer2@wanadoo.fr
web	perso.wanadoo.fr/lemoulindeleymonie/

Map 9 Entry 477

Map 9 Entry 478

Aquitaine

Le Domaine de Foncaudière

Sumptuous, the champagne breakfast with salmon and possibly truffle omelette; opulent, the bright and simple luxury of the big suites; unmissable, the discovery trail through 100 acres of history, caves, fountains, great trees. The warm, leafy, many-eyed face of the lovely old manor draws you in: take time to absorb all the beautiful things inside, carved in wood or stone, wrought in iron or wool, against the calm uncluttered backdrop of vast cut stones. Marcel and his partner care passionately about their guests and their new venture: you will be remarkably well looked after. *Minimum stay two nights.*

rooms	2 suites for 3-4.
price	€150-€175. €185-€210 for 3. €220-€245 for 4.
meals	Restaurants 3km.
closed	Rarely.
directions	From Bergerac N21 for Périgueux 3.5km; left D107 for Maurens 5km; left for Maurens; entrance 300m on right.

Marcel Wils
Le Domaine de Foncaudière,
24140 Maurens,
Dordogne

tel	+33 (0)5 53 61 13 90
fax	+33 (0)5 53 61 03 24
email	info@foncaudiere.com
web	www.foncaudiere.com

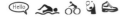

Map 9 Entry 479

Aquitaine

Le Logis Plantagenet

Picture this: a medieval house on a tree-lined square in old Bergerac, a minute's walk from the limpid, lovely river. Your well-travelled, welcoming hosts, he a historian, she a good cook, offer you light-filled bedrooms painted in soft colours with pretty rugs on polished floors, excellent beds, full-length baths and fabulous linen. Breakfasts are served in the flowered courtyard garden in summer and in the big modern kitchen in winter, at one merry table. After a day visiting châteaux and gardens and tasting fine wines, return to two delightful country-house sitting rooms.

rooms	3: 1 doubles, 2 twins.
price	€85-€95.
meals	Restaurants within walking distance.
closed	Never.
directions	From Bergerac to Le Port; owner's house with yellow shutters faces car park at port; Le Logis Plantagenet is directly behind. Ring bell of 6 Quai Salvette.

Bruce & Rosetta Cantlie
Le Logis Plantagenet,
5 rue du Grand Moulin,
24100 Bergerac, Dordogne

tel	+33 (0)5 53 57 15 99
fax	+33 (0)5 53 57 17 91
email	bruce.cantlie@wanadoo.fr
web	www.lelogisplantagenet.com

Map 9 Entry 480

Aquitaine

La Rivière

The large farmhouse auberge sits alone and surrounded by its fields in a hamlet of 12 houses. The Archer family honour tradition; he is a poultry breeder, she is an industrious (non-vegetarian!) cook and the recipes for hand crafting pâtés and foie gras are their heirlooms. The honey stones of the building are impeccably pointed and cleaned, bedrooms have functionality rather than character, shower rooms are large and pristine and there's an open-fired sitting room just for guests. Good for families (a climbing frame in the garden) and utterly, quintessentially French.
Minimum stay two nights.

rooms	2: 1 double, 1 triple.
price	€50.
meals	Dinner with wine, €20.50 (April–mid-Sept).
closed	November–February.
directions	From airport D660 for Sarlat; in Mouleydier over bridge on D21; after bridge 1st left onto D37; Route Balisé 2nd on right; on to house. Don't go into St Agne.

	Marie-Thérèse & Jean-Michel Archer La Rivière, 24520 St Agne, Dordogne
tel	+33 (0)5 53 23 22 26
fax	+33 (0)5 53 23 22 26
mobile	+33 (0)6 84 05 78 69
email	archer.marietherese@wanadoo.fr

Map 9 Entry 481

Aquitaine

Le Relais de Lavergne

Enter the creeper-climbed courtyard through the old arch: looks a touch sophisticated? Francine and Odile will reassure you – ex-Parisian publishers, they are funny, intelligent and wonderful company. They are also keen to preserve the ideal of *chambres d'hôtes* and make a point of eating with their guests. The curvy roof, wafer bricks and ancient timbers may be familiar friends but the long-drop privy is a fascinating rarity. Splendid main rooms combine simplicity and taste; smaller, tempting bedrooms have hand-stencilled doors and quirky touches. There's also a playroom and a garden with a pool.

rooms	5: 3 doubles, 1 twin, 1 family suite.
price	€65.
meals	Dinner with wine, €23.
closed	Rarely.
directions	From Bergerac D660 for Lalinde & Sarlat; right over R. Dordogne at Pont de Couze (still D660); at Bayac right D27 for Issigeac 2km; house on left at top of hill.

	Francine Pillebout & Odile Calmettes Le Relais de Lavergne, Lavergne, 24150 Bayac, Dordogne
tel	+33 (0)5 53 57 83 16
fax	+33 (0)5 53 57 83 16
email	relaisdelavergne@wanadoo.fr

Map 9 Entry 482

Saint Hubert

The long Bergeraçoise farmhouse, in spite of its antique looks, is new. Named after the patron saint of hunting – country pursuits are Madame's passion – protected by tall pine woods yet unremote, Saint Hubert is a calm, inviting, plant-flourished home whose walls are lined with hunting prints and whose coffee tables are laden with books. Guests have a sitting room, washing machine, small kitchen, barbecue and four country-snug bedrooms up in the roof; be cheered by sloped pine ceilings, pretty bathrooms and big bold checks. Muriel is a fine cook – try her *velouté des cèpes*.

rooms	4: 2 doubles, 2 twins.
price	€52–€62.
meals	Dinner with wine, €19. Guest kitchen.
closed	Rarely.
directions	From Bergerac, D32 direction Ste Alvère for approx. 13km. Before Liorac, signed on right.

Muriel Hennion
Saint Hubert,
24520 Liorac sur Louyre,
Dordogne
tel   +33 (0)5 53 63 07 92
fax   +33 (0)5 53 63 07 92
mobile +33 (0)6 22 98 47 96

Map 9 Entry 483

Les Hirondelles

Carine, half-Greek, energetic and fun, makes you feel very welcome in the sunny kitchen of her restored farmhouse on the top of a hill. She enjoys cooking French and international dishes, sometimes organises barbecues round the big pool and makes amazing walnut jam. Each new-bedded, newly-decorated, modern-bathroomed bedroom in the converted barn has its own terrace onto the shady garden (the pool is far enough away not to disturb your siesta). Spend two or three nights and get to know this beautiful village and the whole area; Carine knows the best places to go.

rooms	4: 2 doubles, 2 twins.
price	€48–€52.
meals	Dinner with wine, €17, except July-August.
closed	November-April.
directions	From Le Bugue go to Ste Alvère; at main x-roads there, D30 for Trémolat. House 2nd right, 500m after sign Le Maine at top of hill.

Carine Someritis
Les Hirondelles,
Le Maine,
24510 Ste Alvère, Dordogne
tel   +33 (0)5 53 22 75 40
fax   +33 (0)5 53 22 75 40

Map 9 Entry 484

Aquitaine

Le Moulin Neuf

Robert or Stuart's greeting is the first line of an ode to hospitality written in warm stone and breathtaking gardens, set to the tune of the little stream hurrying by to the lake. Freshly flowery, the immaculate rooms in the guest barn are comfortingly filled with excellent beds; bathrooms are utter luxury. The breakfast room has pretty tables and tea-making kit: have your succulent fruit salad here or on the vine-shaded terrace. All is lovingly tended, in perfect peace; nearby is unspoilt Paunat with its huge church – the whole place is a delight. *Ask about pets; children over 10 welcome.*

Aquitaine

Domaine des Farguettes

Fascinting Françoise is a songwriter and potter, Claude was in the theatre and their home reflects their passions: a baby grand in the salon, pots, paintings, puppets and poetry in every corner. Bedrooms in the house are pleasantly traditional and have spectacular hilltop views, those in the barn are more contemporary (vibrant colours, big glass doors) alongside aged timbers and vaulted ceilings. Both structures were built in 1664 by artisans whose signatures and date are set in stone. The pool is for all and there are great walks round the estate. *Ask about cookery courses. Meeting rooms for big groups.*

rooms	6 twins/doubles.
price	€85–€89.
meals	Restaurant 1km.
closed	Rarely; winter 3 nights minimum.
directions	From Le Bugue D703 & D31 through Limeuil. Past viewpoint to x-roads; D2 for Ste Alvère; after 100m fork left; house 2km on left at small crossroads.

rooms	4 doubles.
price	€70–€110.
meals	Dinner €25. Wine list from €5.
closed	July, August, Christmas & New Year.
directions	From Bergerac for Sarlat exit Le Buisson D25 for Cadouin; right for Paleyrac 4km; on entry to forest 1st house on left, above village.

Robert Chappell & Stuart Shippey
Le Moulin Neuf,
Paunat,
24510 Ste Alvère, Dordogne

tel	+33 (0)5 53 63 30 18
fax	+33 (0)5 53 63 30 55
email	moulin-neuf@usa.net
web	www.the-moulin-neuf.com

Françoise & Claude de Torrenté
Domaine des Farguettes,
24480 Paleyrac,
Dordogne

tel	+33 (0)5 53 23 48 23
fax	+33 (0)5 53 23 48 23
email	clagazel@wanadoo.fr
web	www.farguettes.fr

Map 9 Entry 485

Map 9 Entry 486

Aquitaine

Le Branchat

Waltz in the marble halls of this magnificent manor, sophisticate in its fine new bathrooms, go natural with Richard's ark of roaming animals and gorge on his home-grown fruits. He knows his mushrooms too, and can take you picking. He and Isabelle, happily out of the tourist industry and fervent B&B believers, will share their imaginative cooking with you if you are a small group (book ahead). Simple white bedrooms with plain beds and Richard's excellent paintings are a calm contrast to the opulence below and the pool area is wickedly tempting. Luxury and enthusiasm – special.
Minimum stay two nights July/August.

rooms	7: 2 doubles, 2 twins, 1 triple, (2 connect for family use); 2 suites in separate building.
price	€63–€72.
meals	Dinner €25. Wine €10.50–€19.
closed	20 October-March.
directions	From Périgueux D710 S for Belvès; at r'bout do not fork right to Belvès, stay on D710 500m then left; signed. House 600m on left.

Richard & Isabelle Ginioux
Le Branchat,
24170 Belvès,
Dordogne
tel   +33 (0)5 53 28 98 80
fax   +33 (0)5 53 59 22 52
email info@lebranchat.com
web   www.lebranchat.com

Map 9 Entry 487

Aquitaine

Château de Puymartin

Neither dream nor museum, Puymartin is a chance to act the aristocrat for a spell, and survey the day-trippers from your own wing. The fireplace in the tapestried baronial dining room would take a small tree, painted beams draw the eye, the carved stone staircase asks to be stroked, the furniture is authentic 17th-century Perigordian, history oozes from every corner (possibly a ghost). Bedrooms are vastly in keeping – twin four-posters, a loo in a turret, thick draperies. The ever-elegant Comtesse is friendly and very French; her son helps in the château and speaks good English; both are delightful.

rooms	2: 1 twin, 1 family suite.
price	€115.
meals	Restaurant 5km, choice in Sarlat.
closed	November-March.
directions	From Sarlat D47 for Les Eyzies 8km. Château signposted regularly.

Comtesse de Montbron
Château de Puymartin,
24200 Sarlat la Canéda,
Dordogne
tel   +33 (0)5 53 59 29 97
fax   +33 (0)5 53 29 87 52
email xdemontbron@wanadoo.fr

Map 9 Entry 488

Aquitaine

La Guérinière

Once a charterhouse, this good-looking Périgord house sits squarely in ten hectares of parkland and peace, a tribute to the rich, sober taste of the area. Inside reflects outside: the same dark timbers against pale stone and the new owners have redecorated the bedrooms most charmingly. They are gradually replacing the modern furniture with country antiques and the feel is warmly authentic. Moreover, they used to run a restaurant – do eat in. Sitting at the big table for house guests, you may find more gourmets in the beamed dining room: a few outsiders are occasionally allowed. A gem.

rooms	5: 1 double, 2 twins, 1 triple, 1 quadruple.
price	€75-€90.
meals	Dinner €21. Wine €15.
closed	2 November-March.
directions	From Sarlat D46 to Cénac St Julien. At end of village on for Fumel. House 3rd turning on right.

Brigitte & Christophe Demassougne
La Guérinière, Baccas,
24250 Cénac et St Julien, Dordogne
tel +33 (0)5 53 29 91 97
fax +33 (0)5 53 29 91 97
email contact@la-gueriniere-dordogne.com
web www.la-gueriniere-dordogne.com

Map 9 Entry 489

Aquitaine

Château de Mombette

Built in the 1600s-1700s by the same family, it has the simple, harmonious elegance that natural style brings to an organically-grown house; from its hilltop perch, it gazes across to the splendid medieval fortifications of Domme. Madame is welcoming and easy, has travelled a lot, especially to North Africa, and may even join you for a game of bridge. The character of her house is made of fine, generous spaces and good regional antiques, an attractive library and very lovely gardens. Rooms are comfortable, light and airy and you are within reach of all the delights of the Dordogne. Most relaxing.

rooms	3: 1 double, 1 twin, 1 triple.
price	€90-€95.
meals	Restaurants within walking distance.
closed	15 November-March.
directions	From Sarlat D46 to Cénac & St Julien; D50 right for St Cybranet for 300m; left signposted.

Mme Michèle Jahan
Château de Mombette,
24250 Cénac et St Julien,
Dordogne
tel +33 (0)5 53 28 30 14
fax +33 (0)5 53 28 30 14
email michele.jahan@wanadoo.fr

Map 9 Entry 490

Aquitaine

Le Vignoble

From the wicker-chaired sun room views sweep down the hamlet-studded valley – a blissful spot for breakfasts and dinners. Sue and Nick, who have chosen to swap London for deepest Dordogne, give you lovely bedrooms with big beds and old French linen, white walls and fresh flowers. Two rooms (for one party) share an enchanting lavender bathroom with a swish shower. Seek out a private corner in the elegantly simple garden where the lapping pool is heated to Trinidadian temperatures – Sue was brought up there. Seven hectares for walkers and wild orchids, civilised hosts, privacy and space. Wonderful.

rooms	3: 1 twin/double with separate bath; 2 doubles sharing bath & wc.
price	€65.
meals	Dinner €20. Wine €8.
closed	Rarely.
directions	From Ribérac D708 for Verteillac; over bridge; D99 right to Celles; through village leaving church on right. House sign 2nd right after Peugeot garage.

Sue & Nick Gild
Le Vignoble,
Celles,
24600 Ribérac,
Dordogne
tel   +33 (0)5 53 90 26 60
email   nsgild@orange.fr

Map 9 Entry 491

Aquitaine

Pauliac

The exuberant hillside garden, full of blossom and bamboo, has gorgeous views and an overflowing stone plunge pool, too. John and Jane's talent is a restful atmosphere, their conversion a brilliant marriage of cottage simplicity – simple décor with sparks from African throws and good paintings. Simple bedrooms have a separate entrance off the street. Delightful, energetic Jane offers superb, imaginative food in the sun-splashed veranda with its all-season views, or the bright, rustic dining room with roaring log fire – and early suppers for children. Lovely people in a tranquil view-drenched spot.

rooms	4: 2 doubles, 1 twin, 1 suite for 4.
price	€65.
meals	Dinner €24. Wine €10 per bottle.
closed	Rarely.
directions	From Angoulême D939 for Périgueux 29km; right D12 for Ribérac to Verteillac; left D1 for Lisle 5km; right D99 for Celles for 400m; sign to left.

Jane & John Edwards
Pauliac,
Celles, 24600 Ribérac, Dordogne
tel   +33 (0)5 53 91 97 45
fax   +33 (0)5 53 90 43 46
email   info@pauliac.fr
web   www.pauliac.fr

Map 9 Entry 492

Aquitaine

La Maison des Beaux Arts

The name is well chosen. Delia is a British artist and her striking canvases (from pop art jugs to oversized flowers) set off the house's well-preserved features. Once home to the mayor, the grand 19th-century house faces the main street and backs onto countryside. The only new addition, a glass conservatory, exploits the wonderful valley views. Sumptuous bedrooms are painted in a sizzling array of colours – sunflower yellow, duck-egg blue, Tiffany green – and filled with flowers. Should Delia's enthusiasm and talent inspire, she presents art packages too. *Minimum stay two nights July/August.*

rooms	5: 3 doubles, 2 family rooms for 3.
price	€65–€79.
meals	Restaurant 50m.
closed	Rarely.
directions	From Limoges N21 exit Chalus; right at D6; D85 to Nontron; left over bridge to centre; house opposite post office, next to Tourist Information.

Delia Cavers
La Maison des Beaux Arts,
7 ave du Général Leclerc,
24300 Nontron, Dordogne
tel   +33 (0)5 53 56 39 77
mobile   +33 (0)6 71 09 64 72
email   delia@deliacavers.co.uk
web   www.la-maison-des-beaux-arts.com

Map 9 Entry 493

Aquitaine

La Roche

Such a gorgeous garden on several levels – you breakfast at shaded tables or under a pergola draped in honeysuckle and vines. A convinced vegetarian, Alison produces her own (organic) vegetables, eggs, honey and jams. Two spotless bedrooms, with sloping ceilings, big beams and modern windows, are in a converted barn where they share a comfortable living room furnished with books and hand-crafted furniture. Bathrooms, too, are a good size. It's a marvellous place for children, with donkeys, goats, cats, hens, table tennis and a fenced pool that looks out over heavenly countryside.

rooms	2: 1 double, 1 twin.
price	€65.
meals	Restaurants 12km.
closed	Christmas Day.
directions	From D675 (Nontron to Brantôme), D98 east. La Roche on right about 3km from D675.

Alison Coutanche
La Roche, Quinsac,
24530 Champagnac de Belair,
Dordogne
tel   +33 (0)5 53 54 22 91
email allisons@club-internet.fr
web   perso.club-internet.fr/allisons/

Map 9 Entry 494

Aquitaine

Domaine d'Essendieras

A panorama of apple orchards, river, lakes and two châteaux captures the visitor's eye on this 360-hectare estate. In a modernized outbuilding, each stylish bedroom has an original colour scheme, immaculate wooden floors, the odd country antique and a splendid bathroom with 21st-century shower. You will share breakfast, a sumptuous affair, with the Dutch owners or, in their absence, with charming Véronique. There's so much to do you may never leave: a vast heated pool with sauna and bar, three pool tables and an antique juke box in the baronial hall, cycling and fishing on the estate. A magnificent place.

rooms	5: 3 doubles, 2 twins.
price	€69–€115.
meals	Dinner with wine, €19.
closed	Never.
directions	From Limoges D704 for St Yrieix; 60km right on D705 for Excideuil; 1km, house on right.

Ellen & Jeroen Bakker
Domaine d'Essendieras,
24160 St Médard d'Excideuil,
Dordogne
tel   +33 (0)5 53 55 34 34
fax   +33 (0)5 53 55 34 33
email   info@essendieras.fr
web   www.essendieras.fr

Map 9 Entry 495

Aquitaine

La Licorne

In a tiny, peaceful hamlet, La Licorne is three old buildings with a stream bounding the courtyard. Claire and Marc are from the Alps – she teaches skiing, he works in tourism and is an experienced cook – and are keen to make their home a relaxing place to be. Clutter-free rooms, one in the 13th-century barn overlooking the nut trees and garden, are small, white, with modern furniture and the occasional old carved cupboard door. The dining room is superb with its big fireplace and gallery at each end; food is light and vegetable-orientated. *Arrivals from 5pm. Minimum stay two nights.*

rooms	3: 2 doubles, 1 suite for 4.
price	€55–€58.
meals	Dinner €20. Wine list from €3. Restaurants 500m-6km.
closed	November-Easter.
directions	From Montignac D65 south for 6km; left on minor road to Valojoulx. House in centre of hamlet, left of Mairie.

Claire & Marc Bosse
La Licorne, Valojoulx,
24290 Montignac Lascaux,
Dordogne
tel   +33 (0)5 53 50 77 77
fax   +33 (0)5 53 50 77 77
email   licornelascaux@free.fr
web   www.licorne-lascaux.com

Map 9 Entry 496

Limousin

Limousin

Château de Sannat

The serene 18th-century château stands proud for all to see on the site of an ancient fort – oh, the panorama! Bedrooms are mostly vast, traditionally furnished, regally wallpapered, modern bathroomed; breakfast is seriously good. Madame, full of warmth and enthusiasm, has restored the exceptional, part-hanging gardens, and organises cookery courses. The atmosphere in the spectacular west-facing dining room, with its pale blue and yellow panelling, high-backed tapestried chairs and antique table may be informal, but the surroundings impose civilised dressing for dinner. *Golf couses nearby.*

rooms	5: 3 doubles, 2 twins.
price	€120.
meals	Dinner with wine, €40.
closed	Rarely.
directions	From Poitiers N147 towards Limoges, through Bellac; left D96 for St Junien les Combes. 1st left in village for Rançon approx. 1km.

Comte & Comtesse
Aucaigne de Sainte Croix
Château de Sannat,
St Junien les Combes,
87300 Bellac, Haute-Vienne
tel   +33 (0)8 77 59 56 78
mobile   +33 (0)6 08 02 28 23
email   chateausannat@wanadoo.fr
web   www.chateausannat.com

Map 9   Entry 497

Limousin

Thoveyrat

Plain, simple and real French value. Thoveyrat is a deep-country organic farm (ewes, sows and poultry) run by a sweet young couple who delight in their French country fare, created from home-grown and reared vegetables, lamb, duck, pigeon and rabbit (delicious pâtés). Myriam cares for their baby and guests while Pierre looks after the farm and sees to house improvements. The 18th-century roadside farmhouse has lots of dark old wood – a great old oak staircase, beams and timber framing – family clutter, fireplaces, peaceful, mix-and-match bedrooms and a haphazard garden full of toys.

rooms	4: 1 double, 1 triple, 2 family rooms.
price	€40.
meals	Dinner with wine, €13.
closed	Rarely.
directions	In Bellac follow signs to Limoges; just before leaving Bellac D3 right for Blond 4km to Thoveyrat. House sign on left.

Pierre & Myriam Morice
Thoveyrat,
87300 Blond,
Haute-Vienne
tel   +33 (0)5 55 68 86 86
fax   +33 (0)5 55 68 86 86
email   chambrehote@freesurf.fr

Map 9   Entry 498

Limousin

Château du Fraisse

For 800 years the Monstiers have adapted their château to family needs. It is now mainly a Renaissance gem by the great Serlio, whence warm limestone and a discreetly elegant portico, a Henry II staircase, an astonishing fireplace in the vast salon; a mix of grand and rustic. Your cultured hosts will greet you with warmth, happily tell you about house and history and show you to your room: fine furniture, paintings and prints, traditional furnishings; one bathroom has a fragment of a 16th-century fresco. If you return late at night you must climb the steep old spiral stair to your room as the main door is locked.

rooms	7: 1 double, 3 twins, 1 suite for 3, 2 suites for 4.
price	€92–€114. Suites €145–€154.
meals	Auberge 3km.
closed	15 December–15 January.
directions	From A20 exit 23 to Bellac; Mézières sur Issoire; left to Nouic; château on left.

Comte & Comtesse
des Monstiers Mérinville
Château du Fraisse,
Le Fraisse, 87330 Nouic,
Haute-Vienne

tel	+33 (0)5 55 68 32 68
fax	+33 (0)5 55 68 39 75
email	infos@chateau-du-fraisse.com
web	www.chateau-du-fraisse.com

Map 9 Entry 499

Limousin

Château Ribagnac

Patrick and Colette are as kind, generous, intelligent and thoughtful as they are enthusiastic, and their splendid château, built in 1647, is a treat. This is their dream, and their hands 'show the scars'. The conversion is authentic, attractive and elegantly comfortable: oak floors with rugs, plain walls and papered walls, old and newish furniture, superb new bathrooms (one loo in its turret), views over the parkland and lake, silence but for the birds. Food is grown in their garden, the local meat is succulent, there is a deep commitment. Conversation flows along with the wine. *Swimming lake with beach 1.5km.*

rooms	6: 1 double, 5 suites for 4–5.
price	€100–€140.
meals	Dinner with wine, €45.
closed	December–February.
directions	From Ambazac follow signs for 'gare'. Under bridge for D56 to St Martin Terressus. Château on right after 3km.

Patrick & Colette Bergot
Château Ribagnac,
87400 St Martin Terressus,
Haute-Vienne

tel	+33 (0)5 55 39 77 91
email	patrick-jose.bergot@wanadoo.fr
web	www.chateauribagnac.com

Map 9 Entry 500

Limousin

La Chapelle

Magical walking country, the emphasis here is outside, countryside and woodlands are your garden. With total commitment to the welfare of their region and all natural life systems, your hosts run a bio-dynamic goat farm and are as self-sufficient as possible. The old farmhouse has been modernised inside and the four bedrooms, pine clad and functionally furnished, share a living room and kitchen. Dine with this genuine, unpretentious couple if you can: they're very good company, their food is all home-grown and deliciously nourishing. Children love helping to milk the goats and collect eggs. *Self-catering possible.*

Limousin

Moulin de Marsaguet

The nicest possible people, they have done just enough to this proud old building so it looks as it did 200 years ago when it forged cannon balls. The farm is relaxed and natural, they keep animals (including Lusitanian horses), three small children and a super potager, make pâtés and *confits* by the great mill pond and hang the *magrets* and hams to dry over the magnificent hearth in their big stone sitting room with its tatty sofa. Relish the drive up past tree-framed lake (boating possible) and stone outbuildings and the prospect of dining on home-grown ingredients. It's glorious. *Ask about pets when booking.*

rooms	4: 3 doubles, 1 triple.		rooms	3 doubles.
price	€44.		price	€45.
meals	Dinner €8. Wine list from €5. Guest kitchen.		meals	Dinner with wine, €20, Tuesday, Thursday & Saturday only.
closed	Last week of August.		closed	October–15 April.
directions	From A20 exit 41 to Magnac Bourg; D215 (between Total service station & Brasserie des Sports) SW. Follow signs 4km to La Chapelle.		directions	From A20 exit 39 to Pierre Buffière; cross river D15 & D19 for St Yrieix for 15km. At Croix d'Hervy left D57 for Coussac Bonneval; mill on left after lake (7km).

Patrick & Mayder Lespagnol
La Chapelle,
87380 Château Chervix,
Haute-Vienne

tel   +33 (0)5 55 00 86 67
fax   +33 (0)5 55 00 70 78
email   lespagno@club-internet.fr
web   gite.lachapelle.free.fr

Valérie & Renaud Gizardin
Moulin de Marsaguet,
87500 Coussac Bonneval,
Haute-Vienne

tel   +33 (0)5 55 75 28 29
fax   +33 (0)5 55 75 28 29
email   gizardin.renaud@akeonet.com

Map 9   Entry 501

Map 9   Entry 502

Limousin

La Roche

It's homely yet exciting with Michel's work as artist and handyman everywhere: his sculptures lead you magically through the big, unusual garden; in the old stables, his iron balustrade and carved door frames open onto an abundance of ceiling and bed coverings in generous, painting-hung bedrooms. These are Josette's work, as are the opulent curtains, wall fabric and tented ceiling in the salon. An interesting, likeable couple of ex-Parisians, Michel has a fascinating studio/gallery, Josette loves cooking for vegetarians. The beautiful forested valley alone is worth the visit.

rooms	2 doubles.
price	€55.
meals	Dinner with wine, €18.
closed	Never.
directions	From Eymoutiers D30 for Chamberet. House in village of La Roche, 7km beyond Eymoutiers.

Michel & Josette Jaubert
La Roche,
87120 Eymoutiers,
Haute-Vienne
tel   +33 (0)5 55 69 61 88
web   clos.arts.free.fr

Map 10 Entry 503

Limousin

L'Abbaye du Palais

Everything here is big, beautiful, generous: each marvellous wood-floored bathroom has a rolltop tub and a walk-in shower; high, square bedrooms have delectable old furniture and fine embroidered linen; there are two pianos, some stupendous linden trees and so much heartfelt friendship. Martijn and Saskia left powerful jobs to bring their three young children to a life of nature and creativity in this exceptional old Cistercian abbey. With endless energy and charm, they'll share its wonders with you. Martin's *menu du jour* for your delight, a sprig of rosemary on your pillow for sweet dreams.

rooms	5: 2 doubles, 1 twin, 2 suites for 4.
price	€65-€95.
meals	Dinner with wine, from €32.50, except Wednesdays. Picnic baskets can be arranged.
closed	Rarely.
directions	From Limoges N141 east through Bourganeuf for Pontarion; just after Bourganeuf, left onto D940A. Abbaye with blue gates 5km on right.

Martijn & Saskia
Zandvliet-Breteler
L'Abbaye du Palais,
23400 Bourganeuf, Creuse
tel   +33 (0)5 55 64 02 64
fax   +33 (0)5 55 64 02 63
email   abbayedupalais@wanadoo.fr
web   www.abbayedupalais.com

Map 10 Entry 504

Limousin

Jeanne Maison d'Hotes

Where tree-clad hills surge up from valley bottoms and sprinklings of fortified towns cling gloriously to hilltops is this red-stoned, turreted village. Hidden behind high walls from tourist bustle is a green shady garden, roses in abundance, a 15th-century tower and three floors of living space. Big bedrooms have sisal and sofas, heavy old armoires and one, a stone terrace. White bathrooms sparkle. She was in PR in Paris, he was a restaurateur, both are fine hosts and speak good English. You eat well; mushrooms are gathered in season and Brigitte is proud of her breakfast gâteaux. *Private parking.*

rooms	5: 2 doubles, 3 twins/doubles.
price	€90.
meals	Dinner with wine, €32.
closed	Never.
directions	From Brive A20; exit 52 D38 to Collonges la Rouge; right at 2nd parking sign; follow signs.

Brigitte & Pascal Monteil
Jeanne Maison d'Hotes,
BP 28 Le Bourg,
19500 Collonges la Rouge, Corrèze

tel	+33 (0)5 55 25 42 31
fax	+33 (0)5 55 25 47 80
email	info@jeannemaisondhotes.com
web	www.jeannemaisondhotes.com

Map 9 Entry 505

Limousin

Les Bedaines

The Lardners are loving their brand new house with its high timbers and monumental fireplace. Up above their old hamlet, it gazes over meadows and woods to the Massif Central: one can almost hear the boar, deer, badgers and hares teeming around. Inside, Jim's perfect finishes and Anne's love of texture and colour make for pretty rooms, good modern bathrooms and a splendid sitting gallery beneath the rafters. These two were born to do B&B: interested in others, they genuinely love having visitors, their enthusiasm for this lovely area is infectious, Anne's cooking is superb and the peace unbroken. Great value.

rooms	2: 1 double, 1 twin.
price	€48.
meals	Dinner with wine, €24.
closed	Rarely.
directions	From Argentat N120 for Tulle; thro' St Chammant, left onto D921 for Briue; on for 5km; left into Prézat; thro' hamlet, to top of hill; right, then left; house stands alone.

Anne & Jim Lardner
Les Bedaines,
Prézat,
19380 Albussac, Corrèze

tel	+33 (0)5 55 28 62 36
fax	+33 (0)5 55 28 62 36
email	jim.lardner@aliceadsl.fr

Map 10 Entry 506

Limousin

La Souvigne

Jacquie, half-French, and Ian, half-Hungarian, are fervent Francophiles who know the local people, history, flora and building regs intimately and will tell you all. Indeed, aperitifs and dinner en famille, even breakfast in the separate guest house, are intensely stimulating occasions – not for shrinking violets. A professional chef, Ian serves superb food with a flourish and wines from his cellar. Their clever renovation of the little old village house makes for a communal kitchen, a biggish downstairs room and two cosy rooms under the rafters with Laura Ashley-style décor and some nice furniture.

rooms	3: 2 doubles, 1 twin.
price	€36-€39.
meals	Dinner with wine, €18. Guest kitchen.
closed	Rarely.
directions	From Tulle N120 twds Argentat Aurillac. Left into main square with Mairie on right, park in square on left of church.

Ian & Jacquie Hoare
La Souvigne,
1 impasse La Fontaine,
19380 Forgès, Corrèze
tel +33 (0)5 55 28 63 99
fax +33 (0)5 55 28 65 62
email info@souvigne.com
web www.souvigne.com

Map 10 Entry 507

Limousin

Saulières

The delightful Madame Lafond was born in the area and will never move away – you will soon understand why. With rooms in a modern extension, Saulières is no ancient monument but it's a picture of genuine French rural style, blissfully quiet in its conservation area. Ideal for families, it has masses of space, lots of grass for playing on, a guest kitchen and big, log-fired living room with good old armchairs, magazines and games, plus some fabulous places to visit. The superbly 'family, friends and farming' atmosphere created by this highly likeable couple has been much praised.

rooms	4: 1 double, 1 twin, 1 triple, 1 quadruple.
price	€45. Quadruple €65.
meals	Restaurants 2km. Kitchen available.
closed	Rarely.
directions	From A20 exit Brive. A89 exit Tulle. N120 to Argentat; D12 along R. Dordogne for Beaulieu, past Monceaux to Saulières (6km from Argentat).

Marie-Jo & Jean-Marie Lafond
Saulières,
Monceaux sur Dordogne,
19400 Argentat, Corrèze
tel +33 (0)5 55 28 09 22
fax +33 (0)5 55 28 09 22
email mariejo.lafond@free.fr
web www.chambredhotes-saulieres.com

Map 10 Entry 508

Limousin

La Farge

The stone hamlets take you back to another, slower France as you drive through these rugged valleys. The Archibalds have adopted the stones and the peace, updating them with their English sense of fine finish: an ancient cart carefully restored before being set alight with flowers, old windows fitted with the latest fly screens against sometime bugs, and first-class showers. Pretty pastel rooms have honey-boarded floors and a teddy each; modern pine mixes with antique oak; the kitchen's solid farmhouse table, wood-burning stove and super food are the heart of this welcoming house. *Minimum stay two nights.*

rooms	3: 2 doubles; 1 twin with separate bath.
price	€60.
meals	Dinner with wine, €25.
closed	Rarely.
directions	From Argentat D12; D83E1 for Le Vialard & Moustoulat; 3km right for La Farge; right again; 2nd house on right in village with black gates.

Keith & Helen Archibald
La Farge,
19400 Monceaux sur Dordogne,
Corrèze

tel   +33 (0)5 55 28 54 52
email   archi-at-lafarge@wanadoo.fr
web   www.chezarchi.com

Map 10 Entry 509

Auvergne

Auvergne

Château de Peufeilhoux

Young, full of knowledge about this undiscovered area of the Auvergne, they pay warm attention to both guests and food. Manon loves to cook, Marc is passionate about wine (he has a wine merchant father). Dinner, served in the baronial dining room or on the terrace, is lively. The château on the top of a hill amid pasture, woodland and English gardens is authentic, beamed, wood-panelled and early 20th century. Big bathrooms and bedrooms exude old-fashioned French charm, beds are super-comfy and views sweep over the stunning valley. *Minimum stay two nights mid-January-March & July/August.*

rooms	5: 2 doubles, 2 twins, 1 family room for 3-4.
price	€70-€120.
meals	Dinner, 4 courses with wine, €30, Fri-Sun.
closed	Rarely.
directions	From A71 exit J9 Vallon en Sully & Montluçon; N144 for Vallon; cont. past Vallon for St Amand Montrand; turning on right, signed.

Marc & Manon Beelen & Patries Haberer
Château de Peufeilhoux,
03190 Vallon en Sully, Allier
tel   +33 (0)4 70 06 59 60
fax   +33 (0)4 70 06 60 42
email   info@peufeilhoux.com
web   www.peufeilhoux.com

Map 10 Entry 510

Auvergne

Manoir Le Plaix

Thick, thick walls, great old stones and timbers: the immense age of this gloriously isolated farmhouse (once a fortified manor) is evident but it has been beautifully restored. Big, cosy, subtly-lit rooms, lovingly decorated with family antiques and memorabilia, are reached by a treat of a spiral staircase. A hundred head of cattle graze safely in the surrounding fields – here, you can walk, fish, and hunt mushrooms in season. Easy and good-natured, Madame Raucaz opens her heart, her intelligence and her dining table to all (excellent-value dinners). Relax and feel at home. Great value.

rooms	4: 2 doubles, 1 twin, 1 triple.
price	€45.
meals	Dinner with wine, €18.
closed	Rarely.
directions	From Nevers N7 S 22km; right D978a to Le Veudre; D13 then D234 to Pouzy Mésangy. Chambres d'hôtes signs.

Claire Raucaz
Manoir Le Plaix,
Pouzy Mésangy,
03320 Lurcy Levis,
Allier
tel   +33 (0)4 70 66 24 06
fax   +33 (0)4 70 66 25 82
email   leplaix@yahoo.fr

Map 10 Entry 511

Auvergne

Cognet

Billowing hilly pastures surround the hamlet with sensuality. Here, built in 1886 as a rich man's summer place, is a generous, sophisticated house, informed by Madame's broad cultural interests, her father's paintings and her superb Provençal furniture that sits so well by original panelling and wide fireplace. Alone up steep shiny stairs, the guest space is a sweep of pine floor and ceiling; light floods in past royal blue curtains, big pine bed, old chest; a proud tree shades the splendid shower room. Deep rest, super breakfast and conversation, Romanesque jewels to visit – a must. *Not suitable for children.*

rooms	1 twin/double.
price	€60.
meals	Restaurant in village.
closed	November-February.
directions	From A75 exit Gannat to Vichy; over Allier; immed. right Bd JFK, left for Cusset; over railway; 5 traffic lights, D906 right for Ferrières; right D995 9km; left D121; bear right to Cognet 800m. House with iron gates.

Bénita Mourges
Cognet,
03300 La Chapelle,
Allier

tel	+33 (0)4 70 41 88 28
mobile	+33 (0)6 98 47 54 48
email	maison.cognet@free.fr
web	maison.cognet.free.fr

Map 10 Entry 512

Auvergne

8 route de la Limagne

A generous and handsome family house: the volcanoes gave their lava for dining room and staircase floor slabs; ancestors gave their names to bedrooms, where their faded photographs and intricate samplers now hang on the walls. Others left some fine old *objets* and pieces of furniture and built the stupendous brick barns that shelter the garden; Élisabeth applied all her flair to the décor, marrying vital colour harmonies and soft fabrics. She is dynamic, intelligent and full of wry humour, once a trace of shyness has worn off, and serves her deliciously wholesome breakfast in the flower-decked garden in summer.

rooms	3 doubles.
price	€68-€75.
meals	Restaurants 7km.
closed	November-March, except by arrangement.
directions	From A71, Riom exit, N144 for Combronde & Montluçon; 2.5km after Davayat, right onto D122 to Chaptes.

Mme Élisabeth Beaujeard
8 route de la Limagne,
Chaptes,
63460 Beauregard Vendon,
Puy-de-Dôme

| tel | +33 (0)4 73 63 35 62 |

Map 10 Entry 513

Auvergne

Domaine de Ternant

Grand style – marble, mouldings, gilt frames – and interesting hosts. Madame's astoundingly beautiful patchwork hangings make it utterly personal, the scent of beeswax hovers. All is pure Auvergne: original porcelain basins, third-generation owners, exceptional breakfasts. Bedrooms have antique beds – brass, carved, delicious 1930s – on polished parquet with good rugs and, of course, Madame's artistic needle. The dining room is elegant, the salon, with its well-used piano, sophisticated, the billiard room a library. A good-humoured couple who have lived in foreign lands and enjoy their guests.

rooms	4: 1 double, 1 twin, 2 suites for 4.
price	€86–€90.
meals	Choice of restaurants 3–10km.
closed	15 November–15 March.
directions	From A71 for Clermont Ferrand; exit Riom for Volvic & Puy de Dôme; at Le Cratère, left for Clermont; right for Chanat, 3km Ternant, signposted.

Catherine Piollet
Domaine de Ternant,
Ternant, 63870 Orcines,
Puy-de-Dôme
tel   +33 (0)4 73 62 11 20
fax   +33 (0)4 73 62 29 96
email   domaine.ternant@free.fr
web   domaine.ternant.free.fr

Map 10 Entry 514

Auvergne

La Closerie de Manou

What is B&B perfection? Spring water running from the taps of a huge walk-in shower? La Closerie, a typical old stone-walled and shingled house, sits among the ancient volcanoes of Auvergne where great rivers rise and water is pure. Françoise, called Manou, is a delight, sprightly and elegant, as generous with her time as with her scrumptious embroidered-napkin buffet breakfast, served in the impressive dining room or the garden. Bedrooms are perfect, beamed and ginghem'd, hairdryers hide in bathrooms; in short, every modern comfort against a timeless backdrop of drama and character.

rooms	5: 2 doubles, 1 twin, 2 triples.
price	€75–€80.
meals	Restaurant in village.
closed	15 October–1 April.
directions	From Paris A71; A89 to Bordeaux; exit St Julien Puy Lavèze. At r'bout direction Le Mont Dore; right onto D922 then left for Murat le Quaire; pass Mairie, 3km to Le Genestoux; house signed.

Françoise Larcher
La Closerie de Manou,
Le Genestoux,
63240 Le Mont Dore, Puy-de-Dôme
tel   +33 (0)4 73 65 26 81
fax   +33 (0)4 73 65 58 34
email   lacloseriedemanou@club-internet.fr
web   www.lacloseriedemanou.com

Map 10 Entry 515

Auvergne

Sailles

Perched above Saint Nectaire with views of almost endless forest and mountain, it's a farmhouse in a perfect setting. Inside lives Monique, enthusing her guests with descriptions of the Auvergne in perfect English. She does not pretend to provide luxury, just cosy comfort and the feeling of being in a real home. You stay in an attached but independent cottage and have a kitchen area of your own, but breakfast in Monique and Daniel's vaulted dining room, full of exposed beams and stone; eat copiously and enjoy the humour and zest of a couple who were born to hospitality.

rooms	1 double.
price	€45.
meals	Restaurants in St Nectaire. Kitchen available.
closed	Rarely.
directions	From A75 exit 6 to St Nectaire; at church, D150 for 1.5km; left D643. Last house 300m, signposted.

Monique Deforge
Sailles,
Sailles,
63710 St Nectaire, Puy-de-Dôme
tel   +33 (0)4 73 88 40 08
email   daniel.deforge@wanadoo.fr
web   perso.wanadoo.fr/deforge/lesfrenes

Map 10 Entry 516

Auvergne

Le Chastel Montaigu

The solid reality of this magical tower is deeply moving. Michel's skill in renovation (well, reconstruction from near-ruin) and Anita's decorating talent have summoned a rich and sober mood that makes the 15th-century *chastel* throb with authenticity: only 'medieval' materials; magnificent deep-tinted fabrics, many designed by Anita; antique tapestries, panelling and furniture – nothing flashy, all simply true to the density of the place. Spectacular bedrooms, amazing bathrooms of antique-faced modern perfection and a generous breakfast – this is a treat. *Minimum stay two nights.*

rooms	3 doubles.
price	€125–€130.
meals	Auberge & restaurants 1-4km.
closed	October-April.
directions	From A75 exit 6 for St Nectaire; through Champeix to Montaigut le Blanc; follow signs up to château.

Anita & Michel Sauvadet
Le Chastel Montaigu,
63320 Montaigut le Blanc,
Puy-de-Dôme
tel   +33 (0)4 73 96 28 49
fax   +33 (0)4 73 96 21 60
mobile +33 (0)6 81 61 52 26
web   www.le-chastel-montaigu.com

Map 10 Entry 517

Auvergne

Château de Vaulx

Is this real or a fairy tale? Creak along the parquet, pray in the chapel, swan around the salon, sleep in one tower, bathe in another. It's been in the family for 800 years and room names are as evocative as furnishings are romantic — worthy of the troubadours who surely sang here. Breakfast on home-hive honey, brioche, yogurt, eggs, cheese, get to know your delightfully entertaining hosts, visit the donkey, admire the magnificent trees or, if you're feeling homesick, have a drink in Guy's evocatively vaulted cellar 'pub' with its impressive collection of beer mats. A dream of a place.

Auvergne

Château de Pasredon

Whichever of the splendid rooms is yours — we loved the yellow *Louis Philippe* — you will feel grand: here a canopied bed, there an exquisite little dressing room, everywhere shimmering mirrors, fabulous views of uninterrupted parkland, ancient trees, the Puy-de-Dôme: acres of space for those who like to read in a secluded spot to the magical sound of birdsong. The vast, panelled, period-furnished drawing and dining rooms are quite dramatic. A perfect and relaxed hostess, Madame makes you feel immediately at ease and helps you plan your day over a delicious breakfast. Really very special.

rooms	2: 1 double, 1 triple.
price	€60–€70.
meals	Auberge 3km.
closed	Rarely.
directions	From A72 exit 3 on D7 through Celles sur Durolle to Col du Frissonnet. Château 1st right after Col du Frissonnet.

rooms	5: 3 doubles, 1 twin, 1 suite.
price	€75–€95.
meals	Restaurants 2–8km.
closed	15 October–15 April.
directions	From Clermont Ferrand A75 exit 13 to Parentignat; D999 for St Germain l'Herme 6km; sign on right. (8km from A75 exit.)

Guy & Régine Dumas de Vaulx
Château de Vaulx,
63120 Ste Agathe,
Puy-de-Dôme
tel   +33 (0)4 73 51 50 55
fax   +33 (0)4 73 51 50 55

Henriette Marchand
Château de Pasredon,
63500 St Rémy de Chargnat,
Puy-de-Dôme
tel   +33 (0)4 73 71 00 67
fax   +33 (0)4 73 71 08 72

Map 10 Entry 518

Map 10 Entry 519

Auvergne

Le Relais de la Diligence

Soon after escaping to this pretty village in rugged country, Peter and Laurette opened their doors so guests could enjoy the simplicity of their aptly named house and the local flora and fauna. Peter`s craftsman's skills and their shared passion for restoration come together in this old coaching inn with its carefully restored beams, warm colours and sweet painted furniture. Comfortable beds in sunny bedrooms, cosy sitting room with glorious wood-burner and simple light suppers at a refectory table speak of thoughtful, kind hosts. Next morning, wave to Fleur as she jumps on the school bus, driven by Laurette.

rooms	3: 1 double, 1 family room for 3, 1 family suite for 4.
price	€45. €75 for 4.
meals	Light supper from €6.
closed	Rarely.
directions	From La Chaise Dieu, D906 for Ambert; at Arlanc D999a left for St Germain L'Herm; 13km to St Bonnet; Le Relais on left in middle of village.

Peter & Laurette Eggleton
Le Relais de la Diligence,
Le Bourg,
63630 St Bonnet Le Chastel,
Puy-de-Dôme
tel   +33 (0)4 73 72 57 96
fax   +33 (0)4 73 72 57 96
web   www.relais-diligence.com

Map 10 Entry 520

Auvergne

Ma Cachette

Pierre is the gardener, Johan the cook. Both South African, your charming hosts left the film and television world for this aqua-shuttered village house in the heart of the Regional Park. A few steps from the romantic, private garden, lush with roses, ancient fruit trees and well-tended vegetables, will find you walking some of the most stunning and unspoilt trails through the Massif Central. Rooms are spacious with Persian carpets and garden flowers; walk-in showers are superb; a stylish living room is for guests. Do have dinner: you'll enjoy the conversation as much as the *confit de canard*.

rooms	4: 3 doubles, 1 twin.
price	€55-€60.
meals	Dinner with wine, €25.
closed	Rarely.
directions	From A72 exit 2 for Thiers (west); D906 for Ambert & Le Puy en Velay; 67km, follow chambres d'hôtes signs on entering Arlanc; close to St Pierre Roman church.

Johan Bernard & Pierre Knoesen
Ma Cachette,
10 rue du 11 Novembre,
63220 Arlanc, Puy-de-Dôme
tel   +33 (0)4 73 95 04 88
fax   +33 (0)4 73 95 04 88
email   cachette@club-internet.fr
web   www.ma-cachette.com

Map 10 Entry 521

Auvergne

La Jacquerolle

Built on the ramparts of the ancient town, just below the medieval Abbey whose August music festival draws thousands, the big old house has been lovingly filled with flowers in every fashion and form – carpets, curtains, wallpaper, quilts. It is a soft French boudoir where mother and daughter, quietly attentive, welcome their guests to sleep in pine-slatted bedrooms – ask for the largest – with firm-mattressed divan beds and good little bathrooms (some with wonderful views out to the hills). Gallic cuisine is served on bone china with bohemian crystal before a huge stone fireplace.

rooms	3: 1 double, 1 twin, 1 family room for 4.
price	€57–€60.
meals	Dinner with wine, €24.
closed	Rarely.
directions	From Brioude D19 to La Chaise Dieu. Head for Centre Ville; facing Abbey, right to Place du Monument. Park here; house is off square: bottom right-hand corner then down on left.

Jacqueline & Carole Chailly
La Jacquerolle,
Rue Marchédial,
43160 La Chaise Dieu,
Haute-Loire
tel   +33 (0)4 71 00 07 52
mobile   +33 (0)6 70 73 68 30
email   lajacquerolle@hotmail.com

Map 10 Entry 522

Auvergne

Le Bourg

Simple, unaffected people and keen walkers love this place, with its friendly welcoming atmosphere and new lick of paint. Furniture remains dated and simple, but the home-grown food oozes genuine natural goodness. Éric and his partner Christelle manage a flock of milk-producing sheep and welcome all-comers with a 'cup of friendship' before the great granite hearth. There are sheep and music festivals in August, while walkers are in heaven: join a circuit here and walk from B&B to B&B, or cross-country ski through it in winter. Wonderful value for money in an unknown corner of the Auvergne.

rooms	3: 1 double, 1 twin, 1 triple.
price	€38.
meals	Dinner with wine, €14.
closed	Never.
directions	From Le Puy en Velay, D589 to Saugues; D585 for Langeac, left onto D32 to Venteuges.

Éric Dumas & Christelle Meunier
Le Bourg,
43170 Venteuges,
Haute-Loire
tel   +33 (0)4 71 77 80 66
mobile   +33 (0)6 64 29 14 33
email   meunier-chambresdhotes@wanadoo.fr
web   www.lapastourelle.fr

Map 10 Entry 523

Auvergne

Château de Bassignac

Its front door wide open, Bassignac is real unposh family B&B run, for many years, by charming, active Annie with the support of her artist husband (come and paint with him). She was born in this 16th-century fortified manor built on 13th-century ruins beside what is now a fairly busy road and sold her Parisian furniture shop to come back and... furnish her guest rooms. They are big (two or three windows, fireplace) and small (invitingly womb-like), kempt and clear with Monsieur's watercolours and a dated chintzy charm that draws people back. Son and daughter-in-law run a delicious *ferme auberge* next door.

rooms	6: 4 doubles, 1 family room, 1 family suite for 5.
price	€60-€130.
meals	Occasional dinner with wine, €45. Auberge next door.
closed	Rarely.
directions	D922 from Mauriac for Bort les Orgues Basignac; 16km on right.

Annie & Jean-Michel Besson
Château de Bassignac,
Bassignac,
15240 Saignes,
Cantal

tel	+33 (0)4 71 40 82 82
fax	+33 (0)4 71 40 82 82
email	chateau.bassignac@wanadoo.fr

Map 10 Entry 524

Auvergne

Château de la Vigne

A rare treat, an experience from another age: the deliciously organic old château in pure Cantal style surveying the panorama has been in the family for ever and is utterly lavish. The courtroom is panelled and dazzlingly painted; the fine and formal dining room (do dress for dinner); the Aubusson-hung, chandeliered salon; the Louis XV guest room with its lovely carved fireplace, the darkly four-postered Troubadour room, the bathrooms squeezed into impossible places... a remarkable Dinky Toy collection, and more. Stunning but not overbearing, and yours to share with these gentle, open, aristocratic hosts.

rooms	4: 2 doubles, 1 twin, 1 triple.
price	€132.
meals	Dinner €27. Wine €25.
closed	November-Easter.
directions	From Clermont-Ferrand N89 for Tulle; left D922 to Bort les Orgues; D681 to Mauriac & Ally. Signed.

Bruno & Anne
du Fayet de la Tour
Château de la Vigne,
15700 Ally, Cantal

tel	+33 (0)4 71 69 00 20
fax	+33 (0)4 71 69 00 20
email	la.vigne@wanadoo.fr
web	www.chateaudelavigne.com

Map 10 Entry 525

Auvergne

Ferme des Prades

A real farmhouse – warm and unpretentious. Françoise and Philippe are a sweet, down to earth couple who welcome company: their sons are away at school and this is *la France profonde*! The farm covers 150 hectares; walk for hours and you need not see another soul. The house, destroyed in the French Revolution, was rebuilt by the Abbot of Les Prades (confessor to Napoleon Bonaparte). Outside, ox-blood red shutters give a splash to speckled stone walls, inside are stripped floors, comfortably worn sofas, fine armoires, muslin curtains – and Françoise's bedside tables fashioned from milk churns.

rooms	3: 1 double, 1 triple, 1 family room.
price	€49-€61.
meals	Dinner with wine, €15.
closed	Rarely.
directions	D996 Champeix & Issoire; A75 to Montpellier exit 23 (Massiac); N122 to Murat; D21 Allanche; D679 to Marcenat; Hamlet les Prades, farm on left.

Françoise & Philippe Vauché
Ferme des Prades,
Les Prades, Landeyrat,
15160 Allanche, Cantal
tel +33 (0)4 71 20 48 17
fax +33 (0)4 71 20 91 26
email les-prades@wanadoo.fr
web www.fermedesprades.com

Map 10 Entry 526

Auvergne

Domaine de Luc

Such a heart-filled house, no wonder Olivia, with her husband's support, is battling to keep it in the family. Her ancestor built it in 1900 and grew hay for stagecoach horses. He also planted the lime tree walk to the lake – you can swim, row, fish and picnic all day long. The house is amiable, uncluttered, full of the charm of things imperfect: antique and modern pine beds in parquet-floored family-friendly rooms, big homely bathrooms, the warm kitchen or elegant panelled dining room for meals, lots of light from the rolling Cantal wilds, space for all and their mounts, and real hospitality.

rooms	6: 1 suite; 1 family room, 1 double sharing separate bath; 2 doubles, 1 family room sharing separate bath.
price	€60-€75.
meals	Dinner €20. Wine from €5.
closed	Rarely.
directions	A75 exit 25; for St Poncy. Signposted.

Olivia Brunel
Domaine de Luc,
15500 St Poncy,
Cantal
tel +33 (0)4 71 23 06 79
fax +33 (0)4 71 23 06 79
email ddeluc15@wanadoo.fr
web www.domaine-de-luc.com

Map 10 Entry 527

Auvergne

Lou Ferradou

Your young hosts escaped from heaving, stressful Paris to this rural paradise where their brilliant conversion of an old Cantal farmhouse has preserved the original scullery ledge and sink (vast slabs of stone), the beams, and inglenook. They now aim to convert their neighbours to better environmental (get the scrap metal off the hillside) and social (more respect for your woman?) attitudes. Bedrooms are country comfortable with big oak beds and white counterpanes, the meals are feasts, there are a games room, billiards and books, a sitting room in the barn, and the Balleux are a most interesting and happy couple.

Auvergne

La Roussière

Not another house in sight. Just the Cantal hills and a chattering stream. Brigitte and Christian live here with their young son and have done much of the restoration themselves. Christian is a genius at woodwork: his golden staircase, cupboards and panelling sit happily with mellow stone, old armoires, ancient ceiling hooks... There's an Alpine air to the place. Beds are excellent, sheets crisp and meals en famille a delight: great food, good wine, mineral water from the spring. Be calmed by a serene, rustic elegance. No actual garden but their green rolling hectares, a haven for wildlife, are perfection enough.

rooms	5: 1 double, 1 suite. Cottage: 1 double, 2 suites.
price	€44–€54.
meals	Dinner with wine, €14.
closed	Rarely.
directions	From Aurillac D920 to Arpajon; left on D990 for 10km (don't go to St Étienne de Carlat); left for Caizac; signposted.

rooms	3: 1 double, 1 suite for 2-3, 1 suite for 3-4.
price	€58–€68.
meals	Dinner with wine, €18.
closed	Rarely.
directions	From Massiac N122 for Aurillac; in Vic sur Cère left for Pailherols; D54 for 6km up to col de Curebourse; continue to Pailherols; left before bridge; continue straight on 4km.

Francine & Jacky Balleux
Lou Ferradou,
Caizac,
15130 St Étienne de Carlat, Cantal
tel   +33 (0)4 71 62 42 37
mobile   +33 (0)6 65 25 49 79
email   balleux@louferradou.com
web   www.louferradou.com

Christian Grégoir
& Brigitte Renard
La Roussière,
15800 St Clément,
Cantal
tel   +33 (0)4 71 49 67 34
email   info@laroussiere.fr
web   www.laroussiere.fr

Map 10 Entry 528

Map 10 Entry 529

Auvergne

Château de Lescure

On the southern slope of Europe's largest extinct volcano, where nine valleys radiate, stands a rustic 18th-century château guarded by an 11th-century tower where two vaulted bedrooms soar, one with four-poster. The elegant twin room has the right furbelowed drapery and in the glorious inglenook kitchen Sophie serves home-smoked ham and veg from her organic garden. She and Michel are cultured, bilingual hosts. You play bridge? Bring your tricks. Or you may be invited to volunteer for bread making, cooking, organic gardening, trail blazing...
Minimum stay two nights in summer.

rooms	3: 1 twin; 1 double with separate shower; 1 double with separate shower room downstairs.
price	€60–€65.
meals	Dinner with wine, €25.
closed	Rarely.
directions	From Clermont Ferrand A75 to St Flour; up to old town; left D921 10km; right D990, through Pierrefort to St Martin. Right for Brezons; château 3km on right.

Michel Couillaud
& Phoebe Sophie Verhulst
Château de Lescure,
15230 Saint Martin Sous Vigouroux,
Cantal

tel +33 (0)4 71 73 40 91
email michel.couillaud@wanadoo.fr
web www.multimania.com/psvlescure

Map 10 Entry 530

Midi – Pyrénées

Midi – Pyrénées

Manoir de Malagorse

Passionate eager hosts, a refined old manor in an idyllic setting, magnificent rooms, meals cooked by a master (in winter they run an Alpine restaurant). Abel and Anna's restoration is caring and sophisticated, rooms and bathrooms are statements of simple luxury, and the great kitchen is a dream – its cooker a wonder to behold, its fireplace massive, its ceiling vaulted. There is space for togetherness and privacy, your hosts are unintrusively present and Anna can offer a professional massage after Abel's demanding wine-tastings. You get more than you pay for – enjoy it to the hilt. *'Gastronomic discovery' weekends.*

Midi – Pyrénées

Moulin de Goth

The 13th-century mill – imaginatively, magically restored by its Australian owners – guards a garden of rare peace and beauty. Lily pads and lawns, willows and water – it is ineffably lovely. Coral is humorous and exuberant and cooks like an angel; Bill makes tables and intelligent conversation – join him for snooker in the barn. Big, dramatically raftered rooms have decorative iron beds, soft fabrics, antique chests. The stone-walled dining room, its arrow slits intact, is stunningly barrel-vaulted – but meals are mostly in the enchanting garden. *Children over ten welcome.*

rooms	6 doubles.
price	€100–€140.
meals	Dinner with wine, €45.
closed	Mid-October–May.
directions	From Souillac 6km; N20 for Cressensac, on dual carriageway 1st right to Cuzance, Église de Rignac; 1st right in Rignac, signposted.

rooms	2: 1 double, 1 triple, each with separate bath.
price	€70.
meals	Dinner with wine, €25.
closed	Rarely.
directions	From Martel on N140 D23 for Creysse. After 3km right fork for Le Goth, 1.5km; 1st house on right after stone bridge.

	Anna & Abel Congratel
	Manoir de Malagorse,
	46600 Cuzance, Lot
tel	+33 (0)5 65 27 15 61
mobile	+33 (0)6 89 33 54 45
email	acongratel@manoir-de-malagorse.fr
web	www.manoir-de-malagorse.fr

	Coral Heath-Kauffman
	Moulin de Goth,
	46600 Creysse,
	Lot
tel	+33 (0)5 65 32 26 04
email	coral.heath@wanadoo.fr
web	www.moulindugoth.com

Map 9 Entry 531

Map 9 Entry 532

L'Oustal Nau

This is the house that Colette built when she came back from Paris. And this is the garden that she spent 17 years creating – one glorious hectare overlooking the Dordogne valley. You can spend all day in it if you want to: Colette, who used to work in the diplomatic service, is that sort of hostess, infinitely generous and with a wonderful smile. There's a guest kitchen where you can prepare drinks and snacks and Colette will provide picnics if required. The house is modern but full of character and lovely old pieces; the big, comfortable bedrooms are each named after a flower. A great place for families.

rooms	4: 2 doubles, 1 twin, 1 triple.
price	€80–€100.
meals	Picnic €15 p.p. Guest kitchen.
closed	12 November, 15 December & 6 January–6 February.
directions	From St Céré D20 to Carennac; in village Auberge des Vieux Quercy on right, turn left following Parking sign; top of road left; 200m green gates on right. House just before Parking.

Mme Colette Lemant
L'Oustal Nau,
Les Combes,
46110 Carennac, Lot
tel +33 (0)5 65 10 94 09
fax +33 (0)5 65 50 27 49
email lemant@club-internet.fr
web www.oustalnau-carennac.com

Map 9 Entry 533

La Buissonnière

The converted 18th-century barn with its stone outbuilding feels instantly like home. Élisabeth spent years in America (she's bilingual), loves ceramics and patchwork, uses her creative touch everywhere, including the terrace and garden with its secluded spots, and is a fount of historical and cultural lore. The open-plan living room, where old skylights deliver splashes of sky, is full of artistic character with oak floors, old stove and pretty antiques beneath paintings of all periods. The airy ground-floor guest room has its own antique writing table, watercolours and a glazed stable door to the garden.

rooms	2: 1 double, 1 twin.
price	€55.
meals	Dinner with wine, €18–€20.
closed	Rarely.
directions	From Gramat D840 (previously called N140) for Figeac; left for 'Le Bout du Lieu' after sign for Thémines; house, 200m on right; signposted.

Élisabeth de Lapérouse Coleman
La Buissonnière,
Le Bout du Lieu,
46120 Thémines, Lot
tel +33 (0)5 65 40 88 58
fax +33 (0)5 65 40 88 58
email edelaperouse.coleman@wanadoo.fr
web www.laperouse.fr

Map 10 Entry 534

Midi – Pyrénées

Mas de la Feuille

Charles cooks – the huge kitchen is his domain – and meals, French or Franco-Japanese, are memorable. Kako paints – even the wooden coat hangers bear her flowers. The house is French and spotless. All bedrooms, in the older, lower part of the house, have an exceptionally tranquil rolling view, with superb mattresses; the oldest has an ancient stone fireplace and the original stone sink. They are delightful people, a multi-talented, cosmopolitan couple who keep house here in the summer and live in Japan in the winter. Figeac is said to be one of the best-renovated towns in Europe. Heaven for walkers.

rooms	3: 2 twins, 1 suite for 3.
price	€55.
meals	Dinner with wine, €25.
closed	November-March.
directions	From Gramat N140 for Figeac 17km; through Le Bourg, sharp left immediately after small bridge on edge of village. Sign on left, 1km.

Kako & Charles Larroque
Mas de la Feuille,
46120 Le Bourg,
Lot

tel	+33 (0)5 65 11 00 17
fax	+33 (0)5 65 11 00 17
mobile	+33 (0)6 22 65 37 24
email	larroquecharles@club-internet.fr

Map 10 Entry 535

Midi – Pyrénées

Maison Rouma

Dr Rouma, a distinguished local figure and Consul General, built the house in the 1850s. It was almost a ruin before the Arnetts found it on their return from Japan and restored it, keeping as much of the original as possible, including the wallpaper in the hall where the winding staircase is such a delight. The décor has an oriental tendency, particularly in the enormous dining room. The setting just couldn't be better; there are stunning views over the river and the pretty old town – famous for its medieval music festival which climaxes, by the way, with the "largest firework display in France".
Two bedrooms have sofabeds.

rooms	3: 2 doubles, 1 twin.
price	€50.
meals	Choice of restaurants nearby.
closed	Rarely.
directions	From Cahors D911 for Fumel & Villeneuve sur Lot. At Puy l'Évêque take Rue du Dr Rouma to bridge; house last on right before bridge.

Bill & Ann Arnett
Maison Rouma,
2 rue du Docteur Rouma,
46700 Puy l'Évêque, Lot

tel	+33 (0)5 65 36 59 39
fax	+33 (0)5 65 36 59 39
email	williamarnett@hotmail.com
web	www.puyleveque.com

Map 9 Entry 536

Midi – Pyrénées

Mondounet

The golden Lot stone glows, there are stunning views from the terrace over two valleys, the pool is heated and salt-purified… so what matter if the atmosphere is sometimes a little chaotic. The Scotts labour ever on at their little empire, restoring the 17th-century farmhouse and outbuildings to their original character and adding modern comforts. Zoé will charm you, see you have a good time, serve breakfast whenever. Dinner, sometimes a poolside barbecue, is fun, relaxed and informal and Peter plays the guitar and organises activities. There is a pool-house kitchen for lazy picnic lunches.

rooms	1 double.
price	€50–€55.
meals	Dinner with wine, €20.
closed	Rarely.
directions	From Cahors for Toulouse; at r'bout D653 for Agen 16km; at junc. right D656 for 14km; through Villesèque, Sauzet, Bovila; after Bovila, 3rd left; signposted.

	Peter & Zoé Scott
	Mondounet,
	46800 Fargues, Lot
tel	+33 (0)5 65 36 96 32
fax	+33 (0)5 65 31 84 89
email	scotsprops@aol.com
web	www.mondounetholidaysandhomes.com

Map 14 Entry 537

Midi – Pyrénées

Valrose - Le Poujal

The Italian ambassador, homesick for Florence, built this house and its balustraded terrace overlooking the river in 1805. It has a very lovely garden and a swimming pool in a flowery corner of the lawn (for guests in the mornings) but inside, the first word that comes to mind is 'dramatic': the big, white-beamed dining room – once the kitchen perhaps? – is dominated by a vast fireplace, bold still lifes and red-and-white checks, the bedrooms are delightful, the wonderful terraces have views to the river beyond. A retired teacher who loves people, life, colour, Claude finds B&B the perfect solution.

rooms	2 doubles.
price	€55.
meals	Choice of restaurants nearby.
closed	Rarely.
directions	From Cahors D8 to Pradines; right at roundabout; house 100m down on right through big gates.

	Claude Faille
	Valrose - Le Poujal,
	46090 Pradines,
	Lot
tel	+33 (0)5 65 22 18 52
email	claude.faille@libertysurf.fr
web	valrose.chez.tiscali.fr/

Map 9 Entry 538

Midi – Pyrénées

Flaynac

A heart-warming, genuine *chambres d'hôtes* experience, staying with this lovely cheerful couple who are always ready for a drink and a chat (in French) – their love of life is infectious. Use the peaceful terrace where your hosts are happy for you to sit all day over your breakfast, revelling in the setting, the vast views and the flowering garden. The décor – floral papers and family furniture – is in keeping with the old farmhouse. No dinner but lots of home-grown wine and aperitif, fruit from their trees and *gâteau de noix* (walnut cake) with their own honey – flowing as in paradise.

rooms	1 double.
price	€48.
meals	Restaurant 2km.
closed	Rarely.
directions	From Cahors D8 for Pradines 8km; at sign for Flaynac, follow Chambres d'Hôtes sign on right, then right & right again.

M & Mme Jean Faydi
Flaynac,
46090 Pradines,
Lot
tel   +33 (0)5 65 35 33 36

Map 9   Entry 539

Midi – Pyrénées

Domaine de Lacombe

The elegant, flamboyantly decorated great barn living room reveals Michèle's sense of adventure, the books and baby grand tell of her earlier life as a bookseller and her love of music, the variegated bedrooms in the converted pigsties and stables, from modern simplicity to traditional florality, speak of her eclectic taste. Some have their own patios, one has the original spring welling up behind glass, all have space, privacy and fine bathrooms. Michèle bubbles with delight, encouraging guests to come and chat while she prepares a superb family meal to be shared sitting on rainbow chairs at the deep red table.

rooms	4: 1 double, 1 triple, 1 family room, 1 suite for 4.
price	€62–€92.
meals	Dinner with wine, €28.
closed	Rarely.
directions	From Paris A20 to Cahors Nord exit 58; N20 to Montauban Toulouse; right for Castelnau-Montratier; in Castelnau D19 right to Lauzerte Moissac; 2km, left 100m after brick barn. Lacombe 2nd left.

Michèle Lelourec
Domaine de Lacombe, Lacombe,
46170 Castelnau Monratier, Lot
tel   +33 (0)5 65 21 84 16
mobile +33 (0)6 84 77 07 53
email   michele.lelourec@free.fr
web   www.domaine-lacombe.com

Map 14   Entry 540

Midi – Pyrénées

Château de Termes

Such views! Sublime when the mists hang in the river valleys and the sun glints on the summits. Your hospitable hosts, he a small-plane instructor who offers flying for guests, she quietly busy with her gîtes, have been here two years. More domestic than ostentatious, their 1720s' château promises three gorgeous guest rooms, a garden, a pool, a play area, short tennis, a small bar. Floors are stripped wood or chunky terracotta, furniture 'distressed', two baths are integrated with bedrooms, the suite opens to the garden and the whimsical doubles are in the tower. For families: bliss. *3rd double available 2007.*

rooms	3: 2 doubles, 1 family suite for 3.
price	€65–€85.
meals	Dinner with wine €20–€25, except July & August.
closed	Rarely.
directions	From Martel; D803 to Vayrac St Céré, 4.5km on left.

Pierre & Sophie Nadin
Château de Termes,
St Denis, 46600 Martel, Lot
tel   +33 (0)5 65 32 42 03
fax   +33 (0)5 65 32 27 70
email infos@chateaudetermes.com
web   www.chateaudetermes.com

Map 14 Entry 541

Midi – Pyrénées

Mas de Guerre

Walkers with a taste for magnificent bathrooms and rare orchids (Gary's delight), this is for you. Food lovers too: Sheila always aims to produce a feast – traditional with a twist. They left city jobs for these wild spaces, did a superb restoration of this old house with huge attention to detail and now... B&B: a certain formality still hangs in the air. The big guest rooms in the old stables could scarcely be bettered: original stone flags, white-painted stone walls, classically comfortable new furniture, gorgeous old tiles in the bathrooms. Your attentive hosts do expect you to be out between 11am and 4pm.

rooms	3 doubles.
price	€58–€63.
meals	Dinner €19–€22. Wine list from €5.50.
closed	Rarely.
directions	From Cahors, D911 to Limogne-en-Quercy; D24 to Beauregard; right opposite old 'SPAR' sign & follow signs.

Sheila & Gary Tucknott
Mas de Guerre,
46260 Beauregard,
Lot
tel   +33 (0)5 65 24 32 86
email masdeguerre@freesurf.fr
web   www.masdeguerre.com

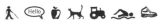

Map 15 Entry 542

Tondes

82400 Castelsagrat, Tarn-et-Garonne

Warm country people, the Sellars left a big Sussex farm for a smallholding in deepest France to breed sheep, goats and poultry the natural way: no pesticides, no heavy machines, animals roaming free. Their enthusiasm and guts have earned them great respect locally and their recipe for a simple, rewarding life includes receiving guests happily under the beams, by the open hearth, in pretty-coloured, country-furnished rooms with super walk-in showers. Julie will welcome you to her wonderful farmhouse kitchen, where she creates feasts of organic veg and homemade marvels. And the garden is a delight.

Hardworking, devoted to the traditional way of life, the Sellars produce almost all of their own food: milk and yogurt from a flock of 150 sheep, eggs from their hens and masses of organic fruit and vegetables. The bread is sourced from outside the farm, arriving fresh each morning from one of the two remaining mills in the *département*. Julie and Mark delight in showing guests around their working farm – children are even invited to join in the early morning milking sessions!

rooms	2: 1 double, 1 family room.
price	€47.
meals	Dinner with wine, €19.
closed	Rarely.
directions	From A62 exit 9. RN113 to Moissac; D7 for Bourg de Visa. At Fourquet, left at r'bout. After 500m, turn right at sign Chambres d'hotes 2km. 2nd sign on left, house at top of drive.

	Julie & Mark Sellars
tel	+33 (0)5 63 94 52 13
fax	+33 (0)5 63 94 52 13

SPECIAL GREEN ENTRY
see page 15

Map 14 Entry 543

Midi – Pyrénées

La Marquise

Quiet Gilbert will take you egg-hunting or goose-feeding of a morning – if you wish. Soft, smiling and big-hearted, Michèle loves doing B&B, has won prizes for her recipes, invents sauces and makes her own aperitif. The quaintly old-fashioned rooms are comfortable (beware waist-low beams) but food is definitely the priority here. Fishing rods on loan for use in the pond; footpaths out from the gate; proper hiking trails a bit further away; the treasures of Moissac, lovely villages, caves, within easy reach. This is an exceptional farm B&B. *Small pets welcome.*

rooms	4: 2 doubles, 2 twins.
price	€44–€45. Singles €41.
meals	Dinner with wine, €19–€20.
closed	Rarely.
directions	From Moissac D7 for Bourg de Visa about 14km; before Brassac, just before bridge, right for Fauroux; farm 2km; signposted.

Gilbert & Michèle Dio
La Marquise,
Brassac, 82190 Bourg de Visa,
Tarn-et-Garonne
tel +33 (0)5 63 94 25 16
fax +33 (0)5 63 94 25 16
email mglamarquise@infonie.fr

Map 14 Entry 544

Midi – Pyrénées

Las Bourdolles

The Quercy light glides through deep window – reveals to dapple the creamy old stones, dark beams and warm floorboards of this 17th-century farmhouse: the pilgrims' welcome cockleshell on the eaves is still deserved; nature-loving walkers and culture vultures flock here. Linda and Erica use a light touch, mixing old and new, cooking with delight, be it hearty game dinners or plum jam. The bedroom is soft and simple, colours pale, the great stone fireplace marvellous in winter. Having thrown over the pinstriped business life they are happily growing vegetables and welcoming visitors to peace.

rooms	1 suite.
price	€70-100.
meals	Lunch €15. Dinner with wine, €30.
closed	Christmas.
directions	A62 exit 8; D953 to Golfech & Lauzerte. Before Lauzerte, right onto D34 to Castelnau-Montratier. Straight on at church x-roads, D57 to Tréjouls. After 1km, sign on left.

Linda Hilton & Erica Lewis
Las Bourdolles,
82110 Tréjouls,
Tarn-et-Garonne
tel +33 (0)5 63 95 80 83
email erica.lewis@wanadoo.fr
web www.frenchbedbreakfast.com

Map 14 Entry 545

Maison des Chevaliers

The door opens onto the bricks and beams of the hall of this huge old house – you're in for a treat. Fascinating proofs of the owners' lives abroad steal your eyes at every turn, their conversation sparkles with anecdotes and interest, their house oozes taste and style. Bedrooms are big, all differently charming with antiques from Spain and Portugal, stencilled wood, superb paint finishes, old lace – it's endlessly, originally beautiful. The courtyard calls for summer breakfast, the secluded pool for cooling dips, the library for contemplation. The crowning glory? Madame once owned a restaurant.

rooms	4: 2 doubles, 2 suites.
price	€75.
meals	Dinner with wine, €22.
closed	Rarely.
directions	From Castelsarrasin for Toulouse, RN113; exit Escatalens; to 'centre du village'; house next to church.

Claudine Choux
Maison des Chevaliers,
82700 Escatalens, Tarn-et-Garonne
tel   +33 (0)5 63 68 71 23
fax   +33 (0)5 63 30 25 90
email   claude.choux@wanadoo.fr
web   www.maisondeschevaliers.com

Map 14 Entry 546

Domaine de Canals

Monsieur is passionate about the garden of his old family home which is a dream of trees, shrubs, lily pond and rare plants (their daughter is a botanist): a pergola awaits the contemplative guest, a maze summons the adventurous. Inside, the suite's gentle country décor is coloured with memories of Egypt, Mexico, India as well as Madame's hand painted furniture. Opening onto the courtyard, the cool, old-fashioned double room has a small tapestry-hung hallway and a wood-burning stove. More tapestries hang in the antique-filled dining room, the atmosphere is safe and friendly, the conversation full of interest.

rooms	2: 1 double, 1 suite for 6.
price	€50–€60. Suite €70–€140.
meals	Dinner with wine, €16–€23.
closed	Rarely.
directions	At Nègrepelisse D64 to Bioule; left after Bioule on D78 for Realville; at La Bouffière, house on right after cemetery.

M & Mme Auréjac
Domaine de Canals,
la Bouffière, 82800 Bioule,
Tarn-et-Garonne
tel   +33 (0)5 63 64 21 07
fax   +33 (0)5 63 64 21 07
email   domainecanals@free.fr
web   domaine-de-canals.fr.st

Map 14 Entry 547

Ferme du Gendre

"Her smile is fabulous." And Le Gendre is pure rural Frenchness, a working farm where fowl and pigs roam. Lively and empathetic, these people share their home easily, without fuss: rustic, cluttered living room with an open fire; simply-furnished, spotless bedrooms with slightly old-fashioned patterns and good beds; breakfast coffee in a bowl and, with that lovely smile, Madame taking you in as family. Her dogs and cats are as friendly as she is. Go lightly on lunch: dinner is uncompromisingly, deliciously 'farmhouse' with portions suitable for a hard-working farmer – she loves feeding her guests.

rooms	2: 1 double, 1 family room for 4.
price	€40.
meals	Dinner with wine, €15.
closed	Rarely.
directions	N20 S from Cahors to Caussade; left D926 to Septfonds; 3km beyond, left for Gaussou. Farm 1km on; signposted.

Françoise & Jean-Louis Zamboni
Ferme du Gendre,
82240 Lavaurette,
Tarn-et-Garonne
tel   +33 (0)5 63 31 97 72

Map 14 Entry 548

La Résidence

Your gentle young hosts love being part of village life – and what a village: medieval to the core and with a joyous Sunday market. It is a pleasure to stay in a townhouse in the centre of it all, with an airy hall and great spiral staircase, views through to an enclosed garden, original tiles and old stone walls. Sunlight dapples over soft colours and uncluttered spaces, modern sculpture and old country pieces. Three of the big tranquil bedrooms overlook the garden, another has a divine terrace with rooftop views. Seriously into food, Sabine and Evert do an excellent *table d'hôtes*. *Studio available.*

rooms	5: 3 doubles, 2 twins.
price	€70-€80.
meals	Dinner, 4 courses, €23. Wine list €10-€20.
closed	Rarely.
directions	From Montauban N20, 22km to Caussade; right D926 for 7km; right D5 to St Antonin Noble Val, 12km; in centre, behind town hall.

Evert & Sabine Weijers
La Résidence, 37 rue Droite,
82140 St Antonin Noble Val,
Tarn-et-Garonne
tel   +33 (0)5 63 67 37 56
fax   +33 (0)5 63 30 18 14
email   info@laresidence-france.com
web   www.laresidence-france.com

Map 15 Entry 549

Midi – Pyrénées

Setzères

An 18th-century Gascon manor, square and generous in its large lush garden boules, badminton, tranquil pool. Beautifully restored, decorated with English antiques and oriental mementoes, breathing charm and peace, it has heart-stopping views to the Pyrenees. Christine is well travelled, her local dishes are made with fresh ingredients and dinner conversation on the star-lit terrace is both cosmopolitan and fun. This is hidden France: old stone hamlets scattered across wide empty countryside, fascinating architecture, fabulous food. A highly civilised place to stay. *Children over ten welcome.*

rooms	3: 1 double, 1 twin, 1 suite for 4.
price	€110.
meals	Dinner €40. Wine €5–€30.
closed	2 weeks December–January.
directions	From Auch N124 for Vic Fézenac 5km; left D943 to Barran, Montesquiou, Bassoues (32km); D943 left for Marciac, sign for Scieurac & Flourès; in village left by church; house on right.

Christine Furney
Setzères,
Scieurac et Flourès,
32230 Marciac, Gers

tel	+33 (0)5 62 08 21 45
fax	+33 (0)5 62 08 21 45
email	setzeres32@aol.com
web	www.setzeres.com

Map 14 Entry 550

Midi – Pyrénées

Lieu Dit Fitan

In 1999, this was just another derelict barn in the glorious Gers countryside. Dido's restoration is inspired: at the door, the whole superb space opens before the eyes, English antiques gleam, the fine modern kitchen sparkles (available for a small fee). Upstairs, one luscious room: raw stones punctuate the soft white wall, patchwork cheers, books tempt. Downstairs, an impeccable full-disabled room. Delightful Dido wants to provide a holiday space for all, loves cooking, has travelled thousands of miles and is highly cultured. A corner of paradise, it even smells heavenly.

rooms	2: 1 double, 1 twin.
price	€65–€73.
meals	Dinner with wine, €35. Use of kitchen €8.
closed	Rarely.
directions	From Marciac D134 north; cross D946, continue to Louslitges church on left, 2nd right, Fitan 3/4 up on right. Pale green shutters.

Dido Streatfeild-Moore
Lieu Dit Fitan,
32230 Louslitges,
Gers

tel	+33 (0)5 62 70 81 88
fax	+33 (0)5 62 70 81 88
email	deedoenfrance@wanadoo.fr
web	www.chezdeedo.com

Map 14 Entry 551

Midi – Pyrénées

Maison de la Porte Fortifiée

Up from the 13th-century fortified archway, peace flows in from ancient stone walls and plunging country views. Welcoming interior designers – outgoing Carsten and his friend who cooks divinely – have clothed these medieval bones and spiralling wooden stair in exquisite classic-contemporary taste. It is sensual and stunning, be it winter by the fire in the cosy study or summer on the tabled terrace with soul-stretching views. Big light bedrooms are simply lovely, pale with colour splashes, lavish touches, gilt mirrors, bowls of flowers, clever little shower rooms, and one with a superb bathroom. Special.

rooms	4: 2 doubles, 2 twins.
price	€79–€110.
meals	Dinner €29. Wine from €9.50.
closed	January-February.
directions	From Auch N21 for Tarbes. At le Trouette D2 to l'Isle de Noé; D943 to Montesquiou. Drive to top of village; park opp. church; house on right near fortified tower.

Carsten Lutterbach
Maison de la Porte Fortifiée,
32320 Montesquiou, Gers
tel   +33 (0)5 62 70 97 06
fax   +33 (0)5 62 70 97 06
email maison@porte-fortifiee.de
web   www.porte-fortifiee.de

Map 14 Entry 552

Midi – Pyrénées

Domaine de Peyloubère

The sober buildings give no inkling of the explosion inside: 80 years ago, an Italian painter spread his heart and love of form and colour over ceilings and doors. 'His' suite has vast space, fine antiques, a dream of a great bathroom and dazzling paintings. Theresa and Ian fell for the romantically wild house and glorious park and left high-pressure London jobs to save the whole place from dereliction – their enthusiasm and sensitive intelligence show in every room. And the waterfall, the Italian garden, the wild bit – there's no other place like it. Wonderful for an anniversary treat.

rooms	2 suites.
price	€80–€105.
meals	Dinner with wine, €24.
closed	Rarely.
directions	From Auch N21 south 3km; left D929 for Lannemezan; in Pavie, left after Mairie, cross old bridge, 1st right, signposted Auterrive; house 1km on left.

Theresa & Ian Martin
Domaine de Peyloubère,
32550 Pavie, Gers
tel   +33 (0)5 62 05 74 97
fax   +33 (0)5 62 05 75 39
email martin@peyloubere.com
web   www.peyloubere.com

Map 14 Entry 553

Midi – Pyrénées

La Garenne

Youthful and enthusiastic, outgoing and warm-hearted, Mireille is an inspired cook and a delight to be with; Olivier is less ebullient but just as warm a presence and beyond the wooden terrace outside your window is a pretty, bird-filled garden. Together, they fill their cosy house with antique plates, prints, pictures and furniture. Their guest room is as family-comfortable and as warm-furnished as the rest. Mareille loves to practise her English – this is a relaxed and happy family home with the essential dogs and cats plus a swimming pool by the gîtes. Perfect for children.

rooms	1 double (& small room for child).
price	€53.
meals	Dinner with wine, €18.
closed	Rarely.
directions	From Auch N21 for Tarbes 2km; left D929 for Lannemezan; in Masseube, left for Simorre 4km; left for Bellegarde; 1st left, before church & castle.

Mireille & Olivier Courouble
La Garenne,
Bellegarde,
32140 Masseube, Gers
tel   +33 (0)5 62 66 03 61
fax   +33 (0)5 62 66 03 61
email   ocourouble@wanadoo.fr
web   www.visitorama.com/32/la-garenne.html

Map 14 Entry 554

Midi – Pyrénées

Maison de L'Évêque

You could weep, this valley is so beautiful; so are the house, its story, garden, owners. A doctor built it (see the caduceus on the great newel post), then it fostered one Bishop Laurence, who 'proved' Bernardette's miracles and set Lourdes up for glory. Arlette, a miracle of industry and human warmth, decorates prettily, cooks simply and brilliantly (you'll never want to eat out) and still finds plenty of time for guests. Quiet and attentive, Robert will take you hiking and fishing in that gorgeous valley (Pyrenean high-mountain trout are the best, naturally). A very special place.

rooms	4: 3 doubles, 1 triple.
price	€46-€55.
meals	Dinner with wine, €20-€28.
closed	November-Easter.
directions	From Lourdes N21 S for 2km; left at bridge; immediately left again D26 to Juncalas; house in village centre on right.

Arlette & Robert Assouère
Maison de L'Évêque,
Impasse Monseigneur Laurence,
65100 Juncalas,
Lourdes, Hautes-Pyrénées
tel   +33 (0)5 62 42 02 04
fax   +33 (0)5 62 42 02 04
email   robert.assouere@wanadoo.fr
web   www.maisondeleveque.com

Map 14 Entry 555

Midi – Pyrénées

La Calèche

Madame paints in the winter, gardens in the summer and loves Giverny. Indeed, the soft pinks and greens of her forest-fringed house are in homage to Monet. Marie-Françoise is also a passionate collector of brocante and her cosy knick-knackery flows as comfortingly as her generosity. Bedrooms reveal striped walls, ornate furniture, florals and lace; pillows are embroidered; bathrooms are strictly modern. Come for a stream in the garden, an orchard with goats, a son who can take you into the mountains (he's a professional guide) and hosts who love to chat over a glass of homemade walnut aperitif.

rooms	2 doubles.
price	€65.
meals	Restaurants 150m–3km.
closed	Rarely.
directions	From Lourdes D937 for Pau 8km to St Pé; left after Peyrouse to hamlet of Rieulliés; house faces church.

Luc & Marie-Françoise L'Haridon
La Calèche,
4 chemin du Bois de Lourdes,
65270 St Pé de Bigorre - Rieulliés,
Hautes-Pyrénées
tel +33 (0)5 62 41 86 71
fax +33 (0)5 62 94 60 50
email luc.lharidon@wanadoo.fr
web www.lacaleche-lourdes.com

Map 14 Entry 556

Midi – Pyrénées

Eth Berye Petit

A magnificent *maison de maître* in a provincial mountain hamlet – amazing. Henri, whose family have lived here for over 1,000 years, is home at weekends, Ione is a gently hospitable mother of two. The grand old house with its wonderful four-sided roof and impressive staircase has stupendous mountain views… the finest in France? Family-comfortable pastel bedrooms, one with the balcony, have antique French sheets; the living room, where a fire roars and dinner is served on winter weekends, is a great space to come back to after a day's white-water rafting, skiing, falconing. A heaven for walkers.

rooms	3: 1 double, 1 twin, 1 suite for 3.
price	€53–€62.
meals	Dinner with wine, €18, November–April.
closed	Rarely.
directions	From Lourdes for Argelès-Gazost; 10km, left at r'bout for Beaucens, follow Eth Berye Petit signs.

Henri & Ione Vielle
Eth Berye Petit,
15 route de Vielle,
65400 Beaucens,
Hautes-Pyrénées
tel +33 (0)5 62 97 90 02
fax +33 (0)5 62 97 90 02
email contact@beryepetit.com
web www.beryepetit.com

Map 14 Entry 557

Midi – Pyrénées

Jouandassou

Standing in rolling farmland on the Gers border – a haven for birds 90 minutes from the mountains – this is the most relaxed house (and jungle-like garden) you could wish for. Expect tiny showers and modest-sized rooms full of bric-a-brac – Dominique's decorative talent runs to bright colours and great flair at auctions. Entertaining, loveable Nick cooks with French, Thai, Latin American flourishes. They are a well-travelled, thoughtful couple, involved in the local music festival – evenings on the terrace, or snug guest room, can be stimulating. Great walks, super food, easy living. *Minimum stay two nights.*

Midi – Pyrénées

Domaine de Jean-Pierre

Madame is gracefully down to earth and her house and garden an oasis of calm where you may share her delight in playing the piano or golf (3km) and possibly make a lifelong friend. Built in Napoleon's time, her house has an elegant hall, big, airy bedrooms and great bathrooms, while fine furniture and linen sheets reflect her pride in her ancestral home – a combination of uncluttered space and character. The huge quadruple has space to waltz in and the smallest bathroom; a beautifully presented breakfast comes with civilised conversation. Come to unwind – you may never want to leave.

rooms	3: 2 doubles, 1 suite for 4.
price	€55.
meals	Dinner €20. Wine list from €4.
closed	Christmas & New Year.
directions	From Tarbes D632 to Trie sur Baïse; through village onto D939 for Mirande 1km; house up little road, sign on left.

rooms	3: 1 double, 1 triple, 1 quadruple.
price	€50.
meals	Restaurants 3-7km.
closed	Rarely.
directions	From Toulouse A64 exit 17 for Montréjeau/Tarbes/Pinas, 11km; at church D158 for Villeneuve. House 1km on right.

Nick & Dominique Collinson
Jouandassou,
65220 Fontrailles,
Hautes-Pyrénées

tel	+33 (0)5 62 35 64 43
mobile	+33 (0)6 88 73 33 03
email	dom@collinson.fr
web	www.collinson.fr

Mme Marie-Sabine Colombier
Domaine de Jean-Pierre,
20 route de Villeneuve,
65300 Pinas, Hautes-Pyrénées

tel	+33 (0)5 62 98 15 08
fax	+33 (0)5 62 98 15 08
email	marie@domainedejeanpierre.com
web	www.domainedejeanpierre.com

Map 14 Entry 558

Map 14 Entry 559

La Souleillane

Fabienne and Jean-Luc have done an amazing restoration, and guest rooms are huge and bright: the cheery yellow family room in the house, the other restful two in the barn. Having two little boys of their own, they make children very welcome and give them the run of the walled garden. Your hosts work so you may be left alone in the morning; come evening, Fabienne enjoys cooking typical local meals and chatting round the table while Jean-Luc, Pyrenean born and bred, is a source of great mountaineering stories. No sitting room but a garden with a large covered terrace. And there's cross-country skiing nearby.

rooms	3: 2 doubles, 1 quadruple.
price	€50. Quadruple €60-€70.
meals	Dinner with wine, €16.
closed	Rarely.
directions	From Toulouse A64, exit 17; D938 west, 7km; signposted. 8km from Lannemezan station.

Fabienne & Jean-Luc Garcia
La Souleillane,
4 rue de l'Ancienne Poste,
65150 St Laurent de Neste,
Hautes-Pyrénées
tel   +33 (0)5 62 39 76 01
mobile   +33 (0)6 87 13 19 45
email   info@souleillane.com
web   www.souleillane.com

Map 14 Entry 560

Gratia

Luscious texture combinations of original floor tiles discovered virgin in the attic, stupendous beam structures – loving hands crafted this place in the 1790s; flair and hard work brought it back from ruin in the 1990s. Jean-Paul's motto 'less is more' informs the wonderful uncluttered bedrooms with their pretty beds and linens; Florence, chic and charming, will do physiotherapy in the great attic studio – mats, music, massage; the ethos is 'polished and cool'. Chill out on the manicured lawn by the saltwater pool, dine in the great kitchen, converse delightfully, depart thoroughly renewed.

rooms	3 doubles.
price	€70-€90.
meals	Dinner with wine, €20.
closed	October-April.
directions	A64 exit 28; at St Sulpice, D919 to Foix; at Lézat-sur-Lèze left onto D19b to Esperce. 200m after Lèze metal bridge, take small road directly in front of you. Gratia at top of hill.

Florence Potey
& Jean-Paul Wallaert
Gratia,
09210 Lézat sur Lèze,
Ariège
tel   +33 (0)5 61 68 64 47
email   ferme.gratia@wanadoo.fr
web   www.ariege.com/gratia/

Map 14 Entry 561

Midi – Pyrénées

Les Clematites

In a pretty, almost Alpine village is this 200-year-old 'peasant dwelling' and hugely artistic home. Goan Teresa was educated in England and paints, Bernard is an expert on water mammals, and André Derain hid here during the war. The guest annexe blends in seamlessly: the double is small but charming, the gallery single, above the lovely dining room, is ideal for an older child, the bathroom is spotless. From the dining room you see straight across to a great snowy peak, a spectacular view for breakfast, and the wild garden is full of flowers. *Children over five & babies only (ladder to mezzanine). Min. stay two nights.*

rooms	1 family suite.
price	€48–€50. Singles €45.
meals	Restaurants within 5km.
closed	Rarely.
directions	From A64 exit 20 to St Girons; right D618 for Castillon 12km; tiny D404 on left to Cescau. Parking 200m, below church on left. Phone & owners will meet you.

Teresa & Bernard Richard
Les Clematites,
09800 Cescau,
Ariège
tel   +33 (0)5 61 96 74 24
fax   +33 (0)5 61 04 98 24
email tizirichard@caramail.com
web   www.ariege.com/les-clematites

Map 14 Entry 562

Midi – Pyrénées

Le Poulsieu

On this remote edge of the world in the breathtaking Pyrenean foothills, the air is clean, the views sharp, the peace tangible. Dutch-born but English-speaking, Hans and Mieke offer great breakfasts, good-value suppers and – in the summer holidays – games galore. Hans, an experienced walker, will also advise on hiking, riding, rafting and fishing. Smallish bedrooms are simple and beamed, there's a kitchen for guests to use, and communal life and dinners are lived on the veranda, or in the garden, under the eye of those blissful serene views. And there's an outdoor pool to return to.

rooms	5: 2 doubles, 1 twin, 1 triple, 1 quadruple (summer only).
price	€55–€65.
meals	Dinner with wine, €22. Guest kitchen.
closed	Rarely.
directions	From Foix D17 towards Col de Marrous 8km; in La Mouline left at Chambres d'Hôtes sign for 1.5km; right C6, tiny but easy track to house.

Mieke van Eeuwijk & Hans Kiepe
Le Poulsieu,
Serres sur Arget,
09000 Foix, Ariège
tel   +33 (0)5 61 02 77 72
fax   +33 (0)5 61 02 77 72
email le.poulsieu@wanadoo.fr
web   www.ariege.com/le-poulsieu

Map 14 Entry 563

La Genade

Up in her beloved mountains with the wild streams splashing and an unbroken view of 13th-century Lordat, Meredith loves sharing her new-found heaven. A passionate climber and skier, she has rebuilt her ruined auberge: old stones and new wood, craggy beams, precious furniture and a cheery fire make it rustic-warm and elegant-formal. Under truly American care, rooms have beautiful bed linens, oriental rugs and books. The en suite bathrooms are large and pretty, the welcome exuberant and genuine, the dinners laid-back. Stay a week: Meredith can reveal some fabulous visits and walks. *Children over seven welcome.*

rooms	3 twins/doubles.
price	€45–€65.
meals	Dinner with wine, €18–€23.
closed	Rarely.
directions	From Toulouse-Montpellier rd; E9 to Andorra. 4-lane road ends Tarascon: E9 & N20; S. to Luzenac, In Luzenac left for Château de Lordat, D55. After Lordat left, Axiat 1km, 1st on left, facing church.

Meredith Dickinson
La Genade,
La Route des Corniches,
09250 Axiat,
Ariège
tel   +33 (0)5 61 05 51 54
email la.genade@wanadoo.fr

Map 14 Entry 564

L'Impasse du Temple

Breakfast among the remains of a Protestant chapel, sleep in a townhouse; it's one of a terrace constructed in 1758 and John and Lee-anne are only its second owners. Sociable Australians, they are restoring their elegant mansion and loving it. Graciously high ceilings, a sweeping spiral staircase, lovely great windows: it's a fine and formal house in an oasis of ancient, stream-kissed oaks made relaxed and welcoming by your fun-loving hosts. The food is fantastic and guest rooms are generous, in pastels and with just enough antiques; one even has the vast original claw-footed bath. Superb.

rooms	5: 2 doubles, 2 triples, 1 suite for 4.
price	€65–€75. Suite €101–€116.
meals	Dinner €22. Wine €6–€18. Restaurant 200m.
closed	Rarely.
directions	From Toulouse A61 for Montpellier; exit 22 at Bram to Mirepoix on D4; D119; D625 to Lavelanet, 11km; at Aigues-Vives left for Léran D28.

John & Lee-anne Furness
L'Impasse du Temple,
09600 Léran, Ariège
tel   +33 (0)5 61 01 50 02
fax   +33 (0)5 61 01 50 02
email john.furness@wanadoo.fr
web   www.chezfurness.com

Map 15 Entry 565

B&B de Figarol

Shutters, balconies and creamy walls give this B&B near the Spanish border the cheerful feel of a mountain chalet. Neil and Jean, who have taken to their new French life with enthusiasm, are warm and hospitable. Climb up the creaking stairs to cosy floral rooms with polished floors and scattered rugs; gaze south, over an exuberant garden, to the snow-capped Pyrenees. The farmhouse dining room with open fire and blue crockery is a great place for breakfast and fine supper, and Jean is at her happiest chatting to guests as she chops and stirs. When the barn owls hoot, Neil takes up his guitar under the stars.

rooms	4: 2 doubles, 1 twin, 1 family room for 4.
price	€55.
meals	Dinner with wine, €18.
closed	Rarely.
directions	From A64 (E80) exit J20; D117 left to Montsaunès; right D26 to Figarol; in village, left fork to Aspet; after 1km signposted on left.

Jean & Neil Adamson
B&B de Figarol,
Chourbaou,
31260 Figarol, Haute-Garonne
tel   +33 (0)5 61 98 25 54
fax   +33 (0)5 61 98 25 54
email info@figarolgites.com
web   www.figarolgites.com

Map 14 Entry 566

Le Moulin

Steve, a wonderful cook, and Kris, a man of the theatre, have achieved a splendid restoration of their remote old mill whose tranquil stream now feeds their organic smallholding: kitchen garden, sheep, poultry, all for your dinner delight. They are deeply involved in the local environment, preserving trees and wildlife and helping farmers. Inside, the fire roars, simple French country furniture glows, home-baked bread is proffered, and they still dream of a turbine to make heat from the river (so rooms may be a little chilly in winter). A wonderfully friendly pair, great value and the Pyrenees so near.

rooms	5: 1 double, 2 triples; 1 double, 1 triple sharing shower & wc.
price	€45.
meals	Dinner with wine, €16.
closed	December-January.
directions	From Toulouse A64 to Boussens, exit 21; D635 to edge of Aurignac; right D8 for Alan 3km; left at sign for Montoulieu, follow D8 to Samouillan then left on D96 follow signs to Le Moulin.

Stephen Callen
& Kris Misselbrook
Le Moulin,
Samouillan, 31420 Aurignac,
Haute-Garonne
tel   +33 (0)5 61 98 86 92
fax   +33 (0)5 61 98 60 77
email kris.steve@free.fr
web   www.moulin-vert.net

Map 14 Entry 567

Midi – Pyrénées

Les Pesques

A quiet lane, a happy family, an old manor decorated in peaceful good taste: it's a delight. Every antique, including cupboard doors, is the right one, bed linen is pretty, most rooms have a gentle blue and white valentine theme; the beautiful new room is in warm yellows, as cheerful as Brigitte's personality and done with her very special feel and an exquisite bathroom. All is soft, mellow, uncluttered; she is smiling, enthusiastic, young; her daughters are adorable and helpful. A dreamy, comfortable, joyful house where you appreciate the skill of Bruno the hard-working kitchen gardener when you sit down to dinner.

rooms	3: 1 double, 1 twin, 1 triple.
price	€48.
meals	Dinner with wine, €17.
closed	Last week in August & Christmas week.
directions	From Toulouse N117 SW for about 50km; exit S D6 to Cazères; over River Garonne, 1st right D7, right D62; after Camping, 2nd left; first house on right-hand side,

Brigitte & Bruno Lebris
Les Pesques,
31220 Palaminy, Haute-Garonne
tel   +33 (0)5 61 97 59 28
fax   +33 (0)5 61 98 12 97
email reserve@les-pesques.com
web   www.les-pesques.com

Map 14 Entry 568

Midi – Pyrénées

La Ferme d'en Pécoul

Kind Élisabeth makes jams and jellies, confit and foie gras, keeps hens *and* surfs the web. Almost-retired Noël gently tends the potager as well as the fields. Wrap yourself in the natural warmth of their Lauragais farmhouse. The first floor is carpeted wall to wall and the airy guest sitting room is sandwiched between two small comfy bedrooms with tiny showers. Summer meals are servd by the goldfish pond. Two dogs, two cats, fields as far as the eye can see – and exquisite medieval Caraman (once rich from the dye cocagne) just down the road. *Minimum stay two nights weekends & summer holidays.*

rooms	2: 1 double, 1 triple.
price	€44. Triple €70.
meals	Dinner with wine, €16-€25, May-October.
closed	Never.
directions	From Toulouse exit 17 Lasbordes to Castres; after approx. 20km, D1 to Caraman; D66 to Cambiac 3km, entrance on right.

Élisabeth & Noël Messal
La Ferme d'en Pécoul,
31460 Cambiac, Haute-Garonne
tel   +33 (0)5 61 83 16 13
fax   +33 (0)5 61 83 16 13
mobile +33 (0)6 70 17 65 49
email   enpecoul@wanadoo.fr

Map 15 Entry 569

Château du Pont Bourguet

You buy a château… and its heart is destroyed by fire on your first Christmas. This is what happened to Davina and her girls in 2003. Friendly, passionate, brave, she has restored its 19th-century glory with charming results. Oak parquet and antique terracotta relaid, mouldings recreated, stylish simplicity introduced. In the elegant bedrooms, no curtains, no pictures, but wonderful views; in the drawing room, fine pieces, a vase of wild flowers. Hidden in woodland on the banks of the Vère, with enticing paths, secret places, pool and maze – captivating. *Minimum stay two nights July/August.*

rooms	2: 1 double, 1 suite.
price	€85–€95. Suite €120–€150.
meals	Dinner with wine, €30.
closed	Rarely.
directions	From Gaillac D964 for Castelnau de Montmiral; stay on D964 for Puycelsi & Larroque. Look out for sign on left for "Campement Préhistorique"; left immed. after, down small track over bridge to Château.

Davina Doughan
Château du Pont Bourguet,
81140 Larroque, Tarn
tel   +33 (0)5 63 40 52 57
mobile   +33 (0)6 89 77 53 85
email   pont-bourguet@aliceadsl.fr
web   www.pontbourguet.com

Map 14 Entry 570

Château de Mayragues

A child's dream become an adult's paradise of history, culture and peace: inside those stern walls you climb old stone stairs to the open sentry's gallery, enter your chamber and gasp at the loveliness of the room and the depth of the view. Beyond the fine old timbers and stonework, glowing floor, furniture and fabrics, your eyes flow out over luscious gardens and woods. Alan is a softly-spoken Scot, Laurence a charming Parisienne; both are passionate about their prize-winning restoration – original materials, expert craftsmen – and they hold musical evenings and produce excellent organic wine. Quite a place.

rooms	2: 1 double, 1 twin.
price	€80.
meals	Restaurants within 5km.
closed	20 December-February.
directions	From Gaillac D964 for Castelnau de Montmiral; at junc. D15 to Château de Mayragues, signposted.

Laurence & Alan Geddes
Château de Mayragues,
81140 Castelnau de Montmiral,
Tarn
tel   +33 (0)5 63 33 94 08
fax   +33 (0)5 63 33 98 10
email   geddes@chateau-de-mayragues.com
web   www.chateau-de-mayragues.com

Map 15 Entry 571

Midi – Pyrénées

La Croix du Sud

A fantastic base for touring the bastide towns or just basking in the garden beneath stunning hilltop Castelnau – even picnics can be arranged. Catherine runs her 19th-century manor farmhouse with quiet sophistication and gentle humour: she wants you to love this place as much as she does. It has table tennis, *pétanque*, a discreetly hidden pool; immaculate rooms with pretty colours, good bedding, scintillating bathrooms; meals in the bright, pleasant dining room or on the terrace. And further afield: fascinating Albi, the Grésigne forest, great walks and a lake complex with all those water sports.

rooms	4: 2 doubles, 1 triple, 1 family room for 4.
price	€75.
meals	Dinner with wine, €27.
closed	Rarely.
directions	From Gaillac D964 to Castelnau de Montmiral, right at bottom of village 100m; right at sign Croix du Sud; fork left for Mazars; on left.

Catherine Sordoillet
La Croix du Sud,
Mazars,
81140 Castelnau de Montmiral,
Tarn
tel +33 (0)5 63 33 18 46
fax +33 (0)5 63 33 18 46
email catherine@la-croix-du-sud.com
web www.la-croix-du-sud.com

Map 15 Entry 572

Midi – Pyrénées

Château La Roussillé

An 18th-century hunting lodge, empty for 45 years, dilapidated but so lovely it captured Duncan and Nicki's hearts and has been stunningly revived. Enter a classical hallway dappled with sunlight – floors slate, antiques French, walls dove-grey and white. Sweep up a walnut stair to bedrooms luxurious with silk, marble, polished wood, great tassel tie-backs, a claw-foot bath, a fabulous shower. Nicki adores cooking for her guests and is fond of animals too: dogs, cats, Shetland ponies, hens; Duncan has created paths for nature lovers through the woods and a bench by the stream. Bliss. *Minimum stay two nights.*

rooms	3: 2 suites for 2, 1 suite for 2-3.
price	€125–€145.
meals	Dinner, 4 courses with wine, €35.
closed	Rarely.
directions	From Cordes sur Ciel D600 to Vaour & St Antonin; thro' Les Cabannes, then Vindrac; left onto D91 to Vaour/Tonnac; under bridge, up hill, 1st right; 2nd drive on left, signed.

Nicki & Duncan Evans
Château La Roussillé,
Vindrac Alayrac,
81170 Nr Cordes sur Ciel,
Tarn
tel +33 (0)5 63 56 58 76
mobile +33 (0)6 21 66 66 42
email la.roussille@wanadoo.fr

Map 15 Entry 573

Aurifat

Good furniture, books and paintings are thoroughly at home in this multi-levelled, history-rich house (the watchtower is 13th-century) and all is serene and inviting. Each freshly decorated room has its own private entrance, balcony or terrace and stupendous views. The house is on the southern slope of hilltop Cordes (ten minutes from both the top and the bottom), the lovely pool is big enough for real exercise and there's a barbecue alongside the superb guest kitchen. Terrace breakfasts (spot the deer) are enchanting and nothing is too much trouble for these lovely hosts. *Minimum stay three nights July/Aug.*

rooms	4: 2 doubles, 2 twins.
price	€66-€74.
meals	Restaurants within walking distance. Kitchen available.
closed	Mid-December-mid-February.
directions	From Albi D600 to Cordes; up 'Cité' road on right of 'Cordes Presse' for 600m; fork left for Le Bouysset; 350m, left at hairpin bend marked Rte de St Jean; house 200m on right.

Ian & Penelope Wanklyn
Aurifat,
81170 Cordes sur Ciel, Tarn

tel	+33 (0)5 63 56 07 03
fax	+33 (0)5 63 56 07 03
email	aurifat@wanadoo.fr
web	www.aurifat.com

Map 15 Entry 574

Mas de Sudre

George and Pippa are ideal B&B folk – relaxed, good-natured, enthusiastic about their corner of France, generous-spirited and adding lots of little extras to make you comfortable. Sudre is a warm, friendly house with beautiful furniture, shelves full of books and big inviting bedrooms. Wine-tastings can be arranged and there is a lovely shady garden set in rolling vineyards and farmland where you can sleep off any excesses. The more energetic may leap to the pool, boules, bikes or several sorts of tennis and you are genuinely encouraged to treat the house as your own. French guests love this very British B&B.

rooms	4: 2 doubles, 2 twins.
price	€70. Singles €50.
meals	Choice of restaurants nearby.
closed	Rarely.
directions	From Gaillac for Cordes; over railway; fork imm'ly left D964 for Castelnau de Montmiral. 1km; left D18 for Montauban 400m; right D4 1.5km; 1st left, 1st house on right.

Pippa & George Richmond-Brown
Mas de Sudre,
81600 Gaillac, Tarn

tel	+33 (0)5 63 41 01 32
fax	+33 (0)5 63 41 01 32
email	masdesudre@wanadoo.fr
web	www.masdesudre.com

Map 15 Entry 575

Midi – Pyrénées

8 place St Michel

Come for an absolutely fabulous French bourgeois experience: a wide stone stair deeply worn, high ceilings, southern colours, antique doors and gorgeousness at every turn. Add the owners' passion for Napoleon III furniture, oil paintings and ornate mirrors and the mood, more formal than family, is unmistakably French. Bedrooms, some with cathedral, some with rooftop views, are antique-furnished and very comfortable; breakfast is on the terrace overlooking the cathedral square. It's good to be in a town with utterly French people. Madame is a sweetheart and it's very good value for money.

rooms	6: 4 doubles, 1 twin, 1 suite.
price	€55.
meals	Restaurants within walking distance.
closed	Rarely.
directions	In centre of Gaillac, directly opposite St Michel abbey church as you come in across bridge from A68 Toulouse-Albi road.

Lucile Pinon
8 place St Michel,
81600 Gaillac, Tarn
tel   +33 (0)5 63 57 61 48
mobile   +33 (0)6 89 70 04 55
email   lucile.pinon@wanadoo.fr
web   lucile.pinon.hotes81.monsite.wanadoo.fr/

Map 15 Entry 576

Midi – Pyrénées

Domaine du Buc

The 17th-century gingerbread château, in landscaped grounds with a pigeon tower, has been in the family for 100 years. Brigitte, bright and smiley, loves this place – and will happily tell you about the family's Toulouse Lautrec connections. The very old arched brick billiards room is now a lovely sitting room; the kitchen preserves its 1900 range. A large white stone stair leads up to bedrooms with original parquet and tiled floors, period furniture and faded, fabulous 19th-century wallpaper. It may be hard to heat the house in winter but these rooms are always cosy. Stay at least a couple of nights.

rooms	3: 2 twins/doubles, 1 single.
price	€75-€90. Single €65.
meals	Dinner with wine, €20-€25.
closed	Rarely.
directions	From Toulouse A68 exit 11 Marssac sur Tarn; left at stop sign, over motorway; left onto D22 for Lagrave & Cadalen; straight on at r'bout and x-roads. Entrance 200m on left.

Brigitte Lesage
Domaine du Buc,
Route de Lagrave,
81150 Marssac sur Tarn, Tarn
tel   +33 (0)5 63 55 40 06
fax   +33 (0)5 63 55 40 06
email   contact@domainedubuc.com
web   www.domainedubuc.com

Map 15 Entry 577

Midi – Pyrénées

Les Buis de Saint Martin

The dogs that greet you are as friendly as their owner, and the banks of the Tarn can be reached from the garden – it's a dream place. Madame has lived here for 25 years and is delighted to please you and practise her English. You will love the softest mushroom hues and white in her bedrooms and bathrooms, the quilting on the high-quality beds, the good paintings on the walls and the floaty muslin at the windows that look over the garden. Meals are served in the luminous white dining room – gleaming antiques on old terracotta tiles – or on the lovely teak-furnished patio. *Minimum stay two nights in summer.*

rooms	2 doubles.
price	€90.
meals	Dinner with wine, €29.
closed	Rarely.
directions	From A68 exit 11 to Marssac; for Lagrave, right after level crossing; 2nd right chemin du Rougé; 2nd right rue St Martin; right at red transformer; left at fork, signposted.

Jacqueline Romanet
Les Buis de Saint Martin,
Rue Saint-Martin,
81150 Marssac sur Tarn, Tarn
tel   +33 (0)5 63 55 41 23
fax   +33 (0)5 63 53 49 65
email   jean.romanet@wanadoo.fr
web   perso.wanadoo.fr/les-buis-de-saint-martin/

Map 15 Entry 578

Midi – Pyrénées

Saint Marcel

Way off the beaten track, 30km from Albi and exceptional. This young couple have recreated the past in their brilliantly authentic restoration of a crumbled old farmhouse. Sylvie's kitchen is a poem: cooking area in the farmer's old fireside bed, shelves groaning with jars of goodies from Pierre's garden. She adores cooking, he loves to chat, has an excellent sense of humour and good English. They have put their hearts into their house with its natural garden, intriguing collection of country antiques and sweetly rustic guest rooms full of beams, armoires, Provençal prints – plus super shower rooms.

rooms	2: 1 double, 1 quadruple.
price	€50–€60.
meals	Dinner with wine, €15.
closed	Rarely.
directions	From Albi for Ambialet to Valence d'Albigeois; left D53 to Tanus 5.5km; left towards St Marcel for 1.5km; Chambres d'Hôtes sign; opposite church (with no bells!).

Sylvie & Pierre Dumetz-Manesse
Saint Marcel,
Padiès, 81340 Valence d'Albi,
Tarn
tel   +33 (0)5 63 76 38 47
email   lamartco@wanadoo.fr
web   www.lamartco.com

Map 15 Entry 579

Midi – Pyrénées

Domaine de la Borie Neuve

Many think about it, this couple have done it — swapped city life for a piece of sweet countryside and a 300-year-old domaine. From each secluded seat — or poolside lounger — farmland stretches for miles. Visit Cordes sur Ciel, Albi, Toulouse, return to grounds full of trees, tennis up the road and a games room in the barn (shared with gîte guests). Bedrooms are in another wing, some big, some small, all fresh, all charming: white ceiling beams, white walls, splashes of russet red and butter yellow. B&Bers eat together at a long table in an open-plan room where glass windows glide open to a sun-drenched terrace.

rooms	7: 5 doubles, 2 suites for 2-4.
price	€46–€54. €76 for 4.
meals	Restaurant in village.
closed	Never.
directions	From Albi D999 to Millau for 10km; after Foncouverte, right for Bellegarde; follow Chambres d'hôte sign.

	Esméralda Francisco
	Domaine de la Borie Neuve,
	81430 Bellegarde,
	Tarn
tel	+33 (0)5 63 55 33 64
fax	+33 (0)5 63 55 33 64
email	laborieneuve@aol.com
web	www.laborieneuve.com

Map 15   Entry 580

Midi – Pyrénées

La Barthe

Your Anglo-French hosts welcome guests as friends to their converted farmhouse. The pastel-painted, stencilled rooms are smallish but beds are good, the hospitality is great and it's a deliciously secluded place to stay and walk or bike out into the country. The Wises grow their own vegetables and summer dinners happen on the terrace (by the raised pool) overlooking the lovely Tarn valley, a largely undiscovered part of France where birds, bees and sheep will serenade you. Watch the farmers milking for roquefort and don't miss Albi, with that fascinating red-brick cathedral — it's no distance at all.

rooms	2: 1 double, 1 family room.
price	€42.
meals	Dinner with wine, €20.
closed	Rarely.
directions	From Albi D999 for Millau 25km; at La Croix Blanche left to Cambon du Temple, up to La Barthe on D163; right; house on left.

	Michèle & Michael Wise
	La Barthe,
	81430 Villefranche d'Albigeois,
	Tarn
tel	+33 (0)5 63 55 96 21
fax	+33 (0)5 63 55 96 27
email	labarthe@chezwise.com
web	www.chezwise.com

Map 15   Entry 581

Midi – Pyrénées

Puech Malou

Pull up at the creeper-clad farmhouse in pretty wooded countryside to a graceful, calming home swimming in crisp light. It's a rustic yet immaculate restoration. Walls are exposed stone or white plaster, floors terracotta or stripped pine, ceiling beams are of heavy oak. The suite has a generous bed and a romantic feel, the sitting room has two huge open fireplaces, the dining room one big country table; there's teak on the terrace and the lawn leads to a lovely pool. Dutch Monique is friendly, hands-on, bakes her bread daily and offers excellent *table d'hôtes. Minimum stay 3 nights. Cookery holidays.*

rooms	5: 1 double, 1 twin, 1 suite for 2; 2 twins sharing bath.
price	€80. Suite €125.
meals	Dinner €20. Wine à la carte.
closed	Never.
directions	From Toulouse A68 for Albi; ring road for Rodez/Millau; D81 to Fauch, D13; left at T-junction; right at r'bout; route de Teillet right. D81 to Teillet. Left before pharmacy, D138 for Alban; right to Terre Basse/Catalanie. House top of road on right.

Monique Moors
Puech Malou,
81120 Teillet, Tarn
tel   +33 (0)5 63 55 79 04
fax   +33 (0)5 63 55 79 88
email   info@maisonpuechmalou.com
web   www.maisonpuechmalou.com

Map 15 Entry 582

Midi – Pyrénées

La Terrasse de Lautrec

Not what you expect to stumble on in a mediaeval village: Le Nôtre-designed gardens backing a graceful house, with terraces overhanging the (stunning) village ramparts. There are secluded shady corners and roses, a box maze, a pond brimming with waterlilies and a pool that looks over the Tarn hills. As you swan through the frescoed dining room and the salon with its 1810 wallpaper you might feel like a Jane Austen character on a French exchange. Dominique, warm and intelligent, treats you to the cuisine of the region. Retire to a stunning salon, or a large, luminous bedroom filled with ochre and gilt.

rooms	4: 2 doubles, 1 twin, 1 suite.
price	€70-€100.
meals	Dinner with wine, €20.
closed	November-March.
directions	From rue Mercadial, Lautrec, past central square on right; continue to monument square, La Terrasse facing monument.

Dominique Ducoudray
La Terrasse de Lautrec,
Rue de L'Église,
81440 Lautrec, Tarn
tel   +33 (0)5 63 75 84 22
mobile   +33 (0)6 07 86 99 10
email   d.ducoudray@wanadoo.fr
web   www.laterrassedelautrec.com

Map 15 Entry 583

Domaine d'en Naudet

Inside and out, such a sense of space! The domaine, surrounded by a patchwork-quilt countryside, was donated by Henri IV to a hunting crony in 1545 – and was in a parlous state when Eliane and Jean fell for it. They have achieved miracles. A converted barn/stable block reveals four vast and beautiful bedrooms (two with private wicker-chaired terraces), sensuous bathrooms and a stunning open-plan breakfast/sitting room. In the grounds, masses for children and energetic adults, while the slothful may bask by the pool. Markets, history and beauty surround you, and Eliane is a lovely hostess.

rooms	4: 2 doubles, 2 twins.
price	€83.
meals	Restaurant 3km. Guest kitchen.
closed	Rarely.
directions	From Lavaur D112 to Castres; right onto D43 to Pratviel. House on left after 2km, signed.

Eliane Barcellini
Domaine d'en Naudet,
81220 Teyssode, Tarn
tel +33 (0)5 63 70 50 59
mobile +33 (0)6 07 17 66 08
email contact@domainenaudet.com
web www.domainenaudet.com

Map 15 Entry 584

La Bousquétarié

Madame Sallier is delightful, running her family château with boundless energy and infectious *joie de vivre*, serving breakfast in her big kitchen in order to chat more easily to you, loving everyone, especially children. Charming bedrooms still have their original personality, and one rare 1850s wallpaper, and turning walk-in cupboards into showers or loos was a stroke of brilliance; antique-filled sitting rooms are totally French; the little reading room holds hundreds of books; even the fresh roses are old-fashioned. It's all comfortably worn around the edges with a tennis court you're welcome to use.

rooms	4: 2 doubles, 2 family suites.
price	€64-€70. Suite €75.
meals	Dinner with wine, €20-€24.
closed	December-February.
directions	From Revel D622 for Castres for 9km; left D12 to Lempaut; right D46 for Lescout; house on left.

Monique & Charles Sallier
La Bousquétarié,
81700 Lempaut,
Tarn
tel +33 (0)5 63 75 51 09
fax +33 (0)5 63 75 51 09
web www.chateau-bousquetarie.com

Map 15 Entry 585

Midi – Pyrénées

Les Abélias

Geneviève moved here from Alsace for more sun and a slower pace of life. As soon as you enter the courtyard and see the mellow old house with little angels guarding the steps you will want to be one of her returning guests – welcomed (in good English) as friends. The chapel in the garden is dedicated to Our Lady of the Angels. Bedrooms are romantic: one soft green with a lace canopy and doors to the garden, another toile de Jouy'd, gently old-fashioned. All the rooms are Geneviève's own work and utterly appealing. Breakfast is on a sunny terrace under the lime trees looking at the garden and fields.

rooms	3: 1 double, 1 twin, 1 suite.
price	€57.
meals	Dinner with wine, €17.
closed	Rarely.
directions	From Revel D84; right V10 for Lamothe; follow signs 'Les Abélias'.

Geneviève Millot
Les Abélias,
Lamothe, 81700 Blan, Tarn
tel   +33 (0)5 63 75 75 14
fax   +33 (0)5 63 75 75 14
email   lesabelias@libertysurf.fr
web   lesabelias.chez.tiscali.fr

Map 15 Entry 586

Midi – Pyrénées

Le Château de Marcenac

The sunny enthusiasm comes from your young, bubbly, hospitable hosts, the history comes from the château and its former occupants, who go back ten centuries. Claire and Ian moved a year ago, she an ex-ballet dancer and spirited cook, he a professional golfer. Loving being in the 'food basket' of France, Claire buys at local markets, then prepares global dishes for a baronial dining room – or outside, overlooking a heavenly valley. Be inspired by vaulted ceilings and sweeping stone stairs to vast dramatic bedrooms that ooze a lavish, almost baroque charm, and bathrooms stylishly new.

rooms	3: 2 doubles, 1 suite for 4.
price	€90. Suite €140.
meals	Dinner €28. Wine from €10.
closed	Rarely.
directions	Before Livinhac le Haut, immediately after bridge right; straight on past pharmacy; follow signs for Marcenac & 1km into château gardens.

Claire & Ian Tyrer
Le Château de Marcenac,
12300 Livinhac le Haut, Aveyron
tel   +33 (0)5 65 64 54 38
fax   +33 (0)5 65 64 54 38
email   enquiries@chateau-marcenac.com
web   www.chateau-marcenac.com

Map 10 Entry 587

Monteillet-Sanvensa

A lovely, old stone mini-hamlet in the calm green Aveyron where there is just so much space. Two compact rooms, each with a nice little terrace, look out over a typical medieval château. One guest room is white and yellow with a walk-in shower, the other washed-pink and white, with a super bathroom and a small kitchenette; both have small terraces. The garden is full of flowers, the rolling views stupendous, and Monique is eager to please. Relax in one of the many shady areas in summer with a drink or a book and enjoy the birdsong. *Well-behaved children & pets welcome.*

rooms	2: 1 double; 1 double & kitchenette.
price	€46.
meals	Dinner with wine, €19.
closed	2 weeks in September.
directions	From Villefranche D922 for Albi; at entrance to Sanvensa, follow signs on right to Monteillet Chambres d'Hôtes.

Monique Bateson
Monteillet-Sanvensa,
12200 Villefranche de Rouergue,
Aveyron
tel   +33 (0)5 65 29 81 01
fax   +33 (0)5 65 65 89 52

Map 15 Entry 588

Montarsès de Tayrac

The rambling farmhouse in the hills is utterly charming; so are its owners. Jacques and Jo love having guests and he is a fountain of knowledge re wildlife and walks (and what walks they are!). Fields, woods, a lake, two donkeys and views that merit several hours of gazing; this swathe of southern Auvergne is sensational. Bedrooms have cream walls, stripped floors, old beams, bathrooms have fluffy towels, and the suite is brilliant for families (two bedrooms, a small salon/dining room, a kitchenette, fresh fabrics). In the living room: logs in the stone fireplace and deep chairs. Marvellous.

rooms	2: 1 double; 1 family suite for 4 & kitchenette.
price	€45. Suite €75.
meals	Restaurant in village, 4km.
closed	Rarely.
directions	From Villefranche de Rouergue for Rodez D911; exit Rieupeyroux for Rodez 2km; right D85 to Tayrac. At La Rode right for La Salvetat Peyralès; towards Montarsès, signs.

Jo & Jacques Rieben
Montarsès de Tayrac,
12440 La Salvetat Peyralès,
Aveyron
tel   +33 (0)5 65 81 46 10
fax   +33 (0)5 65 81 46 10
email montarses@club-internet.fr
web   www.ifrance.com/aveyronvacances

Map 15 Entry 589

Midi – Pyrénées

La Grande Combe

An energetic, lovable Dutch couple live in this astonishing old place, built on a hillside before a heart-stopping view. You go from level to delightful level: the ancient timber frame holds brilliantly restored rooms done in a simple, contemporary style that makes the old stones glow with pride. Superb dining and sitting rooms have original paving, the potager is vast and organic, the atmosphere restful – and there are little terraces and a library for private times. Lovely guest rooms are big (except the singles), pale or bright, and Nelleke's cooking, much of it with a south-western bias, is superb.

rooms	7: 3 doubles, 2 twins, 2 singles.
price	€74. Single €37.
meals	Dinner with wine, €25.
closed	Rarely.
directions	D902 halfway between Brousse-le-chateau and Faveyrolles; turn off at iron bridge onto D200 but do not cross bridge; take forest road, signed.

Hans & Nelleke Versteegen
La Grande Combe,
12480 St Izaire,
Aveyron

tel	+33 (0)5 65 99 45 01
fax	+33 (0)5 65 99 48 41
email	grande.combe@wanadoo.fr
web	www.la-grande-combe.nl

Map 15 Entry 590

Midi – Pyrénées

Quiers - Ferme Auberge

Escape to vast pastures, garden and stunning views. This is an outdoorsy place – you may canoe, climb, hang-glide and hunt orchids. Bedrooms are a short walk from the farm – bring the umbrella! – down a steepish track; sitting snugly in the converted *bergerie*, they vary in size, have shiny terracotta floors, old beams, freshly painted walls and simple pine beds crafted by Jean, your friendly, busy farmer host. In the main house are tapestries and rustic antiques smelling of years of polish; here Véronique serves excellent meals of home-grown organic meat and veg. Good value.

rooms	6: 2 twins, 2 doubles, 1 triple, 1 family room.
price	€48-€50.
meals	Dinner €19-€21. Choice of restaurants in Millau.
closed	Mid-November-March.
directions	From Millau N9 to Aguessac; on way out, D547 right to Compeyre; left in village, follow signs for Ferme Auberge, 3km.

Jean & Véronique
Lombard-Pratmarty
Quiers - Ferme Auberge,
12520 Compeyre, Aveyron

tel	+33 (0)5 65 59 85 10
fax	+33 (0)5 65 59 80 99
email	quiers@wanadoo.fr
web	www.ifrance.com/quiers

Map 15 Entry 591

Montels

The house is modern and rather dark, the rolling Languedoc hills are wild and very ancient; here Monsieur tends his sheep. The views of the new bridge are wonderful – and you watch the paragliders launching off the nearby cliff from the safety of your breakfast table in the garden as you polish off Madame's *lafloune*, a local sheep's-milk cake. It matters little that she speaks no English: she is kind and welcoming and you can get a long way with smiles and sign language. Bright, clean, sweet, spacious bedrooms include one perfect for a family, and the bathrooms are immaculate.

rooms	3: 1 double, 1 triple, 1 family for 4.
price	€45.
meals	Choice of restaurants Millau, 3km.
closed	Rarely.
directions	From Millau D911 for Cahors; just after leaving city limits right after 'Auberge' x-roads. Signposted. Follow small road for about 2km.

Mme Henriette Cassan
Montels,
12100 Millau,
Aveyron
tel +33 (0)5 65 60 51 70

Map 15 Entry 592

Languedoc – Roussillon

Languedoc – Roussillon

La Maison de Marius

Fascinating Quézac: a pilgrimage 'street-village' with a Black Virgin and a lovely old bridge over the Tarn. Amazingly, Marius is a new house: it fits in perfectly with its old stones, beams and doors and its warm, lived-in feel, all light and fresh. Genuine locals, Dany and Pierre adore embellishing their home – delightful country fabrics, hand-painted furniture and murals – and spoiling their guests with homemade and home-grown delicacies from their superb vegetable patch. Their speciality? *Gâteau de noix* made with their own walnuts. Lovely terrace and rose garden where only birds, water and wind are to be heard.

rooms	5: 4 doubles, 1 family suite.
price	€50–€65.
meals	Dinner with wine, €25.
closed	Rarely.
directions	From A75 exit 39 on N88 E for 25km; right N106 for Alès 25km; at Ispagnac right to Quézac; signs in village.

Danièle Méjean
La Maison de Marius,
8 rue du Pontet,
48320 Quézac,
Lozère
tel   +33 (0)4 66 44 25 05
email dany.mejean@wanadoo.fr
web   www.chez.com/maisondemarius

Map 15 Entry 593

Languedoc – Roussillon

Château Massal

Sit in the château's drawing room where a dozen French chairs open their arms. Or wander into the rambling, many-terraced garden with its views across river and red-roofed town. Up a spiral stone stair to big beautiful bedrooms with a château feel; walnut parquet floors and strong-coloured walls set off family furniture to perfection; one has a bathroom in the tower and is enchanting. Madame, one of an old French silk family who have been here for several generations, is as elegant and charming as her house; a fine cook, too. She will show you where to find really good walks, exciting canoeing, and wildlife.

rooms	3: 2 doubles, 1 twin.
price	€68–€88.
meals	Dinner with wine, €28.
closed	15 November-March.
directions	From Millau S on N9 for 19km to La Cavalerie; left D7 for Le Vigan about 50km to Bez; before bridge, sign on left.

Françoise du Luc
Château Massal,
Bez et Esparon,
30120 Le Vigan, Gard
tel   +33 (0)4 67 81 07 60
fax   +33 (0)4 67 81 07 60
email francoiseduluc@aol.com
web   www.cevennes-massal.com

Map 15 Entry 594

Languedoc – Roussillon

Les Asphodèles

It may look unassuming from the street but step into Corine's 18th-century townhouse and you enter a world of light and creativity. A wide stone staircase at its heart leads to airy family rooms full of interest and colour. Corine bubbles with energy; a journalist for years, she now organises workshops in handmade paper and herbalism. The watercolours on the walls are hers, too, and she cooks – delectably. The plant-filled terrace overlooks the hills; close by is the river with its own small beach and rocks to climb (bliss for children). This quiet part of town was once the silk quarter.

rooms	3: 2 doubles, 1 twin.
price	€60–€75.
meals	Dinner with wine, €20–€50.
closed	Never.
directions	From Nîmes N999 for Sauve/Le Vigan; by church in town centre large square for parking; house in small street behind restaurant "Le Plan", 2-minute walk from square.

Corine de Royer
Les Asphodèles,
3 rue Cap de Ville,
30170 St Hippolyte du Fort, Gard

tel	+33 (0)4 66 51 00 54
mobile	+33 (0)6 16 53 49 73
email	corine.deroyer@wanadoo.fr
web	www.lesasphodeles.com

Map 15 Entry 595

Languedoc – Roussillon

Pont d'Ardèche

An ancestor built the fine old fortified farmhouse 220 years ago: it still stands, proudly worn, by the Ardèche and has its own beach. Inside, in sudden contrast, a cavernous entrance hall and a monumental stone staircase lined with portraits... and up to pale, plain rooms, saved from austerity by Madame's painted furniture and friezes. No sitting room but a homely kitchen for good breakfast breads and jams. Best in summer: the squirrelly, tall-treed park invites lingerers, and there's a delicious oval pool. Monsieur can accompany you on canoe trips; expect an attractive, sociable family who enjoy their guests.

rooms	3: 2 doubles, 1 triple.
price	€60. Triple €75.
meals	Dinner with wine, €22.
closed	Rarely.
directions	From A7 Bollène exit D994 to Pont St Esprit; N86 for Bourg St Andéol; sign before bridge across river.

Mme de Verduzan
Pont d'Ardèche,
30130 Pont St Esprit,
Gard

tel	+33 (0)4 66 39 29 80
fax	+33 (0)4 66 39 51 80
email	pontdardeche@aol.com
web	www.pont-dardeche.com

Map 16 Entry 596

Languedoc – Roussillon

La Magnanerie

This happy, artistic pair welcome guests to their open, light-filled, authentically-renovated village silk farm, splashed with Moroccan colour and ethnic *objets*. Such as: pretty ochre-coloured plates, a long wooden table on an uneven stone floor, an ancient sink, beams twisting, glimpses of age-old village rooftops through little windows, a ravishing courtyard, big, uncluttered, attractive bedrooms, a roof terrace looking over Provence. Michèle manages tranquilly and adores cooking, Michel knows his wines and the local community, their talk is deeply cultural and enriching. *Ask about art courses.*

Languedoc – Roussillon

Les Marronniers

They are a delightfully open couple, in love with their life and their 19th-century *maison de maître*, and welcome guests with exuberant gaiety. John is a joiner with a fine eye for interior design while Michel, quieter, softer, does the cooking – beautifully. From the classic black and white tiles of the entrance hall to the art on the walls, every detail counts. A very generous breakfast is served under the chestnut trees; afterwards you can wander off to join in lazy Provençal village life, or visit Avignon, Uzès or Lussan, the fortified Cévenol village. Return to a dreamy pool. *Heated pool.*

rooms	4: 2 doubles, 2 family suites for 3.
price	€50–€55.
meals	Dinner with wine, €18.
closed	Rarely.
directions	From Alès D6 E 27km; left D979 beyond Lussan for Barjac 1km; left D187 to Fons sur Lussan; right at fountain; up on left by church.

rooms	4: 2 doubles, 2 twins.
price	€100–€115.
meals	Dinner with wine, €45.
closed	Rarely.
directions	From A9 exit 23 W to Uzès 19km; D979 N 7.5km; right D238 to La Bruguière. House on big square next to Mairie (vast Micocoulier tree in front).

SAT 13
SUN 14
MON 15.

Michèle Dassonneville
& Michel Genvrin
La Magnanerie,
Place de l'Horloge,
30580 Fons sur Lussan, Gard

tel	+33 (0)4 66 72 81 72
mobile	+33 (0)6 12 83 35 38
email	la-magnanerie@wanadoo.fr

John Karavias & Michel Comas
Les Marronniers,
Place de la Mairie,
30580 La Bruguière, Gard

tel	+33 (0)4 66 72 84 77
mobile	+33 (0)6 14 98 76 93
email	les.marronniers@12stay.co.uk
web	www.les.marronniers.12stay.co.uk

Map 16 Entry 597

Map 16 Entry 598

Languedoc – Roussillon

Mas Vacquières

Thomas and Miriam have restored these lovely old buildings – once a flourishing 18th-century silk farm – with a sure touch, white walls a perfect foil for southern-toned fabrics and materials. Mulberry trees where silk worms once fed still flower; the little vaulted room is intimate and alcoved, the big soft living room a delight. Tables on the verdant terrace under leafy trees and a lawn sloping down to the riverbed make superb spots for silent gazing. Share the pool, subtly hidden in its roofless barn, with your charming hosts. Very pretty, if a touch detached from the owners' quarters.

rooms	3: 2 doubles, 1 twin/double.
price	€77–€102.
meals	Dinner €25. Wine €6.50–€30.
closed	Rarely.
directions	From Alès, D6 for 12km; right on D7; in St Just, left for Vacquières, pink signs to house.

Thomas & Miriam van Dijke
Mas Vacquières,
Hameau de Vacquières,
30580 St Just et Vacquières,
Gard
tel   +33 (0)4 66 83 70 75
fax   +33 (0)4 66 83 74 15
email   info@masvac.com
web   www.masvac.com

Map 16 Entry 599

Languedoc – Roussillon

Mas d'Oléandre

Lovely, long stone buildings enfold the two-tier courtyard, great trees give shade to the pool, the Cévennes hillsides march away behind. It is enchanting. Your young and welcoming Dutch hosts have created a beautiful and unpretentious place to stay; the garden, the lawn around the pool, the glowing old furniture inside. Bedrooms and suites, light and white with splashes of colour, feel separate from each other round the courtyard, and all is utterly pristine, rooms tidied and linen changed every day. Make the most of good regional dishes on the covered terrace in summer.
Minimum stay two nights in winter.

rooms	3: 1 suite for 2-3; 2 doubles, each with separate shower.
price	€65–€120.
meals	Occasional dinner €25. Wine €5–€15.
closed	Rarely.
directions	From Uzès D981 to Montaren for 6km; right at traffic lights onto D337 to St Médiers; in village continue up & around to right. House on left with blue shutters.

Léonard Robberts
& Esther Küchler
Mas d'Oléandre, Hameau St Médiers,
30700 Montaren et St Médiers,
Gard
tel   +33 (0)4 66 22 63 43
fax   +33 (0)4 66 03 14 06
email   info@masoleandre.com
web   www.masoleandre.com

Map 16 Entry 600

Languedoc – Roussillon

Demeure Monte-Arena

Ménélik and Patrick have struck the perfect note. Without compromising the house's austere Protestant beauty, they've lightened it with a minimalist elegance. Whether you're in the airy vaulted dining room, a graceful bedroom or out in the courtyard, the attention to comfort and detail is impressive. All visitors, young and old, are given the kindest of welcomes. An ancient tower overlooks a small walled garden, heady with the scent of roses and cypress trees – a cool retreat. Classical music flows softly, there are concerts in the courtyard in summer, and the dachshund is called Schubert.

Languedoc – Roussillon

La Maison

Old wood, old stone, new ideas. Christian's flair and human touch has revived the grand old stones with opulent Indonesian furniture and hangings, soft lighting and a gentle golden colour – he and Pierre are delighted with their Maison. Beneath the old village church of lovely Blauzac (daytime chimes), the lush walled garden and ancient tower look over wavy red rooftops to blue hills, bedrooms bask in ethnic fabrics and relaxed good taste, the stunning suite has its own roof terrace. Masses of books, a breakfast table by the fire, and good sofas in the salon. Charming. *Watch children with unfenced water.*

rooms	4: 3 doubles, 1 suite.
price	€65–€110.
meals	Dinner with wine, €20–€40.
closed	February.
directions	From Uzès D981 for Alès; 4km to Montaren; right at traffic lights, signed.

rooms	5: 4 doubles, 1 suite for 4.
price	€105–€180.
meals	Bistros in village.
closed	Rarely.
directions	From Nîmes, D979 for Blauzac 16km; after Pont St Nicolas, left for Blauzac; enter village, house behind church.

Plojoux-Demierre & Bühler
Demeure Monte-Arena,
6 place de la Plaine,
Montaren & St Médiers,
30700 Uzès, Gard
tel   +33 (0)4 66 03 25 24
fax   +33 (0)4 66 03 12 49
email info@monte-arena.com
web   www.monte-arena.com

Christian Vaurie
La Maison,
Place de l'Église,
30700 Blauzac, Gard
tel   +33 (0)4 66 81 25 15
fax   +33 (0)4 66 81 25 15
email lamaisondeblauzac@wanadoo.fr
web   www.chambres-provence.com

Map 16 Entry 601

Map 16 Entry 602

Languedoc – Roussillon

La Terre des Lauriers

A path through the woods leads from the house to the river by the Pont du Gard – the setting is special. The house is less historic, and its décor idiosyncratic – a net canopy over one of the beds, hanging hats, splayed fans, silk flowers, etc. Bedrooms are themed, fresh and spotless; one has a connecting room with bunk beds and soft toys. Monsieur works in Nîmes but gives all his remaining time to welcoming and caring for his guests. You get a salon with games for the children, bedrooms with air conditioning and a lovely garden that slopes down to a pool. A reader describes breakfasts as "stupendous".

rooms	5: 2 doubles, 2 twin, 1 suite.
price	€70–€98.
meals	Choice of restaurants within 3km.
closed	Rarely.
directions	From Remoulins follow signs for Pont du Gard 'Rive Droite'. Sign on right.

M & Mme Marianick & Gerard Langlois
La Terre des Lauriers,
Rive Droite - Pont du Gard,
30210 Remoulins, Gard
tel   +33 (0)4 66 37 19 45
fax   +33 (0)4 66 37 19 45
email langlois@laterredeslauriers.com
web   www.laterredeslauriers.com

Map 16 Entry 603

Languedoc – Roussillon

Les Bambous

Circles of delight: the Provençe of vines and umbrella pines, a peaceful typical village, a lovely converted barn and glowing little house, a warm, affectionate couple who genuinely enjoy having guests. Joël paints and Michèle is a keen and good cook. Meal times are flexible, the atmosphere relaxed, the sheltered, well-tended courtyard or cosy dining room conducive to lingering chat. Cottagey, beamed bedrooms have good solid furniture, wooden floors, patchwork, plants and sensible bathrooms. An easy place to be, 10 minutes from Avignon, and in excellent rosé wine, olive and fruit country.

rooms	1 double.
price	€50–€55.
meals	Dinner with wine, €20.
closed	Rarely.
directions	From Avignon & Villeneuve N580 for Bagnols & Cèze; right on D377 & D177 to Pujaut. House opp. town hall; large metal door.

Joël & Michèle Rousseau
Les Bambous,
Rue de la Mairie,
30131 Pujaut, Gard
tel   +33 (0)4 90 26 46 47
fax   +33 (0)4 90 26 46 47
email rousseau.michele@wanadoo.fr
web   lesbambous.monsite.wanadoo.fr

Map 16 Entry 604

Languedoc – Roussillon

Saba'ad

Helen and Jacques met in Africa and are an interesting, committed couple; 10% of their B&B income goes to development projects. Come and share their uncomplicated life in this little old village house with all its stairs, African mementos and pine furniture. There's space in your white-vaulted suite and you won't hear much traffic in enchanting Pujaut. The pretty, peaceful, terraced garden has a summer kitchen for guests but is not really suitable for adventurous toddlers. Super folk with whom to share good conversation over simple suppers and a village worth exploring. *Limited parking.*

rooms	1 suite.
price	€45.
meals	Dinner with wine, €15.
closed	Rarely.
directions	From Avignon N580 for Bagnols & Cèze; right D377 & D177 to Pujaut. In village head for Mairie; house 300m into old village from Mairie & church.

Helen Thompson
& Jacques Sergent
Saba'ad,
Place des Consuls,
30131 Pujaut, Gard
tel   +33 (0)4 90 26 31 68
mobile   +33 (0)6 87 68 83 74
email   sergent.thompson@wanadoo.fr
web   monsite.wanadoo.fr/sabaad

Map 16 Entry 605

Languedoc – Roussillon

Les Écuries des Chartreux

A village or not a village? It feels like one and is a perfect place to stay when Avignon itself is heaving with people. A former stable block next door to a beautiful 13th-century monastery, the house is cool and light inside, its bedrooms polished and appealing with nice touches and a perfect little kitchen for guests. Pascale runs the Écuries as a B&B though in fact you have a fully-equipped studio, so can opt to be independent. But don't think she doesn't want you! She is on hand with breakfast, information and magazines you can borrow, and an aperitif before you head out for the evening.

rooms	3: 2 doubles, 1 suite.
price	€70–€125.
meals	Choice of restaurants nearby. Guest kitchen.
closed	Rarely.
directions	From Avignon cross Rhône for Nîmes & Villeneuve lès Avignon. Just after bridge right for Villeneuve centre, Rue de la République. House next to Pontifical Carthusian monastery, la Chartreux.

Pascale Letellier
Les Écuries des Chartreux,
66 rue de la République,
30400 Villeneuve lès Avignon,
Gard
tel   +33 (0)4 90 25 79 93
email   ecuries-des-chartreux@wanadoo.fr
web   www.ecuries-des-chartreux.com

Map 16 Entry 606

Languedoc – Roussillon

Hôtel de l'Orange

At his *hôtel particulier* (private mansion), Philippe receives with warm refinement. Each very private room is in *maison de famille* style: polished floors, warm-painted walls, white bedcovers, a different and beautiful wall hanging over each bed, super big bathrooms. The magic secluded terrace garden with gasping views over the roofs of the old town is where you swim; breakfast, which to Philippe is *the* moment of the day, is in the old-style dining room or at small tables in the courtyard. Walk into the old town: the river is a charming place. Grand, elegant – but utterly lovable.

Languedoc – Roussillon

La Bastide du Clos d'Ezort

In keeping with traditional bastide proportions, this house marries new and old in crisp Swiss style. Beautiful flowers welcome guests to fresh and colourful poolside rooms, wonderful big showers and blissful towels. Be invigorated and soothed with Romy's natural therapies or a massaging spa bath – and top it off with a generous aperitif, served in a Ferrari tribute bar and made by Juerg's own fair hand (he also sculpts). Dine finely on the terrace or in front of the fireplace in the lovely, spacious dining room; swap travel stories and return with many fond memories of this interesting and happy couple.

rooms	6: 4 doubles, 1 twin, 1 triple.
price	€68–€152.
meals	Dinner with wine, €30.
closed	Rarely.
directions	From Nîmes D40 W 28km to Sommières; from town centre for centre historique; from Post Office follow street up to château; signed.

rooms	3: 2 doubles, 1 twin.
price	€85–€125.
meals	Restaurant in village.
closed	Never.
directions	From Montpellier A9 exit 27 for D34 Sommières; N110 through Sommières; to Alès; right to Calvisson; D107 St Étienne d'Escattes, signed.

Philippe de Frémont
Hôtel de l'Orange,
Chemin du Château Fort,
30250 Sommières,
Gard

tel	+33 (0)4 66 77 79 94
fax	+33 (0)4 66 80 44 87
email	hotel.delorange@free.fr
web	hotel.delorange.free.fr

Juerg & Romy Gross
La Bastide du Clos d'Ezort,
157 chemin du Mas d'Ezort,
St Étienne d'Escattes,
30250 Souvignargues, Gard

tel	+33 (0)4 66 57 07 56
mobile	+33 (0)6 75 08 55 69
email	labastidezort@yahoo.fr
web	www.labastidezort.com

Map 16 Entry 607

Map 16 Entry 608

Languedoc – Roussillon

26 boulevard Saint Louis

A Moorish tang colours Marion's 17th-century townhouse: a fountain in the wall of the deliciously cool walled garden; candlelit dinners that taste of Provence and North Africa; adventurous colours and lovely fabrics; a sunken bath in the air-conditioned suite; beautiful furniture and paintings placed to enhance generous proportions. It isn't grand, just simply elegant. This talented lady is a wonderful hostess who adores having guests, serving superb breakfasts of local produce and *fougasse* (a soft delicate bread) then pointing them to the cultural riches of the area – and the sea. *Secure parking available.*

rooms	4: 3 doubles, 1 suite.
price	€75–€120.
meals	Dinner with wine, €30.
closed	Rarely.
directions	From A9 exit 26 Aimargues Centre. Cross r'bout with fountain down plane tree lane 300m. Entrance opp. Carli Immo, Rue de la Violette (3 cypresses behind garden wall).

Marion Escarfail
26 boulevard Saint Louis,
30470 Aimargues, Gard

tel	+33 (0)4 66 88 52 99
fax	+33 (0)4 66 88 52 99
email	lamaisondemarion@free.fr
web	lamaisondemarion.free.fr

Map 16 Entry 609

Languedoc – Roussillon

Mas de Barbut

Smart, imaginative and decorated with great flair. Bedrooms are Mexican, Mandarin and Provençal: the first vibrant with chunky ethnic touches, the second aesthetically pure with clean lines, the third gracefully, flowingly comfortable. Outstanding bathrooms have fabulous tiles. The Gandons are great travellers, and have brought together fascinating things in a strikingly harmonious way. They also love cosseting guests. The traditional farmhouse protects you from the summer heat; there's a cool pool and a lovely spot for drinks on the river bank. Fifteen minutes from beaches, miles from worldly bustle.

rooms	3: 2 doubles, 1 triple.
price	€92–€102.
meals	Dinner with wine, €30, Monday, Wednesday, Friday.
closed	Rarely.
directions	From A9 exit 26 for Gallargues. D979 for Aigues Mortes, 12.5km. Right at 7th r'bout for Le Vidourle, 2km. House on right.

Danielle & Jean-Claude Gandon
Mas de Barbut,
30220 St Laurent d'Aigouze, Gard

tel	+33 (0)4 66 88 12 09
mobile	+33 (0)6 64 14 28 52
email	gandon.barbut@club-internet.fr
web	www.masdebarbut.com

Map 16 Entry 610

Languedoc – Roussillon

La Ciboulette

The sun-drenched village street with its arched doorways and shuttered windows leads you to the gates of a fine old house where bull-fighting posters hang in the hall. From the garden, your eye leaps from lush bamboos onto braided vines and uneven hills. Monsieur is English; Madame is French, an artist and good company. She has done her house with great sympathy for its original spaces and stone floors; her charming pastels are a bonus on the walls. It is a privilege to be her only guests, enjoy the big unfussy bedroom onto the garden and step out into the morning light for homemade fig jam. *Tennis court in village.*

rooms	1 double.
price	€60.
meals	Choice of restaurants 5km.
closed	Rarely.
directions	From A9 exit 27; D34 Sommières; left to St Christol; right of post office for Cave Coop.; left at r'bout (before small bridge) 800m, left Av. des Bruyères; Rue de l'Église.

Monique Sykes-Maillon
La Ciboulette,
221 rue de l'Eglise,
34400 St Christol, Hérault

tel	+33 (0)4 67 86 81 00
mobile	+33 (0)6 82 37 89 66
email	info@stchristol.com
web	www.stchristol.com

Map 16 Entry 611

Languedoc – Roussillon

Castle's Cottage

On the edge of a wild, unspoilt forest, in a green oasis flooded with mimosa, hibiscus and iris where 46 tortoises roam freely, it's hard to believe you're a short bus ride from lively Montpellier. The house is recent, built with old materials, the vegetation lush, the swimming pool set among atmospheric stone 'ruins'. You sleep in smallish rooms full of family furniture and colour, sharing a very good shower room, and opening onto the terrace. Your hostess, once a city girl in public relations, loves this place and her many tortoises passionately, talks easily and generously shares her fireside and living space.

rooms	2 doubles, sharing shower & separate wc.
price	€78-€99.
meals	Montpellier 3km.
closed	Rarely.
directions	From Mairie in Castelnau le Lez take Rue Jules Ferry; 5th left Chemin de la Rocheuse; last house on left.

Dominique Carabin-Cailleau
Castle's Cottage,
289 chemin de la Rocheuse,
34170 Castelnau le Lez, Hérault

tel	+33 (0)4 67 72 63 08
fax	+33 (0)4 67 72 63 08
email	dpcc@libertysurf.fr
web	castlecottage.free.fr

Map 15 Entry 612

Languedoc – Roussillon

Domaine du Pélican

A perfect B&B on a superb estate with mulberry-lined drive, hills, vineyards and a real family atmosphere: simplicity, peace, fine big rooms and a charming welcome. The owners have four children of their own and run an inn in their beautifully restored old family house. In a separate building, guest rooms have soft-coloured walls, beds on mezzanines, pretty shower rooms. The dining room has old honey-coloured beams – a dream – and gives onto the terrace and rows of vines beyond: just the place for an authentic, and delicious, auberge dinner. New: a lovely guest sitting room and saltwater pool.

rooms	4: 1 double, 1 suite for 4; 1 double, 1 twin, each with fold-out bed.
price	€61-€66. Suite €66.
meals	Dinner with wine, €22.
closed	Last week October.
directions	From Gignac centre towards Montpellier; at edge of town bus stop Pelican on right; right & follow signs for 3km.

Isabelle & Baudouin
Thillaye de Boullay
Domaine du Pélican,
34150 Gignac, Hérault
tel   +33 (0)4 67 57 68 92
fax   +33 (0)4 67 57 68 92
email domaine-de-pelican@wanadoo.fr
web   www.domainedepelican.fr

Map 15 Entry 613

Languedoc – Roussillon

La Missare

A vast and lovely stone winery is the guest wing on this old family property. Your host's sensitive conversion uses old tiles, doors and beams; simple, stylish bedrooms are designed for comfort and privacy, each with an excellent shower room, antique embroidered linen and French windows onto the well-caressed garden courtyard. Jean-François and his mother happily share their living space: go through the big hall, hung with some fine prints, to generous breakfast in the living room where a cabinet of treasures will intrigue. Outside, a discreet pool glimmers under a vast umbrella pine.

rooms	4 doubles.
price	€65-€70.
meals	Restaurants 3-12km.
closed	Rarely.
directions	A75 exit 57 to Clermont L'Hérault; 1st r'bout to Canet; 2nd r'bout to Brignac; at Brignac left to Saint Andre de Sis; house after 20m opp. phone box.

Jean-François Martin
La Missare,
9 route de Clermont,
34800 Brignac, Hérault
tel   +33 (0)4 67 96 07 67
email la.missare@free.fr
web   la.missare.free.fr

Map 15 Entry 614

Languedoc – Roussillon

La Genestière

Madame's work upon the walls,
Monsieur's fine horse in the paddock
the modern house has lots of atmosphere
and your hostess is an open, fun person
who loves getting to know you, even
teaching you to sculpt (do enquire).
Rooms are big and simply furnished,
each with a few lovely things, good
fabrics, mosquito screens (yes!) and a
private terrace onto the lush garden
with great bamboos and aromatic pines,
and a summer kitchen. All in a fabulous
spot near the magnificent Salagou lake
for sailing and swimming on hot days,
and biking and riding in winter. Worth
a good stay. *Minimum stay two nights.*

rooms	2 doubles.
price	€55–€65.
meals	Restaurants 3.5km.
closed	November–March.
directions	A9 exit 34 on D13 N 10km; N9 to Clermont l'Hérault; A75 exit Clermont l'Hérault; D156 left for Lac du Salagou 3km; left to Liausson; 700m along last house on right before woods.

M & Mme Neveu
La Genestière, Route de Liausson,
34800 Clermont l'Hérault, Hérault
tel   +33 (0)4 67 96 30 97
fax   +33 (0)4 99 91 08 89
email lagenestiere@wanadoo.fr
web   www.mediatisse.com/Lac-du-Salagou/genestie/genestie.htm

Map 15 Entry 615

Languedoc – Roussillon

7 Grand Rue

Villeneuvette is a special village, built
under Louis XIV to produce red cloth
for soldiers, and its surrounding wall
and workers' cottages, cobbled streets
and giant plane trees are still intact.
Swedish Anna is a special person doing
real B&B in this phase of her interesting
life. A travel guide, acupuncturist,
gatherer of arts and crafts, she is quiet
and welcoming. Her living room floods
with morning light, crackles with winter
logs, glows with plants, paintings and
books. Looking over rooftops to the
hills, your bedroom is uncluttered and
lovely: Tibetan hangings, one antique
chest, a few stunning colours.

rooms	1 double with separate shower.
price	€50–€60.
meals	Restaurant within walking distance.
closed	Rarely.
directions	From Clermont l'Hérault for Bédarieux; 3km, right to Villeneuvette; enter village, 2nd from last house on right.

Anna Samson
7 Grand Rue,
34800 Villeneuvette,
Hérault
tel   +33 (0)4 67 96 96 67
email anna.samson@tiscali.fr

Map 15 Entry 616

Languedoc – Roussillon
Château de Grézan

An amazing, 19th-century, neo-medieval château built in a troubadour style, with towers, turrets and castellated walls. Yet a very simple welcome from Marie-France – a remarkable, generous lady, a member of the champagne family who organises her own 'taste travels'. Crystal chandeliers, grand piano, original wallpapers, cavernous rooms…you'll forgive the odd imperfect corner. Bedrooms are big and absolutely château, bathrooms fittingly old-fashioned. The evocative inner courtyard is lush with camellias and cyclamen, the gardens are lovely, the swimming pool lies beneath the palms.

rooms	3: 2 doubles, 1 twin.
price	€95–€115.
meals	Restaurant in grounds.
closed	Rarely.
directions	From A75 exit 35 Béziers N112 NW 10km; right D909 for Bédarieux 17km; right to Grézan.

Mme Marie-France Lanson
Château de Grézan,
Au Milieu des Vignes,
34480 Laurens, Hérault

tel	+33 (0)4 67 90 28 03
fax	+33 (0)4 67 90 05 03
email	info@grezan.com
web	www.grezan.com

Map 15 Entry 617

Languedoc – Roussillon
Château de Murviel

The château is perched on the pinnacle of the town, surveying ancient mellow rooftops, sweeping vineyards and hills. Soft, plastered walls, honey-coloured floorboards or pale stone floors and bleached linen curtains around beds give a wonderful feeling of light – unexpected in such an old building. Breakfast, served by the *gardien* (Madame works in Paris), is in a cool courtyard, dotted with lemon trees and oleander and guests can cook supper in their own kitchen. Whether you are interested in wine or the Cathars, this is a comfortable place to lay your head.
Minimum two nights in high season.

rooms	4: 1 double, 2 triples, 1 suite for 4.
price	€80–€100. Whole house €1,950–€3,900 per wk.
meals	Restaurants nearby. Kitchen available.
closed	Rarely.
directions	From A9 exit 35 for Centre Ville; at 1st & 2nd r'bouts: for Bédarieux; 3rd r'bout: for Corneilhan & Murviel; in Murviel centre, next to Mairie.

Yves & Florence Cousquer
Château de Murviel,
1 place Georges Clémenceau,
34490 Murviel lès Béziers, Hérault

tel	+33 (0)4 67 32 35 45
fax	+33 (0)4 67 32 35 25
email	chateaudemurviel@free.fr
web	www.murviel.com

Map 15 Entry 618

Languedoc – Roussillon

Les Mimosas

The O'Rourkes love France, wine, food, their fine house in this enchanting old village and the dazzling countryside around. The red door opens onto a high cool hall and old stone stairs lead to fresh, delicately decorated bedrooms with new shower rooms and art on the walls. Rooms at the back are south-facing with views to the hills. You can walk, ride, climb rocks; swim, canoe in the river; visit the local markets and the unusual succulent garden – and return for a superb, civilised meal on the terrace with your friendly hosts, he a retired-architect and historian, she a creative cook.

Languedoc – Roussillon

La Cerisaie

These new young Dutch owners, their city jobs behind them, are blissfully happy in off-the-beaten-track La Cerisaie. There's a vegetable garden for meals, a trampoline in the orchard and baskets of cherries and walnuts for you. The classically-proportioned rooms decorated with an elegant simplicity, and the proud old staircase mounts to large, light-filled bedrooms, double-glazed against the road (some noise), with views of hills and the truly lovely garden. Luc serves delicious French meals out here, at a huge wicker-chaired table.

rooms	5: 4 doubles; 1 studio & kitchenette.	rooms	6: 3 doubles, 2 twins, 1 studio with kitchenette.
price	€70–€80.	price	€75–€90.
meals	Dinner €28. Wine €8–€30.	meals	Dinner €23 (4 days a week). Occasional lunch à la carte. Wine €10–€25.
closed	November.	closed	November-Easter.
directions	From Béziers N112 W for St Pons for 1/2km; right D14 through Maraussan, Cazouls lès Béziers, Cessenon to Roquebrun; signposted in village.	directions	From A9 exit Béziers Ouest; D64; N112 for Castres, Mazamet & St Pons; 1km before St Pons right D908 to Riols; house on left leaving Riols.

	Martin & Jacqueline O'Rourke		Maija & Luc Simkens
	Les Mimosas,		La Cerisaie,
	Avenue des Orangers,		1 avenue de Bédarieux,
	34460 Roquebrun, Hérault		34220 Riols, Hérault
tel	+33 (0)4 67 89 61 36	tel	+33 (0)4 67 97 03 87
fax	+33 (0)4 67 89 61 36	fax	+33 (0)4 67 97 03 88
email	welcome.lesmimosas@wanadoo.fr	email	info@cerisaie.net
web	www.lesmimosas.net	web	www.cerisaie.net

Map 15 Entry 619   Map 15 Entry 620

Languedoc – Roussillon

La Métairie Basse

In these wild, pastoral surroundings with great walking and climbing trails, you bathe in simplicity, stream-babble and light. Your hosts, hard-working walnut and chestnut growers, have converted to 'bio' and sell delicious pureés and jams. The guest barn is beautifully tended: country antiques, old lace curtains, new bedding and blue tones relax the eye, and there's a fireplace and a full kitchen too. Monsieur has a real, friendly handshake, Madame is gentle and welcoming, and breakfast on the shady terrace includes cheese or walnuts or honey. The wonderful Cathar city of Minerve is a 40-minute drive.

rooms	2 doubles.
price	€49.
meals	Restaurants 3-4km. Guest kitchen.
closed	October-March, except by arrangement.
directions	From A9 exit Béziers Ouest; D64; N112 to Mazamet; N112 for St Pons de Thomières. At Courniou, right to Prouilhe; farm on left.

Éliane & Jean-Louis Lunes
La Métairie Basse,
Hameau de Prouilhe,
34220 Courniou, Hérault

tel	+33 (0)4 67 97 21 59
fax	+33 (0)4 67 97 21 59
email	info@metairie-basse.com
web	www.metairie-basse.com

Map 15 Entry 621

Languedoc – Roussillon

Château de Donos

History upon history, stone upon stone: ruined medieval fortress, Romanesque church, austere 17th-century fortified manor (where guests live) and 200-year-old château (where owners live) are all here, owned astonishingly by just two families in 1,300 years. Bedrooms and bathrooms, huge and beautiful, ooze class; the vineyards give superbly. In the grounds is a delightful lake where you may swim among the fishes (but watch children at all times). Monsieur, whose heart is at Donos, will tell you heroic tales of his forebears. Shyly gracious, Madame is generous to a fault. Both are endlessly interesting.

rooms	6: 4 doubles, 2 family suites for 4.
price	€85-€105.
meals	Restaurant 3km.
closed	October-April.
directions	From Carcassonne for Narbonne exit Lezignan-Corbières. For Ferrals les Corbières; for Villerouge la Crémale; for Thézan des Corbières; D611 through Thézan; 3km, 3rd entrance on right.

M & Mme Chardigny
Château de Donos,
11200 Thézan des Corbières,
Aude

tel	+33 (0)4 68 43 32 11
fax	+33 (0)4 68 43 32 11
email	reservations@chateaudonos.com
web	www.chateaudonos.com

Map 15 Entry 622

Languedoc – Roussillon

La Marelle

What a lovely, starry-eyed team, so young, so enthusiastic about their new venture beneath the château in the middle of this pretty village. They have taken on La Marelle as it was: simple décor in light comfortable rooms (the pale pink 'family' room is very appealing), same huge living room in the old school refectory. They are both wonderful cooks, she with her Polish influence, he with memories of his grandmother's French farm kitchen; she also makes essential oils and natural soaps. Two gardens, and there's an interesting collection of French and English art and travel books in their library.

rooms	5: 4 doubles, 1 family room.
price	€58.
meals	Dinner with wine, €24. Restaurant 0.2km.
closed	Rarely.
directions	Exit A61 at Carcassone Est; D610 for Marseillette & Puichéric; 23.5km, left for La Redorte; after green bridge left; house behind big green iron fence on right.

Philippe & Anna Lizé
La Marelle,
19 avenue du Minervois,
11700 La Redorte,
Aude
tel   +33 (0)4 68 91 59 30
email   la-marelle11@wanadoo.fr
web   perso.wanadoo.fr/lamarelle/

Map 15   Entry 623

Languedoc – Roussillon

Le Domaine aux Quat'Saisons

A quartet of dachshunds adds an engaging touch to this elegant old *maison de maître*, set behind white wrought-iron gates in a friendly and pretty village. The moment you enter the wide hallway with its glowing floor tiles and graceful antiques, you know you are in for a treat. From the immaculately restored rooms to the garden with its lily pond (and a divine pool hidden behind a stone wall), everything is delightful. As are David and Graeme. Enjoy drinks with them both before feasting on David's cooking; Graeme will ensure that meal, wine and conversation flow generously. *Minimum stay two nights.*

rooms	5: 2 doubles, 2 four-posters, 1 twin.
price	€95-€140.
meals	Dinner with wine, €35, Mon, Wed, Fri.
closed	November-Easter. Open Christmas & New Year.
directions	From Rieux Minervois main street, house set back from road behind white wrought iron gates, signed.

David Coles & Graeme McGlasson-West
Le Domaine aux Quat'Saisons,
26 ave Georges Clémenceau,
11160 Rieux Minervois, Aude
tel   +33 (0)4 68 24 49 73
fax   +33 (0)4 68 24 49 10
email   info@auxquatsaisons.com
web   www.auxquatsaisons.com

Map 15   Entry 624

Languedoc – Roussillon

L'Ancienne Boulangerie

In the history- and legend-laden north Minervois, Caunes is one of France's most beautiful medieval towns. Quiet too: the twisting lanes make speed impossible. In a house that baked the abbey's bread from 1500 to 1988, new American owners, easy, interesting people, have kept the steep narrow stairs and the old floors, made five functional guest rooms, one with a kitchenette above – and a tiny, pretty terrace for summer breakfasts. Hugely good conversation – they organise an annual exhibition with artists from San Francisco (Terry was a reporter there) – and all those cobbled streets to explore.

rooms	5: 2 doubles, 1 family suite; 1 double, 1 triple, sharing shower & wc.
price	€45–€68.
meals	Restaurant opposite.
closed	Rarely.
directions	From Carcassonne D620 to Caunes Minervois; cross river & follow to Mairie; house behind Épicerie opp. Place de la Mairie.

Terry & Lois Link
L'Ancienne Boulangerie,
20 Rue St Gènes,
11160 Caunes-Minervois, Aude
tel   +33 (0)4 68 78 01 32
mobile   +33 (0)6 71 11 18 32
email   ancienne.boulangerie@free.fr
web   www.caunes-minervois.com

Map 15   Entry 625

Languedoc – Roussillon

Domaine Saint Pierre de Trapel

Coming in from the magnificent gardens, you catch a wonderful smell of herbs as you walk through the house. The charming owners, educated and well-travelled, moved here from east France for a more relaxing way of life and climate. Using exquisite taste, they have combined original 18th-century elegances with new necessities in big bedrooms and bathrooms of pure luxury, each with its own lovely colour scheme. Best in the summer, with relaxing outdoor spots for all, a superb 150-year-old cedar, olive trees, a swimming pool surrounded by roses and a lovely covered terrace. A place of great beauty.

rooms	5: 1 twin, 3 doubles, 1 suite for 4.
price	€85–€145.
meals	Restaurants in Carcassonne.
closed	November–March.
directions	From A61 exit 23 for Mazamet; at r'bout D620 for Villalier; after 1.5km, towards Villedubert; on right, through wrought-iron gates.

Christophe & Catherine Pariset
Domaine Saint Pierre de Trapel,
11620 Villemoustaussou, Aude
tel   +33 (0)4 68 77 00 68
fax   +33 (0)4 68 77 01 68
email   cpariset@trapel.com
web   www.trapel.com

Map 15   Entry 626

Languedoc – Roussillon

La Plume de ma Tente

It was here that Vercingétorix gathered his advisors before the final stage in the siege that ended his campaign against the Holy Roman Empire. The spot has been semi-sacred ever since – to those true Frenchmen who lament his final failure. This building is all that the planners will allow to rise above the circular gathering place; its shape is that of the gathered group of loyal warriors. Our inspector thought the plastic chairs were a nice touch: reminders of the barbarity that has taken over since the Great Chief's defeat. Yes, it is a bit of a dump – but what an opportunity to sleep in the bosom of French history!

rooms	1 'uni-room' containing all facilities, of which there are few.
price	€1–€1,000, depending on location.
meals	Forage for locally sourceable fodder. BYO.
closed	Only during very bad weather or whilst en route to next destination.
directions	Could be anywhere - ask when trying to book (though don't expect our contact details to help).

M Le Campeur Content
La Plume de ma Tente,
Dans le Jardin,
0.00002 Centre Ville,

tel   +00 00 00 00 02
email   info@accommodation-portable.fr.net/le-camping
web   www.tente-ation.co.fr

Map   Entry 627

Languedoc – Roussillon

Domaine des Castelles

There are space and air galore in this 19th-century gentleman-farmer's house. The freshly decorated bedrooms – with own entrance – are vast, comfortably furnished (plus good mattresses), pine-floored and impeccably clean; the restful gardens cover one whole hectare. Madame, open and welcoming, willingly chats to guests over breakfast – on the terrace in fine weather – and enjoys their travellers' tales. You are in the country yet near the buzz of Carcassonne (and the airport!), while the dreamy Canal du Midi and the vineyards offer their seductively parallel alternatives.

rooms	3: 1 double, 1 triple, 1 suite for 5.
price	€60–€65.
meals	Choice of restaurants nearby.
closed	Rarely.
directions	On A61 exit Carcassonne-West to Salvaza airport; stay on D119 for approx. 4km more. Sign on left.

Isabelle Puaud
Domaine des Castelles,
11170 Caux et Sauzens,
Aude

tel   +33 (0)4 68 72 03 60
fax   +33 (0)4 68 72 03 60

Map 15   Entry 628

Languedoc – Roussillon

Villelongue Côté Jardins

Romantics, painters, poets – paradise. History and romance combine as dark 16th-century passages and uneven stone floors open into heavily beamed rooms stunningly revived. Bedrooms are big and simply refined in their white cotton and fine old armoires, the newest on the ground-floor. Views are to the magic-exotic monastic park or the great courtyard and ruined Cistercian abbey. Sisters Renée and Claude, warm, knowledgable, generous, were born here, and provide marvellous breakfasts and dinners with family linen and silver. There are four retired horses… and so much more. Incomparable.

rooms	4: 1 double, 2 twins, 1 family room for 3.
price	€58.
meals	Dinner with wine, €20, except July-August.
closed	Christmas.
directions	From A61 exit Bram; D4 through Bram & St Martin le Vieil; right on tiny D64 3km to Abbey. Caution: Go to Côté Jardins B&B not Abbey B&B next door.

Claude Antoine
Villelongue Côté Jardins,
11170 St Martin le Vieil, Aude
tel +33 (0)4 68 76 09 03
email avillelongue@free.fr
web avillelongue.free.fr

Map 15 Entry 629

Languedoc – Roussillon

Château de Saint Michel de Lanès

Your admirable hosts have saved this utterly romantic place, a near-ruin of an ancestral château, by dint of sheer crusading aristocratic grit, intelligent research and hard manual work. The Viscount, a self-taught master builder, even regilded the lofty baroque ceilings. There are 40 rooms and four ghosts; Madame can recount pre-Revolutionary family lore for hours; every piece of furniture tells a tale; the cedars are regal, the river peaceful, breakfast luxurious with grandmama's fine silver. Guests have the privilege of the best renovations: two fine salons, huge, elegant bedrooms. Exceptional.

rooms	3: 1 double, 1 twin; 1 double with separate bath & wc.
price	€125-€149.
meals	Restaurant 50m.
closed	Christmas holidays.
directions	A61 for Carcassone; exit Villefranche de Lauragais for Gardouch; cross Canal du Midi; left D625, 10km. In St Michel left cross bridge; château on left.

Vicomte & Vicomtesse
Vincent de La Panouse
Château de Saint Michel de Lanès,
1 rue du Pont de l'Hers,
11410 St Michel de Lanès, Aude
tel +33 (0)4 68 60 31 80
email chateausaintmichel@tiscali.fr
web www.chateausaintmichel.com

Map 14 Entry 630

Languedoc – Roussillon

Domaine de Couchet

It's a pleasure to see this great old farmhouse imbued with new blood: Belgian Justine left high-flying high-pressure Brussels to indulge her love of nature, local markets and organic food (she will cook for you at least once) at Couchet, in heavenly meadows and woodland, and enjoys sharing it with others. Named after Cathar castles, bedrooms and bathrooms have been renovated. The wraparound garden is ever glorious – Martin is a horticulturist – and produces wonders for pot and table, and the French and English library at the top is for all to share. *Minimum stay two nights July/August.*

rooms	3: 2 doubles, 1 twin. Children's room available.
price	€60-€80.
meals	Occasional dinner with wine, €25.
closed	Rarely.
directions	From Limoux D620 for Chalabre 7km; fork right D626 for Mirepoix to Peyrefitte. Signs from village.

Justine Wallington
& Martin Browne
Domaine de Couchet,
11230 Peyrefitte du Razès, Aude

tel	+33 (0)4 68 69 55 06
fax	+33 (0)4 68 69 55 06
email	justine.wallington@wanadoo.fr
web	www.domainedecouchet.com

Map 15 Entry 631

Languedoc – Roussillon

Sanglier Lodge

Jan, a wildlife photographer and film maker, came from Zimbabwe to find a less turbulent life in the south of France. He and his wife Fiona, a lively doctor, have created a cottagey atmosphere with exotic overtones: Zimbabwean teak chairs and a huge antique Spanish table, cast-iron or French teak beds on chestnut floors, original oils on white walls. The old bakery bedroom has the bread oven and the baker's licence; showers are like dinner plates. In an exceptionally beautiful area, it has a kidney-shaped pool and outside space for breakfast, the river Tech below the house and so much more.

rooms	5: 3 doubles, 1 twin, 1 family room.
price	From €68.
meals	Restaurant nearby.
closed	15 November-15 March.
directions	From Perpignan-Barcelona motorway south exit Le Boulou & Céret. Follow signs for Céret, Amélie les Bains & Arles sur Tech; for Prats le Mollo & La Preste, 12 km. Park in village square, go left of post office, Sanglier Lodge is No. 6.

Jan Teede
Sanglier Lodge,
66230 Le Tech,
Pyrénées-Orientales

tel	+33 (0)4 68 39 62 51
fax	+33 (0)4 68 39 62 51
email	jteede@wanadoo.fr
web	www.sanglierlodge.com

Map 15 Entry 632

Languedoc – Roussillon

La Châtaigneraie

The Bethells have created a haven of Pyrenean-Scottish hospitality among some of Europe's wildest, remotest landscapes just 15 minutes' walk from lively Céret. In the magical, lush garden, the family parrot may flit with you among the intimate sitting areas where views dazzle up to snowy Canigou or down to the sea. Super, romantic rooms have original works of art and bright scatter cushions, two even promise the bliss of a private terrace for breakfast, delivered by Kim – a very warm and lovely person. And for dinner, there's the famous Terrasse au Soleil. *Watch children with unfenced pool.*

rooms	6: 3 doubles, 1 twin/double, 2 suites.
price	€75–€165.
meals	Restaurant 400m.
closed	Never.
directions	A9 to Spain, last exit before border; into Céret for Centre Ville then for Hôtel La Terrasse au Soleil. House 400m after hotel, on left.

	Kim & Gill Bethell
	La Châtaigneraie,
	Route de Fontfrède,
	66400 Céret, Pyrénées-Orientales
tel	+33 (0)4 68 87 21 58
fax	+33 (0)4 68 87 77 86
email	kim@ceret.net
web	www.ceret.net

Map 15   Entry 633

Meals, booking and cancelling

Dinner

Do remember that table d'hôtes is a fixed-price set menu that has to be booked. Very few owners offer dinner every day. Once you have booked dinner, it is a question of common courtesy to turn up and partake of the meal prepared for you. Dining in can be a wonderful opportunity to experience both food and company in an authentic French family atmosphere. Or it may be more formal and still utterly French. Some owners no longer eat with their guests for family and waistline reasons.

Rooms

We have heard of chambres d'hôtes hopefuls arriving unannounced at 7pm and being devastated to learn that the house was full. For your own sake and your hosts', do ring ahead: if they can't have you, owners can usually suggest other places nearby. But arriving without warning at the end of the day is asking for disappointment.

Cancelling

As soon as you realise you are not going to take up a booking, even late in the day, please telephone immediately. The owners may still be able to let the room for that night and at least won't stay up wondering whether you've had an accident and when they can give up and go to bed.

By the same token, if you find you're going to arrive later than planned, let your hosts know so that they won't worry unnecessarily or... let your room to someone else.

Rhône Valley – Alps

Rhône Valley – Alps

La Jallat

Lost in the little mountains of the Ardèche, in a garden lovingly landscaped and tended (decorative conifers, birches, fruit trees, manicured lawn) is a refreshing conversion of an old mountain farm. Entrance and guest rooms are on the ground floor, upstairs is a long open living space. Your ex-Parisian hostess – poised and gently spoken – has filled this warm, interesting, light-filled space with books, plants, ethnic pieces and polished antiques. She buys the best local produce and makes her own walnut wine – a delicious aperitif – and greatly enjoys contact with her guests.

rooms	2: 1 double, 1 triple.
price	€50. Triple €69.
meals	Dinner, 4 courses with wine, €19.
closed	Rarely.
directions	D533 from Valence; through Lamastre to St Agrève; D120 to Intres. Follow Gîtes de France signs to house.

Pauline Boyer
La Jallat,
07310 Intres,
Ardèche
tel +33 (0)4 75 30 60 13
email jfrancois-paulineboyer@wanadoo.fr
web perso.wanadoo.fr/jf-boyer/

Map 11 Entry 634

Rhône Valley – Alps

Le Couradou

Diana, bright and gifted, and Jos, a shy geologist, came from cool populous Belgium to empty rustic Ardèche, fell in love with the ghost of a silk worm and set about transforming this fine big silk-farm house into a warm home. Outside, vineyards and the distant Cévennes, inside, wonderful vaulted 15th-century ceilings, split-level living spaces and six super guest rooms. All different, they are simply done with the local gifts of stone walls, country antiques, Provençal patterns and wrought iron. Each room has an armchair or a sofa, all the comforts. They will welcome you like friends.
Minimum stay two nights in high season.

rooms	6: 2 doubles, 1 twin, 2 quadruples, 1 family room.
price	€85–€125.
meals	Dinner with wine, €30.
closed	November–February.
directions	From N86 Bourg St Andeol; D4 to Vallon Pont d'Arc; D579 left for Baryac, 4km; D217 left for Labastide.

Diana Little
& Jos Vandervondelen
Le Couradou,
Le Chambon,
07150 Labastide de Virac, Ardèche
tel +33 (0)4 75 38 64 75
email infos@lecouradou.com
web www.lecouradou.com

Map 16 Entry 635

Les Roudils

07380 Jaujac, Ardèche

A piece of paradise. The climate: Mediterranean. The setting: high, rural, hidden, silent, in the nature-rich Monts d'Ardèche park. The views: long, of mountain peaks, inspiring. The house: of stone, and wood from the surrounding chestnut forests, lovingly restored, light, open. Bedrooms: sunny, just right. Food: organic, home-grown, imaginative, lots of honey. Your hosts warm, trusting are quickly your friends. Marie sings; Gil makes beautiful furniture – see their monumental dining table – and keeps bees; music plays. There's lots more: come up the long narrow road to walk, talk, and believe us.

Harmony and authenticity reign. Furniture-maker Gil crafts tables, staircases and doors from surrounding chestnut, elm, ash and olive, Marie is a member of 'Menus Curieux' and runs cookery courses extolling wild plants. Local produce is promoted and celebrated and breakfasts are entirely organic – poached eggs with paprika, pancakes with heather honey, seasonal fruits, dozens of jams. Walls are limewashed, insulation is from sheep's wool, heating is solar, and all is composted and recycled.

rooms	3: 2 doubles, 1 suite for 5.
price	€54.
meals	Restaurant 4km.
closed	November-Easter.
directions	From Aubenas N102 for Le Puy 8.5km. At Lalevade left to Jaujac centre. By Café des Loisirs cross river & follow signs 4km along narrow mountain road.

	Marie & Gil Florence
tel	+33 (0)4 75 93 21 11
fax	+33 (0)4 75 93 21 11
email	le-rucher-des-roudils@wanadoo.fr
web	www.le-rucher-des-roudils.com

SPECIAL GREEN ENTRY
see page 15

Map 11 Entry 636

Château de La Motte

Alain and Anny welcome you with a gentle warmth to their fairytale turrets and parkland. Their sure, discerning touch has transformed this light-filled château; gleaming old floors, stained glass and antiques rest easily with deep sofas and modern art. Dinner is a cheerful, delicious affair. Guests chat over aperitifs before trooping into the elegant, grey dining room where your hosts, unflustered, present local delicacies, herbs from their garden, great cheeses and wines. Good company, soft music and a turn in the orchard before you climb the creaking old stairs to a divine bedroom and a delicious bed.

Domaine du Château de Marchangy

Down the avenue of oaks and through the grand gates to the perfectly proportioned house. Light pours into intimate but immaculate guest rooms on the first and loft floors of the annexe – big rugs on pale wood floors, harmonious colours, delightful armoires, stylish *objets*, gorgeous fabrics and garden flowers. Rise at your leisure for château breakfasts and fruit from the orchard – served by the pool in summer, in whinnying distance of the horses. Smiling Madame loves having guests; she and her *gardienne* look after you wonderfully. *Mininum stay two nights July/August.*

rooms	6: 5 doubles, 1 twin.
price	€74–€105.
meals	Dinner with wine, €24.
closed	Rarely.
directions	From Roanne D482 to Pouilly sous Charlieu; D4 left through Briennon; just before Noailly, château on left.

rooms	3: 1 double, 2 suites.
price	€85–€98.
meals	Light supper from €15. Wine from €6.
closed	Rarely.
directions	From Roanne D482 north; 5km after Pouilly sous Charlieu right to St Pierre la Noaille. Signed.

	Anny & Alain Froumajou
	Château de La Motte,
	42640 Noailly, Loire
tel	+33 (0)4 77 66 64 60
fax	+33 (0)4 77 66 68 10
email	chateaudelamotte@wanadoo.fr
web	www.chateaudelamotte.net

	Marie-Colette Grandeau
	Domaine du Château de Marchangy,
	42190 St Pierre la Noaille, Loire
tel	+33 (0)4 77 69 96 76
fax	+33 (0)4 77 60 70 37
email	contact@marchangy.com
web	www.marchangy.com

Map 11 Entry 637

Map 11 Entry 638

Rhône Valley – Alps

Il Fut Un Temps

After a two-year trip around the world (and stories told in perfect English), Julien has moved into his old family house in a delicious, reachable corner between the Auvergne and the Loire, keeping the charm and adding his own youthful mark. Lively dinners before a crackling log fire are a seductively rustic mix of modern and traditional; the fruit wine is homemade, the themed stays (massage and relaxation; golf and cross-country skiing; gastronomy) are a treat. Be comforted by cosy rooms – pretty fabrics, new art, rafters and rough stone walls – and shower rooms that sparkle.

rooms	5: 1 double, 2 twins, 2 quadruples.
price	€58–€75.
meals	Dinner with wine, €24.
closed	Rarely.
directions	From A72 exit 4 D53 E to Champoly. D24 E to St Marcel d'Urfé; D20 S for St Martin la Sauveté & follow 'chambres d'hôtes' signs.

Julien Perbet
Il Fut Un Temps,
Les Gouttes,
42430 St Marcel d'Urfé, Loire
tel +33 (0)4 77 62 52 19
fax +33 (0)4 77 62 53 88
email contact@ilfutuntemps.com
web www.ilfutuntemps.com

Map 10 Entry 639

Rhône Valley – Alps

La Gloriette

Over a glass or two of the local beaujolais, discover what pleasant company your hosts are. Originally from Paris, and great travellers (ask about their epic trip to India), they came here in search of the simpler life. And a fine, simple B&B this is – with good country food to match. A woodchip-burner fuels the central heating, the book-filled sitting room has a disarmingly uncoordinated air and the bedrooms are comfortable and bright. It's all cosy and good value. Outside visit La Gloriette, the gardens and the courtyard – all chaotic! – and park a two-minute walk away in the village square.

rooms	3: 1 double, 1 twin, 1 family for 4–6.
price	€42–€47.
meals	Dinner with wine, €17.
closed	28 November 2006–5 March 2007.
directions	From Mâcon N6 south; at Pontanevaux D95 right; through Les Paquelets; D17; D26 to Jullié. House off main square, signed.

Antoinette & Jean-Luc Bazin
La Gloriette,
le Bourg, 69840 Jullié, Rhône
tel +33 (0)4 74 06 70 95
fax +33 (0)4 74 06 70 95
email contact@lagloriette.fr
web www.lagloriette.fr

Map 11 Entry 640

Rhône Valley – Alps

Les Pasquiers

Come and join this family's charming, authentically aristocratic life: no prissiness (two screened-off bathrooms) in their big townhouse, just unselfconscious style. The richly decorated golden salon has a piano, books and open fireplace, the bedrooms are sunny, the beds wear beautiful linen. The richly stocked garden has a pool, a summerhouse, a large terrace, 150 species of trees, an organic vegetable garden and a statue of Grand-père. Madame is too busy cooking to eat with guests but welcomes company as she's preparing dinner – and she is as relaxed and as charming as her house.

rooms	4: 2 doubles, 2 twins.
price	€80.
meals	Dinner with wine, €25.
closed	Rarely.
directions	From A6 exit Macon Sud or Belleville; N6 to Romanèche & Lancié. In Lancié signed.

Jacques & Laurence Gandilhon
Les Pasquiers,
69220 Lancié, Rhône
tel   +33 (0)4 74 69 86 33
fax   +33 (0)4 74 69 86 33
email   welcome@lespasquiers.com
web   www.lespasquiers.com

Map 11   Entry 641

Rhône Valley – Alps

Château de Longsard

Orange trees in the *orangerie*, an obelisk amid the topiary chessmen, two spectacular Lebanon cedars, wine from the estate, beautiful 17th-century beams to guard your sleep. Your Franco-American hosts, sophisticated and well-travelled polyglots, are keen to share their enthusiasm for horticulture (founding a scheme allowing the public to visit private gardens while raising money for local charities). Bedrooms and baths, pure château from faded pastel to bold with hints of modernity, some with fine carved door frames, are eclectically furnished; Olivier's brother is an antique dealer.

rooms	5: 3 doubles, 2 suites.
price	€100–€130.
meals	Dinner with wine, €35 (min. 8 people).
closed	Rarely.
directions	From North A6 exit Villefranche / Saône / Arnas. Straight at r'bout. Through village; château on right after 1.5km.

Alexandra & Olivier du Mesnil
Château de Longsard,
69400 Arnas, Rhône
tel   +33 (0)4 74 65 55 12
fax   +33 (0)4 74 65 03 17
email   longsard@gmail.com
web   www.longsard.com

Map 11   Entry 642

Le Bayard

On a clear day you can see the snow. This marvellous place is clear every day in intention and presence. Gentle people, they have renovated their little old farmhouse with love, different woods (his hobby), pretty lamps. There's sitting space and a wood-burner in the barn guest room, plus two big beds, one on a platform. Delicious, healthy breakfast is at a long table in Marie-Odile's enchanting, light kitchen or on the terrace in their nature garden. She loves all things natural, the house smells of wax and fresh wild flowers, the peace is palpable and you can be as private as you wish.

rooms	1 double.
price	€50.
meals	Restaurants 5km.
closed	Rarely.
directions	South of Lyon leave A7 at Pierre Benite; A45 for Brignais; in Thurins Bourg; for St Martin du Haut; D122 for Yzeron; right at Croix Perrière. Signed.

Marie-Odile Lemoine
Le Bayard,
69510 Thurins,
Rhône
tel   +33 (0)4 78 19 10 83
mobile   +33 (0)6 14 92 45 47
email   mo-lemoine@wanadoo.fr

Map 11   Entry 643

Manoir de Marmont

An amazing avenue of plane trees takes you to this exceptional house and hostess. Madame is a live wire, laughing, enthusing, giving – unforgettable; her house is as elegantly colourful as she is. Climb the grand stairs to your splendid château-style room, revel in Persian carpets, trompe-l'œil walls, antiques, fresh flowers. Beside Shakespeare and the candles, Madame pours tea from silver into porcelain and artfully moves the breakfast butter as the sun rises; at night she'll light your bedside lamp, leaving a book open at a carefully chosen page for you to read after a game of (French) Scrabble. Inimitably fine…

rooms	2 doubles.
price	€85.
meals	Restaurant 3km.
closed	Rarely.
directions	From Bourg en Bresse N83 towards Lyon. At Servas right D64 towards Condeissiat 5km; left at sign Le Marmont: plane-tree avenue. Don't go to St André.

Geneviève & Henri
Guido–Alhéritière
Manoir de Marmont,
01960 St André sur Vieux Jonc,
Ain
tel   +33 (0)4 74 52 79 74

Map 11   Entry 644

Rhône Valley – Alps

Le Châlet

Anne-Marie, outgoing and a delight o talk to, makes this place – come if you want to bathe in genuine French mountain hospitality. She speaks English, keeps horses, and may accompany you on walks to Alpine pastures. The mood here is rustic and characterful; the triple is in the converted cellar. Exceptional walking: you may see chamois and marmots if you go far enough. Dinner (served late to allow you time to settle) is eaten at the long wooden table, with grand-mama's delicious recipes cooked on a wood-fired stove – and the half-board formula includes absolutely everything.

rooms	5: 1 triple; 4 doubles sharing 2 showers & 2 wcs.
price	€79.
meals	Half-board only.
closed	Rarely.
directions	From Thonon les Bains, D26 for Bellevaux. House 2km before Bellevaux on left; sign.

Anne-Marie Félisaz-Denis
Le Châlet,
La Cressonnière,
74470 Bellevaux,
Haute-Savoie
tel +33 (0)4 50 73 70 13
fax +33 (0)4 50 73 70 13

Map 12 Entry 645

Rhône Valley – Alps

La Ferme du Champ Pelaz

It was love at first sight so three generations of Smiths came to the gentle land where distant peaks tantalise, to repair and pamper the 19th-century farmhouse for all: Michael and Linda at one end, daughter Katey and her children at the other, guests to be warmly, privately in between. They are spontaneously hospitable, ever ready to help and know all about the area (Michael specialises in golf breaks). Bedrooms are big, light and softly comfortable without any fuss, ideal for all. A pool for summer heat, and a big log fire and deep sofas in the dayroom for evening cool. Wonderful.

rooms	4: 3 doubles, 1 triple.
price	€70-€90.
meals	Dinner with wine, €27.
closed	Rarely.
directions	A41 exit Annecy south; off N508 for Bourg en Bresse. D17 through Sillingy; D38 through Combe de Sillingy to Thusy; house on right in Le Pesey.

Michael, Linda & Katey Smith
La Ferme du Champ Pelaz,
Le Pesey, 74150 Thusy,
Haute-Savoie
tel +33 (0)4 50 69 25 15
fax +33 (0)4 50 69 25 15
email champ-pelaz@wanadoo.fr
web www.champ-pelaz.com

Map 11 Entry 646

Rhône Valley – Alps

Chalet Odysseus

The village has great character; Chalet Odysseus has much besides. Find comfort in soft sofas, check curtains, bright rugs and open fire, and swishness in sauna and small gym; a French chef who waves his wand over the dining table once a week in winter, and relaxed English hosts to spoil you (Madame also is a fine cook). They have the ground floor of this brand-new chalet; you live above. Cheerfully pretty bedrooms come with the requisite pine garb, two have balconies that catch the sun, the tiniest comes with bunk beds for kids. Marvellous for a family break, whatever the season. *Minimum stay two nights.*

rooms	5: 2 doubles, 2 twins, 1 room with bunkbed.
price	€90. Half-board €100 p.p.
meals	Dinner with wine, €40, six nights only.
closed	Rarely.
directions	After Cuses N205; left D106; 2km before Les Carros red & white-shuttered chalet on left; signed.

Kate & Barry Joyce
Chalet Odysseus,
210 Route de Lachet,
74300 Les Carraz d'Araches,
Haute-Savoie
tel +33 (0)4 50 90 66 00
fax +33 (0)4 50 90 66 01
email chaletodysseus@wanadoo.fr
web www.chaletodysseuslachat.com

Map 12 Entry 647

Rhône Valley – Alps

Proveyroz

Madame has boundless energy, is a great walker, adores her mountain retreat in this lovely valley and cooks very well indeed. Her chalet rooms, all wood-clad of course, are bright and welcoming in blue, white and orange; they have unusually high ceilings, good storage and plenty of space. The open-plan living area has huge windows – opening to a small sun-soaked terrace and little garden – and the mixture of old and modern furniture plus bits and pieces of all sorts gives the whole place a comfortable, family feel. Paragliding is the big thing round here, Annecy is close and Geneva an hour away.

rooms	2 doubles.
price	€48.
meals	Dinner with wine, €18.
closed	Rarely.
directions	From Annecy D909 to Thones; D12 for Serraval & D16 Manigod; 200m after 'Welcome to Manigod' sign, left at cross; chalet on left.

Josette Barbaud
Proveyroz,
74230 Manigod,
Haute-Savoie
tel +33 (0)4 50 44 95 25
fax +33 (0)4 50 44 95 25
web josette.barbaud.free.fr

Map 12 Entry 648

Rhône Valley – Alps

La Touvière

Mountains march past Mont Blanc and over into Italy, cows graze in the foreground – perfect for exploring this walkers' paradise. Myriam, bubbly and easy, adores having guests with everyone joining in the lively, lighthearted family atmosphere. In their typical old unsmart farmhouse, the cosy family room is the hub of life. Marcel is part-time home improver, part-time farmer (just a few cows now). One room has a properly snowy valley view, the other overlooks the owners' second chalet, let as a gîte; both are a decent size, simple but not basic, while shower rooms are spotless. Remarkable value.

rooms	2 doubles.
price	€45.
meals	Dinner with wine, €17.
closed	Rarely.
directions	From Albertville N212 for Megève for 21km; after Flumet, left at Panoramic Hotel & follow signs to La Touvière.

Marcel & Myriam Marin-Cudraz
La Touvière,
73590 Flumet,
Savoie
tel +33 (0)4 79 31 70 11

Map 12 Entry 649

Rhône Valley – Alps

Chessine

Overlooking the valley, vineyards and distant peaks, the 18th-century house, once the château's cottages and stables, has been a country cottage for years. Simone and Henry did some sensitive renovation, using old materials and recreating an authentic atmosphere, then opened for B&B. They are still feeling their way, learning how much contact or privacy their guests expect, hunting for little tables and pieces of character to add to their sparkling, mezzanined guest rooms – each has a small sitting area. Breakfast is in the pretty courtyard garden in summer. Excellent hosts and good value. *Minimum stay two nights.*

rooms	2: 1 double, 1 twin.
price	€84.
meals	Choice of restaurants 2-10km.
closed	November-Easter.
directions	A41 exit Aix les Bains D991 to Viuz; D56 right for Ruffieux; at r'bout head for Chessine & Chambres d'Hôtes.

Simone & Henry Collé
Chessine,
73310 Ruffieux,
Savoie
tel +33 (0)4 79 54 52 35
fax +33 (0)4 79 54 52 35
email chessine@chessine.com
web www.chessine.com

Map 11 Entry 650

Maison Coutin

A year round Alpine dream. In summer it's all flowers, birds and rushing streams... in winter you can ski cross-country, snow-walk or take the ski lift, just 500m away, to the vast ski field of Les Arcs. La Plagne and Val d'Isère are quite close too. Cooking takes place in the outside wood oven and the food is delicious. Your dynamic and friendly young hosts cater for children with early suppers, son Boris and daughter Clémence may be playmates for yours, and Claude will babysit in the evening. Guests have their own comfortable dayroom with a refrigerator. *Discount on ski hire & passes.*

rooms	2: 1 double (extra single bed), 1 suite for 4-6.
price	€52. €64-€68 for 3. Suite €84.
meals	Dinner with wine, €18.
closed	Rarely.
directions	From Albertville N90 to Moutiers; on for Bourg St Maurice. Right D87E to Peisey Nancroix; left to Peisey centre; follow green arrows. 9km from main road to house.

Claude Coutin & Franck Chenal
Maison Coutin,
73210 Peisey Nancroix,
Savoie

tel	+33 (0)4 79 07 93 05
mobile	+33 (0)6 14 11 64 65
email	maison-coutin@wanadoo.fr
web	www.maison-coutin.fr.st

Map 12 Entry 651

Domaine de Gorneton

The most caring and endearing of B&B owners: he, warmly humorous and humble about his excellent cooking; she, generous and outgoing. Built in 1646 as a fort, high on a hill beside a spring that still runs through the shrubby garden, their superb old house is wrapped round a green-clad courtyard. Inside, levels change, staircases abound, vast timbers span the dining room, guest rooms have separate entrances and floral papers, plush chairs and country antiques, impeccable bathrooms – and a bedhead from Hollywood in the best room. Deep country 15 minutes from Lyon.

rooms	4: 3 doubles, 1 suite for 4.
price	€100-€160.
meals	Dinner with wine, €40.
closed	Rarely.
directions	From A7, A46 or A47 exit Chasse & Rhône; through large Centre Commercial; under railway; left for Trembas. (Will fax map or guide you to house.)

M & Mme Fleitou
Domaine de Gorneton,
712 chemin de Violans,
38670 Chasse sur Rhône, Isère

tel	+33 (0)4 72 24 19 15
fax	+33 (0)4 78 07 93 62
email	gorneton@wanadoo.fr
web	www.gorneton.com

Map 11 Entry 652

Longeville

There is a gentle elegance about this house and the people who live in it, including several sleek cats. Originally Scots and Irish, the Barrs have spent their adult years in France and now run a wooden toy business. Their love for this 1750s farmhouse shows in their artistic touch with decorating, their mix of old and modern furniture, their gorgeous big bedrooms done in soft pale colours that leave space for the soaring views coming in from the hills. A high place of comfort and civilised contact where dinner in the airy white living room is a chance to get to know your kind, laid-back hosts more fully.

Le Traversoud

Flowers, ponies and poultry grazing, climbing, tumbling all over courtyard and garden – you can tell the Garniers love living things. Now retired, Albert gardens and plans to be a potter. Jean-Margaret, who is English, grows all her own veg, loves cooking, collects dolls from their worldwide treks, and paints furniture. An interesting, accomplished couple, they welcome you delightedly to their farmhouse, guide you up the outside stairs to colourful, comfortably feminine bedrooms – pretty linen, spotless bathrooms – before serving you excellent French food in their dining room. Sauna and massage shower, too.

rooms	2 twins/doubles.
price	€48-€60.
meals	Dinner with wine, €23.
closed	September-December.
directions	From A43 exit 8, N85 through Nivolas. Left D520 for Succieu. After 2km, left D56 through Succieu for St Victor; 3km; sign for Longeville on right; farm at top of steep hill.

rooms	3: 1 twin, 2 triples.
price	€56.
meals	Dinner with wine, €22.
closed	Rarely.
directions	From A43 exit La Tour du Pin left to N6; right at r'bout for Aix les Bains; left at lights at St Clair de la Tour. 3km for Dolomieu; Chambres d'Hôtes signed.

	Mary & Greig Barr
	Longeville,
	38300 Succieu, Isère
tel	+33 (0)4 74 27 94 07
fax	+33 (0)4 74 92 09 21
email	mary.barr@wanadoo.fr

	Jean-Margaret & Albert Garnier
	Le Traversoud,
	38110 Faverges de la Tour, Isère
tel	+33 (0)4 74 83 90 40
email	garnier.traversoud@free.fr
web	www.le-traversoud.com

Map 11   Entry 653

Map 11   Entry 654

Rhône Valley – Alps

Château de Paquier

Old, mighty, atmospheric – yet so homely. Hélène teaches cookery and spit-roasts poultry in the huge dining room fireplace, then joins you for dinner. Her modernised 17th-century tower kitchen (wood-fired range, stone sink, cobbled floor) is where she makes her bread, honey, jams and walnut aperitif. Wine is from the Rossis' own vineyard near Montpellier. Enormous rooms, high heavy-beamed ceilings, large windows with sensational valley views; terraced gardens and animals; bedrooms (handsome wardrobes, underfloor heating) up an ancient spiral staircase that sets the imagination reeling.

rooms	5: 2 doubles, 2 twins, 1 family room.
price	€65.
meals	Dinner with wine, €22.
closed	Rarely.
directions	From Grenoble A51 or N75 for Sisteron 25km to r'bout; follow signs to St Martin de la Cluze. Château signs in village.

	Jacques & Hélène Rossi
	Château de Paquier,
	38650 St Martin de la Cluze,
	Isère
tel	+33 (0)4 76 72 77 33
fax	+33 (0)4 76 72 77 33
email	hrossi@club-internet.fr
web	chateau.de.paquier.free.fr

Map 11 Entry 655

Rhône Valley – Alps

La Pineraie

A good stopover, this 1970s villa is in something of a time warp, high above the valley outside Valence: floral paper in hall, stairs and bedrooms (the pretty twin with French windows to terrace and rose garden), animal skins on floors and sofas, interesting modern sculptures in many corners. Your hostess is chatty in French, enthusiastic and welcoming, a gift inherited from Armenian parents. Enjoy breakfast with homemade organic jam on the pretty terrace and admire the magnificent chalk escarpments of the Vercors range (beyond less attractive Saint Marcel). Little traffic noise can be heard.

rooms	2: 1 twin, 1 double.
price	€50–€55.
meals	Restaurants in village 500m.
closed	Rarely.
directions	From A7 exit Valence Nord for Grenoble on A49 for 5km; D432 for St Marcel for 3km; left at lights onto Rue des Écoles, under bridge, up hill (total 400m); house on left round hairpin.

	Marie-Jeanne Katchikian
	La Pineraie,
	383 chemin Bel Air,
	26320 St Marcel lès Valence,
	Drôme
tel	+33 (0)4 75 58 72 25
fax	+33 (0)4 75 58 72 25
email	marie.katchikian@minitel.net

Map 11 Entry 656

Le Marais

Opt for the simple country life at this friendly farm which has been in the family for over 100 years and has returned to organic methods; Madame calls it "acupuncture for the land". Four horses, a few hens, and – when there's a full house – meals of regional recipes served family-style, with home-grown veg and *vin de noix* aperitif. Monsieur collects old farming artefacts and Madame, although busy, always finds time for a chat. The bedrooms are in a separate wing with varnished ceilings, antique beds and candlewick covers; baths are old-fashioned pink. At the foot of the Vercors range, utter peace.

rooms	4: 1 double, 1 twin, 1 triple, 1 family room.
price	€45-€50.
meals	Dinner with wine, €16.
closed	Rarely.
directions	From Romans D538 for Chabeuil. Leaving Alixan left by Boulangerie for St Didier; left again, Chambres d'Hôtes St Didier signs for 3km; farm on left.

Christiane & Jean-Pierre Imbert
Le Marais,
26300 St Didier de Charpey, Drôme
tel   +33 (0)4 75 47 03 50
mobile   +33 (0)6 27 32 23 65
email   imbert.jean-pierre@wanadoo.fr
web   perso.wanadoo.fr/les-marais/

Map 11 Entry 657

Chambedeau

Madame's kindliness infuses her home, one that at first glance is coy about its age and charms. Her eventful life has nourished a wicked sense of humour but no bitterness and she is a natural storyteller (she'll show you the photographs too) – she alone is worth the detour. The fading carpets and small shower rooms become incidental after a short while; enjoy, instead, the homely bedrooms, the terraces, the peace and birdlife of the lush leafy garden which shelters the house from the road – and breakfast (organic honeys, homemade jams and cake, cheese) where the table is a picture in itself. Simply unwind.

rooms	2: 1 twin/double; 1 twin with separate shower.
price	€51.
meals	Restaurants 2-7km.
closed	Rarely.
directions	From A7 Valence Sud exit A49 for Grenoble. Exit 33 right D538a for Beaumont, 2.6km; right at sign Chambres d'Hôtes & Chambedeau; 800m on right, tarmac drive.

Mme Lina de Chivré-Dumond
Chambedeau,
26760 Beaumont lès Valence,
Drôme
tel   +33 (0)4 75 59 71 70
email   linadechivredumond@minitel.net

Map 11 Entry 658

Rhône Valley – Alps

Les Péris

Here is the grandmother we all dream of, a delightful woman who cossets her guests, and puts flowers, sweets and fruit in the bedrooms. This old stone farmhouse facing the Vercors mountains is definitely a family home and good meals of regional dishes with local wine, prepared by daughter Élisabeth, can be very jolly with family, friends and guests all sharing the long table in the kitchen. And there's a *menu curieux* using ancient forgotten vegetables! The roomy, old-fashioned bedrooms with walnut armoires breathe a comfortable, informal air. Great for kids, and a duck pond good for splashing in.

rooms	3 triples.
price	€48.
meals	Dinner with wine, €16.
closed	Rarely.
directions	From A7 exit Valence Sud on D68 to Chabeuil. There, cross river; left on D154 for Combovin 5km; signed, on left.

Mme Madeleine Cabanes
Les Péris,
D154 – Route de Combovin,
26120 Châteaudouble,
Drôme
tel   +33 (0)4 75 59 80 51
fax   +33 (0)4 75 59 48 78

Map 11 Entry 659

Rhône Valley – Alps

La Maison du Moulin

Painted beams, pretty *objets trouvés* and informal young Belgians greet you. Deep in lavender and truffle country, their mill has been transformed with style. House and guest outbuildings – slanting roofs, painted shutters – cluster round the courtyard where gorgeous old pottery stands sentinel. Each serene bedroom has its outdoor patch with antique seating. A chandelier tinkles, walls are pastel-washed and white iron beds sport fine linen. Old baths flirt with chic Starck-like basins. After a plop in the pool, wander over the courtyard to supper. And wake to breakfast as dreamy as all the rest.

rooms	5: 4 doubles; 1 suite for 4 & kitchenette.
price	€75–€100.
meals	Dinner with wine, €27.
closed	Rarely.
directions	A7 S; exit Montélimar Sud; D133 to Valaurie; after Valaurie D541 to Grignan. Entrance to house after approx. 8km before entering Grignan.

Bénédicte & Philippe Appels
La Maison du Moulin,
Le Moulin, 26230 Grignan, Drôme
tel   +33 (0)4 75 46 56 94
mobile   +33 (0)6 23 26 23 60
email   info@maisondumoulin.com
web   www.maisondumoulin.com

Map 16 Entry 660

Provence – Alps – Riviera

Provence – Alps – Riviera

Montsalier

Venerable stones in the remote thyme-wafted air of a hillside village: an apparently modest old house unfolds into a place of grandeur with a vast flourish of a dining hall, a tower, a pigeon loft and a well-travelled, fascinating hostess with a fine mix of shyness and humour for company. The courtyard is wisteria-clad, the garden sheltered, the food superb. Two rooms on the 17th-century lower level charm with their simple ancientness, the canopy bed lies in splendour below serried beams; they overflow with character, gentle colours, antique wardrobes. There are two lovely terraces, and hot-air ballooning nearby.

rooms	3 doubles.
price	€100.
meals	Dinner with wine, €40–€45.
closed	Rarely.
directions	From Forcalquier N100 for Apt; at 1st r'bout D950 right to Banon; D51 to Montsalier; house at entrance of village beside Mairie; signed.

Mme Karolyn Kauntze
Montsalier,
Montsalier, 04150 Banon,
Alpes-de-Haute-Provence

tel	+33 (0)4 92 73 23 61
fax	+33 (0)4 92 73 23 61
email	montsalier@infonie.fr
web	maison-karolyn.chez.tiscali.fr

Map 16 Entry 661

Provence – Alps – Riviera

Mas Saint Joseph

Come for the view of row upon row of peaks fading into the distance, the walking, the welcome. Hélène and Olivier bought the *mas* as a holiday home years ago, restored it with loving care, then moved here and began taking guests. Olivier is a walker and can inform you about spectacular walking trails from one B&B to the next. One bedroom has an ancient brick bread oven in a corner; another, once a stable, has a manger to prove it. Breakfast and dinner are on the terrace in warm weather or in the owners' fine old barn, and you can use the biggish pool behind the house. And oh, those views!

rooms	4: 1 double, 1 triple, 2 suites for 4.
price	€48. Triple €65. Suite €82.
meals	Dinner with wine, €17.
closed	Mid-November–March.
directions	From Châteauneuf Val St Donat 1.5km for St Étienne les Orgues; house on bend, on right above road; steep 100m drive to house.

Hélène & Olivier Lenoir
Mas Saint Joseph,
04200 Châteauneuf Val St Donat,
Alpes-de-Haute-Provence

tel	+33 (0)4 92 62 47 54
email	lenoir.st.jo@wanadoo.fr
web	www.provenceweb.fr/04/st-joseph

Map 16 Entry 662

Château d'Esparron

Castellanes built Esparron in the 1400s, both have been pivots of Provençal history. The superb stone stairs lead to vastly luscious bedrooms: plain walls and fresh flowers, tiles and gorgeous fabrics, family antiques with tales to tell. The garden is small but perfect. Slender Charlotte-Anne and her two beautiful children come straight from a Gainsborough portrait. She attends to everyone: family, staff, guests. Bernard, a mine of information with suntan and real manners, adds a touch of 1930s glamour. Wonderful family, splendiferous house, vast breakfast in the cavernously cosy kitchen.

rooms	5: 3 doubles, 1 twin, 1 suite.
price	€130–€200.
meals	Restaurant 5-minute walk.
closed	November–March.
directions	From Aix en Provence A51 exit 18 on D907; D82 to Gréoux les Bains; follow on D952 & D315 to Esparron. Stop & ring at gates (once past, it's impossible to turn).

Bernard & Charlotte-Anne
de Castellane
Château d'Esparron,
04800 Esparron de Verdon,
Alpes-de-Haute-Provence
tel   +33 (0)4 92 77 12 05
fax   +33 (0)4 92 77 13 10
email   chateau@esparron.com
web   www.esparron.com

Map 16 Entry 663

Ferme de Felines

Southern energies, wild evergreen hills and strong light push in through big architect's windows to meet the sober cool of black-white-grey northern design in a thrilling encounter. Small, wiry and full of laughter, Rita has a passion for this house, her land and the wildlife she fights to preserve. She may adorn your space of purity with one perfect flower in a glass cylinder, some fruit and a candle. Linen, beds, taps and towels are all top quality, her generosity is warm, her dog and six cats beautiful, her vast living room a treat. Breakfast at a marble table, then take a swim in the lovely lake. *Minimum stay two-three nights.*

rooms	3 doubles.
price	€125.
meals	Restaurants in Moustiers.
closed	Rarely.
directions	From Aix A51 exit Manosque for Gréoux; D952 to Riez, Moustiers; D952 for Castellane, 6km black sign on right.

Rita Ravez
Ferme de Felines,
04360 Moustiers Ste Marie,
Alpes-de-Haute-Provence
tel   +33 (0)4 92 74 64 19
mobile   +33 (0)6 81 50 60 33
email   ferme-de-felines@wanadoo.fr
web   www.ferme-de-felines.com

Map 16 Entry 664

Provence – Alps – Riviera

La Plantade

No wonder Luc is so passionate about wine: his and Elena's old-stone farm is within the Enclave des Papes, a region purchased by the papacy in the Middle Ages after its wines cured Pope Jean XII. South-facing, La Plantade stands in admiration of its glorious vineyards; a field of sunflowers next to a delicious pool crowns its treasure. Typical of Provençal rural architecture, the house is simple with old beams and small windows. Neat country-style bedrooms are relaxed and informal like your hosts. Belgian Luc is a motorcycle enthusiast, Bulgarian Elena is an accomplished polyglot and maker of fine sorbets.

rooms	4: 2 doubles, 2 twins/doubles.
price	€83–€95.
meals	Dinner €22–€29. Wine list from €8.
closed	Rarely.
directions	From Orange, N7 N for 2km; right onto D576 for Nyons. At La Tulette, left to Visan; right onto D20; house on right after 1.2km opp. Clos du Père Clement.

Luc & Elena Vermeersch
La Plantade,
Route de Vaison,
84820 Visan, Vaucluse
tel   +33 (0)4 90 41 98 80
email laplantadevisan@aol.com
web   www.visanlaplantade.com

Map 16 Entry 665

Provence – Alps – Riviera

L'École Buissonnière

A stone jewel set in southern lushness and miles of green vines and purple hills. Country furniture (a particularly seductive choice of Provençal chairs) is polished with wax and time; big, whitewashed bedrooms are freshly sober; birds sing to the tune of the aviary outside. One balconied bedroom, in the mezzanined old barn, has a saddle and a *gardian's* hat from a spell in the Camargue; ask about John's travels. He rightly calls himself a Provençal Englishman, Monique is warmly welcoming too – theirs is a happy house, where German is also spoken. Wonderful Vaison la Romaine is four miles away.

rooms	3: 2 doubles, 1 family room.
price	€53–€59.
meals	Restaurant in village, 1km. Guest kitchen.
closed	Mid-November–March.
directions	From A7 exit Bollène for Nyons D94; D20 right for Vaison & Buisson; cross River Aygues; left for Villedieu & Cave la Vigneronne D51 & D75 for 2.2km.

Monique Alex & John Parsons
L'École Buissonnière,
D75, 84110 Buisson,
Vaucluse
tel   +33 (0)4 90 28 95 19
email ecole.buissonniere@wanadoo.fr
web   www.buissonniere-provence.com

Map 16 Entry 666

L'Evêché

Narrow, cobbled streets lead to this fascinating and beautifully furnished house that was once part of the 17th-century Bishop's Palace. The Verdiers are charming, relaxed, cultured hosts – he an architect/builder, she a teacher. The white walls of the guests' sitting room-library are lined with modern art and framed posters, and the cosy, quilted bedrooms, all whitewashed beams and terracotta floors, have a serene Provençal feel. Views fly over beautiful terracotta rooftops from the balconied suite, and well-presented breakfasts are served on the terrace, complete with exceptional views to the Roman bridge.

Domaine du Bois de la Cour

A great spot for exploring Provence. The big old house, surrounded by its own vineyards and solid evergreen oaks, within harmless earshot of a road, is very handsome and Madame brings it to life with her special sparkle and enthusiasm for what she has created here. The decoration is all hers – more 'evolved French farmhouse-comfortable' than 'designer-luxurious'. She loves cooking, herbs and flowers; you may be offered her elderflower aperitif. Nothing is too much trouble for Madame or Monsieur – walkers' luggage can be transferred, delicious picnics can be laid on, then there's the wine tasting…

rooms	5: 3 twins/doubles, 2 suites for 2-3.
price	€78-€85. Suite €105-€130.
meals	Choice of restaurants in Vaison.
closed	2 weeks in both November & December.
directions	From Orange, D975 to Vaison. In town, follow 'Ville Médiévale' signs. Parking tricky.

rooms	5: 1 double, 2 triples, 1 quadruple, 1 suite for 5.
price	€60-€84.
meals	Dinner with wine, €23.
closed	Rarely.
directions	A9 exit Bollène for Carpentras 18km; leaving Cairanne, head for Carpentras 1.5km; house on right-hand turn.

	Aude & Jean-Loup Verdier
	L'Evêché,
	Rue de l'Evêché, Cité Médiévale,
	84110 Vaison la Romaine, Vaucluse
tel	+33 (0)4 90 36 13 46
fax	+33 (0)4 90 36 32 43
email	eveche@aol.com
web	www.eveche.com

	Élisabeth & Jerry Para
	Domaine du Bois de la Cour,
	Route de Carpentras,
	84290 Cairanne, Vaucluse
tel	+33 (0)4 90 30 84 68
fax	+33 (0)4 90 30 84 68
email	infos@boisdelacour.com
web	www.boisdelacour.com

Map 16   Entry 667

Map 16   Entry 668

Provence – Alps – Riviera
Les Convenents

For this delightful English couple, refugees from spinning plates in London, welcoming visitors in their haven is as natural as breathing. Five former workers' cottages have become a relaxing Provençal *mas* where space and simplicity leave old stones and timbers to glow and there's a vine-shaded terrace. Small explosions of cushions and paintings bring fresh white walls and fabrics alive; more modernity in good clean bathrooms and superb finishes – Ian's domain. Sarah, who was in catering, rules in the kitchen. They support the local economy, use the village shops, enjoy their community.

rooms	2 doubles.
price	€85–€90. Singles €80–€85.
meals	Dinner €26 with wine, Monday & Friday. Choice of restaurants nearby.
closed	November–March (available on special request).
directions	From Orange D976 to Gap & St Cécile les Vignes; D11 left to Uchaux; through village, between Les Farjons & Rochegude, 3km. Les Covenents on left. Signed.

Sarah Banner
Les Convenents,
84100 Uchaux, Vaucluse
tel +33 (0)4 90 40 65 64
fax +33 (0)4 90 40 65 64
email sarahbanner@wanadoo.fr
web www.lesconvenents.com

Map 16 Entry 669

Provence – Alps – Riviera
La Ravigote

Madame and her house both smile gently. It's a simple, authentic Provençal farmhouse that has escaped the vigorous renovator, its courtyard shaded by a lovely lime tree. Once a teacher in Africa, elegantly shy Madame considers dinners with her guests, in dining room or courtyard, as the best part of B&B – her meals are showcases for local specialities. The interior is a bright version of traditional French country style with old family furniture and tiled floors. Set among vineyards below the Montmirail hills, it has soul-pleasing views across the surrounding unspoilt country. *Minimum stay two nights.*

rooms	4: 1 double, 2 twins, 1 family room.
price	€43–€45.
meals	Dinner with wine, €18.
closed	November–March.
directions	From Carpentras D7 N through Aubignan & Vacqueyras; fork right (still D7) for Sablet; right 500m after 'Cave Vignerons Gigondas'; signed.

Sylvette Gras
La Ravigote,
84190 Gigondas, Vaucluse
tel +33 (0)4 90 65 87 55
fax +33 (0)4 90 65 87 55
email info@laravigote.com
web www.laravigote.com

Map 16 Entry 670

Le Mas de la Pierre du Coq

What's especially nice about this 17th-century farmhouse is that it hasn't been over-prettified. Instead, it has the friendly, informal elegance of a house that's lived in and loved; grey-painted beams, soft open-stone walls, seductive bathrooms. The Lorenzes fell in love with it three years ago; it reminded gentle Stéphan of the home he grew up in. Bustling Martine starts your day with a terrific breakfast, Stéphan shows you the walks from the door. The gardens, sweet with roses, oleanders and lavender, are shaded by ancient trees and the pool and views are glorious. Stay for as long as you can.

rooms	3: 1 double, 1 twin, 1 suite for 4.
price	€120. Suite €170.
meals	Dinner with wine, €30.
closed	Rarely.
directions	From Aubignan to Carpentras; after 2.5km right at junction; immed. right into Chemin de Loriol to Mazan; follow road, house up above on right after bridge.

Stéphan & Martine Lorenz
Le Mas de la Pierre du Coq,
Chemin de Loriol,
84810 Aubignan,
Vaucluse

tel	+33 (0)4 90 67 31 64
mobile	+33 (0)6 76 81 95 09
email	lorenz.stephane@wanadoo.fr
web	www.masdelapierreducoq.com

Map 16 Entry 671

Mas Pichony

Summer evenings are spent beneath the ancient spreading plane tree as the setting sun burnishes the vines beyond the slender cypresses, and the old stones of the 17th-century *mas* breathe gold. Laetitia and Laurent have given the farmhouse style and charm, beautifying it with country antiques, books and vibrant colours. Two children, three horses (a corner of the hall is full of riding gear), a trio of cats and a lone dog complete the charming picture. Laetitia serves good Provençal food at the big, convivial table; a terracotta-roofed area by the pool is a delicious place to sit and soak up the views.

rooms	5: 3 doubles, 1 twin, 1 family room for 5.
price	€78-€88.
meals	Dinner with wine, €28, Friday-Tuesday.
closed	November-February.
directions	From Pernes les Fontaines; D28 for St Didier. House on right, set back from road to St Didier.

Laetitia & Laurent Desbordes
Mas Pichony,
1454 route de Saint Didier,
84210 Pernes les Fontaines,
Vaucluse

tel	+33 (0)4 90 61 56 11
fax	+33 (0)4 90 40 35 02
email	laurent.desbordes@wanadoo.fr
web	www.maspichony.com

Map 16 Entry 672

Provence – Alps – Riviera

Le Mas de Miejour

These are young, easy-going hosts, with a passion for wine and a fine display of Frédéric's pottery, who have escaped from their city pasts. Their guest bedrooms in this converted farmhouse are all different, all serene: one with a white appliquéd bedcover made in Thailand, another with Senegalese bedspreads, and a super family suite with a big brass bed and, on a separate floor, three beds for children. The land here is flat with a high water table so the garden, sheltered by trees and waving maize in summer, is always fresh and green; with its lovely pool, an idyllic retreat after a day's sight-seeing.

rooms	3: 1 double, 1 twin, 1 family suite.
price	€75–€90.
meals	Light supper €16. Wine list from €5.
closed	November–March, except by arrangement.
directions	From A7 exit 23; after toll right at r'bout for Carpentras & Entraigues; 1st exit to Vedène D6 to St Saturnin lès Avignon; left to Le Thor D28 for 2km; right Chemin du Trentin.

Frédéric & Emmanuelle Westercamp
Le Mas de Miejour,
117 chemin du Trentin,
84250 Le Thor, Vaucluse

tel	+33 (0)4 90 02 13 79
mobile	+33 (0)6 68 25 25 06
email	frederic.westercamp@wanadoo.fr
web	www.masdemiejour.com

Map 16 Entry 673

Provence – Alps – Riviera

Villa La Lèbre

Madame is an absolute dear and she and Charles genuinely love doing B&B – they offer an open-hearted welcome and a real guest room in a real home. Charles speaks seven languages and is fascinating. The comfy room has its own dressing room, an extra mezzanine single and a newly tiled shower; you have use of a fridge and are welcome to picnic. The garden is their passion – it is fabulous, with roses, peonies, lavender and more. This is a modern house built of old stone in traditional local style and surrounded by hills, woods and vineyards with lovely valley views towards Goult and the Lubéron. Great value.

rooms	1 triple.
price	€50. Triple €60.
meals	Choice of restaurants 5km.
closed	Rarely.
directions	From Avignon N100 towards Apt. At Coustellet, D2 for Gordes. After Les Imberts right D207 & D148 to St Pantaléon; pass church; small hill on left; 3rd drive on right.

Pierrette & Charles Lawrence
Villa La Lèbre,
Saint Pantaléon,
84220 Gordes,
Vaucluse

tel	+33 (0)4 90 72 20 74
fax	+33 (0)4 90 72 20 74
email	jaclawrav@wanadoo.fr

Map 16 Entry 674

Sous L'Olivier

Old bare stonework rules the scene, big arched openings have become multi-paned dining windows, a stone fire burns immense logs in winter, and all is set around a pretty part-sheltered courtyard. Charming young bon viveur Julien, apron-clad, started his career in the kitchens of Paul Bocuse (breakfasts here are sumptuous affairs, dinners are convivial, the cooking worth a serious detour) while gentle Carole is behind the very fresh, Frenchly decorated bedrooms. Flat agricultural land spreads peacefully out around you; the refreshing pool is arched with canvas shading and surrounded by giant pots and plants.

rooms	6: 2 doubles, 2 triples, 1 suite, 1 suite for 2-6.
price	€90–€130. Apartment €220.
meals	Dinner with wine, €27.
closed	Never.
directions	From Avignon N7 E, then D22 for Apt, Dingé, Sisteron (approx. 29km total), do not go to Lagnes. After Le Petit Palais, sign on right.

Carole, Julien & Hugo Gouin
Sous L'Olivier,
Quartier le Petit Jonquier,
84800 Lagnes,
Vaucluse
tel   +33 (0)4 90 20 33 90
email souslolivier@wanadoo.fr
web   www.chambresdhotesprovence.com

Map 16 Entry 675

Le Mas des Câpriers

The garden is loved and worked at and their own produce abounds: almond milk, olive oil, wine, cherries, saffron, honey. The L-shaped mas once housed silkworms, now it is home to a modest retired couple – surprised owners of such perfection. Wake to orchards, olive groves and long lines of lavender, croissants on white china, dips in a divine pool, spots of privacy and views for all. Be charmed by whitewashed walls, bleached beams, soft hues and gilded touches, cushioned fauteuils and sober chandeliers, delectable bathrooms and a Romany caravan with Art Nouveau panelling. *And* a summer kitchen.

rooms	5: 4 doubles, 1 twin.
price	€95–€140.
meals	Restaurant 2km.
closed	Never.
directions	From Aix A51 to Manosque, exit Pertuis on D956; D9 to Cabrières d'Aigues; thro' village, past church and café, over road, N for hills & Chemin de Raoux. House name at track entrance.

Christine & Bernard Tixier
Le Mas des Câpriers,
Chemin de Raoux,
84240 Cabrières d'Aigues,
Vaucluse
tel   +33 (0)4 90 77 69 68
fax   +33 (0)4 90 77 69 68
email masdescapriers@wanadoo.fr
web   luberon-masdescapriers.com

Map 16 Entry 676

Provence – Alps – Riviera

Villa Saint Louis

Stepping into this typical Provençal townhouse from the busy street one enters a refined, elegant and colourful cocoon of lived-in gentility and old-world charm where period furniture – to each room its style – and a throng of fascinating *objets d'art* create an intrinsically French home unchanged since Balzac. Attentive and cultured, Madame runs the B&B with her daughter, a fluent English speaker. Guest quarters, including breakfast room, are self-contained on the top floor, there's a deep terrace under the plane trees and a cool, fragrant garden for everyone below. *Summer kitchen sometimes available.*

rooms	5: 2 doubles, 3 twins.
price	€60–€70.
meals	Restaurants nearby.
closed	Rarely.
directions	From Aix en Provence N96 & D556 to Pertuis; D973 to Cadenet; D943 for Bonnieux to Lourmarin.

Mme Lassallette
Villa Saint Louis,
35 rue Henri de Savornin,
84160 Lourmarin, Vaucluse

tel	+33 (0)4 90 68 39 18
fax	+33 (0)4 90 68 10 07
email	villasaintlouis@wanadoo.fr
web	www.villasaintlouis.com

Map 16 Entry 677

Provence – Alps – Riviera

Mas de Bassette

Sophisticated simplicity is here: white walls and pale fabrics glow venerably in the sunlight filtering through the greenery outside – an ethereal picture of pure Provence. Your hosts are as quiet and charming, gentle and generous as their 15th-century *mas* with its magical great garden where peacocks dally and a princely doberman keeps watch. Big bedrooms are perfect: old terracotta tiles and wicker chairs, thick towels and soap in a basket. Peer for an eternity at the fascinating framed collection of artists' letters in the handsome salon. Superb value, utter peace.

rooms	2 doubles.
price	€110.
meals	Restaurants 1–20km.
closed	Rarely.
directions	In Barbentane for Abbaye St Michel du Frigoulet; at windmill for tennis club; house entrance near club; signed.

Marie & François Veilleux
Mas de Bassette,
13750 Barbentane,
Bouches-du-Rhône

tel	+33 (0)4 90 95 63 85
fax	+33 (0)4 90 95 63 85
email	bassette2@wanadoo.fr
web	www.masdebassette.com

Map 16 Entry 678

Provence – Alps – Riviera

Le Mas Ferrand

Pure 19th century: house, décor, furniture, all authentic in a slightly chaotic assemblage, all imbued by Jean-Paul's love of life and people, his dedication to his magical wild garden – you will fall beneath the spell. Christine bakes three sorts of bread and croissants each morning, 'Grannie' is part of the equation, you can talk to them about anything, feel at home without trying, leave with new friends to write to. At night, they leave the place to their guests, with two comfortably old-fashioned rooms each with a big simple bathroom at each end of the house let as suites. A place for free spirits.

rooms	3: 1 double, 1 family suite for 2-3, 1 family suite for 2-4.
price	€55.
meals	Restaurants 200m-1km.
closed	Rarely.
directions	Between Avignon & Tarascon & Arnles N570. At r'bout take CD28 to Châteaurenard, direction Graveson centre. Property 300m on right.

Jean-Paul & Christine Ferrand
Le Mas Ferrand,
7 ave Auguste Chabaud,
13690 Graveson,
Bouches-du-Rhône
tel   +33 (0)4 90 95 85 29
fax   +33 (0)4 90 95 86 51
email le-mas.ferrand@wanadoo.fr
web   www.le-mas-ferrand.fr

Map 16 Entry 679

Provence – Alps – Riviera

Le Mas d'Anez

A tree-lined drive and impressive wrought-iron gates welcome you to this impeccable 18th-century mansion. They came here from Paris (a three-hour ride on the TGV, so they can still visit their grandchildren!). He, extrovert and trilingual, swapped wine consultancy for olive oil; she, with a lovely smile, writes books on interior design and runs the odd course. The rooms are decorated with simple, assured elegance; the vast Provençal kitchen is a wonderful place for breakfast. Beyond the stone wall that encloses house, garden and pool stretch Thierry's olive groves. *Minimum stay two nights. Long stays available.*

rooms	2: 1 twin/double, 1 suite for 4.
price	€95. €165 for 4.
meals	Occasional dinner with wine, €31.
closed	Rarely.
directions	Avignon to Tarascon; after Rognonas, N590 to Beaucaire Tarascon; after Graveson r'bout follow Beaucaire & Tarascon signs; on for 7km, house on right; entrance between trees and stone columns.

Thierry & Marie-Laure Mantoux
Le Mas d'Anez,
Route d'Avignon,
13150 Tarascon en Provence,
Bouches-du-Rhône
tel   +33 (0)4 90 91 73 98
fax   +33 (0)4 90 91 73 99
email masdanez@wanadoo.fr
web   www.masdanez.com

Map 16 Entry 680

Provence – Alps – Riviera

24 rue du Château

On a medieval street near one of the loveliest châteaux in France, two *maisons de maître* are joined by an ochre-hued courtyard and a continuity of taste. It's an impeccable renovation that has kept all of the soft patina of stone walls and tiles. No garden, but a courtyard for candlelit evenings and immaculate breakfasts. Calming, gracious bedrooms have fine old furniture and beams, perfect bathrooms, crisp linen. While you can be totally independent, your courteous hostess is relaxed and friendly and thoroughly enjoys her guests. Deeply atmospheric. *Minimum stay two nights July-September.*

rooms	5: 3 doubles, 2 twins.
price	€72-€88.
meals	Choice of restaurants in town.
closed	November-December, except by arrangement.
directions	In Tarascon centre take Rue du Château opposite château (well signed). No. 24 is on right.

Martine Laraison
24 rue du Château,
13150 Tarascon,
Bouches-du-Rhône
tel   +33 (0)4 90 91 09 99
fax   +33 (0)4 90 91 10 33
email ylaraison@wanadoo.fr
web   www.chambres-hotes.com

Map 16 Entry 681

Provence – Alps – Riviera

Le Mas D'Arvieux

Full of chat and laughter, Marie-Pierre is passionate about art and books while Christian loves music, making furniture and pottering in the olive grove; both were journalists travelling the world before settling into the elegant manor, stylishly enhanced by a refined, almost baroque décor. The large bedrooms, one in the tower wing, one with a carved mezzanine, all with personality, have beams and stone walls, fine old armoires, luxurious bathrooms and wonderful views of the Provençal hills. Barn concerts, an exciting menu at supper and some of the best breakfasts in France. *Cookery classes available.*

rooms	5: 2 doubles, 1 triple, 1 suite.
price	€95-€115.
meals	Dinner with wine, €30.
closed	Rarely.
directions	From Avignon D570 to Tarascon; 2nd r'bout after Graveson; now on D970: under bridge; 2km beyond, left on humpback bridge through white gate.

Marie-Pierre Carretier &
Christian Billmann
Le Mas D'Arvieux,
Route d'Avignon, 13150 Tarascon,
Bouches-du-Rhône
tel   +33 (0)4 90 90 78 77
fax   +33 (0)4 90 90 78 68
email mas@arvieux-provence.com
web   www.arvieux-provence.com

Map 16 Entry 682

Provence – Alps – Riviera

Mas Shamrock

A manicured farmhouse whose interior is as southern cool as the welcome from its owners is sincerely Franco-Irish – John is relaxed and direct, Christiane is efficient and helpful. Natural stone, oak beams, terracotta floors and cool colours give a wonderfully fresh and open feel to the house, while bedrooms are light and airy with neat shower rooms. Outside, a delectable garden, centuries-old plane trees, a vine tunnel, three hectares of cypresses and a landscaped, secluded pool add to the magic. An oft-tinkled piano is there for you to play. *Minimum stay two nights July/August.*

rooms	5: 3 doubles, 1 twin, 1 family room for 3-4.
price	€85-€115.
meals	Choice of restaurants in St Rémy.
closed	November-Easter.
directions	From St Rémy D571 for Avignon; over 2 r'bouts, left before 2nd bus stop (Lagoy), opp. 2nd yellow Portes Anciennes sign, Chemin de Velleron; house 6th on right.

Christiane & John Walsh
Mas Shamrock,
Chemin de Velleron & du Prud'homme
13210 St Rémy de Provence,
Bouches-du-Rhône

tel	+33 (0)4 90 92 55 79
fax	+33 (0)4 90 92 55 80
email	mas.shamrock@wanadoo.fr
web	www.masshamrock.com

Map 16 Entry 683

Provence – Alps – Riviera

Le Mas d'Hermès

Uncomplicated country comfort. Danielle and Hugues escaped city life to open this pretty Provençal farmhouse and give you a simple, gentle welcome. Vast airy rooms charm with their sun-faded shutters and unfussy, modern furnishings. Bedroom suites in the separate guest wing have exposed stonework, good bathrooms, sprawling sofas and brocante finds. Choose downstairs for a terrace, upstairs for beams and romance. So much space: guest kitchenette, log-fire sitting room, country-style dining room. A pool and a garden surrounded by pines. Peace and great value – ten minutes from RN7.

rooms	2: 1 suite, 1 family room for 4.
price	€63-€72.
meals	Restaurants 2-5km. Use of kitchenette.
closed	Rarely.
directions	RN7 for Cavaillon; exit Plan d'Orgon; left at r'bout; on for 500m, continue on road 'Chemin Sans Issue'; house 200m on left, signed.

Danielle & Hugues Pelletier
Le Mas d'Hermès,
13750 Plan d'Orgon,
Bouches-du-Rhône

tel	+33 (0)4 90 73 17 13
mobile	+33 (0)6 62 41 32 35
email	chambres@mashermes.com
web	www.mashermes.com

Map 16 Entry 684

Provence – Alps – Riviera

Mas de la Rabassière

Fanfares of lilies at the door, Haydn inside and 'mine host' smiling in his chef's apron. La Rabassière means 'where truffles are found' and epicurean dinners are a must: vintage wines and a sculpted dancer grace the terrace table. Cookery classes with olive oil from his trees, jogging companionship, airport pick-up are all part of the elegant hospitality, aided by Théri, his serene assistant from Singapore. Big bedrooms and drawing room with roaring fire are comfortable in English country-house style: generous beds, erudite bookshelves, a tuned piano, Provençal antiques... and pool, tennis, croquet.

rooms	2 doubles. Extra beds.
price	€125. Singles €70.
meals	Dinner with wine, €40.
closed	Rarely.
directions	From A54 exit 13 to Grans on D19; right on D16 to St Chamas; just before r'way bridge, left for Cornillon, up hill 2km; house on right before tennis court. Map sent on request.

	Michael Frost
	Mas de la Rabassière,
	Route de Cornillon,
	13250 St Chamas,
	Bouches-du-Rhône
tel	+33 (0)4 90 50 70 40
fax	+33 (0)4 90 50 70 40
email	michaelfrost@rabassiere.com
web	www.rabassiere.com

Map 16 Entry 685

Provence – Alps – Riviera

Mas Sainte An

On its hilltop on the edge of pretty Peynier, the old *mas* stands in glory before Cézanne's Mount St Victoire: pull the cowbell, pass the wooden doors and the red-shuttered mass surges up from beds of roses. Beautifully restored, it once belonged to the painter Vincent Roux and memories of his life live on thanks to your gracious hostess. The Roux room is the nicest, with a delicious garden view, beams, terracotta tiles, and a fantastic ochre/green bathroom down the hall. The house has a wonderful patina and the grounds are beautifully kept. *Summer kitchen. Older children welcome. Min. stay two nights.*

rooms	2: 1 triple; 1 double with separate bath.
price	€72-€85.
meals	Restaurants in village.
closed	First three weeks in August.
directions	From Aix on D6, 4km before Trets, right D57 to Peynier; up hill to Trets & Aubagne road; left D908; right between Poste & Pharmacie. House 50m.

	Mme Jacqueline Lambert
	Mas Sainte An,
	3 rue d'Auriol,
	13790 Peynier,
	Bouches-du-Rhône
tel	+33 (0)4 42 53 05 32
fax	+33 (0)4 42 53 05 32
email	stanpeynier@yahoo.fr
web	www.stanpeynier.com

Map 16 Entry 686

Provence – Alps – Riviera

La Royante

The Bishop of Marseille once resided in this delicious corner of paradise and you may sleep in the sacristy, wash by a stained-glass window, nip into the chapel/music room for a quick midnight pray. Your brilliant hosts, a cosmopolitan mix of talent, fantasy and joy – their conversation alone is worth the price – have got every detail right without a hint of pedantry. The stupendous big bedrooms throng with original features and Bernard's beloved antiques (the more old-fashioned St Wlodek is reached through its bathroom) and his leisurely breakfast is fit for a bishop with time to talk about everything.

rooms	4: 3 doubles, 1 triple.
price	€103–€143.
meals	Restaurant 1km.
closed	Never.
directions	From Aix A8 for Nice; A52 Aubagne & Toulon, do not exit at Aubagne; A50 Marseille; exit 5 La Valentine; stay right; for Le Charrel 3km; after 'Legion Etrangère' building on left, 1st left D44a for Eoures; 1st right after bridge, signposted 'Maison de Retraite: Kaliste'; 800m to La Royante.

Xenia Saltiel
La Royante,
Chemin de la Royante,
13400 Aubagne en Provence,
Bouches-du-Rhône
tel   +33 (0)4 42 03 83 42
fax   +33 (0)4 42 03 83 42
email contact@laroyante.com
web   www.laroyante.com

Map 16 Entry 687

Provence – Alps – Riviera

Domaine de la Blaque

Out here among the wild flowers, oak forests and rolling hills you will find a dedication to the genuine, a particular sense of place. Your hosts have that artistic flair which puts the right things together naturally, palest pink-limed walls with white linen; old-stone courtyard walls with massed jasmine and honeysuckle; yoga groups and painters with wide open skies. Indeed, Jean-Luc is passionate about astronomy, Caroline is a photographer, they produce olives, truffles and timber, organise courses and love sharing their remote estate with like-minded travellers. Each pretty, private room has its own little terrace.

rooms	2: 1 double, 1 twin, each with kitchenette.
price	€61–€69.
meals	Restaurants 2.5km.
closed	Rarely.
directions	A8 exit St Maximum; D560 before Barjols; at Brue-Auriac D35 to Varages; sign on left leaving village for Tavernes; follow signs, dirt track part of way.

Caroline & Jean-Luc Plouvier
Domaine de la Blaque,
83670 Varages, Var
tel   +33 (0)4 94 77 86 91
fax   +33 (0)4 94 77 86 91
email ploublaque@hotmail.com
web   www.lablaque.com

Map 16 Entry 688

Le Nichoir

Discreet and exclusive. There is little else to recommend it. The owners flew the nest years ago and the place has been squatted in by the current owners. The circular entrance owes as much to the shape of the original owners as it does to the visionary fenestration ideas of Le Corbusier. They would come and go in an endless orgy of feeding and entertaining their young, oblivious of fattism and modern theories of diet and health. Rumour has it that the food wriggled. Things are marginally better now - but you will be up before the beak if you don't pay your bill.

Domaine de Conillières

In front of a log fire, breakfast is when you like – French pastries, sourdough rolls, delicious cakes, homemade jams, all diligently served by Philippe's elegant aunt. The family have lived in these wonderfully atmospheric buildings for generations. The olive groves and the vines, once part of this remote domaine, are now rented out, but the immense bastide is unchanged. Shapely red floor tiles, pale walls, perhaps a handsome old wardrobe or a red floral quilt – bedrooms are pleasing and extremely spacious, one on the first floor, the other reached via a creeper-covered stone stair. Good solid B&B.

rooms	1 room with nice, soft, circular bed; bath in next door garden.
price	Cheep!
meals	Good grubs & seedy dishes for when you're feeling peckish.
closed	All winter.
directions	As the crow flies, you'll find it near the bottom of the sky, facing east.

rooms	2: 1 suite for 3, 1 suite for 4.
price	€60–€75.
meals	Restaurant 2.5km.
closed	Never.
directions	Chemin du Moulin for 5km; right to Domaine, signed.

M & Mme Nid
Le Nichoir ,
Contremur,
00000 Volière, Var

tel	+33 000 1 00 001
email	courrier@pigeon.co.fr
web	perso-oiseau.intervol.fr/nid

Jacqueline & André Cortez
Domaine de Conillières,
83470 St Maximin la Ste Baume,
Var

tel	+33 (0)4 94 78 92 35
fax	+33 (0)4 94 59 78 57
email	info@domaine-de-conillieres.com
web	www.domaine-de-conillieres.com

Map 16 Entry 690

Provence – Alps – Riviera

La Cordeline

The Counts of Provence lived here in the 1100s: they had style; so does Michel Dyens, a civilised, sociable gentleman. Panache, too. The house lies in the quiet heart of the old town, the châteauesque side over the little street, the other over the walled garden, trees and fountain; it feels almost colonial. Enter to original honeycomb tiles under a grand, arched, embossed ceiling. The elegant comforts of your big, beautifully furnished bedroom include headed paper with the house's 17th-century front door logo. In winter you can snuggle down by a log fire and read in peace.

rooms	5: 3 doubles, 1 twin, 1 triple, all with bath/shower & separate wc.
price	€70–€105.
meals	Dinner with wine, €29.
closed	Rarely.
directions	From A8 exit Brignoles; over river for Centre Ville, immediately right for Hôtel de Claviers; round Pl. Palais de Justice; right Ave. F. Mistral; Rue des Cordeliers on left.

Isabelle Konen
La Cordeline,
14 rue des Cordeliers,
83170 Brignoles, Var
tel   +33 (0)4 94 59 18 66
fax   +33 (0)4 94 59 00 29
email   lacordeline@ifrance.com
web   www.lacordeline.com

Map 16 Entry 691

Provence – Alps – Riviera

Domaine de Saint Ferréol

Readers write: "Armelle is wonderful". Breakfast is the highlight of her hospitality: she full of ideas for excursions, and Monsieur happily sharing his knowledge of the area. Theirs is a warm, lively family – a cultivated couple, four lovely children – and their working vineyard has a timeless feel. Glorious views to Pontevès Castle from the first-class, authentically Provençal bedrooms; they and the breakfast room (with mini-kitchen) are in a separate wing but, weather permitting, breakfast is on the terrace. Peace and privacy in a beautiful old house, superb walking and seriously good value.

rooms	3: 2 twins/doubles, 1 suite for 4.
price	€59–€66. Suite €86.
meals	Restaurant 1.5km. Kitchen available.
closed	Mid-November–mid-March.
directions	From A8 exit St Maximin & Ste Baume D560 to Barjols; D560 2km for Draguignan; entrance opp. D60 turning for Pontevès.

Guillaume & Armelle
de Jerphanion
Domaine de Saint Ferréol,
83670 Pontevès, Var
tel   +33 (0)4 94 77 10 42
fax   +33 (0)4 94 77 19 04
email   saint-ferreol@wanadoo.fr
web   www.domaine-de-saint-ferreol.fr

Map 16 Entry 692

Provence – Alps – Riviera

Mas Saint Maurinet

Simply welcoming, your hosts were born in this unspoilt part of the Var where beautiful, distant views of the Pre-Alps – and genuine human warmth – await you at their modernised farmhouse with 19th-century foundations. The smallish bedrooms have typical Provençal fabrics and antiques and personal touches such as dried-flower arrangements; one has its own big terrace. On the verdant veranda Madame brings you breakfast of wholemeal bread, local honey and homemade jams. Plan a day away or make yourselves at home: you get picnic tables under the linden tree, an excellent summer kitchen and a good pool.

rooms	2: 1 double, 1 twin.
price	€60–€65.
meals	Restaurants 1-3km. BBQ available.
closed	Rarely.
directions	From Barjols to Taverne; to Montmeyan; thro' village to Quinson; house on left 300m after sign saying you have left Montmeyan, signed 'Gîtes de France'.

Dany & Vincent Gonfond
Mas Saint Maurinet,
Route de Quinson,
83670 Montmeyan, Var

tel	+33 (0)4 94 80 78 03
fax	+33 (0)4 94 80 78 03
email	st-maurinet-mosly@wanadoo.fr
web	www.st-maurinet-mosly.fr

Map 16 Entry 693

Provence – Alps – Riviera

Alegria

Belgian Cindy and Dieter, an attractive couple, have performed a masterly French renovation among the gnarled grey olive groves (they press their own). With simplicity and flair, intense colours and minimal furniture, Moroccan lights and repolished brocante, they have created a house of atmosphere, vibrant warmth and easy living. Bedrooms are light with lots of white, pools of colour, total attention to detail, originality (some bathrooms behind bedhead walls, some pure Marrakech). Their enthusiasm is boundless, their breakfast gorgeously Flemish, their food finely fusional.
Minimum stay two nights July/Aug.

rooms	5: 3 doubles, 1 suite for 2, 1 suite for 4.
price	€110–€140.
meals	Dinner with wine, €35.
closed	January.
directions	From Aups take road for Salernes; left opposite Gendarmerie. Signed.

Dieter & Cindy Ruys
Alegria,
59 chemin du Stade,
83630 Aups, Var

fax	+33 (0)4 94 70 00 41
mobile	+33 (0)6 32 20 15 37
email	alegria-aups@wanadoo.fr
web	www.alegria.tk

Map 16 Entry 694

Domaine de Nestuby

Bravo, Nathalie! The children are growing, the guest rooms refreshed, and she's still in calm, friendly control of this gorgeous, well-restored 18th-century bastide. One whole wing is for guests: yours the light, airy, vineyard-view bedrooms, pastel-painted and Provençal-furnished with a happy mix of antique and modern, yours the big bourgeois sitting room (little used: it's too lovely outside), yours a swim in the great spring-fed tank. Jean-François runs the vineyard, the tastings and the wine talk at dinner with sweet-natured ease. Utterly relaxing and very close to perfection. *Minimum stay three nights July/Aug.*

rooms	5: 1 double, 1 twin, 1 triple, 1 family room, 1 suite.
price	€65–€80.
meals	Dinner with wine, €22.
closed	November–February.
directions	From A8 Brignoles exit north D554 through Le Val; D22 through Montfort sur Argens for Cotignac. 5km along left; sign.

	Nathalie & Jean–François Roubaud
	Domaine de Nestuby,
	83570 Cotignac, Var
tel	+33 (0)4 94 04 60 02
fax	+33 (0)4 94 04 79 22
email	nestuby@wanadoo.fr
web	www.sejour-en-provence.com

Map 16 Entry 695

Bastide Notre Dame

The terraced garden, lovely by day (tables and chairs in private corners, a bivouac tent for those escaping the sun), is Moroccan-magical at night as lanterns dot the trees. A treat to start the day by the pool over coffee and *cannelés de Bordeaux* fresh from the oven; the pink, airy 1920s house stands high above the road surveying Entrecasteaux's valley and blue hills beyond. Marie-Thé is proud of her freshly renovated rooms with cool, pale furnishings, three private terraces and sweeping views, ex-farmer Thierry of his putt-perfect lawn. Both give you a courteous and very French welcome.

rooms	4 twins/doubles.
price	€80–€95.
meals	Dinner with wine, €20.
closed	Rarely.
directions	From Aix exit Brignoles; Le Val; Carcès; Lorgues; Entrecasteaux. House on left between chapel and cemetery on entrance to village.

	Thierry & Marie-Thé Bonnichon
	Bastide Notre Dame,
	L'Adrech de Ste Anne,
	83570 Entrecasteaux, Var
tel	+33 (0)4 94 04 45 63
mobile	+33 (0)6 11 42 12 09
email	mariethevalentin@aol.com
web	bastidenotredame.free.fr

Map 16 Entry 696

Bastide des Hautes Moures

Colours rich with Mediterranean sunshine and heat, a sure eye for stunning touches: this lovely house is a celebration of your young hosts' love of colour and brocante. And flawless workmanship. Those delectable bathrooms by North African craftsmen: Moroccan hammams? Roman baths? Bedrooms: there's space to dance round the easy chairs and Catherine's brilliant mix of furniture – into the walk-in wardrobe and out. Dinner? Antoine is an accomplished chef. Butterflies dance to the call of the cicadas beneath the 300-year-old oaks. The wealth of Provence is here. *Children welcome for specific weeks.*

rooms	3 doubles.
price	€80–€130.
meals	Dinner with wine, €30.
closed	Rarely.
directions	From A8 exit Le Luc & Le Cannet des Moures for Le Thoronet. Right on D84 for Vidouban. 4.5km to Les Moures, right & 800m on to house.

Catherine Jobert
& Antoine Debray
Bastide des Hautes Moures,
83340 Le Thoronet, Var
tel   +33 (0)4 94 60 13 36
fax   +33 (0)4 94 73 81 23
email jobertcatherine@aol.com
web   www.bastide-des-moures.com

Map 16 Entry 697

La Canal

Built in 1760 as a silkworm farm, this delicious old manor house in a quiet street in Lorgues still has mulberry trees shading its terrace. Beyond, a large walled garden bursting with lavender and trees, a meadow for children's games, a vast and lovely Roman pool, stupendous view to the distant hills. Inside it is just as authentic: old tiles with good rugs, beams, simple country antiques, bedrooms up a steep stair. Organised, warm-hearted Nicola may not be here all year round but has arranged for a friendly helper to be there when she is away. A house with soul, easy for families. *Minimum stay two nights.*

rooms	4: 1 double, 1 twin; 1 double, 1 twin, sharing shower/bath & wc.
price	€95.
meals	Restaurants within walking distance.
closed	Rarely.
directions	From A8 exit 13 on N7 E to Vidauban; left D48 to Lorgues. In main street, post office on right: right, right again; at T-junction left Pl. Accrarisio. Leave square on left into Rue de la Canal; house on left. Parking tricky.

Nicola d'Annunzio
La Canal,
177 rue de La Canal,
Quartier le Grand Jardin,
83510 Lorgues, Var
tel   +33 (0)4 94 67 68 32
fax   +33 (0)4 94 67 68 69
email lacanallorgues@aol.com
web   www.lacanal-lorgues.com

Map 16 Entry 698

Provence – Alps – Riviera

Les Cancades

Madame lavishes equal amounts of loving care on her guests as her beautiful Mediterranean garden with its tall trees, flowering shrubs and manicured lawn. Indeed, the whole place, designed by Monsieur 20 years ago as a luxurious family villa with thoughtfully concealed pool, is manicured. Comfortable Provençal-style rooms have Salernes bathroom tiles; one has its own piece of garden. Monsieur is shyly welcoming, Madame smilingly efficient; you've the hills full of medieval villages and wine estates to explore. Or make a picnic in the summer kitchen and just laze. *Garden chalet with spa and fitness room.*

rooms	3: 2 twins/doubles, 1 suite for 4.
price	€75. Suite €130.
meals	Restaurants in village.
closed	Rarely.
directions	From Toulon N8 for Aubagne; in Le Beausset cross 2 r'bouts; right opp. Casino supermarket; immediately left by boulangerie, right Chemin de la Fontaine 1.5km; sign on left.

x

Charlotte & Marceau Zerbib
Les Cancades,
1195 chemin de la Fontaine,
83330 Le Beausset, Var
tel   +33 (0)4 94 98 76 93
email charlotte.zerbib@wanadoo.fr
web   www.les-cancades.com

Map 16 Entry 699

Provence – Alps – Riviera

45 boulevard des Pêcheurs

Looking from this perch past umbrella pines out over the town to the marina and the amazing bay is a tonic in itself, served on your private terrace: your many-windowed space feels like a lookout tower, fittingly done in blue and white with a new parquet floor and good bathroom. Breakfast is served under the trumpet vine on the main terrace in the luxuriant garden. The salon, wide, welcoming and uncluttered, has windows to let the view in, old ship's binoculars to look out, nice old French furniture. Claudine is active and attentive, Serge used to work in boats and they are helpful yet unintrusive hosts.

rooms	1 double.
price	€70-€79.
meals	Restaurants nearby.
closed	Rarely.
directions	Into Lavandou centre; left up hill at 2nd lights; 1st left Ave. Bir-Hakem; Ave. des Champs Fleuries; Boulevard des Pêcheurs.

Claudine & Serge Draganja
45 boulevard des Pêcheurs,
Super - Lavandou,
83980 Le Lavandou, Var
tel   +33 (0)4 94 71 46 02
mobile +33 (0)6 16 17 03 83
email   draganja@wanadoo.fr
web   www.draganja-maison-hote.tk

Map 16 Entry 700

21 chemin des Marguerites

The warm-hearted, tireless Didiers seem to have been born to run a happy and hospitable B&B and they do so, enthusiastically, in their quiet 1960s villa with its backdrop of vineyards and hills. Two spotlessly clean bedrooms with real attention to comfort – good cupboards and bedside lights, for example – share the modern shower room and are hung with Amélie's fine paintings. The guest dining room leads to a private outside terrace and thence to the peaceful, beautiful garden; ideal for relaxing after the day's visit, maybe by boat to one of the Îles d'Hyères.

rooms	2: 1 double, 1 twin, sharing shower.
price	€80. €130 for 4.
meals	Restaurant nearby, choice in Le Lavandou.
closed	Rarely.
directions	From Le Lavandou D559 E to La Fossette. In village, left Ave. Capitaine Thorel; left again Chemin des Marguerites. If lost, phone for help!

Robert & Amélie Didier
21 chemin des Marguerites,
La Fossette,
83980 Le Lavandou, Var

tel   +33 (0)4 94 71 07 82
email   ra-didier@tele2.fr
web   www.ra-didier.tk

Map 16 Entry 701

Le Petit Magnan

Georges is retired and runs the B&B with great efficiency, keeping the house and its surprising touches of colour and imagination immaculately. The bedrooms are indisputably pretty; one, the much larger of the two, has floral curtains on a brass rod, peach-coloured 'dragged' walls and a painted bed. Hard to imagine anyone not liking it, especially the doors onto the private terrace. Half a mile up a rough stoney track, it is all immensely peaceful, there's a splendid pool, a woodland of ancient corks, views across tree-laden countryside and generous windows to let the Provençal light stream in.

rooms	2 doubles.
price	€80.
meals	Restaurants nearby.
closed	Rarely.
directions	From A8 exit Le Muy for Ste Maxime & St Tropez. About 5km before Ste Maxime right D74 to Plan de la Tour; entering village left D44 for Grimaud.

M & Mme Georges Ponselet
Le Petit Magnan,
Quartier Saint Sébastien,
83120 Plan de la Tour, Var

tel   +33 (0)4 94 43 72 00
mobile   +33 (0)6 74 85 61 79
email   lepetitmagnan@worldonline.fr
web   lepetitmagnan.free.fr/

Map 16 Entry 702

Les Trois Cyprès

What a view! Sit here, gazing past palms and pool to the plunging sea and enjoying Yvette's speciality of the day (tart, crumble…). She is a wonderful woman, sprightly and endlessly caring; Guy, a gentle and invaluable member of the team, collects the fresh bread and helps you plan your stay; they have travelled lots and simply love people. All three pretty, pastel guest rooms lead off a bright, Moroccan-touched landing – brass lamps, hand-painted mirror – and have lovely rugs on honeycomb-tile floors. The biggest room is definitely the best. And a sandy beach is 10 minutes down the cliff. *Minimum stay two nights.*

rooms	3: 2 doubles, 1 twin.
price	€90–€120.
meals	Restaurants in Les Issambres.
closed	October–May.
directions	From Ste Maxime N98 E through San Piere; after Casino supermarket, 4th left Ave. Belvédère; 1st left into Ave. de l'Ancien Petit Train des Pins; Corniche Ligure; house on junction, green gate.

	Yvette & Guy Pons
	Les Trois Cyprès,
	947 boulevard des Nymphes,
	83380 Les Issambres, Var
tel	+33 (0)4 98 11 80 31
fax	+33 (0)4 98 11 80 31
email	gyjpons@mac.com
web	homepage.mac.com/gyjpons/TOC.html

Map 16 Entry 703

L'Hirondelle Blanche

Monsieur Georges is passionate about painting, music, wine and old houses and has renovated and decorated this typical palm-strewn 1900s Riviera villa all by himself. Each appealing room has a personal touch – a big red parasol over a bed, a fishing net on a wall; some have little balconies for private aperitifs. His own paintings hang in the cosy salon, wines appear for the evening tasting (you can buy them too), the beach is over the road. Despite the nearby road, you don't need a car: fly in, train in, take a taxi or come by bike. A caring couple with two young children in a highly convivial house. *Five bedrooms with air-conditioning.*

rooms	6: 4 doubles, 1 twin/double, 1 family suite for 4.
price	€57–€157.
meals	Dinner €20, July & August. Wine from €5.50.
closed	Rarely.
directions	Autoroute A8 exit 38 Fréjus & St Raphael for St Raphael town centre; from old port follow sea front for 900m after Casino de Jeux heading for Cannes.

	Florence Methout
	L'Hirondelle Blanche,
	533 Bd du Général de Gaulle,
	83700 St Raphaël, Var
tel	+33 (0)4 98 11 84 03
fax	+33 (0)4 98 11 84 03
email	kussler-methout@wanadoo.fr
web	www.hirondelle-blanche.fr

Map 16 Entry 704

La Guillandonne

These lovely, civilised people, former teacher of English and architect, have treated their old house with delicacy and taste. Standing so Italianately red-ochre in its superb *parc* of great old trees by a stream, it could have stepped out of a 19th-century novel yet the interior speaks for your hosts' caring, imaginative approach (polished cement floors, stunning bathrooms). Bedrooms of fine personality, elegant and colourful, are antique, modern and 'ethnic' (heirlooms beside prison-made pieces). After the madding expats in town, you find here a taste of the peace that was the hallmark of inland Var.

rooms	4: 2 doubles, 2 twins.
price	€75.
meals	Restaurants 1.5km.
closed	Rarely.
directions	From A8 'Les Adrets' exit 39 for Fayence; left after lake, D562 for Fayence/Tourrettes; at Intermarché r'bout, D19 to Fayence; after 2km D219 right to Tourrettes; 200m black gate on right.

	Marie-Joëlle Salaün
	La Guillandonne,
	Chemin du Pavillon,
	83440 Tourrettes, Var
tel	+33 (0)4 94 76 04 71
fax	+33 (0)4 94 76 04 71
mobile	+33 (0)6 24 20 73 09
email	guillandonne@wanadoo.fr

Map 16 Entry 705

Chemin de la Fontaine d'Aragon

On an ancient hillside steeply studded with rows of gnarled, sentry-like olives, this generous modern house is an oasis of cool peace between sophisticated Monte Carlo and the wild Verdon gorges. The sheer pleasure your hosts find in giving hospitality fills the serene place and its comfortable new and 'medieval' furnishings. Monsieur made perfume for 35 years, now he makes prize-winning and equally delicious organic jam. Like Monsieur, sweetly smiling Madame loves walking and both will help you discover the Esterel hills. The spotless airy double room shares a big pink shower room with the small twin.

rooms	2: 1 double, 1 twin, sharing shower & wc (let to same party only).
price	€50. €100 for 4.
meals	Restaurant within walking distance.
closed	Rarely.
directions	From A8 exit 39 on D37 N for 8.5km; cross D562; continue 200m; house on right; signed.

	Pierre & Monique Robardet
	Chemin de la Fontaine d'Aragon,
	Quartier Narbonne,
	83440 Montauroux, Var
tel	+33 (0)4 94 47 71 39
fax	+33 (0)4 94 47 71 39
email	p.robardet@wanadoo.fr

Map 16 Entry 706

Les Palmiers

Don't be deceived by the Seventies façade; this ground-floor studio apartment is a gem. There are books, music, fresh flowers, warm colours, cream curtains, a seagrass floor, a velours fauteuil. Sliding doors lead to a tiny, canopied patio; from your bed you can watch the glistening waters of the Bay of Cannes. Youthful Édith, once a model, charming and kind, lives on the other side of the door and brings you morning croissants and coffee. The beach, markets and glamour of central Cannes are ten minutes by bus and Édith will update you on the local goings-on. Delightful. *Minimum stay three nights.*

rooms	1 twin & kitchenette.
price	€100–€120.
meals	Restaurants within walking distance.
closed	Rarely.
directions	A8; exit 42 for 'Cannes centre'; N285 to Le Cannet; right Ave. Notre Dame des Anges; right Bd. Paul Doumer; left Ave. des Broussailles; left Ave. de Lattre de Tassigny; at top of hill on right.

	Édith Lefay
	Les Palmiers,
	86 ave de Lattre de Tassigny,
	06400 Cannes, Alpes-Maritimes
tel	+33 (0)4 93 69 25 67
fax	+33 (0)4 93 69 25 67
mobile	+33 (0)6 64 68 25 67

Map 16 Entry 707

Mas du Mûrier

The paradise of a garden, blending into the pine-clothed hillside, is a lesson in Mediterranean flora, aeons away from the potteries and madding fleshpots of nearby Vallauris, and Madame makes marmalade with the oranges. The Roncés restored this old building on a terraced vineyard: such peace. Pamper yourself by the pool, relax to the sound of chirruping cicadas. The bedrooms in this multi-levelled house – one looking over the garden, one the pool – have in common their modern paintings, cheery textiles and old brocante. A remote and deeply restorative place. *Minimum two nights in summer.*

rooms	2: 1 twin; 1 double with separate shower.
price	€75–€95.
meals	Bistro within walking distance.
closed	Rarely.
directions	From A8 Antibes exit 44 to Vallauris; Chemin St Bernard, then Chemin des Impiniers; right into Montée des Impiniers; left at Auberge Bleue; sharp right into picnic area and right up track, signed.

	M & Mme G. Roncé
	Mas du Mûrier,
	1407 route de Grasse,
	06220 Vallauris, Alpes-Maritimes
tel	+33 (0)4 93 64 52 32
fax	+33 (0)4 93 64 52 32
email	fcwhronce@free.fr

Map 16 Entry 708

Provence – Alps – Riviera

Villa Panko

The exotic dream of a (no-smoking) garden is full of tropical crannies and secluded corners, while real and fake flowers invade the living room and fight with the cheerful pictures that cover the variegated walls. Upstairs are rainbow sheets, patchwork bedcovers, painted furniture and *objets* galore, fine big towels and myriad toiletries; exceptional breakfasts are served on colourful china. Madame's energy drives it all – she'll organise your stay to a tee, gardens and galleries a speciality. It is quiet, exclusive, minutes from beaches, and massages can be arranged. *Minimum three to five nights depending on season.*

rooms	2 twins/doubles, one with kitchenette.
price	€100–€115.
meals	Choice of restaurants 10-minute walk.
closed	August, Christmas & New Year.
directions	From Antibes for Cap d'Antibes; palm tree r'bout for 'Cap d'Ant. Juan Les Pins'; next junc. for Cap d'Ant.; 1st right Ch. du Crouton; 1st left cul-de-sac; at end, left on drive; 2nd house on right.

Clarisse & Bernard Bourgade
Villa Panko,
17 chemin du Parc Saramartel,
06160 Cap d'Antibes,
Alpes-Maritimes

tel	+33 (0)4 93 67 92 49
fax	+33 (0)4 93 61 29 32
email	capdantibes.panko@wanadoo.fr
web	www.villapanko.com

Map 16 Entry 709

Provence – Alps – Riviera

Villa Maghoss

Cascades of bougainvillea and pelargonium tumble over the terrace of this 1910 villa, and grapes dangle into your hand at breakfast. From the pretty garden you enter your delightful little sitting room with its country antiques, then through a basic shower room to a rather cramped bedroom. But your hosts take such great care of you – fresh flowers in the rooms, delicious breakfast – that this is a minor thorn among the roses. Although this is a quiet, dull piece of suburbia, sweet old seaside Antibes is only a 20-minute walk away – or borrow the bikes. *Minimum stay two nights. Madame will pick you up from airport/train.*

rooms	1 double & sitting room.
price	€75.
meals	Choice of restaurants in Antibes.
closed	Rarely.
directions	In Antibes centre from Place de Gaulle take Rue Aristide Briand; left at r'bout, follow railway 600m; right Impasse Lorini with barrier marked 'Privé'; house at end on right.

Martine & Pierre Martin
Villa Maghoss,
8 impasse Lorini,
06600 Antibes,
Alpes-Maritimes

tel	+33 (0)4 93 67 02 97
fax	+33 (0)4 93 67 02 97
email	maghoss@voila.fr

Map 16 Entry 710

Provence – Alps – Riviera

Le Cheneau

This very appealing Provençal-type villa is a happy marriage of modern technique and traditional design; the setting is entrancing, with umbrella pines, palms, the southern skies and Mediterranean heat. In the cool interior all is well-ordered and smart. Your charming, efficient and enthusiastic hosts have created old out of new, paved their generous terrace with lovely old squares, and furnished the rooms with a mix of the antique and the contemporary – and big beds. There is a dayroom/kitchen for guests and a beautifully tended garden with breakfast terrace – and ten golf courses within a three-mile radius!

rooms	3: 1 double, 2 twins/doubles.
price	€70–€80.
meals	Restaurants 300m. Guest kitchen.
closed	Rarely. Book ahead.
directions	From A8 exit Antibes; at Bouillides r'bout twds Valbonne village 3km, D103; 100m after Bois Doré res't on rt., before Petite Ferme bus stop, ring at iron gate No. 205; up lane, on lft at top.

Alain & Christine Ringenbach
Le Cheneau,
205 route d'Antibes,
06560 Valbonne,
Alpes-Maritimes

tel	+33 (0)4 93 12 13 94
fax	+33 (0)4 93 12 13 94
mobile	+33 (0)6 68 15 82 64
email	ringbach@club-internet.fr

Map 16 Entry 711

Provence – Alps – Riviera

Lou Candelou

Terracotta roofs peep over lush foliage in this residential area, to hills and the heavenly Med. A huge mimosa guards this friendly small house of soft local stone and light blue shutters; arrive by narrow private road to a warm (multi-lingual) welcome from Boun. Fresh, colourwashed ground-floor rooms with ethnic cottons, painted furniture and immaculate bathrooms lead directly to a potted terrace. Breakfast on the balcony: a joy of pastries, fresh fruit, exotic conserves – and views; pull yourself away and hop on a train to the coast. Grasse, Cap d'Antibes and the pink poochies of Nice await.

rooms	3 doubles.
price	€50–€70.
	Summer +20% if one night only.
meals	Restaurant 1km.
closed	Rarely.
directions	A8 Nice to Cannes; exit 47 for Villeneuve Loubet; to Grasse; after Le Rouret, over r'bout; Pré du Lac r'bout, for Palais de Justice; 2nd exit at Les Roumégons r'bout, thro' tunnel to lights; house 1st on right.

M & Mme Bougie
Lou Candelou,
57 ave St Laurent,
06520 Magagnosc,
Alpes-Maritimes

tel	+33 (0)8 70 41 90 16
fax	+33 (0)4 93 36 90 16
email	bounb@club-internet.fr
web	www.loucandelou.com

Map 16 Entry 712

Les Coquelicots

Annick, a well-travelled, kind and restful person, is a former riding instructor, now more likely to be helping people into hammocks than onto horses. Her peaceful garden, with its awesomely ancient olive trees dotted about the terraces and among the lush grass, is ideal for a siesta. Over this looks the garden suite, a treat for those who want to self-cater: its delightful kitchen is light-filled and quarry-tiled. The smaller blue room is charming with its own entrance, a vast antique wardrobe, fine linen, an old wooden bed. If it's too hot for the terrace, breakfast is in the lovely saffron-yellow living room.

rooms	2: 1 double; 1 suite & kitchenette.
price	€55–€80.
meals	Restaurants in village; self-catering available.
closed	November–mid-December.
directions	From Grasse D2085 to Le Rouret; through village, left D7 for La Colle sur Loup & Cagnes; on leaving village, hard right down steep track; house on right; call to meet Mme at *La Mairie*.

Annick Le Guay
Les Coquelicots,
30 route de Roquefort,
06650 Le Rouret,
Alpes-Maritimes

tel	+33 (0)4 93 77 40 04
fax	+33 (0)4 93 77 40 04
email	annick.coquelicot@tiscali.fr

Map 16 Entry 713

Le Clos de St Paul

A young Provençal house (built in 1975) on a lushly planted and screened piece of land where boundary hedging is high. In a separate guest wing, each smallish bedroom has its own patio and shares the guest sitting space with kettle and fridge. Smiling Madame has furnished with taste, simple floral fabrics, plain pale walls, beautifully tiled bathrooms. She is genuinely interested to see that you enjoy yourself, offers a welcome glass of rosé on her stunning shaded terrace and serves very fresh breakfast on yours. The mosaic-lined pool is refreshingly discreet. *Minimum stay two nights. Children over seven welcome.*

rooms	3: 1 double, 2 twins/doubles.
price	€70–€85.
meals	Restaurant 1km.
closed	Rarely.
directions	From A8 exit 48 for St Paul de Vence, 3km; fork right on D536/D7 to La Colle. Right at flashing light, cont. down hill; 100m after telephone box on right; right into chemin de la Rouguière; 1st house on left.

Béatrice Ronin Pillet
Le Clos de St Paul,
71 chemin de la Rouguière,
06480 La Colle sur Loup,
Alpes-Maritimes

tel	+33 (0)4 93 32 56 81
fax	+33 (0)4 93 32 56 81
email	leclossaintpaul@hotmail.com
web	perso.wanadoo.fr/leclossaintpaul

Map 16 Entry 714

Provence – Alps – Riviera

13 Montée de la Citadelle

Both Alain and Michelle, a delightfully happy and enthusiastic couple, are rightly proud of this attractive and lovingly renovated old house. It has an ideal setting on the upper fringe of a very pretty village, with the woods behind and wild boar who snuffle into the garden at night. The charming bedrooms, each with its own terrace onto the garden, and the suite on two floors, are separate from yet cleverly integrated with the rest of the lovely, white, uncluttered space. Dinners are amazing, with delicious wines and patisserie by Alain; breakfast is under the plum tree. *Minimum stay two nights.*

rooms	2: 1 double, 1 suite.
price	€60–€70.
meals	Dinner with wine, €20.
closed	October–March.
directions	From Cagnes sur Mer centre D18 to La Gaude; left 100m after Cupola; Place des Marronniers; Rue des Marronniers to house. (Alain will fetch luggage.)

Alain & Michelle Martin
13 Montée de la Citadelle,
06610 La Gaude,
Alpes-Maritimes

tel	+33 (0)4 93 24 71 01
fax	+33 (0)4 93 24 71 01

Map 16 Entry 715

Provence – Alps – Riviera

L'Olivier Peintre

In a 14th-century hilltop village, breakfast in heaven on Michelle's finely laid spread before a distant sea view, birdsong thrilling from the subtropical vegetation and Beethoven from the house. The luscious garden drops down to the sheltered pool, bedrooms are in French 1950s style – comfy beds, some antiques. Your hosts, a devoted couple who adore children, make all who come near them feel happier: he makes olive-wood carvings and interesting conversation; she is a management consultant. And they have a super dog called Oomba. Genuine B&B. *Minimum stay two nights. Parking can be tricky.*

rooms	4: 2 doubles, 1 twin/double, 1 family suite.
price	€90–€110. Under 10s free.
meals	Dinner with wine, €20.
closed	Occasionally in winter.
directions	From A8 exit St Laurent du Var; over r'bout for Zone Ind.; over 2nd r'bout; 3rd r'bout left D118 to St Jeannet; through village to top, Rue St Claude. (Owners will send map.)

Guy & Michelle Benoît Sère
L'Olivier Peintre,
136 rue Saint Claude,
06640 St Jeannet, Alpes-Maritimes

tel	+33 (0)4 93 24 78 91
fax	+33 (0)4 93 24 78 77
mobile	+33 (0)6 11 30 45 36
email	mbenoitsere@aol.com

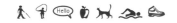

Map 16 Entry 716

Provence – Alps – Riviera

Un Ange Passe

Serenity, forests and views. The Deloupys used to have a Special Place in Nice Old Town; now they've moved from the hum of the city to the jingle of goats' bells and the splash of the stream. The old sheepfold is palm-lush on the outside, freshly modern within: open-stone walls, polished terracotta, plants, cushions, gliding glass doors to a flood-lit pool. Light, airy, air-conditioned bedrooms have tree-top views, showers have delicious towels. You are five minutes from St Paul de Vence, and your hosts are cosmopolitan people who delight in sharing their knowledge of the area. *Minimum stay two nights.*

rooms	5: 2 doubles, 2 suites, 1 family room.
price	€80–€110.
meals	Restaurants 1km.
closed	Rarely.
directions	From La Colle sur Loup for Bar sur Loup bypass; at sports stadium right; 1st left after pharmacy; follow Chambres d'Hôtes signs.

Bernard & Martine Deloupy
Un Ange Passe,
419 ave Jean Leonardi,
06480 La Colle sur Loup,
Alpes-Maritimes

tel   +33 (0)4 93 32 60 39
fax   +33 (0)4 93 82 45 29
email contact@unangepasse.fr
web   www.unangepasse.fr

Map 16 Entry 717

Provence – Alps – Riviera

Villa L'Aimée

In one of the most authentic parts of Nice, a short bus ride from the city's rich culture (buses stop virtually at the gate), Villa L'Aimée is a belle époque villa constructed in 1929 and Toni's decoration has restored its wonderful shapes and details to their original opulence. Warm, cultured and much-travelled – one of her lives was in the art world – she has created delightful bedrooms in subtle colours with damasks and silks, fine linen, tulle canopies and beautiful furnishings, exuding an air of old luxury. The original parquet is breathtaking, and breakfasts are superb. *Babies & children over ten welcome.*

rooms	3: 2 twins/doubles, 1 twin.
price	€100–€125.
meals	Restaurants within walking distance.
closed	December–January.
directions	From A8 exit 54 Nice Nord for Nice & centre ville; left Ave. du Ray; r'bout right; over 2nd r'bout; Place Alex Medicin left; left into Ave. Henri Durant; 1st left at Garage Auto Bilan; immed. right Vieux Chemin de Gairaut; 1st right Ave. Piatti.

Toni Redding
Villa L'Aimée,
5 ave Piatti,
06100 Nice,
Alpes-Maritimes

tel   +33 (0)4 93 52 34 13
fax   +33 (0)4 93 52 34 13
email bookings@villa-aimee.co.uk
web   www.villa-aimee.co.uk

Map 16 Entry 718

Provence – Alps – Riviera

La Tour Manda

Such engaging hosts – nothing is too much trouble. Set well back from the busy dual carriageway, the house is convenient for airport and town. And what a classic Côte d'Azur setting: look from your elegant bedroom over immaculate lawns and palms imported from Egypt. Inside, light, space and heaps of southern style – family antiques, Persian carpets, gorgeous paintings, pristine bathrooms yet not the least intimidating. "Super inside, super outside and super people" – and do visit the Fondation Maeght in hilltop St Paul de Vence for fabulous modern art. *Open by request during carnival. Min two nights.*

rooms	3: 2 doubles, 1 suite for 4.
price	€100. €170 for 4.
meals	Restaurants in Nice.
closed	Rarely.
directions	From Nice airport for Digne Grenoble; past centre commercial Carrefour; right onto small road just before 'Cuisine Number 1'.

Jean-Claude & Brigitte Janer
La Tour Manda,
682 route de Grenoble,
06200 Nice, Alpes-Maritimes
tel   +33 (0)4 93 29 81 32
fax   +33 (0)4 93 29 81 32
email latourmanda@wanadoo.fr
web   www.bb-tourmanda.com

Map 16 Entry 719

Provence – Alps – Riviera

Le Castel Enchanté

Way, way above Nice (the drive up is an adventure), drowned in bougainvillea, the Italianate villa with 70s additions stands in a jungle of scented garden – the 'enchanted' tag is not usurped. Your hosts are extremely engaging and enjoy meeting guests. Rooms, all big, one very big with its own veranda, are almost lavish in their Provençal colours, excellent furnishings and bathrooms unmatched by many hotels. Served on the sunny terrace, a brilliant breakfast includes cheese, cereals and fresh fruit salad. A super pool and three big docile dogs finish the picture. *Expensive taxi ride into town.*

rooms	3: 2 doubles, 1 twin/double, 1 suite for 4.
price	€100. Suite €180.
meals	Restaurants 2km.
closed	Rarely.
directions	From Pl. St Philippe, under expressway, left Ave. Estienne d'Orves 600m, over level crossing, after sharp right-hand bend, hard back left, tricky track up to house.

Mme Martine Ferrary
Le Castel Enchanté,
61 route de Saint Pierre de Féric,
06000 Nice, Alpes-Maritimes
tel   +33 (0)4 93 97 02 08
fax   +33 (0)4 93 97 13 70
email contact@castel-enchante.com
web   www.castel-enchante.com

Map 16 Entry 720

Provence – Alps – Riviera

151 route de Castellar

Delightful Paul and English Dorothy have been here since the 60s and have made the most of every square inch of the steep site (not for the infirm or elderly!). He is proud of his handiwork, his latest creation being a bridge over the water garden. The views – of wooded valley leading to distant sea – are stupendous and make it entirely worth braving the narrow approach roads from Old Menton. Bedrooms open off a south-facing terrace, have satin bedspreads, simple furniture and good bathrooms. Breakfast may be on that pretty shaded terrace and it's breezy by the pool in summer. *Min stay two nights.*

rooms	4 doubles.
price	€60.
meals	Choice of restaurants in Menton, 2km.
closed	December-January, except by arrangement.
directions	From Autoroute exit Menton; for Centre Ville & Hotel de Ville; right for Castellar; up narrow road; 151 on left.

M & Mme Paul Gazzano
151 route de Castellar,
06500 Menton,
Alpes-Maritimes
tel   +33 (0)4 93 57 39 73
email   natie06@yahoo.fr

Map 16 Entry 721

Provence – Alps – Riviera

Domaine du Paraïs

Set in gentle isolation just a dramatic drive up from hot Riviera vulgarity, the slightly faded Italianate mansion is home to a trio of highly cultured, artistic, English-fluent people who have re-awakened its 19th-century magic. No clutter, either of mind or matter, here. Breakfast is in the atmospheric old kitchen. White bedrooms have pretty fabrics, simple antiques and views of trees where birds burst their lungs and Marcel Mayer's superb sculptures await you. Come for dreamy space, natural peace, intelligent conversation. And ride a horse into the hills for a day.

rooms	2 doubles.
price	€55-€65.
meals	Restaurants in Sospel, 1-2km.
closed	Rarely.
directions	From Menton D2566 to Sospel; at entrance to village left for Col de Turini 1.9km; left for 'La Vasta' & 'Campings'. Paraïs 1.3km along, hard back on right after ranch & sharp bend.

Marie Mayer & Marcel Mayer
Domaine du Paraïs,
La Vasta Supérieure,
06380 Sospel, Alpes-Maritimes
tel   +33 (0)4 93 04 15 78
fax   +33 (0)4 93 04 15 78
email   domaine.du.parais@wanadoo.fr
web   domaineduparais.monsite.wanadoo.fr

Map 16 Entry 722

Monaco

Villa Nyanga

Looking east over the yacht-studded bay, south over the onion domes of a *fin de siècle* Persian palace, here is a warmly human refuge from the fascinating excesses that are Monaco. Michelle's sober, white-painted flat is decorated with wood, marble and lots of contemporary art, her own and her friends'. Living room: arched doors, little fireplace, little breakfast table, wide balcony; guest room: white candlewick bedcover, big gilt-framed mirror, sea view; bathroom: gloriously old-fashioned beige. Space everywhere, and Michelle is as good a hostess as she is an artist.

rooms	1 twin/double.
price	€100.
meals	Choice of restaurants in Monaco.
closed	August.
directions	From A8 exit 56 Monaco for centre (tunnel); past Jardin Exotique; on right-hand bend (pharmacy on corner) left; left at end Malbousquet; park opposite no. 26 to unload.

Michelle Rousseau
Villa Nyanga,
26 rue Malbousquet,
98000 Monaco,

tel	(00) 377 93 50 32 81
fax	(00) 377 93 50 32 81 *Please note this includes code for Monaco.*
email	michelle.rousseau@mageos.com
web	www.bbfrance.com/rousseau.html

Map 16   Entry 723

French Holiday Homes

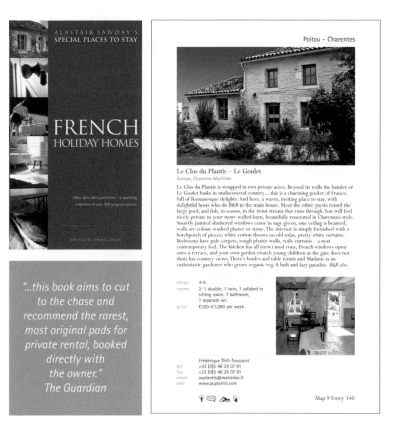

ALASTAIR SAWDAY'S
SPECIAL PLACES TO STAY

FRENCH
HOLIDAY HOMES

Villas, gîtes and apartments – a sparkling
collection of over 350 gorgeous places

EDITED BY EMMA CAREY

"...this book aims to cut
to the chase and
recommend the rarest,
most original pads for
private rental, booked
directly with
the owner."
The Guardian

Poitou – Charentes

Le Clos du Plantis – Le Goulet
Sonnac, Charente-Maritime

Le Clos du Plantis is wrapped in two private acres. Beyond its walls the hamlet of
Le Goulet basks in undiscovered country... this is a charming pocket of France,
full of Romanesque delights. And here, a warm, inviting place to stay, with
delightful hosts who do B&B in the main house. Meet the other guests round the
large pool; and fish, in season, in the trout stream that runs through. You will feel
nicely private in your stone-walled barn, beautifully renovated in Charentais style.
Smartly painted shuttered windows come in sage green, one ceiling is beamed,
walls are colour-washed plaster or stone. The interior is simply furnished with a
hotchpotch of pieces; white cotton throws on old sofas, pretty white curtains.
Bedrooms have pale carpets, rough plaster walls, voile curtains - a neat
contemporary feel. The kitchen has all (new) mod cons, French windows open
onto a terrace, and your own garden (watch young children as the gate does not
shut) has country views. There's boules and table tennis and Madame is an
enthusiastic gardener who grows organic veg. A lush and lazy paradise. B&B also.

sleeps	4-6.
rooms	2: 1 double, 1 twin, 1 sofabed in sitting room; 1 bathroom, 1 separate wc.
price	€320-€1,090 per week.

	Frédérique Thill-Toussaint
tel	+33 (0)5 46 25 07 91
fax	+33 (0)5 46 25 07 91
email	auplantis@wanadoo.fr
web	www.auplantis.com

Map 9 Entry 140

The B&Bs below also have self-
catering accommodation in our
French Holiday Homes guide (£12.99)

French gardens

Interesting that 'Capability' Brown and André le Nôtre, Britain and France's most celebrated gardeners, stand at opposite ends of the horticultural spectrum. The English garden, no matter how grand, is an extension of nature – Levens Hall, Stourhead, Hatfield House – while the traditional French garden is a place of formality and grandeur. And even though French gardening has undergone profound changes in recent years, the great classical heritage lives on, renovated and revived in the châteaux gardens as well as in new, and sometimes stunning, contemporary forms.

and symmetry, alleys of pleached lime and parterres of box, canals, cascades, fountains and statuary, viewpoints, vistas and paths cut with mathematical accuracy through woods, few inclines and even fewer flowers: the French 17th-century nobility expressed power through the grandeur of its gardens and its châteaux. It all culminated in the gardens of the palace of Versailles, designed by Le Nôtre, employed by the Sun King. The orangery housed 1,200 orange trees, the fountains were the most dazzling ever seen. Extravagant topiary, stonework and statuary existed in 15th-century Italy, but never on this scale.

The Château de Brecy in Normandy is one of the earliest examples of the architectural garden; its charming walled topiary sits the other side of meadows grazed by cows. The Château de Courances, an hour from Paris, is a more grandiose garden of the period, and includes beautiful arabesque *parterres de broderie*. But the garden of which Le Nôtre himself was most proud was the Château de Chantilly, austerely elegant with its lawn parterres, pools with water jets, canals and 'hamlet' – a precursor of picturesque Englishness to come.

All that hedge-clipping was dauntingly impressive, cost a fortune and served its purpose: to impress the neighbours. Geometric design

photo Painton Cowen

In the 18th century the English landscape garden – the clumps of trees, the meandering paths, the temples, grottos, lakes and hills, seemingly so random yet so artfully composed, came to the fore, and soon 'le jardin anglais' was all the rage.

The Parc Canon in Normandy is one such natural garden, created by a Parisian barrister in the late 1700s: a broad path cutting through woods, a temple at one end and open excursions into idyllic nature. Le Désert de Retz near Paris is another; its follies were to seduce the Surrealists two centuries later. Thirty miles from Paris the philosopher Rousseau, inventor of "the noble savage", lies buried in the arborous landscape of the Parc de Jean-Jacques Rousseau. His tomb rests under poplars on an island in a lake – suitably far from the corrupting influences of civilisation.

The Modern Garden
Little by little the characteristics of the traditional garden have given way to a new, modern eclecticism, as worldwide exchanges of knowledge and increased accessibility of unusual plants have led to new takes on old fashions. A flood of rhododendron introductions began in the 19th century when botanists started foraging in the Himalayas; willows followed from Japan and roses from China. The best of today's gardens are, in effect, an anthology of garden styles, from ornamental to wild – and there's equal artifice in both. At the same time the fascination with plantmanship has resulted in a mushrooming of nurseries on both sides of the channel and (in tribute to global warming?) a recent interest in Australasian exotics. Garden fashions come and go, from the rock garden craze of the Thirties to the 'colour my garden' approach of the Sixties to our modern predilection for foliage of every red, silver and green... while 'wild' drifts of alliums and grasses are the essence of current garden chic.

Twentieth-century French gardens worth a detour include Kerdalo, a glorious garden in Brittany, planted in the Sixties; Le Vasterival in Normany, a shrub connoisseur's delight; the Villa Nouailles in Provence, with its softly hedged 'rooms' a la Gertrude Jekyll; La Chèvre d'Or near Antibes, with its canopies of wisteria and clouds of blue ceanothus. Perhaps most special of all are the gardens of the Château de Villandry, west of Tours, restored to their Renaissance glory in the early 1900s. The vast potager, divided into nine equal squares, is stuffed with ornamental cabbages, radishes, peas, strawberries, sorrel, leeks, forget-me-nots and daisies, replanted twice a year. It has a dazzling beauty.

Jo Boissevain

B&Bs with gorgeous gardens

photo Villa Panko, entry 709

Cycling and walking in France

Cycling in France

France offers rich rewards to the cyclist: plenty of space, a superb network of minor roads with little traffic, and a huge diversity of landscapes.

When to go

Avoid July and August! The south is good from mid-March, except on high ground which may be snow-clad until the end of June. The north can be lovely from May onwards. Most other areas are suitable from April until October.

Getting bikes to and through France

Ferries carry bikes free or for a small fee. British Airways and Air France take bikes free if you don't exceed their weight allowance. If you travel by Eurostar, you should be able to store your bike in one of the guards' vans if you reserve and pay extra. Some mainline and most regional trains accept bikes, sometimes free, most for a fee. Information is contradictory so check details before you depart. Insist on a ticket *avec réservation d'un emplacement vélo*. If you are two or more make sure the reservation is multiple.

Maps

The two big names are Michelin and the Institut Géographique National (IGN). For route-planning, IGN publishes a map of the whole of France showing mountain-biking and cycle tourism (No. 906). The best on-the-road reference maps are Michelin's Yellow 1:200,000 Series. IGN publishes a Green Series at a scale of 1:100,000. For larger scale maps, go for IGN's excellent 1:25,000 Top 25 and Blue Series (which you will also use for walking). You can buy maps at most Maisons de la Presse newsagents in France, or at Stanfords in the UK.

Walking in France

With over 60,000km of clearly marked long distance footpaths, or sentiers de Grandes Randonnées (GRs), and a fantastic variety of landscapes and terrains, France is a superb country in which to walk.

Maps

The IGN maps are likely to be of most use for walkers. A useful map for planning walks is the IGN's France: Grande Randonnée sheet No. 903 which shows all the country's long distance footpaths. For walking, the best large-scale maps are the IGN's 1:25,000 Serie Bleue and Top 25 series.

Books

The FFRP produces more than 180 topo-guides – guidebooks for walkers which include walking instructions and IGN maps (usually 1:50,000). Most of these are now translated into English so it's worth buying one before you leave.

Order form

All these books are available in major bookshops or you may order them direct.
Post and packaging are FREE within the UK.

Bed & Breakfast for Garden Lovers	£14.99
British Hotels, Inns & Other Places	£14.99
British Bed & Breakfast	£14.99
Croatia	£11.99
French Bed & Breakfast	£15.99
French Hotels, Châteaux & Other Places	£14.99
French Holiday Homes	£12.99
Greece	£11.99
Green Places to Stay	£13.99
India	£11.99
Ireland	£12.99
Italy	£14.99
London	£9.99
Morocco	£11.99
Mountains of Europe	£9.99
Paris Hotels	£9.99
Portugal	£10.99
Pubs & Inns of England & Wales	£13.99
Spain	£14.99
Turkey	£11.99
One Planet Living	£4.99
The Little Food Book	£6.99
The Little Money Book	£6.99
Six Days	£12.99

Please make cheques payable to Alastair Sawday Publishing   Total £ _____

Please send cheques to: Alastair Sawday Publishing, The Old Farmyard, Yanley
Lane, Long Ashton, Bristol BS41 9LR. For credit card orders call 01275 395431
or order directly from our web site www.specialplacestostay.com

Title   First name   Surname

Address

Postcode   Tel

FBB10

If you do not wish to receive mail from other like-minded companies, please tick here ☐
If you would prefer not to receive information about special offers on our books, please tick here ☐

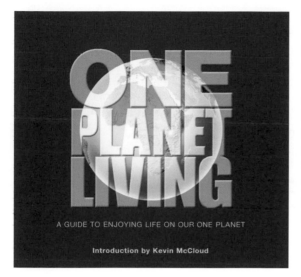

If everyone in the world consumed the planet's natural resources at the same rate as people in the UK, we would need THREE planets to support us

The Solution?
One Planet Living

One Planet Living   Edition 1, £4.99

A practical guide providing us with easy, affordable and attractive alternatives for achieving a higher quality of life while using our fair share of the planet's capacity. Two environmental organisations, BioRegional and WWF, have come together to promote a simple set of principles to make sustainable living achievable.

The Little Food Book   Edition 1, £6.99

By Craig Sams, Chairman of the Soil Association
An explosive account of the food we eat today. Never have we been at such risk – from our food. This book will help clarify what's at stake.

The Little Money Book   Edition 1, £6.99

By David Boyle, associate of the New Economics Foundation
This pithy, wry little guide will tell you where money comes from, what it means, what it's doing to the planet and what we might be able to do about it.

www.fragile-earth.com

www.special-escapes.co.uk
Self-catering from Alastair Sawday's

ALASTAIR SAWDAY'S
SPECIAL ESCAPES

Home • Search • Hotlist • Owners • Links

The Flat, Sloane Square
London, England

You're in the heart of town, yet tucked up in a smart residential street. Sloane Square tube is on your doorstep, you can be on the King's Road within three minutes and the No. 19 bus whisks you off to Knightsbridge and beyond. The apartment is dreamy: you will linger in the morning, then find an excuse to bolt home in the afternoon. Climb up to the third floor to discover an enormous glass roof flooding the hall with light. Glittering elegance comes in the form of Farrow & Ball paints, a 1793 Chatelet great-grandfather clock, a walnut dining table, a gilded Venetian bedhead and halogen lights. The sofa, covered in raw silk, was too big to come through the door so the delivery man pulled it up single-handedly, tottering on the tiny balcony. Best of all is the exquisite art that hangs on the walls (Frederique represents several artists and holds shows in New York). A super-comfy double bed wears crisp Egyptian cotton, a leaf from a Burmese bible graces the sitting room wall and a mellow marble bathroom pampers. The kitchen is similarly resplendent with dishwasher, hanging pots and stainless steel oven. Exceptional.

Sloane Gardens.

Hall.

Living area in Flat 4.

Details for The Flat

Contact Frederique Browne	**sleeps:**
tel: 020 7823 4704	**rooms:** 2: 1 double, 1 single, sharing bathroom.
@ Send E-mail Enquiry	**price:** £0 – £850.
» Visit Web Site	**closed:** Never.
	changeover: Flexible.

? Details Explanation

€ Currency Converter

✖ 🛁   ? Symbol Explanations

Why Come Here?

Checklist

✔ Dishwasher
✔ Electricity included
✔ Washing machine

✔ Television
✔ Land line telephone**
✔ Restaurant nearby
✔ Iron & ironing board
✔ Public transport
✔ Music system***

** May only be for incoming calls
*** Not necessarily including CD player

More details here »

Points Of Interest

◉ Two minutes away from Royal Court Theatre.
◉ Near to Peter Jones department store.
◉ Battersea Park a 10-minute walk away.
◉ 5 minutes from the river and the Chelsea Flower Show.

This information is provided by owners and is not endorsed by ASP. If you have questions about it, please contact the owners.

Master bedroom in Flat 4.

Now what?

◉ Add The Flat to your Hotlist »

◉ Find other Special Escapes in London »

◉ Booking Advice for Special Escapes »

Cosy cottages • Sumptuous castles • City apartments • Hilltop bothies • Tipis and more

A whole week self-catering in Britain with your friends or family is precious, and you dare not get it wrong. To whom do you turn for advice and who on earth do you trust when the web is awash with advice from strangers? We launched Special Escapes to satisfy an obvious need for impartial and trustworthy help – and that is what it provides. The criteria for inclusion are the same as for our books: we have to like the place and the owners. It has, quite simply, to be 'special'. The site, our first online-only publication, is featured on www.thegoodwebguide.com and is growing fast.

www.special-escapes.co.uk

Where on the web?

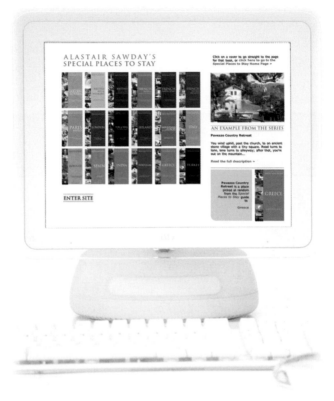

The World Wide Web is big – very big. So big, in fact, that it can be a fruitless search if you don't know where to find reliable, trustworthy, up-to-date information about fantastic places to stay in Europe, India, Morocco and beyond....

Fortunately, there's www.specialplacestostay.com, where you can dip into all of our guides, find special offers from owners, catch up on news about the series and tell us about the special places you've been to.

www.specialplacestostay.com

Report form

If you have any comments on entries in this guide, please let us have them. If you have a favourite house, hotel, inn or other new discovery, please let us know about it. You can return this form, email info@sawdays.co.uk, or visit www.specialplacestostay.com and click on 'contact'.

Existing entry
Property name:_____

Entry number: _____ Date of visit: ___ / ___ / ___

New recommendation
Property name:_____

Address: _____

_____

Tel: _____

Your comments
What did you like (or dislike) about this place? Were the people friendly? What was the location like? What sort of food did they serve?

_____

_____

_____

_____

_____

_____

_____

_____

Your details
Name: _____

Address: _____

Postcode: _____ Tel: _____

Please send completed form to ASP, The Old Farmyard, Yanley Lane, Long Ashton, Bristol BS41 9LR

Wheelchair-friendly

These owners have told us they have facilities for people in wheelchairs.

No car?

Owners of these B&Bs have told us that it is feasible to stay here without a car. Also, dinner is available at these places or there is a restaurant within 1km.

Wine

Owners can organise wine-tastings or tours of vineyards.

Quick reference indices

Art courses
Painting or sculpture courses available.

Language courses available
These places offer French language courses.

Quick reference indices

Our offices

Beautiful as they were, our old offices leaked heat, used electricity to heat water and rooms, flooded whole rooms with light to illuminate one person, and were not ours to alter. We failed our eco-audit in spite of using recycled cooking oil in one car and gas in another, recycling everything we could and gently promoting 'greenery' in our travel books. (Our Fragile Earth series takes a harder line.)

After two eco-audits we leaped at the chance to buy some old barns closer to Bristol, to create our own eco-offices and start again. Our accountants thought we were mad and there was no time for proper budgeting. The back of every envelope bore the signs of frenzied calculations, and then I shook hands and went off on holiday.
Two years later we moved in.

As I write, swallows are nesting in our wood-pellet store, the fountain plays in the pond, the grasses bend

Photos above Quentin Craven

before a gentle breeze and the solar panels heat water too hot to touch. We have, to our delight, created an inspiring and serene place.

The roof was lifted to allow us to fix thick insulation panels beneath the tiles. More panels were fitted between the rafters and as a separate wall inside the old ones, and laid under the underfloor heating pipes. We are insulated for the Arctic, and almost totally air-tight. Ventilation is natural, and we open windows. An Austrian boiler sucks wood-pellets in from an outside store and slowly consumes them, cleanly and – of course – without using any fossil fuels. Rain-water is channelled to a 6,000-litre underground tank and then, filtered, flushes loos and fills basins. Sun-pipes funnel the daylight into dark corners, and double-glazed velux windows, most facing north, pour it into every office.

We built a small green-oak barn between two old barns, and this has become the heart of the offices, warm, light and beautiful. Wood plays a major role: our simple oak desks were made by a local carpenter, my office floor is of oak, and there is oak panelling. Even the carpet tiles tell a story; they are made from the wool of Herdwick sheep from the Lake District.

Our electricity consumption is extraordinarily low. We set out not to flood the buildings with light, but to provide attractive, low background lighting and individual 'task' lights to be used only as needed. Materials, too, have been a focus: we used non-toxic paints and finishes.

Events blew our budgets apart, but we have a building of which we are proud and which has helped us win two national awards this year. Architects and designers are fascinated and we are all working with a renewed commitment. But, best of all, we are now in a better position to encourage our 'owners' and readers to take 'sustainability' more seriously.

I end by answering an obvious question: our office carbon emissions will be reduced by about 75%. We await our bills, but they will be low and, as time goes by, relatively lower – and lower. It has been worth every penny and every ounce of effort.

Alastair Sawday

Photo above Paul Groom
Photo below Tom Germain

Index by place name

Index by place name

Index by place name

Index by surname

Index by surname

Index by surname

① Poitou – Charentes

A l'Ombre du Figuier

② The old farmhouse, lovingly restored and decorated, is simple, pristine, with biggish, comfortable rooms overlooking a pretty garden where you may picnic (there's a guest kitchen too). They are an interesting couple of anglophiles. Madame knows about nutrition and serves generous breakfasts with homemade jam, cheese, yogurt and cereals, all on local pottery. Monsieur teaches engineering in beautiful La Rochelle: follow his hints and discover the lesser-known treasures there. They love children of any age – there's some baby kit, table tennis and country peace. Good value. *No pets in rooms.*

Poitou – Charentes

Le Clos de la Garenne

In this lovingly restored 16th-century house lives a lively young family: three children to entertain young visitors, and sophisticated parents, avid collectors, to decorate with elegance and eclectic flair, cook with exotic inspiration and organics, and talk with passion. Old and modern rub happy shoulders: traditional armoires and new beds, disabled facilities in the newer-style cottage, antique treasures and a tennis court. The air is full of warm smiles, harmony breathes from walls and woodwork, your hosts are endlessly thoughtful, families are positively welcome. *Minimum stay three nights July / Aug.*

③ rooms	2: 1 double, 1 room for 2-4. Rooms interconnect.	
④ price	€50-€57.	
⑤ meals	Occasional dinner with wine, €20. Guest kitchen.	
⑥ closed	Rarely.	
⑦ directions	From La Rochelle N11 E for 11km exit Longèves; D112, signed to village. In village, past church; right at 'bar-pizzas', 1st left, signed. 700m on left.	

rooms	2 + 1: 1 triple, 1 suite for 6. Cottage for 5.
price	€65. Triple €75. Cottage €125.
meals	Dinner with wine, €25.
closed	Rarely.
directions	From Surgères Gendarmerie & fire station, D115 for Marans & Puyravault 5km, following signs.

M-Christine & J-François Prou
A l'Ombre du Figuier,
43 rue du Marais, 17230 Longèves,
Charente-Maritime
tel   +33 (0)5 46 37 11 15
fax   +33 (0)5 46 37 11 15
email   mcprou@wanadoo.fr
web   www.alombredufiguier.com

Brigitte & Patrick François
Le Clos de la Garenne,
9 rue de la Garenne, 17700
Puyravault, Charente-Maritime
tel   +33 (0)5 46 35 47 71
fax   +33 (0)5 46 35 47 91
email   info@closdelagarenne.com
web   www.closdelagarenne.com

⑨ ⚐ ✗ Hello 🌿 👟

⑧ Map 8 Entry 415

Map 8 Entry 416